Lecture Notes in Computer Science 7141

Commenced Publication in 1973
Founding and Former Series Editors:
Gerhard Goos, Juris Hartmanis, and Jan van Leeuwen

Farhad Arbab   Marjan Sirjani (Eds.)

Fundamentals of Software Engineering

4th IPM International Conference, FSEN 2011
Tehran, Iran, April 20-22, 2011
Revised Selected Papers

 Springer

Volume Editors

Farhad Arbab
Centre for Mathematics
and Computer Science (CWI)
Science Park 123
1098 XG Amsterdam
The Netherlands
E-mail: farhad@cwi.nl

Marjan Sirjani
Reykjavik University
Menntavegur 1
Reykjavik 101
Iceland
E-mail: marjan@ru.is

ISSN 0302-9743   e-ISSN 1611-3349
ISBN 978-3-642-29319-1   e-ISBN 978-3-642-29320-7
DOI 10.1007/978-3-642-29320-7
Springer Heidelberg Dordrecht London New York

Library of Congress Control Number: 2012935110

CR Subject Classification (1998): D.2, D.2.4, F.4.1, D.2.2, F.3

LNCS Sublibrary: SL 2 – Programming and Software Engineering

Typesetting: Camera-ready by author, data conversion by Scientific Publishing Services, Chennai, India

Printed on acid-free paper

Springer is part of Springer Science+Business Media (www.springer.com)

Preface

The present volume contains the proceedings of the 4th IPM International Conference on Fundamentals of Software Engineering (FSEN), held in Tehran, Iran, during April 20–22, 2011. This event, FSEN 2011, was organized by the School of Computer Science at the Institute for Studies in Fundamental Sciences (IPM) in Iran, in cooperation with the ACM SIGSOFT and IFIP WG 2.2.

The topics of interest of FSEN span all aspects of formal methods, especially those related to advancing the application of formal methods in the software industry and promoting their integration with practical engineering techniques. The Program Committee of FSEN 2011 consisted of 35 top researchers from 24 different academic institutes in 13 countries. We received a total of 64 submissions from 28 countries out of which the Program Committee selected 19 as regular papers, 5 as short papers, and three as poster presentations in the conference program. Each submission was reviewed by at least three independent referees, for its quality, originality, contribution, clarity of presentation, and its relevance to the conference topics. This volume contains the post-event versions of the regular and the short papers of FSEN 2011.

Three distinguished keynote speakers delivered their lectures at FSEN 2011: "Proposition Algebra and Short-Circuit Logic" by Jan Bergstra, "Towards Specification Inference" by Carlo Ghezzi, and "Model Checking—One Can Do Much More Than You Think" by Joost-Pieter Katoen.

We thank the Institute for Studies in Fundamental Sciences (IPM), Tehran, Iran, for their financial support and local organization of FSEN 2011. We thank the members of the Program Committee for their time, effort, and contributions to making FSEN a quality conference. We thank Hossein Hojjat for his help in preparing this volume. Last but not least, our thanks go to our authors and conference participants, without whose submissions and participation, FSEN would not have been possible.

October 2011

Farhad Arbab
Marjan Sirjani

Conference Organization

General Chair

Hamid Sarbazi-azad   IPM, Iran
Sharif University of Technology, Iran

Steering Committee

Farhad Arbab   CWI, The Netherlands
Leiden University, The Netherlands
Christel Baier   University of Dresden, Germany
Frank de Boer   CWI, The Netherlands
Leiden University, The Netherlands
Ali Movaghar   IPM, Iran
Sharif University of Technology, Iran
Jan Rutten   CWI, The Netherlands
Radboud University Nijmegen,
The Netherlands
Hamid Sarbazi-azad   IPM, Iran
Sharif University of Technology, Iran
Marjan Sirjani   Reykjavík University, Iceland
University of Tehran, Iran

Program Chairs

Farhad Arbab   CWI, The Netherlands
Leiden University, The Netherlands
Marjan Sirjani   Reykjavík University, Iceland
University of Tehran, Iran

Program Committee

Luca Aceto   Reykjavík University, Iceland
Gul Agha   University of Illinois at Urbana - Champaign,
USA
Farhad Arbab   CWI, The Netherlands
Leiden University, The Netherlands
Jos Baeten   Eindhoven University of Technology,
The Netherlands
Christel Baier   University of Dresden, Germany
Frank de Boer   CWI, The Netherlands
Leiden University, The Netherlands

Marcello M. Bonsangue	CWI, The Netherlands
	Leiden University, The Netherlands
Mario Bravetti	University of Bologna, Italy
James C. Browne	University of Texas at Austin, USA
Einar Broch Johnsen	University of Oslo, Norway
Michael Butler	University of Southampton, UK
Dave Clarke	Katholieke University Leuven, Belgium
Wan Fokkink	Vrije Universiteit Amsterdam, The Netherlands
Masahiro Fujita	University of Tokyo, Japan
Maurizio Gabbrielli	University of Bologna, Italy
Jan Friso Groote	Technical University of Eindhoven, The Netherlands
Radu Grosu	State University of New York at Stony Brook, USA
Ramtin Khosravi	University of Tehran, Iran
Joost Kok	Leiden University, The Netherlands
Kim Larsen	Aalborg University, Denmark
Zhiming Liu	United Nations University, Macao, China
Sun Meng	Peking University, China
Seyyed Hassan Mirian	Sharif University of Technology, Iran
Ugo Montanari	University of Pisa, Italy
Peter Mosses	Swansea University, UK
Mohammadreza Mousavi	Technical University of Eindhoven, The Netherlands
Ali Movaghar	IPM, Iran
	Sharif University of Technology, Iran
Andrea Omicini	University of Bologna, Italy
Saeed Parsa	Iran University of Science and Technology, Iran
Hiren Patel	University of Waterloo, Canada
Jan Rutten	CWI, The Netherlands
	Radboud University Nijmegen, The Netherlands
Davide Sangiorgi	University of Bologna, Italy
Marjan Sirjani	Reykjavík University, Iceland
	University of Tehran, Iran
Carolyn Talcott	SRI International, USA
Erik De Vink	Technical University of Eindhoven, The Netherlands

Local Organization

Hamidreza Shahrabi	IPM, Iran

External Reviewers

Amadio, Roberto M.
Andova, Suzana
Astefanoaei, Lacramioara
Atif, Muhammad
Bartocci, Ezio
Beek, Bert Van
Bella, Giampaolo
Bertolini, Cristiano
Birgisson, Arnar
Bodei, Chiara
Bonifacio, Adilson
Buchanan, Nathan
Colley, John
Corradini, Andrea
Costa, David
Davari, Iman
Dixit, Ketan
Dovland, Johan
Edmunds, Andy
Ferrari, Gian Luigi
Gadducci, Fabio
Ghamarian, Amir Hossein
Ghassemi, Fatemeh
Giachino, Elena
Grabe, Immo
Haghighi, Hassan
Hansen, Helle Hvid
Helvensteijn, Michiel
Hooman, Jozef
Huang, Xiaowan
Izadi, Mohammad
Jaghoori, Mohammad Mahdi
Jahangard, Amir
Karmani, Rajesh
Kashif, Hany
Katoen, Joost-Pieter
Keiren, Jeroen J.A.
Keramati, Hossein

König, Barbara
Kop, Cynthia
Korthikanti, Vijay Anand
Kyas, Marcel
Lanese, Ivan
Li, Xiaoshan
Lienhardt, Michael
Lluch Lafuente, Alberto
Markovski, Jasen
Mauro, Jacopo
Melgratti, Hernan
Montesi, Fabrizio
Moon, Young-Joo
Murthy, Abhishek
Mller, Mikael H.
Nyman, Ulrik
Osaiweran, Ammar
Palomino, Miguel
Papaspyrou, Nikolaos
Prakash, Aayush
Raffelsieper, Matthias
Rafnsson, Willard
Reniers, Michel
Rezazadeh, Abdolbaghi
Sabouri, Hamideh
Schlatte, Rudolf
Schäf, Martin
Shu, Qin
Silva, Alexandra
Sinha, Rohit
Snook, Colin
Stolz, Volker
Valencia, Frank
Wang, Hao
Willemse, Tim
Zhao, Liang
Zuppiroli, Sara

Table of Contents

Model Checking:
One Can Do Much More Than You Think!

Joost-Pieter Katoen[1,2]

[1] RWTH Aachen University, Software Modelling and Verification Group, Germany
[2] University of Twente, Formal Methods and Tools, The Netherlands

Abstract. Model checking is an automated verification technique that actively is applied to find bugs in hardware and software designs. Companies like IBM and Cadence developed their in-house model checkers, and acted as driving forces behind the design of the IEEE-standardized temporal logic PSL. On the other hand, model checking C-, C#- and .NET-program code is an intensive research topic at, for instance, Microsoft and NASA. In this short paper, we briefly discuss three non-standard applications of model checking. The first example is taken from systems biology and shows the relevance of probabilistic reachability. Then, we show how to determine the optimal scheduling policy for multiple-battery systems so as to optimize the system's lifetime. Finally, we discuss a stochastic job scheduling problem that —thanks to recent developments— can be solved using model checking.

1 Introduction

Despite the scepticism in the early eighties, it is fair to say that model checking is scientifically a big success. Important prizes have been awarded to prominent researchers in model checking. Examples are the Paris Kanellakis Award 1998 which was awarded to Bryant, Clarke, Emerson, and McMillan for their invention of "symbolic model checking", the Gödel prize 2000 —the equivalent of the Nobel prize in Mathematics— that was awarded to Vardi and Wolper for their work on model checking with finite automata, and last but not least, the Nobel prize in Computer Science, the ACM Turing Award 2007, that was granted to the inventors of model checking, Clarke, Emerson, and Sifakis. The impact of model checking tools is clearly demonstrated by the ACM System Software Award 2001, granted to Holzmann, for his model checker SPIN, "a popular open-source software tool, used by thousands of people worldwide, that can be used for the formal verification of distributed software systems". Other winners of this prestigious award are, e.g., TeX, Postscript, unix, TCP/IP and Java, to mention a few.

Model checking is based on an exhaustive state space search; in fact, checking whether a set of target states is reachable from a given state is at the heart of various model-checking algorithms. The prime usage of model checking [6,2,8] is bug hunting: finding flaws in software programs, hardware designs, communication protocols, and the like. The feature of model checkers to generate a

F. Arbab and M. Sirjani (Eds.): FSEN 2011, LNCS 7141, pp. 1–14, 2012.

counterexample in case a property is refuted is extremely useful and turns model checking into an intelligent and powerful debugging technique. This feature combined with an abstraction-refinement loop is currently main stream in software verification. Success stories include the demonstration of conceptual bugs in an international standard proposal for a cache coherence protocol, catching a fatal flaw in the Needham-Schröder authentication protocol, but also the usage of model checking in designing device drivers in recent Microsoft operating systems, and highly safety-critical NASA space missions. The fact that the Property Specification Language (PSL), basically a derivative of linear temporal logic enriched with regular expressions, has become an IEEE standard since 2005 for specifying properties or assertions about hardware designs, is a clear sign that formal verification techniques such as model checking have significantly gained popularity and importance.

Model checking can however be applied to various problems of a completely different nature. It can be used for instance to solve combinatorial puzzles such as the famous Chapman puzzle [7] and Sudoku problems. In the rest of this short paper, we will discuss three non-standard applications of model checking. The first example is taken from systems biology and shows the relevance of probabilistic reachability. Then, we show how to determine the optimal scheduling policy for multiple-battery systems. Finally, we discuss a stochastic scheduling problem that—thanks to quite recent developments—can be solved using model checking. All examples share that the models and properties that we will check are *quantitative*. This is an important deviation from traditional model checking that focuses on functional correctness of models. It is our firm belief that quantitative model checking will gain importance in the (near) future and will become a technique that is highly competitive in comparison to standard solution techniques for quantitative problems.

2 Systems Biology: Enzyme Kinetics

Enzyme kinetics investigates of how enzymes (E) bind substrates (S) and turn them into products (P). About a century ago, Henri considered enzyme reactions to take place in two stages. First, the enzyme binds to the substrate, forming the enzyme-substrate complex. This substrate binding phase catalyses a chemical reaction that releases the product. Enzymes can catalyse up to several millions of reactions per second. Rates of kinetic reactions are obtained from enzyme assays, and depend on solution conditions and substrate concentration. The enzyme-substrate catalytic substrate conversion reaction is described by the stoichiometric equation:

$$E + S \underset{k_2}{\overset{k_1}{\rightleftharpoons}} C \xrightarrow{k_3} E + P$$

where k_i is the Michaelis-Menten constant for reaction i, which is the substrate concentration required for an enzyme to reach one-half of its maximum reaction rate. Now let us suppose we have N different types of molecules that randomly collide. The state $X(t)$ of the biological system at time instant $t \in \mathbb{R}_{\geqslant 0}$ is given by $X(t) = (x_1, \ldots, x_N)$ where x_i denotes the number of species of sort i. In the enzyme-catalytic substrate conversion case, $N{=}4$ and $i \in \{C, E, P, S\}$. Let us number the types of reaction, e.g., $E{+}S \to C$ and $C \to E{+}S$ could be the first and second reaction, respectively. The reaction probability of reaction m within the infinitesimally small time-interval $[t, t{+}\Delta)$ with $\Delta \in \mathbb{R}_{\geqslant 0}$ is given by:

$$\alpha_m(\boldsymbol{x}) \cdot \Delta \;=\; \Pr\{\text{reaction } m \text{ in } [t, t{+}\Delta) \mid X(t) = \boldsymbol{x}\}$$

where $\alpha_m(\boldsymbol{x}) = k_m \cdot$ the number of possible combinations of reactant molecules in $\boldsymbol{x}$. For instance, in state (x_E, x_S, x_C, x_P) where $x_i > 0$ for all $i \in \{E, S, C, P\}$, the reaction $E{+}S \to C$ happens with rate $\alpha_m(\boldsymbol{x}) = k_1 {\cdot} x_E {\cdot} x_S$ and yields the state $(x_E{-}1, x_S{-}1, x_C{+}1, x_P)$. This stochastic process possesses the Markov property, i.e., its future is completely described by the current state of the system. Moreover, it is time-homogeneous, i.e., its behaviour is invariant with respect to time shifts. In fact, it is a *continuous-time Markov chain* (CTMC, for short).

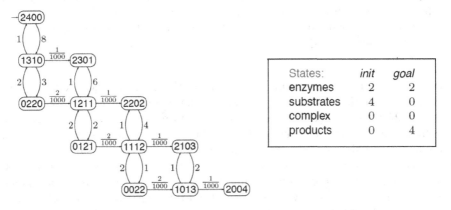

States:	init	goal
enzymes	2	2
substrates	4	0
complex	0	0
products	0	4

Fig. 1. CTMC for enzyme-catalytic substrate conversion for initially 2 enzyme and 4 substrate species with $k_1 = k_2 = 1$ and $k_3 = 0.001$. The transition labels are rates of exponential distributions, i.e., the reciprocal of the average duration of a reaction.

Let us now consider the following question: given a certain concentration of enzymes and substrates, what is the likelihood that after four days all substrates have engaged in a catalytic step and resulted in products? In terms of the CTMC, this boils down to determining the probability that starting from the state $(x_E, x_S, 0, 0)$ we can reach a state of the form $(x_E, 0, 0, x_P)$ within four days. This is a so-called *time-bounded reachability* property that we can tackle by model checking thanks to the following result:

Theorem 1. *[3] The following reachability problem is efficiently computable:*

Input: a finite CTMC, a target state, accuracy $0 < \epsilon < 1$, and deadline $d \in \mathbb{R}_{\geqslant 0}$
Output: an ϵ-approximation of the probability to reach the target in d time.

This result suggests to use an off-the-shelf probabilistic model checker for CTMCs such as `prism` [14] or `mrmc` [12]. Due to the large difference between the rates in the CTMC —the rates between states within one column is about a factor 1,000 times larger than the rates between columns— many iterations are needed to obtain results for a reasonable ϵ, say 10^{-4} or 10^{-6}. Verifying a configuration with 200 substrates and 20 enzymes yielding a CTMC of about 40,000 states, e.g., takes many hours. In order to deal with this problem, we apply aggressive abstraction techniques that are based on partitioning the state space. This manual step is guided by the following rule of thumb: group states that are quickly connected, i.e., group the states in a column-wise manner. This yields a chain structure as indicated in Fig. 2. Now the next step of the abstraction is to take

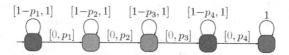

Fig. 2. Abstract CTMC for enzyme-catalytic substrate conversion for 2 enzyme and 4 substrate species after a state partitioning. The transition labels are probability intervals. Rates are omitted, as the residence times of all states has been normalised prior to abstraction, cf. [12].

several transitions into account. For instance, the lower bound probability of moving from the leftmost abstract state to the one-but-leftmost state is 0, as the state 2400 cannot move to any state of the form $(x_E, x_S, x_C, 1)$ in one step, i.e., by taking a single transition. This yields rather course lower bounds. To overcome this deficiency, we consider several steps. That is to say, in addition to the state partitioning, we consider an abstraction of sequences of transitions. The resulting structure is sketched in Fig. 3 where the most important change is the amendment of the lower bounds in the probability intervals, and the addition of transitions. The length k of the sequences that are abstracted from is a

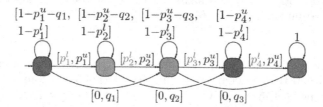

Fig. 3. Abstract CTMC for enzyme-catalytic substrate conversion for 2 enzyme and 4 substrate species after a state and transition sequence abstraction. The transition labels are probability intervals. State residence times now are Erlang distributions.

parameter of the abstraction procedure. The state residence times now become sequences of (equal) exponential distributions, i.e., they become Erlang distributions of length k. As a result of the intervals on the transition probabilities, the analysis of the abstract CTMC yields lower and upper bounds of the real probability. On increasing the parameter k, the difference between these bounds becomes smaller. This effect is illustrated in Fig. 4(a). Our method is accurate

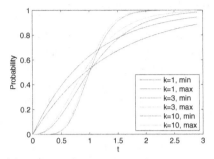

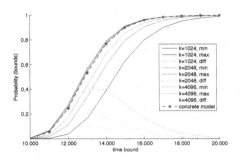

(a) The influence of k on the accuracy of bounds.

(b) Time-bounded reachability bounds for enzyme-catalysed substrate conversion.

if the obtained intervals are small, e.g., for $x_S = 200$, $k = 2^{12}$, and time-bound $t = 14,000$, the relative interval width between the lower and upper bounds is about 10%. The column-wise abstraction results in a state space reduction by a factor 20 and reduces the run-times with several orders of magnitude. For further details on this case study we refer to [11]. The results have been obtained using the **mrmc** model checker [12].

To conclude, model checking combined with novel aggressive abstraction techniques yield a powerful technique to check interesting properties of biological systems. The technique is highly competitive with existing techniques such as solving chemical master equations and Monte Carlo simulation. Recent experiments indicate that these techniques are also very helpful for a completely different application area—queueing theory. By means of abstraction we were able to analyse timed reachability properties for so-called tree-based quasi-birth-death processes with state spaces of up to 10^{278} states by abstractions of about 1.2 million states with an accuracy of $\epsilon = 10^{-6}$, see [13]. To our knowledge, this was the first time ever that tree-shaped Markov models of this size have been analysed numerically.

3   Optimal Battery Scheduling

As argued in the introduction, an important feature of model checking is the possibility to generate counterexamples in case a property is refuted. For instance, for the property $\Box(x > 2)$, expressing that along a path any state should satisfy $x > 2$ for integer variable x, a counterexample is a finite path reaching a state for which $x \leqslant 2$. Counterexamples can be used for scheduling problems in the following way. Suppose that we are interested in finding a schedule that steers a system from a starting to a target state, G, say. Then we model the possible non-deterministic moves of the system by means of a finite transition system, and check whether the property $\neg\Diamond G$, or equivalently, $\Box\neg G$, holds. If there exists a schedule leading to G, the model checker will refute the property $\Box\neg G$ and yields a finite schedule as counterexample. A similar strategy can be applied to real-time systems extended with costs where schedules are sought that minimize the total costs. This will be briefly illustrated in the following example where we will use costs to model energy consumption.

It is well-known that the battery lifetime determines system uptime and heavily depends on the battery capacity, the level of discharge current, and the usage profile. We consider the following problem: given a number of batteries and a usage profile, what is the optimal policy to empty the batteries such that the multiple-battery system's lifetime is maximized. It is certainly far from optimal to solve this off-line scheduling problem by emptying the batteries in a sequential fashion due to the recovery effect: during idle periods, the battery regains some of its capacity, cf. Fig. 4(d). There is an electro-chemical explanation for this recovery effect. Ions have to diffuse from the anode to the cathode of the battery. At high currents, the internal diffusion is too slow and the reaction sites at the cathode surface get blocked. During idle periods, ions get time to diffuse again and accordingly the battery's capacity increases. Alternative scheduling strategies that can exploit this recovery during idle periods are round-robin (empty the batteries according to fixed total order), or best-of-N strategies (use the mostly charged battery among the available N ones). We will show that optimal scheduling policies can be obtained using model checking of *priced timed automata*.

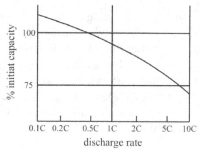

(c) The rate-capacity effect: the battery capacity (y-axis) drops for high discharge currents (x-axis). A discharge rate of 0.5 C means that the total discharge takes 2 hours.

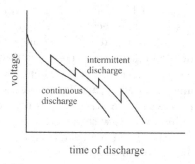

(d) The recovery effect: battery regains capacity during idle periods. This yields the saw-tooth curve.

A second non-linear effect of batteries that has to be taken into account is the so-called rate-capacity effect, see Fig. 4(c). One would think that the ideal capacity would be constant for all discharge currents, and all energy stored in the battery would be used. However, in reality for a real battery the voltage slowly drops during discharge and the effective capacity is lower for high discharge currents. The discharge rate in Fig. 4(c) is given in terms of C rating, a C rating of $2C$ means that the battery is discharged in $1/2$ hour. The measured capacities are given relatively to the capacity at the 2 hour discharge rate, 0.5 C.

The battery model we use is based on the kinetic battery model for lead-acid batteries as developed by Manwell & McGowan [15]. In this model, the charge of the battery is distributed over two wells, the available charge with height h_1 and the bound charge with height h_2, see Fig. 4. The available charge represents the charge that is currently available for usage. Discharging leads to a decrease of h_1. The battery is empty if and only if $h_1 = 0$. When the battery is idle, i.e., not being discharged, charge flows from the bound charge to the available charge. The speed depends on the height difference $h_2 - h_1$ and the resistance k between the two wells. This models the recovery effect. The rate capacity effect is captured by the fact that at higher discharge levels, there is less time to recover. Let y_1 be the volume of the available charge well and y_2 the volume of the

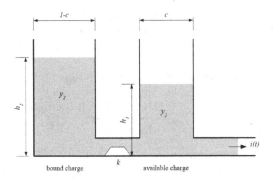

Fig. 4. The kinetic battery model with a boundary and available charge well of height $h_1(t)$ and $h_2(t)$ at time t, respectively. The discharge $i(t)$ at time point t is depicted on the right and will lead to a decrease of the available charge. Recovery is modelled by a charge flow between the boundary and available well when $i(t) = 0$.

boundary charge well. The behaviour of the kinetic battery model is captured by the following set of linear differential equations:

$$h_1(t) = \frac{y_1(t)}{c} \qquad \dot{y}_1(t) = -i(t) + k \cdot (h_2(t) - h_1(t))$$
$$h_2(t) = \frac{y_2(t)}{1-c} \qquad \dot{y}_2(t) = -k \cdot (h_2(t) - h_1(t))$$

with initial conditions $y_1(0) = c \cdot C$ and $y_2(0) = (1 - c) \cdot C$ where C is the total capacity and $0 < c < 1$ for constant c. The constant c indicates the fraction of capacity that is initially present in the available charge well. Here, $i(t)$ represents the discharge process.

The kinetic battery model can naturally be described by a network of *priced timed automata*. Intuitively speaking, clocks in timed automata are used to model the advancement of time t, whereas cost variables are used to model the battery charge (in fact, the reverse). A timed automaton is in fact a finite-state automaton equipped with real-valued clocks that can be used as timers to measure the elapse of time. Constraints on these clocks can be used to guard state-transitions, and clocks can be set to zero while taking a transition. In priced timed automata, states are equipped with a cost rate r such that the accumulated cost in that state over a time period d grows with $r \cdot d$.

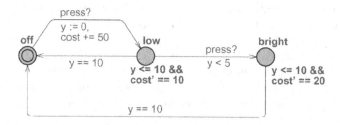

Fig. 5. Example priced timed automaton of a lamp. The cost rate is 0 in state *off*, 10 in state *low* and 20 in state *bright*. Cost represents energy consumption.

We now model the battery scheduling problem as:

$$\underbrace{(DC_1 \,\|\, RC_1)}_{\text{battery } 1} \,\|\, \ldots\ldots \,\|\, \underbrace{(DC_n \,\|\, RC_n)}_{\text{battery } n} \,\|\, Load \,\|\, Scheduler$$

where DC_i describes the discharging process of the battery i, RC_i the recovery effect during idle periods of battery i, *Load* the usage profile and *Scheduler* an automaton that non-deterministically selects one of the batteries for discharging once the usage profile demands a discharge. Then we exploit the following result:

Theorem 2. *[4,1] The following reachability problem is effectively computable:*

Input: a priced timed automaton, an initial state, and a target state
Output: the minimum cost of runs from the initial state to the target.

The complexity of the reachability problem is however exponential. As a by-product of the computation of the minimal cost run, an optimal schedule is obtained that achieves this minimal-cost run.

Our objective is to minimize the bound charge levels (of all batteries) once all batteries are empty, i.e., once all available charges are empty. Table 1 presents the results for two batteries for several usage profiles (the rows) and several battery scheduling disciplines (columns). The last column presents the battery lifetimes obtained by model checking our priced timed automaton. These results have been obtained using the `uppaal cora` model checker[1]. The recovery effect becomes clearly apparent when comparing, e.g., the rows for the usage profiles

---
[1] `www.uppaal.com`

Table 1. Lifetimes of a multi-battery system under various usage profiles (first column) and various scheduling disciplines (second to fourth column). The optimal lifetimes obtained by model checking are listed in the last column.

test load	sequential lifetime (min)	round robin lifetime (min)	best-of-two lifetime (min)	optimal lifetime (min)
CL_250	9.12	11.60	11.60	12.04
CL_500	4.10	4.53	4.53	4.58
CL_alt	5.48	6.10	6.12	6.48
ILs_250	22.80	38.96	38.96	40.80
ILℓ_250	45.84	76.00	76.00	78.96
ILs_500	8.60	10.48	10.48	10.48
ILℓ_500	12.94	15.96	15.96	18.68
ILs_alt	12.38	12.82	16.30	16.91
ILs_r1	12.80	16.26	16.26	20.52

ILs_250 and ILℓ_250. Both profiles have a peak charge of 250 Amin^2 the and peak with equal duration, but the idle time between successive discharging periods is small and long, respectively. This almost doubles the battery lifetime. A similar phenomenon appears for profiles ILs_500 and ILℓ_500. The optimal battery lifetimes obtained by model checking (last column) clearly outperform round-robin and best-of-two scheduling. Note that best-of-two is not much better than round-robin, and requires the ability to measure the remaining capacity of the batteries. Sequential scheduling is far from attractive. An example schedule that is obtained by model checking (lower part), and compared to a best-of-two schedule (middle part) for a given usage profile (uppermost block curve, in black) is provided in Fig. 6.

To conclude, model checking allows for computing the optimal battery scheduling policy. Alternative techniques to obtain such policies are by solving nonlinear optimisation problems. It is fair to say, that the obtained optimal schedules using this technique are not easily implementable in realistic battery-powered systems such as PDAs or sensor nodes. By means of model checking, one can however determine the quality of a given scheduling policy by comparing it to the optimal one. The above experiments show that round-robin scheduling is mostly behaving quite good. For further details on this case study, see [9,10].

4 Stochastic Scheduling

The third application example is slightly more theoretical, and aims to illustrate how state-of-the-art stochastic model checking techniques can be used to solve stochastic scheduling problems. Stochastic scheduling is important in the field of optimization [19], and is motivated by problems of priority assignment in various

---

^{2} Amin stands for ampere minute and is the equivalent of one ampere for one minute.

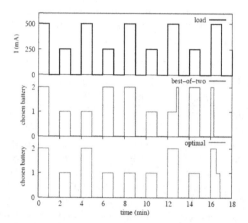

Fig. 6. Example of obtained optimal schedule for two batteries (lowermost curve) for a given usage profile (uppermost curve), compared to a best-of-two scheduling policy (middle curve).

systems where jobs with random features, such as random durations, or arrival processes, are considered, or in which machines are present that are subject to random failures.

More concretely, we consider the scheduling of N jobs on K identical machines, where $K \ll N$. Every job has a random duration such that job i has a mean duration of $d_i > 0$ time units. The most appropriate stochastic approximation is to model the duration of job i by a negative exponential distribution with rate $\lambda_i = \frac{1}{d_i}$. (Technically speaking, given that only the mean of a random event is known, the probability distribution that maximizes the entropy is an exponential one with exactly this mean; intuitively, maximizing entropy minimizes the amount of prior information built into the probability distribution.) Jobs are scheduled on the machines such that job scheduling is pre-emptive. The pre-emptive scheduling allows us to assign each machine one of the n remaining jobs giving rise to $\binom{n}{K}$ possible choices. This means that on finishing of a job on machine j, every job on any other machine can be pre-empted. This scheme is illustrated by a decision tree for 4 jobs and 2 machines in Fig. 7. Every node in the tree is labelled with the set of remaining, i.e., unfinished jobs. The underlined job numbers are those that are selected for execution; if one of the jobs, i say, finishes in a situation where n jobs have not been processed yet, an event that happens with probability $\frac{\lambda_i}{\lambda_i + \lambda_j}$ (where j is the number of the other selected, but unfinished job), $n-1$ jobs remain, and a new selection is made. The time that has elapsed is determined by the rate λ_i. Due to the memoryless property of the exponential distribution, the remaining execution time of the pre-empted job j remains exponentially distributed with rate λ_j.

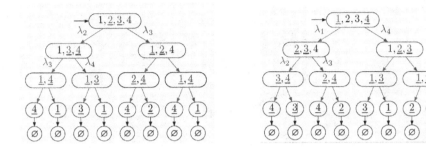

Fig. 7. Two possible schedules of 4 jobs on 2 machines with pre-emptive scheduling policy. In the left one, jobs 2 and 3 are selected first; in the right one, jobs 1 and 4 are initially picked.

It is well-known that the LEPT policy —the longest expected processing time-first policy— yields the minimal expected finishing time of the last job (also called the expected makespan), cf. [5]. As [5] however argues, "it is hard to calculate these expected values". We will show how probabilistic model checking can be applied to address a harder question, namely: which policy maximizes the probability to finish all jobs on time? (The alerted reader might argue that this question is somehow related to the biology case study, and indeed it is. The difference is that the biology example is fully deterministic, that is, in fact an instance of the above case in which there is only a single possible choice in every node of the decision tree.)

This stochastic job scheduling problem naturally gives rise to a *continuous-time Markov decision process* (CTMDP, for short)[3]. This model is a generalisation of CTMCs, the model used in the first case study, with non-determinism. In every state, an action (ranged over by α) is selected non-deterministically, see Fig. 8. In our setting, an action corresponds to a scheduling decision of which jobs to process next. The residence time in a state is exponentially distributed. The problem of determining the policy that maximizes the probability to finish all jobs within d time units now reduces to the following question: what is the maximal probability to reach the sink state within d time units? This can be solved by means of model checking using the following result.

Theorem 3. *[18] The following reachability problem is effectively computable:*

Input: a finite CTMDP, a target state, accuracy $0 < \epsilon < 1$, and deadline $d \in \mathbb{R}_{\geqslant 0}$
Output: an ϵ-approximation of the maximal (or dually, minimal) probability to reach the target in d time.

Importantly though is that as a by-product of determining this ϵ-approximation, one obtains an ϵ-optimal policy that yields this maximal probability (up to an accuracy of ϵ). The main complication of this timed reachability problem is that the optimal policies are time-dependent. This is an important difference with

---

[3] In fact, a locally uniform continuous-time Markov decision process [17].

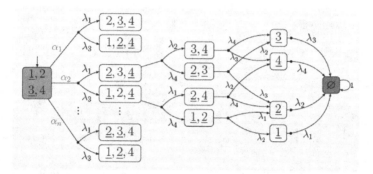

Fig. 8. Possible schedules for 4 jobs on 2 machines, modelled as a continuous-time Markov decision process

reachability questions for discrete-time Markov decision processes (MDPs) for which time-independent policies suffice, e.g., policies that in any state always take the same decision. The decisions of time-dependent policies may vary over time and may for instance depend on the remaining time until the deadline d. Their computation is done via a discretisation yielding an MDP on which a corresponding step-bounded reachability problem is solved using value iteration. The smallest number of steps needed in the discretised MDP to guarantee an accuracy of ϵ is $\frac{\lambda^2 \cdot d^2}{2\epsilon}$, where λ is the largest rate of a state residence time in the CTMDP at hand. In a similar way, minimal timed reachability probabilities can be obtained as well as their corresponding policies.

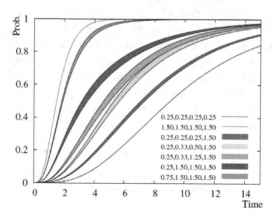

Fig. 9. Minimal and maximal reachability probabilities for finishing 4 jobs on 2 machines under a pre-emptive scheduling strategy

The results of applying this discretization on the example with 4 jobs and two machines is shown in Fig. 9 where the deadline d is given on the x-axis and the reachability probability on the y-axis. For equally distributed job durations, i.e., $\lambda_i = \lambda_j$ for all i, j, the maximal and minimal probabilities coincide. Otherwise, the probabilities depend on the scheduling policy. It turns out that the ϵ-optimal scheduler that maximizes the reachability probabilities adheres to the SEPT (shortest expected processing time first) strategy; moreover, the optimal ϵ-scheduler for the minimum probabilities obeys the LEPT strategy. These results have been obtained by a vanilla version of the model checker mrmc [12]. The case study is described in more detail in [16].

5   Concluding Remarks

By means of three examples from different application fields, we have attempted to argue that model checking is applicable to problems of a quite different nature than what is typically considered as verification problems. All problems have a quantitative flavor, i.e., non-functional aspects such as timing, randomness, and costs (energy) are essential to adequately model the applications at hand. We believe that there is an increased need for quantitative model checking as the importance of non-functional aspects is growing at staggering rate. We stress that in the last two examples we used model checking to *synthesize* an optimal schedule.

The battery example can certainly also be handled with existing techniques such as mixed integer linear programming. Dynamic programming techniques using Bellman equations can be used to tackle the stochastic planning example. The systems biology example can be handled using the chemical master equation or by Gillespie's simulation algorithm. Truly so. Our take-home message is not that model checking is the best and most efficient technique to tackle the described problems here; it is a valuable and interesting alternative that in some cases might be well competitive with existing traditional solution techniques. Model checking is on its way to become ubiquitous!

Acknowledgement. I thank all co-workers on the discussed case studies: Henrik Bohnenkamp, Boudewijn Haverkort, Marijn Jongerden, Daniel Klink, Alexandru Mereacre, Martin Neuhäusser, Martin Leucker, Verena Wolf, and Lijun Zhang. Part of this work has been established in the context of the EU FP7 QUASIMODO project, the NWO-DFG bilateral ROCKS project and the DFG Research Training Group ALGOSYN.

References

1. Alur, R., Torre, S.L., Pappas, G.J.: Optimal paths in weighted timed automata. Theor. Comput. Sci. 318(3), 297–322 (2004)
2. Baier, C., Katoen, J.-P.: Principles of Model Checking. MIT Press (2008)
3. Baier, C., Katoen, J.-P., Hermanns, H.: Approximate Symbolic Model Checking of Continuous-Time Markov Chains (Extended Abstract). In: Baeten, J.C.M., Mauw, S. (eds.) CONCUR 1999. LNCS, vol. 1664, pp. 146–161. Springer, Heidelberg (1999)

4. Behrmann, G., Fehnker, A., Hune, T., Larsen, K.G., Pettersson, P., Romijn, J., Vaandrager, F.W.: Minimum-Cost Reachability for Priced Timed Automata. In: Di Benedetto, M.D., Sangiovanni-Vincentelli, A.L. (eds.) HSCC 2001. LNCS, vol. 2034, pp. 147–161. Springer, Heidelberg (2001)
5. Bruno, J.L., Downey, P.J., Frederickson, G.N.: Sequencing tasks with exponential service times to minimize the expected flow time or makespan. J. ACM 28(1), 100–113 (1981)
6. Clarke, E.M., Grumberg, O., Peled, D.A.: Model Checking. MIT Press (1999)
7. Clarke, E.M., Schlingloff, H.: Model checking. In: Robinson, A., Voronkov, A. (eds.) Handbook of Automated Reasoning, vol. II, ch.24, pp. 1635–1790 (2000)
8. Grumberg, O., Veith, H. (eds.): 25 Years of Model Checking. LNCS, vol. 5000. Springer, Heidelberg (2008)
9. Jongerden, M.R., Haverkort, B.R., Bohnenkamp, H.C., Katoen, J.-P.: Maximizing System Lifetime by Battery Scheduling. In: 39th IEEE/IFIP Conf. on Dependable Systems and Networks (DSN), pp. 63–72. IEEE Computer Society (2009)
10. Jongerden, M.R., Mereacre, A., Bohnenkamp, H.C., Haverkort, B.R., Katoen, J.-P.: Computing optimal schedules for battery usage in embedded systems. IEEE Trans. Industrial Informatics 5(3), 276–286 (2010)
11. Katoen, J.-P., Klink, D., Leucker, M., Wolf, V.: Abstraction for Stochastic Systems by Erlang's Method of Stages. In: van Breugel, F., Chechik, M. (eds.) CONCUR 2008. LNCS, vol. 5201, pp. 279–294. Springer, Heidelberg (2008)
12. Katoen, J.-P., Zapreev, I.S., Hahn, E.M., Hermanns, H., Jansen, D.N.: The ins and outs of the probabilistic model checker MRMC. Perform. Eval. 68(2), 90–104 (2011)
13. Klink, D., Remke, A., Haverkort, B.R., Katoen, J.-P.: Time-bounded reachability in tree-structured QBDs by abstraction. Perform. Eval. 68(2), 105–125 (2011)
14. Kwiatkowska, M.Z., Norman, G., Parker, D.: PRISM: probabilistic model checking for performance and reliability analysis. SIGMETRICS Performance Evaluation Review 36(4), 40–45 (2009)
15. Manwell, J., McGowan, J.: Lead acid battery storage model for hybrid energy systems. Solar Energy 50(5), 399–405 (1993)
16. Neuhäußer, M.R.: Model Checking Nondeterministic and Randomly Timed Systems. PhD thesis, RWTH Aachen University and University of Twente (2010)
17. Neuhäußer, M.R., Stoelinga, M., Katoen, J.-P.: Delayed Nondeterminism in Continuous-Time Markov Decision Processes. In: de Alfaro, L. (ed.) FOSSACS 2009. LNCS, vol. 5504, pp. 364–379. Springer, Heidelberg (2009)
18. Neuhäußer, M.R., Zhang, L.: Time-bounded reachability probabilities in continuous-time Markov decision processes. In: 7th Int. Conf. on the Quantitative Evaluation of Systems (QEST), pp. 209–218. IEEE Computer Society (2010)
19. Nino-Mora, J.: Stochastic scheduling. In: Encyclopedia of Optimization, vol. V, pp. 367–372. Springer, Heidelberg (2001)

Proposition Algebra and Short-Circuit Logic

Jan A. Bergstra and Alban Ponse

Section Theory of Computer Science,
Informatics Institute, Faculty of Science,
University of Amsterdam, The Netherlands
www.science.uva.nl/{~janb/,~alban/}

Abstract. Short-circuit evaluation denotes the semantics of propositional connectives in which the second argument is only evaluated if the first argument does not suffice to determine the value of the expression. In programming, short-circuit evaluation is widely used.

We review proposition algebra [2010], an algebraic approach to propositional logic with side effects that models short-circuit evaluation. Proposition algebra is based on Hoare's conditional [1985], which is a ternary connective comparable to if-then-else. Starting from McCarthy's notion of sequential evaluation [1963] we discuss a number of valuation congruences on propositional statements and we introduce Hoare-McCarthy algebras as the structures that model these congruences. We also briefly discuss the associated short-circuit logics, i.e., the logics that define these congruences if one restricts to sequential binary connectives.

Keywords: Conditional composition, reactive valuation, sequential connective, short-circuit evaluation, side effect.

1 Introduction

Short-circuit evaluation is a folk term[1] that describes how the common propositional connectives are evaluated in a setting of programming languages: evaluation stops as soon as the value T (*true*) or F (*false*) of the expression is determined. In particular, the "conjunction" of x and y in a notation commonly used to prescribe short-circuit evaluation, is often explained by the identity

$$\text{x \&\& y} = \text{if x then y else } F,$$

and the connective *or* in short-circuit interpretation, notation || , is then explained by the identity

$$\text{x || y} = \text{if x then } T \text{ else y.}$$

So, evaluation of x && y stops if x yields F and then y is not evaluated, and similarly, evaluation of x || y stops if x yields T and then y is not evaluated. In the most general case, both && and || are not commutative.

---

[1] Other names used for short-circuit evaluation are *Minimal evaluation* and *McCarthy evaluation*.

F. Arbab and M. Sirjani (Eds.): FSEN 2011, LNCS 7141, pp. 15–31, 2012.

Following this lay-out, the evaluation of a "conditional expression" is considered a natural candidate for short-circuit evaluation, and hence justifies our choice for Hoare's ternary connective

$$x \triangleleft y \triangleright z,$$

i.e., the *conditional* connective that represents if y then x else z, as a basic connective. Hoare's conditional connective is introduced in 1985 in the paper [9] (accounts of a similar ternary connective can be found in [7, 8]). So,

$$x \ \&\& \ y = y \triangleleft x \triangleright F \quad \text{and} \quad x \ || \ y = T \triangleleft x \triangleright y. \tag{1}$$

The conditional connective satisfies the three equational laws

$$x \triangleleft T \triangleright y = x, \quad x \triangleleft F \triangleright y = y \quad \text{and} \quad T \triangleleft x \triangleright F = x. \tag{2}$$

Interestingly, in the most general case the conditional connective cannot be defined in terms of the common binary connectives, where by "most general" we refer to a semantics in which all possible "side effects" can occur, and thus a semantics that identifies least. As an example, in many imperative-based programming languages, assignments such as x=x+1 when interpreted as atoms (i.e., atomic propositions) yield upon evaluation the interpretation of the assigned value next to having the intended side effect. It is trivial to find a propositional statement P such that $P \neq P \triangleleft (\text{x=x+1}) \triangleright F$, or equivalently, $P \neq (\text{x=x+1}) \ \&\& \ P$, e.g.,

$$(\text{x==2}) \neq (\text{x==2}) \triangleleft (\text{x=x+1}) \triangleright F$$

if the initial value of x is either 1 or 2, == is interpreted as an equality test, and the interpretation of values different from zero is T. However, the three laws for the conditional (2) are valid in this most general case.

In case side effects do *not* occur, the conditional can be defined:[2] using the common notation for connectives, a definition is

$$y \triangleleft x \triangleright z = (x \wedge y) \vee (\neg x \wedge z),$$

which is easily seen by substituting T respectively F for x. An example in a setting *with* side effects that refutes this translation is

$$(\text{y==2}) \triangleleft ((\text{x=x+1}) \wedge (\text{x==2})) \triangleright (\text{y=y+1}).$$

This follows easily: if both x and y have initial value 1, the interpretation of this conditional expression yields F with the side effect that x has final value 2, while the above-mentioned translation yields T with the side effect that the final value of x is 3 and the final value of y is 2 (note that this argument holds irrespective of the question whether $\wedge$ is interpreted as a short-circuit operator).

---

[2] This is the semantical setting in Hoare's paper [9], where the conditional was introduced to provide an equational basis for propositional logic.

A way to settle whether side effects have impact, and if so, to what extent, is to distinguish various types of *valuation semantics*. Typically, and illustrated by the above examples, a valuation may return different values for the same atom during the sequential evaluation of a propositional statement (a closed term), and valuation semantics is about such reactive valuations. We adopt the conditional connective as a primitive connective and both T and F as constants. A *proposition algebra* is a model of the three axioms mentioned in (2) and an axiom for decomposing a compound central condition c in $x \lhd c \rhd z$. By adding more axioms, more propositional statements are identified, and all proposition algebras we consider are defined by concise equational axiomatizations. Given some proposition algebra, a valuation semantics can be defined that is constructed from so-called valuation functions, that is, functions defined on sequences of atoms that return either T or F. Propositional statements are identified if they yield in each context for each valuation function the same result. This context requirement refers to the fact that upon the evaluation of an atom that yields a side effect, the valuation value of future atoms in the propositional statement under evaluation is possibly flipped, as is clear from the previous examples.

Concerning conjunction and disjunction, we will consider *sequential* versions of these connectives that by their notation prescribe short-circuit evaluation and that are defined with the conditional (cf. the equations in (1)). Also, negation can be easily defined in terms of the conditional:

$$\neg x = F \lhd x \rhd T.$$

Given some axiomatization of a proposition algebra, a *short-circuit logic* is a logic that implies all consequences that can be expressed using only binary sequential conjunction, negation and the constant T. Typical examples are the associativity of sequential conjunction and the double negation shift $\neg \neg x = x$.

In this paper we present a survey of our work based on proposition algebra [4]. In the next section we briefly discuss so-called *Hoare-McCarthy algebras* (HMAs). HMAs were introduced in [6] in order to provide a more elegant and generic framework for the valuation semantics associated with proposition algebra (we return to this point in Section 7). We construct an HMA that identifies least and characterizes *structural congruence*. In Section 3 we consider the short-circuit logic that is associated with structural congruence (short-circuit logics were introduced in [5]). Section 4 is about *contractive congruence*, a congruence that identifies more propositional statements than structural congruence. We construct a characterizing HMA and we briefly consider the short-circuit logic associated with contractive congruence. In Section 5 we discuss *memorizing congruence*, a congruence that identifies more than contractive congruence and less than propositional logic, and we argue that the associated short-circuit logic also defines this congruence because the conditional is definable in this setting (whereas it is not in contractive congruence, see Section 7). In Section 6 we consider *static congruence* and its short-circuit logic; apart from the notation, this is the setting of conventional propositional logic and no side effects are possible. In Section 7 we end the paper with a brief summary and discussion about our work described in [4–6].

Table 1. The set CP of axioms for proposition algebra

$$x \triangleleft T \triangleright y = x \qquad \text{(CP1)}$$

$$x \triangleleft F \triangleright y = y \qquad \text{(CP2)}$$

$$T \triangleleft x \triangleright F = x \qquad \text{(CP3)}$$

$$x \triangleleft (y \triangleleft z \triangleright u) \triangleright v = (x \triangleleft y \triangleright v) \triangleleft z \triangleright (x \triangleleft u \triangleright v) \qquad \text{(CP4)}$$

2 Proposition Algebras and HMAs

In this section we define proposition algebras, and in order to capture their valuation semantics we briefly discuss *Hoare-McCarthy algebras*, a certain type of two-sorted algebras that we introduced in [6].

Throughout this paper let A be a non-empty, denumerable set of atoms (atomic propositions) with typical elements $a, b, \ldots$. Define C as the sort of conditional expressions with signature

$$\Sigma_{ce}^{A} = \{a : C, \ T : C, \ F : C, \ . \triangleleft . \triangleright . : C \times C \times C \to C \mid a \in A\},$$

thus each atom in A is a constant of sort C. In Σ_{ce}^{A}, ce stands for "conditional expressions". We write $\mathcal{T}_{\Sigma_{ce}^{A}}$ for the set of closed terms over Σ_{ce}^{A}. Given an expression $t_1 \triangleleft t_2 \triangleright t_3$ we will sometimes refer to t_2 as the *central condition*. We assume that conditional composition satisfies the axioms in Table 1 and we refer to this set of axioms with CP (Conditional Propositions). Axiom (CP4) also stems from [9] and defines decomposition of the central condition by distributivity. We argue in Section 3 that CP characterizes all valid identities in the case that unrestricted side effects occur.

Definition 1. *A Σ_{ce}^{A}-algebra is a **proposition algebra** if it is a model of* CP.

A non-trivial initial algebra $I(\Sigma_{ce}^{A}, \text{CP})$ exists. This can be easily shown in the setting of term rewriting [12]. It is not hard to show that directing all CP-axioms from left to right yields a strongly normalizing TRS (term rewriting system) for closed terms. However, the normal forms resulting from this TRS are not particularly suitable for systematic reasoning, and we introduce another class of closed terms for this purpose.

Definition 2. *A term $t \in \mathcal{T}_{\Sigma_{ce}^{A}}$ is a **basic form** if for $a \in A$,*

$$t ::= T \mid F \mid t \triangleleft a \triangleright t.$$

Lemma 1. *For each closed term $t \in \mathcal{T}_{\Sigma_{ce}^{A}}$ there exists a unique basic form t' with* CP $\vdash t = t'$.

Proof. Let t'' be the unique normal form of t. Replace in t'' each subterm that is a single atom a and occurs as an outer argument by $T \triangleleft a \triangleright F$. This results in a unique basic form t' and clearly CP $\vdash t = t'$. $\qquad\square$

Let S be a sort of states with constant c. We extend the signature Σ_{ce}^A to

$$\Sigma_{sce}^A = \Sigma_{ce}^A \cup \{c : S, \ .\triangleleft.\triangleright. : S \times C \times S \to S\},$$

where sce stands for "states and conditional expressions".

Definition 3. *A Σ_{sce}^A-algebra is a **two-sorted proposition algebra** if its Σ_{ce}^A-reduct is a proposition algebra, and if it satisfies the following axioms where x ranges over conditional expressions and s, s' range over states:*

$$s \triangleleft T \triangleright s' = s, \tag{TS1}$$

$$s \triangleleft F \triangleright s' = s', \tag{TS2}$$

$$x \neq T \wedge x \neq F \to s \triangleleft x \triangleright s' = c. \tag{TS3}$$

So, the state set of a two-sorted proposition algebra can be seen as one that is equipped with an if-then-else construct and conditions that stem from CP. We extend the signature Σ_{sce}^A to

$$\Sigma_{spa}^A = \Sigma_{sce}^A \cup \{\,!\, : C \times S \to S, \ \bullet : C \times S \to C\},$$

where spa stands for "stateful proposition algebra" (see below). The operator $!$ is called "reply" and the operator $\bullet$ is called "apply" and we further assume that these operators bind stronger than conditional composition. The reply and apply operator are taken from [3].

Definition 4. *A Σ_{spa}^A-algebra is a **stateful proposition algebra**, SPA for short, if its reduct to Σ_{sce}^A is a two-sorted proposition algebra, and if it satisfies the following axioms where x, y, z range over conditional expressions and s ranges over states:*

$$T\,!\,s = T, \tag{SPA1}$$

$$F\,!\,s = F, \tag{SPA2}$$

$$(x \triangleleft y \triangleright z)\,!\,s = x\,!\,(y \bullet s) \triangleleft y\,!\,s \triangleright z\,!\,(y \bullet s), \tag{SPA3}$$

$$T \bullet s = s, \tag{SPA4}$$

$$F \bullet s = s, \tag{SPA5}$$

$$(x \triangleleft y \triangleright z) \bullet s = x \bullet (y \bullet s) \triangleleft y\,!\,s \triangleright z \bullet (y \bullet s), \tag{SPA6}$$

$$x\,!\,s = T \vee x\,!\,s = F, \tag{SPA7}$$

$$\forall s(x\,!\,s = y\,!\,s \wedge x \bullet s = y \bullet s) \to x = y. \tag{SPA8}$$

*We refer to (SPA7) as **two-valuedness** and we write CTS (abbreviating CP and TS and SPA) for the set that exactly contains all fifteen axioms involved.*

In a stateful proposition algebra $\mathbb{S}$ with domain C' of conditional expressions and domain S' of states, a propositional statement $t \in \mathcal{T}_{\Sigma_{ce}^A}$ can be associated with a 'valuation function' $t\,! \, : S' \to \{T, F\}$ (the evaluation of t according to some initial valuation function or 'state') and a 'state transformer' $t \bullet : S' \to S'$.

Definition 5. *A **Hoare-McCarthy algebra**, HMA for short, is the Σ_{ce}^A-reduct of a stateful proposition algebra.*

For each HMA $\mathbb{A}$ we have by definition $\mathbb{A} \models CP$. In Theorem 1 below we prove the existence of an HMA that characterizes CP in the sense that a closed equation is valid only if it is derivable from CP.

We define *structural congruence*, notation $=_{sc}$, on $\mathcal{T}_{\Sigma_{ce}^A}$ as the congruence generated by CP.

Theorem 1. *An HMA that characterizes CP exists: there is an HMA $\mathbb{A}^{sc}$ such that for all $t, t' \in \mathcal{T}_{\Sigma_{ce}^A}$, $CP \vdash t = t' \iff \mathbb{A}^{sc} \models t = t'$.*

Proof. We construct the Σ_{spa}^A-algebra $\mathbb{S}^{sc}$ with $C' = \mathcal{T}_{\Sigma_{ce}^A}/_{=sc}$ as its set of conditional expressions and, writing A^+ for the set of finite, non-empty strings over the set A of atoms, the function space

$$S' = \{T, F\}^{A^+}$$

as its set of states. For each state f and atom $a \in A$ define $a\,!\,f = f(a)$ and $a \bullet f$ as the function defined for $\sigma \in A^+$ by

$$(a \bullet f)(\sigma) = f(a\sigma).$$

The state constant c is given an arbitrary interpretation, and the axioms (TS1)–(TS3) define $.\lhd.\rhd. : S' \times C' \times S'$ in $\mathbb{S}^{sc}$. The axioms (SPA1)–(SPA6) fully determine the functions $!$ and $\bullet$, and this is well-defined: if $t =_{sc} t'$ then for all f, $t\,!\,f = t'\,!\,f$ and $t \bullet f = t' \bullet f$ (this follows by inspection of the CP axioms). The axiom (SPA7) holds by construction of S'. In order to prove that $\mathbb{S}^{sc}$ is a SPA it remains to be shown that axiom (SPA8) holds, i.e., for all $t, t' \in \mathcal{T}_{\Sigma_{ce}^A}$,

$$\forall f(t\,!\,f = t'\,!\,f \wedge t \bullet f = t' \bullet f) \to t =_{sc} t'.$$

This follows by contraposition. By Lemma 1 we may assume that t and t' are basic forms, and we apply induction on the complexity of t, where we use $\equiv$ to denote syntactic equivalence:

1. Suppose $t \equiv T$, then $t' \equiv F$ yields $t\,!\,f \neq t'\,!\,f$ for any f, and if $t' \equiv t_1 \lhd a \rhd t_2$ then consider f with $f(a) = T$ and $f(a\sigma) = F$ for $\sigma \in A^+$. We find $t \bullet f = f$ and $t' \bullet f \neq f$ because $(t' \bullet f)(a) = (t_1 \bullet f)(a\sigma) = F$.
2. If $t \equiv F$ a similar argument applies.
3. Suppose $t \equiv t_1 \lhd a \rhd t_2$, then the cases $t' \in \{T, F\}$ can be dealt with as above.
   If $t' \equiv t_3 \lhd a \rhd t_4$ then assume $t_1 \lhd a \rhd t_2 \neq_{sc} t_3 \lhd a \rhd t_4$ because $t_1 \neq_{sc} t_3$. By induction there exists f with $t_1 \bullet f \neq t_3 \bullet f$ or $t_1\,!\,f \neq t_3\,!\,f$. Take some g such that $a \bullet g = f$ and $a\,!\,g = T$, then g distinguishes $t_1 \lhd a \rhd t_2$ and $t_3 \lhd a \rhd t_4$.
   If $t_1 =_{sc} t_3$, then a similar argument applies for $t_2 \neq_{sc} t_4$.
   If $t' \equiv t_3 \lhd b \rhd t_4$ with a and b different, then $(t_1 \lhd a \rhd t_2) \bullet f \neq (t_3 \lhd b \rhd t_4) \bullet f$ for f defined by $f(a) = f(a\sigma) = T$ and $f(b) = f(b\sigma) = F$ because $((t_1 \lhd a \rhd t_2) \bullet f)(a) = (t_1 \bullet (a \bullet f))(a) = f(a\rho a) = T$, and $((t_3 \lhd b \rhd t_4) \bullet f)(a) = (t_4 \bullet (b \bullet f))(a) = f(b\rho' a) = F$ (where ρ, ρ' possibly equal the empty string).

So $\mathbb{S}^{sc}$ is a SPA. Define the HMA $\mathbb{A}^{sc}$ as the Σ_{ce}^{A}-reduct of $\mathbb{S}^{sc}$. The validity of axiom (SPA8) proves $\Longleftarrow$ as stated in the theorem (the implication $\Longrightarrow$ holds by definition of a SPA). $\square$

Observe that $\mathbb{A}^{sc} \cong I(\Sigma_{ce}^{A}, \text{CP})$ and that by the proof of the above theorem we find for all $t, t' \in \mathcal{T}_{\Sigma_{ce}^{A}}$,

$$\text{CP} \vdash t = t' \iff \mathbb{S}^{sc} \models t = t'.$$

In [10] it is shown that the axioms of CP are independent, and also that they are ω-complete if the set of atoms involved contains at least two elements.

3 Free Short-Circuit Logic: FSCL

In this section we recall our generic definition of a short-circuit logic introduced in [5] and discuss *free short-circuit logic* (FSCL), the least identifying short-circuit logic we consider and that is associated with CP.

We first return to our discussion of short-circuit evaluation started in the Introduction. Our interest can be captured by the following question: Given some programming language, what is the logic that implies the equivalence of conditions, notably in if-then-else and while-do constructs and the like? In [5] we study sequential variants of propositional logic that are based on *left-sequential conjunction*, i.e., conjunction that prescribes short-circuit evaluation and that is defined by

$$x \mathbin{\mathop{\wedge}\limits^{\circ}} y = y \triangleleft x \triangleright F$$

where the fresh symbol $\mathbin{\mathop{\wedge}\limits^{\circ}}$ is taken from [1] (the small circle indicates that the left argument must be evaluated first). It is not hard to find examples that show that the laws $x \mathbin{\mathop{\wedge}\limits^{\circ}} x$ and its weaker version $a \mathbin{\mathop{\wedge}\limits^{\circ}} a = a$ are not valid in the most general case (cf. the examples discussed in the Introduction), which is the case characterized by CP. We define a set of equations that is sound in FSCL and raise the question of its completeness.

We define short-circuit logics such as FSCL in a generic way. Intuitively, a short-circuit logic is a logic that implies all consequences of CP that can be expressed in the signature $\{T, \neg, \mathbin{\mathop{\wedge}\limits^{\circ}}\}$. The definition below uses the export-operator $\square$ of module algebra [2] to define this in a precise manner, where it is assumed that CP satisfies the format of a module specification. In module algebra, $\Sigma \square X$ is the operation that exports the signature Σ from module X while declaring other signature elements hidden. In this case it declares conditional composition to be an auxiliary operator.

Definition 6. *A **short-circuit logic** is a logic that implies the consequences of the module expression*

$$\text{SCL} = \{T, \neg, \mathbin{\mathop{\wedge}\limits^{\circ}}\} \ \square \ (\text{CP} + \langle \neg x = F \triangleleft x \triangleright T \rangle + \langle x \mathbin{\mathop{\wedge}\limits^{\circ}} y = y \triangleleft x \triangleright F \rangle).$$

For example, $\text{SCL} \vdash \neg\neg x = x$ can be easily shown. Following Definition 6, the most basic (least identifying) short-circuit logic we distinguish is this one:

Table 2. EqFSCL, a set of equations for FSCL

$$F = \neg T \tag{SCL1}$$

$$x \mathbin{\vphantom{V}^{\text{\tiny Q}}\mkern-4mu\vee} y = \neg(\neg x \mathbin{\wedge\mkern-11mu{\diagup}} \neg y) \tag{SCL2}$$

$$\neg\neg x = x \tag{SCL3}$$

$$T \mathbin{\wedge\mkern-11mu{\diagup}} x = x \tag{SCL4}$$

$$x \mathbin{\wedge\mkern-11mu{\diagup}} T = x \tag{SCL5}$$

$$F \mathbin{\wedge\mkern-11mu{\diagup}} x = F \tag{SCL6}$$

$$(x \mathbin{\wedge\mkern-11mu{\diagup}} y) \mathbin{\wedge\mkern-11mu{\diagup}} z = x \mathbin{\wedge\mkern-11mu{\diagup}} (y \mathbin{\wedge\mkern-11mu{\diagup}} z) \tag{SCL7}$$

$$(x \mathbin{\vphantom{V}^{\text{\tiny Q}}\mkern-4mu\vee} y) \mathbin{\wedge\mkern-11mu{\diagup}} (z \mathbin{\wedge\mkern-11mu{\diagup}} F) = (\neg x \mathbin{\vphantom{V}^{\text{\tiny Q}}\mkern-4mu\vee} (z \mathbin{\wedge\mkern-11mu{\diagup}} F)) \mathbin{\wedge\mkern-11mu{\diagup}} (y \mathbin{\wedge\mkern-11mu{\diagup}} (z \mathbin{\wedge\mkern-11mu{\diagup}} F)) \tag{SCL8}$$

$$(x \mathbin{\vphantom{V}^{\text{\tiny Q}}\mkern-4mu\vee} y) \mathbin{\wedge\mkern-11mu{\diagup}} (z \mathbin{\vphantom{V}^{\text{\tiny Q}}\mkern-4mu\vee} T) = (x \mathbin{\wedge\mkern-11mu{\diagup}} (z \mathbin{\vphantom{V}^{\text{\tiny Q}}\mkern-4mu\vee} T)) \mathbin{\vphantom{V}^{\text{\tiny Q}}\mkern-4mu\vee} (y \mathbin{\wedge\mkern-11mu{\diagup}} (z \mathbin{\vphantom{V}^{\text{\tiny Q}}\mkern-4mu\vee} T)) \tag{SCL9}$$

$$((x \mathbin{\wedge\mkern-11mu{\diagup}} F) \mathbin{\vphantom{V}^{\text{\tiny Q}}\mkern-4mu\vee} y) \mathbin{\wedge\mkern-11mu{\diagup}} z = (x \mathbin{\wedge\mkern-11mu{\diagup}} F) \mathbin{\vphantom{V}^{\text{\tiny Q}}\mkern-4mu\vee} (y \mathbin{\wedge\mkern-11mu{\diagup}} z) \tag{SCL10}$$

Definition 7. FSCL *(free short-circuit logic) is the short-circuit logic that implies no other consequences than those of the module expression* SCL.

Although the constant F does not occur in the exported signature of SCL, we discuss FSCL using this constant to enhance readability. This is not problematic because

$$\text{CP} + \langle\, \neg x = F \mathbin{\vartriangleleft} x \mathbin{\vartriangleright} T \,\rangle \vdash F = \neg T,$$

so F can be used as a shorthand for $\neg T$ in FSCL.

In Table 2 we provide equations for FSCL and we use the name EqFSCL for this set of equations. Some comments: equation (SCL1) defines the constant F, and equation (SCL2) defines $\mathbin{\vphantom{V}^{\text{\tiny Q}}\mkern-4mu\vee}$, so-called *left-sequential disjunction*. Equations (SCL3) − (SCL7) need no comment. Equation (SCL8) defines a property of the mix of negation and the sequential connectives, and its soundness can perhaps be easily grasped by considering the evaluation values of x (observe that $z \mathbin{\wedge\mkern-11mu{\diagup}} F = (z \mathbin{\wedge\mkern-11mu{\diagup}} F) \mathbin{\wedge\mkern-11mu{\diagup}} ...$). Equation (SCL9) defines a restricted form of right-distributivity of $\mathbin{\wedge\mkern-11mu{\diagup}}$, and so does equation (SCL10) (because $(x \mathbin{\wedge\mkern-11mu{\diagup}} F) \mathbin{\wedge\mkern-11mu{\diagup}} z = x \mathbin{\wedge\mkern-11mu{\diagup}} F$).

We note that equations (SCL2) and (SCL3) imply sequential versions of De Morgan's laws, which allows us to use sequential versions of the duality principle. Furthermore, we note that the equation $x \mathbin{\wedge\mkern-11mu{\diagup}} F = F$ should not be a consequence of EqFSCL: it is easily seen that $\mathbb{A}^{sc} \not\models F \mathbin{\vartriangleleft} a \mathbin{\vartriangleright} F = F$ (see Theorem 1). A simple consequence of equation (SCL8) is

$$x \mathbin{\wedge\mkern-11mu{\diagup}} F = \neg x \mathbin{\wedge\mkern-11mu{\diagup}} F \tag{SCL8*}$$

(take $y = z = F$), which we will use in Section 5, and another interesting EqFSCL-consequence is $(x \mathbin{\vphantom{V}^{\text{\tiny Q}}\mkern-4mu\vee} T) \mathbin{\wedge\mkern-11mu{\diagup}} y = (x \mathbin{\wedge\mkern-11mu{\diagup}} F) \mathbin{\vphantom{V}^{\text{\tiny Q}}\mkern-4mu\vee} y$ (for a proof see [5]).

Proposition 1 (Soundness). *The equations in EqFSCL (see Table 2) are derivable in FSCL.*

While not having found any equations that are derivable in FSCL but not from EqFSCL, we failed to prove completeness of EqFSCL in the following sense (of course, $\Longrightarrow$ follows from Proposition 1):

$$\text{For all SCL-terms } t \text{ and } t', \quad \text{EqFSCL} \vdash t = t' \iff \text{FSCL} \vdash t = t'. \quad (3)$$

4   Contractive Congruence

In this section we consider the congruence defined by the axioms of CP and these axiom schemes ($a \in A$):

$$(x \lhd a \rhd y) \lhd a \rhd z = x \lhd a \rhd z, \quad (\text{CPcr1})$$

$$x \lhd a \rhd (y \lhd a \rhd z) = x \lhd a \rhd z. \quad (\text{CPcr2})$$

Following [4], we write CP_{cr} for this set of axioms. Typically, successive equal atoms are contracted according to the axiom schemes (CPcr1) and (CPcr2).

Let *contractive congruence*, notation $=_{cr}$, be the congruence on $\mathcal{T}_{\Sigma^A_{ce}}$ generated by the axioms of CP_{cr}.

Definition 8. *A term $t \in \mathcal{T}_{\Sigma^A_{ce}}$ is a **cr-basic form** if for $a \in A$,*

$$t ::= T \mid F \mid t_1 \lhd a \rhd t_2$$

and t_i ($i = 1, 2$) is a cr-basic form with the restriction that the central condition (if present) is different from a.

Lemma 2. *For each $t \in \mathcal{T}_{\Sigma^A_{ce}}$ there exists a cr-basic form t' with $\text{CP}_{cr} \vdash t = t'$.*

Proof. By structural induction; see [4] for a full proof. $\square$

Theorem 2. *For $|A| > 1$, an HMA that characterizes CP_{cr} exists, i.e. there is an HMA $\mathbb{A}^{cr}$ such that for all $t, t' \in \mathcal{T}_{\Sigma^A_{ce}}$, $\quad \text{CP}_{cr} \vdash t = t' \iff \mathbb{A}^{cr} \models t = t'$.*

Proof. Let $A^{cr} \subset A^+$ be the set of strings that contain no consecutive occurrences of the same atom. Construct the Σ^A_{spa}-algebra $\mathbb{S}^{cr}$ with $\mathcal{T}_{\Sigma^A_{ce}}/{=_{cr}}$ as its set of conditional expressions and the function space

$$S' = \{T, F\}^{A^{cr}}$$

as its set of states. For each state f and atom $a \in A$ define $a \,!\, f = f(a)$ and $a \bullet f$ by

$$(a \bullet f)(\sigma) = \begin{cases} f(\sigma) & \text{if } \sigma = a \text{ or } \sigma = a\rho, \\ f(a\sigma) & \text{otherwise.} \end{cases}$$

Clearly, $a \bullet f \in \{T, F\}^{A^{cr}}$ if $f \in \{T, F\}^{A^{cr}}$. Similar as in the proof of Theorem 1, the state constant c is given an arbitrary interpretation, and the axioms (TS1)–(TS3) define the function $s \lhd f \rhd s'$ in $\mathbb{S}^{cr}$. The axioms (SPA1)–(SPA6) fully determine the functions $!$ and $\bullet$, and this is well-defined: if $t =_{cr} t'$ then for all

$f, t \,!\, f = t' \,!\, f$ and $t \bullet f = t' \bullet f$ follow by inspection of the CP_{cr} axioms. We show soundness of the axiom scheme (CPcr1): note that $a \,!\, (a \bullet f) = a \,!\, f$ and $a \bullet (a \bullet f) = a \bullet f$, and derive

$$((t_1 \lhd a \rhd t_2) \lhd a \rhd t) \,!\, f = (t_1 \lhd a \rhd t_2) \,!\, (a \bullet f) \lhd a \,!\, f \rhd t \,!\, (a \bullet f)$$
$$= t_1 \,!\, (a \bullet (a \bullet f)) \lhd a \,!\, f \rhd t \,!\, (a \bullet f)$$
$$= (t_1 \lhd a \rhd t) \,!\, f,$$

and

$$((t_1 \lhd a \rhd t_2) \lhd a \rhd t) \bullet f = (t_1 \lhd a \rhd t_2) \bullet (a \bullet f) \lhd a \,!\, f \rhd t \bullet (a \bullet f)$$
$$= t_1 \bullet (a \bullet (a \bullet f)) \lhd a \,!\, f \rhd t \bullet (a \bullet f)$$
$$= (t_1 \lhd a \rhd t) \bullet f.$$

The soundness of (CPcr2) follows in a similar way. The axiom (SPA7) holds by construction of S'. In order to prove that $\mathbb{S}^{cr}$ is a SPA it remains to be shown that axiom (SPA8) holds. This follows by contraposition: by Lemma 2 we may assume that both t and t' are cr-basic forms, and apply induction on the complexity of t (for a detailed proof of this, see [6]). Now define the HMA $\mathbb{A}^{cr}$ as the Σ_{ce}^A-reduct of $\mathbb{S}^{cr}$. The above argument on the soundness of the axiom schemes (CPcr1) and (CPcr2) proves $\Longrightarrow$ as stated in the theorem, and the validity of axiom (SPA8) proves $\Longleftarrow$. Finally, note that $\mathbb{A}^{cr} \cong I(\Sigma_{ce}^A, \mathrm{CP}_{cr})$. □

In the proof above we defined the SPA $\mathbb{S}^{cr}$ and we found that if $|A| > 1$, then for all $t, t' \in \mathcal{T}_{\Sigma_{ce}^A}$,

$$\mathrm{CP}_{cr} \vdash t = t' \iff \mathbb{S}^{cr} \models t = t'. \tag{4}$$

If $A = \{a\}$ then $A^{cr} = A$ and $\mathbb{S}^{cr}$ as defined above has only two states, say f and g with $f(a) = T$ and $g(a) = F$. It easily follows that

$$\mathbb{A}^{cr} \models T \lhd a \rhd T = T,$$

so $\mathbb{A}^{cr} \not\cong I(\Sigma_{ce}^A, \mathrm{CP}_{cr})$ if $A = \{a\}$. The following corollary is related to Theorem 2 and characterizes contractive congruence in terms of a quasivariety of SPAs that satisfy an extra condition.

Corollary 1. *Let $|A| > 1$. Let $\mathcal{C}_{cr}$ be the class of SPAs that satisfy for all $a \in A$ and $s \in S$,*

$$a \,!\, (a \bullet s) = a \,!\, s \,\wedge\, a \bullet (a \bullet s) = a \bullet s.$$

Then for all $t, t' \in \mathcal{T}_{\Sigma_{ce}^A}$, $\mathcal{C}_{cr} \models t = t' \iff \mathrm{CP}_{cr} \vdash t = t'.$

Proof. By its definition, $\mathbb{S}^{cr} \in \mathcal{C}_{cr}$, which by (4) implies $\Longrightarrow$. For the converse, it is sufficient to show that the axioms (CPcr1) and (CPcr2) hold in any SPA that is in $\mathcal{C}_{cr}$. Let such $\mathbb{S}$ be given. Consider (CPcr1): if for an interpretation of s in $\mathbb{S}$, $a \,!\, s = F$ the proof is trivial, and if $a \,!\, s = T$, then $a \,!\, (a \bullet s) = T$ and thus

$$((t_1 \lhd a \rhd t_2) \lhd a \rhd t) \,!\, s = t_1 \,!\, (a \bullet (a \bullet s))$$
$$= t_1 \,!\, (a \bullet s)$$
$$= (t_1 \lhd a \rhd t) \,!\, s,$$

and $((t_1 \lhd a \rhd t_2) \lhd a \rhd t) \bullet s = (t_1 \lhd a \rhd t) \bullet s$ can be proved in a similar way. □

Finally, we briefly discuss a variant of short-circuit logic that is based on CP_{cr}. We write $\mathrm{CP}_{cr}(A)$ to denote CP_{cr} in a notation close to module algebra [2].

Definition 9. CSCL *(Contractive Short-Circuit Logic)* is the short-circuit logic that implies no other consequences than those of the module expression

$$\{T, \neg, \wedge\!\!\!\wedge, a \mid a \in A\} \; \square \; (\mathrm{CP}_{cr}(A) + \langle\, \neg x = F \triangleleft x \triangleright T \,\rangle + \langle\, x \wedge\!\!\!\wedge y = y \triangleleft x \triangleright F \,\rangle).$$

The equations defined by CSCL include those derivable from EqFSCL, and

$$a \wedge\!\!\!\wedge (a \vee\!\!\!\vee x) = a,$$
$$a \vee\!\!\!\vee (a \wedge\!\!\!\wedge x) = a.$$

It is an open question whether the extension of EqFSCL with these two equations yields an axiomatization of CSCL. Observe that the following equations are consequences in CSCL:

$$a \wedge\!\!\!\wedge a = a, \qquad\qquad\qquad a \vee\!\!\!\vee a = a,$$
$$\neg a \wedge\!\!\!\wedge (\neg a \vee\!\!\!\vee x) = \neg a, \qquad \neg a \vee\!\!\!\vee (\neg a \wedge\!\!\!\wedge x) = \neg a,$$
$$\neg a \wedge\!\!\!\wedge \neg a = \neg a, \qquad\qquad \neg a \vee\!\!\!\vee \neg a = \neg a.$$

An example that illustrates the use of CSCL concerns atoms that define manipulation of Boolean registers:

- Consider atoms $\mathtt{set}{:}i{:}j$ and $\mathtt{eq}{:}i{:}j$ with $i \in \{1, ..., n\}$ (the number of registers) and $j \in \{T, F\}$ (the value of registers).
- An atom $\mathtt{set}{:}i{:}j$ can have a side effect (it sets register i to value j) and yields upon evaluation always T.
- An atom $\mathtt{eq}{:}i{:}j$ has no side effect but yields upon evaluation only T if register i has value j.

Clearly, the CSCL-consequences mentioned above are valid in the setting of this example, but $x \wedge\!\!\!\wedge x = x$ is not: assume register 1 has value F and let $t = \mathtt{eq}{:}1{:}F \wedge\!\!\!\wedge \mathtt{set}{:}1{:}T$. Then t yields T upon evaluation in this state, while $t \wedge\!\!\!\wedge t$ yields F.

5   Memorizing Congruence

In this section we consider the congruence defined by the axioms of CP and this axiom:

$$x \triangleleft y \triangleright (z \triangleleft u \triangleright (v \triangleleft y \triangleright w)) = x \triangleleft y \triangleright (z \triangleleft u \triangleright w). \qquad \text{(CPmem)}$$

Following [4], we write CP_{mem} for this set of axioms. Axiom (CPmem) defines how the central condition y may recur in a propositional statement, and defines a general form of contraction: with $u = F$ we find

$$x \triangleleft y \triangleright (v \triangleleft y \triangleright w) = x \triangleleft y \triangleright w. \qquad (5)$$

The symmetric variants of (CPmem) and (5) all follow easily with $y \lhd x \rhd z = (z \lhd F \rhd y) \lhd x \rhd (z \lhd T \rhd y) = z \lhd (F \lhd x \rhd T) \rhd y$ (which is a CP-derivation), e.g.,

$$(x \lhd y \rhd (z \lhd u \rhd v)) \lhd u \rhd w = (x \lhd y \rhd z) \lhd u \rhd w. \tag{6}$$

Let *memorizing congruence*, notation $=_{mem}$, be the congruence on $\mathcal{T}_{\Sigma_{ce}^A}$ generated by the axioms of CP_{mem}. As in the preceding cases, a special type of basic forms can be used to construct a SPA $\mathbb{S}^{mem}$ that defines the HMA $\mathbb{A}^{mem}$, which in turn characterizes $=_{mem}$ (for closed terms). Because this construction is quite involved, we here only define the state set of $\mathbb{S}^{mem}$ in order to illustrate the valuation semantics that goes with CP_{mem}, and refer to [6] for all further details and proofs. Let $A^{core} \subset A^+$ be the set of strings in which each element of A occurs at most once. Then the function space

$$M = \{T, F\}^{A^{core}}$$

is the state set of $\mathbb{S}^{mem}$. Define for $f \in M$ the following: $a \,!\, f = f(a)$ and for $\sigma \in A^{core}$,

$$(a \bullet f)(\sigma) = \begin{cases} f(a) & \text{if } \sigma = a \text{ or } \sigma = \rho a, \\ f(a(\sigma - a)) & \text{otherwise, where } (\sigma - a) \text{ is as } \sigma \text{ but with } a \text{ left out.} \end{cases}$$

For example, $(a \bullet f)(a) = (a \bullet f)(ba) = f(a)$ and $(a \bullet f)(b) = (a \bullet f)(ab) = f(ab)$. In [6] we proved the following result.

Theorem 3. *For $|A| > 1$, an HMA that characterizes CP_{mem} exists, i.e. there is an HMA $\mathbb{A}^{mem}$ such that for all $t, t' \in \mathcal{T}_{\Sigma_{ce}^A}$,*

$$\text{CP}_{mem} \vdash t = t' \iff \mathbb{A}^{mem} \models t = t'.$$

Note that if $A = \{a\}$ then M has only two states, say f and g with $f(a) = T$ and $g(a) = F$. It then easily follows that $\mathbb{A}^{mem} \models T \lhd a \rhd T = T$ so in that case $\mathbb{A}^{mem} \not\cong I(\Sigma_{ce}^A, \text{CP}_{mem})$. Furthermore, note that if $A \supseteq \{a, b\}$, it easily follows that $\mathbb{S}^{mem} \not\models a \wedge b = b \wedge a$: take f such that $f(a) = f(ab) = T$ and $f(b) = F$. The following corollary is related to Theorem 3 and characterizes memorizing congruence in terms of a quasivariety of SPAs that satisfy an extra condition.

Corollary 2. *Let $|A| > 1$. Let $\mathcal{C}_{mem}$ be the class of SPAs that satisfy for all $a \in A$ and $s \in S$,*

$$a \,!\, (x \bullet (a \bullet s)) = a \,!\, s \ \wedge \ a \bullet (x \bullet (a \bullet s)) = x \bullet (a \bullet s).$$

(Note that with $x = T$ this yields the axiom scheme from Corollary 1 that characterizes contractive congruence.) Then for all $t, t' \in \mathcal{T}_{\Sigma_{ce}^A}$,

$$\mathcal{C}_{mem} \models t = t' \iff \text{CP}_{mem} \vdash t = t'.$$

Proof. Somewhat involved; see [6]. □

Table 3. EqMSCL, a set of axioms for MSCL

$$F = \neg T \qquad \text{(SCL1)}$$

$$x \vee y = \neg(\neg x \wedge \neg y) \qquad \text{(SCL2)}$$

$$\neg\neg x = x \qquad \text{(SCL3)}$$

$$T \wedge x = x \qquad \text{(SCL4)}$$

$$x \wedge T = x \qquad \text{(SCL5)}$$

$$F \wedge x = F \qquad \text{(SCL6)}$$

$$(x \wedge y) \wedge z = x \wedge (y \wedge z) \qquad \text{(SCL7)}$$

$$x \wedge F = \neg x \wedge F \qquad \text{(SCL8}^*\text{)}$$

$$x \wedge (x \vee y) = x \qquad \text{(MSCL1)}$$

$$x \wedge (y \vee z) = (x \wedge y) \vee (x \wedge z) \qquad \text{(MSCL2)}$$

$$(x \vee y) \wedge (\neg x \vee z) = (\neg x \vee z) \wedge (x \vee y) \qquad \text{(MSCL3)}$$

$$((x \wedge y) \vee (\neg x \wedge z)) \wedge u = (x \vee (z \wedge u)) \wedge (\neg x \vee (y \wedge u)) \qquad \text{(MSCL4)}$$

We conclude with a brief discussion about the short-circuit logic that is based on CP_{mem}. In this logic, only *static side effects* can occur: during the evaluation of a propositional statement, the value of each atom remains fixed after its first evaluation, which is a typical property axiomatized by CP_{mem}. A major difference with the short-circuit logics discussed in the previous sections is that in CP_{mem} the conditional is definable:

$$
\begin{aligned}
(y \wedge x) \vee (\neg y \wedge z) &= T \lhd (x \lhd y \rhd F) \rhd (z \lhd (F \lhd y \rhd T) \rhd F) \\
&= T \lhd (x \lhd y \rhd F) \rhd (F \lhd y \rhd z) \\
&= (T \lhd x \rhd (F \lhd y \rhd z)) \lhd y \rhd (F \lhd y \rhd z) \\
&= (T \lhd x \rhd F) \lhd y \rhd (F \lhd y \rhd z) && \text{by (6)} \\
&= x \lhd y \rhd z. && \text{by (5)}
\end{aligned}
$$

Definition 10. MSCL *(Memorizing Short-Circuit Logic) is the short-circuit logic that implies no other consequences than those of the module expression*

$$\{T, \neg, \wedge\} \,\square\, (CP_{mem} + \langle \neg x = F \lhd x \rhd T \rangle + \langle x \wedge y = y \lhd x \rhd F \rangle).$$

In Table 3 we present a set of axioms for MSCL and we refer to this set by EqMSCL. Axioms (SCL1) − (SCL7) occur in EqFSCL (see Table 2) and thus need no further comment, and neither does axiom (SCL8*). The EqFSCL-equations (SCL8) − (SCL10) are derivable from EqMSCL. For any further comments, intuitions and proofs on MSCL we refer to [5], and we end this section by recalling the main result from that paper:

Theorem 4 (Completeness). *For all SCL-terms t and t',*

$$\text{EqMSCL} \vdash t = t' \iff \text{MSCL} \vdash t = t'.$$

An interesting aspect of this result is that we have a complete axiomatization EqMSCL of a logic in which $\wedge$ is not commutative and in which $x \wedge F = F$ does not hold, but that is otherwise very close to propositional logic.

6   Static Congruence (Propositional Logic)

In this section we consider *static congruence* defined by the axioms of CP and the axioms

$$(x \lhd y \rhd z) \lhd u \rhd v = (x \lhd u \rhd v) \lhd y \rhd (z \lhd u \rhd v), \qquad \text{(CPstat)}$$
$$(x \lhd y \rhd z) \lhd y \rhd u = x \lhd y \rhd u. \qquad \text{(CPcontr)}$$

Following [4], we write CP_{stat} for this set of axioms. Note that the symmetric variants of the axioms (CPstat) and (CPcontr), say

$$x \lhd y \rhd (z \lhd u \rhd v) = (x \lhd y \rhd z) \lhd u \rhd (x \lhd y \rhd v), \qquad \text{(CPstat')}$$
$$x \lhd y \rhd (z \lhd y \rhd u) = x \lhd y \rhd u, \qquad \text{(CPcontr')}$$

easily follow with the (derivable) identity $y \lhd x \rhd z = z \lhd (F \lhd x \rhd T) \rhd y$. Moreover, in CP_{stat} it follows that

$$\begin{aligned} x &= (x \lhd y \rhd z) \lhd F \rhd x \\ &= (x \lhd F \rhd x) \lhd y \rhd (z \lhd F \rhd x) \qquad \text{by (CPstat)} \\ &= x \lhd y \rhd x. \end{aligned}$$

We define *static congruence* $=_{stat}$ on $\mathcal{T}_{\Sigma_{ce}^A}$ as the congruence generated by CP_{stat}. Let $t, t' \in \mathcal{T}_{\Sigma_{ce}^A}$. Then under static congruence, t and t' can be rewritten into the following special type of basic form: assume the atoms occurring in t and t' are $a_1, ..., a_n$, and consider the full binary tree with at level i only occurrences of atom a_i (there are 2^{i-1} such occurrences), and at level $n+1$ only leaves that are either T or F (there are 2^n such leaves). Then the axioms in CP_{stat} are sufficient to rewrite both t and t' into exactly one such special basic form.

Theorem 5. *There exists an HMA that characterizes static congruence, i.e. there is an HMA $\mathbb{A}^{stat}$ such that for all $t, t' \in \mathcal{T}_{\Sigma_{ce}^A}$,*

$$\text{CP}_{stat} \vdash t = t' \iff \mathbb{A}^{stat} \models t = t'.$$

Proof. Construct the Σ_{spa}^A-algebra $\mathbb{S}^{stat}$ with $\mathcal{T}_{\Sigma_{ce}^A}/{=_{stat}}$ as the set of conditional expressions and the function space

$$S' = \{T, F\}^A$$

as the set of states. For each state f and atom $a \in A$ define $a \mathbin{!} f = f(a)$ and $a \bullet f = f$. Similar as in the proof of Theorem 1, the state constant c is given an arbitrary interpretation, and the axioms (TS1)–(TS3) define the function $s \lhd f \rhd s'$ in $\mathbb{S}^{stat}$. The axioms (SPA1)–(SPA6) fully determine the functions $!$ and $\bullet$, and this is well-defined: if $t =_{stat} t'$ then for all f, $t!f = t'!f$ and $t \bullet f = t' \bullet f$ follow by inspection of the CP_{stat} axioms. The axiom (SPA7) holds by construction of S'. In order to prove that $\mathbb{S}^{stat}$ is a SPA it remains to be shown that axiom (SPA8) holds. This follows by contraposition. We may assume that both t and t' are in the basic form described above: if t and t' are different in some leaf then the reply function f leading to this leaf satisfies $t \, ! \, f \neq t' \, ! \, f$.

Define the HMA $\mathbb{A}^{stat}$ as the Σ_{ce}^A-reduct of $\mathbb{S}^{stat}$. The above argument on the soundness of the axioms (CPstat) and (CPcontr) proves $\Longrightarrow$ as stated in the theorem, and the soundness of axiom (SPA8) proves $\Longleftarrow$. Moreover, $\mathbb{A}^{stat} \cong I(\Sigma_{ce}^A, \mathrm{CP}_{stat})$.

From the proof above it follows that for all $t, t' \in \mathcal{T}_{\Sigma_{ce}^A}$,

$$\mathrm{CP}_{stat} \vdash t = t' \iff \mathbb{S}^{stat} \models t = t'. \tag{7}$$

Corollary 3. *Let $\mathcal{C}_{stat}$ be the class of SPAs that satisfy for all $a \in A$ and $s \in S$,*

$$a \bullet s = s.$$

Then for all $t, t' \in \mathcal{T}_{\Sigma_{ce}^A}$, $\mathcal{C}_{stat} \models t = t' \iff \mathrm{CP}_{stat} \vdash t = t'$.

Proof. By its definition, $\mathbb{S}^{stat} \in \mathcal{C}_{stat}$, which by (7) implies $\Longrightarrow$. For the converse, it is sufficient to show that the axioms (CPstat) and (CPcontr) hold in each SPA in $\mathcal{C}_{stat}$. This follows easily from the $\mathcal{C}_{stat}$-identity $t \bullet s = s$ that holds for all $t \in \mathcal{T}_{\Sigma_{ce}^A}$ (see [6] for a detailed proof). $\qquad\square$

Finally, we return to short-circuit logic. It appears to be the case that the axiom

$$x \, {\wedge\!\!\!\!\circ} \, F = F \tag{8}$$

marks the distinction between MSCL and propositional logic (PL): adding this axiom to EqMSCL yields an equational characterization of PL (be it in sequential notation and defined with short-circuit evaluation).

We write SSCL (static short-circuit logic) for the extension of the short-circuit logic MSCL obtained by adding the associated axiom $F \triangleleft x \triangleright F = F$ to CP_{mem}, and we write EqSSCL for the extension of the axiom set EqMSCL with axiom (8). It easily follows that

$$\mathrm{EqSSCL} \vdash x \, {\wedge\!\!\!\!\circ} \, \neg x = F,$$

and hence F and T are definable in SSCL. Also, commutativity of ${\wedge\!\!\!\!\circ}$ is derivable from EqSSCL (see [5]). By duality it follows that full distributivity holds in EqSSCL, and it is not difficult to see that EqSSCL defines the mentioned variant of PL: this follows for example immediately from [11] in which equational bases for Boolean algebra are provided, and each of these bases can be easily derived from EqSSCL (we return to this point in Section 7).

7   Discussion

In this section we further discuss our papers on proposition algebra and short-circuit logic and briefly mention some issues not considered earlier.

In [4] we introduce 'proposition algebra' as a generic term for algebras that model four basic axioms for Hoare's conditional connective $x \triangleleft y \triangleright z$ (introduced in [9]). We define valuation semantics using valuation algebras (VAs), which are algebras over a signature that contains the Boolean constants and valuations as sorts, and that satisfy axioms comparable to those that define a stateful proposition algebra (a SPA). A valuation variety defines a valuation equivalence by identifying all propositional statements that yield the same evaluation result in all VAs in that variety. For example, T and $T \triangleleft a \triangleright T$ are valuation equivalent in all valuation varieties we consider. The largest congruence contained in a given valuation equivalence is then the 'valuation congruence' to be considered. Main results in [4] are the concise axiomatizations of various valuation congruences (some more than discussed in this paper), and a proof that modulo contractive congruence (or any finer congruence), the conditional, in particular $a \triangleleft b \triangleright c$ with a, b and c atoms, is not definable by sequential binary operators. The axiom set CP characterizes the least identifying valuation congruence we consider, and CP extended with the axiom (CPmem) characterizes memorizing congruence, the most identifying valuation congruence below propositional logic that we distinguish. These valuation congruences are ordered in an incremental way, gradually identifying more propositional statements, and have axiomatizations that all share the axioms of CP.[3] In [4] we also consider some complexity issues: in each VA the satisfiability problem SAT can be defined in a natural way and in all valuation congruences defined thus far, SAT is in NP, and in some cases even in P: in the free CP-algebra SAT is polynomial, while in memorizing congruence the complexity of SAT is increased to NP-complete.

In our report [6] we provide an alternative valuation semantics for proposition algebra in the form of HMAs that appears to be more elegant: HMA-based semantics has the advantage that one can define a valuation congruence without first defining the valuation equivalence it is contained in. Furthermore, we show in [6] that not all proposition algebras are HMAs. In particular, we prove that $\text{CP} + \langle T \triangleleft x \triangleright T = T \rangle$ has a non-trivial initial algebra (which by definition is a proposition algebra) that is not an HMA because each HMA satisfies the conditional equation $((T \triangleleft x \triangleright T = T) \wedge (T \triangleleft y \triangleright T = T)) \to T \triangleleft x \triangleright y = T \triangleleft y \triangleright x$, while $\text{CP} + \langle T \triangleleft x \triangleright T = T \rangle \not\vdash T \triangleleft a \triangleright b = T \triangleleft b \triangleright a$ for distinct atoms a and b.

In [5] we introduce *short-circuit logic*: we show that the extension of CP_{mem} with $\neg$ and $\wedge\!\!\!/$ (and with F and $\vee\!\!\!/$ being definable) characterizes a reasonable logic if one restricts to identities defined over the signature $\{T, \neg, \wedge\!\!\!/\}$. As recalled in the present paper, we provide an axiomatization of MSCL (memorizing short-circuit logic) and we define FSCL (free short-circuit logic) as the most basic (least identifying) short-circuit logic. Each valuation congruence defines a

---

[3] In [10] it is noted that if the set A of atoms contains one element, all valuation congruences other than structural congruence coincide with static valuation congruence.

short-circuit logic, and these logics are put forward for modeling conditions as used in programming with short-circuit evaluation and for that reason we named them "short-circuit logics". Typical axioms that are valid in FSCL (and thus in each short-circuit logic) are the associativity of $\require{enclose}\wedge\!\!\!\!\!\_$, the double negation shift and $F \wedge\!\!\!\!\!\_\, x = F$, and we conjecture that FSCL is axiomatized by the equations in Table 2. Furthermore, as noted in Section 5, a typical non-validity is $x \wedge\!\!\!\!\!\_\, F = F$, which does not hold modulo memorizing congruence (or any finer congruence). The extension of CP_{mem} with the axiom $F \triangleleft x \triangleright F = F$ that defines SSCL (static short-circuit logic, comprising $x \wedge\!\!\!\!\!\_\, F = F$), or equivalently, the extension of CP_{mem} with the axiom $T \triangleleft x \triangleright T = T$, yields an axiomatization of static valuation congruence that is perhaps more elegant than our axiomatization CP_{stat}: using the expressibility of conditional composition and the commutativity of $\wedge\!\!\!\!\!\_$ and $\vee\!\!\!\!\!\_$ (and hence full distributivity), it is not hard to derive the axiom (CPstat). In [5, Appendix C] we provide another axiomatization of static valuation congruence that is even more elegant than $CP_{mem} + \langle F \triangleleft x \triangleright F = F \rangle$. This axiomatization consists of the five axioms (CP1), (CP2), (CP4) (see Table 1),

$$T \triangleleft x \triangleright y = T \triangleleft y \triangleright x \quad \text{and} \quad (x \triangleleft y \triangleright z) \triangleleft y \triangleright F = x \triangleleft y \triangleright F,$$

and we also prove that it is independent.

References

1. Bergstra, J.A., Bethke, I., Rodenburg, P.H.: A propositional logic with 4 values: true, false, divergent and meaningless. Journal of Applied Non-Classical Logics 5(2), 199–218 (1995)
2. Bergstra, J.A., Heering, J., Klint, P.: Module algebra. Journal of the ACM 37(2), 335–372 (1990)
3. Bergstra, J.A., Middelburg, C.A.: Instruction sequence processing operators (2009), http://arxiv.org/:ArXiv:0910.5564v2 [cs.LO]
4. Bergstra, J.A., Ponse, A.: Proposition algebra. ACM Transactions on Computational Logic 12(3), Article 21 (36 pages) (2011)
5. Bergstra, J.A., Ponse, A.: Short-circuit logic (2010/2011), http://arxiv.org/abs/1012.3674v3 [cs.LO]
6. Bergstra, J.A., Ponse, A.: On Hoare-McCarthy algebras (2010), http://arxiv.org/abs/1012.5059v1 [cs.LO]
7. Bloom, S.L., Tindell, R.: Varieties of "if-then-else". SIAM Journal of Computing 12(4), 677–707 (1983)
8. Mekler, A.H., Nelson, E.M.: Equational bases for if-then-else. SIAM Journal of Computing 16(3), 465–485 (1987)
9. Hoare, C.A.R.: A couple of novelties in the propositional calculus. Zeitschrift für Mathematische Logik und Grundlagen der Mathematik 31(2), 173–178 (1985)
10. Regenboog, B.C.: Reactive valuations. MSc. thesis Logic, University of Amsterdam. December 2010, http://arxiv.org/abs/1101.3132v1 [cs.LO] (2011)
11. Sioson, F.M.: Equational bases of Boolean algebras. Journal of Symbolic Logic 29(3), 115–124 (1964)
12. Terese. Term Rewriting Systems. Cambridge Tracts in Theoretical Computer Science, vol. 55. Cambridge University Press (2003)

Decompositional Reasoning about the History of Parallel Processes*

Luca Aceto[1], Arnar Birgisson[2],
Anna Ingólfsdóttir[1], and MohammadReza Mousavi[3]

[1] School of Computer Science, Reykjavik University, Iceland
[2] Department of Computer Science and Engineering,
Chalmers University of Technology, Sweden
[3] Department of Computer Science, TU/Eindhoven, The Netherlands

Abstract. This paper presents a decomposition technique for Hennessy-Milner logic with past and its extension with recursively defined formulae. In order to highlight the main ideas and technical tools, processes are described using a subset of CCS with parallel composition, nondeterministic choice, action prefixing and the inaction constant. The study focuses on developing decompositional reasoning techniques for parallel contexts in that language.

1 Introduction

State-space explosion is a major obstacle in model checking logical properties. One approach to combat this problem is compositional reasoning, where properties of a system as a whole are deduced in a principled fashion from properties of its components. The study of compositional proof systems for various temporal and modal logics has attracted considerable attention in the concurrency-theory literature and several compositional proof systems have been proposed for such logics over (fragments of) process calculi. (See, e.g., [6,36,37,41].) A related line of research is the one devoted to (de)compositional model checking [5,19,25,31,42]. Decompositional reasoning aims at automatically decomposing the global property to be model checked into local properties of (possibly unknown) components—a technique that is often called *quotienting*. In the context of process algebras, as the language for describing reactive systems, and (extensions of) Hennessy-Milner logic (HML), as the logical specification formalism for describing their properties, decompositional reasoning techniques date back to the seminal work of Larsen and Liu in the 1980's and early 1990's [29,31], which is further developed in,

---

* The work of Aceto, Birgisson and Ingólfsdóttir has been partially supported by the projects "New Developments in Operational Semantics" (nr. 080039021) and "Metatheory of Algebraic Process Theories" (nr. 100014021) of the Icelandic Research Fund. Birgisson has been further supported by research-student grant nr. 080890008 of the Icelandic Research Fund and by grants from the Swedish research agencies SSF and VR.

F. Arbab and M. Sirjani (Eds.): FSEN 2011, LNCS 7141, pp. 32–47, 2012.
© Springer-Verlag Berlin Heidelberg 2012

e.g., [7,9,10,12,18,23,25,26,35]. However, we are not aware of any such decomposition technique that applies to reasoning about the "past". This is particularly interesting in the light of recent developments concerning reversible processes [13,34] and knowledge representation (epistemic aspects) inside process algebra [14,20], all of which involve some notion of specification and reasoning about the past. Moreover, a significant body of evidence indicates that being able to reason about the past is useful in program verification [22,28,32].

In this paper, we address the problem of developing a decomposition technique for Hennessy-Milner logic with past [16,17,27] and for its extension with recursively defined formulae. This way, we obtain a decomposition technique for the modal μ-calculus with past [21,33]. Apart from its intrinsic interest, the decompositionality results we present in this paper also shed light on the expressiveness of the logics we consider. For example, as shown in, e.g., [2,3], the closure of a logic with respect to quotienting is closely tied to its ability to express properties that can be tested by performing reachability analysis of processes in the context of so-called test automata. As the language for describing processes, in order to highlight the main ideas and technical tools in our approach, we use a subset of CCS with parallel composition, nondeterministic choice, action prefixing and the inaction constant. Our results, however, extend naturally to other classic parallel composition operators from the realm of process algebra, such as the general one considered in the literature on ACP [8], and to a setting where (possibly infinite) synchronization trees [40] are used as a model of process behaviour.

As the work presented in this paper shows, the development of a theory of decompositional reasoning in a setting with past modalities involves subtleties and design decisions that do not arise in previous work on HML and Kozen's μ-calculus [24]. For instance, the decompositionality result for HML with past and its extension with recursively defined formulae rests on a decomposition of computations of parallel processes into *sets* of pairs of computations of their components, whose concurrent execution might have produced the original parallel computations. Moreover, as explained in detail in the main body of the paper, the presence of past modalities leads us to consider computations of the components of a parallel process that may explicitly include *stuttering steps*—that is, steps where the component under consideration is idle, while a computation step takes place elsewhere in the parallel system. The main results of the paper (Theorems 1 and 2) roughly state that if a computation π of a parallel process $p \parallel q$ satisfies a formula φ in one of the logics we study then, no matter what decomposition of π we pick, the contribution of p to the computation π will satisfy the "quotient of φ with respect to the contribution of q to π." Conversely, if there is *some way* of decomposing π, in such a way that the contribution of p to the computation π satisfies the "quotient of φ with respect to the contribution of q to π", then the computation π of the parallel process $p \parallel q$ is guaranteed to satisfy φ.

The rest of this paper is structured as follows. Section 2 introduces preliminary definitions and the extension of Hennessy-Milner logic with past. Section 3 discusses how parallel computations are decomposed into their components. Section 4 presents the decompositional reasoning technique and the first main theorem of the paper. Section 5 extends the theory to recursively defined formulae, and Section 6 discusses related work and possible extensions of our results. Due to space limitation, the proofs of the results are included in the extended version of this paper [1].

2   Preliminaries

A *labelled transition system* (LTS) is a triple $\langle P, A, \longrightarrow \rangle$ where

- P is a set of process names,
- A is a finite set of action names, not including a *silent action* τ (we write A_τ for $A \cup \{\tau\}$), and
- $\longrightarrow \subseteq P \times A_\tau \times P$ is the *transition relation*; we call its elements *transitions* and usually write $p \xrightarrow{\alpha} p'$ to mean that $(p, \alpha, p') \in \longrightarrow$.

We let $p, q, \ldots$ range over P, $a, b, \ldots$ over A and $\alpha, \beta, \ldots$ over A_τ.

For any set S, we let S^* be the set of finite sequences of elements from S. Concatenation of sequences is represented by juxtaposition. λ denotes the empty sequence and $|w|$ stands for the length of a sequence w.

Given an LTS $\mathcal{T} = \langle P, A, \longrightarrow \rangle$, we define a *path from* p_0 to be a sequence of transitions $p_0 \xrightarrow{\alpha_0} p_1$, $p_1 \xrightarrow{\alpha_1} p_2$, $\ldots$, $p_{n-1} \xrightarrow{\alpha_{n-1}} p_n$ and usually write this as $p_0 \xrightarrow{\alpha_0} p_1 \xrightarrow{\alpha_1} p_2 \xrightarrow{\alpha_2} \cdots \xrightarrow{\alpha_{n-1}} p_n$.

We use $\pi, \mu, \ldots$ to range over paths. A *computation from* p is a pair (p, π), where π is a path from p, and we use $\rho, \rho', \ldots$ to range over computations. $\mathcal{C}_\mathcal{T}(p)$, or simply $\mathcal{C}(p)$ when the LTS $\mathcal{T}$ is clear from the context, is the set of computations from p and $\mathcal{C}_\mathcal{T}$ is the set of all computations in $\mathcal{T}$.

For a computation $\rho = (p_0, \pi)$, where $\pi = p_0 \xrightarrow{\alpha_0} p_1 \xrightarrow{\alpha_1} p_2 \xrightarrow{\alpha_2} \cdots \xrightarrow{\alpha_{n-1}} p_n$, we define $\mathrm{first}(\rho) = \mathrm{first}(\pi) = p_0$, $\mathrm{last}(\rho) = \mathrm{last}(\pi) = p_n$, and $|\rho| = |\pi| = n$.

Concatenation of computations ρ and ρ' is denoted by their juxtaposition $\rho\rho'$ and is defined iff $\mathrm{last}(\rho) = \mathrm{first}(\rho')$. When $\mathrm{last}(\rho) = p$ we write $\rho(p \xrightarrow{\alpha} q)$ as a shorthand for the slightly longer $\rho(p, p \xrightarrow{\alpha} q)$. We also use $\rho \xrightarrow{\alpha} \rho'$ to denote that there exists a computation $\rho'' = (p, p \xrightarrow{\alpha} p')$, for some processes p and p', such that $\rho' = \rho\rho''$.

Definition 1 (Hennessy-Milner logic with past). *Let* $\mathcal{T} = \langle P, A, \rightarrow \rangle$ *be an LTS. The set* $HML_\leftarrow(A)$, *or simply* $HML_\leftarrow$, *of Hennessy-Milner logic formulae with past is defined by the following grammar, where* $\alpha \in A_\tau$.

$$\varphi, \psi ::= \top \mid \varphi \wedge \psi \mid \neg\varphi \mid \langle\alpha\rangle\varphi \mid \langle\leftarrow\alpha\rangle\varphi.$$

We define the satisfaction relation $\vDash \subseteq \mathcal{C}_\mathcal{T} \times HML_\leftarrow$ *as the least relation that satisfies the following clauses:*

- $\rho \vDash \top$ *for all* $\rho \in \mathcal{C}_\mathcal{T}$,
- $\rho \vDash \varphi \wedge \psi$ *iff* $\rho \vDash \varphi$ *and* $\rho \vDash \psi$,
- $\rho \vDash \neg\varphi$ *iff not* $\rho \vDash \varphi$,

$-\ \rho \vDash \langle \alpha \rangle \varphi$ iff $\rho \xrightarrow{\alpha} \rho'$ and $\rho' \vDash \varphi$ for some $\rho' \in \mathcal{C}_T$, and

$-\ \rho \vDash \langle \leftarrow \alpha \rangle \varphi$ iff $\rho' \xrightarrow{\alpha} \rho$ and $\rho' \vDash \varphi$ for some $\rho' \in \mathcal{C}_T$.

For a process $p \in P$, we take $p \vDash \varphi$ to mean $(p, \lambda) \vDash \varphi$.

We make use of some standard short-hands for Hennessy-Milner-type logics, such as $\bot = \neg \top$, $\varphi \lor \psi = \neg(\neg \varphi \land \neg \psi)$, $[\alpha]\varphi = \neg \langle \alpha \rangle(\neg \varphi)$ and $[\leftarrow \alpha]\varphi = \neg \langle \leftarrow \alpha \rangle(\neg \varphi)$. For a finite set of actions B, we also use the following notations.

$$\langle \leftarrow B \rangle \varphi = \bigvee_{\alpha \in B} \langle \leftarrow \alpha \rangle \varphi \qquad\qquad [\leftarrow B]\varphi = \bigwedge_{\alpha \in B} [\leftarrow \alpha]\varphi$$

It is worth mentioning that the operators $\langle \cdot \rangle$ and $\langle \leftarrow \cdot \rangle$ are not entirely symmetric. The future is nondeterministic; the past is, however, always deterministic. This is by design, and we could have chosen to model the past as nondeterministic as well, i.e., to take a possibilistic view where we would consider all possible histories. Overall, the deterministic view is more appropriate for our purposes. See, e.g., [28] for a clear discussion of possible approaches in modelling the past and further references.

3   Decomposing Computations

In this section, following [5,25,31], we aim at defining a notion of "formula quotient with respect to a process in a parallel composition" for formulae in $HML_\leftarrow$. In our setting, this goal translates into a theorem of the form $\rho \vDash \varphi$ iff $\rho_1 \vDash \varphi / \rho_2$, where ρ, ρ_1, ρ_2 are computations such that ρ is a computation of a "parallel process" that is, in some sense, the "parallel composition" of ρ_1 and ρ_2.

In the standard setting, definitions of "formula quotients" are based on local information that can be gleaned from the operational semantics of the chosen notion of parallel composition operator. In the case of computations, however, such local information does not suffice. A computation arising from the evolution of two processes run in parallel has the form $(p \parallel q, \pi)$, where $p \parallel q$ is a syntactic representation of the initial state and π is the path leading to the current state. The path π, however, may involve contributions from both of the parallel components. Separating the contributions of the components for the purposes of decompositional model checking requires us to unzip these paths into separate paths that might have been observed by considering only one argument of the composition. This means that we have to find two paths π_p and π_q such that (p, π_p) and (q, π_q) are, in some sense, independent computations that run in parallel will yield $(p \parallel q, \pi)$.

CCS Computations and Their Decomposition. For this study, in order to highlight the main ideas and technical tools in our approach, we restrict ourselves to a subset of CCS, namely CCS without renaming, restriction or recursion.

(We discuss possible extensions of our results in Section 6.) Processes are thus defined by the grammar

$$p, q \quad ::= \quad 0 \mid \alpha.p \mid p + q \mid p \parallel q$$

and their operational semantics is given by the following rules.

$$\frac{}{\alpha.p \xrightarrow{\alpha} p} \qquad \frac{p \xrightarrow{\alpha} p'}{p + q \xrightarrow{a} p'} \qquad \frac{q \xrightarrow{\alpha} q'}{p + q \xrightarrow{a} q'}$$

$$\frac{p \xrightarrow{\alpha} p'}{p \parallel q \xrightarrow{\alpha} p' \parallel q} \qquad \frac{q \xrightarrow{\alpha} q'}{p \parallel q \xrightarrow{\alpha} p \parallel q'} \qquad \frac{p \xrightarrow{a} p' \quad q \xrightarrow{\bar{a}} q'}{p \parallel q \xrightarrow{\tau} p' \parallel q'}$$

We write $p \xrightarrow{\alpha} q$ to denote that this transition is provable by these rules. We assume also that $\bar{} : A \to A$ is a bijective function on action names such that $\bar{\bar{a}} = a$.

The decomposition of a computation resulting from the evolution of two parallel components must retain the information about the order of steps in the interleaved computation. We do so by modelling the decomposition using *stuttering computations*. These are computations that are not only sequences of transition triplets, but may also involve pseudo-steps labelled with $\dashrightarrow$. Intuitively, $p \dashrightarrow p$ means that process p has remained idle in the last transition performed by a parallel process having p as one of its parallel components. We denote the set of stuttering computations with $\mathcal{C}_T^*$ or simply $\mathcal{C}^*$. For example, the computation $(a.0 \parallel b.0, a.0 \parallel b.0 \xrightarrow{a} 0 \parallel b.0 \xrightarrow{b} 0 \parallel 0)$ is decomposed into the stuttering computations $(a.0, a.0 \xrightarrow{a} 0 \dashrightarrow 0)$ and $(b.0, b.0 \dashrightarrow b.0 \xrightarrow{b} 0)$. However, the decomposition of a parallel computation is not in general unique, as there may be several possibilities stemming from different synchronization patterns. For example consider a computation with path $(a.0 + b.0) \parallel (\bar{a}.0 + \bar{b}.0) \xrightarrow{\tau} 0 \parallel 0$. From this computation it is not possible to distinguish if the transition labelled with τ was the result of communication of the a and $\bar{a}$ actions, or of the b and $\bar{b}$ actions. We thus consider *all* possibilities simultaneously, i.e., a decomposition of a computation is actually *a set* of pairs of components.

The following function over paths defines the decomposition of a computation.

$$D(\lambda) = \{(\lambda, \lambda)\}$$
$$D(\pi(p \parallel q \dashrightarrow p \parallel q)) = \{(\mu_1(p \dashrightarrow p), \mu_2(q \dashrightarrow q)) \mid (\mu_1, \mu_2) \in D(\pi)\}$$

$$D(\pi(p \parallel q \xrightarrow{\alpha} p' \parallel q')) = \begin{cases} \{(\mu_1(p \xrightarrow{\alpha} p'), \mu_2(q \dashrightarrow q)) \\ \quad \mid (\mu_1, \mu_2) \in D(\pi)\} & \text{if } q = q' \\[2mm] \{(\mu_1(p \dashrightarrow p), \mu_2(q \xrightarrow{\alpha} q')) \\ \quad \mid (\mu_1, \mu_2) \in D(\pi')\} & \text{if } p = p' \\[2mm] \{(\mu_1(p \xrightarrow{a} p'), \mu_2(q \xrightarrow{\bar{a}} q')) \\ \quad \mid (\mu_1, \mu_2) \in D(\pi), a \in A, \\ \quad \quad p \xrightarrow{a} p', q \xrightarrow{\bar{a}} q'\} & \text{otherwise} \end{cases}$$

Note that if (μ_1, μ_2) is a decomposition of a computation π, then the three computations have the same length. Furthermore $\mathrm{last}(\pi) = \mathrm{last}(\mu_1) \parallel \mathrm{last}(\mu_2)$.

Another notable property of path decomposition is that it is injective, i.e., a pair (μ_1, μ_2) can only be the decomposition of at most one path.

Lemma 1. *Let π_1 be a path of a parallel computation and $(\mu_1, \mu_2) \in D(\pi_1)$. If π_2 is a path such that $(\mu_1, \mu_2) \in D(\pi_2)$ also, then $\pi_1 = \pi_2$.*

We now aim at defining the quotient of an $HML_\leftarrow$-formula φ with respect to a computation (q, μ_2), written $\varphi/(q, \mu_2)$, in such a way that a property of the form

$$(p \parallel q, \pi) \vDash \varphi \quad \Leftrightarrow \quad (p, \mu_1) \vDash \varphi/(q, \mu_2)$$

holds when $(\mu_1, \mu_2) \in D(\pi)$. However, since we are dealing with sets of decompositions, we need to quantify over these sets. It turns out that a natural way to do so, which also gives a strong result, is as follows. Given that a composed computation satisfies a formula, we prove in Section 4 that one component of *every* decomposition satisfies a formula quotiented with the other component:

$$(p \parallel q, \pi) \vDash \varphi \implies \forall (\mu_1, \mu_2) \in D(\pi) : (p, \mu_1) \vDash \varphi/(q, \mu_2).$$

On the other hand, to show the implication from right to left, we need only one witness of a decomposition that satisfies a quotiented formula to deduce that the composed computation satisfies the original one:

$$\exists (\mu_1, \mu_2) \in D(\pi) : (p, \mu_1) \vDash \varphi/(q, \mu_2) \implies (p \parallel q, \pi) \vDash \varphi.$$

In order to define the quotienting transformation, we need a logic that allows us to describe properties of computations involving explicit pseudo-steps. To this end, we now extend $HML_\leftarrow$ with two additional modal operators.

Definition 2 (Stuttering Hennessy-Milner logic with past). *Consider an LTS $\mathcal{T} = \langle P, A, \rightarrow \rangle$. The set $HML_\leftarrow^*(A)$, or simply $HML_\leftarrow^*$, of stuttering Hennessy-Milner logic formulae with past is defined by the grammar*

$$\varphi, \psi ::= \top \mid \varphi \wedge \psi \mid \neg \varphi \mid \langle \alpha \rangle \varphi \mid \langle \leftarrow \alpha \rangle \varphi \mid \langle \dashrightarrow \rangle \varphi \mid \langle \leftarrow\!\dashleftarrow \rangle \varphi$$

where $\alpha \in A_\tau$. The satisfaction relation $\vDash^* \subseteq \mathcal{C}_\mathcal{T}^* \times HML_\leftarrow^*$ is defined in the same manner as for Hennessy-Milner logic with past, by extending Definition 1 with the following two items.

- *$\rho \vDash^* \langle \dashrightarrow \rangle \varphi$ iff $\rho(p \dashrightarrow p) \vDash^* \varphi$ where $p = \mathrm{last}(\rho)$.*
- *$\rho \vDash^* \langle \leftarrow\!\dashleftarrow \rangle \varphi$ iff $\rho' \vDash^* \varphi$ where $\rho = \rho'(p \dashrightarrow p)$ for some p.*

Similarly, $\vDash^* \in P \times HML_\leftarrow^*$ is defined by $p \vDash^* \varphi$ if and only if $(p, \lambda) \vDash^* \varphi$.

The satisfaction relations $\vDash^*$ and $\vDash$ coincide over $\mathcal{C}_\mathcal{T} \times HML_\leftarrow$.

Why Are the Pseudo-steps Necessary? One may ask why we need to extend both the computations and the logic to include the notion of pseudo-steps. The reason for doing so is to capture information about the interleaving order in component computations. This in turn is necessary because the original logic can differentiate between different interleavings of parallel processes. For an example, consider the computation $(a.0 \parallel b.0, \pi)$, where $\pi = a.0 \parallel b.0 \xrightarrow{a} 0 \parallel b.0 \xrightarrow{b} 0 \parallel 0$. Clearly this computation does *not* satisfy the formula $\langle \leftarrow a \rangle \top$.

Another interleaving of the same parallel composition is the computation $(a.0 \parallel b.0, \pi')$, where $\pi' = a.0 \parallel b.0 \xrightarrow{b} a.0 \parallel 0 \xrightarrow{a} 0 \parallel 0$. This computation, on the other hand, does satisfy $\langle \leftarrow a \rangle \top$. Since the logic can distinguish between different interleaving orders of a parallel computation, it is vital to maintain information about the interleaving order in our decomposition. If the decomposition of the above computations only considered the actions contributed by each component, this information would be lost and the two paths would have the same decomposition. As a result, we could not reasonably expect to test if they satisfy the formula $\langle \leftarrow a \rangle \top$ in a decompositional manner.

4   Decompositional Reasoning

We now define the quotienting construction over formulae structurally. The complete quotienting transformation is given in Table 1. Below we limit ourselves to discussing the quotienting transformation for formulae of the form $\langle \leftarrow \alpha \rangle \varphi$.

To define the transformation for formulae of that form, we examine several cases separately. First we consider the case when ρ has the empty path. In this case it is obvious that no backward step is possible and therefore:

$$(\langle \leftarrow \alpha \rangle \varphi)/(p, \lambda) = \bot.$$

The second case to consider is when ρ ends with a pseudo-transition. In this case the only possibility is that the other component (the one we are testing) is able to perform the backward transition.

$$(\langle \leftarrow \alpha \rangle \varphi)/\rho'(p' \dashrightarrow p') = \langle \leftarrow \alpha \rangle (\varphi/\rho')$$

The third case applies when ρ does indeed end with the transition we look for. In this case the other component must end with a matching pseudo-transition.

$$(\langle \leftarrow \alpha \rangle \varphi)/\rho'(p'' \xrightarrow{\alpha} p') = \langle \leftarrow \dashrightarrow \rangle (\varphi/\rho') \tag{1}$$

The only remaining case to consider is when ρ ends with a transition different from the one we look for. We split this case further and consider again separately the cases when $\alpha \in A$ and when $\alpha = \tau$. The former case is simple: if ρ indicates that the last transition has a label other than the one specified in the diamond operator, the composite computation cannot satisfy $\langle \leftarrow a \rangle \varphi$ because the other component must have performed a pseudo-step.

$$(\langle \leftarrow a \rangle \varphi)/\rho'(p'' \xrightarrow{\beta} p') = \bot \quad \text{where } a \neq \beta$$

Table 1. Quotienting transformations of formulae in $HML_\leftarrow^*$, where $p' = \text{last}(\rho)$

$\top/\rho = \top$

$(\varphi_1 \wedge \varphi_2)/\rho = \varphi_1/\rho \wedge \varphi_2/\rho$

$(\neg\varphi)/\rho = \neg(\varphi/\rho)$

$(\langle a \rangle \varphi)/\rho = \langle a \rangle (\varphi/\rho(p' \dashrightarrow p')) \vee \left(\bigvee_{\rho' : \rho \xrightarrow{a} \rho'} \langle \dashrightarrow \rangle (\varphi/\rho') \right)$

$(\langle \tau \rangle \varphi)/\rho = \langle \tau \rangle (\varphi/\rho(p' \dashrightarrow p')) \vee \left(\bigvee_{\rho' : \rho \xrightarrow{\tau} \rho'} \langle \dashrightarrow \rangle (\varphi/\rho') \right) \vee \left(\bigvee_{\rho', a : \rho \xrightarrow{a} \rho'} \langle \bar{a} \rangle (\varphi/\rho') \right)$

$(\langle \leftarrow\alpha \rangle \varphi)/(p, \lambda) = \bot$

$(\langle \leftarrow\alpha \rangle \varphi)/\rho'(p' \dashrightarrow p') = \langle \leftarrow\alpha \rangle (\varphi/\rho')$

$(\langle \leftarrow\alpha \rangle \varphi)/\rho'(p'' \xrightarrow{\alpha} p') = \langle \leftarrow\!\text{-} \rangle (\varphi/\rho')$

$(\langle \leftarrow a \rangle \varphi)/\rho'(p'' \xrightarrow{\beta} p') = \bot \quad \text{where } a \neq \beta$

$(\langle \leftarrow\tau \rangle \varphi)/\rho'(p'' \xrightarrow{b} p') = \langle \leftarrow\bar{b} \rangle (\varphi/\rho')$

$(\langle \dashrightarrow \rangle \varphi)/\rho = \langle \dashrightarrow \rangle (\varphi/\rho(p' \dashrightarrow p'))$

$(\langle \leftarrow\!\text{-} \rangle \varphi)/\rho = \begin{cases} \langle \leftarrow\!\text{-} \rangle (\varphi/\rho') & \text{if } \rho = \rho'(p' \dashrightarrow p') \\ \bot & \text{otherwise} \end{cases}$

If however the diamond operator mentions a τ transition, then we must look for a transition in the other component that can synchronise with the last one of ρ. Note that this case does not include computations ending with a τ transition, as that case is covered by Equation (1).

$$(\langle \leftarrow\tau \rangle \varphi)/\rho'(p'' \xrightarrow{b} p') = \langle \leftarrow\bar{b} \rangle (\varphi/\rho')$$

This covers all possible cases for $\langle \leftarrow\alpha \rangle \varphi/\rho$.

We are now ready to prove the main theorem in this section, to the effect that the quotienting of a formula φ with respect to a computation ρ is properly defined.

Theorem 1. *For CCS processes p, q and a computation $(p \parallel q, \pi) \in \mathcal{C}(p \parallel q)$ and a formula $\varphi \in HML_\leftarrow^*$, we have*

$$(p \parallel q, \pi) \vDash^* \varphi \Rightarrow \forall(\mu_1, \mu_2) \in D(\pi) : (p, \mu_1) \vDash^* \varphi/(q, \mu_2) \tag{2}$$

and, conversely,

$$(p \parallel q, \pi) \vDash^* \varphi \Leftarrow \exists(\mu_1, \mu_2) \in D(\pi) : (p, \mu_1) \vDash^* \varphi/(q, \mu_2). \tag{3}$$

Theorem 1 uses the existential quantifier in the right-to-left direction. This makes it easy to show that a computation of a process of the form $p \parallel q$ satisfies a formula, given only one witness of a decomposition with one component satisfying the corresponding quotient formula. Note, however, that the set of decompositions of any given process is never empty, i.e., every parallel computation has a decomposition. This allows us to write the above theorem in a more symmetric form.

Corollary 1. *For CCS processes p, q, a parallel computation $(p \parallel q, \pi)$ and a formula $\varphi \in HML_\leftarrow^*$, we have $(p \parallel q, \pi) \vDash^* \varphi$ iff $(p, \mu_1) \vDash^* \varphi/(q, \mu_2)$, for each $(\mu_1, \mu_2) \in D(\pi)$.*

5   Adding Recursion to $HML^*_\leftarrow$

In this section, we extend the results from Section 4 to a version of the logic $HML^*_\leftarrow$ that includes (formula) variables and a facility for the recursive definition of formulae. Following, e.g., [30], the intended meaning of a formula variable is specified by means of a declaration, i.e., a mapping from variables to formulae, which may themselves contain occurrences of variables. A declaration is nothing but a system of equations over the set of formula variables.

By using the extension of the logic $HML^*_\leftarrow$ discussed in this section, we can reason about properties of processes and computations that go beyond one step of lookahead or look-back. For example we can phrase the question "Has the action α ever happened in the past?" as the least model of a suitable recursive logical property.

Definition 3. *Let A be a finite set of actions and let $\mathcal{X}$ be a finite set of identifiers. The set $HML^*_{\leftarrow,\mathcal{X}}(A)$, or simply $HML^*_{\leftarrow,\mathcal{X}}$, is defined by the grammar*

$$\varphi, \psi ::= \top \mid \varphi \wedge \psi \mid \neg\varphi \mid \langle\alpha\rangle\varphi \mid \langle\leftarrow\alpha\rangle\varphi \mid \langle\text{--}\rightarrow\rangle\varphi \mid \langle\leftarrow\text{--}\rangle\varphi \mid X$$

where $X \in \mathcal{X}$. A declaration over $\mathcal{X}$ is a function $\mathcal{D} : \mathcal{X} \to HML^*_{\leftarrow,\mathcal{X}}$, assigning a formula to each variable contained in $\mathcal{X}$, with the restriction that each occurrence of a variable in a formula in the range of $\mathcal{D}$ is positive, i.e., any variable is within the scope of an even number of negations.

When reasoning about recursive formulae, it is technically convenient to define their meaning (i.e., the set of computations that satisfy them) denotationally, because well-definedness of the semantics of recursive formulae relies on Tarski's fixed point theory. This in turn, depends on a notion of *monotone function* over a lattice, which is best described by the denotation function and the usual subset ordering on the set of states satisfying a formula. For the sake of clarity, we rephrase Definition 2 in a denotational setting. As it is customary, the following definition makes use of a notion of environment to give meaning to formula variables. An *environment* is a function $\sigma : \mathcal{X} \to \mathcal{P}(\mathcal{C}^*)$. Intuitively, an environment assigns to each variable the set of computations that are assumed to satisfy it. We write $\mathcal{E}_\mathcal{X}$ for the set of environments over the set of (formula) variables $\mathcal{X}$. It is well-known that $\mathcal{E}_\mathcal{X}$ is a complete lattice when environments are ordered pointwise using set inclusion.

Definition 4 (Denotational semantics of $HML^*_{\leftarrow,\mathcal{X}}$). *Let $\mathcal{T} = \langle P, A, \rightarrow\rangle$ be an LTS. Let φ be a $HML^*_{\leftarrow,\mathcal{X}}$ formula and let σ be an environment. The denotation of φ with respect to σ, written $[\![\varphi]\!]\sigma$, is defined structurally as follows:*

$$
\begin{aligned}
[\![\top]\!]\sigma &= \mathcal{C}^*_\mathcal{T} & [\![\neg\varphi]\!]\sigma &= \mathcal{C}^*_\mathcal{T} \setminus [\![\varphi]\!]\sigma \\
[\![X]\!]\sigma &= \sigma(X) & [\![\varphi \wedge \psi]\!]\sigma &= [\![\varphi]\!]\sigma \cap [\![\psi]\!]\sigma \\
[\![\langle\alpha\rangle\varphi]\!]\sigma &= \langle\cdot\alpha\cdot\rangle[\![\varphi]\!]\sigma & [\![\langle\leftarrow\alpha\rangle\varphi]\!]\sigma &= \langle\cdot\leftarrow\alpha\cdot\rangle[\![\varphi]\!]\sigma \\
[\![\langle\text{--}\rightarrow\rangle\varphi]\!]\sigma &= \langle\cdot\text{--}\rightarrow\cdot\rangle[\![\varphi]\!]\sigma & [\![\langle\leftarrow\text{--}\rangle\varphi]\!]\sigma &= \langle\cdot\leftarrow\text{--}\cdot\rangle[\![\varphi]\!]\sigma,
\end{aligned}
$$

where the operators $\langle \cdot\alpha\cdot \rangle, \langle \cdot \leftarrow\alpha\cdot \rangle, \langle \cdot \dashrightarrow \cdot \rangle, \langle \cdot \leftdasharrow \cdot \rangle \ : \ \mathcal{P}(\mathcal{C}_T^*) \to \mathcal{P}(\mathcal{C}_T^*)$ *are defined thus:*

$$
\begin{aligned}
\langle \cdot\alpha\cdot \rangle S &= \{\rho \in \mathcal{C}_T^* \mid \exists \rho' \in S : \rho \xrightarrow{\alpha} \rho'\} \\
\langle \cdot \leftarrow\alpha\cdot \rangle S &= \{\rho \in \mathcal{C}_T^* \mid \exists \rho' \in S : \rho' \xrightarrow{\alpha} \rho\} \\
\langle \cdot \dashrightarrow \cdot \rangle S &= \{\rho \in \mathcal{C}_T^* \mid \exists \rho' \in S : \rho \dashrightarrow \rho'\} \quad \text{and} \\
\langle \cdot \leftdasharrow \cdot \rangle S &= \{\rho \in \mathcal{C}_T^* \mid \exists \rho' \in S : \rho' \dashrightarrow \rho\}.
\end{aligned}
$$

The satisfaction relation $\vDash_\sigma \, \subseteq \mathcal{C}_T^* \times HML^*_{\leftarrow,\mathcal{X}}$ *is defined by*

$$\rho \vDash_\sigma \varphi \quad \Leftrightarrow \quad \rho \in [\![\varphi]\!]\sigma.$$

It is not hard to see that, for formulae in $HML^*_\leftarrow$, the denotational semantics is independent of the chosen environment and is equivalent to the satisfaction relation offered in Definition 2.

The semantics of a declaration $\mathcal{D}$ is given by a *model* for it, namely by an environment σ such that $\sigma(X) = [\![\mathcal{D}(X)]\!]\sigma$, for each variable $X \in \mathcal{X}$. For every declaration there may be a variety of models. However, we are usually interested in either the greatest or the least models, since they correspond to safety and liveness properties, respectively. In the light of the positivity restrictions we have placed on the formulae in the range of declarations, each declaration always has least and largest models by Tarski's fixed-point theorem [38]. See, e.g., [4,30] for details and textbook presentations.

Decomposition of Formulae in $HML^*_{\leftarrow,\mathcal{X}}$. We now turn to the transformation of formulae, so that we can extend Theorem 1 to include formulae from $HML^*_{\leftarrow,\mathcal{X}}$. Our developments in this section are inspired by [23], but the technical details are rather different and more involved.

In Section 4 we defined how a formula φ is quotiented with respect to a computation ρ. In particular, the quotiented formula $\top/\rho$ is $\top$ for any computation ρ. This works well in the non-recursive setting, but there is a hidden assumption that we must expose before tackling recursive formulae. In Theorem 1, the satisfaction relations are actually based on two different transition systems. By way of example, consider the expression on the right-hand side of (2), namely

$$\forall(\mu_1, \mu_2) \in D(\pi) : \ (p, \mu_1) \vDash \varphi/(q, \mu_2).$$

When establishing this statement, we have implicitly assumed that we are working within the transition system of computations from p that are *compatible* with the computations from q—i.e., above, μ_1 really is a path that is the counterpart of μ_2 in a decomposition of the path π.

Intuitively, the set of computations that satisfy a quotient formula φ/ρ is the set of computations that *are compatible with* ρ and whose *composition with* ρ satisfies the formula φ. However, defining $\top/\rho = \top$ does not match this intuition, if we take the denotational viewpoint of the formula $\top$ on the right-hand side as representing *all* possible computations. In fact, we expect $\top/\rho$ to represent only those computations that are compatible with ρ. We formalize the notion of pairs of compatible computations and refine our definition of $\top/\rho$.

Definition 5. *Paths μ_1 and μ_2 are* compatible with each other *if and only if they have the same length and one of the following holds if they are non-empty.*

- *If $\mu_1 = \mu_1'(p'' \xrightarrow{\tau} p')$ then $\mu_2 = \mu_2'(q' \dashrightarrow q')$ and μ_1' and μ_2' are compatible.*
- *If $\mu_1 = \mu_1'(p'' \xrightarrow{a} p')$ then either $\mu_2 = \mu_2'(q'' \xrightarrow{\bar{a}} q')$ or $\mu_2 = \mu_2'(q' \dashrightarrow q')$; and in both cases μ_1' and μ_2' are compatible.*
- *If $\mu_1 = \mu_1'(p'' \dashrightarrow p')$ then either $\mu_2 = \mu_2'(q'' \xrightarrow{\alpha} q')$, for some action α, or $\mu_2 = \mu_2'(q' \dashrightarrow q')$; and in both cases μ_1' and μ_2' are compatible.*

We say that two computations are compatible with each other *if their paths are compatible.*

We now revise our transformation of the formula $\top$. We want $\top/\rho$ to be a formula that is satisfied by the set of all computations that are compatible with ρ. It turns out this can be expressed in $HML_{\leftarrow}^*$ as described below.

Definition 6. *Let π be a path of transitions in the LTS $\mathcal{T} = \langle P, A, \rightarrow \rangle$. Then the $HML_{\leftarrow}^*$ formula $\top_\pi$ is defined as follows.*

$$\top_\lambda = [\leftarrow A_\tau]\bot \wedge [\leftarrow\!\text{-}\text{-}]\bot$$
$$\top_{\pi'(p \xrightarrow{\tau} p')} = \langle\leftarrow\!\text{-}\text{-}\rangle\top_{\pi'}$$
$$\top_{\pi'(p \xrightarrow{a} p')} = \langle\leftarrow\bar{a}\rangle\top_{\pi'} \vee \langle\leftarrow\!\text{-}\text{-}\rangle\top_{\pi'}$$
$$\top_{\pi'(p \dashrightarrow p')} = \langle\leftarrow A_\tau\rangle\top_{\pi'} \vee \langle\leftarrow\!\text{-}\text{-}\rangle\top_{\pi'}$$

Our reader may notice that this is a rewording of Definition 5, and it is easy to see that the computations satisfying $\top_\pi$ are exactly the computations that have paths compatible with π. Now the revised transformation of $\top$ is

$$\top/(p, \pi) = \top_\pi, \tag{4}$$

which matches our intuition. For the constructs in the logic $HML_{\leftarrow}^*$, we can reuse the transformation defined in Section 4. We therefore limit ourselves to highlighting how to quotient formulae of the form X. However, instead of decomposing formulae of this form, we treat the quotient X/ρ as a variable, i.e., we use the set $\mathcal{X} \times \mathcal{C}$ as our set of variables. The intuitive idea of such variables is as follows:

$$(p, \mu_1) \vDash_{\sigma'} X/(q, \mu_2) \Leftrightarrow (p \parallel q, \pi) \vDash_\sigma X \Leftrightarrow (p \parallel q, \pi) \in \sigma(X),$$

where σ is an environment for a declaration $\mathcal{D}$ over the variables $\mathcal{X}$, σ' is an environment for a declaration $\mathcal{D}'$ over the variables $\mathcal{X} \times \mathcal{C}$, and $(\mu_1, \mu_2) \in D(\pi)$. We explain below the relation between $\mathcal{D}$ and $\mathcal{D}'$ as well as the one between σ and σ'.

Formally, the variables used in quotienting our logic are pairs $(X, \rho) \in \mathcal{X} \times \mathcal{C}$. Formulae of the form X are simply rewritten as $X/\rho = (X, \rho)$, where the X/ρ on the left-hand side denotes the transformation (as in Section 4) and the pair on the right-hand side is the variable in our adapted logic. When there is no risk of ambiguity, we simply use the notation X/ρ to represent *the variable (X, ρ).*

Transformation of Declarations. Generating the transformed declaration $\mathcal{D}'$ from a declaration $\mathcal{D}$ is done as follows:

$$\mathcal{D}'(X/\rho) = \mathcal{D}(X)/\rho. \tag{5}$$

Note that the rewritten formula on the right-hand side may introduce more variables which obtain their values in $\mathcal{D}'$ in the same manner.

Transformation of Environments. The function Φ maps environments over $\mathcal{X}$ to environments over $\mathcal{X} \times \mathcal{C}$ thus:

$$\begin{aligned}
\sigma'(X/(q,\mu_2)) &= \Phi(\sigma)(X/(q,\mu_2)) \\
&= \{(p,\mu_1) \mid (p \parallel q, \pi) \in \sigma(X) \\
&\quad \text{for some } \pi \text{ with } (\mu_1,\mu_2) \in D(\pi)\}.
\end{aligned}$$

Our order of business now is to show that if σ is the least (respectively, largest) model for a declaration $\mathcal{D}$, then σ' is the least (respectively, largest) model for $\mathcal{D}'$ and vice versa. In particular, we show that there is a bijection relating models of $\mathcal{D}$ and models of $\mathcal{D}'$, based on the mapping Φ. First we define its inverse. Consider the function Ψ, which maps an environment over $\mathcal{X} \times \mathcal{C}$ to one over $\mathcal{X}$.

$$\Psi(\sigma')(X) = \{(p \parallel q, \pi) \mid \forall(\mu_1,\mu_2) \in D(\pi) : (p,\mu_1) \in \sigma'(X/(q,\mu_2))\}$$

It is not hard to see that Φ and Ψ are both monotonic.

We now use the model transformation functions Φ and Ψ to prove an extended version of Theorem 1.

Theorem 2. *Let p,q be CCS processes, $(p \parallel q, \pi) \in \mathcal{C}^*(p \parallel q)$. For a formula $\varphi \in HML^*_{\leftarrow,\mathcal{X}}$ and an environment σ, we have*

$$(p \parallel q, \pi) \vDash_\sigma \varphi \Leftrightarrow \forall(\mu_1,\mu_2) \in D(\pi) : (p,\mu_1) \vDash_{\Phi(\sigma)} \varphi/(q,\mu_2). \tag{6}$$

Conversely, for an environment σ',

$$(p \parallel q, \pi) \vDash_{\Psi(\sigma')} \varphi \Leftrightarrow \forall(\mu_1,\mu_2) \in D(\pi) : (p,\mu_1) \vDash_{\sigma'} \varphi/(q,\mu_2). \tag{7}$$

We can now show that the functions Φ and Ψ are inverses of each other.

Lemma 2. $\Psi \circ \Phi = \mathrm{id}_{\mathcal{E}_\mathcal{X}}$ *and* $\Phi \circ \Psi = \mathrm{id}_{\mathcal{E}_{\mathcal{X} \times \mathcal{C}}}$.

This means that Φ is a bijection between the collections of environments over the variable spaces $\mathcal{X}$ and $\mathcal{X} \times \mathcal{C}$, and Ψ is its inverse. The last theorem of this section establishes soundness of the decompositional reasoning for $HML^*_{\leftarrow,\mathcal{X}}$ by showing that Φ and Ψ preserve models of $\mathcal{D}$ and $\mathcal{D}'$, respectively.

Theorem 3. *Let $\mathcal{D}$ be a declaration over $\mathcal{X}$, and let $\mathcal{D}'$ be its companion declaration over $\mathcal{X} \times \mathcal{C}$ defined by (5). If σ is a model for $\mathcal{D}$, then $\Phi(\sigma)$ is a model for $\mathcal{D}'$. Moreover, if σ' is a model for $\mathcal{D}'$, then $\Psi(\sigma')$ is a model for $\mathcal{D}$.*

Theorem 3 allows us to use decompositional reasoning for $HML^*_{\leftarrow,\chi}$. Assume, for example, that we want to find the least model for a declaration $\mathcal{D}$. We start by constructing the declaration $\mathcal{D}'$ defined by (5). Next, we find the least model $\sigma'_{\min}$ of $\mathcal{D}'$ using standard fixed-point computations. (See, e.g., [4] for a textbook presentation.) We claim that $\Psi(\sigma'_{\min})$ is the least model of the declaration $\mathcal{D}$. Indeed, let σ be any model of $\mathcal{D}$. Then, by the above theorem, $\Phi(\sigma)$ is a model of $\mathcal{D}'$ and thus $\sigma'_{\min} \subseteq \Phi(\sigma)$ holds, where $\subseteq$ is lifted pointwise to environments. Then the monotonicity of Ψ and Lemma 2 ensure that $\Psi(\sigma'_{\min}) \subseteq \Psi(\Phi(\sigma)) = \sigma$. To conclude, note that $\Psi(\sigma'_{\min})$ is a model of $\mathcal{D}$ by the above theorem.

6   Extensions and Further Related Work

In this paper, we have developed techniques that allow us to apply decompositional reasoning for history-based computations over CCS and Hennessy-Milner logic with past modalities. Moreover, we extended the decomposition theorem to a recursive extension of that logic. The contribution of this paper can thus be summarized as follows. For each modal formula φ (in the μ-calculus with past) and each parallel computation π, in order to check whether $(p \parallel q, \pi) \vDash_\sigma \varphi$, it is sufficient to check $(p, \mu_1) \vDash_{\Phi(\sigma)} \varphi/(q, \mu_2)$, where (μ_1, μ_2) is a decomposition of π and $\varphi/(q, \mu_2)$ is the quotient of φ with respect to the component (q, μ_2). (The implication holds in the other direction, as well; however, the application of this theorem is expected in the aforementioned direction.) In the presentation of the decomposition of computations that is at the heart of our approach, we rely on some specific properties of CCS at the syntactic level, namely to detect which rule of the parallel operator was applied. By tagging a transition with its proof [11,15], or even just with the last rule used in the proof, we could eliminate this restriction and extend our approach to other languages involving parallel composition. Another possibility is to construct a rule format that guarantees the properties we use at a more general level, inspired by the work of [18]. However, all our results apply without change to CCS parallel composition over (possibly infinite) synchronization trees.

In this work we have only considered contexts built using parallel composition. However, decompositionality results have been shown for the more general setting of *process contexts* [31] and for rule formats [10,18]. In that work, one considers, for example, a unary context $C[\cdot]$ (a process term with a *hole*) and a process p with which to instantiate the context. A property of the instantiated context $C[p]$ can then be transformed into an equivalent property of p, where the transformation depends on C. As the state space explosion of model-checking problems is often due to the use of the parallel construct, we consider our approach a useful first step towards a full decomposition result for more general contexts. In general, the decomposition of computations will be more complex for general contexts.

The initial motivation for this work was the application of epistemic logic to behavioural models, following the lines of [14]. We therefore plan to extend our results to logics that include epistemic operators, reasoning about the knowledge of agents observing a running system. This work depends somewhat on the results presented in Section 5.

As we already mentioned in the introduction, there is by now a substantial body of work on temporal and modal logics with past operators. A small sample is given by the papers [21,27,39]. Of particular relevance for our work in this paper is the result in [27] to the effect that Hennessy-Milner logic with past modalities can be translated into ordinary Hennessy-Milner logic. That result, however, is only proved for the version of the logic without recursion and does not directly yield a quotienting construction for the logics we consider in this paper.

References

1. Aceto, L., Birgisson, A., Ingolfsdottir, A., Mousavi, M.R.: Decompositional reasoning about the history of parallel processes. Technical Report CSR-10-17, TU/Eindhoven (2010)
2. Aceto, L., Bouyer, P., Burgueño, A., Larsen, K.G.: The power of reachability testing for timed automata. TCS 300(1–3), 411–475 (2003)
3. Aceto, L., Ingólfsdóttir, A.: Testing Hennessy-Milner Logic with Recursion. In: Thomas, W. (ed.) FOSSACS 1999. LNCS, vol. 1578, pp. 41–55. Springer, Heidelberg (1999)
4. Aceto, L., Ingolfsdottir, A., Larsen, K.G., Srba, J.: Reactive Systems: Modelling, Specification and Verification, Cambridge (2007)
5. Andersen, H.R.: Partial model checking (extended abstract). In: LICS 1995, pp. 398–407. IEEE CS (1995)
6. Andersen, H.R., Stirling, C., Winskel, G.: A compositional proof system for the modal mu-calculus. In: LICS 1994, pp. 144–153. IEEE CS (1994)
7. Arnold, A., Vincent, A., Walukiewicz, I.: Games for synthesis of controllers with partial observation. TCS 303(1), 7–34 (2003)
8. Baeten, J.C.M., Basten, T., Reniers, M.A.: Process Algebra: Equational Theories of Communicating Processes, Cambridge (2009)
9. Basu, S., Kumar, R.: Quotient-based control synthesis for non-deterministic plants with mu-calculus specifications. In: IEEE Conference on Decision and Control 2006, pp. 5463–5468. IEEE (2006)
10. Bloom, B., Fokkink, W., van Glabbeek, R.J.: Precongruence formats for decorated trace semantics. ACM Trans. Comput. Log. 5(1), 26–78 (2004)
11. Boudol, G., Castellani, I.: A non-interleaving semantics for CCS based on proved transitions. Fundamenta Informaticae 11(4), 433–452 (1988)
12. Cassez, F., Laroussinie, F.: Model-Checking for Hybrid Systems by Quotienting and Constraints Solving. In: Emerson, E.A., Sistla, A.P. (eds.) CAV 2000. LNCS, vol. 1855, pp. 373–388. Springer, Heidelberg (2000)
13. Danos, V., Krivine, J.: Reversible Communicating Systems. In: Gardner, P., Yoshida, N. (eds.) CONCUR 2004. LNCS, vol. 3170, pp. 292–307. Springer, Heidelberg (2004)
14. Dechesne, F., Mousavi, M., Orzan, S.: Operational and Epistemic Approaches to Protocol Analysis: Bridging the Gap. In: Dershowitz, N., Voronkov, A. (eds.) LPAR 2007. LNCS (LNAI), vol. 4790, pp. 226–241. Springer, Heidelberg (2007)

15. Degano, P., Priami, C.: Proved Trees. In: Kuich, W. (ed.) ICALP 1992. LNCS, vol. 623, pp. 629–640. Springer, Heidelberg (1992)
16. De Nicola, R., Montanari, U., Vaandrager, F.W.: Back and Forth Bisimulations. In: Baeten, J.C.M., Klop, J.W. (eds.) CONCUR 1990. LNCS, vol. 458, pp. 152–165. Springer, Heidelberg (1990)
17. De Nicola, R., Vaandrager, F.W.: Three logics for branching bisimulation. JACM 42(2), 458–487 (1995)
18. Fokkink, W., van Glabbeek, R.J., de Wind, P.: Compositionality of Hennessy-Milner logic by structural operational semantics. TCS 354(3), 421–440 (2006)
19. Giannakopoulou, D., Pasareanu, C.S., Barringer, H.: Component verification with automatically generated assumptions. Automated Software Engineering 12(3), 297–320 (2005)
20. Halpern, J.Y., O'Neill, K.R.: Anonymity and information hiding in multiagent systems. Journal of Computer Security 13(3), 483–512 (2005)
21. Hennessy, M., Stirling, C.: The power of the future perfect in program logics. I & C 67(1-3), 23–52 (1985)
22. Henzinger, T.A., Kupferman, O., Qadeer, S.: From pre-historic to post-modern symbolic model checking. Formal Methods in System Design 23(3), 303–327 (2003)
23. Ingólfsdóttir, A., Godskesen, J.C., Zeeberg, M.: Fra Hennessy-Milner logik til CCS-processer. Technical report, Aalborg Universitetscenter (1987)
24. Kozen, D.: Results on the propositional mu-calculus. TCS 27, 333–354 (1983)
25. Laroussinie, F., Larsen, K.G.: Compositional Model Checking of Real Time Systems. In: Lee, I., Smolka, S.A. (eds.) CONCUR 1995. LNCS, vol. 962, pp. 27–41. Springer, Heidelberg (1995)
26. Laroussinie, F., Larsen, K.G.: CMC: A tool for compositional model-checking of real-time systems. In: FORTE 1998. IFIP Conference Proceedings, vol. 135, pp. 439–456. Kluwer (1998)
27. Laroussinie, F., Pinchinat, S., Schnoebelen, P.: Translations between modal logics of reactive systems. TCS 140(1), 53–71 (1995)
28. Laroussinie, F., Schnoebelen, P.: Specification in CTL+past for verification in CTL. I & C 156(1), 236–263 (2000)
29. Larsen, K.G.: Context-dependent bisimulation between processes. PhD thesis, University of Edinburgh (1986)
30. Larsen, K.G.: Proof systems for satisfiability in Hennessy–Milner logic with recursion. TCS 72(2–3), 265–288 (1990)
31. Larsen, K.G., Xinxin, L.: Compositionality through an operational semantics of contexts. Journal of Logic and Computation 1(6), 761–795 (1991)
32. Lichtenstein, O., Pnueli, A., Zuck, L.D.: The Glory of the Past. In: Parikh, R. (ed.) Logic of Programs 1985. LNCS, vol. 193, pp. 196–218. Springer, Heidelberg (1985)
33. Nielsen, M.: Reasoning about the Past. In: Brim, L., Gruska, J., Zlatuška, J. (eds.) MFCS 1998. LNCS, vol. 1450, pp. 117–128. Springer, Heidelberg (1998)
34. Phillips, I.C.C., Ulidowski, I.: Reversing algebraic process calculi. JLAP 73(1–2), 70–96 (2007)
35. Raclet, J.-B.: Residual for component specifications. Electr. Notes Theor. Comput. Sci. 215, 93–110 (2008)
36. Simpson, A.K.: Sequent calculi for process verification: Hennessy-Milner logic for an arbitrary GSOS. JLAP 60-61, 287–322 (2004)
37. Stirling, C.: A Complete Compositional Modal Proof System for a Subset of CCS. In: Brauer, W. (ed.) ICALP 1985. LNCS, vol. 194, pp. 475–486. Springer, Heidelberg (1985)

38. Tarski, A.: A lattice-theoretical fixpoint theorem and its applications. Pacific Journal of Mathematics 5, 285–309 (1955)
39. Vardi, M.Y.: Reasoning about the Past with Two-Way Automata. In: Larsen, K.G., Skyum, S., Winskel, G. (eds.) ICALP 1998. LNCS, vol. 1443, pp. 628–641. Springer, Heidelberg (1998)
40. Winskel, G.: Synchronization trees. TCS 34, 33–82 (1984)
41. Winskel, G.: A complete proof system for SCCS with modal assertions. Fundamenta Informaticae IX, 401–420 (1986)
42. Xie, G., Dang, Z.: Testing Systems of Concurrent Black-Boxes—an Automata-Theoretic and Decompositional Approach. In: Grieskamp, W., Weise, C. (eds.) FATES 2005. LNCS, vol. 3997, pp. 170–186. Springer, Heidelberg (2006)

A Model-Based Development Approach for Model Transformations

Shekoufeh Kolahdouz-Rahimi and Kevin Lano

Dept. of Informatics, King's College London, Strand, London, UK

Abstract. Model transformations have become a key element of model-driven software development, being used to transform platform-independent models (PIMs) to platform-specific models (PSMs), to improve model quality, to introduce design patterns and refactorings, and to map models from one language to another. A large number of model transformation notations and tools exist, however, there remain substantial problems concerning the analysis and verification of model transformations. In particular, there is no systematic development process for model transformations.

In this paper, we provide a unified semantic treatment of model transformations, and show how correctness properties of model transformations can be defined. We define a systematic model-driven development process for model transformations based on this semantics, and we describe case studies using this process.

1 Introduction

Model transformations are mappings of one or more software engineering models (*source* models) into one or more *target* models. The models considered may be graphically constructed using graphical languages such as the Unified Modelling Language (UML) [18], or can be textual notations such as programming languages or formal specification languages.

The research area of model transformations remains very active, and certain fundamental issues have as yet only partially been solved:

Specification Issues. Semantically, model transformations can be considered to be relations between (the sets of models of) languages, ie., in the binary case, they identify for a pair (M_1, M_2) of models of two languages, if M_1 is related by the transformation to M_2.

But for convenience transformations are usually defined by sets of transformation rules which relate specific elements of M_1 to specific elements of M_2. This introduces problems of dependency and consistency between rules, and the overall effect of the set of rules may be difficult to deduce from the rules themselves, either for a human reader, or for analysis and verification tools [23].

These problems are akin to those of other software technologies, such as rewrite-rule based systems and knowledge-based systems, which describe global processes by collections of localised rules.

F. Arbab and M. Sirjani (Eds.): FSEN 2011, LNCS 7141, pp. 48–63, 2012.
© Springer-Verlag Berlin Heidelberg 2012

Development Issues. At present, construction of model transformations is focussed upon the implementation of a transformation in a particular model transformation language [6], the transformation is described only at a relatively low level of abstraction, without a separate specification. The development process may be ad-hoc, without systematic guidelines on how to structure transformations. The plethora of different transformation languages creates problems of migration and reuse of transformations from one language to another.

Ironically, the model transformation community has recreated the development problems, for this specialised form of software, which model-driven development (MDD) was intended to ameliorate: the inability to reuse and migrate systems due to the lack of platform-independent specifications, and an excessive implementation focus [7].

The solution which we propose to these problems is to adopt a general model-driven software development approach, UML-RSDS (Reactive System Development Support) [14], for model transformation development. UML-RSDS provides the necessary specification notations for model transformation definition, at different levels of abstraction, and provides support for verification and the synthesis of executable code. UML-RSDS uses standardised UML notation and concepts, so permitting reuse and communication of models.

We consider the following kinds of model transformation: *Refinement* transformations are used to refine a model towards an implementation. For example, PIM to PSM transformations in the Model-driven Architecture (MDA). *Re-expressions* translate a model in one language into its 'nearest equivalent' in a different language. This includes model migration. Transformations which perform some analysis upon the source model and construct analysis results, such as checking or model comparison transformations, can be considered as *abstractions*. *Quality improvement* transformations transform a model to improve its structure.

Within each category, further subcategories can be distinguished, for example *refactoring* is a particular subcategory of quality improvement transformation.

Section 2 defines a general semantics for model transformations and defines concepts of correctness for model transformations. Section 3 surveys techniques for the definition of transformations. Section 4 describes the UML-RSDS language and the elements of our model transformation development process using UML-RSDS. Section 5 describes the application of the process to the specification and design of transformation case studies. Finally in Section 7 we summarise our recommendations for improving the development of model transformations.

2   Semantic Framework for Model Transformations

2.1   Metamodelling Framework

We will consider transformations between languages specified using the Meta-Object Framework (MOF). Figure 1 shows the four-level metamodelling framework of UML using MOF. At each level, a model or structure can be considered to be an instance of a structure at the next higher level.

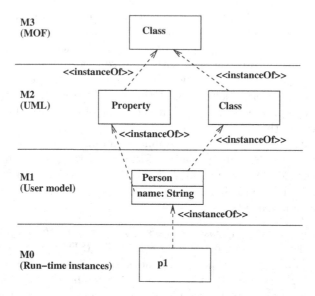

Fig. 1. UML metamodel levels

In discussing model transformation correctness, we will refer to the M2 level as the *language level* (the models define the languages which the transformation relates) and to the M1 level as the *model level* (the models which the transformation operates upon).

For each model M at levels M2 and M3, we can define (i) a logical language $\mathcal{L}_M$ that corresponds to M, and (ii) a logical theory Γ_M in $\mathcal{L}_M$, which defines the semantic meaning of M, including any internal constraints of M. If an M1 model is also a UML model, it can also be assigned such a language and theory. $\mathcal{L}_M$ and Γ_M are defined using the axiomatic semantics for UML given in Chapter 6 of [16], based upon structured theories and theory morphisms in a real-time temporal logic.

$\mathcal{L}_M$ consists of type symbols for each type defined in M, including primitive types such as integers, reals, booleans and strings which are normally included in models, and each classifier defined in M. There are attribute symbols $att(c : C) : T$ for each property att of type T in the feature set of C. There are attributes $\overline{C}$ to denote the instances of each classifier C (corresponding to $C.allInstances()$ in the UML object constraint language (OCL)), and action symbols $op(c : C, p : P)$ for each operation $op(p : P)$ in the features of C [15]. Collection types and operations on these and the primitive types are also included. The OCL logical operators *and*, *implies*, *forAll*, *exists* are interpreted as $\wedge$, $\Rightarrow$, $\forall$, $\exists$, etc.

Γ_M includes axioms expressing the multiplicities of association ends, the mutual inverse property of opposite association ends, deletion propagation through composite aggregations, the existence of generalisation relations, and the logical semantics of any explicit constraints in M, including pre/post specifications of operations.

For a sentence φ in $\mathcal{L}_M$, there is the usual notion of logical consequence:

$$\Gamma_M \vdash \varphi$$

means the sentence is provable from the theory of M, and so holds in M. $\vdash_L$ is used to emphasise that the deduction takes place within language L.

If M is at the M1 level and is an instance of a language L at the M2 level, then it satisfies all the properties of Γ_L, although these cannot be expressed within $\mathcal{L}_M$ itself. We use the notation $M \models \varphi$ to express satisfaction of an $\mathcal{L}_L$ sentence φ in M.

For example, any particular UML class diagram satisfies the language-level property that there are no cycles in the inheritance hierarchy.

2.2   Model Transformation Semantics

As discussed above, transformations can be regarded as relations between models. The models may be in the same or in different modelling languages. Let $\mathcal{L}_1$ and $\mathcal{L}_2$ be the languages concerned. We assume these are defined as metamodels using MOF. A transformation τ then describes which models M_1 of $\mathcal{L}_1$ correspond to (transform to) which models M_2 of $\mathcal{L}_2$.

Let $Models_{\mathcal{L}}$ be the set of models which interpret the language (metamodel) $\mathcal{L}$ and satisfy ($\models$) any logical properties defined for $\mathcal{L}$. We may simply write $M : \mathcal{L}$ instead of $M : Models_{\mathcal{L}}$.

A model transformation τ from language $\mathcal{L}_1$ to language $\mathcal{L}_2$ can therefore be expressed as a relation

$$Rel_\tau : Models_{\mathcal{L}_1} \leftrightarrow Models_{\mathcal{L}_2}$$

Sequential composition τ; σ of transformations corresponds to relational composition of their representing relations.

2.3   Model Transformation Correctness

The following notions of transformation correctness have been defined [24,3]: *Syntactic correctness, Definedness, Completeness* and *Semantic correctness*. The first three properties are termed *Strong executability, Totality* and *Determinism* in [3].

In our semantics for transformations, we can precisely define these criteria as follows for a model transformation τ from $\mathcal{L}_1$ to $\mathcal{L}_2$:

Syntactic Correctness. For each model which conforms to (is a model in the language) $\mathcal{L}_1$, and to which the transformation can be applied, the transformed model conforms to $\mathcal{L}_2$:

$$\forall M_1 : \mathcal{L}_1; \; M_2 \cdot Rel_\tau(M_1, M_2) \;\Rightarrow\; M_2 : \mathcal{L}_2$$

Definedness. This means that the applicability condition of Rel_τ is *true*: its domain is the complete collection of models of $\mathcal{L}_1$.

Uniqueness. This means that Rel_τ is functional in the source to target direction.

Completeness. The specification of τ is complete with respect to the requirements, if when a model M_1 of $\mathcal{L}_1$ should be related to a model M_2 of $\mathcal{L}_2$ by the transformation, then $Rel_\tau(M_1, M_2)$ holds.

Semantic Correctness. 1. (Language-level correctness): each language-level property $\varphi : \mathcal{L}_{\mathcal{L}_1}$ satisfied by source model M_1 is also satisfied, under an interpretation χ on language-level expressions, in M_2:

$$\forall M_1 : \mathcal{L}_1;\ M_2 : \mathcal{L}_2 \cdot Rel_\tau(M_1, M_2)\ \wedge\ M_1 \models \varphi\ \Rightarrow\ M_2 \models \chi(\varphi)$$

This shows that $\mathcal{L}_2$ is at least as expressive as $\mathcal{L}_1$, and that users of M_2 can continue to view it as a model of $\mathcal{L}_1$, because the data of M_1 can be expressed in terms of that of M_2. In particular, no information about M_1 is lost by τ.

2. (Model-level correctness): each model-level property $\varphi : \mathcal{L}_{M_1}$ of a source model M_1 is also true, under an interpretation ζ on model-level expressions, in M_2:

$$\forall M_1 : \mathcal{L}_1;\ M_2 : \mathcal{L}_2 \cdot Rel_\tau(M_1, M_2)\ \wedge\ \Gamma_{M_1} \vdash \varphi\ \Rightarrow\ \Gamma_{M_2} \vdash \zeta(\varphi)$$

for $\varphi \in \Gamma_{M_1}$.

This means that internal constraints of M_1 remain valid in interpreted form in M_2, for example, that subclassing in a UML model is mapped to subsetting of sets of table primary key values, in a transformation from UML to relational databases [20].

Model-level semantic correctness should be expected for refinement, specialisation, enhancement and quality improvement transformations. For re-expression transformations there may be cases where M_1 properties cannot be expressed in M_2 (ζ will be a partial interpretation), but all expressible properties should be preserved from M_1 to M_2.

If transformations τ and σ are semantically correct at a particular level, so is their composition $\tau; \sigma$, using the composition of the corresponding interpretations.

At the model level, the OCL constraints φ of a model should be transformed to $\zeta(\varphi)$ or to a predicate which implies this. This will ensure model-level semantic correctness in many cases, although if the types or classifiers of the source language are changed by the transformation (such as by amalgamating subclasses of a class), additional steps need to be taken.

Further correctness properties can also be considered concerning collections of model transformations which may be used together (for example, individual model transformation rules within a transformation specification):

No Conflicts. Two rules conflict if they can both be applied to the same elements in a particular model, and their results are different.

Confluence. That where different orders of application of transformation rules to a model are possible, the resulting model is the same regardless of the order of applications. In particular, the result of an individual transformation rule applied repeatedly to different elements within a model does not depend on the order in which these applications occur.

One recommendation that could be made is that within each group of transformation rules which may be executed without ordering restrictions, that no rules conflict with each other, and that there is confluence within the group. Such a group could constitute a single phase in a transformation algorithm. The correctness of a transformation could then be demonstrated from that of its individual phases or rulesets.

A model transformation implementation is said to be *change propagating* if changes Δs to the source model s can be used to compute a necessary change Δt to the target model, without the need to re-execute the transformation on the new source model $s + \Delta s$. Two change-propagating transformations compose to form a change-propagating transformation.

3   Specification Techniques for Model Transformations

A large number of formalisms have been proposed for the definition of model transformations: the *pure relational* approach of [2,1], *graphical* description languages such as graph grammars [5,22] or the visual notation of QVT-Relations [19], hybrid approaches such as Epsilon [11] and implementation-oriented languages such as Kermeta [10].

In each approach, model transformations are specified and implemented as rules specific to particular kinds of elements in the source model(s) and individual elements in the target model(s). The model-to-model relation is then derived from some composition of these individual rules.

This raises the question of how it can be shown that the composition of the rules achieves the intended global relation, and what semantics should be used to carry out the composition. In the case of languages such as ATL [8] and QVT-Relations, the order of invocations of rules may be only implicitly defined, and may be indeterminate.

4   Transformation Specification in UML-RSDS

UML-RSDS is a UML-based specification language, consisting of UML class diagrams, state machines, activities, sequence diagrams, and a subset of OCL. It is used as the specification language of an automated Model-Driven Development approach, Constraint-Driven Development (CDD) [15], by which executable systems can be synthesised from high-level specifications.

The most abstract form of specification in UML-RSDS consists of class diagrams together with constraints, the constraints serve to define both the static state and dynamic behaviour of the system, and executable code is synthesised from such constraints using the principle that any operation *op* that changes the state of the model must have an executable implementation which ensures that all the model constraints remain true in the modified state.

It is also possible to use a lower level of abstraction, and to explicitly specify operations using pre and post-conditions in OCL, and define activities or state machines to specify the order of execution of operations within a class, or of individual steps of specific operations.

Both styles may be used to specify model transformations. The first style inherently supports bidirectional (invertible) and change-propagating model transformations, the second only directly supports unidirectional mappings, but can produce more efficient implementations of the transformation.

4.1 Development Process for Model Transformations

Our general recommended development process for model transformations is as follows:

Requirements. The requirements of the transformation are defined, the source and target metamodels are specified, including which constraints need to be established or preserved by the transformation, and what assumptions can be made about the input models. A use case diagram can be used to describe the top-level capabilities of the system, and non-functional requirements can be identified.

Abstract Specification. Constraints can be used to define the overall relation Rel_τ between source and target models for each use case (transformation). We will usually express the precondition of a transformation (considered as a single operation) as a predicate Asm, and the postcondition as a predicate $Cons$, both Asm and $Cons$ may be expressed in the union of the languages of the source and target models. Asm defines the domain of Rel_τ, and $Cons$ defines which pairs of models are in Rel_τ. Informal diagrams in the concrete syntax of the source and target languages can be used to explain the key aspects of this relation, as in the CGT model transformation approach [7].

It should be possible to show at this stage that $Cons$ establishes the required properties Ens of the result models:

$$Cons, \Gamma_{L1} \vdash_{\mathcal{L}_{L1 \cup L2}} Ens$$

where $L1$ is the source language, $L2$ the target language.

Likewise, $Cons$ should prove that $Pres$ are preserved, via a suitable interpretation χ from the source language to the target language:

$$Cons, Pres, \Gamma_{L1} \vdash_{\mathcal{L}_{L1 \cup L2}} \chi(Pres)$$

Explicit Specification and Design. The transformation can be broken down into phases, each with its own source and target language and specification. Phases should be independent of each other, except that the assumptions of a non-initial phase should be ensured by the preceeding phase(s).

For each phase, define transformation rules (as operations specified by pre/postconditions), and an activity to specify the order of execution of the rules. Recursion between rules should be avoided if possible. Again, informal diagrams can supplement the formal definition of the rules. For each phase, verification that the activity combination of the rules satisfies the overall specification of the phase can be carried out. It can also be checked that the rule operations are deterministic and well-defined, and that the activities are confluent and terminating under the precondition of the phase. Finally, it should be checked that the composition of the phases achieves the specified relation *Cons* and required property preservation/establishment conditions of the overall transformation:

$$\Gamma_{L1} \vdash_{\mathcal{L}_{L1 \cup L2}} Asm \Rightarrow [activity] Cons$$

where *activity* is the design decomposition of the transformation into phases. [*stat*]*P* is the weakest precondition of predicate P with respect to statement/activity *stat* (Chapter 6 of [16]).

The relative independence of particular rules and phases will enhance the possibilities for reuse of these in other transformations.

Implementation. Code can be generated in a particular transformation implementation language, such as Java, ATL or Kermeta. Different phases can be implemented in different languages.

The emphasis in this development approach is on simplicity and verifiability. Even if fully formal verification is not attempted, the decomposition of a transformation into phases and activities supports the systematic composition of local pre/post specifications of individual rules to establish the specifications of phases and then of the complete transformation. The specification of the transformation can then be used (independently of the details of phases) to prove the required preservation and establishment properties of the use case corresponding to the transformation.

5   Case Studies

The first case study that we consider is a re-expression transformation from trees to graphs. Figure 2 shows the source and target metamodels of this transformation. We will carry out all reasoning in this example directly upon OCL constraints, rather than upon the formal semantics of these constraints. Such reasoning can be recast in a fully formal version.

The *identity* constraint in the metamodels means that tree nodes must have unique names, and likewise for graph nodes.

5.1   Requirements

The requirements of the case study consist of the metamodels, and two use cases, one to check the validity of the source model and the other to carry out the mapping upon a valid model.

The checking transformation has no assumptions, and should return *true* if the source model is valid (no duplicate names, and no undefined *parent* trees), and *false* otherwise.

Fig. 2. Tree to graph transformation metamodels

The mapping transformation has as its assumption *Asm* these validity conditions *Asm*1:

$\forall t1, t2 : Tree \cdot t1.name = t2.name$ *implies* $t1 = t2$
$\forall t : Tree \cdot t.parent : Tree$

together with the emptiness of the target model (*Asm*2):

$Node = \{\}$ *and* $Edge = \{\}$

The following *Pres* property of the tree metamodel is to be preserved: that there are no non-trivial cycles in the *parent* relationship:

$t : Tree$ *and* $t \neq t.parent$ *implies* $t \notin t.parent^+$

where r^+ is the non-reflexive transitive closure of r. Trees may be their own parent if they are the root node of a tree.

There are two properties of the graph metamodel which should be ensured: *Ens*1 is the constraint that edges must always connect different nodes:

$e : Edge$ *implies* $e.source \neq e.target$

*Ens*2 states that edges are uniquely defined by their source and target, together:

$e1 : Edge$ *and* $e2 : Edge$ *and*
$e1.source = e2.source$ *and* $e1.target = e2.target$ *implies* $e1 = e2$

Pres is a predicate in OCL over the source metamodel (considered as a UML class diagram), and *Ens* is a predicate in OCL over the target metamodel. *Asm* may in general be a predicate over both metamodels (for example, to assert that the target model is empty at the start of a mapping transformation).

5.2   Abstract Specification

We will consider the use case to map trees to graphs. The transformation relates tree objects in the source model to node objects in the target model with the same name, and defines that there is an edge object in the target model for each non-trivial relationship from a tree node to its parent.

The formal specification *Cons* of the transformation as a single global relation between the source and target languages can be split into five separate constraints:

C1. "For each tree node in the source model there is a graph node in the target model with the same name":

$$t : Tree \; implies \; \exists \, n : Node \cdot n.name = t.name$$

C2. "For each non-trivial parent relationship in the source model, there is an edge representing the relationship in the target model":

$$t : Tree \; and \; t.parent \neq t \; implies$$
$$\exists \, e : Edge \cdot e.source = Node[t.name] \; and \; e.target =$$
$$Node[t.parent.name]$$

The notation *Node*[x] refers to the node object with primary key (in this case name) value equal to x, it is implemented in the UML-RSDS tools by maintaining a map from the key values to nodes. In OCL it would be expressed as

$$Node.allInstances() \rightarrow select(n \;\; | \;\; n.name \;\; = \;\; x) \rightarrow any()$$

C3. "For each graph node in the target model there is a tree node in the source model with the same name":

$$g : Node \; implies \; \exists \, t : Tree \cdot t.name = g.name$$

C4. "For each edge in the target model, there is a non-trivial parent relationship in the source model, which the edge represents":

$$e : Edge \; implies \; \exists \, t : Tree \cdot t.parent \neq t \; and$$
$$t = Tree[e.source.name] \; and$$
$$t.parent = Tree[e.target.name]$$

C5. The same as *Ens2*.

$C3$ and $C4$ are duals of $C1$ and $C2$, defining a reverse direction, from graphs to trees, of the transformation, so that it is (in principle) bidirectional. $C1$ and $C3$ together with the metamodels ensure that there is a 1-1 mapping from trees to nodes, which facilitates change propagation in both directions. Because *Ens2* is not provable from $C1$ to $C4$, we have included it in *Cons*, so requiring that the design ensures this property.

$C4$ together with the uniqueness of names, establishes *Ens1*, and $C5$ establishes *Ens2*.

For refinement and re-expression transformations in particular, it is important that the transformation preserves semantic meaning. That is, the information of the source model is preserved in the target model, possibly under some interpretation. In our example, a logical interpretation χ from trees to graphs can be defined, in OCL notation, as follows.

$$Tree.allInstances() \longmapsto Node.allInstances()$$
$$name \longmapsto name$$
$$parent \longmapsto if\ Edge.allInstances() \rightarrow select(e \mid e.source = self) \rightarrow notEmpty()$$
$$then\ Edge.allInstances() \rightarrow select(e \mid e.source = self) \rightarrow any().target$$
$$else\ self$$

This is well-defined since all edges with the same source must also have the same target. The parent relation of the source model is therefore recoverable from the edges of the target model. The property *Pres* has interpretation $\chi(Pres)$ which states that nodes in the graph which are not linked to themselves in the graph are never reachable from themselves by following edges from source to target.

This is provable from $C3$ and $C4$ and from *Pres* in $L1$, since if there was such a cycle in the graph, it must have been produced from a corresponding cycle of trees, contradicting *Pres*.

5.3   Explicit Specification and Design

This example is small enough that a single phase is sufficient for its design, however we can split the mapping transformation into two phases:

1. *phase*1: map all tree elements to corresponding nodes;
2. *phase*2: map *parent* links to corresponding edges.

These are composed as *phase*1; *phase*2 to achieve the overall mapping.

*phase*1 can be treated as a new transformation with its own specification and design. Its global specification is $C1$ *and* $C3$, its assumption is *Asm*.

*phase*2 has the global specification $C2$ *and* $C4$ *and* $C5$, its assumption is $C1$ *and* $C3$ *and* $Asm1$ *and* $Edge = \{\}$.

In turn, a set of specific rules can be defined to carry out each phase, together with an activity which defines the order of application of the rules within the phase.

For *phase*1 the mapping from a particular tree to a new graph node could be expressed by the operation:

$$mapTreeToNode(t\ :\ Tree)$$
$$\texttt{post:}$$
$$\exists\ n\ :\ Node\ \cdot\ n.name\ =\ t.name$$

The activity for this phase is a simple unordered iteration over all tree elements:

$$for\ t : Tree\ do\ mapTreeToNode(t)$$

This iteration executes $mapTreeToNode(t)$ exactly once for each t in *Tree* at the start of the loop execution.

For *phase2* the rule is:

mapTreeToEdge(t : *Tree*)
pre:
   $t.name$ $\in$ *Node.name*   and
   $t.parent.name$ $\in$ *Node.name*
post:
   t $\neq$ $t.parent$ *implies* $\exists$ e : *Edge* ·
      $e.source$ = $Node[t.name]$ and
      $e.target$ = $Node[t.parent.name]$

Node.name abbreviates *Node.allInstances*()→*collect*(*name*).

Note that the rules are very close in form to the constraints $C1$ and $C3$ of *Cons*, indeed for specifications in *conjunctive-implicative* form as for *Cons* in this example, the rules can be generated from the forward constraints in *Cons*.

The activity for this phase is:

for t : *Tree* **do** *mapTreeToEdge*(t)

The explicit unidirectional rules generally permit more efficient implementation than the purely constraint-based specifications. They can be related to the requirements *Cons* by showing, using reasoning in the axiomatic semantics (Chapter 6 of [16]) of UML, that they do establish the constraints:

$$t : Tree \;\Rightarrow\; [mapTreeToNode(t)](\exists\, n : Node \cdot n.name = t.name)$$

and hence

$$[for\ t : Tree\ do\ mapTreeToNode(t)](\forall\, t : Tree \cdot \exists\, n : Node \cdot n.name = t.name)$$

because the individual applications of *mapTreeToNode*(t) are independent and non-interfering, so the iteration is confluent.

We can also reason that *phase1* establishes $C3$ because nodes are only created by the execution of *mapTreeToNode*(t), and hence each is derived from a corresponding tree element. Therefore the design of this phase is correct wrt its specification.

Similarly we can verify the correctness of the second phase.

A *ruleset* in UML-RSDS is a set of rules (operations), it is defined as a UML class with a behaviour defined by an activity. This controls the allowed order of application of the rules. In this example we can therefore have one ruleset for each phase, each with a single operation.

By composing the two phases in sequence, we can also establish the overall correctness of the transformation:

$$Asm \Rightarrow [phase1;\ phase2]\,Cons$$

This is the case because *phase1* establishes the assumptions of *phase2*, and *phase2* does not invalidate the effects $C1$ and $C3$ achieved by *phase1*.

The syntactic correctness of individual phases can be formally proved by using an automated translation from UML-RSDS to the B formal notation [13,17], and applying proof within B. The B module produced represents the union of the theories of the source and target languages. It is linear in size with respect to these languages.

Definedness can be checked by ensuring that sufficient conditions hold (eg, that the precondition of each called operation is true at the point of call, and that no undefined expression evaluations can occur) to ensure definedness of each transformation activity. Loop termination for unbounded loops requires the definition of a loop variant and proof that this integer expression is decreased in value on each loop iteration and is bounded below.

The UML-RSDS tools check completeness of rules by checking that all data features of an object are set in the operation which creates it. For example, in the operation *mapTreeToEdge*, an error message would be given if there was no assignment to the *target* of the new edge. In addition it is checked that in a postcondition formed from conjunctions of E *implies* P implications, that the disjunction of the E conditions is implied by the precondition.

There are rules to determine when unordered iterations are confluent, for example, if they update disjoint sets of elements [17].

Determinacy of an operation is checked by ensuring that there are no disjunctions or other indeterminate operators on the right-hand side of implications in the postcondition. Consistency is checked by ensuring that in conjunctions of E *implies* P implications, that the E conditions are pairwise disjoint.

5.4   Implementation

Using the UML-RSDS tools, executable Java code can be generated for the transformation, from the explicit activities and rules, this code operates upon Java representations of the source and target metamodels.

5.5   Other Case Studies

The process has also been applied to several larger case studies, including the mapping of activities from UML 1.4 to UML 2.2, in the 2010 transformation tool competition [21], and the mapping of UML class diagrams, including both single and multiple inheritance, and association classes, to relational database schemas.

An example of a constraint from the *Cons* specification of the migration case study is the mapping of a simple state in UML 1.4 activities to *AcceptEventAction* instances in UML 2.2:

$$s : SimpleState \ and \ s.outgoing.size = 1 \ and \ s.outgoing.trigger.size = 1 \ implies$$
$$\exists n : AcceptEventAction \ \cdot \ n.name = s.name \ and \ n.trigger = s.outgoing.trigger$$

Figure 3 shows the mapping of a signal-triggered transition from a UML 1.4 *SimpleState* to a semantically equivalent UML 2.2 diagram with an *AcceptEventAction* to consume the triggering event.

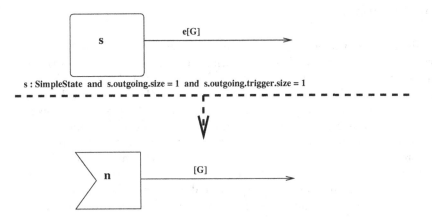

n : AcceptEventAction and n.name = s.name and n.trigger = s.outgoing.trigger

Fig. 3. Mapping of signal-triggered transitions

The transformation design consists of three phases:

1. *phase*1: establishes the correspondences between each kind of state vertex and activity node.
2. *phase*2: establishes the correspondences of guards and transitions with opaque expressions and activity edges, assuming the correspondences of states from *phase*1.
3. *phase*3: establishes the correspondences of partitions and activity graphs with activity partitions and activities, assuming the correspondences of states from *phase*1 and transitions from *phase*2.

The mapping of simple states is implemented as an operation

toActivity()
post:
$\quad$ *outgoing.size* $= 1$ *and outgoing.trigger.size* $= 1$ *implies*
$\quad\quad \exists \ n \ : \ AcceptEventAction \ \cdot \ n.name \ = \ name \ and$
$\quad\quad\quad\quad\quad\quad\quad\quad n.trigger \ = \ outgoing.trigger$

in *SimpleState*.

6   Related Work

The paper [6] introduces a language, transML, to support the development of model transformations. This however introduces a set of novel notations for requirements, specification and design. We consider that it is preferable to use standardised and familier notations where possible, particularly UML, with which most model transformation developers can be assumed to be already familiar.

Other MDD languages and processes could also be used to systematically develop model transformations using the development process described here, for example, executable UML [9].

7 Conclusions

We have defined a development process and specification technique for model transformations, using UML-RSDS. Modularity is based upon the object-oriented modularity of UML models (class diagrams and behaviour models). Model transformation tools generally lack support for semantic analysis. UML-RSDS provides a completeness check on objects created by rules. Other semantic checks, such as the detection of potentially unbounded recursion between rules, would also be beneficial for developers. Proof that metamodel constraints are established or preserved by transformations (syntactic and semantic correctness) is important in maintaining the integrity and correctness of a system. By decomposing transformations into phases, compositional proof that the transformation establishes a required global relationship between the source and target models can be carried out.

Acknowledgement. The work presented here was carried out in the EPSRC HoRTMoDA project at King's College London.

References

1. Akehurst, D., Howells, W., McDonald-Maier, K.: Kent Model Transformation Language. Model Transformations in Practice (2005)
2. Akehurst, D.H., Caskurlu, B.: A Relational Approach to Defining Transformations in a Metamodel. In: Jézéquel, J.-M., Hussmann, H., Cook, S. (eds.) UML 2002. LNCS, vol. 2460, pp. 243–258. Springer, Heidelberg (2002)
3. Cabot, J., Clariso, R., Guerra, E., De Lara, J.: Verification and Validation of Declarative Model-to-Model Transformations Through Invariants. Journal of Systems and Software (2009) (preprint)
4. Cuadrado, J., Molina, J.: Modularisation of model transformations through a phasing mechanism. Software Systems Modelling 8(3), 325–345 (2009)
5. Ehrig, H., Engels, G., Rozenberg, H.-J. (eds.): Handbook of Graph Grammars and Computing by Graph Transformation, vol. 2. World Scientific Press (1999)
6. Guerra, E., de Lara, J., Kolovos, D.S., Paige, R.F., dos Santos, O.M.: *transML*: A Family of Languages to Model Model Transformations. In: Petriu, D.C., Rouquette, N., Haugen, Ø. (eds.) MODELS 2010. LNCS, vol. 6394, pp. 106–120. Springer, Heidelberg (2010)
7. Grønmo, R., Møller-Pedersen, B., Olsen, G.K.: Comparison of Three Model Transformation Languages. In: Paige, R.F., Hartman, A., Rensink, A. (eds.) ECMDA-FA 2009. LNCS, vol. 5562, pp. 2–17. Springer, Heidelberg (2009)
8. Jouault, F., Kurtev, I.: Transforming Models with ATL. In: Bruel, J.-M. (ed.) MoDELS 2005. LNCS, vol. 3844, pp. 128–138. Springer, Heidelberg (2006)
9. Carter, K.: Executable UML (2010), http://www.kc.com/XUML
10. Kermeta (2010), http://www.kermeta.org
11. Kolovos, D., Paige, R., Polack, F.: The Epsilon Transformation Language. In: Vallecillo, A., Gray, J., Pierantonio, A. (eds.) ICMT 2008. LNCS, vol. 5063, pp. 46–60. Springer, Heidelberg (2008)

12. Kurtev, I., Van den Berg, K., Joualt, F.: Rule-based modularisation in model transformation languages illustrated with ATL. In: Proceedings 2006 ACM Symposium on Applied Computing (SAC 2006), pp. 1202–1209. ACM Press (2006)
13. Lano, K.: The B Language and Method. Springer, Heidelberg (1996)
14. Lano, K.: Constraint-Driven Development. Information and Software Technology 50, 406–423 (2008)
15. Lano, K.: A Compositional Semantics of UML-RSDS. SoSyM 8(1), 85–116 (2009)
16. Lano, K. (ed.): UML 2 Semantics and Applications. Wiley (2009)
17. Lano, K., Kolahdouz-Rahimi, S.: Specification and Verification of Model Transformations using UML-RSDS. In: Méry, D., Merz, S. (eds.) IFM 2010. LNCS, vol. 6396, pp. 199–214. Springer, Heidelberg (2010)
18. OMG, UML superstructure, version 2.1.1. OMG document formal/2007-02-03, (2007)
19. OMG, Query/View/Transformation Specification, ptc/05-11-01, (2005)
20. OMG, Query/View/Transformation Specification, annex A (2010)
21. Rose, L., Kolovos, D., Paige, R., Polack, F.: Model Migration Case for TTC 2010, Dept. of Computer Science, University of York (2010)
22. Schurr, A.: Specification of Graph Translators with Triple Graph Grammars. In: Mayr, E.W., Schmidt, G., Tinhofer, G. (eds.) WG 1994. LNCS, vol. 903, pp. 151–163. Springer, Heidelberg (1995)
23. Stevens, P.: Bidirectional model transformations in QVT. SoSyM 9(1) (2010)
24. Varro, D., Pataricza, A.: Automated Formal Verification of Model Transformations. In: CSDUML 2003 Workshop (2003)

Analyzing Component-Based Systems
on the Basis of Architectural Constraints

Christian Lambertz and Mila Majster-Cederbaum

Department of Computer Science, University of Mannheim, Germany
lambertz@informatik.uni-mannheim.de

Abstract. Component-based development (CBD) is a promising approach to master design complexity. In addition, the knowledge about the architecture of a component system can help in establishing important system properties, which in general is computationally hard because of the state space explosion problem. Extending previous work, we here investigate the novel class of *disjoint circular wait free* component systems and show how we can use the architectural information to establish a condition for the important property of deadlock-freedom in polynomial time. A running example is included. We use the framework of interaction systems, but our result carries over to other CBD models.

1 Introduction

The design complexity of modern software systems is only reasonably controllable with structured approaches such as component-based development (CBD) that separate the concerns of software architecture from individual component behavior and that allow for reusability of components. Thereby, the application of formal methods (FM) can guarantee and foster the fault-free development of such systems and supports the software engineer with reliable information about this process. For a successful marriage of CBD and FM, a formal component model needs to be defined, i.e., the behavior of the components and the cooperation by means of so-called ports needs to be specified, which then allows for verification of system properties. Various formalisms have been used as such a model, e.g., process algebras [2, 10, 25, 26, 27], channel-based methods [3, 4], interface theories [7, 15, 16, 19], Petri nets [1, 5, 14], and interaction systems [6, 11, 18]. Since all these models suffer from the well-known state space explosion problem, a global state space analysis for property verification is often unfeasible, and it has been shown that many important properties such as deadlock-freedom or liveness are PSPACE-complete in, e.g., interaction systems [23] or 1-safe Petri nets [13].

One way to master this complexity problem is to restrict the architecture of the system, i.e., the way the components are allowed to cooperate, and exploit this information to derive polynomial time checkable conditions that imply the validity of the property in question. Here, we show how we can use the architectural information to establish a condition for the property of deadlock-freedom. Note that deadlock-freedom is an important property in itself, and in addition, the verification of safety properties can be reduced to deadlock detection [17]. Unfortunately, all we can aim for with such an approach is to find *conditions* since, as we argue in a moment, our architectural restriction does not affect the complexity of deadlock-freedom verification in general.

F. Arbab and M. Sirjani (Eds.): FSEN 2011, LNCS 7141, pp. 64–79, 2012.

For all our considerations in this paper, we use *interaction systems* as introduced by Gössler and Sifakis [18] as the formal component model. Note that our approach does not rely on this model; our ideas carry over to other CBD models as well. In interaction systems, data and I/O operations are completely abstracted away and every single operation is called an action. Each component's behavior is modeled as a labeled transition system (LTS), where the set of labels equals the set of actions and each action is understood as a port of the associated component. Actions of different components are then grouped into sets called *interactions* to model cooperation among the components. Thereby, any action can only be executed if all other actions contained in an appropriate interaction are also executable. The global behavior is then derived by executing the interactions nondeterministically according to their executability. The multiway cooperation, that interaction systems allow for, facilitates a very compact and convenient modeling on a certain level of abstraction. Note that more complex glueing mechanisms can be realized by means of special glue components.

In order to restrict the architecture as motivated above, we consider a novel architectural constraint called *disjoint circular wait freedom* that excludes certain waiting situations among the components. Our restriction is based on the acyclicity of the underlying cooperation structure, which is typically defined by means of a graph where the nodes represent the components and edges exist between any cooperating components. Similar requirements of acyclicity exist for many formalisms under various names, e.g., acyclic topologies [19], acyclic architectural types [10], tree networks [12], or tree-like architectures [21]. Note that only restricting the architecture to be acyclic is in general not sufficient to ensure the existence of efficient verification algorithms, e.g., it has been shown that deciding deadlock-freedom of interaction systems with tree-like architectures, which restrict the architecture in a strictly stronger way than we do in this paper, is PSPACE-complete [24]. Nevertheless, the verification of many instances of CBD models can be tackled with polynomial time checkable conditions that rely on an architectural restriction and ensure the property validity. In the following, we consider such a conditional approach.

Typically, one drawback of the definition of acyclic architectures is that all cooperations must be binary—otherwise the induced architecture is cyclic, e.g., if three components cooperate together each pair of them is connected in the topology of [12, 21]. Therefore, Majster-Cederbaum and Martens [22] improved their notion of a tree-like architecture to also work with multiway cooperation in the setting of interaction systems. They defined a special graph—called *cooperation graph* in the following—in which nodes represent all sets of components that are able to cooperate and whose graph-theoretical property of being a forest defines tree-like interaction systems in [22].

. Due to this definition and the assumption of a deadlock in the system, the authors were able to make observations regarding waiting situations between deadlocked components and the corresponding nodes that represent these components in the cooperation graph. Their central observation is that if a component i waits for a component j because of an interaction α which again waits for a component k because of an interaction β then at least two components exist that participate in both α and β. This observation can be checked for all pairs of components, and the authors introduced a notion called "problematic states" to reason about the reachability of states satisfying the observation in polynomial time. Thereby, this reachability analysis depends on a property called "exclusive communication" which requires that no action is used for cooperation with different sets of components. They also present a transformation technique that is able to ensure this property for an arbitrary interaction system in polynomial time.

Here, we extend the approach of Majster-Cederbaum and Martens [22] in several ways. Our contribution is threefold:

1. We define a novel architectural constraint that disallows circular waiting of three or more components such that the reasons of the single waits are unrelated. As we will see, this constraint is especially useful in systems with multiway cooperations when, e.g., one component i cooperates with components $j_1, \ldots, j_n$ (individually and all $n + 1$ together) but no j_k cooperates with a j_l without i (for $k \neq l$). To the best of our knowledge such a constraint has not been studied in a formal setting.
2. We show how to use this architectural information to establish an efficiently checkable condition for deadlock-freedom of interaction systems. The class of systems that satisfy our condition extends the class of systems studied in [10, 12, 19, 21, 22].
3. We improve the approach of [22] by avoiding a polynomial time preprocessing step that ensures a property of interaction systems called "exclusive communication", which is important for the technique presented by the authors. Thereby, this preprocessing possibly enlarges the behavior of the components for the verification process. We show that this step is completely unnecessary as the required information can already be extracted beforehand. We demonstrate the effect of this avoidance with an evaluation for two example systems in Section 5.

As an illustration of our considerations, we present a running example in the next section. Note that our architectural constraint of disjoint circular wait freedom can be found in many settings in which multiway cooperations occur that are restricted in the following way: Components modeling clients cooperate with a server component such that no binary cooperations between two clients are allowed. Additionally, any set of clients can cooperate with the server. Typically, such settings occur in many practical applications such as, e.g., broadcasting, global commits, and barrier synchronization.

The paper is organized as follows: In Section 2 we introduce the definition of interaction systems, deadlock-freedom, and our architectural constraint. Next, we show how this information can be used to establish a condition for deadlock-freedom (Section 3) and how we can further refine this idea in case the first approach fails (Section 4). As already mentioned, in Section 5 we evaluate our approach with respect to the approach of [22]. Finally, we conclude the paper and take a look at related work in Section 6.

2   Modeling Interacting Components

We first define the setting of all our considerations: interaction systems as a model for component-based system design. Afterwards, we directly introduce a running example that supports each definition and theorem with a concrete application in the following.

Definition 1 (Interaction System). *An* interaction system *is defined by a tuple* $Sys :=$ $(Comp, \{A_i\}_{i \in Comp}, Int, Beh)$. *Here,* $Comp$ *is a finite set of* components, *which are* *referred to as* $i \in Comp$. *The* actions *of each component* i *are given by the* action set A_i—*where* $a_i \in A_i$ *denotes an action*—*and are assumed to be disjoint, i.e.,* $\forall i, j \in Comp$: $i \neq j \implies A_i \cap A_j = \emptyset$. *The union of all action sets is called the* global action set $Act := \bigcup_{i \in Comp} A_i$.

A nonempty finite set $\alpha \subseteq Act$ *of actions is called an* interaction, *if it contains at most one action of every component, i.e.,* $|\alpha \cap A_i| \leq 1$ *for all* $i \in Comp$. *For any interaction* α *and component* i *we put* $i(\alpha) := A_i \cap \alpha$ *and say that* i participates *in* α *if* $i(\alpha) \neq \emptyset$. *The* interaction set Int *is a set of interactions which covers all actions, i.e., we require that* $\bigcup_{\alpha \in Int} \alpha = Act$ *holds.*

Finally, the behavior model Beh *of* Sys *contains for every component* i *a* labeled transition system (LTS) $\llbracket i \rrbracket := (S_i, A_i, \{\xrightarrow{a_i}_i\}_{a_i \in A_i}, I_i)$ *describing the* local behavior *of* i *where* S_i *is the* local state space, *action set* A_i *contains the labels,* $\{\xrightarrow{a_i}_i\}_{a_i \in A_i}$ *is a family of* transition relations with $\xrightarrow{a_i}_i \subseteq S_i \times S_i$, *and* $I_i \subseteq S_i$ *is the set of* local initial states. *Whenever* $(s_i, s_i') \in \xrightarrow{a_i}_i$ *we write* $s_i \xrightarrow{a_i}_i s_i'$ *instead. For a local state* $s_i \in S_i$ *of a component* i *we put* $Int(s_i) := \{\alpha \in Int \mid \exists a_i \in A_i \cap \alpha \; \exists s_i' \in S_i : s_i \xrightarrow{a_i}_i s_i'\}$ *and say for an interaction* $\alpha \in Int(s_i)$ *that* i wants to perform α *in* s_i. *Local state* s_i *is called* independent *if* $\exists \alpha \in Int(s_i): |\alpha| = 1$, *otherwise* s_i *is called* dependent[1].

We now introduce an interaction system that will serve as a running example throughout the paper. Consider the interaction system Sys_{DB} depicted in Figure 1. The system models a database server and a fixed number of clients that are allowed to read and write to the database. In order to avoid inconsistencies if one of the clients wants to write, the database provides a locking mechanism that ensures that read requests are not answered once a client is granted writing access and starts to write. Additionally, all clients are informed about the data change and a global commit among all clients ensures the consistency with any local data. After this commit, the database performs an internal backup step; however, an appropriate storage component is not part of the example. Here, we will consider n clients with the property that client i with $1 \leq i \leq n$ is able to write up to w_i times in a row (because of local memory constraints), i.e., the client can decide how many times it wants to write to the database as long as this number does not exceed w_i. Thus, the database d allows for an arbitrary number of write operations but at least one has to be performed if a client is granted write access.

We have $Comp = \{d, 1, \ldots, n\}$, and the action sets and interactions are defined as in Figure 1: Figure 1(a) depicts the behavior $\llbracket d \rrbracket$ of the database d and Figure 1(b) the behavior $\llbracket i \rrbracket$ of client i with $1 \leq i \leq n$. We omit unnecessary state information in the figure, e.g., state s_d^0 of d is depicted as a circled 0. Note that the states s_i^0 of all clients i and state s_d^3 are independent. Before we define the cooperation graph—Figure 1(c) shows it for Sys_{DB}—we define the *global behavior* of an interaction system.

Definition 2 (Global Behavior). *The* global behavior *of an interaction system* Sys *is a* LTS $\llbracket Sys \rrbracket := (S, Int, \{\xrightarrow{\alpha}\}_{\alpha \in Int}, I)$ *where the set of* global states $S := \prod_{i \in Comp} S_i$ *is given by the product of the local state spaces, which we consider to be order independent. Global states are denoted by tuples* $s := (s_1, \ldots, s_n)$ *with* $n = |Comp|$, *and the set of* global initial states *is* $I := \prod_{i \in Comp} I_i$. *The family of* global transition relations

---

[1] This state property is called "complete" respectively "incomplete" in the work of [22]. Originally, this notion was introduced by Gössler and Sifakis [18].

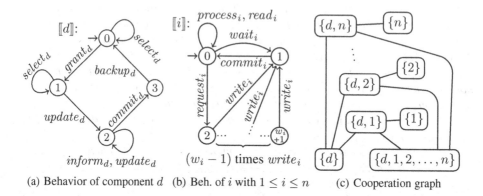

(a) Behavior of component d (b) Beh. of i with $1 \leq i \leq n$ (c) Cooperation graph

Fig. 1. Inter. sys. Sys_{DB} with $Int = \bigcup_{1 \leq i \leq n} \{\{select_d, read_i\}, \{grant_d, request_i\}, \{process_i\}, \{update_d, write_i\}, \{inform_d, wait_i\}\} \cup \{\{commit_d, commit_1, \ldots, commit_n\}, \{backup_d\}\}$

$\{\xrightarrow{\alpha}\}_{\alpha \in Int}$ *is defined canonically where for any* $\alpha \in Int$ *and any* $s, s' \in S$ *we have* $s \xrightarrow{\alpha} s'$ *iff* $\forall\, i \in Comp$*: if* $i(\alpha) = \{a_i\}$ *then* $s_i \xrightarrow{a_i}_i s_i'$ *and if* $i(\alpha) = \emptyset$ *then* $s_i = s_i'$.

The global state space that is computed for the global behavior is typically very large because of the well-known state space explosion problem, i.e., $|\prod_{i \in Comp} S_i| \in O(|S_{max}|^n)$ with $n = |Comp|$ and S_{max} being the largest local state space. Note that the global behavior $[\![Sys_{DB}]\!]$ of our running example already contains more than one hundred thousand reachable states and roughly ten times more transitions for $n = 12$ clients[2] and each $w_i = i$. Thus, even this simple example suffers from state space explosion for relatively small parameters. But, as motivated in the introductory part, the construction of the global state space can be avoided if the architectural information of the components is exploited. For this exploitation, we need access to the *partial behavior* of a subset of the set of components.

Definition 3 (Partial Behavior). *Let Sys be an interaction system and* $C \subseteq Comp$ *a set of components. The* partial behavior *of Sys with respect to* C *is a LTS* $[\![C]\!] := (S_C, Int_C, \{\xrightarrow{\alpha_C}_C\}_{\alpha_C \in Int_C}, I_C)$ *where* $S_C := \prod_{i \in C} S_i$, $I_C := \prod_{i \in C} I_i$, $Int_C := \{\alpha \cap (\bigcup_{i \in C} A_i) \mid \alpha \in Int\} \setminus \{\emptyset\}$, *and* $\{\xrightarrow{\alpha_C}_C\}_{\alpha_C \in Int_C}$ *is defined analogously to the family of global transition relations (cf. Definition 2). For a state* $s_C \in S_C$ *we put* $Int(s_C) := \{\alpha \in Int \mid \exists\, \alpha_C \in Int_C\ \exists\, s_C' \in S_C : \alpha_C \subseteq \alpha \wedge s_C \xrightarrow{\alpha_C}_C s_C'\}$. *If* s_C *is reachable from an initial state in* $[\![C]\!]$, *we denote this by* $s_C \in [\![C]\!]$.

Before we define and exploit any architectural constraint on interaction systems, we have to define our goal of *deadlock-freedom* more precisely.

Definition 4 (Deadlock). *A* deadlock *in an interaction system Sys is a global state* $s \in S$ *such that no interaction is performable in s. If no such state is reachable from an initial state in* $[\![Sys]\!]$ *we call Sys* deadlock-free.

---

[2] The exact numbers are 139277 states and 1784121 transitions. Note that for $n \geq 15$ there are more than one million reachable states and over 25 million transitions.

As already mentioned in the introduction, a deadlock induces a circular waiting among the involved components. Next, we formalize this information about deadlocks. Thereby and in the following, we reasonably assume that the local behavior of every component is "locally deadlock-free", i.e., at least one outgoing transition is present in any local state of the corresponding LTS.

Lemma 1 (Deadlock Properties). *For every deadlock s in an interaction system Sys, there is a set $D \subseteq Comp$ such that the components in D can be ordered in such a way that each component is waiting for the next one in a circular way, i.e., each component $d \in D$ wants to perform an interaction α_d in its local state s_d of the deadlock ($\alpha_d \in Int(s_d)$), but α_d is not enabled in s because the next component is unable to perform it.*

Note that for any deadlock, we can find a set D as in Lemma 1 that is minimal among all suitable sets. In the following, we assume that D is such a minimal set.

In order to introduce architectural constraints on interaction systems, we define the *cooperation graph*[3] as an undirected graph with two types of nodes. One type represents each component as a singleton. The other one models any (partial) cooperation situation among the components, i.e., for any two interactions there is a node representing the set of components participating in both of them. The edges between the nodes correspond to containment among the sets of components, i.e., possible cooperation situations that rely on each other. Note that Figure 1(c) depicts this graph for our running example.

Definition 5 (Cooperation Graph and Disjoint Circular Wait Freedom). *Given an interaction system Sys. For an interaction $\alpha \in Int$, let $\mathrm{compset}(\alpha) := \{i \in Comp \mid i(\alpha) \neq \emptyset\}$ denote the set of components participating in α. The cooperation graph $G := (V, E)$ of Sys is defined by the set of nodes $V := V_1 \cup V_2$ where $V_1 := \{\{i\} \mid i \in Comp\}$ and $V_2 := \{\mathrm{compset}(\alpha) \cap \mathrm{compset}(\beta) \mid \alpha, \beta \in Int \wedge \mathrm{compset}(\alpha) \cap \mathrm{compset}(\beta) \neq \emptyset\}$ and the set of edges $E := \{\{u, v\} \mid u, v \in V \wedge u \subset v \wedge \forall w \in V : u \subset w \implies w \not\subset v\}$. If on any simple cycle in G at most one node v is an element of V_1, i.e., $|v| = 1$, then Sys is called* disjoint circular wait free.

Note that other approaches, e.g., [12, 19], typically define the architecture based on the set V_1 of nodes where two nodes are adjacent if the corresponding components cooperate. The acyclicity of the resulting graph then defines the acyclicity of the architecture. However with such a definition, any cooperation of three or more components induces a cycle in the corresponding graph, and thus disqualifies the system for analysis. Here, we allow for the existence of certain cycles that can be analyzed efficiently.

Our definition of the cooperation graph can be motivated in the following way: For the verification of deadlock-freedom, we have to consider any way the components are able to cooperate. Lemma 1 shows that a deadlock induces a circular waiting among some of the involved components. Since these components are also related in the cooperation graph, the superimposition of the waiting and cooperation information will allow us to exclude those waiting situations where the reason of each single wait is completely independent from the other ones. Thereby, the nodes of the graph represent all possible cooperation sets, i.e., any node whose size is greater than two indicates a

---

[3] This graph is called "interaction graph" by Majster-Cederbaum and Martens [22].

possible (partial) cooperation. As we will see in the next section, the exclusion of the above mentioned waiting situations then allows for the establishment of a condition for deadlock-freedom of the whole system by an analysis of the partial behaviors of systems of size two, which results in a polynomial time bound of the approach.

Note that we assume that the cooperation graph is connected in the following, otherwise each connected component of the graph can be treated separately. Figure 1(c) depicts the cooperation graph of our running example Sys_{DB}. Note that Sys_{DB} is disjoint circular wait free because on any simple cycle of Sys_{DB}'s cooperation graph at most one node represents a component. Further note that the running example is not tree-like in the sense of [22] because it contains a simple cycle.

3   Exploiting Disjoint Circular Wait Freedom

Before we exploit the disjoint circular wait freedom of interaction systems, we formalize the ideas mentioned at the end of the previous section. This lets us derive a polynomial time checkable condition for deadlock-freedom of interaction systems. The following definition of *cooperation paths* corresponds to the mentioned transfer of a waiting caused by a deadlock to the cooperation graph.

Definition 6 (Cooperation Path). *Let Sys be an interaction system and G its cooperation graph. A simple path in G is called* cooperation path $\pi_{i,j}^{\alpha}$ *for components $i, j \in Comp$ and interaction $\alpha \in Int$ with $\{i, j\} \subseteq \text{compset}(\alpha)$ if it connects the corresponding nodes $\{i\}, \{j\}$, and $\text{compset}(\alpha)$ in G, i.e., $\pi_{i,j}^{\alpha} := (v_0, \ldots, v_k)$ with $k \in \mathbb{N}$, $v_0 = \{i\}$, $v_k = \{j\}$, $v_{k'} = \text{compset}(\alpha)$ for a $k' \in \mathbb{N}$ with $0 < k' < k$, and $\forall l \in \mathbb{N}: 0 \le l < k \implies \{v_l, v_{l+1}\} \in E$.*

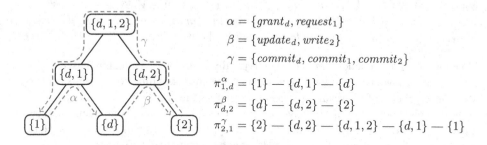

$$\alpha = \{grant_d, request_1\}$$
$$\beta = \{update_d, write_2\}$$
$$\gamma = \{commit_d, commit_1, commit_2\}$$
$$\pi_{1,d}^{\alpha} = \{1\} - \{d, 1\} - \{d\}$$
$$\pi_{d,2}^{\beta} = \{d\} - \{d, 2\} - \{2\}$$
$$\pi_{2,1}^{\gamma} = \{2\} - \{d, 2\} - \{d, 1, 2\} - \{d, 1\} - \{1\}$$

Fig. 2. Three cooperation paths of our running example Sys_{DB} with $n = 2$. Additionally, possible "waiting for" situations are shown as dashed lines, e.g., $\{1\} \overset{\alpha}{\dashrightarrow} \{d\}$ means component 1 waits for component d because of interaction α. Observe that each dashed line corresponds to the sequence of edges of a cooperation path, e.g., $\{1\} \overset{\alpha}{\dashrightarrow} \{d\}$ corresponds to $\pi_{1,d}^{\alpha}$.

Figure 2 illustrates cooperation paths for the running example. Since we are interested in using the cooperation paths to derive information about disjoint circular wait free interaction systems, we state three simple observations about cooperation paths between cooperating components in the following lemma.

Lemma 2 (Cooperation Path Properties). *Let Sys be an interaction system and G its cooperation graph. For all components $i, j \in Comp$ and interactions $\alpha \in Int$ with $\{i, j\} \subseteq \text{compset}(\alpha)$ exists a cooperation path $\pi^\alpha_{i,j}$ with the following properties:*

1. *Every node on the path is a subset of the set of components participating in α, i.e., $\forall v \in \pi^\alpha_{i,j}: v \subseteq \text{compset}(\alpha)$.*
2. *Every node on the path except the ones that represent components i and j contain at least two components, i.e., $\forall v \in \pi^\alpha_{i,j}: v \neq \{i\} \wedge v \neq \{j\} \implies |v| \geq 2$.*
3. *The cooperation path consists of at least three nodes, i.e., $|\pi^\alpha_{i,j}| \geq 3$.*

In the following, we only consider cooperation paths that have the properties of Lemma 2. We will now use the information about deadlocks of Lemma 1 to conclude the existence of a certain node in the cooperation graph. Intuitively, this node provides the information that at least two components have to (partially) wait for *each other* if the corresponding interaction system is disjoint circular wait free but not deadlock-free.

Lemma 3. *Let Sys be an interaction system and $G = (V, E)$ its cooperation graph. Assume that Sys is disjoint circular wait free and not deadlock-free. There exist components $i, j, k \in Comp$ and interactions $\alpha, \beta \in Int$ with $i \neq j$, $j \neq k$, $\{i, j\} \subseteq \text{compset}(\alpha)$, $\{j, k\} \subseteq \text{compset}(\beta)$, and $\alpha \neq \beta$ such that two cooperation paths $\pi^\alpha_{i,j}$ and $\pi^\beta_{j,k}$ exist that have a node in common that does not represent a component, i.e., $\exists v \in V: v \in \pi^\alpha_{i,j} \wedge v \in \pi^\beta_{j,k} \wedge |v| \geq 2$.*

Next, we combine our knowledge about cooperation paths from Lemma 2 and the existence of a common node in at least two such paths (if a deadlock exists) of Lemma 3 in order to prove a condition that is checkable among two components without considering whole cooperation paths, i.e., in the theorem we do not need to access elements of the cooperation graph.

Theorem 1. *Let Sys be an interaction system. Assume that Sys is disjoint circular wait free and contains a deadlock s. There exist components $i, j \in Comp$ and interactions $\alpha, \beta \in Int$ with $i \neq j$, $\{i, j\} \subseteq \text{compset}(\alpha)$, $\{j\} \subseteq \text{compset}(\beta)$, $\alpha \in Int(s_i)$, $\alpha \notin Int(s_j)$, $\beta \in Int(s_j)$, and $|\text{compset}(\alpha) \cap \text{compset}(\beta)| \geq 2$ (where s_i and s_j are the local states of the components i and j in the global state s).*

Theorem 1 offers a sufficient condition to verify the deadlock-freedom of interaction systems. To see this, consider the negation of the statement of the theorem, that we formalize as the following corollary. We also simplify the statement such that we only need to consider one interaction α instead of every pair of distinct interactions.

Corollary 1. *Given a disjoint circular wait free interaction system Sys. For a component $i \in Comp$ and a state $s_i \in S_i$, let $\text{coopset}(s_i) := \bigcup_{\alpha \in Int(s_i)} \text{compset}(\alpha) \setminus \{i\}$ denote the set of components that i wants to cooperate with in s_i. If no two components $i, j \in Comp$, interaction $\alpha \in Int$, and local states $s_i \in S_i$ and $s_j \in S_j$ with $i \neq j$, $\{i, j\} \subseteq \text{compset}(\alpha)$, $\alpha \in Int(s_i)$, $\alpha \notin Int(s_j)$, and $\text{compset}(\alpha) \cap \text{coopset}(s_j) \neq \emptyset$ exist, then Sys is deadlock-free.*

Observe that the statement of the corollary corresponds to the negation of the statement of Theorem 1 with the following adjustment: Instead of requiring that there is an interaction $\beta \in Int(s_j)$ with $|\text{compset}(\alpha) \cap \text{compset}(\beta)| \geq 2$, we can simply check whether $\text{compset}(\alpha) \cap \text{coopset}(s_j) \neq \emptyset$ holds, since this implies that there is such an interaction β.

We use the information provided by Corollary 1 to define the notion of problematic states as follows. As already mentioned, a similar definition can be found in [22].

Definition 7 (Problematic States). *For component $i \in Comp$, dependent local state $s_i \in S_i$, interaction $\alpha \in Int(s_i)$, and component $j \in \text{compset}(\alpha) \setminus \{i\}$, we define* $\text{PS}_j(s_i, \alpha) := \{s_j \in S_j \mid \alpha \notin Int(s_j) \ \wedge \ \text{compset}(\alpha) \cap \text{coopset}(s_j) \neq \emptyset \ \wedge \ s_j \text{ dependent} \ \wedge \ \forall \beta \in Int((s_i, s_j)): \text{compset}(\beta) \neq \{i, j\} \ \wedge \ (s_i, s_j) \in [\![\{i, j\}]\!]\}.$

Note that we incorporated two observations to refine these sets with respect to Corollary 1: States are only problematic regarding deadlock-freedom to each other, if both states are dependent—otherwise, they can execute a singleton interaction globally and thus never are involved in a deadlock. Similarly, since we compute the partial behaviors of systems of size two, if an interaction in which only components i and j participate is enabled in a state combination, it is also globally enabled. The second observation regards the reachability of state combinations: If the combination (s_i, s_j) of two states is not reachable in the partial behavior of the components i and j, it is clear that this combination is not part of any reachable global state. With this definition, we are able to state the following efficiently checkable result regarding deadlock-freedom.

Theorem 2. *Let Sys be a disjoint circular wait free interaction system. Sys contains no deadlock if for all components $i \in Comp$ and dependent local states $s_i \in S_i$ holds*

$$\bigcup_{\alpha \in Int(s_i)} \bigcup_{j \in \text{compset}(\alpha) \setminus \{i\}} \text{PS}_j(s_i, \alpha) = \emptyset$$

Note that computing the sets of problematic states can be done in polynomial time since there are at most $|S_{\max}| \times |Comp| \times |Int|$ such sets and each of them requires a reachability analysis that is bounded by $O(|S_{\max}|^2)$.

We now compute the problematic states of our example system according to Definition 7. For state $s_d^2 \in S_d$ and all components $i, j \in Comp \setminus \{d\}$ with $1 \leq i, j \leq n$ and $i \neq j$ and states $s_i^1 \in S_i$ we get (all other combinations are empty):

$$\text{PS}_i(s_d^2, \{update_d, write_i\}) = \{s_i^1\} \qquad \text{PS}_i(s_d^2, \{inform_d, wait_i\}) = \{s_i^1\}$$
$$\text{PS}_j(s_i^1, \{commit_d, \dots\}) = \{s_j^k \mid 2 \leq k \leq w_j + 1\}$$

Note that these states are also intuitively problematic to each other, e.g., if the database d is in state s_d^2 and wants to inform client i which is already in state s_i^1, this is not possible since i does not offer its wait action in this state and wants to cooperate with d.

Since not all sets of problematic states are empty, we cannot conclude the deadlock-freedom of the example with Theorem 2. In the next section, we will further refine the information provided by problematic states.

4 Refinement: Problematic States Reachability

We use a similar observation as Majster-Cederbaum and Martens [22] to refine the information provided by problematic states. We motivate this refinement with the help of our running example.

Consider Sys_{DB} with $n = 2$ and the global state (s_d^1, s_1^2, s_2^2). We want to exclude its reachability by only considering partial behaviors of size two. In state s_d^1, component d wants to cooperate with client 1 and 2, i.e., $\mathrm{coopset}(s_d^1) = \{1, 2\}$—cf. Corollary 1 for the definition of $\mathrm{coopset}(\cdot)$. Therefore, we take a look at $[\![\{d, 1\}]\!]$ and see that the state (s_d^1, s_1^2) is *only* reachable by performing interaction $\{grant_d, request_1\}$ and analogously in $[\![\{d, 2\}]\!]$ the state (s_d^1, s_2^2) is *only* reachable by $\{grant_d, request_2\}$. Comparing these two interactions, we see that they are not consistent, i.e., only one of them can be used to enter either (s_d^1, s_1^2, s_2^0) or (s_d^1, s_1^0, s_2^2).

We will use this observation to exclude the reachability of problematic state combinations. Similar to the notion of "backward search" of Majster-Cederbaum and Martens [22], we first compute for each local state the set of states from which it can be reached without cooperating with any of its cooperation partners. In the comparison of the interactions which lead to a certain global state, these can be reached as intermediate steps without affecting the reachability of a state combination in question. Note that as already mentioned in the introduction, we here adjust the techniques of [22] in order to work without previously establishing the property of exclusive communication.

Definition 8 (Non-interfering Backward Reachable Set). *We define the* non-interfering backward reachable set (NBRS) *of a state s_i of component i as the set of all states from which s_i is reachable without using actions that are only used for cooperation with components that i wants to cooperate with in s_i:*

$$\mathrm{NBRS}^0(s_i) := \{s_i\}$$

$$\mathrm{NBRS}^{l+1}(s_i) := \{s_i' \in S_i \mid \exists s_i'' \in \mathrm{NBRS}^l(s_i): s_i' \in \mathrm{Pre}(s_i'', \{a_i \in A_i \mid$$

$$\exists \alpha \in Int: a_i \in \alpha \ \wedge \ \mathrm{compset}(\alpha) \cap \mathrm{coopset}(s_i) = \emptyset\})\}$$

$$\mathrm{NBRS}(s_i) := \bigcup_{l \in \mathbb{N}} \mathrm{NBRS}^l(s_i)$$

where $\mathrm{Pre}(s_i, A) := \{s_i' \in S_i \mid \exists a \in A: s_i' \xrightarrow{a}_i s_i\}$ *denotes the A-predecessors of a state $s_i \in S_i$ for any subset $A \subseteq A_i$ of component i's actions.*

Computing the NBRSs for our running example yields for all clients i and states $s_i \in S_i$: $\mathrm{NBRS}(s_i) = \{s_i\}$ and for the states of the database: $\mathrm{NBRS}(s_d^0) = \{s_d^0, s_d^3\}$, $\mathrm{NBRS}(s_d^1) = \{s_d^1\}$, $\mathrm{NBRS}(s_d^2) = \{s_d^2\}$, and $\mathrm{NBRS}(s_d^3) = \{s_d^3, s_d^2, s_d^1, s_d^0\} = S_d$. Note that the NBRS of state s_d^3 is d's whole state space since in this state the component only "cooperates" with itself. However, the NBRS of state s_d^0 shows that for reachability concerns also combinations involving s_d^3 have to be considered, since component d can transit from this state to s_d^0 without affecting any cooperation partners.

Next, we formalize the set of actions relevant for such comparisons as the entry combinations of state combinations.

Definition 9 (Entry Combinations). *We define the* entry combinations (EC) *of a state* s_i *of component* i *and a state* s_j *of component* j *as the combinations of actions* a_i *of* i *and interactions* α *such that* a_i *is used for cooperation with components that* i *wants to cooperate with in* s_i *and* a_i *is also used in* α *to enter a reachable state in the partial behavior of* i *and* j *from which the state* (s_i, s_j) *can be reached without using actions that are only used for cooperation with components that* i *respectively* j *wants to cooperate with in* s_i *respectively* s_j:

$$\mathrm{EC}(s_i, s_j) := \big\{ (\{a_i\}, \alpha) \in 2^{A_i} \times Int \mid a_i \in \alpha$$
$$\wedge \; \exists \beta \in Int : a_i \in \beta \; \wedge \; \mathrm{compset}(\beta) \cap \mathrm{coopset}(s_i) \neq \emptyset$$
$$\wedge \; \exists (s_i', s_j') \in \mathrm{NBRS}(s_i) \times \mathrm{NBRS}(s_j) \; \exists (s_i'', s_j'') \in [\![\{i, j\}]\!] :$$
$$(s_i'', s_j'') \in \mathrm{Pre}((s_i', s_j'), \{\alpha \cap (A_i \cup A_j)\}) \big\}$$

Note that we use the singleton $\{a_i\}$ in the definition of the pairs of actions a_i and interactions α as entry combinations in order to identify a_i with the corresponding action of component i in the interaction α via the function $i(\alpha)$. This makes the use of entry combinations in the following theorem more readable.

We are not interested in computing these combinations for all states, i.e., only the ones that are problematic to each other are of interest. Thereby, we exploit the following observation similar to Majster-Cederbaum and Martens [22]: A state $s_i \in S_i$ of any component $i \in Comp$ is only part of a global deadlock if all interactions $\alpha \in Int(s_i)$ that s_i wants to perform are blocked by the corresponding cooperation partners, i.e., for all such α there is a component $j \in \mathrm{compset}(\alpha) \setminus \{i\}$ that is in a state $s_j \in S_j$ where α in not performable.

Thus, since we want to determine which entry combinations of i may lead to a state where α is not performable, we take the union of all entry combinations of problematic states of components participating in α. Since this argument may only result in a global deadlock if it holds for all interactions that s_i wants to perform, i.e., if there is an entry combination that is part of the union as above for all $\alpha \in Int(s_i)$, we compare these sets: In order to determine whether such a combination exists, we compute the intersection of all these unions, which corresponds to the interaction comparison mentioned before Definition 8.

The following theorem formalizes this observation. Thereby, the first condition ensures that we actually are able to perform the described comparison, because if a state can be reached from any initial state without using actions that are only needed for cooperation with its cooperation partners, we cannot rely on any entry information of this state. Therefore, we simply demand that no such state is reachable or otherwise that no corresponding problematic state of another component is also reachable in this way.

Theorem 3. *Let Sys be a disjoint circular wait free interaction system. If the following two conditions hold then Sys contains no deadlock:*

1. *For all components* $i \in Comp$ *and dependent local states* $s_i \in S_i$ *holds that* $\mathrm{NBRS}(s_i) \cap I_i = \emptyset$ *or there is an interaction* $\alpha \in Int(s_i)$ *such that for all components* $j \in \mathrm{compset}(\alpha) \setminus \{i\}$ *holds* $\big(\bigcup_{s_j \in \mathrm{PS}_j(s_i, \alpha)} \mathrm{NBRS}(s_j) \big) \cap I_j = \emptyset$.

2. *For all interactions* $\alpha \in Int$ *with* $|\text{compset}(\alpha)| \geq 2$ *exists a component* $i \in$ compset(α) *such that for all dependent local states* $s_i \in S_i$ *holds*

$$(i(\alpha), \alpha) \notin \bigcap_{\beta \in Int(s_i)} \bigcup_{j \in \text{compset}(\beta) \setminus \{i\}} \bigcup_{s_j \in \text{PS}_j(s_i, \beta)} EC(s_i, s_j)$$

Note that computing the entry combinations of problematic states can be done in polynomial time since there are at most $|S_{\max}| \times |Comp| \times |Int|$ such problematic state sets and only $O(|Comp|^2)$ reachability analyses bounded by $O(|S_{\max}|^2)$ are performed.

For enhanced readability and for a state $s_i \in S_i$ and an interaction $\beta \in Int$, we use the abbreviation $\text{PEC}(s_i, \beta) := \bigcup_{j \in \text{compset}(\beta) \setminus \{i\}} \bigcup_{s_j \in \text{PS}_j(s_i, \beta)} EC(s_i, s_j)$ for the union of entry combinations and $\text{CUTS}(s_i) := \bigcap_{\beta \in Int(s_i)} \text{PEC}(s_i, \beta)$ for the corresponding intersections in the following (cf. Theorem 3).

We continue with our running example where we get (all other sets are empty):

$$\text{PEC}(s_d^2, \{update_d, write_i\}) = \text{PEC}(s_d^2, \{inform_d, wait_i\})$$
$$= \bigcup_{1 \leq j \leq n} \{(\{inform_d\}, \{inform_d, wait_j\}), (\{update_d\}, \{update_d, write_j\})\}$$
$$\text{PEC}(s_i^1, \{commit_d, \dots\}) = \{(\{wait_i\}, \{inform_d, wait_i\}), (\{write_i\}, \{update_d, write_i\})\}$$

Again, these combinations correspond to the intuition, e.g., the entry combinations $EC(s_d^2, s_i^1)$ of state s_d^2 of d and state s_i^1 of a client i are that d informs the client or updates its database.

This results in the following intersections: For all $i \in Comp \setminus \{d\}$ and $s_i^1 \in S_i$ we get (all other sets are empty):

$$\text{CUTS}(s_i^1) = \{(\{wait_i\}, \{inform_d, wait_i\}), (\{write_i\}, \{update_d, write_i\})\}$$

Now, we see that for all $s_d \in S_d$ the set $\text{CUTS}(s_d)$ is empty. Since component d participates in every interaction $\alpha \in Int$ with $|\text{compset}(\alpha)| \geq 2$, and $(d(\alpha), \alpha) \notin \text{CUTS}(s_d)$ for all s_d, the second part of Theorem 3 holds. Note that also the first condition holds, since for all dependent local states s_i of all components $i \in Comp$ holds $\text{NBRS}(s_i) \cap I_i = \emptyset$—except for state s_d^0 but there the corresponding problematic state sets are empty. Thus, we can conclude that Sys_{DB} is deadlock-free.

5   Evaluation of the Exclusive Communication Factor

As already mentioned in the introduction, our approach of deadlock verification is based on an earlier approach by Majster-Cederbaum and Martens [22]. In their work, the property of "exclusive communication" is needed in order to establish the deadlock-freedom of interaction systems. Roughly speaking, exclusive communication requires that no action is used for cooperation with different sets of components. Here, we showed how we can drop this requirement by comparing more information in our entry combinations than Majster-Cederbaum and Martens [22] in their corresponding entry information called "problematic actions". In order to verify systems without exclusive communication, Majster-Cederbaum and Martens [22] provide a construction technique that transforms an arbitrary interaction system into one with exclusive communication in polynomial time. Thereby, their construction introduces fresh actions for any action that is used non-exclusively and multiplies the affected transitions in any LTSs.

However, since we showed that this transformation is not necessary, we are interested in the time savings that our approach allows for. In order to evaluate the savings, we used a prototype implementation for interaction systems that is able to verify the conditions of Theorem 3. Figure 3(a) depicts the verification time for the running example system Sys_{DB} for various numbers of clients. It shows a slight performance increase if we do not transform the system into one with exclusive communication beforehand. Note that the database d is the only component that needs adjustment.

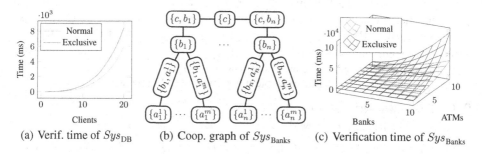

(a) Verif. time of Sys_{DB} (b) Coop. graph of Sys_{Banks} (c) Verification time of Sys_{Banks}

Fig. 3. Verification time of Sys_{DB} ($w_i = i$ for client i) and Sys_{Banks} and its cooperation graph

In order to better illustrate the exclusive communication factor, we also evaluated the interaction system Sys_{Banks} that has the cooperation graph depicted in Figure 3(b). This system was introduced by Baumeister et al. [7] and modeled as an interaction system by Majster-Cederbaum and Martens [21] for an earlier version of their approach that does not support multiway cooperation—note that only binary cooperations occur in the cooperation graph. The system consists of a clearing company c that cooperates with n banks b_i which again cooperate with m ATMs a_i^j. The nested structure of the cooperation graph already indicates that a lot of cooperations are not exclusive, i.e., the transformation of the system requires adjustments of many more components than of Sys_{DB}. Figure 3(c) depicts our evaluation for different numbers of banks and ATMs. Here, the transformation factor is better visible since the verification of the systems with exclusive communication requires much more time. Note that the transformation time is not included in the measured verification times.

This lets us conclude that also from a performance point of view, the exclusive communication factor should not be underestimated and it is beneficial to have a technique such as our entry combinations to completely circumvent this requirement.

6 Conclusion and Related Work

In this paper, we showed how component-based systems with multiway cooperation can be analyzed on the basis of an architectural constraint. The presented analysis focuses on the property of deadlock-freedom of interaction systems and provides a polynomial time checkable condition that ensures deadlock-freedom by exploiting a restriction of the architecture called disjoint circular wait freedom. Roughly speaking, this architectural constraint disallows any circular waiting situations among the components such that the reason of one waiting is independent from any other one.

We want to point out that we only derived a *condition* for deadlock-freedom. For instance, our approach fails in situations where a set of components blocks each other but other components not involved in this blocking are able to proceed globally. But, it should be clear that by only considering sets of components of size two—which yields a very efficient approach—not all such situations can be covered.

On the other hand, if our approach fails then the information provided by the entry combinations gives a hint of which components are involved in a possible deadlock. With this information, a software engineer can take a closer look at this potentially small set of components and either resolve the reason manually or encapsulate this set in a new composite component that has equivalent behavior, is verified deadlock-free with another technique, and now causes no problems in the remaining system. Such a hierarchical approach comparable to ideas of Hennicker et al. [19] is currently studied in the setting of interaction systems. Considering other properties, e.g., progress of components, or weaker architectural constraints are also left for future work.

As mentioned in the introduction, acyclic architectures are also exploited in the work of Bernardo et al. [10] and Hennicker et al. [19]. Thereby, both approaches rely on behavioral equivalences among certain key components in the architecture, i.e., if the behavior of such a key component is not influenced by the cooperation with the remaining components (which is checked with weak bisimilarity), the question of deadlock-freedom is answerable by only looking at the behavior of the key component. Apart from the fact that such equivalences can be found in many systems—we also considered a comparable approach for interaction systems [20]—however also numerous examples with no behavioral equivalences at all exist modeling realistic scenarios that are still verifiable with our approach, e.g., such an example can be found in [22].

The work of Brookes and Roscoe [12] considers tree-like networks in the context of CSP restricted to binary communication. For such networks, the authors additionally require that cooperating components (or processes in this case) have at most one cooperation partner in every state. This directly allows to imply the deadlock-freedom of the whole network by the analysis of all cooperating pairs of components. However, for networks without this additional property, a tedious case analysis is required to exclude certain waitings among the components.

For interaction systems, also several approaches for proving deadlock-freedom exist, e.g., Bensalem et al. [9] in the context of BIP [6] (for which interaction systems are a theoretical model), that also exploit the compositional structure of the system. Their approach is based on finding invariants for the components, which must be provided for each property, and for the interactions, which are computed automatically. Unfortunately, according to Bensalem et al. [8], for this computation "there is a risk of explosion, if exhaustiveness of solutions is necessary in the analysis process." Thus, this approach is not guaranteed to be polynomial in the number and size of the components which is an important property of our approach.

References

[1] van der Aalst, W.M.P., van Hee, K.M., van der Toorn, R.A.: Component-based software architectures: a framework based on inheritance of behavior. Science of Computer Programming 42(2-3), 129–171 (2002)

[2] Allen, R., Garlan, D.: A formal basis for architectural connection. ACM Transactions on Software Engineering and Methodology 6(3), 213–249 (1997)

[3] Arbab, F.: Reo: a channel-based coordination model for component composition. Mathematical Structures in Computer Science 14(3), 329–366 (2004)

[4] Baier, C., Blechmann, T., Klein, J., Klüppelholz, S.: A Uniform Framework for Modeling and Verifying Components and Connectors. In: Field, J., Vasconcelos, V.T. (eds.) COORDINATION 2009. LNCS, vol. 5521, pp. 247–267. Springer, Heidelberg (2009)

[5] Barboni, E., Bastide, R.: Software components: a formal semantics based on coloured Petri nets. In: Proceedings of the 2nd International Workshop on Formal Aspects of Component Software (FACS 2005). Electronic Notes in Theoretical Computer Science, vol. 160, pp. 57–73. Elsevier (2006)

[6] Basu, A., Bozga, M., Sifakis, J.: Modeling heterogeneous real-time components in BIP. In: Proceedings of the 4th International Conference on Software Engineering and Formal Methods (SEFM 2006), pp. 3–12. IEEE Press (2006)

[7] Baumeister, H., Hacklinger, F., Hennicker, R., Knapp, A., Wirsing, M.: A component model for architectural programming. In: Proceedings of the 2nd International Workshop on Formal Aspects of Component Software (FACS 2005). Electronic Notes in Theoretical Computer Science, vol. 160, pp. 75–96. Elsevier (2006)

[8] Bensalem, S., Bozga, M., Sifakis, J., Nguyen, T.-H.: Compositional Verification for Component-Based Systems and Application. In: Cha, S(S.), Choi, J.-Y., Kim, M., Lee, I., Viswanathan, M. (eds.) ATVA 2008. LNCS, vol. 5311, pp. 64–79. Springer, Heidelberg (2008)

[9] Bensalem, S., Bozga, M., Nguyen, T.-H., Sifakis, J.: D-finder: A Tool for Compositional Deadlock Detection and Verification. In: Bouajjani, A., Maler, O. (eds.) CAV 2009. LNCS, vol. 5643, pp. 614–619. Springer, Heidelberg (2009)

[10] Bernardo, M., Ciancarini, P., Donatiello, L.: Architecting families of software systems with process algebras. ACM Transactions on Software Engineering and Methodology 11(4), 386–426 (2002)

[11] Bozga, M.D., Sfyrla, V., Sifakis, J.: Modeling synchronous systems in BIP. In: Proceedings of the 7th International Conference on Embedded software (EMSOFT 2009), pp. 77–86. ACM Press (2009)

[12] Brookes, S.D., Roscoe, A.W.: Deadlock analysis in networks of communicating processes. Distributed Computing 4(4), 209–230 (1991)

[13] Cheng, A., Esparza, J., Palsberg, J.: Complexity Results for 1-Safe Nets. In: Shyamasundar, R.K. (ed.) FSTTCS 1993. LNCS, vol. 761, pp. 326–337. Springer, Heidelberg (1993)

[14] da Silva, L.D., Perkusich, A.: Composition of software artifacts modelled using colored Petri nets. Science of Computer Programming 56(1-2), 171–189 (2005)

[15] de Alfaro, L., Henzinger, T.: Interface Theories for Component-Based Design. In: Henzinger, T.A., Kirsch, C.M. (eds.) EMSOFT 2001. LNCS, vol. 2211, pp. 148–165. Springer, Heidelberg (2001)

[16] Doyen, L., Henzinger, T.A., Jobstmann, B., Petrov, T.: Interface theories with component reuse. In: Proceedings of the 8th International Conference on Embedded Software (EMSOFT 2008), pp. 79–88. ACM Press (2008)

[17] Godefroid, P., Wolper, P.: Using Partial Orders for the Efficient Verification of Deadlock Freedom and Safety Properties. In: Larsen, K.G., Skou, A. (eds.) CAV 1991. LNCS, vol. 575, pp. 332–342. Springer, Heidelberg (1992)

[18] Gößler, G., Sifakis, J.: Composition for Component-Based Modeling. In: de Boer, F.S., Bonsangue, M.M., Graf, S., de Roever, W.-P. (eds.) FMCO 2002. LNCS, vol. 2852, pp. 443–466. Springer, Heidelberg (2003)

[19] Hennicker, R., Janisch, S., Knapp, A.: On the observable behaviour of composite components. In: Proceedings of the 5th International Workshop on Formal Aspects of Component Software (FACS 2008). Electronic Notes in Theoretical Computer Science, vol. 260, pp. 125–153. Elsevier (2010)

[20] Lambertz, C.: Exploiting architectural constraints and branching bisimulation equivalences in component-based systems. In: Proceedings of the Doctoral Symposium of the 2nd World Congress on Formal Methods (FM 2009-DS), no. 0915 in Eindhoven University of Technology Technical Report, Eindhoven, pp. 1–7 (2009)

[21] Majster-Cederbaum, M., Martens, M.: Compositional analysis of deadlock-freedom for tree-like component architectures. In: Proceedings of the 8th International Conference on Embedded Software (EMSOFT 2008), pp. 199–206. ACM Press (2008)

[22] Majster-Cederbaum, M., Martens, M.: Using architectural constraints for deadlock-freedom of component systems with multiway cooperation. In: Proceedings of the 3rd International Symposium on Theoretical Aspects of Software Engineering (TASE 2009), pp. 225–232. IEEE Press (2009)

[23] Majster-Cederbaum, M., Minnameier, C.: Everything is PSPACE-Complete in Interaction Systems. In: Fitzgerald, J.S., Haxthausen, A.E., Yenigun, H. (eds.) ICTAC 2008. LNCS, vol. 5160, pp. 216–227. Springer, Heidelberg (2008)

[24] Majster-Cederbaum, M., Semmelrock, N.: Reachability in tree-like component systems is PSPACE-complete. In: Proceedings of the 6th International Workshop on Formal Aspects of Component Software (FACS 2009). Electronic Notes in Theoretical Computer Science, vol. 263, pp. 197–210. Elsevier (2010)

[25] Montesi, F., Sangiorgi, D.: A Model of Evolvable Components. In: Wirsing, M., Hofmann, M., Rauschmayer, A. (eds.) TGC 2010, LNCS, vol. 6084, pp. 153–171. Springer, Heidelberg (2010)

[26] Ramos, R., Sampaio, A., Mota, A.: Systematic Development of Trustworthy Component Systems. In: Cavalcanti, A., Dams, D.R. (eds.) FM 2009. LNCS, vol. 5850, pp. 140–156. Springer, Heidelberg (2009)

[27] Plášil, F., Višňovský, S.: Behavior protocols for software components. IEEE Transactions on Software Engineering 28(11), 1056–1076 (2002)

Constructive Development
of Probabilistic Programs[*]

Hassan Haghighi and Mohammad Mahdi Javanmard

Faculty of Electrical and Computer Engineering, Shahid Beheshti University,
Tehran, Iran
h_haghighi@sbu.ac.ir,
ma.javanmard@Mail.sbu.ac.ir

Abstract. Probabilistic techniques in computer programs are becoming
more and more widely used. Therefore, there is a big interest in methods
for formal specification, verification, and development of probabilistic
programs. In this paper, we present a constructive framework to develop
probabilistic programs formally. To achieve this goal, we first introduce
a Z-based formalism that assists us to specify probabilistic programs
simply. This formalism is mainly based on a new notion of Z operation
schemas, called probabilistic schemas, and a new set of schema calculus
operations that can be applied on probabilistic schemas as well as ordinary operation schemas. We show the resulting formalism can be used to
specify any discrete-time Markov chain. We also reason how one can derive functional probabilistic programs from correctness proofs of formal
specifications written in the new formalism. In this way, a completely
formal solution to develop probabilistic programs will be proposed.

Keywords: formal program development, probabilistic specification,
functional probabilistic program, CZ set theory, type theory.

1 Introduction

Probabilistic techniques in computer programs are becoming more and more
widely used; examples are in *random algorithms* to increase efficiency, in concurrent systems for *symmetry breaking*, and in hybrid systems when the low-level
hardware might be represented by probabilistic programs that model quantitative unreliability [11]. Therefore, there has been a renewed interest in methods
for formal specification, verification, and development of probabilistic programs.

Methods for modelling probabilistic programs go back to the early work in
[7] introducing *probabilistic predicate transformers* as a framework for reasoning
about *imperative* probabilistic programs. From that time on, a wide variety of
logics have been developed as possible bases for verifying probabilistic systems.
A survey of this work can be found in [10].

---

[*] This research has been done using research credits of Shahid Beheshti University,
G.C. under Contract Number: 600/177.

F. Arbab and M. Sirjani (Eds.): FSEN 2011, LNCS 7141, pp. 80–95, 2012.
© Springer-Verlag Berlin Heidelberg 2012

In [11] and [13], Morgan et al. introduced probabilistic nondeterminism into Dijkstra's *GCL* (*Guarded Command Language*) and thus provided a means with which probabilistic programs can be rigorously developed and verified. Although the semantics has been designed to work at the level of program code, it has an in-built notion of program refinement which encourages a prover to move between various levels of abstraction. Unlike publications of Morgan et al. handling probabilistic choice in *imperative* settings, there are several studies considering probabilistic choice in *functional* languages; for example, see [2,15,16].

As far as we know, much of the work in the literature, such as the above mentioned work, has focused on the *verification* of probabilistic programs; however, besides a considerable trend in *verifying* probabilistic programs, there is a big interest in the *formal specification and development* of such programs. In this paper, we introduce a *constructive* framework allowing us to write probabilistic specifications formally and then drive functional probabilistic programs from *correctness proofs of these specifications*.

In this framework, we use a *Z-based* formalism to write specifications of probabilistic programs. Then, we translate the resulting probabilistic specifications into their counterparts in Z itself. Of course, to interpret the obtained specifications in Z, we use an existing, *constructive* set theory, called CZ set theory [12], instead of the classical set theory Z. We choose CZ since it has an interpretation [12] in *Martin-Löf's theory of types* [9]; this enables us to translate our Z-style specification of a probabilistic program into its counterpart in Martin-Löf's theory of types and then drive a functional probabilistic program from a correctness proof of the resulting type theoretical specification.

The main contribution of the current paper is to introduce the Z-based formalism that will be used in the mentioned constructive framework. We interpret this formalism in the conventional Z and then show the given interpretation will constructively lead to functional programs which preserve the initially specified probabilistic behavior. To build the new formalism, we first augment the Z notation with a new notion of operation schemas, called *probabilistic schema*, intended to specify probabilistic operations. Also, since the schema calculus operations of Z do not work on probabilistic schemas anymore, we define a new set of operators for the schema calculus operations *negation, conjunction, disjunction, existential quantifier, universal quantifier*, and *sequential composition* which properly work on probabilistic schemas as well as ordinary operation schemas.

The paper is organized in the following way. In section 2, we give a brief overview of the CZ set theory and its interpretation in Martin-Löf's theory of types. We assume that the reader has some familiarity with Z [17] and constructive type theory [9,14]. In section 3, we begin to introduce our formalism by defining the notion of probabilistic schemas and showing how they can be used to model probabilistic operations. We also give an interpretation of probabilistic schemas in conventional Z. Since the proposed interpretation of probabilistic schemas is not sufficient for the purpose of program construction, in section 4 we give a new interpretation of probabilistic schemas that constructively yield functional programs implementing the initially specified probabilistic behavior.

In section 5, we introduce a new set of schema calculus operations into the resulting Z-based formalism. We then show how one can apply the resulting formalism to specify Markov chains which themselves are widely used to model stochastic processes with the Markov property and discrete (finite or countable) state space [8]. Of course, since usually a Markov chain would be defined for a discrete set of times, we will concentrate on discrete-time Markov chains. The last section is devoted to the conclusion and directions for future work.

2   Preliminaries

To employ both the facilities of Z as a specification medium and the abilities of constructive theories in program development, in [12], the CZ set theory has been introduced which provides constructive interpretations for the specification constructs of the Z notation. In this section, we give a brief description of the CZ set theory and its interpretation in Martin-Löf's theory of types.

2.1   CZ Set Theory

All proof rules of the *classical* set theory *ZF* (*Zermelo-Fraenkel*) can be used in CZ except *classical negation* since this rule is derived from the axiom of *excluded middle*. The axioms of CZ shadow those of the classical theory; indeed, most axioms remain intact. However, three axioms including *separation, foundation,* and *power set* have been modified to satisfy *constructive* scruples. Also, modifying the power set axiom yields a new axiom concerning the *cartesian product* set constructor. To indicate the constructive nature of CZ, we give the modified version of the power set axiom here. Other axioms of CZ can be found in [12].

decidable power set: $\forall x \cdot \exists z \cdot \forall y \cdot y \in z \Leftrightarrow y \sqsubseteq x$

In the above axiom, the relation $y \sqsubseteq x$ indicates that y is a *decidable subset* of x. $y \sqsubseteq x$ iff $y \subseteq x$ and $\forall u \in x \cdot u \in y \vee \neg(u \in y)$. In the Z (ZF without the axiom of *replacement* [12]) set theory, the power set is not restricted: any kind of subset is permitted, not just the decidable ones. It is the most important difference between Z and CZ set theories. CZ only permits subsets which can be constructed in the sense that we can determine their membership relative to their superset. Intuitively, the decidable subsets can be identified with decision procedures which test for membership.

The CZ set theory can be considered as a *constructive* interpretation of the Z language. Specially, replacing instances of the power set by decidable ones provides a way for determining whether specifications specify decidable problems. In [12], it has been shown that the CZ set theory is enough for the purposes of program specification in the style of Z. In other words, the common set theoretical constructions employed in Z can be interpreted using CZ.

2.2   Interpretation of CZ in Martin-Löf's Theory of Types

In [12], a model $\nu = \langle V, \dot{\in}, \doteq \rangle$ of CZ in Martin-Löf's theory of types has been built in which each set is associated with a pair consisting of a base type together with a family of types, i.e., its elements. In the model ν, $V \cong Wx \in U.x$, where U is the *universe* whose elements are themselves types, and W is the type constructor for recursive data types [14]. To complete the description of the model ν, we need to define two binary relations $\dot{=}$ and $\dot{\in}$:

$$\alpha \dot{=} \beta \cong (\Pi x \in \alpha^- \cdot \tilde{\alpha} x \dot{\in} \beta) \otimes (\Pi x \in \beta^- \cdot \tilde{\beta} x \dot{\in} \alpha)$$
$$\alpha \dot{\in} \beta \cong \Sigma x \in \beta^- \cdot \tilde{\beta} x \dot{=} \alpha$$

In the above definition, the equality between sets is explained according to the extensional equality in set theories, stated by the *extensionality* axiom. In [12], the type theoretical interpretations of the empty set and the set of natural numbers as two basic sets of CZ have been also given using the model ν. Also, a mapping function, called ξ, has been defined which assigns elements of V to well-formed and atomic formulas of CZ as follows:

$$[\Omega]_\xi = \Omega$$
$$[x = y]_\xi = \xi(x) \dot{=} \xi(y)$$
$$[x \in y]_\xi = \xi(x) \dot{\in} \xi(y)$$
$$[\phi \wedge \psi]_\xi = [\phi]_\xi \otimes [\psi]_\xi$$
$$[\phi \vee \psi]_\xi = [\phi]_\xi \oplus [\psi]_\xi$$
$$[\phi \Rightarrow \psi]_\xi = [\phi]_\xi \Rightarrow [\psi]_\xi$$
$$[\forall x \in y \cdot \phi]_\xi = \Pi \alpha \in (\xi(y))^- \cdot [\phi]_{\xi[(\xi(y))^-\alpha/x]}$$
$$[\exists x \in y \cdot \phi]_\xi = \Sigma \alpha \in (\xi(y))^- \cdot [\phi]_{\xi[(\xi(y))^-\alpha/x]}$$

The translation given in [12] is not still sufficient to transform a Z specification into a type theoretical one: we need to interpret schemas, as a distinctive feature of the Z notation, in type theory. In [3], we extended the work of [12] to handle Z schemas. Here, we only mention our solution for operation schemas. Suppose that an operation schema has the following general form:

$$Op\_Schema \cong [x_1 \in A_1;\ ...;\ x_m \in A_m;\ y_1 \in B_1;\ ...;\ y_n \in B_n \mid \phi],$$

where $x_i (i : 1..m)$ are input or before state variables, $y_j (j : 1..n)$ are output or after state variables, and ϕ denotes the pre- and postconditions of the operation being specified. Now we extend the function ξ to translate Op_Schema into an element of V:

$$[Op\_Schema]_\xi = (\Pi \alpha_1 \in (\xi(A_1))^-, ..., \alpha_m \in (\xi(A_m))^- \cdot$$
$$\Sigma \beta_1 \in (\xi(B_1))^-, ..., \beta_n \in (\xi(B_n))^- \cdot [\phi]_\xi)_{[(\xi(A_i))^\neg \alpha_i/x_i][(\xi(B_j))^\neg \beta_j/y_j]}$$

Now, we can use the function ξ to translate any Z specification into a type in type theory and then extract a program (a term in type theory) which meets the initial specification (more precisely, meets its representation in type theory).

3   Specifying Probabilistic Operations

In this section, we begin to introduce a Z-based formalism to specify probabilistic programs formally. To achieve this goal, we first define the notion of *probabilistic schema* by which one can simply model probabilistic operations.

Definition 3.1. The general form of probabilistic schemas is as follows:

$$P\_Schema \cong [x_1 \in A_1;\ ...;\ x_m \in A_m;\ y_1 \in B_1;\ ...;\ y_n \in B_n \mid$$
$$\phi \wedge (p_1 : \phi_1;\ ...;\ p_l : \phi_l)],$$

where $x_i(i : 1..m)$ are input or before state variables, and $y_j(j : 1..n)$ are output or after state variables. Some part of the schema predicate, shown as ϕ, specifies those functionalities of the operation that are *non-probabilistic*; it specially includes the preconditions of the operation being specified. The remainder of the predicate is separated into l predicates $\phi_1, ..., \phi_l$; $p_k \in \mathbb{R}(k : 1..l)$ are (constant) probabilities and by the notation $p_k : \phi_k$, we want to say that the predicate ϕ_k holds with probability p_k. In other words, the relationship between the variables of *P_Schema* is stated by ϕ_k with probability p_k. For a given probabilistic schema, we assume that $p_1 + ... + p_l = 1$ and for each $k : 1..l$, $p_k \geq 0$. Notice that in the predicate part of *P_Schema*, l may be equal to 0, i.e., ordinary operation schemas are considered as special cases of probabilistic schemas.   △

In the next example, we use the notion of probabilistic schema to specify a simple probabilistic operation.

Example 3.2. Suppose that the state of the weather tomorrow depends on only weather status today and not on past weather conditions. For example, suppose that if today is rainy in a specific area, tomorrow is rainy too with probability 0.5, dry with probability 0.4, and finally snowy with probability 0.1. By the following probabilistic schema, we specify the weather forecast for tomorrow provided that today is rainy. In this schema, $x?$ and $y!$ are the weather status for today and tomorrow, respectively. Also, suppose that we use values 1, 2 and 3 to specify *dry*, *rainy* and *snowy* statuses, respectively.

$$P\_WF \cong [x?, y! \in \mathbb{N} \mid x? = 2 \wedge (0.4 : y! = 1; \ 0.5 : y! = 2; \ 0.1 : y! = 3)]   △$$

The next definition introduces a function $[]^P$ that maps probabilistic schemas into ordinary operation schemas of Z. We will show later that this interpretation of probabilistic schemas is not enough for the purpose of constructive program development. Thus, in section 4, we change this interpretation to provide a constructive way to extract probabilistic programs from their Z-like specifications.

Definition 3.3. Recall *P_Schema*, given in definition 3.1 as the general form of probabilistic schemas. If for all real numbers $p_1, ..., p_l$, the maximum number of digits to the right of the decimal point is d, then we have:

if *P_Schema* is an ordinary operation schema (i.e., when $l = 0$),
then $[P\_Schema]^P = P\_Schema$;
otherwise, $[P\_Schema]^P \cong [x_1 \in A_1; \ ...; \ x_m \in A_m; \ y_1 \in B_1; \ ...; \ y_n \in B_n \mid$
$\phi \wedge (\exists p \in \mathbb{N} \cdot ((0 \leq p < p_1 * 10^d \wedge \phi_1) \vee (p_1 * 10^d \leq p < (p_1 + p_2) * 10^d \wedge \phi_2) \vee ... \vee$
$((p_1 + ... + p_{l-1}) * 10^d \leq p < (p_1 + ... + p_l) * 10^d \wedge \phi_l)))]   △$

$[]^P$ behaves as an identity function when applied to an ordinary operation schema, i.e., when $l = 0$; otherwise, an auxiliary variable $p \in \mathbb{N}$ is introduced into the predicate part helping us to implement the probabilistic choice between l predicates $\phi_1, ..., \phi_l$. The variable p ranges nondeterministically from 0 to $10^d - 1$, and the length of each allowable interval of its values determines how many times (of 10^d times) a predicate $\phi_k(k : 1..l)$ holds (or in fact describes the relationship between the schema variables). More precisely, in $p_k * 10^d$ cases per 10^d times, the predicate $\phi_k(k : 1..l)$ determines the behavior of the final program. In the next example, we apply the above defined interpretation to the probabilistic schema P_WF, given in example 3.2. We then use the interpretation of CZ in type theory to extract a functional program from the resulting specification.

Example 3.4. We first use the function $[]^P$ to transform P_WF into an ordinary operation schema of Z as follows:

$$[P\_WF]^P \cong [x?, y! \in \mathbb{N} \mid x? = 2 \land (\exists p \in \mathbb{N} \cdot ((0 \le p < 4 \land y! = 1)$$
$$\lor (4 \le p < 9 \land y! = 2) \lor (9 \le p < 10 \land y! = 3)))]$$

By the above schema, p *nondeterministically* takes one of 10 values $0, 1, ..., 9$. For four (i.e., in 4 cases per 10) possible values of p (i.e., $0, 1, 2$, and 3), it has been specified that the weather is dry tomorrow. For other five (i.e., in 5 cases per 10) possible values of p (i.e., $4, 5, 6, 7$, and 8), it has been described that the weather is rainy tomorrow. Finally, for the remaining (i.e., in 1 case per 10) possible value of p (i.e., 9), it has been indicated that the weather is snowy tomorrow. Thus, it seems that if one makes a uniform choice to select one of the values $0, 1, ..., 9$ for p, s/he will be provided with a correct implementation of P_WF. Nevertheless, we now show that the schema $[P\_WF]^P$ cannot *constructively* lead to a program which implements the probabilistic behavior specified by P_WF.

To extract a program from a correctness proof of $[P\_WF]^P$, we first use the function ξ (see subsection 2.2) to interpret the operation schema $[P\_WF]^P$ into type theory. The resulting type theoretical specification is as follows:

$$\Pi\alpha \in \mathbb{N} \cdot \Sigma\beta \in \mathbb{N} \cdot (\alpha \doteq 2 \otimes$$
$$(\Sigma\delta \in \mathbb{N} \cdot ((0 \dot{\le} \delta \dot{<} 4 \otimes \beta \doteq 1) \oplus (4 \dot{\le} \delta \dot{<} 9 \otimes \beta \doteq 2) \oplus (9 \dot{\le} \delta \dot{<} 10 \otimes \beta \doteq 3)))),$$

where α, β, and δ correspond to the variables $x?$, $y!$, and p existing in $[P\_WF]^P$, respectively. Also, $b \dot{\le} a$ and $b \dot{<} a$ are abbreviations for $\Sigma\rho \in \mathbb{N} \cdot b + \rho \doteq a$ and $\Sigma\rho \in \mathbb{N}_1 \cdot b + \rho \doteq a$, respectively. Now we can use the inference rules of type theory to prove the correctness of the above specification (or in other words, construct an object of its corresponding type). This object can be viewed as a program satisfying the schema P_WF. A part of such a proof is shown in Fig. 1. At the end of the proof, the following functional program has been obtained:

$$prog = \lambda\alpha.(1, q),$$

where q is an intermediate proof object in the proof tree (see Fig. 1). For each valuation of $\alpha \in \mathbb{N}$, the program *prog* *always* provides the value 1 for β, provided that $\alpha = 2$. In this way, *prog* cannot implement the probabilistic behavior specified by P_WF: according to *prog*, the weather will be *absolutely* dry tomorrow, provided that it is rainy today. Notice that if we select another path in the proof tree (i.e., if we prove the correctness of $(4 \dot{\le} \delta \dot{<} 9 \otimes \beta \doteq 2)$ or $(9 \dot{\le} \delta \dot{<} 10 \otimes \beta \doteq 3)$, rather than $(0 \dot{\le} \delta \dot{<} 4 \otimes \beta \doteq 1)$), we will again obtain a program that cannot implement the probabilistic behavior specified by P_WF. This problem is due to the fact that in the proof tree, we can replace each of the variables β and δ by *only one* of their possible values. This occurs when we use the introduction rule for dependent sum (Σ_i); see two circled Σ_i in Fig. 1. As it can be seen in the proof tree, this finally results in single value 0 for δ and single value 1 for β. $\triangle$

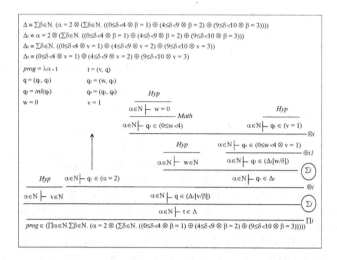

Fig. 1. Program extraction from the probabilistic schema P_WF

As it was shown in example 3.4, using the function $[]^P$ to interpret the probabilistic schema P_WF and then proving the correctness of the resulting specification did not *constructively* lead to a probabilistic program being enable to implement the probabilistic behavior initially specified by P_WF. We can investigate this problem in the general case by applying functions $[]^P$ and ξ to the schema P_Schema, the general form of probabilistic schemas, in turn:

$$[[P\_Schema]^P]_\xi = \Pi\alpha_1 \in (\xi(A_1))^-, ..., \alpha_m \in (\xi(A_m))^- \cdot$$
$$\Sigma\beta_1 \in (\xi(B_1))^-, ..., \beta_n \in (\xi(B_n))^- \cdot$$
$$([\phi \wedge (\exists\, p \in \mathbb{N} \cdot ((0 \leq p < p_1 * 10^d \wedge \phi_1) \vee ...\vee$$
$$((p_1 + ... + p_{l-1}) * 10^d \leq p < (p_1 + ... + p_l) * 10^d \wedge \phi_l)))]_\xi)$$
$$[(\xi(A_i))\check{~}\alpha_i/x_i][(\xi(B_j))\check{~}\beta_j/y_j],$$

where $[[P\_Schema]^P]_\xi$ is the type theoretical equivalent of $[P\_Schema]^P$. Using the conventions

$$A'_i = (\xi(A_i))^- \ (i : 1..m), \ B'_j = (\xi(B_j))^- \ (j : 1..n), \text{ and}$$
$$\phi' = ([\phi \wedge (\exists\, p \in \mathbb{N} \cdot ((0 \leq p < p_1 * 10^d \wedge \phi_1) \vee ...\vee$$
$$((p_1 + ... + p_{l-1}) * 10^d \leq p < (p_1 + ... + p_l) * 10^d \wedge \phi_l)))]_\xi)$$
$$[(\xi(A_i))\check{~}\alpha_i/x_i][(\xi(B_j))\check{~}\beta_j/y_j],$$

$[[P\_Schema]^P]_\xi$ is equal to the following type in type theory:

$$\Pi\alpha_1 \in A'_1, ..., \alpha_m \in A'_m \cdot \Sigma\beta_1 \in B'_1, ..., \beta_n \in B'_n \cdot \phi'$$

We can now derive a program from a correctness proof of the above type theoretical specification. An initial part of such a proof is shown in Fig. 2. The extracted program is as follows:

$$prog = \lambda(\alpha_1, ..., \alpha_m) \cdot ((v_1, ..., v_n), q),$$

For each valuation of $\alpha_1 \in A'_1, ..., \alpha_m \in A'_m$, this program *always* produces the single n-ary $(v_1, ..., v_n)$. In this way, the probabilistic behavior specified by P_Schema cannot be implemented by *prog*. The origin of this problem can be

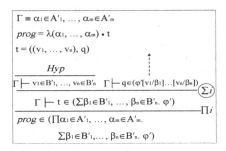

Fig. 2. Program extraction from the probabilistic schema *P_Schema*

realized considering the proof tree, specially where we used the introduction rule for dependent sum (Σ_i) (see the circled Σ_i in Fig. 2): according to the definition of Σ_i, we could replace the n-ary $(\beta_1, ..., \beta_n)$ by *only one* of its possible values. Although the problem originates from the rules of type theory, in the next section, we change the given interpretation of probabilistic schemas such that without the need to modify the proof rules of type theory, we will be able to construct functional programs which preserve the specified probabilistic choice.

4   A New Interpretation of Probabilistic Schemas

We change the current interpretation of probabilistic schemas such that it *explicitly* models *all* possible values of the variable p and also all possible values of the after state and output variables of *P_Schema*, allowed according to the predicate part of this schema.

In this way, the process of proving correctness is forced to construct a program that involves *all* possible values of p and also all possible values of the after state and output variables; such a program will be able to implement the probabilistic behavior, initially specified by the probabilistic choice between l predicates $\phi_1, ..., \phi_l$. This approach is similar to what we presented in [4] and [5] to specify nondeterminism *explicitly* in Z. The next definition introduces a new function $[]^{NP}$ that interprets probabilistic schemas according to the new idea.

Definition 4.1. Recall *P_Schema*, given in definition 3.1 as the general form of probabilistic schemas. If for all real numbers $p_1, ..., p_l$, the maximum number of digits to the right of the decimal point is d, we have:

if *P_Schema* is an ordinary operation schema, $[P\_Schema]^{NP} = P\_Schema$; otherwise, $[P\_Schema]^{NP} \cong [x_1 \in A_1; \; ...; \; x_m \in A_m;$
$pvar \in seq(B_1 \times ... \times B_n \times \mathbb{N}) \mid$
$\forall (y_1, ..., y_n, p) \in (B_1 \times ... \times B_n \times \mathbb{N}) \cdot (y_1, ..., y_n, p) \in pvar \Leftrightarrow \psi]$,
where
$\psi \equiv \phi \wedge ((0 \leq p < p_1 * 10^d \wedge \phi_1) \vee (p_1 * 10^d \leq p < (p_1 + p_2) * 10^d \wedge \phi_2) \vee ...\vee$
$((p_1 + ... + p_{l-1}) * 10^d \leq p < (p_1 + ... + p_l) * 10^d \wedge \phi_l))$
Like $[]^P$, the function $[]^{NP}$ behaves as an identity function when applied to an ordinary operation schema; otherwise, it promotes the *combination* of the

after state and output variables and an auxiliary variable $p \in \mathbb{N}$ to a *sequence* *pvar* of *all* possible combinations of these variables that satisfy the predicates of the schema. We have combined all of the above mentioned variables using the cartesian product of their types in order to preserve the relationship between them after the interpretation. The next theorem shows the recent interpretation of probabilistic schemas constructively leads to programs which can implement the probabilistic behavior initially specified by probabilistic schemas.

Theorem 4.2. Assume that for every predicate $\phi_k (k : 1..l)$ existing in the predicate part of P_Schema, each combination of values of before state and input variables with one and only one combination of values of after state and output variables satisfies ϕ_k. A program extracted from the correctness proof of the type theoretical counterpart of $[P\_Schema]^{NP}$ can implement the probabilistic behavior specified by P_Schema.

Proof. Based on the predicate part of $[P\_Schema]^{NP}$, a program satisfies $[P\_Schema]^{NP}$ iff when applied to a combination of input values, it produces a sequence consisting of all allowable values of $y_1, ..., y_n, p$ and not anything else. Therefore, any formal program development method that is sound (such as the *constructive* method of extracting programs from correctness proofs of type theoretical counterparts of Z specifications; see the soundness proof in [12]) absolutely extracts a program from $[P\_Schema]^{NP}$ that for each combination of input values, produces a sequence consisting of all possible values of $y_1, ..., y_n, p$ and not anything else. On the other hand, by the assumption of the theorem, the resulting sequence includes 10^d elements from which $p_k * 10^d$ $(k : 1..l)$ elements implement the behavior specified by ϕ_k. Thus, if we make a uniform choice over the elements of this sequence, we will be provided with a correct implementation of the probabilistic behavior, initially specified by P_Schema. $\triangle$

In the next example, we apply the function $[]^{NP}$ to the probabilistic schema P_WF, given in example 3.2.

Example 4.3. We use the function $[]^{NP}$ to translate the probabilistic schema P_WF, given in example 3.2, into an ordinary operation schema of Z:

$[P\_WF]^{NP} \cong [x? \in \mathbb{N};\ pvar \in seq(\mathbb{N} \times \mathbb{N})\ |$
$\forall (y!, p) \in (\mathbb{N} \times \mathbb{N}) \cdot (y!, p) \in pvar \Leftrightarrow$
$(x? = 2 \wedge ((0 \le p < 4 \wedge y! = 1) \vee (4 \le p < 9 \wedge y! = 2) \vee (9 \le p < 10 \wedge y! = 3)))]$

If we apply the function ξ (see subsection 2.2) to the above resulting schema, the following type theoretical specification is obtained:

$\Pi \alpha \in \mathbb{N} \cdot \Sigma \beta \in List^1\ (\mathbb{N} \otimes \mathbb{N}) \cdot \Pi (\tau, \delta) \in (\mathbb{N} \otimes \mathbb{N}) \cdot (\tau, \delta) \dot{\in} \beta \Leftrightarrow$
$(\alpha \dot{=} 2 \otimes ((0 \dot{\le} \delta \dot{<} 4 \otimes \tau \dot{=} 1) \oplus (4 \dot{\le} \delta \dot{<} 9 \otimes \tau \dot{=} 2) \oplus (9 \dot{\le} \delta \dot{<} 10 \otimes \tau \dot{=} 3))),$

where α, β, τ, and δ correspond to the variables $x?$, $pvar$, $y!$, and p existing in $[P\_WF]^{NP}$, respectively. Due to the space limitation, we do not give the correctness proof of the above type theoretical specification here. Nevertheless, such

---

[1] In [12], it has been shown that $seqX$ of CZ is equivalent to $List(X)$ of type theory.

a proof will result in a functional program that produces a sequence consisting of all allowable values of τ and δ, provided that $\alpha = 2$. More precisely, this program produces the sequence

$$< (1,0), (1,1), (1,2), (1,3), (2,4), (2,5), (2,6), (2,7), (2,8), (3,9) >$$

Selecting any of the first four elements of the above sequence results in $\tau = 1$ which means that the weather will be dry tomorrow. Similarly, selecting any of the five elements $(2,4),(2,5), (2,6), (2,7)$ and $(2,8)$ yields $\tau = 2$ which means that the weather will be rainy tomorrow. Finally, selecting the element $(3,9)$ results in $\tau = 3$ which means that the weather will be snowy tomorrow. Now, it is enough to have a programming construct in the final functional language which *uniformly* chooses between the elements existing in the above sequence.

Fortunately, there is considerable work to model probabilistic choice in functional languages and λ-calculus (for example, see [2,15,16]). In most of this work, a simple notation like $P_1 \oplus_p P_2$ is introduced to model probabilistic choice. Based on this construct, two expressions P_1 and P_2 are occurred with probabilities $1 - p$ and p, respectively. Now, having this probabilistic construct, we define a λ function, called UC, which receives a sequence consisting of n elements and then implements the *uniform* choice among these elements. More precisely, UC is equivalent to a probabilistic construct in which each element of the input sequence is occurred with probability $\frac{1}{n}$. UC is recursively defined as follows:

$$UC(h :: t) = h \oplus_{\frac{\#t}{\#t+1}} (UC(t)) \mid UC(nil) = \bot,$$

where nil represents the empty sequence, and $\bot$ indicates the *undefined* or *error* state. Also, $\#$ can be easily defined to calculate the sequence size.

Now, we can use UC to make a *uniform* choice over elements existing in the above obtained sequence. Making such a choice, tomorrow is dry with probability 0.4, rainy with probability 0.5, and snowy with probability 0.1. This behavior exactly corresponds to the probabilistic choice specified initially by P_WF. $\triangle$

We have so far proposed to use probabilistic schemas in order to specify probabilistic operations in our Z-based notation. A distinctive feature of Z is its *schema calculus operations*. In the next section, we show these operations do not work in the presence of probabilistic schemas anymore. We thus introduce a new set of schema calculus operations into the new formalism that can be applied to probabilistic schemas as well as ordinary operation schemas.

5   A Calculus for Probabilistic Schemas

We first investigate wether we can use the operations of the Z schema calculus to manipulate probabilistic schemas. It seems that a simple way to do this is to transform probabilistic schemas into ordinary ones (using the function $[]^{NP}$) before applying the schema calculus operations of Z; in this way, we will have ordinary operation schemas that can be manipulated by the Z schema calculus operations in the conventional way. However, we show that this approach may result in *unwanted* specifications; it even may make the applications of operations to schemas *undefined*. For instance, consider the probabilistic schema P_WF, given in example 3.2. This schema specifies a *partial* operation [17] since the effect of the operation is undefined for some input values, i.e., when $x? <> 2$. To describe a *total* operation, we give a new specification:

$Res ::= OK \mid ERROR$

$P\_P\_WF \cong [x?, y! \in \mathbb{N};\ r! \in Res \mid$

$x? = 2 \wedge r! = OK \wedge (0.4 : y! = 1;\ 0.5 : y! = 2;\ 0.1 : y! = 3)]$

$Exception \cong [x?, y! \in \mathbb{N};\ r! \in Res \mid x? <> 2 \wedge r! = ERROR \wedge y! = 0],$

where $y! = 0$ indicates an unknown weather state for tomorrow. Now, we can describe a total operation by applying a disjunction between two schemas P_P_WF and $Exception$ above. Before doing this, however, we first translate P_P_WF into an ordinary operation schema as follows:

$[P\_P\_WF]^{NP} \cong [x? \in \mathbb{N};\ pvar \in seq(\mathbb{N} \times Res \times \mathbb{N}) \mid$

$\forall (y!, r!, p) \in (\mathbb{N} \times Res \times \mathbb{N}) \cdot (y!, r!, p) \in pvar \Leftrightarrow (x? = 2 \wedge r! = OK \wedge$

$((0 \leq p < 4 \wedge y! = 1) \vee (4 \leq p < 9 \wedge y! = 2) \vee (9 \leq p < 10 \wedge y! = 3)))]$

Since two schemas $[P\_P\_WF]^{NP}$ and $Exception$ are *type compatible* [17], we can apply the operator $\vee$ to these schemas. However, in the resulting schema, there is no relationship between the variables $y!$ and $r!$ coming from $Exception$ and the sequence $pvar$ coming from $[P\_P\_WF]^{NP}$ whereas all the elements of $pvar$ involve instances of $y!$ and $r!$. In this way, the resulting specification is unwanted, or in other words, does not correspond to what is intended by the initial specification. The problem originates from the fact that using $[]^{NP}$ forces the output variables $y!$ and $r!$ existing in P_P_WF to be combined into a new variable, and the resulting variable to be promoted to a sequence.

Interpreting probabilistic schemas before applying the schema calculus operations may even yield undefined operations. For instance, suppose that we use $\exists y! \in \mathbb{N} \cdot P\_P\_WF$ to hide $y!$ in the resulting schema. If we use the function $[]^{NP}$ to interpret P_P_WF before applying the existential quantifier, we miss $y!$ since it is combined with some other schema variables and then promoted to a sequence; in this way, the quantification over $y!$ becomes undefined.

Similar problems occur when we transform probabilistic schemas into ordinary ones before applying the other schema calculus operations, such as conjunction, universal quantifier, and sequential composition: By using $[]^{NP}$ to interpret probabilistic schemas, the relationship between instances of a variable that exist in the declaration part of various schemas (or exist in the list of quantified variables and the declaration part of the quantified schema when using quantifiers) may be lost; hence, applying schema calculus operations to the resulting schemas may be undefined or result in unwanted specifications.

Unfortunately, another problem will occur if we try the reverse path, i.e., applying the schema calculus operations to probabilistic schemas before interpreting them by $[]^{NP}$. For instance, suppose that we apply the operator $\vee$ to the schemas P_P_WF and $Exception$ before interpreting P_P_WF:

$P\_T\_WF \cong P\_P\_WF \vee Exception \cong [x?, y! \in \mathbb{N};\ r! \in Res \mid$

$(x? = 2 \wedge r! = OK \wedge (0.4 : y! = 1;\ 0.5 : y! = 2;\ 0.1 : y! = 3)) \vee$

$(x? <> 2 \wedge r! = ERROR \wedge y! = 0)]$

P_T_WF does not correspond to the general form of probabilistic schemas (see definition 3.1). Therefore, we are not allowed to apply the function $[]^{NP}$ to interpret P_T_WF. It seems that we can solve this problem by manually transforming the resulting schema into the general form of probabilistic schemas or even changing the definition of $[]^{NP}$ to cover schemas such as P_T_WF; however, having such a method in mind, in various situations we encounter various cases for each of which we must provide a special, manual way.

We have so far shown any of the mentioned paths (interpreting probabilistic schemas before applying the schema calculus operations or the reverse path) to employ the operations of the Z schema calculus in our formalism do not work when we want to manipulate probabilistic schemas. Now, we present another approach in which the application of operations and the interpretation of probabilistic schemas occur in an interleaved manner. Suppose that $[]^{NP}$ operates in a two-step process, or in other words, $[]^{NP}$ is equivalent to the composition of two functions $[]^{NP_1}$ and $[]^{NP_2}$; the former approximately behaves like the function $[]^{P}$ introduced by definition 3.3, but unlike $[]^{P}$, $[]^{NP_1}$ introduces the variable p into the declaration part of the schema. Here is the formal definition of $[]^{NP_1}$:

Definition 5.1. Recall P_Schema, given in definition 3.1 as the general form of probabilistic schemas. Also assume that for all real numbers $p_1, ..., p_l$, the maximum number of digits to the right of the decimal point is d. Thus we have:

if P_Schema is an ordinary operation schema, $[P\_Schema]^{NP_1} = P\_Schema$; otherwise,

$[P\_Schema]^{NP_1} \cong$
$[x_1 \in A_1; \ ...; \ x_m \in A_m; \ y_1 \in B_1; \ ...; \ y_n \in B_n; \ p! \in \&\mathbb{N} \ |$
$\phi \wedge ((0 \leq p! < p_1 * 10^d \wedge \phi_1) \vee (p_1 * 10^d \leq p! < (p_1 + p_2) * 10^d \wedge \phi_2) \vee ... \vee$
$((p_1 + ... + p_{l-1}) * 10^d \leq p! < (p_1 + ... + p_l) * 10^d \wedge \phi_l))]$.

In definition 5.1, we have used the symbol & when declaring $p!$ in order to be able to distinguish between probabilistic schemas and ordinary operation schemas when we want to apply $[]^{NP_2}$ later. Based on the next definition, $[]^{NP_2}$ takes a schema and promotes the combination of its output and after state variables to a sequence, provided that it includes an output variable declared by &.

Definition 5.2. Suppose that $[]^{NP_2}$ applies to the following operation schema:

$Op\_Schema \cong [x_1 \in A_1; \ ...; \ x_m \in A_m; \ y_1 \in B_1; \ ...; \ y_n \in B_n \ | \ \phi]$,

where $x_i (i : 1..m)$ are input or before state variables, and $y_j (j : 1..n)$ are output or after state variables. Now, we have:

if OP_Schema has no output variable declared by &,
then $[OP\_Schema]^{NP_2} = OP\_Schema$;
otherwise,
$[OP\_Schema]^{NP_2} \cong [x_1 \in A_1; \ ...; \ x_m \in A_m;$
$pvar \in seq(B_1 \times ... \times B_n) \ |$
$\forall (y_1, ..., y_n) \in (B_1 \times ... \times B_n) \cdot (y_1, ..., y_n) \in pvar \Leftrightarrow \phi]$

It can be easily justified that $[]^{NP} = [[]^{NP_1}]^{NP_2}$. Now, to manipulate probabilistic schemas by the operations of the Z schema calculus, we propose to apply these operations between the applications of $[]^{NP_1}$ and $[]^{NP_2}$. An informal illustration of the correctness of this approach is as follows: $[]^{NP_1}$ transforms a probabilistic schema into an ordinary one according to the probabilities involved in its predicate part; however, $[]^{NP_1}$ does not promote the combination of the output and after state variables to a sequence. Therefore, we can apply the operations of the Z schema calculus to the resulting schema in the usual way; this does not yield unwanted specifications or undefined operations. At the final stage, we apply $[]^{NP_2}$ to the resulting schema in order to enable the final program to implement the initially specified probabilistic behavior.

To implement the above idea, we introduce a new set of schema calculus operations into our Z-based formalism that can be applied to probabilistic schemas appropriately. In the Z notation [17], there exist operators $\neg$, $\wedge$, $\vee$, $\exists$, $\forall$, and $\mathring{9}$ for the schema calculus operations *negation*, *conjunction*, *disjunction*, *existential quantifier*, *universal quantifier*, and *sequential composition*, respectively. Here, we define a new set of operators consisting of $\neg_p$, $\wedge_p$, $\vee_p$, $\exists_p$, $\forall_p$, and $\mathring{9}_p$:

Definition 5.3. Let PS_1 and PS_2 be two probabilistic schemas. Now, we have:

$$\neg PS_1 \cong [\neg [PS_1]^{NP_1}]^{NP_2}$$
$$PS_1 \, \wp_p \, PS_2 \cong [([PS_1]^{NP_1} \, \wp \, [PS_2]^{NP_1})]^{NP_2} \quad \wp \in \{\wedge, \vee, \mathring{9}\}$$
$$\varrho_p \, d_h \cdot PS_1 \cong [\varrho \, d_h \cdot [PS_1]^{NP_1}]^{NP_2} \quad \varrho \in \{\exists, \forall\},$$

where d_h is the declaration of quantified variables.

To show the usability of the new operations, we apply $\vee_p$ to P_P_WF and *Exception*. By this example, we also show that in the case of disjunction between a probabilistic schema and an ordinary one, we must apply a slight change to the ordinary schema after using $[]^{NP_1}$ and before using $\vee$:

$$P\_P\_WF \vee_p Exception \cong [([P\_P\_WF]^{NP_1} \vee [Exception]^{NP_1})]^{NP_2} \cong$$
$$[x?, pvar \in (\mathbb{N} \times Res \times \mathbb{N}) \mid \forall (y!, r!, p!) \in (\mathbb{N} \times Res \times \mathbb{N}) \cdot (y!, r!, p!) \in pvar \Leftrightarrow$$
$$((x? = 2 \wedge r! = OK \wedge$$
$$((0 \le p! < 4 \wedge y! = 1) \vee (4 \le p! < 9 \wedge y! = 2) \vee (9 \le p! < 10 \wedge y! = 3))) \vee$$
$$(x? <> 2 \wedge r! = ERROR \wedge y! = 0))]$$

The above resulting schema specifies a total operation. When $x? = 2$, this operation produces a sequence consisting of all allowable values of $y!$ and $p!$ and also reports OK. When $x? <> 2$, the operation assigns 0 to $y!$ and reports $ERROR$; however, the possible values of $p!$ has not been determined for this case, and $p!$ can take any natural number; it violates producing a *finite* sequence for $pvar$.

To solve this problem, it is enough to introduce $p!$ into the declaration part of *Exception* and add a conjunct such as $p! = 0$, limiting the possible values of $p!$, into the predicate part of *Exception* before using $\vee$ between P_P_WF and *Exception*. Notice that this modification is not required when we use conjunction or sequential composition operators between a probabilistic schema and an ordinary one since in these cases, we apply a conjunction between the predicate parts of two schemas; this scenario automatically limits the possible values of $p!$.

Before ending this subsection, we show the resulting formalism can be used to specify any discrete-time Markov chain. Markov chains are widely used to model stochastic processes with the Markov property (the next state of the system depends only on the current state) and discrete (finite or countable) state space [8]. Of course, since usually a Markov chain would be defined for a discrete set of times, we concentrate on discrete-time Markov chains.

Now, suppose that we are going to specify an arbitrary discrete-time Markov chain with n states $S_1, ..., S_n$ $(n \geq 1)$. Also, suppose that for each S_i and S_j $(1 \leq i, j \leq n)$, p_{ij} denotes the fixed probability that the system process will next be in state S_j, provided that it is in state S_i now. The state schema of the system and its initialization schema are as follows:

$DTMC \cong [s \in \mathbb{N} \mid 1 \leq s \leq n]$

$DTMCInit \cong [DTMC' \mid s' = m]$,

where s and m indicate the current and initial states of the system, respectively.

Now, for each system state S_i $(1 \leq i \leq n)$, we consider a probabilistic schema to model transitions from S_i to all system states (including S_i itself) as follows:

$P\_TransFrom_i \cong [\Delta DTMC \mid s = i \wedge (p_{i1} : s' = 1; \; ...; \; p_{in} : s' = n)]$

Finally, having the above defined probabilistic schemas, the following specification describes the stochastic process formally:

$P\_SP \cong P\_TransFrom_1 \vee_p P\_TransFrom_2 \vee_p ... \vee_p P\_TransFrom_n$

6 Conclusions and Future Work

In this paper, we have presented a Z-based formalism by which one can specify probabilistic programs formally. We have also reviewed a *constructive* approach for formal program development that is well integrated with the new formalism: since we have interpreted all the new constructs of this formalism in Z itself, we can still use the translation of the CZ set theory into type theory [12] to derive functional programs from correctness proofs of probabilistic specifications written in the new formalism. In this way, we are provided with a completely constructive framework for developing probabilistic programs formally.

However, the current framework suffers from a main drawback: Recall that we have proved that using the interpretation function $[]^{NP}$ can lead to appropriate programs, provided that this function is applied to those probabilistic schemas

$P\_Schema \cong [x_1 \in A_1; \; ...; \; x_m \in A_m;$
$y_1 \in B_1; \; ...; \; y_n \in B_n \mid \phi \wedge (p_1 : \phi_1; \; ...; \; p_l : \phi_l)]$

that obey the following law:

for every predicate $\phi_k (k : 1..l)$, each combination of values of before state and input variables with one and only one combination of values of after state and output variables satisfies ϕ_k.

Notice that the above law is in fact what has been explicitly assumed in theorem 4.2. For instance, consider the following probabilistic schema:

$P\_GetLEQ \cong [x? \in \mathbb{N}; \; y! \in \mathbb{N} \mid 0.5 : y! < x?; \; 0.5 : y! = x?]$

P_GetLEQ does not obey the above mentioned law (consider predicate $y! < x?$). Now, applying the function $[]^{NP}$ to P_GetLEQ yields the following schema:

$[P\_GetLEQ]^{NP} \cong [x? \in \mathbb{N}; \; pvar \in seq(\mathbb{N} \times \mathbb{N}) \mid \forall (y!, p!) \in (\mathbb{N} \times \mathbb{N}) \cdot$
$(y!, p!) \in pvar \Leftrightarrow ((0 \leq p! < 5 \wedge y! < x?) \vee (5 \leq p! < 10 \wedge y! = x?))]$

A program satisfying the above obtained specification is not what the initial schema, i.e., P_GetLEQ, specifies. For example, for the input value 2, such a program produces the sequence

$< (0,0), (1,0), (0,1), (1,1), (0,2), (1,2), (0,3), (1,3), (0,4), (1,4),$
$(2,5), (2,6), (2,7), (2,8), (2,9) >$

Selecting any of the first 10 elements of the above sequence results in an output value less than 2. In other words, a uniform choice over the elements of this sequence selects an output value less than 2 with probability $\frac{2}{3}$. It also selects the output value 2 with probability $\frac{1}{3}$; however, who wrote the initial specification wants both the above sorts of output to be produced with the same probability. This problem is due to the nondeterministic relationship between possible values of $x?$ and $y!$ allowed by the predicate $y! < x?$ in P_GetLEQ.

A similar problem occurs when a probabilistic schema involves a predicate $\phi_k(k : 1..l)$ that is unsatisfiable for a combination of values of before state and input variables. For instance, consider the following probabilistic schema by which we specify an operation that for each input value x, produces $x + 1$ with probability 0.5 and produces $x - 1$ with probability 0.5:

$$P\_GetAdj \cong [x? \in \mathbb{N}; \; y! \in \mathbb{N} \mid 0.5 : y! = x? + 1; \; 0.5 : y! = x? - 1]$$

Notice that for the input value $x? = 0$, there exists no value for the output variable $y!$ which satisfies the predicate $y! = x? - 1$. Now, using $[]^{NP}$ to interpret P_GetAdj results in a program that for input value $x? = 0$, produces $< (1,0), (1,1), (1,2), (1,3), (1,4) >$. A uniform choice over the elements of this sequence $always$ results in the value 1 for the output variable $y!$ while the specification writer wants the program to produce the output value 1 with probability 0.5 and $aborts$ (without producing anything) with probability 0.5. Therefore, we have again obtained a program that does not satisfy the initial specification. Introducing a new interpretation of probabilistic schemas that solves the above mentioned problem can be an interesting topic in continuing this work.

To compare our work with other approaches in the literature which apply formal methods to probabilistic systems, it is worth mentioning that, as we have stated in section 1, most of the contributions in the literature have focused on the verification of probabilistic programs, and there is too little work on the formal program development of probabilistic systems. As one of contributions regarding formal program development, we can point to [1] in which a rewrite-based specification language, called PMAUDE, has been proposed for specifying probabilistic concurrent and real-time systems. Specifications in PMAUDE are based on a probabilistic rewrite theory which has both a rigorous formal basis and the characteristics of a high-level programming language. In other words, this theory allows us to express both specifications and programs within the same formalism.

While our specification language in this paper is based on a different theory in comparison to that of [1] (i.e., set theory in comparison to rewrite theory), we are going to utilize one advantage of [1] in our future work; this advantage is that PMAUDE allows specifications to be easily written in a way that they have no un-quantified nondeterminism. More precisely, all occurrences of nondeterminism are replaced by quantified nondeterminism such as probabilistic choices and stochastic real-time; hence, this work does not have the problem of ours when both nondeterminism and probability exist in the specification simultaneously. As another related work, we can point to [6] in which a formalism that is based on the notion of state-transition is proposed to specify probabilistic processes. In this work, Jonsson and Larsen define a refinement relation between probabilistic specifications as inclusion between the sets of processes that satisfy the respective specifications. One of the most advantages of [6] is the ability to consider variable probabilities for each transition. More precisely, each transition is labelled by an appropriate interval of probabilities. Although we use a different theory (set theory instead of state-transition) as the basis of our specification language, we are going to employ the idea of [6] to enrich our framework to support variable probabilities.

References

1. Agha, G., Meseguer, J., Sen, K.: PMaude: Rewrite-based Specification Language for Probabilistic Object Systems. ENTCS 153(2), 213–239 (2006)
2. Di Pierro, A., Hankin, C., Wiklicky, H.: Probabilistic λ-calculus and Quantitative Program Analysis. Journal of Logic and Computation 15(2) (2005)
3. Haghighi, H., Mirian-Hosseinabadi, S.H.: An Approach to Nondeterminism in Translation of CZ Set Theory into Type Theory. In: FSEN 2005. ENTCS, vol. 159 (2006)
4. Haghighi, H., Mirian-Hosseinabadi, S.H.: Nondeterminism in Constructive Z. Fundamenta Informaticae 88(1-2), 109–134 (2008)
5. Haghighi, H.: Nondeterminism in CZ Specification Language. Ph.D. dissertation, Sharif Univ. of Technology, Iran (2009)
6. Jonsson, B., Larsen, K.G.: Specification and Refinement of Probabilistic Processes. In: Sixth Annual IEEE Symposium on Logic in Computer Science (1991)
7. Kozen, D.: Semantics of Probabilistic Programs. Journal of Computer and System Sciences, 328–350 (1981)
8. Meyn, S., Tweedie, R.L.: Markov Chains and Stochastic Stability, 2nd edn. Cambridge University Press (2008)
9. Martin-Löf, P.: An Intuitionistic Theory of Types: Predicative Part. In: Rose, H.E., Sheperdson, J.C. (eds.), pp. 73–118. North Holland (1975)
10. McIver, A., Morgan, C.: Abstraction and Refinement in Probabilistic Systems. ACM SIGMETRICS Performance Evaluation Review 32(4), 41–47 (2005)
11. McIver, A., Morgan, C.: Developing and Reasoning About Probabilistic Programs in pGCL. In: Cavalcanti, A., Sampaio, A., Woodcock, J. (eds.) PSSE 2004. LNCS, vol. 3167, pp. 123–155. Springer, Heidelberg (2006)
12. Mirian-Hosseinabadi, S.H.: Constructive Z. Ph.D. dissertation, Essex Univ. (1997)
13. Morgan, C., McIver, A., Hurd, J.: Probabilistic Guarded Commands Mechanised in HOL. Theoretical Computer Science, pp. 96–112 (2005)
14. Nordstrom, B., Petersson, K., Smith, J.M.: Programming in Martin-Löf's Type Theory: An Introduction. Oxford University Press (1990)
15. Park, S., Pfenning, F., Thrun, S.: A Probabilistic Language Based Upon Sampling Functions. In: ACM Symp. on Principles of Prog. Lang., pp. 171–182 (2005)
16. Ramsey, N., Pfeffer, A.: Stochastic Lambda Calculus and Monads of Probability Distributions. In: 29th ACM Symp. on Principles of Prog. Lang. (2002)
17. Woodcock, J., Davies, J.: Using Z, Specifications, Refinement and Proof. Prentice-Hall (1996)

Composing Real-Time Concurrent Objects
Refinement, Compatibility and Schedulability*

Mohammad Mahdi Jaghoori

LIACS, Leiden, The Netherlands
CWI, Amsterdam, The Netherlands
jaghoori@cwi.nl

Abstract. Concurrent objects encapsulate a processor each and communicate by asynchronous message passing; therefore, they can be composed to naturally model distributed and embedded systems. We model real-time concurrent objects using timed automata and provide each object with a context-specific scheduling policy. The envisioned usage and guaranteed deadlines of each object is specified in its behavioral interface, given also in timed automata. Furthermore, multiple objects can be composed only if they are compatible, i.e., if they respect the expected use patterns given in the behavioral interfaces of each other. In this paper, we define refinement of timed automata with inputs and outputs from a new perspective and we take account of deadlines in the refinement theory. Within this framework, we study composition and compatibility of real-time concurrent objects, and apply it in the context of compositional schedulability analysis of multiple-processor systems.

1 Introduction

Object oriented paradigm is a good basis for modular modeling and compositional analysis. A distributed system can be modeled as the composition of a set of concurrent objects where each concurrent object conceptually has a dedicated processor. We use timed I/O automata to model the real-time behavior of concurrent objects at an abstract level, as in our previous work [11]. Automata theory provides a rich basis for analysis; nevertheless, we need compositional techniques to overcome the complexity of large asynchronous distributed systems. A concurrent object is both the unit of concurrency and distribution; it is also a natural point for compositional analysis.

In this paper, we aim at compositional schedulability analysis of multiple-processor distributed systems specified with concurrent objects; a real-time system is schedulable if it can finish all of its tasks within their deadlines. While an object comprises a queue, a scheduling policy and several methods and is thus modeled in several automata, the abstract behavior of the object is given in one automaton, called the behavioral interface. A behavioral interface specifies at a high level and in the most general terms how an object may be used; thus it is used as the key to compositional analysis. Each object is analyzed individually

---

* This work is supported by the EU FP7-231620 project: HATS.

F. Arbab and M. Sirjani (Eds.): FSEN 2011, LNCS 7141, pp. 96–111, 2012.

for schedulability with respect to its behavioral interface. As in modular verification [15], which is based on assume-guarantee reasoning, individually schedulable objects can be used in systems *compatible* with their behavioral interfaces. The schedulability of such systems is then guaranteed [13].

In interface-based design, refinement is usually used as the means for compositional analysis. Given a set of components C_j with interfaces I_j, C_j is considered a correct implementation if it refines I_j. Then ideally, when the interfaces are *compatible* their implementations should also be able to work together. To capture all incompatibilities, any behavior not allowed in the interfaces should lead to an error (e.g., [8], cf. related work); however, this is too restrictive in practice because interfaces are abstract and easily produce spurious counterexamples to compatibility. An optimistic approach (e.g., [2]) considers two interfaces compatible if there exists a common behavior that allows them to work together. This is useful if we can make sure the implementation of evey components indeed follows this common behavior. We formalized this last step in [13] by requiring the composition of the components $C = \|_j C_j$ to be a refinement of $I = \|_j I_j$.

In this paper, we give a compositional solution to checking the refinement between $C = \|_j C_j$ and $I = \|_j I_j$. The idea is that the outputs of each component C_j should be expected as an input by the interface of the receiving component; this is formalized as every C_j being a refinement of I. Traditional views on refinement do not allow this relation because C_j and I have incompatible sets of inputs and outputs. A contribution of this paper is generalizing refinement such that it considers the common set of actions as the observable behavior. Thus, I is comparable to each C_j with respect to the inputs and outputs of C_j.

The second contribution of the paper is adding deadlines, as parameters to actions, to the refinement theory. A deadline on an output specifies when the task is required to finish. A deadline on an input specifies the guaranteed time before which the task is finished. Usually parameters are not included in the theory of refinement; instead, they are handled by expansion, i.e., an action is expanded to several actions considering different valuations of the parameter. Deadline parameters cannot be treated by expanding. A component may require weaker deadlines than its interface on the outputs and provide stronger guarantees for the inputs. We redefine refinement giving deadlines this special treatment.

Another contribution of this paper is applying the developed refinement theory in checking compatibility of concurrent objects in a compositional way. In [13], we have defined compatibility in terms of refinement: a closed system made up of individually schedulable objects is schedulable if it is a refinement of the composition of the behavioral interfaces. With our general definition of refinement, we can apply our method in *open systems* of multiple concurrent objects, too. The behavioral interface of the composite open system is the composition of the behavioral interfaces of individual objects.

We will explain how to automate refinement checking in the tool UPPAAL [16]. We show further how to check schedulability and compatibility in UPPAAL.

Related Work. Compatibility of real-time systems in automata theory has been studied for timed interfaces [2] and timed I/O automata [8]. Alfaro et al. [2] take an optimistic approach in which two interfaces are compatible if there is a possible way for them to work properly. This leads to a simpler theory but to implement these interfaces, one needs to adhere to these possibilities to end up with a working system. David et al. [8] suggest to make specifications input-enabled by adding an Error state and directing every undesired behavior to that state. They define two specifications to be compatible if their composition does not reach the Error state. This is unfortunately too restrictive for high-level specifications; abstract behavioral interfaces easily fall into spurious incompatibilities whereas their implementations may still work together. Our approach bridges the gap between these two methods. In fact, we check whether the implementations at hand, when composed, indeed follow the behavior that makes their interfaces compatible (w.r.t. the optimistic approach of [2]).

Analyzing the composition of the concurrent objects is subject to state space explosion because of their asynchronous nature and all their queues. We proposed a testing technique for compatibility in [13]. In present paper, we will model check compatibility in a compositional way with our generalized refinement theory.

Schedulability has been studied for actor languages [18] and event driven distributed systems [10]. Unlike these works, we work with non-uniformly recurring tasks as in task automata [9] which fits better the nature of message passing in object-oriented languages. The advantage of our work, as in [12,5], over task automata is that tasks are specified and may in turn create new tasks. Furthermore, we address schedulability analysis of multiple-processor systems. Compared to [14] we deal with the problem in a compositional way.

A characteristic of our work is modularity. A behavioral interface models the most general message arrival pattern for an object. A behavioral interface can be viewed as a contract as in 'design by contract' [17] or as a most general assumption in modular model checking [15] (based on assume-guarantee reasoning); schedulability is guaranteed if the real use of the object satisfies this assumption. In the literature, a model of the environment is usually the task generation scheme in a specific situation. For example in TAXYS [6], different models of the environment can be used to check schedulability of the application in different situations. However, a behavioral interface in our analysis covers all allowable usages of the object, and is thus an over-approximation of all environments in which the object can be used. This adds to the modularity of our approach; every use of the object foreseen in the interface is verified to be schedulable.

2   Timed Automata

Suppose $\mathcal{B}(C)$ is the set of all clock constraints on the set of clocks C. A *timed automaton*, as defined by Alur and Dill [3], over actions Σ and clocks C is a tuple $\langle L, l_0, \longrightarrow, I \rangle$ representing

- a finite set of locations L (including an initial location l_0);
- the set of edges $\longrightarrow \subseteq L \times \mathcal{B}(C) \times \Sigma \times 2^C \times L$; and,
- a function $I : L \mapsto \mathcal{B}(C)$ assigning an invariant to each location.

An edge (l, g, a, r, l') implies that action 'a' may change the location l to l' by resetting the clocks in r, if the clock constraints in g (as well as the invariant of l') hold. When we use UPPAAL [16] for analysis, we allow defining variables of type boolean and bounded integers. Variables can appear in guards and updates.

A timed automaton is called *deterministic* if and only if for each $a \in \Sigma$, if there are two edges (l, g, a, r, l') and (l, g', a, r', l'') from l labeled by the same action a then the guards g and g' are disjoint (i.e., $g \wedge g'$ is unsatisfiable).

Semantics. A timed automaton defines a possibly infinite labeled transition system whose states have the form (l, u) with $l \in L$ and $u : C \rightarrow \mathbb{R}_+$ is a *clock assignment*. We write $\mathbf{0}$ for the assignment mapping every clock in C to 0. Initial state is $s_0 = (l_0, \mathbf{0})$. There are two types of transitions from a given state (l, u):

- action transitions $(l, u) \xrightarrow{a} (l', u')$ where $a \in \Sigma$, if there exists (l, g, a, r, l') such that u satisfies the guard g, u' is obtained by resetting all clocks in r and leaving the others unchanged and u' satisfies the invariant of l';
- delay transitions $(l, u) \xrightarrow{d} (l, u')$ where $d \in \mathbb{R}_+$, if u' is obtained by delaying every clock for d time units and for each $0 \leq d' \leq d$, u' satisfies the invariant of location l.

Refinement. Traditionally, two timed automata are considered comparable if they have the same set of (observable) actions. We do not define observable and hidden actions explicitly for timed automata. Given two timed automata A and B, we consider them comparable if their common set of actions $\Sigma_A \cap \Sigma_B$ is not empty. A meaningful use of this definition is when there is a meaningful relation between the sets of actions of the two automata.

Definition 1 (TA Refinement). *Given two timed automata A and B, we say A refines B (written $A \sqsubseteq B$) iff there is a relation R between their underlying transition systems such that $(s_0^A, s_0^B) \in R$, and if $(s, t) \in R$ then*

- *for $a \in \Sigma_A \cap \Sigma_B$, if $s \xrightarrow{a}_A s'$ then $t \xrightarrow{a}_B t'$ and $(s', t') \in R$;*
- *if A can delay: $s \xrightarrow{d}_A s'$, then B can also delay: $t \xrightarrow{d}_B t'$ and $(s', t') \in R$.*

3 Timed I/O Automata

In timed I/O automata, the action set Σ is partitioned into inputs (Σ^I), outputs (Σ^O) and internal actions (Σ^τ). This allows us to model different components of a real-time system using automata while their communication is modeled by synchronization on matching input and output actions. Internal actions are not necessarily hidden; as we will see in composition, internal actions may model internal communication which may still be observable, i.e., included in refinement checking.

We consider timed I/O automata as a superclass of timed automata such that in normal timed automata $\Sigma^I = \Sigma^O = \emptyset$. For an action a we will write $a!$, $a?$ and a to denote that it is treated as an output, input or internal action, respectively.

Composition Composition of two timed I/O automata A and B is written as $S = A \parallel B$. The set of locations of S is the Cartesian product of those of A and B, denoted $L(S) = L(A) \times L(B)$ where invariants are defined as $I(l_A, l_B) = I(l_A) \wedge I(l_B)$. The composed automata synchronize on the set of sync actions $\Sigma_\cap = (\Sigma_A^I \cap \Sigma_B^O) \cup (\Sigma_A^O \cap \Sigma_B^I)$, which are made internal in S:

- input actions: $\Sigma_S^I = (\Sigma_A^I \cup \Sigma_B^I) \setminus \Sigma_\cap$
- output actions: $\Sigma_S^O = (\Sigma_A^O \cup \Sigma_B^O) \setminus \Sigma_\cap$
- internal actions: $\Sigma_S^\tau = \Sigma_A^\tau \cup \Sigma_B^\tau \cup \Sigma_\cap$

The set of transitions of S is computed as follows:

- $(l, k) \xrightarrow{g,a,r}_S (l', k)$ when $l \xrightarrow{g,a,r}_A l'$ and $a \notin \Sigma_\cap$
- $(l, k) \xrightarrow{g,a,r}_S (l, k')$ when $k \xrightarrow{g,a,r}_B k'$ and $a \notin \Sigma_\cap$
- $(l, k) \xrightarrow{g \wedge g',a,r \wedge r'}_S (l', k')$ when $l \xrightarrow{g,a,r}_A l'$ and $k \xrightarrow{g',a,r'}_B k'$ and $a \in \Sigma_\cap$

where by $r \wedge r'$ we mean updating both r and r'. Semantically, S can delay if both A and B can delay; S can perform a sync action $a \in \Sigma_\cap$ if both A and B can perform a; S can do any other action if either A or B can do that action.

For a finite set of timed I/O automata A_i ($1 \le i \le n$) to be *composable*, they should have disjoint observable actions: $\forall_{1 \le i,j \le n}\ \Sigma_{A_i}^I \cap \Sigma_{A_j}^I = \Sigma_{A_i}^O \cap \Sigma_{A_j}^O = \emptyset$. In this case, composition is associative, i.e., $(A \parallel B) \parallel C = A \parallel (B \parallel C)$. Thus, one could simply write $S = A_1 \parallel \cdots \parallel A_n$ to describe the composition of several composable timed I/O automata communicating with each other. The composition is called a *closed* system when $\Sigma_S^I = \Sigma_S^O = \emptyset$.

3.1   Refinement for Timed I/O Automata

A recent work by David et al. [8] gives a game-theoretic solution for checking refinement of timed I/O automata, but they assume input-enabled specifications. Our definition of refinement for timed automata and timed I/O automata does not assume input-enabledness; this leads to a more precise notion of compatibility (cf. [2,8]). This is more practical and will be used in Section 6 for schedulability analysis.

Two timed I/O automata A and B are traditionally (e.g., in [8]) considered comparable if they have the same sets of input and output actions, i.e., $\Sigma_A^I = \Sigma_B^I$ and $\Sigma_A^O = \Sigma_B^O$. Since we want to consider refinement in the context of composition where inputs and outputs may need to be compared to internal actions (which are in turn the result of synchronization), we need to be more liberal with the relation of the action sets. We say the timed I/O automata A and B are comparable for the relation $A \sqsubseteq B$ if:

$$\Sigma_A^I \subseteq \Sigma_B^I \cup \Sigma_B^\tau \ \wedge \ \Sigma_A^O \subseteq \Sigma_B^O \cup \Sigma_B^\tau \ \wedge \ \Sigma_A^\tau \cap (\Sigma_B^I \cup \Sigma_B^O) = \emptyset$$

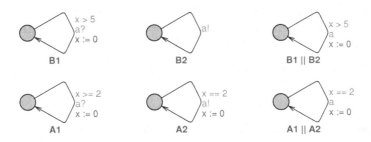

Fig. 1. Composition and refinement: $A_1 \sqsubseteq B_1$ and $A_2 \sqsubseteq B_2$ but $A_1 \parallel A_2 \not\sqsubseteq B_1 \parallel B_2$. This result is expected because $A_1 \sqsubseteq B_1 \parallel B_2$ but $A_2 \not\sqsubseteq B_1 \parallel B_2$.

In refinement between timed I/O automata, inputs and outputs are treated differently, as in alternating refinement [4]. Intuitively, when A refines B, the refined model A must accept any input that is acceptable in B; and, A may produce an output only if it is allowed at the abstract level B (e.g., see Fig. 1).

As timed IO automata are used in component-based design, we would like to be able to use them in compositional analysis, too. Given $A_1 \sqsubseteq B_1$ and $A_2 \sqsubseteq B_2$, B_1 and B_2 could be abstract interfaces for components A_1 and A_2, and one might expect that $A_1 \parallel A_2 \sqsubseteq B_1 \parallel B_2$. Such a compositional reasoning does not hold for timed I/O automata; this is illustrated in the counterexample in Fig. 1. In this example, A_1 admits the input a? in a bigger time interval than B_1; it becomes an internal action after synchronization with a! in A_2 (cf. composition in Section 3), this action would exist in $A_1 \parallel A_2$ but not necessarily in $B_1 \parallel B_2$. To compositionally infer $A_1 \parallel A_2 \sqsubseteq B_1 \parallel B_2$, we suggest an extra sufficient step $A_1 \sqsubseteq B_1 \parallel B_2$ and $A_2 \sqsubseteq B_1 \parallel B_2$. Here, we give a definition for refinement of timed I/O automata that supports such compositional analysis.

Definition 2 (TIOA Refinement). *Given two comparable timed I/O automata A and B, we say A refines B iff there is a relation R between their underlying transition systems such that $(s_0^A, s_0^B) \in R$, and if $(s, t) \in R$*

- *for $a \in \Sigma_A^I$, if $t \xrightarrow{a}_B t'$, then $s \xrightarrow{a}_A s'$ and $(s', t') \in R$;*
- *for $a \in \Sigma_A^O \cup (\Sigma_A^\tau \cap \Sigma_B)$, if $s \xrightarrow{a}_A s'$, then $t \xrightarrow{a}_B t'$ and $(s', t') \in R$;*
- *if A can delay: $s \xrightarrow{d}_A s'$ then B can also delay: $t \xrightarrow{d}_B t'$ and $(s', t') \in R$.*

It is easy to see that when A and B are normal timed automata, i.e., the input and output action sets are empty, Def. 2 simplifies to Def. 1. Furthermore, we do not require any direct relation between the inputs (resp. outputs) of A and B; we may compare inputs or outputs of A with internal actions of B. Thus we can compare arbitrary automata which helps us check refinement in a compositional way, described below.

Theorem 1. *Given the timed I/O automata A_1, A_2 and B, we have:*

$$A_1 \sqsubseteq B \land A_2 \sqsubseteq B \implies A_1 \parallel A_2 \sqsubseteq B$$

In the example in Figure 1, we can make A_2 to be a refinement of $B_1 \parallel B_2$ by changing the guard on $a!$, for example, to $x == 6$. It is easy to see that in this case $A_1 \parallel A_2$ is also a refinement of $B_1 \parallel B_2$.

Corollary 1. *Given a finite set of timed I/O automata A_i ($1 \leq i \leq n$) and B, we have:*

$$A_1 \sqsubseteq B \wedge \ \ldots \ \wedge A_n \sqsubseteq B \implies A_1 \parallel \cdots \parallel A_n \sqsubseteq B$$

In a component-based design where different components A_i implement the behavioral interfaces B_i, this corollary helps us check the refinement relation $A \sqsubseteq B$ in a compositional way, where $A = A_1 \parallel \cdots \parallel A_n$ and $B = B_1 \parallel \cdots \parallel B_n$. Having checked this refinement, one could prove safety properties at the abstract level for B, which then carries over to the refined and more complex system A. In Section 6 we use this approach for compositional schedulability analysis of a multiple processor system modeled in concurrent objects.

4   Timed I/O Automata with Deadlines

A deadline specifies the time before which a task must be done. A common property to check for real-time systems is schedulability, i.e., whether all tasks finish within their deadlines. We associate a *relative* deadline $d \in \mathbb{N}$ to input and output actions, i.e., the deadline is d time units after the action is taken. The interpretation of a deadline depends on the action type:

- An automaton with an input action $a(d)?$ guarantees the deadline d; therefore, it naturally also guarantees $d + 1$.
- An output action $a(d)!$ requires a deadline d; naturally, a deadline d is a stronger requirement than $d + 1$.

At the lowest level of abstraction, the tasks are implemented and one needs to check whether they indeed meet their deadlines, as explained in Section 5.

Composition. In presence of deadlines, we restrict composition of timed I/O automata by allowing only compatible actions to synchronize; two actions $a(d)?$ and $a(d')!$ are compatible if $d \leq d'$, i.e., the required deadline is not stronger than the guaranteed one. As a result of this synchronization, the composed automaton will have an internal action $a(d, d')$. A deadline interval $[d..d']$ associated to an internal action a is stronger than $[\delta..\delta']$ if the interval $[d..d']$ is included in $[\delta..\delta']$, i.e., $\delta \leq d$ and $d' \leq \delta'$. When two transitions have a sync action as input and output with incompatible deadlines, they do not synchronize and they do not appear in the composed automaton.

Refinement. When considering deadlines in refinement, the refined model must provide the same (or stronger) deadline guarantees on its inputs compared to the abstract model; the refined model may not require stronger deadlines on its outputs than the abstract model. A common internal action cannot have a stronger deadline interval than the abstract one. Below, Def. 2 is extended to include deadlines with the abovementioned considerations. Taking deadline intervals for internal actions makes this definition of refinement transitive, i.e., given $A \sqsubseteq B$ and $B \sqsubseteq C$ we have $A \sqsubseteq C$.

Definition 3 (Refinement with Deadlines). *Given two comparable timed I/O automata, we say A refines B iff there is a relation R between their underlying transition systems such that $(s_0^A, s_0^B) \in R$, and if $(s, t) \in R$*

- *for $a \in \Sigma_A^I$, if $t \xrightarrow{a(d)?}_B t'$ then $s \xrightarrow{a(\delta)?}_A s'$ with $d \geq \delta$ and $(s', t') \in R$;*
- *for $a \in \Sigma_A^I$, if $t \xrightarrow{a(d,d')}_B t'$ then $s \xrightarrow{a(\delta)?}_A s'$ with $d \geq \delta$ and $(s', t') \in R$;*
- *for $a \in \Sigma_A^O$, if $s \xrightarrow{a(\delta)!}_A s'$ then*
  - *$t \xrightarrow{a(d)!}_B t'$ with $d \leq \delta$ and $(s', t') \in R$; or,*
  - *$t \xrightarrow{a(d,d')}_B t'$ with $d' \leq \delta$ and $(s', t') \in R$;*
- *for $a \in \Sigma_A^\tau \cap \Sigma_B$, if $s \xrightarrow{a(\delta,\delta')}_A s'$ then $t \xrightarrow{a(d,d')}_B t'$ and $\delta \leq d$ and $d' \leq \delta'$ and $(s', t') \in R$;*
- *if A can delay: $s \xrightarrow{d}_A s'$ then B can also delay: $t \xrightarrow{d}_B t'$ and $(s', t') \in R$.*

4.1   Checking Refinement in UPPAAL

It has been shown for timed automata that checking refinement $A \sqsubseteq B$ is decidable when B is deterministic [3]. For input-enabled timed I/O automata, David et al. [8] use a game-theoretic approach. We gave in [13] a simple algorithm to test refinement of timed automata, in the flavor of Def. 1, using reachability analysis in UPPAAL. Below, we show how to check refinement for timed I/O automata with deadlines (cf. Def. 2) again using reachability analysis in UPPAAL. The idea of using reachability analysis to tackle verification problems is not new (cf. [1]); what is new in this section is how we encode checking for refinement (as defined in this paper) as a reachability check, especially including deadlines.

To check the refinement relation $A \sqsubseteq B$, first, we assume no deadlines in checking refinement (cf. Def. 2). We start from A^* and B^* being copies of A and B, respectively, and continue as below:

- First, we repartition the action sets: $\Sigma_{A^*}^I = \Sigma_{B^*}^O = \Sigma_A^I$ and $\Sigma_{A^*}^O = \Sigma_{B^*}^I = \Sigma_A^O \cup (\Sigma_A^\tau \cap \Sigma_B)$; other actions are treated as internal. Considering the requirements that make A and B comparable for the relation $A \sqsubseteq B$ (cf. Section 3.1), it is easy to see that the assignments above do not change the action set of B^*, i.e., $\Sigma_B = \Sigma_{B^*}$.
- We add an Error location to each of A^* and B^*.

Next, with the algorithms in Fig. 2, we produce $A_E^* = \text{NegGuard}(A^*)$ and $B_E^* = \text{NegGuard}(\text{NegInv}(B^*))$. A_E^* and B_E^* basically have the same behavior as A^* and B^* but they are made input-enabled such that every incompatible action in A or B leads to a designated Error location, i.e., intuitively, unexpected inputs in A

Algorithm NegGuard

 for every location $l \in L(A)$ **do**
  for every action $m \in \Sigma_A^I$ **do**
   let $g_f = \bigvee\limits_i g_i$ for all transitions $l \xrightarrow{g_i, m, r_i} l'$ in A
   add $l \xrightarrow{\neg g_f, m, \emptyset} Error$
  endfor
 endfor

Algorithm NegInv

 for every location $l \in L(A)$ **do**
  let h be the invariant of l in A
  add $l \xrightarrow{\neg h, \tau, \emptyset} Error$
  change every transition $l \xrightarrow{g, m, r} l'$ to $l \xrightarrow{g \wedge h, m, r} l'$
 endfor
 Remove all location invariants

Fig. 2. Adding transitions to the Error Location to find incompatibilities

and unexpected output or delay in B. Finally, A_E^* and B_E^* have matching inputs and outputs and thus their composition can be analyzed in a tool like UPPAAL. The Error locations of A_E^* and B_E^* is not reachable iff $A \sqsubseteq B$. To sketch the proof of this, NegInv and NegGuard help detect the possible incompatibilities between delay and action transitions, respectively, with respect to Def. 2.

In order to consider deadlines in UPPAAL, we add an extra step in computing A^* and B^*:

- For every $a \in \Sigma_A^I$, we change $a(d)$ to $a(d, 0)$ in both A^* and B^*.
- For every $a \in \Sigma_A^O$, we change $a(d)$ to $a(0, d)$ in both A^* and B^*.

Obviously, the above rules leave the internal actions of B (which already have the form $a(d, d')$) unchanged. Thus, every input and output action of A^* and B^* has two deadline values. Next, we add two fresh global variables δ and δ'; in UPPAAL, global variables are used to pass parameter values. We transform input and output actions to UPPAAL format as follows:

- We change every output transition $s \xrightarrow{g, a(d, d')!, r}_{A^*} s'$ to $s \xrightarrow{g, a!, r \wedge \delta := d \wedge \delta' := d'}_{A^*} s'$.
- We change every output transition $s \xrightarrow{g, a(d, d')!, r}_{B^*} s'$ to $s \xrightarrow{g, a!, r \wedge \delta := d}_{B^*} s'$.
- We change every input transition $s \xrightarrow{g, a(d, d')?, r}_{A^*} s'$ to $s \xrightarrow{g \wedge d \leq \delta, a?, r}_{A^*} s'$.
- We change every input transition $s \xrightarrow{g, a(d, d')?, r}_{B^*} s'$ to $s \xrightarrow{g \wedge d \leq \delta \wedge \delta' \leq d', a?, r}_{B^*} s'$.

The outputs set the values of δ and δ' to their deadline values which are checked against the input deadline guarantees in the input actions. This way the deadline values and the corresponding checks are integrated into the guards and updates of the automata. Then we can continue in the same way as explained above without deadlines, i.e., compute A_E^* and B_E^* and check for the reachability of the Error locations. An example of computing B_E^* is given in the next section.

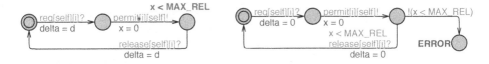

Fig. 3. The abstract behavioral interface of a resource and applying NegInv on it

5   Real-Time Concurrent Objects

Concurrent objects encapsulate a processor each and communicate by asynchronous message passing; therefore, they can be composed to naturally model distributed and embedded systems. An object is an instance of a class with a context-specific scheduler; a class implements a behavioral interface. In this section, we use timed I/O automata with deadlines to model behavioral interfaces, classes and schedulers.

The observable actions of concurrent objects are the messages they communicate. For their automata models to be composable, they should have disjoint sets of inputs (resp. outputs). To achieve this, we consider an action to be a triple (m, r, s) where m is the message name, r is the receiver object identity, and s is the sender object identity. The keyword *self* refers to the identity of the owner object itself. Given an object A, its input and output actions are $\Sigma_I^A = \{(m, r = A, s)\}$ and $\Sigma_O^A = \{(m, r, s = A)\}$. For simplicity in presentation, we may write an action (m, r, s) only as the message name m.

Behavioral Interfaces. A behavioral interface provides an abstract overview of the object behavior in a single automaton in terms of the messages it may receive and send. We assume a finite global set $\mathcal{M}$ for method names; sending and receiving messages are written as $m!$ and $m?$, respectively. We use natural values $d \in \mathbb{N}$ to represent deadlines. A behavioral interface B providing a set of method names $M_B \subseteq \mathcal{M}$ is formally defined as a deterministic timed I/O automaton over alphabet Σ^B which is partitioned into two sets of actions:

- object outputs received by the environment: $\Sigma_O^B = \{m! | m \in \mathcal{M} \wedge m \notin M_B\}$
- object inputs sent by the environment: $\Sigma_I^B = \{m(d)? | m \in M_B \wedge d \in \mathbb{N}\}$

We allow underspecified actions where no deadline is given, e.g., for output actions above. An underspecified deadline is potentially stronger than any specified deadline value $d \in \mathbb{N}$; therefore, to be able to reuse the definition of refinement, we assume that underspecified actions have a deadline zero.

A behavioral interface abstracts from specific method implementations, the queue in the object and the scheduling strategy. It can also be seen as the highest level of abstraction (i.e., an over-approximation) of the environments that can communicate with the object.

Fig. 3 (left) gives the behavioral interface of a resource object which guarantees the deadline d on its inputs *req* and *release*. Furthermore, when a requester

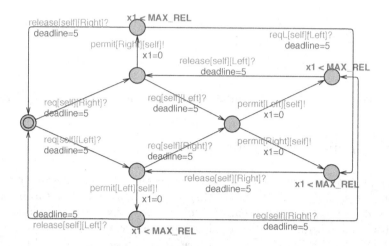

Fig. 4. A mutually exclusive resource

is permitted to take the resource, it has to release it before MAX_REL time units. This automaton is parameterized in i which must be instantiated with the identity of the requester object when the requester and the resource objects are composed. If there are two requesters, the behavioral interface of the resource can be obtained by composing two instances of this automaton with different values for i.

Fig. 4 gives the behavioral interface of a mutually exclusive resource shared by two objects Right and Left. When there are two requests at a time, only one of them is granted in this model. This model is a refinement of the unrestricted model in Fig. 3 if $5 <= d$. To check refinement, we must apply the algorithm NegGuard to Fig. 4 and both algorithms NegGuard and NegInv to Fig. 3 (the result of the latter is shown in Fig. 3 right).

Classes. One can define a class R as a set of methods implementing a specific behavioral interface B, which must include at least the methods M_B. For an input action $m(d)!$ in the behavioral interface, a correct implementation should be able to finish method m before d time units. A class R implementing the behavioral interface B is a set $\{(m_1, A_1), \ldots, (m_n, A_n)\}$ of methods, where

- $M_R = \{m_1, \ldots, m_n\} \subseteq \mathcal{M}$ is a set of method names such that $M_B \subseteq M_R$;
- for all i, $1 \leq i \leq n$, A_i is a timed I/O automaton representing method m_i with the output alphabet $\Sigma_i = \{m! | m \in M_R\} \cup \{m(d)! \mid m \in \mathcal{M} \land d \in \mathbb{N}\}$ and no explicit inputs.

Classes have an *initial* method which is implicitly called upon initialization and is used for the system startup. Method automata only send messages while computations are abstracted into time delays. Sending a message $m \in M_R$ is called a self call. Self calls may or may not be assigned an explicit deadline. The self calls with no explicit deadline are called *delegation*. Delegation implies that the internal task (triggered by the self call) is in fact the continuation of the parent task; therefore, the delegated task inherits the (remaining) deadline of the task that triggers it.

Schedulers. Receiving and buffering messages and executing the corresponding methods is handled by the scheduler automata. A *scheduler automaton* implements a queue for storing messages and their deadlines. The scheduler of a concurrent object is input enabled, i.e., it can receive any message in M_R at any time; this is to model the asynchronous nature of communication between the objects. Whenever a method is finished, the scheduler selects another message from the queue (based on its scheduling strategy) and starts the corresponding method (called context-switch).

Since the object is strongly input-enabled, i.e., it may accept any input at any time, it is not per se a refinement of the behavioral interface; because the object may wait (i.e., have a delay transition) for an input while it is not allowed (i.e., expected) in the behavioral interface. Next, we describe how we may restrict the object behavior so that it is schedulable; in this case, it is a correct refinement of its behavioral interface.

Schedulable Objects. An object is an instance of a class together with a scheduler automaton. An object is called *schedulable* if it can finish all of its tasks within their deadlines. An unrestricted object is trivially non-schedulable, because it may accept too many inputs in a short time. To restrict the possible ways in which the methods of an object could be called, we consider only the incoming messages specified in its behavioral interface. To check an object for schedulability (e.g., in UPPAAL), the inputs of B are changed to outputs $m!$ so that they match the inputs in the scheduler written as $m?$ and the outputs of B are changed to inputs written as $m?$ so that they match outputs of method automata written as $m!$.

The scheduler automaton moves to an Error location with no outgoing transitions when a task in the queue misses its deadline. Furthermore, as shown in [11], a schedulable object never puts more than $\lceil d_{max}/b_{min} \rceil$ messages in the queue, where d_{max} is the longest deadline for any method called on any transition of the automata (method automata or the input actions of the behavioral interface) and b_{min} is the shortest termination time of any of the method automata. Thus we can put a finite bound on the queue length such that queue overflow implies non-schedulability. We can calculate the best case runtime for timed automata as shown in [7].

We explained in [11] how the restricted behavioral model of an object can be constructed as one automaton. The action set of this automaton are the same as its behavioral interface. We have also shown in [11] how to model an object in UPPAAL. To capture possible design errors, one can start with checking for deadlock in UPPAAL. A deadlock may be caused by a mismatching invariant and guards in a method implementation, or if the Error location in the scheduler is reached. To ensure schedulability at the same time, one should add a check for queue overflow. This can be written in UPPAAL as "A□ not deadlock and tail ≤ MAX".

Furthermore, one may check other properties on the restricted object behavior. It is easy to see that when the restricted object model is schedulable, it is also a true refinement of the behavioral interface.

6   Real-Time Distributed Systems

Once an object is checked for schedulability with respect to its behavioral interface, it can be used as an off-the-shelf component to compose distributed systems. If the assumptions in the behavioral interface of the object are satisfied, the correct behavior of the object is guaranteed (with respect to the properties already checked for the object, e.g., its schedulability). Checking this is usually referred to as *compatibility* check.

In an optimistic approach [2] two interfaces are considered compatible when there is a way that they can work together. In this case, there exists at least one implementation of those interfaces that are compatible, too. What actually needs to be done next is to check whether the implementations at hand indeed follow the traces that make their interfaces work together.

For concurrent objects, the composition of their behavioral interfaces shows the acceptable sequences of messages that may be communicated between the objects. As compatibility is defined in [13], the system implementation at hand must be a refinement of the composition of the behavioral interfaces. It is shown in [13] that, assuming individually schedulable concurrent objects, their composition is schedulable if they are compatible.

Since our definition of refinement in this paper is not restricted to closed systems, we can generalize compatibility to any open or closed system. When compatible concurrent objects form an open component, the composition of their behavioral interfaces serves as the behavioral interface of their composition. Below, we write $A : B$ to denote an object A with its input behavior restricted to a behavioral interface B (as explained in the previous section).

Definition 4 (Compatibility). *We define the set of concurrent objects $A_i : B_i$ $(1 \leq i \leq n)$ to be compatible iff $A_1 \parallel \cdots \parallel A_n \sqsubseteq B_1 \parallel \cdots \parallel B_n$.*

Since the compsition of concurrent objects is usually too big (due to their asynchrony and message queues), model checking compatibility is subject to state-space explosion; therefore, a testing method has been proposed in [13]. Here, we propose to use the compositional refinement check to verify compatibility in this sense.

Given $A_i : B_i$ $(1 \leq i \leq n)$ when $A_i : B_i \sqsubseteq B_1 \parallel \cdots \parallel B_n$ for all $1 \leq i \leq n$, it follows from Theorem 1 that the composition of the restricted objects $A' = A_1 : B_1 \parallel \cdots \parallel A_n : B_n$ is a refinement of $B = B_1 \parallel \cdots \parallel B_n$. We still need to show that the composition of the unrestricted objects $A = A_1 \parallel \cdots \parallel A_n$ is also a refinement of B; in fact, in this setting the behavior of A and A' is the same.

Theorem 2. *The closed system $A_1 \parallel \cdots \parallel A_n$ is trace equivalent to the restricted system $A_1 : B_1 \parallel \cdots \parallel A_n : B_n$ if $\forall_{1 \leq i \leq n} A_i : B_i \sqsubseteq B_1 \parallel \cdots \parallel B_n$.*

Theorems 1 and 2 result in the following corollary:

Corollary 2. *The concurrent objects $A_i : B_i$ ($1 \leq i \leq n$) are compatible iff $A_i : B_i \sqsubseteq B_1 \parallel \cdots \parallel B_n$ for all $1 \leq i \leq n$.*

This implies that given individually schedulable objects, their composition is also schedulable if we can show that each object is a refinement of the composition of the behavioral interfaces of all objects. This method will be complementary to the testing method we had already proposed in [13].

7   Conclusions and Future Work

We bridge the gap between automata theory and object orientation. In previous work, we developed schedulability analysis techniques for concurrent objects modeled in timed I/O automata. In this work, we further developed the related automata theory such that we can check compatibility in a compositional way.

To be able to argue about schedulability, we extended timed I/O automata with deadlines. Furthermore, we extended the definition of composition and refinement to include deadlines. On the other hand, our definition of refinement is not restricted to automata with the same sets of inputs and outputs; this allows us to compare a component, modeled as an automaton, with a composition of components for refinement.

We applied the refinement theory for timed I/O automata with deadlines to compositional schedulability analysis of systems modeled with concurrent objects. Each concurrent object is model checked to be schedulable when its input behavior is restricted as specified in its behavioral interface; a system is schedulable when all objects receive inputs as they expect according to their behavioral interface. This *compatibility* can be ensured by checking whether the system is a refinement of the composition of the behavioral interfaces. We showed in this paper how to model check this in a compositional way.

Currently, we are considering network delays between concurrent objects when composed. Network delays both affect the deadlines of messages and the input assumptions of the object receiving that message. Moreover, complex network structures can also be added to coordinate distributed schedulable services; for example, to balance the load of a fast client between multiple slow servers.

References

1. Aceto, L., Bouyer, P., Burgueño, A., Larsen, K.G.: The power of reachability testing for timed automata. Theor. Comput. Sci. 300(1-3), 411–475 (2003)
2. de Alfaro, L., Henzinger, T.A., Stoelinga, M.: Timed Interfaces. In: Sangiovanni-Vincentelli, A.L., Sifakis, J. (eds.) EMSOFT 2002. LNCS, vol. 2491, pp. 108–122. Springer, Heidelberg (2002)
3. Alur, R., Dill, D.L.: A theory of timed automata. Theoretical Computer Science 126(2), 183–235 (1994)
4. Alur, R., Henzinger, T.A., Kupferman, O., Vardi, M.Y.: Alternating Refinement Relations. In: Sangiorgi, D., de Simone, R. (eds.) CONCUR 1998. LNCS, vol. 1466, pp. 163–178. Springer, Heidelberg (1998)

5. de Boer, F.S., Jaghoori, M.M., Johnsen, E.B.: Dating Concurrent Objects: Real-Time Modeling and Schedulability Analysis. In: Gastin, P., Laroussinie, F. (eds.) CONCUR 2010. LNCS, vol. 6269, pp. 1–18. Springer, Heidelberg (2010)
6. Closse, E., Poize, M., Pulou, J., Sifakis, J., Venter, P., Weil, D., Yovine, S.: TAXYS: A Tool for the Development and Verification of Real-Time Embedded Systems. In: Berry, G., Comon, H., Finkel, A. (eds.) CAV 2001. LNCS, vol. 2102, pp. 391–395. Springer, Heidelberg (2001)
7. Courcoubetis, C., Yannakakis, M.: Minimum and maximum delay problems in real-time systems. Formal Methods in System Design 1(4), 385–415 (1992)
8. David, A., Larsen, K.G., Legay, A., Nyman, U., Wasowski, A.: Timed I/O automata: a complete specification theory for real-time systems. In: Proc. Hybrid Systems: Computation and Control (HSCC 2010), pp. 91–100. ACM (2010)
9. Fersman, E., Krcal, P., Pettersson, P., Yi, W.: Task automata: Schedulability, decidability and undecidability. Information and Computation 205(8), 1149–1172 (2007)
10. Garcia, J.J.G., Gutierrez, J.C.P., Harbour, M.G.: Schedulability analysis of distributed hard real-time systems with multiple-event synchronization. In: Proc. 12th Euromicro Conference on Real-Time Systems, pp. 15–24. IEEE (2000)
11. Jaghoori, M.M., de Boer, F.S., Chothia, T., Sirjani, M.: Schedulability of asynchronous real-time concurrent objects. J. Logic and Alg. Prog. 78(5), 402–416 (2009)
12. Jaghoori, M.M., Chothia, T.: Timed automata semantics for analyzing Creol. In: Proc. Foundations of Coordination Languages and Software Architectures (FOCLASA 2010). EPTCS, vol. 30, pp. 108–122 (2010)
13. Jaghoori, M.M., Longuet, D., de Boer, F.S., Chothia, T.: Schedulability and compatibility of real time asynchronous objects. In: Proc. RTSS 2008, pp. 70–79. IEEE CS (2008)
14. Krcal, P., Stigge, M., Yi, W.: Multi-Processor Schedulability Analysis of Preemptive Real-Time Tasks with Variable Execution Times. In: Raskin, J.-F., Thiagarajan, P.S. (eds.) FORMATS 2007. LNCS, vol. 4763, pp. 274–289. Springer, Heidelberg (2007)
15. Kupferman, O., Vardi, M.Y., Wolper, P.: Module checking. Information and Computation 164(2), 322–344 (2001)
16. Larsen, K.G., Pettersson, P., Yi, W.: UPPAAL in a nutshell. STTT 1(1-2), 134–152 (1997)
17. Meyer, B.: Eiffel: The language. Prentice-Hall (1992)
18. Nigro, L., Pupo, F.: Schedulability Analysis of Real Time Actor Systems using Coloured Petri Nets. In: Agha, G., De Cindio, F., Rozenberg, G. (eds.) APN 2001. LNCS, vol. 2001, pp. 493–513. Springer, Heidelberg (2001)

Proofs Omitted from Text

Theorem 1. Given the timed I/O automata A_1, A_2 and B, we have:

$$A_1 \sqsubseteq B \wedge A_2 \sqsubseteq B \implies A_1 \parallel A_2 \sqsubseteq B$$

Proof. For simplicity, we give the proof without considering deadlines. Deadlines can be added to the proof in a straightforward way.

We write the states of (the underlying transition system of) $A = A_1 \parallel A_2$ as (s_1, s_2) where s_i is a state in (the underlying transition system of) A_i. We write $(s_1, s_2)R(t)$ to relate a state (s_1, s_2) in A to t in B using a relation R. We assume $A_1 \sqsubseteq B$ and $A_2 \sqsubseteq B$ with the refinement relations R_1 and R_2, respectively, as defined in Def. 2. We define R such that $(s_1, s_2)R(t)$ if and only if $(s_1, t) \in R_1$ or $(s_2, t) \in R_2$. We show below that the relation R satisfies the requirements put forward in Def. 2 and therefore $A \sqsubseteq B$.

Obviously R relates the initial states of A and B. Let's assume that $(s_1, s_2)R(t)$. The set of sync actions of A_1 and A_2 are $\Sigma_\cap = (\Sigma^I_{A_1} \cap \Sigma^O_{A_2}) \cup (\Sigma^O_{A_1} \cap \Sigma^I_{A_2})$. By definition of composition, we have $\Sigma_\cap \subseteq \Sigma^\tau_A$.

- For $a \in \Sigma^I_A$, we know that $a \in \Sigma^I_{A_1}$ or $a \in \Sigma^I_{A_2}$ and a is not a sync action. Without loss of generality, we take $a \in \Sigma^I_{A_1}$. Since $A_1 \sqsubseteq B$, by Def. 2, we know that if $t \xrightarrow{a} t'$ in B there is a transition $s_1 \xrightarrow{a} s'_1$ in A_1 and $(s'_1, t') \in R_1$. Since a is not a sync action, there is a transition $(s_1, s_2) \xrightarrow{a} (s'_1, s_2)$ in A, too. Since $(s'_1, t') \in R_1$, we have $(s'_1, s_2)R(t')$.

- For $a \in \Sigma^O_A \cup ((\Sigma^\tau_A \cap \Sigma_B) \setminus \Sigma_\cap)$, i.e., excluding sync actions, we assume, without loss of generality, that $a \in \Sigma^O_{A_1} \cup (\Sigma^\tau_{A_1} \cap \Sigma_B)$. In this case, A may have a transition $(s_1, s_2) \xrightarrow{a} (s'_1, s_2)$ only if there is $s_1 \xrightarrow{a} s'_1$ in A_1. From $A_1 \sqsubseteq B$, we can say that there is also a transition $t \xrightarrow{a} t'$ in B and $(s'_1, t') \in R_1$. Since $(s'_1, t') \in R_1$, we have $(s'_1, s_2)R(t')$.

- For $a \in \Sigma^\tau_A \cap \Sigma_B \cap \Sigma_\cap$, A may have a transition $(s_1, s_2) \xrightarrow{a} (s'_1, s'_2)$ only if there are $s_1 \xrightarrow{a} s'_1$ in A_1 and $s_2 \xrightarrow{a} s'_2$ in A_2. Without loss of generality, we assume $a \in \Sigma^O_{A_1} \cap \Sigma^I_{A_2}$. By considering $A_1 \sqsubseteq B$ and $s_1 \xrightarrow{a} s'_1$, we can conclude that there is a transition $t \xrightarrow{a} t'$ in B and $(s'_1, t') \in R_1$. Since $(s'_1, t') \in R_1$, we have $(s'_1, s'_2)R(t')$.

- Finally, if A can delay for d time units, both A_1 and A_2 can delay and therefore B can delay for d time units. It is easy to see that the target states are related by R. □

To extend this proof with deadlines, consider the case when an input with deadline d synchronizes with an output with deadline d'. The generated internal action has the deadline interval (d, d'). Considering the definition of refinement, we can easily show that the corresponding interval in B is stronger than (d, d').

Theorem 2. The closed system $A_1 \parallel \cdots \parallel A_n$ is trace equivalent to the restricted system $A_1 : B_1 \parallel \cdots \parallel A_n : B_n$ if $\forall_{1 \leq i \leq n} A_i : B_i \sqsubseteq B_1 \parallel \cdots \parallel B_n$.

Proof (idea). It is easy to see that every trace in A' also exists in A, because every $A_i : B_i$ is a in fact restriction of A_i.

To show the other direction, take a trace $\sigma = (t_1, a_1) \ldots (t_n, a_n)$ from A. We use induction to show that σ is also a trace in A'. As the base case, since A and A' start in the same initial states, they can generate the same initial outputs. Therefore, A' can output a_1 at time t_1. Assume that for $j < n$, $\sigma_j = (t_1, a_1) \ldots (t_{j-1}, a_{j-1})$ exists in A' and furthermore A' can output a_j at time t_j. We must show that a_j is also an acceptable input at time t_j.

Suppose a_j is an output action of A_{j1} and an input action of A_{j2}. Since $A_{j1} : B_{j1}$ is a refinement of B, the action a_j exists in B; and since $A_{j2} : B_{j2}$ is also a refinement of B, the action a_j is acceptable in $A_{j2} : B_{j2}$ at time t_j. Next, A' can produce the output action a_{j+1} at time t_{j+1} because it has the same methods as A. □

Specification Guidelines to Avoid the State Space Explosion Problem

Jan Friso Groote, Tim W.D.M. Kouters, and Ammar Osaiweran

Eindhoven University of Technology
Department of Computer Science
P.O. Box 513, 5600 MB Eindhoven, The Netherlands
{J.F.Groote,A.A.H.Osaiweran}@tue.nl,
T.W.D.M.Kouters@student.tue.nl

Abstract. During the last two decades we modelled the behaviour of a large number of systems. We noted that different styles of modelling had quite an effect on the size of the state spaces of the modelled system. The differences were so substantial that some specification styles led to far too many states to verify the correctness of the model, whereas with other styles the number of states was so small that verification was a straightforward activity. In this paper we summarise our experience by providing seven specification guidelines, of which five are worked out in more detail.

Keywords: Design for verifications, specification guidelines, state space explosion, model checking.

1 Introduction

These days, we and others have ample experience in system design through discrete behavioural specification of computer systems. The primary lesson is that, although, behavioural specification is extremely helpful, it is not enough. We need to verify that the designed behaviour is correct, in the sense that it either satisfies certain behavioural requirements or that it matches a compact external description. It turns out that discrete behaviour is so complex, that a flawless design without verification is virtually impossible.

When verifying system behaviour, the state space explosion problem kicks in. This means that the behaviour of any real system quickly has so many states that despite the use of clever verification algorithms and powerful computers, verification is often problematic. Three decades of improvements of verification technology did not provide the means to overcome the state space explosion problem.

We believe that the state space explosion problem must, therefore, also be dealt with in another way, namely by designing models such that their behaviour can be verified. We call this *design for verifiability* or *modelling for verifiability*. Compared to the development of state space reduction techniques, design for verifiability is a barely addressed issue. The best we could find is [11], but

F. Arbab and M. Sirjani (Eds.): FSEN 2011, LNCS 7141, pp. 112–127, 2012.

it primarily addresses improvements in verification technology, too. Specification styles from the perspective of expressiveness have been addressed [14], but verifiability is also not really an issue here.

In this article we provide five specification guidelines that we learned by specifying complex realistic systems (e.g. traffic control systems, medical equipment, domestic appliances, communication protocols). For each guideline we give two examples. The first one does not take the guideline into account and the second does. We show by a transition system or a table that the state space that is using the guideline is much smaller. The 'bad' and the 'good' specifications are in general not behaviourally equivalent (for instance in the sense of branching bisimulation) but as we will see, they both capture the application's intent. All specifications are written in mCRL2, which is a process specification formalism based on process algebra [8,15]. A detailed version of this paper that contains a concise introduction of mCRL2 and two more guidelines can be found in [6].

In hindsight, we can say that it is quite self evident why the guidelines have a beneficial effect on the size of the state spaces. Some of the guidelines are already quite commonly used, such as reordering information in buffers, if the ordering is not important. The use of synchronous communication, although less commonly used, also falls in this category. Other guidelines such as information polling are not really surprising, but specifiers appear to have a natural tendency to use information pushing instead. The use of external specifications may be foreign to most specifiers.

Although we provide a number of guidelines that we believe are really important for the behavioural modellist, we do not claim completeness. Without doubt we have overlooked a number of specification strategies that are helpful in keeping state spaces small. Furthermore, a systematic or formal approach to relate the specification pairs for each guideline are beyond the interest of this paper. Hopefully this document will be an inspiration to investigate state space reduction from this perspective, which ultimately can be accumulated in effective teaching material, helping both students and working practitioners to avoid the pitfalls of state space explosion.

2   Overview of Design Guidelines

In this section we give a short description of the five guidelines that we present in this paper.

I **Information Polling**. This guideline advises to let processes ask for information, whenever it is required. The alternative is to share information with other components, whenever the information becomes available. Although, this latter strategy clearly increases the number of states of a system, it appears to prevail over information polling in most specifications that we have seen.

II **Global Synchronous Communication**. If more parties communicate with each other, it can be that a component 1 communicates with a component 2, and subsequently, component 2 informs a component 3. This requires two consecutive communications and therefore two state transitions. By using multi-actions it is possible to let component 1 communicate with component 2 that synchronously communicates with a component 3. This only requires one transition. By synchronising communication over different components, the number of states of the overall system can be substantially reduced.

III **Avoid Parallelism Among Components.** If components operate in parallel, the state space grows exponentially in the number of components. By sequentialising the behaviour of these components, the size of the total state space is only the sum of the sizes of the state spaces of the individual components. In this latter case state spaces are small and easy to analyse, whereas in the former case analysis might be quite hard. Sequentialising the behaviour can for instance be done by introducing an arbiter, or by letting a process higher up in the process hierarchy to allow only one sub-process to operate at any time.

IV **Restrict the use of Data.** The use of data in a specification is a main cause for state-space explosion. Therefore, it is advisable to avoid using data whenever possible. If data is essential, try to categorise it, and only store the categories. For example, instead of storing a height in millimetres, store *too_low*, *right_height* and *too_high*. Finally, take care that data is only stored in one way. E.g., storing the names of the files that are open in an unordered buffer is a waste. The buffer can be ordered without losing information.

V **Specify the External Behaviour of Sets of Sub-components.** If the behaviour of sets of components are composed, the external behaviour tends to be overly complex. In particular the state space is often larger than needed. A technique to keep this behaviour small is to separately specify the expected external behaviour first. Subsequently, the behaviours of the components are designed such that they meet this external behaviour.

3   Guideline I: Information Polling

One of the primary sources of many states is the occurrence of data in a system. A good strategy is to only read data when it is needed and to decide upon this data, after which the data is directly forgotten. In this strategy data is polled when required, instead of pushed to those that might potentially need it. An obvious disadvantage of polling is that much more communication is needed. This might be problematic for a real system, but for verification purposes it is attractive, as the number of states in a system becomes smaller when using polling.

Currently, it appears that most behavioural specifications use information pushing, rather than information polling. E.g., whenever some event happens, this information is immediately shared with neighbouring processes.

In order to illustrate the advantage of information polling, we provide two specifications. The first one is 'bad' in the sense that there are more states than in the second specification. We are now interested in a system that can be triggered by two sensors $trig_1$ and $trig_2$. After both sensors fire a trigger, a traffic light must switch from red to green, from green to yellow, and subsequently back

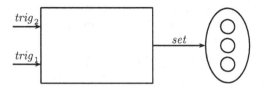

Fig. 1. A simple traffic light with two sensors

to red again. For setting the colour of the traffic light, the action *set* is used. One can imagine that the sensors are proximity sensors that measure whether cars are waiting for the traffic light. Note that it can be that a car activates the sensors, while the traffic light shows another colour than red. In figure 1 this system is drawn.

First, we define a data type *Colour* which contains the three aspects of a traffic light.

sort *Colour* = **struct** *green* | *yellow* | *red*;

The pushing controller is very straightforward. The occurrence of $trig_1$ and $trig_2$ indicate that the respective sensors have been triggered. In the pushing strategy, the controller must be able to always deal with incoming signals, and store their occurrence for later use. In the specification below, the pushing process has two booleans b_1 and b_2 for this purpose. Initially, these booleans are false, and the traffic light is assumed to be red. The booleans become *true* if a trigger is received, and are set to *false*, when the traffic light starts with a *green*, *yellow* and *red* cycle. Note that we underline all external actions in the specification (but not in the text or in the diagrams) and we use the same style throughout the paper. External actions are those actions communicating with entities outside the described system, whereas internal actions happen internally in components of the system or are communications among those components.

proc $Push(b_1, b_2{:}\mathbb{B}, c{:}\,Colour)$
$\quad = \quad \underline{trig_1} \cdot Push(true, b_2, c)$
$\quad + \quad \underline{trig_2} \cdot Push(b_1, true, c)$
$\quad + \quad (b_1 \wedge b_2 \wedge c \approx red) \rightarrow \underline{set}(green) \cdot Push(false, false, green)$
$\quad + \quad (c \approx green) \rightarrow \underline{set}(yellow) \cdot Push(b_1, b_2, yellow)$
$\quad + \quad (c \approx yellow) \rightarrow \underline{set}(red) \cdot Push(b_1, b_2, red);$
init $Push(false, false, red);$

The polling controller differs from the pushing controller in the sense that the actions $trig_1$ and $trig_2$ now have a parameter. It checks whether the sensors have been triggered using the actions $trig_1(b)$ and $trig_2(b)$. The boolean b indicates whether the sensor has been triggered (*true*: triggered, *false*: not triggered). In *Poll*, sensor $trig_1$ is repeatedly polled, and when it indicates by a *true* that it has been triggered, the process goes to $Poll_1$. In $Poll_1$ sensor $trig_2$ is polled, and when both sensors have been triggered $Poll_2$ is invoked. In $Poll_2$ the traffic light goes through a colour cycle and back to $Poll$.

proc $Poll = \underline{trig_1}(false){\cdot}Poll + \underline{trig_1}(true){\cdot}Poll_1$;
$\quad\quad Poll_1 = \underline{trig_2}(false){\cdot}Poll_1 + \underline{trig_2}(true){\cdot}Poll_2$;
$\quad\quad Poll_2 = \underline{set}(green){\cdot}\underline{set}(yellow){\cdot}\underline{set}(red){\cdot}Poll$;
init $Poll$;

The transition systems of both systems are drawn in figure 2. At the left the diagram for the pushing system is drawn, and at the right the behaviour of the polling traffic light controller is depicted. The diagram at the left has 12 states while the diagram at the right has 5, showing that even for this very simple system polling leads to a smaller state space.

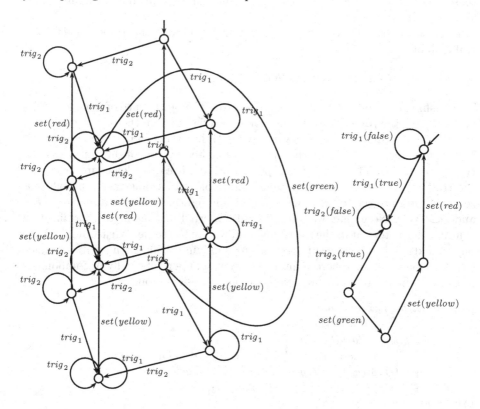

Fig. 2. Transition systems of push/poll processes

4   Guideline II: Use Global Synchronous Communication

Communication along different components can sometimes be modelled by synchronising the communication over all these components. For instance, instead of modelling that a message is forwarded in a stepwise manner through a number of components, all components engage in one big action that says that the message travels through all components at once. In the first case there is a new state for every time the message is forwarded. In the second case the total communication only requires one extra state. The use of global synchronous communication can be justified if passing this message is much faster than the other activities of the components, or if passing such a message is insignificant relative to the other activities.

Several formalisms use global synchronous interactions as a way to keep the state space of a system small. The co-ordination language REO uses the concept very explicitly [2]. A derived form can be found in Uppaal, which uses committed locations [10].

To illustrate the effectiveness of global synchronous communication, we provide the system in figure 3. A trigger signal enters at a, and is non-deterministically forwarded via b_c or c_c to one of the two components at the right. One might for instance think that there is a complex algorithm that determines whether the information is forwarded via b_c or c_c, but we do not want to model the details of this algorithm. After being passed via b_c or c_c, the message is forwarded to the outside world via d or e. To illustrate the effect on state spaces, it is not necessary that we pass an actual message, and therefore it is left out.

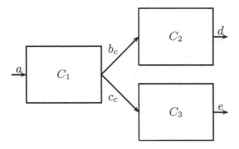

Fig. 3. Synchronous/asynchronous message passing

The asynchronous variant is described below. Process C_1 performs a, and subsequently performs b_s or c_s, i.e. sending via b or c. The process C_2 reads via b by b_r, and then performs a d. The behaviour of C_3 is similar. The whole system consists of the processes C_1, C_2 and C_3 where b_r and b_s synchronise via the Γ_s operator to become b_c, and c_r and c_s become c_c. The ∇_v operator allows multi-actions in v to happen, and blocks all others. The behaviour of this system contains 8 states and is depicted in figure 4 at the left.

proc $C_1 = \underline{a} \cdot (b_s + c_s) \cdot C_1$;
$\quad C_2 = b_r \cdot \underline{d} \cdot C_2$;
$\quad C_3 = c_r \cdot \underline{e} \cdot C_3$;

init $\nabla_{\{\underline{a}, b_c, c_c, \underline{d}, \underline{e}\}}(\Gamma_{\{b_r | b_s \to b_c, c_r | c_s \to c_c\}}(C_1 || C_2 || C_3))$;

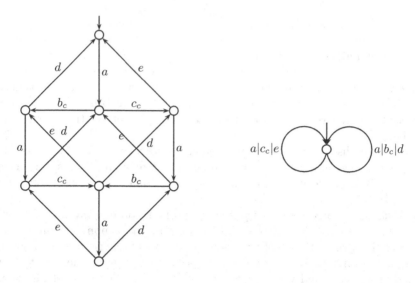

Fig. 4. Transition systems of a synchronous and an asynchronous process

The synchronous behaviour of this system can be characterised by the following mCRL2 specification. Process C_1 can perform a multi-action $a|b_s$ (i.e. action a and b_s happen exactly at the same time) or a multi-action $a|c_s$. This represents the instantaneous receiving and forwarding of a message. Similarly, C_2 and C_3 read and forward the message instantaneously. The effect is that the state space only consists of one state as depicted in figure 4 at the right.

proc $C_1 = \underline{a}|b_s{\cdot}C_1 + \underline{a}|c_s{\cdot}C_1$;
   $C_2 = b_r|\underline{d}{\cdot}C_2$;
   $C_3 = c_r|\underline{e}{\cdot}C_3$;
init $\nabla_{\{\underline{a}|c_c|\underline{e},\underline{a}|b_c|\underline{d}\}}(\Gamma_{\{b_r|b_s \to b_c, c_r|c_s \to c_c\}}(C_1\|C_2\|C_3))$;

The operator $\nabla_{\{a|c_c|e, a|b_c|d\}}$ allows the two multi-actions $a|c_c|e$ and $a|b_c|d$, enforcing in this way that in both cases these three actions must happen simultaneously.

5   Guideline III: Avoid Parallelism among Components

When models have many concurrent components that can independently perform an action, then the state space of the given model can be reduced by limiting the number of components that can simultaneously perform activity. Ideally, only one component can perform activity at any time. This can for instance be achieved by one central component that allows the other components to do an action in a round robin fashion.

It very much depends on the nature of the system whether this kind of modelling is allowed. If the primary purpose of a system is the calculation of values, sequentialising appears to be defendable. If on the other hand the sub-components are controlling all kinds of devices, then the parallel behaviour of the sub-components might be the primary purpose of the system and sequentialisation can not be used.

In some specification languages explicit avoidance of parallel behaviour between components has been used. For instance Esterel [3] uses micro steps which can be calculated per component. In Promela there is an explicit atomicity command, grouping behaviour in one component that is executed without interleaving of actions of other components [9].

As an example we consider M traffic lights guarding the same number of entrances of a parking lot. See figure 5 for a diagrammatic representation where $M = 3$. A sensor detects that a car arrives at an entrance. If there is space in the garage, the traffic light shows green for some time interval. There is a detector at the exit, which indicates that a car is leaving. The number of cars in the garage cannot exceed N.

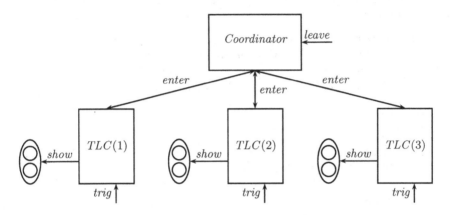

Fig. 5. A parking lot with three entrances

The first model is very simple, but has a large state space. Each traffic light controller (TLC) waits for a trigger of its sensor, indicating that a car is waiting. Using the $enter_s$ action it asks the *Coordinator* for admission to the garage. If a car can enter, this action is allowed by the co-ordinator and a traffic light cycle starts. Otherwise the $enter_s$ action is blocked. The *Coordinator* has an internal counter, counting the number of cars. When a *leave* action takes place, the counter is decreased. When a car is allowed to enter (via $enter_r$), the counter is increased.

proc *Coordinator*($count$:$\mathbb{N}$)
$\quad = (count>0)\rightarrow\underline{leave} \cdot Coordinator(count-1)$
$\quad + (count<N)\rightarrow enter_r \cdot Coordinator(count+1);$

$\quad TLC(id:\mathbb{N}^+)$
$\quad = \underline{trig}(id)\cdot enter_s \cdot \underline{show}(id, green)\cdot\underline{show}(id, red)\cdot TLC(id);$

init $\nabla_{\{\underline{trig},\underline{show},enter_c,\underline{leave}\}}(\Gamma_{\{enter_s\mid enter_r \rightarrow enter_c\}}(Coordinator(0)\|$
$\quad\quad\quad\quad\quad\quad\quad\quad\quad TLC(1)\| TLC(2)\| TLC(3)));$

The state space of this control system grows exponentially with the number of traffic light controllers. In columns 2 and 4 of table 1 the sizes of the state spaces for different M are shown. It is also clear that the number of parking places N only contributes linearly to the state space.

Following the guideline, we try to limit the amount of parallel behaviour in the traffic light controllers. So, we put the initiative in the hands of the co-ordinator in the second model. It assigns the task of monitoring a sensor to one of the traffic light controllers at a time. The traffic controller will poll the sensor, and only if it has been triggered, switch the traffic light to green. After it has done its task, the traffic light controller will return control to the co-ordinator. Of course if the parking lot is full, the traffic light controllers are not activated. Note that in this second example, only one traffic light can show green at any time, which might not be desirable.

proc $Coordinator(count{:}\mathbb{N}, active\_id{:}\mathbb{N}^+)$
$$= (count{>}0){\rightarrow}\underline{leave}{\cdot}Coordinator(count{-}1, active\_id)$$
$$+ (count{<}N){\rightarrow}enter_s(active\_id){\cdot}\textstyle\sum_{b{:}\mathbb{B}} enter_r(b){\cdot}$$
$$Coordinator(count{+}\mathrm{if}(b,1,0), \mathrm{if}(active\_id{\approx}M,1, active\_id{+}1));$$

$TLC(id{:}\mathbb{N}^+)$
$$= enter_r(id){\cdot}$$
$$(\underline{trig}(id, true){\cdot}\underline{show}(id, green){\cdot}\underline{show}(id, red){\cdot}enter_s(true){+}$$
$$\underline{trig}(id, false){\cdot}enter_s(false)$$
$$){\cdot}$$
$$TLC(id);$$

init $\nabla_{\{\underline{trig},\underline{show},enter_c,\underline{leave}\}}(\Gamma_{\{enter_s|enter_r{\rightarrow}enter_c\}}$
$$(Coordinator(0,1)\| TLC(1)\| TLC(2)\| TLC(3)));$$

As can be seen in table 1 the state space of the second model only grows linearly with the number of traffic lights.

Table 1. State space sizes of parking lot controllers (N: no. of traffic lights, M: no. of parking places)

M	parallel ($N = 10$)	restricted ($N = 10$)	parallel ($N = 100$)	restricted ($N = 100$)
1	44	61	404	601
2	176	122	1,616	1,202
3	704	183	6,464	1,803
4	2,816	244	25,856	2,404
5	11,264	305	103,424	3,005
6	45,056	366	413,696	3,606
10	$11.5\,10^6$	610	$106\,10^6$	6,010

6   Guideline IV: Restrict the Use of Data

The use of data in behavioural models can quickly blow up a state space. Therefore, data should always be looked at with extra care, and if its use can be avoided, this should be done. If data is essential (and it almost always is), then there are several methods to reduce its footprint. Below we give two examples, one where data is categorised and one where buffers are ordered.

In order to reduce the state space of a behavioural model, it sometimes helps to categorise the data in categories, and formulate the model in terms of these categories, instead of individual values. From the perspective of verification, this technique is called abstract interpretation [5]. Using this technique, a given data domain is interpreted in categories, in order to assist the verification process. Here, we advice that the modeller uses the categories in the model, instead of letting the values be interpreted in categories during the verification process. As the modeller generally knows his model best, he also has a good intuition about the appropriate categories.

Fig. 6. An advanced approach controller

Consider for example an intelligent approach controller which measures the distance of an approaching car as depicted in figure 6. If the car is expected to pass distance 0 before the next measurement, a trigger signal is forwarded. The farthest distance the approach controller can observe is M. A quite straightforward description of this system is given below. Using the action $dist$ the distance to a car is measured, and the action $trig$ models the trigger signal. The $\diamond$ operator denotes the else part of a condition.

map $M : \mathbb{N}$;
eqn $M = 100$;
proc $AC(d_{prev}{:}\mathbb{N}) = \sum_{d:\mathbb{N}}(d{<}M){\rightarrow}(\underline{dist}(d){\cdot}(2d{<}d_{prev}){\rightarrow}\underline{trig}{\cdot}AC(M)\diamond AC(d))$;
init $AC(M)$;

The state space of this system is a staggering $M^2{+}1$ states big, or more concretely 10001 states. This is of course due to the fact that the values of d and d_{prev} must be stored in the state space to enable the evaluation of the condition $2d{<}d_{prev}$. But only the information needs to be recalled whether this condition holds, instead of both values of d and d_{prev}. So, a first improvement is to move the condition backward as is done below, leading to a required $M{+}1$ states, or 101 in this concrete case.

proc $AC_1(d_{prev}{:}\mathbb{N}) = \sum_{d:\mathbb{N}}(d{<}M){\rightarrow}((2d{<}d_{prev}){\rightarrow}\underline{dist}(d){\cdot}\underline{trig}{\cdot}AC_1(M)$
$\diamond\underline{dist}(d){\cdot}AC_1(d))$;

init $AC_1(M)$;

But we can go much further, provided it is possible to abstract from the concrete distances. Let us assume that the only relevant information that we obtain from the individual distances is whether the car is far from the sensor or nearby. Note that we abstract from the concrete speed of the car which was used above. The specification of this abstract approach controller AAC is given by:

sort $Distance = $ **struct** $near \mid far$;
proc $AAC = \sum_{d:Distance} \underline{dist}(d) \cdot ((d \approx near) \rightarrow \underline{trig} \cdot AAC \diamond AAC)$;
init AAC;

Note that M does not occur anymore in this specification. The state space is now reduced to two states.

Table 2. Number of states of an non ordered/ordered buffer with max. N elements

N	non ordered	ordered
1	2	2
2	5	4
3	16	8
4	65	16
5	326	32
6	$2.0 \ 10^3$	64
7	$14 \ 10^3$	128
8	$110 \ 10^3$	256
9	$986 \ 10^3$	512
10	$9.9 \ 10^6$	$1.02 \ 10^3$
11	$109 \ 10^6$	$2.05 \ 10^3$
12	$1.30 \ 10^9$	$4.10 \ 10^3$

As a last example we show the effect of ordering buffers. With queues and buffers different contents can represent the same data. If a buffer is used as a set, the ordering in which the elements are put into the buffer is irrelevant. In such cases it helps to maintain an order on the data structure. As an example we provide a simple process that reads arbitrary natural numbers smaller than N and puts them in a set. The process doing so is given below. The operator $\triangleright$ puts an element in front of a list.

map $N : \mathbb{N}$;
$\quad$ $insert, ordered\_insert : \mathbb{N} \times List(\mathbb{N}) \rightarrow List(\mathbb{N})$;

var $n, n' : \mathbb{N}; b : List(\mathbb{N})$;
eqn $insert(n, b) = if(n \in b, b, n \triangleright b)$;
$\quad$ $ordered\_insert(n, []) = [n]$;
$\quad$ $ordered\_insert(n, n' \triangleright b) = if(n < n', n \triangleright n' \triangleright b, if(n \approx n', n' \triangleright b, n' \triangleright$
$\qquad\qquad\qquad\qquad\qquad\qquad\qquad\qquad ordered\_insert(n, b)))$;
$\quad$ $N = 10$;
proc $B(buffer:List(\mathbb{N})) = \sum_{n:\mathbb{N}}(n < N) \rightarrow \underline{read}(n) \cdot B(insert(n, buffer))$;

init $B([])$;

If the function *insert* is used, the elements are put into a set in an arbitrary order (more precisely, the elements are prepended). If the function *ordered_insert* is used instead of *insert*, the elements occur in ascending order in the buffer. In table 2 the effect of ordering is shown. Although the state spaces with ordering also grow exponentially, the beneficial effect of ordering does not need further discussion.

7 Guideline V: Specify External Behaviour of Sets of Sub-components

We observed that sometimes the composed behaviour of sets of components can be overly complex, and contains far too many states, even after applying a behavioural reduction. In order to keep the behaviour of such sets of components small, it is useful to first design the desired external behaviour of this set of components, and to subsequently design the behaviour of the components such that they meet this external behaviour. The situation is quite comparable to the implementation of software. If the behaviour is governed by the implementation, a system is often far less understandable and usable, than when a precise specification of the software has been provided first, and the software has been designed to implement exactly the specified behaviour.

The use of external behaviour for various purposes was most notably defended in the realm of protocol specification [13], although keeping the state space small was not one of these purposes. The word service was commonly used in this setting for the external behaviour. More recently, the ASD development method has been proposed, where a system is to be defined by first specifying the external behaviour of a system, which is subsequently implemented [4]. The purpose here is primarily to allow a designer to keep control over his system.

In order to illustrate how specifications can be used to keep external behaviour small, we provide a simple example, and we show how a small difference in the behaviour of the components has a distinctive effect on the complexity in terms of states. From the perspective of the task that the components must perform, the difference in the description looks relatively minor. The example is inspired by the third sliding window protocol in [12] which is a fine example of a set of components that provides the intended task but has a virtually incomprehensible external behaviour.

Our system is depicted in figure 7. The first specification has a complex external behaviour whereas the external behaviour of the second is straightforward. The system consists of a device-monitor and a controller that can be started (*start*) or stopped (*stop*) by an external source. The device-monitor observes the status of a number of devices and sends the defected device number to the controller via the action *broken*. The controller comprises a buffer that stores the status of the devices.

The first specification can be described as follows. The device monitor is straightforward in the sense that it continuously performs actions $broken_s(n)$ for numbers $n < M$. The parameter *buff* represents the buffer by a function from

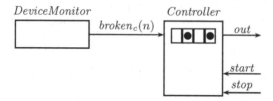

Fig. 7. A system comprises a controller and a device-monitor

natural numbers to booleans. If $buff(i)$ is true, it indicates that a fault report
has been received for device i. The boolean parameter $bool$ indicates whether the
controller is switched on or off and the natural number i is the current position
in the buffer, which the controller uses to cycle through the buffer elements. It
sends an action out whenever it encounters an element that is set to $true$. The
internal action int takes place when the controller moves to investigate the next
buffer place.

map $M{:}\mathbb{N}^+$;
eqn $M=2$;
map $buff_0{:}\mathbb{N}{\rightarrow}\mathbb{B}$;
eqn $buff_0 = \lambda n{:}\mathbb{N}.false$;
proc $DeviceMonitor = \sum_{n:\mathbb{N}} (n{<}M){\rightarrow}broken_s(n).DeviceMonitor$;
$\quad Controller(buff{:}\mathbb{N}{\rightarrow}\mathbb{B}, bool{:}\mathbb{B}, i{:}\mathbb{N})$
$\quad\quad = \quad \sum_{n:\mathbb{N}} broken_r(n)\cdot Controller(buff[n{\rightarrow}true], bool, i)$
$\quad\quad + \quad (\neg buff(i)\wedge bool){\rightarrow}\underline{stop}\cdot Controller(buff, false, i)$
$\quad\quad + \quad (\neg bool){\rightarrow}\underline{start}\cdot Controller(buff, true, i)$
$\quad\quad + \quad (buff(i)\wedge bool){\rightarrow}\underline{out}\cdot Controller(buff[i{\rightarrow}false], bool, (i{+}1)\bmod M)$
$\quad\quad + \quad (\neg buff(i)\wedge bool){\rightarrow}int\cdot Controller(buff, bool, (i{+}1)\bmod M)$
init $\tau_{\{broken_c, int\}}(\nabla_{\{broken_c, \underline{out}, \underline{start}, \underline{stop}, int\}}(\Gamma_{\{broken_r | broken_s \rightarrow broken_c\}}($
$\quad\quad Controller(buff_0, false, 0)\| DeviceMonitor)))$;

The total number of devices is denoted by M. All positions of $buff$ are initially
set to $false$ as indicated by the lambda expression $\lambda n{:}\mathbb{N}.false$. In this specification the controller blocks the $stop$ request if there is a defected device at index i
of the buffer forming a dependency between external and internal behaviour. If
we calculate the state space of the external behaviour of this system with $M = 2$
and apply a branching bisimulation reduction [7], we obtain the state space depicted in figure 8 at the left. Note that the behaviour is remarkably complex. In
particular a number of τ-transitions complicate the transition system. But they
cannot be removed as they are essential for the perceived external behaviour of
the system. Table 3 provides the number of states produced as a function of the
number of devices monitored in the system. The table shows that the state space
of the original system and the state space capturing the external behaviour are

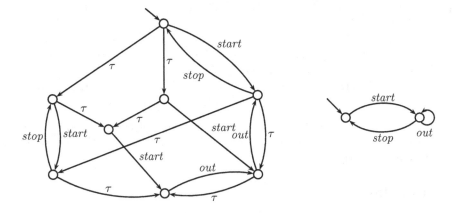

Fig. 8. The system external behaviour

comparable. This indicates a complex external behaviour that might complicate verification with external parties and makes understanding the behaviour quite difficult. It might be amazing that the external state space of the system is large. Actual expectation is that it should be small, matching the specification below, depicted in the transition system in figure 8 at the right.

proc *Stopped* = <u>*start*</u>·*Started*;
     Started = <u>*out*</u>·*Started* + <u>*stop*</u>·*Stopped*;
init *Stopped*;

Investigation of the cause of the difference between the actual and the expected sizes of the transition systems leads to the conclusion that blocking the *stop* action when *buff*(*i*) is true is the cause of the problem. If we remove this from the condition of the stop action, we obtain the mCRL2 specification of the *DeviceMonitor* process below. In this specification the *stop* request is processed independently from the rest of the behaviour.

Table 3. Sizes of the original and external state space of the monitor controllers

M	No. of original states		No. of external states	
	1st spec	2nd spec	1st spec	2nd spec
1	4	4	2	2
2	16	16	8	2
3	48	48	16	2
4	128	128	32	2
5	320	320	64	2
6	768	768	128	2
10	$20.5 \ 10^3$	$20.5 \ 10^3$	$2.48 \ 10^3$	2

proc $DeviceMonitor = \sum_{n:\mathbb{N}}(n<M)\rightarrow broken_s(n).DeviceMonitor;$
$Controller(buff:\mathbb{N}\rightarrow\mathbb{B}, bool:\mathbb{B}, i:\mathbb{N})$

$$= \sum_{n:\mathbb{N}} broken_r(n)\cdot Controller(buff[n\rightarrow true], bool, i)$$
$$+ \quad bool\rightarrow\underline{stop}\cdot Controller(buff, false, i)$$
$$+ \quad (\neg bool)\rightarrow\underline{start}\cdot Controller(buff, true, i)$$
$$+ \quad (buff(i)\wedge bool)\rightarrow\underline{out}\cdot Controller(buff[i\rightarrow false], bool, (i+1)\bmod M)$$
$$+ \quad (\neg buff(i)\wedge bool)\rightarrow int\cdot Controller(buff, bool, (i+1)\bmod M)$$

As can be seen from table 3, the number of states of the non-reduced model remains the same. However, the reduced behaviour is exactly the one depicted in figure 8 at the right for any constant M.

8   Conclusion

We have shown that different specification styles can substantially influence the number of states of a system. We believe that an essential skill of a behavioural modellist is to make models such that the insight that is required can be obtained. If a system is to be designed such that it provably satisfies a number of behavioural requirements, then the behaviour must be sufficiently small to be verified. If an existing system is modelled to obtain insight in its behaviour, then on the one hand the model should reflect the existing system sufficiently well, but on the other hand the model of the system should be sufficiently simple to allow to answer relevant questions about the behaviour of the system.

As far as we can see hardly any attention has been paid to the question how to make behavioural models such that they can be analysed. All attention appears to be directed to the question of how to analyse given models better. But it is noteworthy that it is very common in other modelling disciplines to let models be simpler than reality. For instance in electrical engineering models are as much as possible reduced to sets of linear differential equations. In queueing theory, only a few queueing models can be studied analytically, and therefore, it is necessary to reduce systems to these standard models if analytical results are to be obtained.

We provided five guidelines, based on our experience with building models of various systems. There is no claim that this set is complete, or even that these five guidelines are the most important model reduction techniques. What we hope is that this paper will induce research such that more reduction techniques will be uncovered, described, classified and subsequently become a standard ingredient in teaching behavioural modelling.

Acknowledgements. We thank Sjoerd Cranen, Helle Hansen, Jeroen Keiren, Matthias Raffelsieper, Frank Stappers, Ron Swinkels, Marco van der Wijst, and Tim Willemse for their useful comments on the text.

References

1. Acharya, S., Franklin, M., Zdonik, S.: Balancing push and pull for data broadcast. In: Proceedings of the 1997 ACM SIGMOD International Conference on Management of Data, pp. 183–194 (1997)

2. Arbab, F.: Reo: A Channel-based coordination model for component composition. Mathematical Structures in Computer Science 14(3), 329–366 (2004)
3. Berry, G., Gonthier, G.: The ESTEREL synchronous programming language: design, semantics, implementation. Science of Computer Programming 19, 87–152 (1992)
4. Broadfoot, G.H.: ASD Case Notes: Costs and Benefits of Applying Formal Methods to Industrial Control Software. In: Fitzgerald, J.S., Hayes, I.J., Tarlecki, A. (eds.) FM 2005. LNCS, vol. 3582, pp. 548–551. Springer, Heidelberg (2005)
5. Dams, D., Gerth, R., Grumberg, O.: Abstract interpretation of reactive systems. ACM Transactions on Programming Languages and Systems (TOPLAS) 19(2), 253–291 (1997)
6. Groote, J.F., Kouters, T.W.D.M., Osaiweran, A.A.H.: Specification Guidelines to avoid the State Space Explosion Problem. Technical Report 10-14, Computer Science Reports, Department of Computer Science, Eindhoven University of Technology, Eindhoven, The Netherlands (2010)
7. van Glabbeek, R.J., Weijland, W.P.: Branching time and abstraction in bisimulation semantics. Journal of the ACM 43(3), 555–600 (1996)
8. Groote, J.F., Mathijssen, A.H.J., Reniers, M.A., Usenko, Y.S., van Weerdenburg, M.J.: Analysis of distributed systems with mCRL2. In: Alexander, M., Gardner, W. (eds.) Process Algebra for Parallel and Distributed Processing, pp. 99–128. Chapman and Hall (2009)
9. Holzmann, G.J.: The SPIN model checker. Primer and reference manual. Addison-Wesley (2003)
10. Larsen, K.G., Pettersson, P., Yi, W.: Uppaal in a nutshell. Int. Journal on Software Tools for Technology Transfer 1(12), 134–152 (1997)
11. Lin, F.J., Chu, P.M., Liu, M.T.: Protocol verification using reachability analysis: The state space explosion problem and relief strategies. ACM SIGCOMM Computer Communication Review 17(5), 126–135 (1987)
12. Tanenbaum, A.S.: Computer networks, 2nd edn. Prentice Hall (1988)
13. Vissers, C.A., Logrippo, L.: The importance of the service concept in the design of data communications protocols. In: Diaz, M. (ed.) Protocol Specification, Testing and Verification (Proc. of the IFIP WG 6.1 Fifth International Workshop on Protocol Sepcification, Testing and Verification), pp. 3–17. Elsevier North Holland (1986)
14. Vissers, C.A., Scollo, G., van Sinderen, M., Brinksma, E.: Specification styles in distributed systems design and verification. Theoretical Computer Science 89, 179–206 (1991)
15. (2010), http://www.mcrl2.org

Strong Normalisation
in λ-Calculi with References

Romain Demangeon[1], Daniel Hirschkoff[1], and Davide Sangiorgi[2]

[1] ENS Lyon, Université de Lyon, CNRS, INRIA, France
[2] INRIA/Università di Bologna, Italy

Abstract. We present a method for ensuring termination of lambda-calculi with references. This method makes it possible to combine measure-based techniques for termination of imperative languages with traditional approaches to termination in purely functional languages, such as logical relations. More precisely, the method lifts any termination proof for the purely functional simply-typed lambda-calculus to a termination proof for the lambda-calculus with references. The method can be made parametric on the termination technique employed for the functional core.

1 Motivations

This paper studies strong normalisation in λ_{ref}, a call-by-value λ-calculus with (higher-order) references. It is well-known that, even in the simply-typed calculus, the problem is difficult, because references allow one to program loops "via the memory". We refer to Boudol's [3] for a discussion on existing works on this question.

Boudol [3] has proposed a type and effect system for a calculus whose core is very similar to λ_{ref}; the system guarantees termination by means of the realisability technique. That work is revisited and generalised in [1], where the closely related technique of reducibility candidates is exploited to establish soundness of the type and effect system. In both these works, the type and effect system relies on a stratification of memory into regions; the stratification is used to control interactions between the functional and the imperative constructs, in order to prevent "loops via the memory". The stratification plays also a key role in the structure of the soundness proof, to support the induction argument. Boudol's approach has also been investigated by Tranquilli [9], who proposes an analysis of the stratification imposed by the type and effect system, by means of a monadic translation. The target of this translation, in the general case, is a lambda-calculus with recursive types. Tranquilli however shows that when applying the translation to well-typed source terms, one can avoid the use of recursive types. By combining this observation with a simulation result, the author concludes that well-typed terms terminate.

In this paper, we propose a different proof strategy for strong normalisation in λ_{ref}. Our approach is adapted from [7], where we introduced a type system for termination of mobile processes. The crux in defining types in that work is to

F. Arbab and M. Sirjani (Eds.): FSEN 2011, LNCS 7141, pp. 128–142, 2012.

distinguish between functional and imperative channels, and to exploit a stratification of imperative channel names. Soundness of the type system is established by defining a projection of an *impure calculus*, that is, a calculus featuring imperative and functional features, into a purely functional core calculus (in the context of the π-calculus, the functional subcalculus is given, intuitively, by the image of the encoding of the λ-calculus in the π-calculus). The proof then relies on termination of the functional core, which is treated like a "black box" in the proof: since our projection function preserves divergences, and the target calculus is terminating, we can reason by contradiction to show that the source of the translation only consists of terminating terms.

In the present paper we show that we can transport the strategy from [7] onto $\lambda_{\texttt{ref}}$. In contrast with π-calculus, $\lambda_{\texttt{ref}}$ is purely sequential and higher-order (it involves substitutions of variables with terms); both these features have a substantial impact on the details of the technique. In this sense, another goal of the paper is to show that the technique in [7] is not specific to a concurrent scenario, and can be used on different kinds of impure languages. The "black box" property for the purely functional subcalculus in [7] remains: the technique for $\lambda_{\texttt{ref}}$ is essentially parametric on the method employed for ensuring termination of the pure λ-calculus (realisability, reducibility candidates or other methods). The present paper is devoted to the presentation of our technique in a rather simple setting, where the core functional language is the simply typed λ-calculus.

With respect to [7], several modifications have to be made in order to handle $\lambda_{\texttt{ref}}$. Many of them are related to the definition of the projection function, which in the present work maps λ-terms with references to purely functional terms. In the π-calculus the projection acts on prefixed terms, simply by replacing some of them with the inactive process $\mathbf{0}$; this crucially relies on the operators of parallel composition and $\mathbf{0}$ of the process calculus. In the λ-calculus the situation is more intricate. Consider for instance a $\lambda_{\texttt{ref}}$ term of the form $T = (\lambda z.\star)\,(\texttt{ref}\,M)$, where $\star$ is the unique element of type $\mathbb{1}$ (the unit type), and $\texttt{ref}\,M$ denotes the allocation of a reference holding the value of M (the – slightly more involved – syntax and operational semantics of $\lambda_{\texttt{ref}}$ will be introduced formally below). The idea is to project T into some purely functional term T', in such a way that: (i) if T is typable in our type and effect system, then T' is typable according to simple types; (ii) the projection function is defined compositionally on the structure of terms, and preserves divergences. In a call-by-value strategy, if the evaluation of M terminates, the evaluation of T yields $\star$. In order to preserve divergences, because of a potential divergence in M, we cannot define T' by simply erasing the subterm $\texttt{ref}\,M$. Instead, we set $T' \overset{\text{def}}{=} (\lambda x_1.\lambda x_2.\,x_1)\,\star\,M'$, where M' is the purely functional term obtained by applying recursively the projection to M. This way, T' diverges if M' does so, and eventually returns $\star$, in case M' converges. This shows how the projection acts at an operational level. In the proof, we also take care of condition (i) above, by defining the translation both on terms and on types, in such a way as to preserve typability.

Building on the projection function, we derive soundness of the type and effect system by contradiction: suppose a well-typed $\lambda_{\texttt{ref}}$ term T diverges, then its projection T' is diverging too, which contradicts the fact that T' belongs to a terminating calculus. Termination of T' is obtained by an external argument, namely the strong normalisation proof for the functional subcalculus (here, the simply typed call by value λ-calculus).

Other technical differences with respect to the technique in the setting of the π-calculus [7] are discussed later in the paper.

Comparison with [3,1,9]. As we hinted above, the question we address in this paper has been studied in a very similar setting in other works. In contrast with the works by Boudol and Amadio, where soundness of the type system is obtained by a 'semantic' approach (be it realisability or reducibility candidates), which is applied to the whole (impure) calculus, we somehow factor out the imperative part of the calculus, which allows us to lift a termination proof of $\lambda_{\mathbf{ST}}$ to a termination proof of $\lambda_{\mathtt{ref}}$.

Tranquilli [9] proceeds similarly, in two steps: a translation into a purely functional calculus, followed by a termination argument about the latter. However, technically, our approach and his differ considerably, in particular because we project into a subcalculus, using a translation function which seems unrelated to Tranquilli's.

Outline. We introduce $\lambda_{\mathtt{ref}}$ and its type and effect system in Section 2. Section 3 is devoted to the soundness proof, where we present in particular the projection function on $\lambda_{\mathtt{ref}}$. In Section 4, we discuss how the proof can be extended to calculi richer than simple types.

2 $\lambda_{\mathtt{ref}}$: A λ-Calculus with References

2.1 Syntax and Semantics for $\lambda_{\mathtt{ref}}$

We now define the calculi we manipulate in this work. The standard, simply-typed, λ-calculus with the constant $\star$ and the base type $\mathbb{1}$ is called $\lambda_{\mathbf{ST}}$ in the following. The reduction relation in $\lambda_{\mathbf{ST}}$ is full β-reduction, and is denoted using $\twoheadrightarrow$.

$\lambda_{\mathtt{ref}}$ is a call-by-value λ-calculus extended with imperative operations (read, write and update) acting on a store (sometimes called a *memory* in the following). The store is stratified into regions, which are referred to using natural numbers, i.e., we suppose that the store is divided into a finite number of regions, and that there exists an enumeration of these regions. Constructs of the language involving imperative operations are annotated by a region — thus, by a natural number. For instance, $\mathtt{deref}_n(M)$ is the operator that reads the value stored at the address which is returned by the evaluation of M; n denotes the fact that this address belongs to the region n of the memory.

To define terms of $\lambda_{\mathtt{ref}}$, we rely on a set of *addresses*, which are distinct from the variables used in the syntax of the standard λ-calculus. Addresses are written $u_{(n,T)}$: they are explicitly associated both to a region n and to a type T (types are described below). These annotations are not mandatory in order to obtain

$$M ::= \quad (M\ M) \mid x \mid \lambda x.\,M \mid \star$$
$$\mid \mathbf{ref}_n\ M \mid \mathbf{deref}_n(M) \mid M \mathbin{:=}_n M \mid u_{(n,T)}$$
$$T ::= \mathbb{1} \mid T\ \mathbf{ref}_n \mid T \to^n T$$
$$V ::= \lambda x.\,M \mid x \mid u_{(n,T)} \mid \star$$
$$R ::= \quad (\lambda x.\,M)\ V$$
$$\mid \mathbf{deref}_n(u_{(n,T)}) \mid \mathbf{ref}_n\ V \mid u_{(n,T)} \mathbin{:=}_n V$$
$$\mathbf{E} ::= \quad [\,] \mid V\ \mathbf{E} \mid \mathbf{E}\ M$$
$$\mid \mathbf{deref}_n(\mathbf{E}) \mid \mathbf{ref}_n\ \mathbf{E} \mid \mathbf{E} \mathbin{:=}_n M \mid V \mathbin{:=}_n \mathbf{E}$$

Fig. 1. Syntax for terms, types, values, redexes and evaluation contexts

the results we state in this paper, but they improve the readability of our proofs. Note in passing that values of different types can be stored in the same region. We suppose that there exists an infinite number of addresses for a given pair consisting of a type and a region.

Stores, ranged over using δ, are formally defined as partial mappings from addresses to values. The (finite) support of δ is written $\mathrm{supp}(\delta)$, $\emptyset$ is the empty store $(\mathrm{supp}(\emptyset) = \emptyset)$, and $\delta\langle u_{(n,T)} \rightsquigarrow V\rangle$ denotes the store δ' defined by $\delta'(u_{(n,T)}) = V$ and $\delta'(v) = \delta(v)$ for every $v \in \mathrm{supp}(\delta)$ such that $v \neq u_{(n,T)}$.

Figure 1 presents the grammar definitions for (respectively) terms, types, values, redexes and evaluation contexts.

The standard λ-calculus syntax is extended with the unit value $(\star)$, addresses and three imperative operators. $\mathbf{ref}_n\ M$ stands for the creation of a new cell in the store, at region n, and containing the result of the evaluation of M; $\mathbf{deref}_n(M)$ yields the value that is stored at the address given by the evaluation of M (in region n); finally, $M \mathbin{:=}_n N$ updates the value stored at the address given by the evaluation of M with the value of N.

Types extend the simple types of $\lambda_{\mathbf{ST}}$ with unit $(\mathbb{1})$ and a reference type: $T\ \mathbf{ref}_n$ is the type of an address in region n containing values of type T. To record the latent effect of a function, arrow types are annotated with regions: intuitively, $T_1 \to^n T_2$ is the type of a function taking arguments of type T_1, returning a term of type T_2, and such that evaluation of the body accesses regions in the memory *lower than* the region n.

Stratification. We impose a well-formedness condition on types that reflects the stratification of the store: a term acting at region n cannot be stored in a region smaller than $n + 1$. For this, we define $\mathrm{reg}(T)$, an integer describing the set of regions associated to a type T, by:

$$\mathrm{reg}(\mathbb{1}) = 0 \qquad \mathrm{reg}(T\ \mathbf{ref}_n) = \max(n, \mathrm{reg}(T))$$
$$\mathrm{reg}(T_1 \to^n T_2) = \max(n, \mathrm{reg}(T_2))$$

Definition 1 (Well-formed types). *A type T is well-formed if for all its subtypes of the form T' $\mathtt{ref}_n$, we have $\mathrm{reg}(T') < n$.*

In the following, we shall implicitly assume that all types we manipulate are well-formed. Well-formedness of types is the condition that ensures the termination of the imperative part of a term. This in particular ensures that each time we reduce a redex $\mathtt{deref}_n(u_{(n,T)})$, the obtained value does not create new operations acting at region n.

Comparison with [3]. The type system we present in the next section is actually very close to the one given in [3], which in turn is close to the one of [1].

In our presentation, regions, defined in [3] as abstract parts of the store, are denoted by natural numbers. The two presentations are equivalent. In [3], when the stratification condition (which is inductively defined on sets of regions) is met, a partial order between regions can be extracted, and thus integers can be assigned to regions so that each typable term can be given a well-formed type using our definitions. Conversely, from a set of regions indexed by natural numbers we can derive easily a set of corresponding abstract regions satisfying the stratification condition.

Another difference between the two settings is that our well-formedness condition for types is actually looser than the one found in [3], allowing us to typecheck more terms. Indeed, in Definition 1, in the case of an arrow type, we do not impose the well-formedness condition in the type of the argument, making terms like $(\lambda x.(\mathtt{deref}_2(x)\ u_{(3,1)}))\ (\mathtt{ref}_2\ \lambda y.\star)$ acceptable in our setting, while they are not in [3]. In this example, x has type $\mathbb{1}\ \mathtt{ref}_3 \to^0 \mathbb{1}$ (detailed typing rules can be found in the following section), which gives type $(\mathbb{1}\ \mathtt{ref}_3 \to^0 \mathbb{1})\ \mathtt{ref}_2$ for $\mathtt{ref}_2\ \lambda y.\star$. Note that this example is phrased using natural numbers for regions: it is not difficult to translate it into Boudol's framework, and insert the term in an appropriate context in order to enforce that the (abstract) region corresponding to 3 dominates the region corresponding to 2.

We think that the works [3] and [1] can easily be adapted with this small refinement in our definition of well-formedness in order to obtain the same expressiveness as our system.

2.2 Types and Reduction

Typing. Figure 2 defines two typing judgements, of the form $\Gamma \vdash M : (T, n)$ for terms and $\Gamma \vdash \delta$ for stores. Our type system is presented *à la Church*, and we write $\Gamma(x) = T$ when variable x has type T according to type environment Γ.

In a typing judgement $\Gamma \vdash M : (T, n)$, n defines a bound on the *effect* of the evaluation of M, which intuitively corresponds to the highest region accessed when evaluating M. Effects can be thought of as sets of regions (the part of the store manipulated by the evaluation of a term), and are denoted by a single natural number, which stands for the maximum region in the effect.

As explained above, in type $T_1 \to^n T_2$, n refers to the effect of the body of the function. As a consequence, in rule (**App**), the effect of the application $M\ N$

Typing rules for terms

$$(\mathbf{App}) \frac{\Gamma \vdash M : (T_1 \rightarrow^n T_2, m) \qquad \Gamma \vdash N : (T_1, k)}{\Gamma \vdash M \; N : (T_2, \max(m, n, k))}$$

$$(\mathbf{Abs}) \frac{\Gamma \vdash M : (T_2, n) \qquad \Gamma(x) = T_1}{\Gamma \vdash \lambda x.\, M : (T_1 \rightarrow^n T_2, 0)}$$

$$(\mathbf{Ref}) \frac{\Gamma \vdash M : (T_1, m)}{\Gamma \vdash \mathbf{ref}_n \; M : (T_1 \; \mathbf{ref}_n, \max(n, m))} \qquad\qquad (\mathbf{Var}) \frac{\Gamma(x) = T_1}{\Gamma \vdash x : (T_1, 0)}$$

$$(\mathbf{Uni}) \frac{}{\Gamma \vdash \star : (\mathbb{1}, 0)} \qquad\qquad (\mathbf{Add}) \frac{}{\Gamma \vdash u_{(n, T_1)} : (T_1 \; \mathbf{ref}_n, 0)}$$

$$(\mathbf{Asg}) \frac{\Gamma \vdash M : (T_1 \; \mathbf{ref}_n, m) \qquad \Gamma \vdash N : (T_1, k)}{\Gamma \vdash M :=_n N : (\mathbb{1}, \max(m, n, k))}$$

$$(\mathbf{Drf}) \frac{\Gamma \vdash M : (T \; \mathbf{ref}_n, m)}{\Gamma \vdash \mathbf{deref}_n(M) : (T, \max(m, n))}$$

Typing rules for stores

$$(\mathbf{Emp}) \frac{}{\Gamma \vdash \emptyset} \qquad\qquad (\mathbf{Sto}) \frac{\Gamma \vdash \delta \qquad \Gamma \vdash V : (T, 0)}{\Gamma \vdash \delta \langle u_{(n, T)} \rightsquigarrow V \rangle}$$

Fig. 2. λ_{ref}: Type and Effect System

where M has type $T_1 \rightarrow^n T_2$ is the maximum between the effect of M, the effect of N, and n. Indeed the maximum region accessed during the evaluation of $M \; N$ is accessed during either the evaluation of M to some function $\lambda x.M_2$, or the evaluation of N to some value V_1, or during the evaluation of $M_2\{V_1/x\}$, whose effect is n.

We notice that values have an effect 0: values cannot reduce and, as explained above, the effect of a term stands for the maximum region accessed during its evaluation.

We extend typing to evaluation contexts by treating the hole as a term variable which can be given any type and has effect 0.

Reduction. The execution of programs is given by a reduction relation, written $\mapsto$, relating *states* (a state is given by a pair consisting of a term and a store), and which is defined on Figure 3. We write $\mapsto_{\mathrm{F}}^n$ for a *functional* reduction, obtained using rule (β); n refers to the effect of the β-redex, that is, in this call-by-value setting, the region that decorates the type of the function being triggered. In other words, we suppose in rule (β) that $\Gamma \vdash \lambda x.\, M : (T_V \rightarrow^n T, m)$ holds for some T_V, T, m. We introduce similarly *imperative* reductions, noted $\mapsto_{\mathrm{I}}^n$, for reductions obtained using rules (**ref**), (**deref**) or (**store**) (in these cases, the

$$(\beta) \frac{}{(\lambda x.\, M\ V, \delta) \mapsto (M\{V/x\}, \delta)}$$

$$(\text{ref}) \frac{u_{(n,T)} \notin \text{supp}(\delta) \qquad \Gamma \vdash V : (T, \_)}{(\mathbf{ref}_n\ V, \delta) \mapsto (u_{(n,T)},\ \delta\langle u_{(n,T)} \rightsquigarrow V\rangle)}$$

$$(\text{deref}) \frac{\delta(u_{(n,T)}) = V}{(\mathbf{deref}_n(u_{(n,T)}), \delta) \mapsto (V, \delta)}$$

$$(\text{store}) \frac{\Gamma \vdash V : (T, \_)}{(u_{(n,T)} :=_n V, (\delta)) \mapsto (\star,\ \delta\langle u_{(n,T)} \rightsquigarrow V\rangle)}$$

$$(\text{context}) \frac{(M, \delta) \mapsto (M', \delta')}{(\mathbf{E}[M], \delta) \mapsto (\mathbf{E}[M'], \delta')}$$

Fig. 3. λ_{ref}: Reduction Rules

accessed region n appears explicitly in the rules of Figure 3). We will call a reduction according to $\mapsto_{\mathrm{F}}^n$ (resp. $\mapsto_{\mathrm{I}}^n$) "a functional reduction on level n" (resp. "an imperative reduction on level n").

Definition 2. *We define an* infinite computation starting from M *as an infinite sequence* $(M_i, \delta_i)_{0 \le i}$ *such that* $M_0 = M$, $\delta_0 = \emptyset$ *and* $\forall i, (M_i, \delta_i) \mapsto (M_{i+1}, \delta_{i+1})$.

We say that a term M diverges *when there exists an infinite sequence starting from M and that M* terminates *when it does not diverge.*

The following result will be useful to prove Proposition 5. It says that we can replace a term inside an evaluation context with a term of the same type but with a smaller effect, while preserving typability. The effect of the whole term can decrease (in the case where $\mathbf{E} = [\,]$ for instance).

Lemma 3. *If* $\begin{cases} \Gamma \vdash \mathbf{E}[M] : (T, n) \\ \Gamma \vdash M : (T_0, m) \\ \Gamma \vdash M' : (T_0, m') \\ m' \le m \end{cases}$ *then* $\Gamma \vdash \mathbf{E}[M'] : (T, n')$ *with* $n' \le n$.

Our type and effect system enjoys the two standard properties of subject substitution and subject reduction. Notice that in the statement of Lemma 4, the effect associated to $M\{V/x\}$ is the same as the one associated to M. This holds as the term V is a value and thus does not introduce new operations on the memory which are not handled by the type system. Should we have used a call-by-name setting, the statement of this proposition would have been: "If $\Gamma \vdash M : (T, n)$, $\Gamma(x) = T'$ and $\Gamma \vdash N : (T', m)$ then $\Gamma \vdash M\{N/x\} : (T, \max(m, n))$".

Lemma 4 (Subject Substitution).
If $\Gamma \vdash M : (T, n)$, $\Gamma(x) = T'$ *and* $\Gamma \vdash V : (T', m)$ *then* $\Gamma \vdash M\{V/x\} : (T, n)$.

We only sketch proofs for some results. The proof for Lemma 4, as well as detailed proofs for all other results, can be found in [5].

Proposition 5 (Subject Reduction).
  $\Gamma \vdash M : (T, n)$, $\Gamma \vdash \delta$ and $(M, \delta) \mapsto (M', \delta')$ entail that $\Gamma \vdash \delta'$ and $\Gamma \vdash M' : (T, n')$ for some $n' \leq n$.

Proof (Sketch). The proof is done by induction on the derivation of $(M, \delta) \mapsto (M', \delta')$. If the rule (**context**) is used, we rely on Lemma 3. If the rule (**beta**) is used, we use Lemma 4. Cases (**ref**) and (**store**) are easy. Case (**deref**) is done using the hypothesis that δ is well-typed.

3 Termination of $\lambda_{\texttt{ref}}$ Programs

3.1 Defining a Projection from $\lambda_{\texttt{ref}}$ to $\lambda_{\textbf{ST}}$

The technique of projection and simulation works as follows. First, we define a projection function, parametrised upon a region p (we will refer to a "projection on level p"), which strips a $\lambda_{\texttt{ref}}$ term from its imperative constructs (and some of its functional parts), in order to obtain a $\lambda_{\textbf{ST}}$ term.

Then, we prove a simulation result (Lemma 14 below), stating that when a well-typed state (M, δ) reduces to (M', δ') by a functional reduction on level p, the projection on level p of M reduces in at least one step to the projection on level p of M'; moreover, when (M, δ) reduces to (M', δ') by another type of reduction then either the projections on level p of M and M' are equal, or the projection of M reduces in at least one step to the projection of M'. This result is what makes the projection function divergence preserving, as announced in Section 1.

With these results at hand, we suppose, toward a contradiction, the existence of a diverging process M_0, and we show the existence of a region p such that an infinite computation starting from M_0 contains an infinite number of functional reductions on level p. Using the simulation lemma, we obtain by projection a diverging $\lambda_{\textbf{ST}}$ term (as a functional reduction on level p is mapped to at least one step of reduction), which contradicts strong normalisation of $\lambda_{\textbf{ST}}$.

Before turning to the formal definition of the projection function, let us explain informally how it acts on $\texttt{deref}_n(M)$ — we already gave some ideas about the projection of $\texttt{ref}_n\ M$ in Section 1. Again, the purpose of the projection is to remove the imperative command. Because we cannot just throw away M (this would invalidate the simulation lemma), we apply the projection function recursively to M. Once the projected version of M is executed, we replace the result with a value of the appropriate type, which we call a *generic value*.

More precisely, generic values are canonical terms that are used to replace a given subterm *once we know that no divergence can arise due to the evaluation of the subterm* (this would correspond either to a divergence of the subterm, or to a contribution to a more general divergence). They are defined as follows:

Definition 6. *Given a type T without the* **ref** *construct, the* generic value V_T *of type T is defined by:* $V_{T\ \mathtt{ref}_n} = V_{\mathbb{1}} = \star$, *and* $V_{T_1 \to^n T_2} = \lambda x.V_{T_2}$ *(x being of type T_1 in the latter term).*

In order to program the evaluation of a projected subterm and its replacement with a generic value, the definition of projection makes use of the following (families of) projectors:

$$\Pi^{(1,2)} = \lambda x.\lambda y.\, x \qquad\qquad \Pi^{(1,3)} = \lambda x.\lambda y.\lambda z.\, x \ .$$

In the following, we shall use these projectors in a well-typed fashion (that is, we pick the appropriate instance in the corresponding family).

In order to present the definition of the projection function, we need a last notion, that conveys the intuition that a given term M can be involved in a reduction on level p. This can be the case for two reasons. Either M is able to perform (maybe after some preliminary reduction steps) a reduction on level p, in which case, by the typing rules, the effect of M is greater than p, or M is a function that can receive some arguments and eventually perform a reduction on level p, in which case the type system ensures that its type T satisfies $\mathrm{reg}(T) \geq p$.

Definition 7. *Suppose $\Gamma \vdash M : (T,n)$. We say that M is* related to p *if either $n \geq p$ or $\mathrm{reg}(T) \geq p$. In the former (resp. latter) case, we say that M is related to p* via its effect *(resp.* via its type*).*

We extend this notion to evaluation contexts by treating the hole like a term variable, for a given typing derivation for a context (this is useful in particular in the statement of Lemma 13).

Notice that a term containing a subterm whose effect is p is not necessarily related to p: for instance, we can derive $\Gamma \vdash (\lambda x.\star)\ \lambda y.\mathtt{deref}_3(u_{(3,\mathbb{1})}) : (\mathbb{1},0)$ for an appropriate Γ, but this term is not related to 3, although we can derive $\Gamma' \vdash \mathtt{deref}_3(u_{(3,\mathbb{1})}) : (\mathbb{1},3)$ for some Γ' — one can easily check that this term cannot be used to trigger a reduction on level 3.

Definition 8. *Given a typable M of type T, we define the* projection on level p *of M, written $\mathrm{pr}^p_\Gamma(M)$, as follows:*

> *If M is not related to p:*
> $$\mathrm{pr}^p_\Gamma(M) = V_T$$
> *Otherwise:*
> $$\mathrm{pr}^p_\Gamma(M_1\ M_2) = \mathrm{pr}^p_\Gamma(M_1)\ \mathrm{pr}^p_\Gamma(M_2)$$
> $$\mathrm{pr}^p_\Gamma(x) = x$$
> $$\mathrm{pr}^p_\Gamma(\lambda x.M_1) = \lambda x.\mathrm{pr}^p_\Gamma(M_1)$$
> $$\mathrm{pr}^p_\Gamma(\mathtt{ref}_n\ M_1) = (\Pi^{(1,2)}\ \star\ \mathrm{pr}^p_\Gamma(M_1))$$
> $$\mathrm{pr}^p_\Gamma(\mathtt{deref}_n(M_1)) = (\Pi^{(1,2)}\ V_T\ \mathrm{pr}^p_\Gamma(M_1))$$
> $$\mathrm{pr}^p_\Gamma(M_1 :=_n M_2) = (\Pi^{(1,3)}\ \star\ \mathrm{pr}^p_\Gamma(M_1)\ \mathrm{pr}^p_\Gamma(M_2))$$
> $$\mathrm{pr}^p_\Gamma(u_{(n,T_1)}) = \star$$

We extend this definition to evaluation contexts in the following way: we always propagate the projection inductively in a context $\mathbf{E}$, without checking if the context is related to p or not. For instance, $\mathsf{pr}_\Gamma^p(\mathbf{E}_1\ M) = \mathsf{pr}_\Gamma^p(\mathbf{E}_1)\ \mathsf{pr}_\Gamma^p(M)$ even if $(\mathbf{E}_1\ M)$ is not related to p.

The projection function maps $\lambda_{\mathtt{ref}}$ terms to $\lambda_{\mathbf{ST}}$ terms, where $\lambda_{\mathbf{ST}}$ is the simply typed λ-calculus: this is stated in Lemma 10.

Definition 9. *We extend the projection function to act on types as follows:*

$$\mathsf{pr}_\Gamma^p(\mathbb{1}) = \mathbb{1} \qquad \mathsf{pr}_\Gamma^p(T\ \mathtt{ref}_n) = \mathbb{1} \qquad \mathsf{pr}_\Gamma^p(T_1 \to^n T_2) = \mathsf{pr}_\Gamma^p(T_1) \to \mathsf{pr}_\Gamma^p(T_2)\ .$$

Observe that for any type T, $\mathsf{pr}_\Gamma^p(T)$ is a simple type, and V_T is a simply-typed λ-term of type $\mathsf{pr}_\Gamma^p(T)$.

Lemma 10. *Take $p \in \mathbb{N}$, and suppose $\Gamma \vdash M : (T, n)$. Then $\mathsf{pr}_\Gamma^p(M)$ belongs to $\lambda_{\mathbf{ST}}$, and has type $\mathsf{pr}_\Gamma^p(T)$.*

Proof (Sketch). We reason by induction on the typing judgement in $\lambda_{\mathtt{ref}}$. If M is not related to p, the result follows directly from the remarks above. Otherwise, we reason by cases on the last rule used to type M and conclude using the induction hypothesis.

3.2   Simulation Result

In order to reason about the transitions of projected terms, the first step is to understand how projection interacts with the decomposition of a term into an evaluation context and a redex.

The lemma below explains how the projection function is propagated within a term of the form $\mathbf{E}[M]$. There are, intuitively, two possibilities, depending only on the context and on the level (p) of the projection:

– either $\mathbf{E}$ is such that $\mathsf{pr}_\Gamma^p(\mathbf{E}[M]) = \mathsf{pr}_\Gamma^p(\mathbf{E})[\mathsf{pr}_\Gamma^p(M)]$ for all M, that is, the projection is always propagated in the hole to M,
– or this is not the case and the context is such that, if the effect of M is too small, the projection inserts a generic value before reaching the hole in $\mathbf{E}$. In this case $\mathsf{pr}_\Gamma^p(\mathbf{E}[M]) = \mathsf{pr}_\Gamma^p(\mathbf{E}_1)[V]$, where $\mathbf{E}_1$ is an 'initial part' of $\mathbf{E}$, and this equality holds independently from M (as long as, like said above, the effect of M is sufficiently small in some sense).

In the former case, the projection is propagated inductively inside the context to the hole, no matter the effect of M, whereas in the latter case, if the effect of M is small enough, the projection does not stop before reaching the hole in $\mathbf{E}$.

Lemma 11. *Take $p \in \mathbb{N}$, and consider a well-typed context $\mathbf{E}$. We have:*

1. *Either for all well-typed process M, $\mathsf{pr}_\Gamma^p(\mathbf{E}[M]) = \mathsf{pr}_\Gamma^p(\mathbf{E})[\mathsf{pr}_\Gamma^p(M)]$,*
2. *or there exist $\mathbf{E}_1$ and $\mathbf{E}_2 \neq []$ s.t. $\mathbf{E} = \mathbf{E}_1[\mathbf{E}_2]$ and, for all M, if k stands for the effect of M, we are in one of the two following cases:*

(a) If $k \geq p$, then $\mathsf{pr}_\Gamma^p(\mathbf{E}[M]) = \mathsf{pr}_\Gamma^p(\mathbf{E})[\mathsf{pr}_\Gamma^p(M)]$.
(b) If $k < p$, then $\mathsf{pr}_\Gamma^p(\mathbf{E}[M]) = \mathsf{pr}_\Gamma^p(\mathbf{E}_1)[\mathsf{V}_{T''}]$ (where T'' is the type of $\mathbf{E}_2$).

Proof (Sketch). We proceed by structural induction on $\mathbf{E}$ and distinguish two cases:

1. Either the context is not related to p. This means that $\mathbf{E}_1 = [\,]$ and $\mathbf{E}_2 = \mathbf{E}$. If $k < p$ then the projection of the whole term returns a generic value. If $k \geq p$ then we discuss on the structure of $\mathbf{E}$, use the induction hypothesis and the definition of projection.
2. If the context is related to p we discuss on the structure of the context and use the induction hypothesis, constructing at each step the outer context $\mathbf{E}_1$. When we reach a context not related to p, we conclude using case 1.

The properties we now establish correspond to the situation, in the previous lemma, where M is an imperative redex acting on region p. The typing rules of Figure 2 insure that firing the redex yields a term which is not related to p via its effect: depending on the kind of imperative operator that is executed, this term might either be related to p via its type, or not related to p at all.

In the latter case, we are able to show that the projected versions of the two terms are related by $\twoheadrightarrow^+$ (the transitive closure of reduction in $\lambda_{\mathbf{ST}}$), which allows us to establish a simulation property.

Fact 12. *If $\mathbf{E}_2$ is not related to p, then:*

1. *If $\mathbf{E}_2 = (V_3\ \mathbf{E}_3)$ then V_3 is not related to p.*
2. *If $\mathbf{E}_2 = (\mathbf{E}_3\ M_3)$ then $\mathbf{E}_3$ is not related to p.*

Lemma 13. *If $\Gamma \vdash \mathbf{E}_2 : (T'', m)$ and $\mathbf{E}_2$ is not related to p, then for any well-typed M, M',*

1. $\mathsf{pr}_\Gamma^p(\mathbf{E}_2)[(\Pi^{(1,2)}\ \mathsf{V}_T\ M)] \twoheadrightarrow^+ \mathsf{V}_{T''}$;
2. $\mathsf{pr}_\Gamma^p(\mathbf{E}_2)[(\Pi^{(1,3)}\ \mathsf{V}_T\ M\ M')] \twoheadrightarrow^+ \mathsf{V}_{T''}$.

Proof (Sketch). We proceed by structural induction on $\mathbf{E}_2$. Fact 12 is necessary: for instance, if $\mathbf{E}_2 = \mathbf{E}_3\ M_3$, we have

$$\mathsf{pr}_\Gamma^p(\mathbf{E}_2)[(\Pi^{(1,2)}\ \mathsf{V}_T\ N)] = (\mathsf{pr}_\Gamma^p(\mathbf{E}_3)[(\Pi^{(1,2)}\ \mathsf{V}_T\ N)]\ \mathsf{pr}_\Gamma^p(M_3))$$

with $\mathbf{E}_3$ of type $T_3 \to T''$. Thus, we can use Fact 12 and the induction hypothesis on $\mathbf{E}_3$ to get $\mathsf{pr}_\Gamma^p(\mathbf{E}_3)[(\Pi^{(1,2)}\ \mathsf{V}_T\ N)] \twoheadrightarrow^+ \mathsf{V}_{T_3 \to T''}$, from which we conclude.

Lemmas 11 and 13 allow us to derive the desired simulation property for λ_{ref}, the main point being that a functional reduction on level p is projected into one reduction in the target calculus (case 4 below).

Lemma 14 (Simulation). *Consider $p \in \mathbb{N}$, and suppose $\Gamma \vdash M : (T, m)$.*

1. *If $(M, \delta) \mapsto_{\mathsf{I}}^n (M', \delta')$ and $n < p$, then $\mathsf{pr}_\Gamma^p(M) = \mathsf{pr}_\Gamma^p(M')$.*
2. *If $(M, \delta) \mapsto_{\mathsf{I}}^p (M', \delta')$, then $\mathsf{pr}_\Gamma^p(M) \twoheadrightarrow^+ \mathsf{pr}_\Gamma^p(M')$.*

3. If $(M, \delta) \mapsto_F^n (M', \delta')$ and $n < p$, then $\mathsf{pr}_\Gamma^p(M) = \mathsf{pr}_\Gamma^p(M')$.

4. If $(M, \delta) \mapsto_F^p (M', \delta')$, then $\mathsf{pr}_\Gamma^p(M) \twoheadrightarrow \mathsf{pr}_\Gamma^p(M')$.

Proof (Sketch). The structure of the proof is as follows. For cases 1 and 2, terms are decomposed in the same way but the arguments invoked are different. In case 1, we use the definition of projection on terms not related to p to conclude; in case 2, projection yields an "actual term" (not a generic value) and we use Lemma 13 to conclude.

In these reasonings, the proofs for rules (**ref**) and (**deref**) differ, as in the former case the more complex term appears before the reduction (we have $\mathtt{ref}_n \, V$ which reduces to $u_{(n,T)}$) whereas in the latter case the more complex term appears after the reduction (we have $\mathtt{deref}_n(u_{(n,T)})$ which reduces to V).

Cases 3 and 4 are treated along the lines of cases 1 and 2, except that Lemma 13 is not required.

3.3   Deriving Soundness

To obtain soundness, we need to show that a diverging term performs an infinite number of functional reductions on level p, for some p. For this we introduce a measure that decreases along imperative reductions on level p and does not increase along reductions on level $< p$. The measure is given by counting the *active imperative operators* of a term, which are the imperative operators (reference creations, dereferencings and assignments) that do not occur under a λ.

Definition 15. *Take M in λ_{ref}. The number of active imperative operators on region p in M, written $\mathbf{Ao}^p(M)$ is defined inductively as follows:*

$$\mathbf{Ao}^p(x) = \mathbf{Ao}^p(\lambda x.M) = \mathbf{Ao}^p(u_{(n,T)}) = 0 \qquad \mathbf{Ao}^p(M \, N) = \mathbf{Ao}^p(M) + \mathbf{Ao}^p(N)$$

$$\mathbf{Ao}^p(\mathtt{deref}_n(M)) = \mathbf{Ao}^p(\mathtt{ref}_n \, M) = \mathbf{Ao}^p(M) \qquad \text{if } n \neq p$$
$$\mathbf{Ao}^p(\mathtt{deref}_p(M)) = \mathbf{Ao}^p(\mathtt{ref}_p \, M) = 1 + \mathbf{Ao}^p(M)$$

$$\mathbf{Ao}^p(M :=_n N) = \mathbf{Ao}^p(M) + \mathbf{Ao}^p(N) \qquad \text{if } n \neq p$$
$$\mathbf{Ao}^p(M :=_p N) = 1 + \mathbf{Ao}^p(M) + \mathbf{Ao}^p(N)$$

$\mathbf{Ao}^p(M)$ and the effect of M are related as follows:

Lemma 16. *If $\Gamma \vdash M : (T, m)$ and $m < p$ then $\mathbf{Ao}^p(M) = 0$.*

We are finally able to show that $\mathbf{Ao}^p(M)$ yields the measure we need.

Lemma 17. *If $\Gamma \vdash M : (T, m)$ then:*

1. if $(M, \delta) \mapsto_F^n (M', \delta')$ with $n < p$ then $\mathbf{Ao}^p(M') \leq \mathbf{Ao}^p(M)$,
2. if $(M, \delta) \mapsto_I^n (M', \delta')$ with $n < p$ then $\mathbf{Ao}^p(M') \leq \mathbf{Ao}^p(M)$,
3. and if $(M, \delta) \mapsto_I^p (M', \delta')$ then $\mathbf{Ao}^p(M') < \mathbf{Ao}^p(M)$.

Proof (Sketch). We reason by cases on the reduction rules and use Lemma 16 to show that new imperative operators on region p can only be generated by functional reductions on level $\geq p$ or by imperative reductions on level $> p$, and that each imperative reduction on level p erases one active imperative operator on region p.

The following lemma states that there exists a maximum region p on which an infinite number of reductions takes place. With the previous result, we can deduce that an infinite number of functional reductions take place on level p.

Lemma 18. *Suppose that $\Gamma \vdash M : (T, l)$, and that there exists $(M_i, \delta_i)_{i \in \mathbb{N}}$, an infinite reduction sequence starting from M. Then:*

1. *For all i, M_i is typable.*
2. *There exist p and i_o s.t.*
   (a) *if $i > i_0$ and $(M_i, \delta_i) \mapsto^n_I (M_{i+1}, \delta_{i+1})$ then $n \leq p$,*
   (b) *if $i > i_0$ and $(M_i, \delta_i) \mapsto^n_F (M_{i+1}, \delta_{i+1})$ then $n \leq p$,*
   (c) *There exists an infinite set of indexes $\mathcal{I}$ s.t. for each $i \in \mathcal{I}$, either $(M_i, \delta_i) \mapsto^p_F (M_{i+1}, \delta_{i+1})$ or $(M_i, \delta_i) \mapsto^p_I (M_{i+1}, \delta_{i+1})$.*
   (d) *There are infinitely many $i \in \mathcal{I}$ s.t. $(M_i, \delta_i) \mapsto^p_F (M_{i+1}, \delta_{i+1})$.*

Proof (Sketch).

1. Follows from Proposition 5.
2. The set of different regions is finite, so we easily find a p satisfying 2a, 2b and 2c. Lemma 17 ensures that 2d holds.

Theorem 19 (Soundness). *If $\Gamma \vdash M : (T, m)$ then M terminates.*

Proof. Consider, by absurd, an infinite computation $(M_i, \delta_i)_i$ starting from $M = M_0$ and δ_0. By Lemma 18, all the M_i's are well-typed, and there is a maximal p s.t. for infinitely many i, $(M_i, \delta_i) \mapsto^p_F (M_{i+1}, \delta_{i+1})$. Furthermore, there exists i_0 such that every reduction on an index greater than i_0 is performed on region $n \leq p$. Consider the sequence $(\mathsf{pr}^p_\Gamma(M_i))_{i > i_0}$. By Lemma 14, we obtain that for every $i > i_0$, $\mathsf{pr}^p_\Gamma(M_i) \twoheadrightarrow^* \mathsf{pr}^p_\Gamma(M_{i+1})$. Moreover, $\mathsf{pr}^p_\Gamma(M_i) \twoheadrightarrow^+ \mathsf{pr}^p_\Gamma(M_{i+1})$ for an infinite number of i. Thus $\mathsf{pr}^p_\Gamma(M_{i_0})$ is diverging. This contradicts the termination of $\lambda_{\mathbf{ST}}$.

Remark 20 (Raising the effect). *The results we present in this paper still hold if we add the rule:*

$$\textbf{(Sub)} \frac{\Gamma \vdash M : (T, n) \qquad n \leq n'}{\Gamma \vdash M : (T, n')}$$

to the type system.

This rule allows us to be more liberal when typing terms, thus obtaining a greater expressiveness. For instance, it allows one to store at the same address functions whose bodies do not have the same effect.

Example 21 (Landin's Trick). *The standard example of diverging term in λ_{ref}, known as Landin's trick, is given by:*

$$(\lambda f.[(\lambda t.(\mathtt{deref}_1(f) \, \star)) \, (f :=_1 \lambda z.(\mathtt{deref}_1(f) \, z))]) \, (\mathtt{ref}_1 \, \lambda x.x) \ .$$

In order to try and type this term, we are bound to manipulate non well-formed types.

In the call by value setting of λ_{ref}, a first address $u_{(1,\mathbb{1} \to {}^1\mathbb{1})}$ (we use Remark 20 here, as the identity has no effect) is created when evaluating the argument ($\mathtt{ref}_1 \, \lambda x.x$); this address instantiates f in the body of the outer function. Then $u_{(1,\mathbb{1} \to {}^1\mathbb{1})}$ is updated using the function $\lambda z.(\mathtt{deref}_1(f) \, z)$, whose type is $\mathbb{1} \to^1 \mathbb{1}$, at which point the term enters a loop. It is easy to see that the type of $u_{(1,\mathbb{1} \to {}^1\mathbb{1})}$ (which is also the type of f) is $(\mathbb{1} \to^1 \mathbb{1}) \, \mathtt{ref}_1$ and is not well-formed, as $\mathrm{reg}(\mathbb{1} \to^1 \mathbb{1}) = 1 \not< 1$.

On the other hand, consider the following terminating term:

$$(\lambda f.[(\lambda t.(\mathtt{deref}_1(f) \, \star)) \, (f :=_1 \lambda z.(\Pi^{(1,2)} \, I \, (\lambda y.\mathtt{deref}_1(f) \, y)) \, z)]) \, (\mathtt{ref}_1 \, \lambda x.x)$$

where $I = \lambda t.t$. This term is close to the example given above, except that $\lambda z.(\mathtt{deref}_1(f) \, z)$ is replaced with $\lambda z.(\Pi^{(1,2)} \, I \, (\lambda y.\mathtt{deref}_1(f) \, y) \, z$. This new subterm, stored at address f, contains a dereferencing of f. Yet the term terminates because the dereferencing never comes in redex position. Indeed, the term $(\lambda z.(\Pi^{(1,2)} \, I \, (\lambda y.\mathtt{deref}_1(f) \, y)) \, z)$ reduces to $(\Pi^{(1,2)} \, I \, (\lambda y.\mathtt{deref}_1(f) \, y))$ which, in turn, reduces in two steps to I.

Here the type system assigns to $(\Pi^{(1,2)} \, I \, (\lambda y.\mathtt{deref}_1(f) \, y))$ the type $\mathbb{1} \to^0 \mathbb{1}$ and the effect 0. Thus the type of x is $\mathbb{1} \to^0 \mathbb{1} \, \mathtt{ref}_1$, which is well-formed.

4 Parametricity

As is the case in [7] for the π-calculus, the method we have presented for the λ-calculus with references is parametric with respect to a terminating purely functional core, and does not examine the corresponding termination proof. Other core calculi could be considered. Moreover, if the functional calculus corresponds to a subset of the simply typed terms, then the result holds directly.

We believe that it is possible to extend our work to polymorphic types, although this extension is not trivial if we consider adding region polymorphism: for instance, we would have to guarantee that a type like $(\forall A.A \to^0 A) \, \mathtt{ref}_n$ cannot have its A component instantiated with a type containing a region strictly greater than n.

Another idea is to apply this termination technique to a language containing both references and a recursion operator on integers. By restricting the use of the latter (in order not to create loops based on recursion), we think that one could be able to enrich the system we have presented.

By taking as functional core a λ-calculus with complexity bounds (such as, for instance, [2]), we believe that one can use our technique in order to lift complexity bounds for impure languages. The main idea is to rely on the projection function to provide bounds on the number of reductions a terminating typed term can make.

Note, to conclude, that references can be encoded in a standard way in the π-calculus (as well as the call-by-value λ-calculus). One could then wonder if the method presented in [7] can recognise as terminating the subset of π-processes corresponding to encodings of $\lambda_{\mathbf{ref}}$ terms. The question is challenging, as weight-based methods for termination in π [8] cannot be used to prove termination of the encoding of $\lambda_{\mathbf{ST}}$ [6,4].

Acknowledgements. Support from the french ANR projects "CHoCo", "AEO-LUS" and "Complice" (ANR-08-BLANC-0211-01), and by the European Project "HATS" (contract number 231620) is acknowledged.

References

1. Amadio, R.M.: On Stratified Regions. In: Hu, Z. (ed.) APLAS 2009. LNCS, vol. 5904, pp. 210–225. Springer, Heidelberg (2009)
2. Amadio, R.M., Baillot, P., Madet, A.: An affine-intuitionistic system of types and effects: confluence and termination. CoRR, abs/1005.0835 (2010)
3. Boudol, G.: Fair Cooperative Multithreading. In: Caires, L., Vasconcelos, V.T. (eds.) CONCUR 2007. LNCS, vol. 4703, pp. 272–286. Springer, Heidelberg (2007)
4. Cristescu, I., Hirschkoff, D.: Termination in a π-calculus with Subptying (in preparation, 2011)
5. Demangeon, R.: Termination for Concurrent Systems. PhD thesis, Ecole Normale Superieure de Lyon (2010),
   http://perso.ens-lyon.fr/romain.demangeon/phd.pdf
6. Demangeon, R., Hirschkoff, D., Sangiorgi, D.: Mobile Processes and Termination. In: Palsberg, J. (ed.) Semantics and Algebraic Specification. LNCS, vol. 5700, pp. 250–273. Springer, Heidelberg (2009)
7. Demangeon, R., Hirschkoff, D., Sangiorgi, D.: Termination in Impure Concurrent Languages. In: Gastin, P., Laroussinie, F. (eds.) CONCUR 2010. LNCS, vol. 6269, pp. 328–342. Springer, Heidelberg (2010)
8. Deng, Y., Sangiorgi, D.: Ensuring Termination by Typability. Information and Computation 204(7), 1045–1082 (2006)
9. Tranquilli, P.: Translating types and effects with state monads and linear logic (submitted, 2011)

Compositional Reasoning
for Markov Decision Processes
(Extended Abstract)

Yuxin Deng[1,2,*] and Matthew Hennessy[3,**]

[1] Dept. Comp. Sci. & Eng. and MOE-Microsoft Key Lab for Intell. Comp. & Syst.,
Shanghai Jiao Tong University, China
[2] State Key Lab of Comp. Sci., Inst. of Software, Chinese Academy of Sciences
[3] Trinity College Dublin, Ireland

Abstract. Markov decision processes (MDPs) have long been used to model qualitative aspects of systems in the presence of uncertainty. However, much of the literature on MDPs takes a monolithic approach, by modelling a system as a particular MDP; properties of the system are then inferred by analysis of that particular MDP. In this paper we develop compositional methods for reasoning about the qualitative behaviour of MDPs. We consider a class of labelled MDPs called weighted MDPs from a process algebraic point of view. For these we define a coinductive simulation-based behavioural preorder which is compositional in the sense that it is preserved by structural operators for constructing MDPs from components.

For finitary convergent processes, which are finite-state and finitely branching systems without divergence, we provide two characterisations of the behavioural preorder. The first uses a novel qualitative probabilistic logic, while the second is in terms of a novel form of testing, in which benefits are accrued during the execution of tests.

1 Introduction

Markov decision processes (MDPs) have long been used to model qualitative aspects of systems in the presence of uncertainty [12,13,1]. A comprehensive account of analysis techniques may be found in [12], while [13] provides a good account of *model-checking*.

However, much of the literature on MDPs takes a monolithic view of systems; essentially a system is modelled using a particular MDP, and properties of the system are then inferred by analysis of that MDP. In this paper, instead, we would like to develop compositional methods for reasoning about qualitative behaviour of Markov decision processes. This involves defining an appropriate method for comparing the behaviour MDPs which is susceptible to compositional analysis; the behaviour of a composite system should be determined by that of its components.

Our starting point is the idea of one system being able to *simulate* another. For example consider the following three systems:

---

* Supported by the National Natural Science Foundation of China (61033002, 61011140074).
** Supported by SFI project SFI 06 IN.1 1898.

F. Arbab and M. Sirjani (Eds.): FSEN 2011, LNCS 7141, pp. 143–157, 2012.

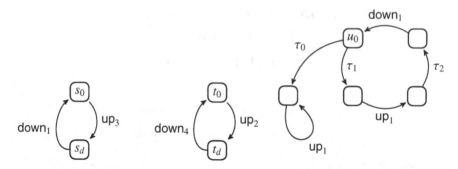

The first, a two-state machine, continually performs an up action, which accrues a benefit of 3 units, followed by a down action, which accrues a benefit of 1. The second machine performs the same actions but with benefits 2 and 4 respectively. In some sense t_0 is an improvement on s_0; intuitively t_0 can simulate the behaviour of s_0 but in so doing accrue more benefits; this is true even if one of its actions up is less beneficial than the corresponding action of s_0. The same is true for the machine u_0; it can also simulate the behaviour of s_0, with more benefit, although in this case some internal weighted actions, denoted by τ, participate in the simulation and add to the accumulation of benefits. In our terminology we will write $s_0 \sqsubseteq_{sim} t_0$, $s_0 \sqsubseteq_{sim} u_0$. However, we will have $t_0 \not\sqsubseteq_{sim} u_0$ because although u_0 can simulate the behaviour of t_0 it accumulates less benefit.

Similar informal reasoning can also be applied to probabilistic systems. Consider the following systems:

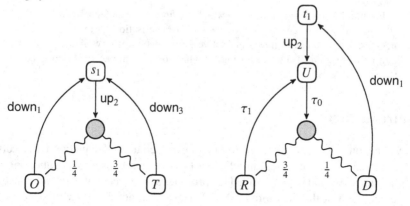

The first, from state s_1, can perform the up action with benefit 2 and a quarter of the time it ends up in a state in which down can be performed with benefit only 1. But for the remaining three-quarters it ends up in a state in which down can be performed for the larger benefit 3. The circular darkended node represents a distribution of states, with its outgoing edges describing the associated probabilities. Again intuitively we can see that s_1 is an improvement on s_0 because it can simulate s_0 and on average accrue slightly more benefits; in our theory we will have $s_0 \sqsubseteq_{sim} s_1$.

The mixture of probabilistic behaviour and internal actions introduces complications. Consider the system t_1 above which after performing an up probabilistically decides internally whether to perform a down action for benefit 1, or branch back to make another probabilistic choice. However, each time it reverts back it accumulates a non-zero benefit via the internal weighted action τ_1, albeit with diminishing probability. Nevertheless, it will turn out that $s_0 \sqsubseteq_{sim} t_1$ and indeed $s_1 \sqsubseteq_{sim} t_1$.

Systems exhibiting both probabilistic and nondeterministic behaviour require more complicated analysis. Consider the following system:

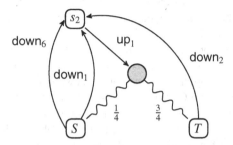

After performing the action **up** it finds itself either in a state in which the action **down** will accrue the benefit 2, or 25% of the time there will be a nondeterministic choice between it accruing either 1 or 6. In the literature there are numerous mechanisms, such as policies, schedulers, adversaries, etc. [12,14,13] for resolving such choices. Here one can see if this choice systematically leads to the lower benefit 1 then s_2 will not simulate s_0 as it does not accrue sufficient benefits. This is a pessimistic outlook; an optimistic outlook means that the best choices are systematically made. If this is assumed then we will have $s_0 \sqsubseteq_{sim} s_2$; in s_2 one execution of **up** followed by **down** will yield on average the benefit $1 + (\frac{3}{4} \cdot 2 + \frac{1}{4} \cdot 6) = 4$.

The main contribution of the paper is a coinductively defined behavioural preorder $\sqsubseteq_{sim}$ between MDPs based on simulations which validate the examples discussed informally above. We confine our attention to the optimistic approach to the resolution of nondeterministic choices, although in a later paper we hope to investigate the pessimistic approach. We also show that this preorder is compositional in the sense that it is preserved by structural operators for constructing MDPs from components. The main operator is one for composing two MDPs in parallel. In $P \mid Q$ the two MPDs P and Q remain independent, execute in parallel and may communicate by synchronising on complementary actions; these internal synchronisations accrue the combined benefits of the associated complementary actions.

For finitary convergent MDPs, which are finite-state and finitely branching systems without divergence, we also provide two characterisations for the behavioural preorder $\sqsubseteq_{sim}$. The first is in terms of a *qualitative probabilistic logic* $\mathcal{L}_Q$. In addition to the standard logical connectives $\wedge$, $\vee$ and both maximal and minimal fixpoints this contains a novel qualitative *possibility* modality $\langle \alpha \rangle_w (\phi_1 \,{}_p\oplus \phi_2)$, where p is some probability between 0 and 1. Intuitively this is satisfied by an MDP which can accrue at least the benefit w by performing the action α, and subsequently satisfy the probabilistic assertion $\phi_1 \,{}_p\oplus \phi_2$. It turns out that the simulation preorder is completely determined by the logic $\mathcal{L}_Q$. Further evidence of the compatibility between the logic and the simulation relation is the fact that every system P has a *characteristic formula* $\phi(P)$ in the logic which captures its behaviour; informally system Q can simulate P if and only if it satisfies the characteristic formula $\phi(P)$.

Our second characterisation is in terms of a novel form of testing called *benefits* testing. Intuitively a system P can be tested by running it in parallel with another testing system T, and seeing the possible accrued benefits. In the presence of nondeterminism the execution of the combined system $(T \mid P)$ will result in a non-empty set of benefits, **Benefits**$(T \mid P)$. Then systems P and Q can be compared by comparing the associated benefit sets **Benefits**$(T \mid P)$ and **Benefits**$(T \mid Q)$ where T ranges over some collection of possible tests. We show that the simulation preorder $\sqsubseteq_{sim}$ is also determined in this manner by a suitable collection of tests T.

The rest of this paper is organised as follows. In Section 2 we introduce the model of weighted MDPs, the notation of hyper-derivations and some important properties. Then we define a behavioural preorder based on amortised weighted simulations, which turns out to be a precongruence in a CCS-like process calculus for MDPs. Next, we provide logical and testing characterisations of the behavioural preorder over finitary convergent processes. In Section 3 we present a qualitative probabilistic logic whose formulae completely determine the behavioural preorder. We also show that characteristic formulae can be constructed for any state in such an MDP. In Section 4 we propose a testing framework where our behavioural preorder is sound and complete for may testing preorder. Finally, we conclude in Section 5.

Due to lack of space, we omit all detailed proofs: they are reported in [4].

2   Simulations for Weighted Markov Decision Processes

There is considerable variation in the literature in the formal definition of a (labelled) Markov decision process [13,12]. For the purpose of this paper we use Definition 1.

We first fix some notation. A (discrete) probability subdistribution over a countable set S is a function $\Delta : S \to [0,1]$ with $\sum_{s \in S} \Delta(s) \leq 1$; the support of such an Δ is the set $\lceil \Delta \rceil = \{ s \in S \mid \Delta(s) > 0 \}$. A subdistribution is a (total, or full) distribution if $\sum_{s \in S} \Delta(s) = 1$. The point distribution $\overline{s}$ assigns probability 1 to s and 0 to all other elements of S, so that $\lceil \overline{s} \rceil = s$. We use $\mathcal{D}_{sub}(S)$ to denote the set of subdistributions over S, and $\mathcal{D}(S)$ its subset of full distributions.

Let $\{\Delta_k \mid k \in K\}$ be a set of subdistributions, possibly infinite. Then $\sum_{k \in K} \Delta_k$ is the real-valued function in $S \to \mathbb{R}$ defined by $(\sum_{k \in K} \Delta_k)(s) := \sum_{k \in K} \Delta_k(s)$. This is a partial operation on subdistributions because for some state s the sum of $\Delta_k(s)$ might exceed 1. If the index set is finite, say $\{1..n\}$, we often write $\Delta_1 + \ldots + \Delta_n$. For p a real number from $[0,1]$ we use $p \cdot \Delta$ to denote the subdistribution given by $(p \cdot \Delta)(s) := p \cdot \Delta(s)$. Finally we use ε to denote the everywhere-zero subdistribution that thus has empty support. These operations on subdistributions do not readily adapt themselves to distributions; yet if $\sum_{k \in K} p_k = 1$ for some collection of $p_k \geq 0$, and the Δ_k are distributions, then so is $\sum_{k \in K} p_k \cdot \Delta_k$.

Definition 1 (Weighted Markov decision process). *A* weighted Markov decision process *or wMDP is a 4-tuple* $\langle S, A, W, \longrightarrow \rangle$ *where S is a set of states,* A *a set of actions,* W *a set of weights, and* $\longrightarrow \; \subseteq \; S \times A \times W \times \mathcal{D}(S)$. *We normally write* $s \xrightarrow{\alpha}_w \Delta$ *to mean* $(s, \alpha, w, \Delta) \in \longrightarrow$. *In this paper we set* W *to be* $\mathbb{R}_{\geq 0}$, *the set of non-negative real numbers, and we assume* A *has the structure* $\mathsf{Act}_\tau = \mathsf{Act} \cup \{\tau\}$ *where, for the purpose of communication, each a in* Act *has an inverse $\overline{a}$ satisfying $\overline{\overline{a}} = a$.*   □

A wMDP is

- *finite-state* if S is a finite set;
- *finitely branching* if for each state s, the set $\{(\alpha, w, \Delta) \mid s \xrightarrow{\alpha}_w \Delta\}$ is finite;
- *finitary* if it is both finite-state and finitely branching.

In the Introduction we have used a straightforward graphical representation for wMDPs; a state s is represented by a node $\boxed{s}$ while darkened circular nodes are used for distributions, and arrows between nodes and distributions are annotated with their weights. Often a point distribution is represented by the unique state in its support; see the first series of examples with initial states s_0, t_0 and u_0.

2.1 Hyper-derivations

As we have seen in the Introduction, when reasoning informally that t_1 can simulate s_0, the limiting behaviour of internal computations must be taken into account. We formalise this by extending the approach originally given in [5].

In a wMDP actions are only performed by states, in that actions are given by relations from states to distributions. But formally, systems or processes in general correspond to distributions over states, so in order to define what it means for a process to perform an action, we need to *lift* these relations so that they also apply to distributions. In fact we will find it convenient to lift them to subdistributions.

Definition 2. *Let* $\mathcal{R} \subseteq S \times (\mathbb{R}_{\geq 0} \times \mathcal{D}_{sub}(S))$ *be a relation from states to pairs of weights and subdistributions. Then* $\overline{\mathcal{R}} \subseteq \mathcal{D}_{sub}(S) \times (\mathbb{R}_{\geq 0} \times \mathcal{D}_{sub}(S))$ *is the smallest relation that satisfies:*

(i) $s \, \mathcal{R} \, \langle r, \Theta \rangle$ *implies* $\overline{s} \, \overline{\mathcal{R}} \, \langle r, \Theta \rangle$, *and*

(ii) *(Linearity)* $\Delta_i \, \overline{\mathcal{R}} \, \langle r_i, \Theta_i \rangle$ *for* $i \in I$ *implies* $(\sum_{i \in I} p_i \cdot \Delta_i) \, \overline{\mathcal{R}} \, (\sum_{i \in I} p_i \cdot \langle r_i, \Theta_i \rangle)$ *for any* $p_i \in [0, 1]$ *(*$i \in I$*) with* $\sum_{i \in I} p_i \leq 1$. $\qquad\square$

An application of Definition 2 to the arrow relation $\xrightarrow{\alpha}$ in a wMDP gives a relation $\overline{(\xrightarrow{\alpha})} \subseteq \mathcal{D}(S) \times (W \times \mathcal{D}(S))$; for convenience we also denote elements of this relation as $\Delta \xrightarrow{\alpha}_w \Theta$. Thus, as source of a relation $\xrightarrow{\alpha}$ we now also allow distributions, and even subdistributions.

Definition 3 (Hyper-derivations). *A hyper-derivation consists of a collection of subdistributions* $\Delta, \Delta_k^{\rightarrow}, \Delta_k^{\times}$, *for* $k \geq 0$, *with the following properties:*

$$
\begin{aligned}
\Delta &= \Delta_0^{\rightarrow} + \Delta_0^{\times} \\
\Delta_0^{\rightarrow} &\xrightarrow{\tau}_{w_0} \Delta_1^{\rightarrow} + \Delta_1^{\times} \\
&\;\;\vdots \\
\Delta_k^{\rightarrow} &\xrightarrow{\tau}_{w_k} \Delta_{k+1}^{\rightarrow} + \Delta_{k+1}^{\times} \\
&\;\;\vdots \\
\Delta' &= \sum_{k=0}^{\infty} \Delta_k^{\times}
\end{aligned}
\tag{1}
$$

Then we call $\Delta' = \sum_{k=0}^{\infty} \Delta_k^{\times}$ *a hyper-derivative of* Δ, *and write* $\Delta \overset{\tau}{\Longrightarrow}_w \Delta'$, *where* $w = \sum_{k\geq 0} w_k$. *Note that in general* $w \in \mathbb{R}_{\geq 0} \cup \{\infty\}$; *that is there is no guarantee that the sum* $\sum_{k\geq 0} w_k$ *has a finite limit.* $\square$

The reader is referred to [5] for a detailed discussion of the concept of hyper-derivation.

Example 1. Consider the wMDP with initial state t_1 discussed in the Introduction. Then we have the following hyper-derivation:

$$\overline{U} = \overline{U} + \varepsilon$$

$$\overline{U} \overset{\tau}{\longrightarrow}_0 \frac{3}{4} \cdot \overline{R} + \frac{1}{4} \cdot \overline{D}$$

$$\frac{3}{4} \cdot \overline{R} \overset{\tau}{\longrightarrow}_{\frac{3}{4}} \frac{3}{4} \cdot \overline{U} + \varepsilon$$

$$\frac{3}{4} \cdot \overline{U} \overset{\tau}{\longrightarrow}_0 (\frac{3}{4})^2 \cdot \overline{R} + (\frac{3}{4})\frac{1}{4} \cdot \overline{D}$$

$$(\frac{3}{4})^2 \cdot \overline{R} \overset{\tau}{\longrightarrow}_{(\frac{3}{4})^2} (\frac{3}{4})^2 \cdot \overline{U} + \varepsilon$$

$$\vdots$$

$$(\frac{3}{4})^k \cdot \overline{U} \overset{\tau}{\longrightarrow}_0 (\frac{3}{4})^{(k+1)} \cdot \overline{R} + (\frac{3}{4})^k \frac{1}{4} \cdot \overline{D}$$

$$(\frac{3}{4})^{(k+1)} \cdot \overline{R} \overset{\tau}{\longrightarrow}_{(\frac{3}{4})^{(k+1)}} (\frac{3}{4})^{(k+1)} \cdot \overline{U} + \varepsilon$$

$$\vdots$$

That is, $\overline{U} \overset{\tau}{\Longrightarrow}_w \sum_{k\geq 0} (\frac{3}{4})^k (\frac{1}{4} \cdot \overline{D})$ where $w = \sum_{k\geq 1} (\frac{3}{4})^k$. However this weight evaluates to 3, while the sum of the sub-distributions is the full point distribution $\overline{D}$. In other words $\overline{U} \overset{\tau}{\Longrightarrow}_3 \overline{D}$. $\square$

Hyper-derivations satisfy the transitivity property: if $\Delta \overset{\tau}{\Longrightarrow}_{w_1} \Delta_1$ and $\Delta_1 \overset{\tau}{\Longrightarrow}_{w_2} \Delta_2$ then $\Delta \overset{\tau}{\Longrightarrow}_{w_1+w_2} \Delta_2$. The generation of a hyper-derivative is in general highly nondeterministic. In (1) of Definition 3 the calculation of $\Delta_{k+1}^{\rightarrow}$ and $\Delta_{k+1}^{\times}$ from $\Delta_k^{\rightarrow}$ involves making nondeterministic choices. But these choices can be governed by *policies*.

Definition 4 (Static policies). *A static policy for a wMDP is a partial function* $\mathsf{pp} : S \rightarrow \mathbb{R}_{\geq 0} \times \mathcal{D}(S)$ *such that if* $\mathsf{pp}(s) = \langle w, \Delta \rangle$ *then* $s \overset{\tau}{\longrightarrow}_w \Delta$. $\square$

Let us write $\Delta \overset{\tau}{\Longrightarrow}_{\mathsf{pp},w} \Delta'$ to mean that the hyper-derivative Δ' is generated with weight w from Δ using the policy pp. Formally this means that in (1) of Definition 3 the weights w_k and subdistributions $\Delta_k^{\rightarrow}$, $\Delta_k^{\times}$ are calculated as follows:

- $s \in \lceil \Delta_k^{\times} \rceil$ if and only if $\mathsf{pp}(s)$ is undefined
- $s \in \lceil \Delta_k^{\rightarrow} \rceil$ if and only if $\mathsf{pp}(s)$ is defined
- $\langle w_{k+1}, \Delta_{k+1}^{\rightarrow} + \Delta_{k+1}^{\times} \rangle = \sum_{s \in \lceil \Delta_k^{\rightarrow} \rceil} \Delta_k^{\rightarrow}(s) \cdot \mathsf{pp}(s)$ for all $k \geq 0$.

Theorem 1 (Finite generability). *Let* $\mathsf{pp}_1, ..., \mathsf{pp}_n$ ($n \geq 1$) *be all the static policies in a finitary wMDP. Suppose* $\Delta \overset{\tau}{\Longrightarrow}_{\mathsf{pp}_i, w_i} \Delta_i'$ *and* $w_i < \infty$ *for all* $1 \leq i \leq n$. *If* $\Delta \overset{\tau}{\Longrightarrow}_w \Delta'$ *then there are probabilities* p_i *for all* $1 \leq i \leq n$ *with* $\sum_{i=1}^n p_i = 1$ *such that* $\langle w, \Delta' \rangle = \sum_{i=1}^n p_i \cdot \langle w_i, \Delta_i' \rangle$. $\square$

In later developments it will be important to rule out the possibility of hyper-derivatives generating an infinite weight.

Definition 5. *A wMDP is* convergent *if* $\bar{s} \overset{\tau}{\Longrightarrow}_w \varepsilon$ *for no state s and weight w; in other words there is no divergent internal computation from any state. A wMDP is* bounded *if it is finitary and whenever* $\Delta \overset{\tau}{\Longrightarrow}_w \Delta'$ *then* $w \in \mathbb{R}_{\geq 0}$. □

A simple source of unboundedness is divergence. Consider the trivial wMDP consisting of one state s and one arrow $s \overset{\tau}{\longrightarrow}_1 \bar{s}$. This is not a bounded wMDP because $\bar{s} \overset{\tau}{\Longrightarrow}_\infty \bar{s}$. In fact for finitary wMDPs, this is the only source of unboundedness:

Theorem 2. *Every finitary convergent wMDP is also bounded.* □

The proof of the above theorem relies on Theorem 1. Another important consequence of Theorem 1 is the following.

Corollary 1. *In a bounded wMDP, for every Δ the set $\{\langle w, \Delta' \rangle \mid \Delta \overset{\tau}{\Longrightarrow}_w \Delta'\}$ is compact, in the standard Euclidean topology.* □

2.2 (Amortised Weighted) Simulations

Here we assume some wMDP $\langle S, \mathsf{Act}_\tau, \mathbb{R}_{\geq 0}, \longrightarrow \rangle$. Our simulation relation is parametrised on an initial investment $r \in \mathbb{R}_{\geq 0}$ and relates states to distributions, rather than states to states. It also uses *weak* arrow relations, defined using hyper-derivations: we write $\Delta \overset{a}{\Longrightarrow}_w \Theta$ whenever $\Delta \overset{\tau}{\Longrightarrow}_{w_1} \Delta' \overset{a}{\longrightarrow}_{w_2} \Theta' \overset{\tau}{\Longrightarrow}_{w_3} \Theta$, where $w = w_1 + w_2 + w_3$.

Definition 6. *Given a relation $\mathcal{R} \subseteq S \times (\mathbb{R}_{\geq 0} \times \mathcal{D}(S))$, let $\mathcal{S}(\mathcal{R}) \subseteq S \times (\mathbb{R}_{\geq 0} \times \mathcal{D}(S))$ be the relation defined by letting $s\, \mathcal{S}(\mathcal{R}) \langle r, \Theta \rangle$ whenever*

$$s \overset{\alpha}{\longrightarrow}_v \Delta \text{ implies the existence of some } w \text{ and } \Theta' \text{ with } \Theta \overset{\alpha}{\Longrightarrow}_w \Theta' \text{ and } \Delta\, \overline{\mathcal{R}} \langle r{+}w{-}v, \Theta' \rangle.$$

We say $\mathcal{R}$ is an (amortised weighted) simulation if $\mathcal{R} \subseteq \mathcal{S}(\mathcal{R})$. The operator $\mathcal{S}(-)$ is (pointwise) monotonic and so it has a maximal fixpoint, which is also a simulation, and which we denote by $\vartriangleleft$. We often write $s \vartriangleleft_r \Theta$ for $s \vartriangleleft \langle r, \Theta \rangle$ and use $\Delta \sqsubseteq_{sim} \Theta$ to mean that there is some initial investment r such that $\Delta \overline{\vartriangleleft}_r \Theta$. □

The basic idea here is that $s \vartriangleleft_r \Theta$ intuitively means that Θ can simulate the actions of s but with *more benefit*, or at least not less benefit. The parameter r should be viewed as compensation which Θ has accumulated and can be used in local comparisons between the benefits of individual actions. Thus when we simulate $s \overset{\alpha}{\longrightarrow}_v \Delta$ with $\Theta \overset{\alpha}{\Longrightarrow}_w \Theta'$ there are two possibilities:

   (i) $w > v$; here the accumulated compensation is increased from r to $r + (w - v)$. In subsequent rounds this extra compensation may be used to successfully simulate a heavier action with a lighter one.

  (ii) $w \leq v$; here the compensation is decreased from r to $r - (v - w)$.

Finally it is important that $r \geq 0$, and remains greater than or equal to zero, or otherwise the presence of weights would have no effect. Thus in case (ii) if $(v - w) > r$ then the attempted simulation is not successful.

   We now show that with this formal definition of the relation $\sqsubseteq_{sim}$ the various statements asserted in the Introduction are true:

(L-ACT)

$$\alpha_w.(\oplus_{i \in I} p_i \cdot P_i) \xrightarrow{\alpha}_w Dist(\{(p_i, P_i) \mid i \in I\})$$

(L-ALT)

$$\frac{P_1 \xrightarrow{\alpha}_w \Delta}{P_1 + P_2 \xrightarrow{\alpha}_w \Delta}$$

(L-COMM)

$$\frac{P_1 \xrightarrow{a}_{w_1} \Delta_1, \quad P_2 \xrightarrow{\bar{a}}_{w_2} \Delta_2}{P_1 \mid P_2 \xrightarrow{\tau}_w \Delta_1 \mid \Delta_2} \quad w = w_1 + w_2$$

(L-PAR)

$$\frac{P_1 \xrightarrow{\alpha}_w \Delta}{P_1 \mid P_2 \xrightarrow{\alpha}_w \Delta \mid \overline{P_2}}$$

(L-HIDE)

$$\frac{P \xrightarrow{\alpha}_w \Delta}{P \backslash a \xrightarrow{\alpha}_w \Delta \backslash a} \quad \alpha \neq a, \bar{a}$$

(L-DEF)

$$\frac{P_A \xrightarrow{\alpha}_w \Delta}{A \xrightarrow{\alpha}_w \Delta} \quad A \Leftarrow P_A$$

Fig. 1. Weighted actions for CCMDP

Example 2. Consider the first two systems, s_0 and t_0, viewed as wMDPs. Then the relation $\mathcal{R}$ given by $\mathcal{R} = \{(s_0, \langle r, \overline{t_0} \rangle) \mid r \geq 1\} \cup \{(s_d, \langle r, \overline{t_d} \rangle) \mid r \geq 0\}$ is a simulation. Thus $s_0 \vartriangleleft_r \overline{t_0}$ for any $r \geq 1$. As pointed out in [11] this example shows the need for the parametrisation with respect to initial investments r; Because of the weights associated with the action up an initial investment of at least one is required in order for $\overline{t_0}$ to be able to match s_0.

We also have $s_0 \vartriangleleft_r \overline{s_1}$ for any $r \geq 1$ because of the following simulation:
$$\mathcal{R} = \{(s_0, \langle r, \overline{s_1} \rangle) \mid r \geq 1\} \cup \{(s_d, \langle r, \Delta \rangle) \mid r \geq 0\}$$
where Δ is the distribution $\frac{1}{4} \cdot \overline{O} + \frac{3}{4} \cdot \overline{T}$. Note that this is indeed a simulation because $\Delta \xrightarrow{down}_{2.5} \overline{s_1}$. Incidently this example shows the necessity of relating states to distributions, rather than states; no individual state accessible from s_1 can simulate s_d.

Similarly $s_1 \vartriangleleft_r \overline{t_1}$ for every $r \geq 0$ because of the simulation:
$$\mathcal{R} = \{(s_1, \langle r, \overline{t_1} \rangle) \mid r \geq 0\} \cup \{(O, \langle r, \overline{U} \rangle) \mid r \geq 0\} \cup \{(T, \langle r, \overline{U} \rangle) \mid r \geq 0\}$$
This relies on the fact that $\overline{U} \xrightarrow{down}_4 \overline{t_1}$, which follows by transitivity, since we have already seen in Example 1 that $\overline{U} \xrightarrow{\tau}_3 \overline{D}$.

Finally $s_0 \vartriangleleft_2 s_2$ because of the following simulation:
$$\mathcal{R} = \{(s_0, \langle r, \overline{s_2} \rangle) \mid r \geq 2\} \cup \{(s_d, \langle r, \overline{\Delta} \rangle) \mid r \geq 0\}$$
where Δ is the distribution $\frac{1}{4} \cdot \overline{S} + \frac{3}{4} \cdot \overline{T}$. Note that $\Delta \xrightarrow{down}_3 \overline{s_2}$ although it is also possible for it to do the down action for much less benefit. □

The simulation relations $\vartriangleleft_r$ are defined coinductively. But in bounded wMDPS they can also be characterised inductively.

Definition 7. *For every* $k \geq 0$ *we define the relation* $\vartriangleleft^k \subseteq S \times (\mathbb{R}_{\geq 0} \times \mathcal{D}(S))$ *as follows:*
(i) $\vartriangleleft^0 = S \times (\mathbb{R}_{\geq 0} \times \mathcal{D}(S))$
(ii) $\vartriangleleft^{k+1} = \mathcal{S}(\vartriangleleft^k)$ *for every* $k \geq 0$.
Finally we let $\vartriangleleft^\infty$ *be* $\bigcap_{k=0}^{\infty} \vartriangleleft^k$. □

Theorem 3. *In a bounded wMDP, the two relations* $\vartriangleleft$ *and* $\vartriangleleft^\infty$ *coincide.* □

Corollary 1 plays a crucial role in proving the above theorem.

The simplest approach to discussing compositionality is, as in [8], to introduce a process calculus-like syntax for wMDPs. Our calculus, CCMDP, is based on CCS:

$$P ::= \alpha_w.(\oplus_{i \in I} p_i \cdot P_i) \mid P \mid P \mid P + P \mid \mathbf{0} \mid P \backslash a \mid A \tag{2}$$

The main operator is prefixing, $\alpha_w.(\oplus_{i\in I} p_i \cdot P_i)$. Here α is taken from Act_τ, w from $\mathbb{R}_{\geq 0}$, I is a non-empty finite index set and p_i are probabilities satisfying $\sum_{i\in I} p_i = 1$. We also assume a set of definitional constants, ranged over by A, and each such A has a definition associated with it, a process term P_A. We often write these definitions as $A \Leftarrow P_A$.

Intuitively, we view each process term as describing a wMDP. Formally we describe one overarching wMDP where the states are all terms P in the grammar (2) and the weighted actions $P \xrightarrow{\alpha}_w \Delta$ are those which can be derived by the rules in Figure 1; obvious symmetric counterparts to the rules (L-ALT) (L-PAR) are omitted. In rule (L-ACT) we use the obvious notation $\mathcal{D}ist(\{(p_i, P_i) \mid i \in I\})$ for constructing a distribution from the formal term $\oplus_{i\in I} p_i \cdot P_i$. In rules (L-COMM) and (L-PAR) we use an abbreviation for distributing parallel composition over a distribution: e.g. $\Delta_1 \mid \Delta_2$ is the distribution given by $(\Delta_1 \mid \Delta_2)(R) = \Delta_1(P_1) \cdot \Delta_2(P_2)$ if $R = P_1 \mid P_2$ and 0 otherwise. Similar is the hiding operator in (L-HIDE). Note that all of the wMDPs described graphically in the Introduction can be described in CCMDP. In the sequel we will not distinguish between the syntactic term P, its interpretation as a state in the wMDP defined in Figure 1, and the wMDP it induces by considering only those states accessible from it.

Theorem 4 (Compositionality). *The preorders $\overline{\vartriangleleft}_r$, for each $r \in \mathbb{R}_{\geq 0}$, are preserved by each of the operators in the language* CCMDP. □

Example 3. Let P, Q be two processes with $P \vartriangleleft_0 \overline{Q}$. Consider the following processes:
$$U \Leftarrow \tau_0.(\tau_1.U \tfrac{3}{4}\oplus \mathsf{down}_1.Q)$$
$$P' \equiv \mathsf{up}_2.(\mathsf{down}_1.P \tfrac{1}{4}\oplus \mathsf{down}_3.P)$$
$$Q' \equiv \mathsf{up}_2.U$$
By the analysis in Example 1 we know that $\overline{U} \overset{\tau}{\Longrightarrow}_3 \overline{\mathsf{down}_1.Q}$, thus $\overline{U} \overset{\mathsf{down}}{\Longrightarrow}_4 \overline{Q}$. Then it is easy to see that $\mathsf{down}_1.P \vartriangleleft_0 \overline{U}$ and $\mathsf{down}_3.P \vartriangleleft_0 \overline{U}$. It follows from the compositionality of $\overline{\vartriangleleft}_0$ that $(\mathsf{down}_1.P \tfrac{1}{4}\oplus \mathsf{down}_3.P) \overline{\vartriangleleft}_0 \overline{U}$ and furthermore $\overline{P'} \overline{\vartriangleleft}_0 \overline{Q'}$. □

3   A Qualitative Probabilistic Logic

Let Var be a set of variables, ranged over by X. We define the set of formulae as follows:
$$\phi ::= \mathsf{tt} \mid \mathsf{ff} \mid \langle \alpha \rangle_w (\phi_1 \,_p\oplus \phi_2), \ \alpha \in \mathsf{Act}_\tau, w \in \mathbb{R}_{\geq 0}, p \in [0, 1]$$
$$\mid \phi_1 \wedge \phi_2 \mid \phi_1 \vee \phi_2 \mid X \mid \min X. \phi \mid \max X. \phi$$

The two fixpoint operators $\min X. -$ and $\max X. -$ act as binders in the standard manner; we use $\mathcal{L}_Q$ to denote the set of *closed* formulae, that is containing no free variables. As a shorthand, we write $\langle \alpha \rangle_w \phi$ for $\langle \alpha \rangle_w (\phi_1 \oplus \phi')$ for any ϕ'.

Let *Con* denote the set of *configurations*, pairs $\langle r, \Delta \rangle$ where $r \in \mathbb{R}_{\geq 0}$ and $\Delta \in \mathcal{D}(S)$, with S denoting the state space of some wMDP. Intuitively this represents a system which has accumulated compensation r which it can use to satisfy formulae in the future. A formula from $\mathcal{L}_Q$ determines a set of configurations, those which satisfy it; their calculation is standard, apart from the novel qualitative possibility operator. An environment ρ is a function that maps each variable in Var to a subset of *Con*. For a set $V \subseteq \mathbb{R}_{\geq 0} \times \mathcal{D}(S)$ and a variable $X \in$ Var, we write $\rho[X \mapsto V]$ for the environment that maps X to V and Y to $\rho(Y)$ for all $Y \neq X$. The semantics of a formula ϕ is given by the set of configurations $\llbracket \phi \rrbracket_\rho$ defined as follows:

- $[\![tt]\!]_\rho = Con,$ $[\![ff]\!]_\rho = \emptyset$
- $[\![\phi_1 \wedge \phi_2]\!]_\rho = [\![\phi_1]\!]_\rho \cap [\![\phi_2]\!]_\rho,$ $[\![\phi_1 \vee \phi_2]\!]_\rho = [\![\phi_1]\!]_\rho \cup [\![\phi_2]\!]_\rho$
- $[\![\langle \alpha \rangle_v (\phi_1 \,_p\oplus \phi_2)]\!]_\rho = \{\langle r, \Delta \rangle \mid \Delta \overset{\alpha}{\Longrightarrow}_w \Theta$ where
  $\langle (r + w - v), \Theta \rangle = \langle r_1, \Theta_1 \rangle \,_p\oplus \langle r_2, \Theta_2 \rangle$ and $\langle r_i, \Theta_i \rangle \in [\![\phi_i]\!]_\rho \}$
- $[\![X]\!]\rho = \rho(X)$
- $[\![\min X. \phi]\!]_\rho = \bigcap \{V \mid [\![\phi]\!]_{\rho[X \mapsto V]} \subseteq V\}$
- $[\![\max X. \phi]\!]_\rho = \bigcup \{V \mid V \subseteq [\![\phi]\!]_{\rho[X \mapsto V]}\}$

When ϕ is closed the set $[\![\phi]\!]_\rho$ is independent of the environment ρ, and in this case we use the standard notation $C \models \phi$ in place of $C \in [\![\phi]\!]$.

The novel qualitative formula $\langle \alpha \rangle_v (\phi_1 \,_p\oplus \phi_2)$ represents the ability to do an α action with benefit at least v and then probabilistically satisfy the property $\phi_1 \,_p\oplus \phi_2$; we have $\langle r, \Delta \rangle \models \langle \alpha \rangle_v (\phi_1 \,_p\oplus \phi_2)$ whenever $\Delta \overset{\alpha}{\Longrightarrow}_w \Theta_1 \,_p\oplus \Theta_2$ and $\langle r_i, \Theta_i \rangle \models \phi_i$ for some r_i satisfying $(r + w - v) = p \cdot r_1 + (1 - p) \cdot r_2$. Here there are two possibilities:

(i) $v > w$: here the compensation comes into play. The action may be accepted despite being too heavy but the compensation for future use is reduced from r to $r - (v - w)$; this is split into r_1, r_2 via the probability p. Note this possibility will only exist if $r - (v - w) \geq 0$.

(ii) $v \leq w$: The action is accepted and then the compensation is increased from r to $r + (w - v)$, which again is split proportionally into r_1, r_2, to satisfy ϕ_1 and ϕ_2 respectively.

Example 4. Both liveness and safety properties can be expressed in $\mathcal{L}_Q$. For example, suppose AB denote the formula $\langle a \rangle_0 (\langle b \rangle_{10} tt \,_{\frac{9}{10}}\oplus tt)$ and C is a configuration. Then $C \models AB$ means that C can perform an a action such that at least 90% of the time it can subsequently perform a b action with a benefit of at least 10. So the formula

$$\min X. \langle up \rangle_0 (\langle down \rangle_{10} X \,_{\frac{9}{10}}\oplus tt) \vee \langle up \rangle_0 X$$

expresses the liveness property of being able to perform a sequence of up actions to arrive at a state where at least 90% of the time a down action for benefit at least 10 can be performed. On the other hand, the formula

$$\max X. \langle up \rangle_0 (\langle down \rangle_{10} X \,_{\frac{9}{10}}\oplus tt) \wedge \langle stay \rangle_0 X$$

expresses the safety property of always being able to perform a stay action and at the same time to perform an up action to arrive at a state where at least 90% of the time a down action for benefit at least 10 can be performed.   □

Let $\mathcal{L}_Q(r, \Delta) = \{\phi \in \mathcal{L}_Q \mid \langle r, \Delta \rangle \models \phi\}$. We have the following logical characterisation of simulations.

Theorem 5 (Logical characterisation). *In a bounded wMDP, $s \lhd_r \Theta$ if and only if $\mathcal{L}_Q(0, \bar{s}) \subseteq \mathcal{L}_Q(r, \Theta)$.*   □

The proof of Theorem 5 exploits Theorem 3, which says that $\lhd$ can be approximated by a family of stratified relations $\lhd^k$ for $k \in \mathbb{N}$. So it suffices to prove that each approximant $\lhd^k$ is completely determined by the finite fragment of the qualitative probabilistic logic.

The import of Theorem 5 is that if $s \lhd_r \Theta$ does not hold then there is a formula ϕ from $\mathcal{L}_Q$ which $\bar{s}$ satisfies but Θ does not. Furthermore, it turns out that in a bounded wMDP this distinguishing formula will always be finite; that is contains no occurrence of a

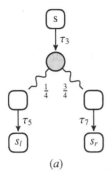
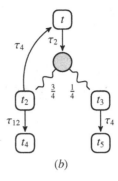

$$(a) \qquad\qquad\qquad (b)$$

Fig. 2. Testing systems

fixpoint operator. For example, $\overline{s_2} \not\blacktriangleleft_0 \overline{s_0}$, where these are defined in the Introduction, because of the distinguishing formula $\langle \mathsf{up}\rangle_1(\langle \mathsf{down}\rangle_6\mathsf{tt} \; {}_1\!\oplus\; \langle \mathsf{down}\rangle_2\mathsf{tt})$.

Our logic is expressive enough so that the whole behaviour of a state in a bounded wMDP can be captured by one formula in the logic:

Theorem 6 (Characteristic formula). *In a bounded wMDP, for every state s there is a characteristic formula* $\phi(s) \in \mathcal{L}_Q$ *such that* $s \vartriangleleft_r \Theta$ *if and only if* $\langle r, \Theta \rangle \models \phi(s)$.   □

For example, the state s_1 in the Introduction has the following characteristic formula:
$$\phi(s_1) \;=\; \max X.\, \langle \mathsf{up}\rangle_2(\langle \mathsf{down}\rangle_1 X \; {}_{\frac{1}{4}}\!\oplus\; \langle \mathsf{down}\rangle_3 X).$$

4   Benefits Based Testing

Standard theories of testing involve the idea of applying tests to processes and seeing if the result is a *success*. With the presence of weights in wMDPs we have a more elementary way of testing; we run them in parallel with other wMDPs and calculate the possible benefits which can be accrued. Then two wMDPs can be compared by examining the resulting sets of possible accrued benefits.

Consider the simple fully probabilistic wMDP in Figure 2(a), which results from running the test $T = \overline{\mathsf{up}}_1.\mathsf{down}_4.\,\mathbf{0}$ in parallel with the system s_1 from the Introduction. Formally this is the sub-wMDP of the wMDP $(\overline{s_1} \mid T)$ obtained by concentrating on the internal actions τ_w; this is just the wMDP represented by $(\overline{s_1} \mid T)\backslash\mathsf{Act}$ that we denote by $\overline{s_1} \parallel T$. Every time the experiment runs we get the initial benefit 3; three-quarters of the time we also get the benefit 7 while a quarter of time we get 5. So the total benefit is $3 + \frac{3}{4} \cdot 7 + \frac{1}{4} \cdot 5 = 9.5$. In the presence of nondeterminism there will in general be a set of possible benefits, depending on the way in which the nondeterminism is resolved. Traditionally this resolution is expressed in terms of a scheduler, or adversary, which for each state decides which of its successors is chosen for execution, with the resulting set of benefits consequently depending on the choice of scheduler. Here we take a more abstract approach, following [5], and essentially allow arbitrary schedulers.

Definition 8 (Extreme derivatives). *For any* Δ *in a wMDP we write* $\Delta \overset{\tau}{\Longrightarrow}_w \Phi$ *if*

- $\Delta \Longrightarrow_w \Phi$, *that is* Φ *is a hyper-derivative of* Δ
- Φ *is* stable, *that is* $s \overset{\tau}{\nrightarrow}$ *for every s in* $\lceil \Phi \rceil$

where $s \stackrel{\tau}{\nrightarrow}$ means that s cannot enable any τ-transition. We say Φ is an extreme
derivative of Δ, with weight w.   □

Intuitively every extreme derivation $\Delta \stackrel{\tau}{\Longrightarrow}_w \Phi$ represents a computation from the initial
distribution Δ guided by some implicit scheduler. For example, consider the hyper-
derivation of an extreme derivative:

$$
\begin{aligned}
\Delta &= \Delta_0^{\rightarrow} + \Delta_0^{\times} \\
\Delta_0^{\rightarrow} &\stackrel{\tau}{\longrightarrow}_{w_0} \Delta_1^{\rightarrow} + \Delta_1^{\times} \\
&\vdots \\
\Delta_k^{\rightarrow} &\stackrel{\tau}{\longrightarrow}_{w_k} \Delta_{k+1}^{\rightarrow} + \Delta_{k+1}^{\times} \\
&\vdots \\
\Phi &= \sum_{k=0}^{\infty} \Delta_k^{\times}
\end{aligned}
\tag{3}
$$

where $w = \sum_{k \geq 0} w_k$. Initially, since $\Delta_0^{\times}$ is stable, $\Delta_0^{\rightarrow}$ contains (in its support) all states
which can proceed with the computation. The implicit scheduler decides for each of
these states which step to take, cumulating in the first move, $\Delta_0^{\rightarrow} \stackrel{\tau}{\longrightarrow}_{w_0} \Delta_1^{\rightarrow} + \Delta_1^{\times}$. At an
arbitrary stage, $\Delta_k^{\rightarrow}$ contains all states which can continue; the scheduler decides which
step to take for each individual state and the overall result of the schedulers decision for
this stage is captured in the step $\Delta_k^{\rightarrow} \stackrel{\tau}{\longrightarrow}_{w_k} \Delta_{k+1}^{\rightarrow} + \Delta_{k+1}^{\times}$.

Example 5. Referring to Figure 2(a) it is easy to see that $\overline{s}$ has a unique (degenerate)
extreme derivative, $\overline{s_1} \stackrel{\tau}{\Longrightarrow}_{9.5} (\frac{1}{4}\overline{s_l} + \frac{3}{4}\overline{s_r})$, intuitively representing the unique weighted
computation from $\overline{s_1}$. However, consider the wMDP in Figure 2(b), in which there is
a nondeterministic choice from state t_2; here the extreme derivatives generated from $\overline{t}$,
and their associated weights, will depend on the choices made during the computation
by the implicit scheduler.

First suppose that the scheduler uses the static policy which maps t_2 to $\langle 12, \overline{t_4} \rangle$. Then
it is easy to see that the generated extreme derivative, which is degenerate, is $\overline{t} \stackrel{\tau}{\Longrightarrow}_{12}$
$(\frac{3}{4}\overline{t_4} + \frac{1}{4}\overline{t_5})$. However using the static policy which maps t_2 to $\langle 4, \overline{t_1} \rangle$ we generate, using
(3), a non-degenerate extreme derivative; after some calculations this can be seen to be
$\overline{t_1} \stackrel{\tau}{\Longrightarrow}_{24} \overline{t_5}$.

However there are many other possible implicit schedulers, for example at different
times in the computations employing either of these static policies, or even choosing
nondeterministically between them. But these are the only static policies and therefore
we know from Theorem 1 that if $\overline{t_1} \stackrel{\tau}{\Longrightarrow}_w \Delta$ then w must take the form $p \cdot 12 + (1-p) \cdot 24$
for some $0 \leq p \leq 1$. That is the set of benefits which can be generated from $\overline{t_1}$ is
$\{24 - 12 \cdot p \mid 0 \leq p \leq 1\}$.   □

Definition 9 (May testing). *In a wMDP, for any $\Delta \in \mathcal{D}(S)$, let*

$$\mathbf{Benefits}(\Delta) = \{\, w \in \mathbb{R}_{\geq 0} \mid \Delta \overset{\tau}{\Longrightarrow}_w \Phi, \text{ for some } \Phi \in \mathcal{D}_{sub}(S)\,\}$$

Benefit sets are compared as follows:

$$B_1 \leq^r_{\mathrm{Ho}} B_2 \text{ if for every } r_1 \in B_1 \text{ there exists some } r_2 \in B_2 \text{ such that } r_1 \leq r + r_2$$

For any two distributions Δ, Θ we write $\Delta \sqsubseteq^r_{may} \Theta$ if for every finite (testing) process T, **Benefits**$(\Delta \parallel T) \leq^r_{\mathrm{Ho}}$ **Benefits**$(\Theta \parallel T)$. *We write $\Delta \sqsubseteq_{may} \Theta$ to mean that there is some $r \in \mathbb{R}_{\geq 0}$ such that $\Delta \sqsubseteq^r_{may} \Theta$.*   □

This interpretation of processes is optimistic; $\Delta \sqsubseteq^r_{may} \Theta$ means that, given the investment r, every possible benefit produced by Δ can in principle be improved upon by Θ.

Note that in a bounded wMDP **Benefits**(Δ) cannot contain ∞. Moreover we can show that the parallel composition of a bounded wMDP with a finite wMDP is also bounded. This means that if we confine our attention to bounded wMDPs then benefit sets will always only contain real numbers. One way of restricting to bounded wMDPS is, by Theorem 2, to only use finitary convergent wMDPs.

Our first result shows that simulations can be used as a sound proof technique for this semantics:

Theorem 7 (Soundness). $\Delta \overline{\lessdot}_r \Theta$ *implies* $\Delta \sqsubseteq^r_{may} \Theta$.   □

The converse is not true in general:

Example 6. Consider the two distributions $\Delta = \mathbf{0} \,_{\frac{1}{2}}\!\oplus a_1.\mathbf{0}$ and $\Theta = \tau_2.\mathbf{0} \,_{\frac{1}{2}}\!\oplus a_0.\mathbf{0}$. It is easy to see that $\Delta \overline{\lessdot}_0 \Theta$ because there is no way to decompose Θ into $\Theta_1 \,_{\frac{1}{2}}\!\oplus \Theta_2$ for some Θ_1, Θ_2 such that $a_1.\mathbf{0} \lessdot_0 \Theta_2$. However, one can show that $\Delta \sqsubseteq^0_{may} \Theta$. This follows from the observations below:

  (i) For all weights w and tests T, **Benefits**$(\tau_w.\mathbf{0} \parallel T) = \{v + w \mid v \in$ **Benefits**$(\mathbf{0} \parallel T)\}$.
  (ii) For all weights w and tests T, **Benefits**$(a_w.\mathbf{0} \parallel T) \leq^w_{\mathrm{Ho}}$ **Benefits**$(a_0.\mathbf{0} \parallel T)$.

Both assertions can be proved by structural induction on T.

Now suppose $w \in$ **Benefits**$(\Delta \parallel T)$ for an arbitrary test T. There is some stable derivative Γ such that $\Delta \parallel T \overset{\tau}{\Longrightarrow}_w \Gamma$. It can be shown that there are some $w_1, w_2, \Gamma_1, \Gamma_2$ with $\mathbf{0} \parallel T \overset{\tau}{\Longrightarrow}_{w_1} \Gamma_1$, $a_1.\mathbf{0} \parallel T \overset{\tau}{\Longrightarrow}_{w_2} \Gamma_2$, $w = \frac{1}{2}w_1 + \frac{1}{2}w_2$, and $\Gamma = \frac{1}{2} \cdot \Gamma_1 + \frac{1}{2} \cdot \Gamma_2$, where both Γ_1 and Γ_2 are stable. In other words, we have $w_1 \in$ **Benefits**$(\mathbf{0} \parallel T)$ and $w_2 \in$ **Benefits**$(a_1.\mathbf{0} \parallel T)$. By (i) above, $w_1 + 2 \in$ **Benefits**$(\tau_2.\mathbf{0} \parallel T)$; by (ii) above, there exists some $w'_2 \in$ **Benefits**$(a_0.\mathbf{0} \parallel T)$ with $w_2 \leq w'_2 + 1$. Thus, we can infer that

$$\begin{aligned}
w &= \tfrac{1}{2}w_1 + \tfrac{1}{2}w_2 \\
&< \tfrac{1}{2}(w_1 + 2) + \tfrac{1}{2}(w_2 - 1) \\
&\leq \tfrac{1}{2}(w_1 + 2) + \tfrac{1}{2}w'_2
\end{aligned}$$

It turns out that $\frac{1}{2}(w_1 + 2) + \frac{1}{2}w'_2 \in$ **Benefits**$(\Theta \parallel T)$. Therefore, we have

$$\mathbf{Benefits}(\Delta \parallel T) \leq^0_{\mathrm{Ho}} \mathbf{Benefits}(\Theta \parallel T).$$

Since this reasoning is carried out for an arbitrary test T, it follows that $\Delta \sqsubseteq^0_{may} \Theta$.   □

Nevertheless we do have a testing characterisation for the unannotated simulation preorder:

Theorem 8 (Testing characterisation). *In a bounded wMDP,* $\bar{s} \sqsubseteq_{may} \Theta$ *if and only if* $\bar{s} \sqsubseteq_{sim} \Theta$.

Proof (Outline). One direction follows from Theorem 7. For the converse we carry out the proof in two steps: we first prove that $\bar{s} \sqsubseteq_{may}^{r} \Theta$ implies the existence of some compensation $r' \geq r$ with $\mathcal{L}_Q(0, \bar{s}) \subseteq \mathcal{L}_Q(r', \Theta)$, then appeal to Theorem 5. In the first step we proceed by constructing, for each formula ϕ, a *characteristic test* $T(\phi)$, such that if a process satisfies ϕ then it passes test $T(\phi)$ with some threshold benefit. $\square$

An alternative approach to testing would be to use one special action ω in a test to report success and when applying such a test to a system to report the weighted average of the weight of each path leading to an occurrence of the success action; this we refer to as *expected benefits testing*. Here we will not give the formal definition of how these *expected benefits* are calculated, which is provided in [4], but simply give an informal argument to show that our simulation preorder is not sound with respect to it.

Example 7 (Simulation is unsound for expected benefits testing). Consider the following processes:
$$P = \tau_2.(\mathbf{0}_{\frac{1}{4}} \oplus a_0.\mathbf{0})$$
$$Q = \tau_1.(\tau_2.(\mathbf{0}_{\frac{1}{2}} \oplus a_0.\mathbf{0})_{\frac{1}{2}} \oplus a_0.\mathbf{0})$$
It is easy to see that $P \lhd_0 Q$ as the transition $P \overset{\tau}{\longrightarrow}_2 \mathbf{0}_{\frac{1}{4}} \oplus a_0.\mathbf{0}$ can be simulated by the hyper-derivative $Q \overset{\tau}{\Longrightarrow}_2 \mathbf{0}_{\frac{1}{4}} \oplus a_0.\mathbf{0}$. Now let T be the test $\bar{a}_0.\omega$. Both $P \parallel T$ and $Q \parallel T$ give rise to fully probabilistic wMDPs. The unique expected benefit resulted from $P \parallel T$ is $\frac{1}{4} \cdot 0 + \frac{3}{4} \cdot 2$, i.e. $\frac{3}{2}$. On the other hand, the unique expected benefit obtained from $Q \parallel T$ is $\frac{1}{2} \cdot 1 + \frac{1}{2}(\frac{1}{2} \cdot 0 + \frac{1}{2} \cdot 3)$, i.e. $\frac{5}{4}$. As $\{\frac{3}{2}\} \not\sqsubseteq_{Ho}^0 \{\frac{5}{4}\}$, we have that P is not related to Q under expected benefits may testing; thus $\lhd$ is unsound for expected benefits testing. Note that if we consider total benefits, then **Benefits**$(P \parallel T) = \{2\} = $ **Benefits**$(Q \parallel T)$. $\square$

5   Concluding Remarks

We have proposed the model of weighted Markov decision processes for compositional reasoning about the behaviour of systems with uncertainty. Amortised weighted simulation is coinductively defined to be a behavioural preorder for comparing different wMDPs. It is shown to be a precongruence relation with respect to all structural operators for constructing wMDPs from components. For finitary convergent wMDPs, we have also given logical and testing characterisations of the simulation preorder: it can be completely determined by a qualitative probabilistic logic and for each system we can find a characteristic formula to capture its behaviour; the simulation preorder also coincides with a notion of may testing preorder.

The dual of may testing is must testing. It would be interesting to investigate the must preorder given by our testing approach. We leave it as future work to provide a coinductive formulation of the preorder and study its logical characterisations.

There is a very limited literature on compositional theories of Markov decision processes particularly in the presence of weights. There is however an extensive literature on probabilistic variations of bisimulation equivalence for Markov chains; see Chapter 10 of [1] for an elementary introduction and [10] for a survey. Bisimulation equivalence has also been defined in [8] for *Interactive Markov Chains (IMCs)*, and it is shown to be compositional, in the sense of our Theorem 4: it is preserved by the operators of a process calculus interpreted as IMCs. Bisimulation and testing equivalence for Markovian process algebras are also investigated in [9,2], but the analysis was mainly restricted to models free of nondeterminism. Recently a combination of probabilistic automata and IMCs has been studied in [7], where a notation of weak bisimulation is proposed. Since time rates are treated essentially as action names, some intuitively equivalent processes are differentiated by the weak bisimulation.

There is also an extensive literature on weighted automata [6], and probabilistic variations have also been studied [3]. However there the focus is on traditional language theoretic issues, rather than our primary concern, compositionality.

References

1. Baier, C., Katoen, J.-P.: Principles of Model Checking. The MIT Press (2008)
2. Bernardo, M., Cleaveland, R.: A Theory of Testing for Markovian Processes. In: Palamidessi, C. (ed.) CONCUR 2000. LNCS, vol. 1877, pp. 305–319. Springer, Heidelberg (2000)
3. Chatterjee, K., Doyen, L., Henzinger, T.A.: Probabilistic Weighted Automata. In: Bravetti, M., Zavattaro, G. (eds.) CONCUR 2009. LNCS, vol. 5710, pp. 244–258. Springer, Heidelberg (2009)
4. Deng, Y., Hennessy, M.: Compositional reasoning for Markov decision processes (full version) (2010), `http://basics.sjtu.edu.cn/~yuxin/temp/mdp.pdf`
5. Deng, Y., van Glabbeek, R., Hennessy, M., Morgan, C.: Testing Finitary Probabilistic Processes. In: Bravetti, M., Zavattaro, G. (eds.) CONCUR 2009. LNCS, vol. 5710, pp. 274–288. Springer, Heidelberg (2009)
6. Droste, M., Kuich, W., Vogler, H. (eds.): Handbook of Weighted Automata. Springer, Heidelberg (2009)
7. Eisentraut, E., Hermanns, H., Zhang, L.: On probabilistic automata in continuous time. In: Proc. LICS 2010, pp. 342–351. IEEE Computer Society (2010)
8. Hermanns, H. (ed.): Interactive Markov Chains. LNCS, vol. 2428. Springer, Heidelberg (2002)
9. Hillston, J.: A Compositional Approach to Performance Modelling. Cambridge University Press (1996)
10. Jonsson, B., Larsen, K.G., Wang, Y.: Probabilistic Extensions of Process Algebras. In: Handbook of Process Algebra, pp. 685–710. Elsevier (2001)
11. Kiehn, A., Arun-Kumar, S.: Amortised Bisimulations. In: Wang, F. (ed.) FORTE 2005. LNCS, vol. 3731, pp. 320–334. Springer, Heidelberg (2005)
12. Puterman, M.: Markov Decision Processes. Wiley (1994)
13. Rutten, J., Kwiatkowska, M., Norman, G., Parker, D.: Mathematical Techniques for Analyzing Concurrent and Probabilistic Systems. American Mathematical Society (2004)
14. Segala, R.: Modeling and verification of randomized distributed real-time systems. Technical Report MIT/LCS/TR-676, PhD thesis, MIT, Dept. of EECS (1995)

Safe Locking for Multi-threaded Java[*]

Einar Broch Johnsen, Thi Mai Thuong Tran, Olaf Owe, and Martin Steffen

Department of Informatics, University of Oslo, Norway
{einarj,tmtran,olaf,msteffen}@ifi.uio.no

Abstract. There are many mechanisms for concurrency control in high-level programming languages. In Java, the original mechanism for concurrency control, based on synchronized blocks, is lexically scoped. For more flexible control, Java 5 introduced non-lexical operators, supporting lock primitives on re-entrant locks. These operators may lead to run-time errors and unwanted behavior; e.g., taking a lock without releasing it, which could lead to a deadlock, or trying to release a lock without owning it. This paper develops a static type and effect system to prevent the mentioned lock errors for non-lexical locks. The effect type system is formalized for an object-oriented calculus which supports non-lexical lock handling. Based on an operational semantics, we prove soundness of the effect type analysis. Challenges in the design of the effect type system are dynamic creation of threads, objects, and especially of locks, aliasing of lock references, passing of lock references between threads, and reentrant locks as found in Java.

1 Introduction

With the advent of multiprocessors, multi-core architectures, and distributed web-based programs, effective parallel programming models and suitable language constructs are needed. Many concurrency control mechanisms for high-level programming languages have been developed, with different syntactic representations. One option is lexical scoping; for instance, `synchronized` blocks in Java, or protected regions designated by an *atomic* keyword. However, there is a trend towards more flexible concurrency control where protected critical regions can be started and finished freely. Two proposals supporting flexible, non-lexical concurrency control are lock handling via the `ReentrantLock` class in Java 5 [13] and transactional memory, as formalized in *Transactional Featherweight Java* (TFJ) [9]. While Java 5 uses `lock` and `unlock` operators to acquire and release re-entrant locks, TFJ uses `onacid` and `commit` operators to start and terminate transactions. Even if these proposals take quite different approaches towards dealing with concurrency —"pessimistic" or lock-based vs. "optimistic" or based on transactions— the additional flexibility of non-lexical control mechanisms comes at a similar price: *improper use leads to run-time exceptions and unwanted behavior.*

A static *type and effect* system for TFJ to prevent unsafe usage of transactions was introduced in [12]. This paper applies that approach to a calculus which supports *lock*

---

[*] The author list is written in alphabetical order. The work is partly funded by the EU project FP7-231620 HATS: Highly Adaptable and Trustworthy Software using Formal Models (http://www.hats-project.eu).

F. Arbab and M. Sirjani (Eds.): FSEN 2011, LNCS 7141, pp. 158–173, 2012.

handling as in Java 5. Our focus is on *lock errors*; i.e., taking a lock without releasing it, which could lead to a deadlock, and trying to release a lock without owning it.

Generalizing our approach for TFJ to lock handling, however, is not straightforward: In particular, locks are re-entrant and have identities available at the program level. Our analysis technique needs to take identities into account to keep track of which lock is taken by which thread and how many times it has been taken. Furthermore, the analysis needs to handle dynamic lock creation, aliasing, and passing of locks between threads. As transactions have no identity at program level and are not re-entrant, these problems are absent in [12]. Fortunately, they can be solved under reasonable assumptions on lock usage. In particular, aliasing can be dealt with due to the following observation: for the analysis it is sound to assume that all variables are non-aliases, even if they may be aliases at run-time, provided that, per variable, each interaction history with a lock is lock error free in itself. This observation allows us to treat soundness of lock-handling *compositionally*, i.e., individually per thread. So the contribution of the paper is a static analysis preventing lock-errors for non-lexical use of re-entrant locks. A clear separation of local and shared memory allows the mentioned simple treatment of aliasing.

The paper is organized as follows. Sections 2 and 3 define the abstract syntax and the operational semantics of our language with non-lexically scoped locks. Section 4 presents the type and effect system for safe locking, and Section 5 shows the correctness of the type and effect system. Sections 6 and 7 conclude with related and future work.

2   A Concurrent, Object-Oriented Calculus

Consider a variant of Featherweight Java (FJ) [7] with concurrency and explicit lock support, but without inheritance and type casts. Table 1 shows the abstract syntax of this calculus. A program consists of a sequence $\vec{D}$ of class definitions. Vector notation refers to a list or sequence of entities; e.g., $\vec{D}$ is a sequence $D_1, \ldots, D_n$ of class definitions and $\vec{x}$ a sequence of variables. A class definition class $C(\vec{f}:\vec{T})\{\vec{f}:\vec{T};\vec{M}\}$ consists of a name C, fields $\vec{f}$ with corresponding types $\vec{T}$ (assuming that all f_i's are different), and method definitions $\vec{M}$. Fields get values when instantiating an object; $\vec{f}$ are the formal parameters of the constructor C. When writing $\vec{f}:\vec{T}$ (and in analogous situations) we assume that the lengths of $\vec{f}$ and $\vec{T}$ correspond, and let $f_i : T_i$ refer to the i'th pair of field and type. We omit such assumptions when they are clear from the context. For simplicity, the calculus does not support overloading; each class has exactly one constructor and all fields and methods defined in a class have different names. A method definition $m(\vec{x}:\vec{T})\{t\} : T$ consists of a name m, the typed formal parameters $\vec{x}:\vec{T}$, the method body t, and the declaration of the return type T. Types are class names C, (unspecified) basic types B, and Unit for the unit value. Locks have type L, which corresponds to Java's Lock-interface, i.e., the type for instances of the class ReentrantLock.

The syntax distinguishes expressions e and threads t. A thread t is either a value v, the terminated thread stop, error representing exceptional termination, or sequential composition. The let-construct generalizes sequential composition: in let $x:T = e$ in t, e is first executed (and may have side-effects), the resulting value after termination is bound to x and then t is executed with x appropriately substituted. (Standard sequential composition $e;t$ is syntactic sugar for let $x:T = e$ in t where x does not occur

Table 1. Abstract syntax

$$
\begin{array}{lll}
D ::= \text{class } C(\vec{f}{:}\vec{T})\{\vec{f}{:}\vec{T};\vec{M}\} & & \text{class definitions} \\
M ::= m(\vec{x}{:}\vec{T})\{t\} : T & & \text{methods} \\
t ::= \text{stop} \mid \text{error} \mid v \mid \text{let } x{:}T = e \text{ in } t & & \text{threads} \\
e ::= t \mid \text{if } v \text{ then } e \text{ else } e \mid v.f \mid v.f := v \mid v.m(\vec{v}) \mid \text{new } C(\vec{v}) & & \text{expressions} \\
\quad\mid \text{spawn } t \mid \text{new } L \mid v.\,\text{lock} \mid v.\,\text{unlock} \mid \text{if } v.\,\text{trylock then } e \text{ else } e & & \\
v ::= r \mid x \mid () & & \text{values} \\
T ::= C \mid B \mid \text{Unit} \mid L & &
\end{array}
$$

free in t.) Values v are expressions that can not be evaluated further. We ignore standard values like booleans and integers, so values are references r, variables x (including this), and the unit value (). We distinguish references o to objects and references l to locks. This distinction is for notational convenience; the type system can distinguish both kinds of references. Conditionals if v then e_1 else e_2, field access $v.f$, field update $v_1.f := v_2$, method calls $v.m(\vec{v})$ and object instantiation new $C(\vec{v})$ are standard. The language is multi-threaded: spawn t starts a new thread which evaluates t in parallel with the spawning thread. The expression new L dynamically creates a new lock, like instantiating Java's ReentrantLock class. The operations $v.$ lock and $v.$ unlock denote lock acquisition and release. The conditional if $v.$ trylock then e_1 else e_2 checks the availability of a lock v for the current thread, in which case v is taken.

3   Operational Semantics

The operational semantics of the calculus is split into steps at the local level of one thread and at the global level. We focus here on global rules which concern more than one sequential thread or lock-manipulating steps. See [10] for the full semantics. Local configurations are written as $\sigma \vdash e$ and local reduction steps as $\sigma \vdash e \rightarrow \sigma' \vdash e'$, where σ is the *heap*, a finite mapping from references to objects and locks. Re-entrant locks are needed for recursive method calls. A lock is either *free* (represented by the value 0), or *taken* by a thread p (represented by $p(n)$ for $n \geq 1$ where n specifies that p holds the lock n times). A global configuration $\sigma \vdash P$ consists of a shared heap σ and a "set" of processes, where the processes are given by the following grammar:

$$ P ::= \mathbf{0} \mid P \parallel P \mid p\langle t \rangle \qquad \text{processes/named threads} \tag{1} $$

$\mathbf{0}$ represents the empty process, $P_1 \parallel P_2$ the parallel composition of P_1 and P_2, and $p\langle t \rangle$ a process (or named thread), where p is the process identity and t the thread being executed. The binary $\parallel$-operator is associative and commutative with $\mathbf{0}$ as neutral element. Furthermore, thread identities must be *unique*. Global steps are of the form

$$ \sigma \vdash P \rightarrow \sigma' \vdash P' . \tag{2} $$

The corresponding rules are given in Table 2. Rule R-LIFT lifts the local reduction steps to the global level and R-PAR expresses interleaving of the parallel composition of threads. Spawning a new thread is covered in rule R-SPAWN. The new thread gets a fresh identity and runs in parallel with the spawning thread. Rule R-NEWL creates a new lock and extends the heap with a fresh identity l and the lock is initially free. The lock can be taken, if it is free, or a thread already holding the lock can execute the locking statement once more, increasing the lock-count by one (cf. R-LOCK$_1$ and R-LOCK$_2$). The R-TRYLOCK-rules describe conditional lock taking. If the lock l is available for a thread, the expression l. trylock evaluates to true and the first branch of the conditional is taken (cf. the first two R-TRYLOCK-rules). Additionally, the thread acquires the lock. If the lock is unavailable, the else-branch is taken and the lock is unchanged (cf. R-TRYLOCK$_3$). Unlocking works dually and only the thread holding the lock can execute the unlock-statement on that lock. If the lock has value 1, the lock is free afterwards, and with a lock count of 2 or larger, it is decreased by 1 in the step (cf. R-UNLOCK$_1$ and R-UNLOCK$_2$). The R-ERROR-rules formalize misuse of a lock: unlocking a non-free lock by a thread that does not own it or unlocking a free lock (cf. R-ERROR$_1$ and R-ERROR$_2$). Both steps result in an error-term.

4 The Type and Effect System

A type and effect system combines rules for *well-typedness* with an *effect* part [1]. Here, effects track the use of locks and capture how many times a lock is taken or released. The underlying typing part is standard (the syntax for types is given in Table 1) and ensures, e.g., that actual parameters of method calls match the expected types for that method and that an object can handle an invoked method.

The type and effect system is given in Table 3 (for the thread local level) and Table 4 (for the global level). At the local level, the derivation system deals with expressions (which subsume threads). Judgments of the form

$$\Gamma; \Delta_1 \vdash e : T :: \Delta_2[\&v] \tag{3}$$

are interpreted as follows: Under the type assumptions Γ, an expression e is of type T. The effect part is captured by the effect or lock contexts: With the lock-status Δ_1 before the e, the status after e is given by Δ_2. The typing contexts (or type environments) Γ contain the type assumptions for variables; i.e., they bind variables x to their types, and are of the form $x_1:T_1,\ldots,x_n:T_n$, where we silently assume the x_i's are all different. This way, Γ is also considered a finite mapping from variables to types. By $dom(\Gamma)$ we refer to the domain of that mapping and write $\Gamma(x)$ for the type of variable x. Furthermore, we write $\Gamma,x:T$ for extending Γ with the binding $x:T$, assuming that $x \notin dom(\Gamma)$. To represent the effects of lock-handling, we use *lock environments* (denoted by Δ). At the local level of one single thread, the lock environments are of the form $v_1:n_1,\ldots,v_k:n_k$, where a value v_i is either a variable x_i or a lock reference l_i, but not the unit value. Furthermore, all v_i's are assumed to be different. The natural number n_i represents the lock status, and is either 0 in case the lock is marked as free, or n (with $n \geq 1$) capturing that the lock is taken n times by the thread under consideration. We use the same notations as for type contexts, i.e., $dom(\Delta)$ for the domain of Δ, further $\Delta(v)$ for looking up the lock status of the lock v in Δ, and $\Delta,v:n$ for extending Δ with a new binding, assuming $v \notin dom(\Delta)$. We write $\bullet$ for the empty context, containing no bindings.

Table 2. Global semantics

$$\frac{\sigma \vdash t \rightarrow \sigma' \vdash t'}{\sigma \vdash p\langle t \rangle \rightarrow \sigma' \vdash p\langle t' \rangle} \text{ R-Lift} \qquad \frac{\sigma \vdash P_1 \rightarrow \sigma' \vdash P_1'}{\sigma \vdash P_1 \parallel P_2 \rightarrow \sigma' \vdash P_1' \parallel P_2} \text{ R-Par}$$

$$\frac{p' \text{ fresh}}{\sigma \vdash p\langle \text{let } x{:}T = \text{spawn } t' \text{ in } t \rangle \rightarrow \sigma \vdash p\langle \text{let } x : T = () \text{ in } t \rangle \parallel p'\langle t' \rangle} \text{ R-Spawn}$$

$$\frac{l \notin dom(\sigma) \qquad \sigma' = \sigma[l \mapsto 0]}{\sigma \vdash p\langle \text{let } x{:}T = \text{new } \text{L } \text{in } t \rangle \rightarrow \sigma' \vdash p\langle \text{let } x{:}T = l \text{ in } t \rangle} \text{ R-NewL}$$

$$\frac{\sigma(l) = 0 \qquad \sigma' = \sigma[l \mapsto p(1)]}{\sigma \vdash p\langle \text{let } x : T = l. \text{ lock in } t \rangle \rightarrow \sigma' \vdash p\langle \text{let } x : T = l \text{ in } t \rangle} \text{ R-Lock}_1$$

$$\frac{\sigma(l) = p(n) \qquad \sigma' = \sigma[l \mapsto p(n+1)]}{\sigma \vdash p\langle \text{let } x : T = l. \text{ lock in } t \rangle \rightarrow \sigma' \vdash p\langle \text{let } x : T = l \text{ in } t \rangle} \text{ R-Lock}_2$$

$$\frac{\sigma(l) = 0 \qquad \sigma' = \sigma[l \mapsto p(1)]}{\sigma \vdash p\langle \text{let } x : T = \text{if } l. \text{ trylock then } e_1 \text{ else } e_2 \text{ in } t \rangle \rightarrow \sigma' \vdash p\langle \text{let } x : T = e_1 \text{ in } t \rangle} \text{ R-Trylock}_1$$

$$\frac{\sigma(l) = p(n) \qquad \sigma' = \sigma[l \mapsto p(n+1)]}{\sigma \vdash p\langle \text{let } x : T = \text{if } l. \text{ trylock then } e_1 \text{ else } e_2 \text{ in } t \rangle \rightarrow \sigma' \vdash p\langle \text{let } x : T = e_1 \text{ in } t \rangle} \text{ R-Trylock}_2$$

$$\frac{\sigma(l) = p'(n) \qquad p \neq p'}{\sigma \vdash p\langle \text{let } x : T = \text{if } l. \text{ trylock then } e_1 \text{ else } e_2 \text{ in } t \rangle \rightarrow \sigma \vdash p\langle \text{let } x : T = e_2 \text{ in } t \rangle} \text{ R-Trylock}_3$$

$$\frac{\sigma(l) = p(1) \qquad \sigma' = \sigma[l \mapsto 0]}{\sigma \vdash p\langle \text{let } x : T = l. \text{ unlock in } t \rangle \rightarrow \sigma' \vdash p\langle \text{let } x : T = l \text{ in } t \rangle} \text{ R-Unlock}_1$$

$$\frac{\sigma(l) = p(n+2) \qquad \sigma' = \sigma[l \mapsto p(n+1)]}{\sigma \vdash p\langle \text{let } x : T = l. \text{ unlock in } t \rangle \rightarrow \sigma' \vdash p\langle \text{let } x : T = l \text{ in } t \rangle} \text{ R-Unlock}_2$$

$$\frac{\sigma(l) = p'(n) \qquad p \neq p'}{\sigma \vdash p\langle \text{let } x : T = l. \text{ unlock in } t \rangle \rightarrow \sigma \vdash p\langle \text{error} \rangle} \text{ R-Error}_1$$

$$\frac{\sigma(l) = 0}{\sigma \vdash p\langle \text{let } x : T = l. \text{ unlock in } t \rangle \rightarrow \sigma \vdash p\langle \text{error} \rangle} \text{ R-Error}_2$$

A lock context Δ corresponds to a local view on the heap σ in that Δ contains the status of the locks from the perspective of one thread, whereas the heap σ in the global semantics contains the status of the locks from a global perspective. See also Definition 3 of projection later, which connects heaps and lock contexts. The final component of the judgment from Equation 3 is the value v after the &-symbol. If the type T of e is the type L for lock-references, type effect system needs information in which variable resp. which lock reference is returned. If $T \neq$ L, that information is missing; hence we write $[\&v]$ to indicate that it's "optional". In the following we concentrate mostly on the rules dealing with locks, and therefore with an $\&v$-part in the judgment.

At run-time, expressions do not only contain variables (and the unit value) as values but also references. They are stored in the heap σ. To check the well-typedness of configurations at run-time, we extend the type and effect judgment from Equation 3 to

$$\sigma; \Gamma; \Delta_1 \vdash e : T :: \Delta_2[\&v] \tag{4}$$

The rules of Table 3 are mostly straightforward. We concentrate on the rules relevant for lock handling, the full set of rules is shown in [10]. To define the rules, we need two additional auxiliary functions. We assume that the definition of all classes is given. As this information is static, we do not explicitly mention the corresponding "class table" in the rules; relevant information from the class definitions is referred to in the rules by $\vdash C : \vec{T} \rightarrow C$ (the constructor of class C takes parameters of types $\vec{T}$ as arguments; the "return type" of the constructor corresponds to C), $\vdash C.m : \vec{T} \rightarrow T :: \Delta_1 \rightarrow \Delta_2$ (method m of class C takes input of type $\vec{T}$ and returns a value of type T). Concerning the effects, the lock status of the parameters must be larger or equal as specified in the pre-condition Δ_1, and the effect of method m is the change from Δ_1 to Δ_2. Similarly, $\vdash C.f : T$ means that the field f of instances of class C is of type T. Because fields simply contain values, they have no effect.

Values have no effect and thus $\Delta_1 = \Delta_2$ (cf. the rule T-VAL). A conditional expression is well-typed with type T if the conditional expression is a boolean and if both branches have the common type T. Also for the effect, rule T-COND insists that both branches are well-typed with the same pre- and post-condition. Field update in rule T-ASSIGN has no effect, and the type of the field must coincide with the type of the value on the right-hand side of the update.

For looking up a field containing a lock reference (cf. T-FIELD), the local variable used to store the reference is assumed with a lock-counter of 0. Rule T-LET, dealing with the local variable scopes and sequential composition, requires some explanation. First, it deals only with the cases not covered by T-NEWL or T-FIELD, which are excluded by the first premise. The two recursive premises dealing with the sub-expressions e and t basically express that the effect of e precedes the one for t: The post-condition Δ_2 of e is used in the pre-condition when checking t, and the post-condition Δ_3 after t in the premise then yields the overall postcondition in the conclusion. Care, however, needs to be taken in the interesting situation where e evaluates to a lock reference: In this situation the lock can be referenced in t by the local variable x *or* by the identifier which is handed over having evaluated e, i.e., via v' in the rule. Note that the body is analysed under the assumption that originally x, which is an alias of v', has the lock-counter 0. The last side condition deals with the fact that after executing e, only *one* lock reference can be handed over to t, all others have either been existing *before* the let-expression or become "garbage" after e, since there is no way in t to refer to them. To avoid hanging locks, the rule therefore requires that all lock values *created* while executing e must end free, i.e., they must have a lock count of 0 in Δ_2. This is formalized in the predicate $FE(\Delta_1, \Delta_2, v)$ in the rule's last premise where $FE(\Delta_1, \Delta_2, v)$ holds if $\Delta_2 = \Delta_1', \vec{v}{:}\vec{0}, v{:}n$ for some Δ_1' such that $dom(\Delta_1') = dom(\Delta_1)$ or $dom(\Delta_1', v{:}n) = dom(\Delta_1)$.

As for method calls in rule T-CALL, the premise $\vdash C.m : \vec{T} \rightarrow T :: \Delta_1' \rightarrow \Delta_2'$ specifies $\vec{T} \rightarrow T$ as the type of the method and $\Delta_1' \rightarrow \Delta_2'$ as the effect; this corresponds to looking up the definition of the class including their methods from the class table. To be well-typed, the actual parameters must be of the required types $\vec{T}$ and the type of the call itself is T, as declared for the method. For the effect part, we can conceptually think of the pre-condition Δ_1' of the method definition as the *required* lock balances and Δ_1 the *provided* ones at the control point before the call. For the post-conditions, Δ_2' can be seen as the promised post-condition and Δ_2 the actual one. The premise $\Delta_1 \geq \Delta_1'[\vec{v}/\vec{x}]$ of the rule requires that the provided lock status of the locks passed as formal parameters must be larger or equal to those required by the precondition Δ_1' declared for the method. The lock status *after* the method is determined by adding the effect (as the *difference* between the promised post-condition and the required pre-condition) to the provided lock status Δ_1 before the call. In the premises, we formalize those checks and calculations as follows:

Definition 1. *Assume two lock environments Δ_1 and Δ_2. The sum $\Delta_1 + \Delta_2$ is defined point-wise, i.e., $\Delta = \Delta_1 + \Delta_2$ is given by: $\Delta \vdash v : n_1 + n_2$ if $\Delta_1 \vdash v : n_1$ and $\Delta_2 \vdash v : n_2$. If $\Delta_1 \vdash v : n_1$ and $\Delta_2 \nvdash v$ then $\Delta \vdash v : n_1$, and dually $\Delta \vdash v : n_2$, when $\Delta_1 \nvdash v$ and $\Delta_2 \vdash v : n_2$. The comparison of two contexts is defined point-wise, as well: $\Delta_1 \geq \Delta_2$ if $dom(\Delta_1) \supseteq dom(\Delta_2)$ and for all $v \in dom(\Delta_2)$, we have $n_1 \geq n_2$, where $\Delta_1 \vdash v : n_1$ and $\Delta_2 \vdash v : n_2$. The difference $\Delta_1 - \Delta_2$ is defined analogously. Furthermore we use the following short-hand: for $v \in dom(\Delta)$, $\Delta + v$ denotes the lock context Δ', where $\Delta'(v) = 1$ if $\Delta(v) = 0$, and $\Delta'(v) = n + 1$, if $\Delta(v) = n$. $\Delta - v$ is defined analogously.*

For the effect part of method specifications $C.m :: \Delta_1 \rightarrow \Delta_2$, the lock environments Δ_1 and Δ_2 represent the pre- and post-conditions for the lock parameters. We have to be careful how to *interpret* the assumptions and commitments expressed by the lock environments. As usual, the formal parameters of a method have to be unique; it's not allowed that a formal parameter occurs twice in the parameter list. Of course, the assumption of uniqueness does not apply to the *actual* parameters; i.e., at run-time, two different actual parameters can be *aliases* of each other. The consequences of that situation are discussed in the next example.

Example 1 (Method parameters and aliasing). Consider the following code:

Listing 1.1. Method with 2 formal parameters

```
m(x₁:L, x₂:L) {
   x₁.unlock ;x₂.unlock
}
```

Method m takes two lock parameters and performs a lock-release on each one. As for the effect specification, the precondition Δ_1 should state that the lock stored in x_1 should have at least value 1, and the same for x_2, i.e.,

$$\Delta_1 = x_1{:}1, x_2{:}1 \tag{5}$$

With Δ_1 as pre-condition, the effect type system accepts the method of Listing 1.1 as type correct, because the effects on x_1 and x_2 are checked *individually*. If at run-time the actual parameters, say l_1 and l_2 happen to be *not aliases*, and if each of them satisfies the precondition of Equation 5 *individually*, i.e., at run-time, the lock environment $\Delta_1' = \Delta_1[l_1/x_1][l_2/x_2]$ i.e.,

$$\Delta_1' = l_1{:}1, l_2{:}1 \tag{6}$$

executing the method body does not lead to a run-time error. If, however, the method is called such that x_1 and x_2 become aliases, i.e., called as $o.m(l,l)$, where the lock value of l is 1, it results in a run-time error. That does *not* mean that the system works *only* if there is no aliasing on the actual parameters. The lock environments express *resources* (the current lock balance) and if x_1 and x_2 happen to be aliases, the resources must be *combined*. This means that if we substitute in Δ_1 the variables x_1 and x_2 by the same lock l, the result of the substitution is

$$\Delta_1' = \Delta_1[l/x_1][l/x_2] = l{:}(1+1)$$

i.e., l is of balance 2.   □

This motivates the following definition of substitution for lock environments.

Definition 2 (Substitution for lock environments). *Given a lock environment Δ of the form $\Delta = v_1{:}n_1,\ldots,v_k{:}n_k$, with $k \geq 0$, and all the natural numbers $n_i \geq 0$. The result of the* substitution *of a variable x by a value v in Δ is written $\Delta[v/x]$ and defined as follows. Let $\Delta' = \Delta[v/x]$. If $\Delta = \Delta'', v{:}n_v, x{:}n_x$, then $\Delta' = \Delta'', v{:}(n_v + n_x)$. If $\Delta = \Delta'', x{:}n$ and $v \notin dom(\Delta'')$, then $\Delta' = \Delta'', v{:}n$. Otherwise, $\Delta' = \Delta$.*

Example 2 (Aliasing). The example continues from Example 1, i.e., we are given the method definition of Listing 1.1. Listing 1.2 shows the situation of a *caller* of m where first, the actual parameters are *without* aliases. Before the call, each lock (stored in the fields f_1 and f_2) has a balance of 1, as required in m's precondition, and the method body individually unlocks each of them once.

Listing 1.2. Method call, no aliasing

```
f₁ := new L;
f₂ := new L;         // f₁ and f₂: no aliases
f₁.lock; f₂.lock;
o.m(f₁,f₂);
```

If we change the code of the call site by making f_1 and f_2 aliases, setting $f_2 := f_1$ in the second line, instead of $f_2 :=$ new L, again there is *no* run-time error, as after executing $f_1.$ lock and $f_2.$ lock, the actual balance of the single lock stored in f_1 as well as in f_2 is 2.   □

Why aliasing f_1 and f_2 in the situation of Example 2 is unproblematic is illustrated in Figure 1. Figures 1(a) and 1(b) show the change of two different locks over time, where the y-axis represents the lock balance. The behavior of each lock is that it starts at a lock-count of zero, counts up and down according to the execution of lock and unlock and at the end reaches 0 again. It is important that at no point in time the lock balance can be *negative,* as indicated by the red, dashed arrow in the left sub-figure.

Connecting the figures to the example above, the two lock histories correspond to the situation of Listing 1.2 where f_1 and f_2 are *no* aliases. When they *are* aliases, the overall history looks as shown in Figure 1(c). This combined history, clearly, satisfies the mentioned condition for a lock behavior: it starts and ends with a lock balance of 0 and it never reaches a negative count as it is simply the "sum" of the individual lock histories.

The identity of a new thread is irrelevant, i.e., spawning carries type Unit (cf. T-SPAWN). Note for the effect part of T-SPAWN that the pre-condition for checking the thread t in the premise of the rule is the empty lock context $\bullet$. The reason is that the new thread starts without holding any lock. Note further that for the post-condition of the newly created thread t, all locks that may have been acquired while executing t must have been released again; this is postulated by $\Delta' \vdash \textit{free}$. Typing for new locks is covered by T-NEWL. As for the effect, the pre-context Δ_1 is extended by a binding for the new lock initially assumed to be free, i.e., the new binding is $x{:}0$. The two operations for acquiring and releasing a lock carry the type L. The type rules here are formulated on the thread-local level, i.e., irrespective of any other thread. Therefore, the lock contexts also contain no information about which thread is currently in possession of a non-free lock, since the rules are dealing with one local thread only. The effect of taking a lock is unconditionally to increase the lock counter in the lock context by one (cf. Definition 1). Dually in rule T-UNLOCK, $\Delta - v$ decreases v's lock counter by one. To do so safely, the thread must hold the lock before the step, as required by the premise $\Delta \vdash v : n+1$. The expression for tentatively taking a lock is a two-branched conditional. The first branch e_1 is executed if the lock is held, the second branch e_2 is executed if not. Hence, e_1 is analysed in the lock context $\Delta_1 + v$ as precondition, whereas e_2 uses Δ_1 unchanged (cf. T-TRYLOCK). As for ordinary conditionals, both branches coincide concerning their type and the post-condition of the effects, which in turn also are the type, resp. the post-condition of the overall expression.

The type and effect system in Table 3 dealt with expressions at the local level, i.e., with expression e and threads t of the abstract syntax of Table 1. We proceed analysing the language "above" the level of one thread, and in particular of global configurations as given in Equation 1.

The effect system at the local level uses lock environments to approximate the effect of the expression on the locks (cf. Equation 4). Lock environments Δ are thread-local views on the status of the locks, i.e., which locks the given thread holds and how often. In the reduction semantics, the locks are allocated in the (global) heap σ, which contains the status of all locks (together with the instance states of all allocated objects). The thread-local view can be seen as a *projection* of the heap to the thread, as far as the locks are concerned. This projection is needed to connect the local part of the effect system to the global one (cf. T-THREAD of Table 4).

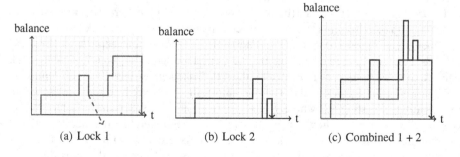

Fig. 1. Two lock histories

Table 3. Type and effect system (thread-local)

$$\frac{\sigma;\Gamma \vdash v : L \quad \Delta \vdash v}{\sigma;\Gamma;\Delta \vdash v : L :: \Delta\&v} \text{ T-VAL} \qquad \frac{\sigma;\Gamma \vdash v : \text{Bool} \quad \sigma;\Gamma;\Delta_1 \vdash e_1 : T :: \Delta_2\&v \quad \sigma;\Gamma\Delta_1 \vdash e_2 : T :: \Delta_2\&v}{\sigma;\Gamma;\Delta_1 \vdash \text{if } v \text{ then } e_1 \text{ else } e_2 : T :: \Delta_2\&v} \text{ T-COND}$$

$$\frac{\sigma;\Gamma \vdash v' : C \quad \vdash C.f : L \quad \sigma;\Gamma,x{:}L;\Delta_1,x{:}0 \vdash t : T :: \Delta_2\&v}{\sigma;\Gamma;\Delta_1 \vdash \text{let } x : L = v'.f \text{ in } t : T :: \Delta_2\&v} \text{ T-FIELD}$$

$$\frac{\sigma;\Gamma;\Delta \vdash v_1 : C :: \Delta \quad \vdash C.f_i : T_i \quad \sigma;\Gamma;\Delta \vdash v_2 : T_i :: \Delta\&v_2}{\sigma;\Gamma;\Delta \vdash v_1.f := v_2 : T_i :: \Delta\&v_2} \text{ T-ASSIGN}$$

$$\frac{e \notin \{\text{new } L, v.f\} \quad \sigma;\Gamma;\Delta_1 \vdash e : T_1 :: \Delta_2\&v' \quad (\sigma;\Gamma,x{:}T_1;\Delta_2,x{:}0 \vdash t : T_2 :: \Delta_3\&v'')[v'/x] \quad FE(\Delta_1,\Delta_2,v')}{\sigma;\Gamma;\Delta_1 \vdash \text{let } x : T_1 = e \text{ in } t : T_2 :: \Delta_3[v'/x]\&v''[v'/x]} \text{ T-LET}$$

$$\frac{\vdash C.m = \lambda \vec{x}.t \quad \sigma;\Gamma \vdash \vec{v} : \vec{T} \quad \sigma;\Gamma \vdash v : C \quad \vdash C.m : \vec{T} \to T :: \Delta_1' \to \Delta_2' \quad \Delta_1 \geq \Delta_1'[\vec{v}/\vec{x}] \quad \Delta_2 = \Delta_1 + (\Delta_2' - \Delta_1')[\vec{v}/\vec{x}] \quad T \neq L}{\sigma;\Gamma;\Delta_1 \vdash v.m(\vec{v}) : T :: \Delta_2} \text{ T-CALL}$$

$$\frac{\sigma;\Gamma,x{:}L;\Delta_1,x{:}0 \vdash t : T :: \Delta_2\&v}{\sigma;\Gamma;\Delta_1 \vdash \text{let } x{:}L = \text{new } L \text{ in } t : T :: \Delta_2\&v} \text{ T-NEWL} \qquad \frac{\sigma;\Gamma;\bullet \vdash t : T :: \Delta' \quad \Delta' \vdash free}{\sigma;\Gamma;\Delta \vdash \text{spawn } t : \text{Unit} :: \Delta} \text{ T-SPAWN}$$

$$\frac{\Delta \vdash v \quad \sigma;\Gamma \vdash v : L}{\sigma;\Gamma;\Delta \vdash v.\text{lock} : L :: \Delta + v\&v} \text{ T-LOCK} \qquad \frac{\Delta \vdash v : n+1 \quad \sigma;\Gamma \vdash v : L}{\sigma;\Gamma;\Delta \vdash v.\text{unlock} : L :: \Delta - v\&v} \text{ T-UNLOCK}$$

$$\frac{\sigma;\Gamma \vdash v : L \quad \sigma;\Gamma;\Delta_1 + v \vdash e_1 : T :: \Delta_2\&v' \quad \sigma;\Gamma;\Delta_1 \vdash e_2 : T :: \Delta_2\&v'}{\sigma;\Gamma;\Delta_1 \vdash \text{if } v.\text{trylock} \text{ then } e_1 \text{ else } e_2 : T :: \Delta_2\&v'} \text{ T-TRYLOCK}$$

Definition 3 (Projection). *Assume a heap σ with $\sigma \vdash ok$ and a thread p.*[1] *The projection of σ onto p, written $\sigma \downarrow_p$ is inductively defined as follows:*

$$\bullet \downarrow_p = \bullet$$
$$(\sigma, l{:}0) \downarrow_p = \sigma \downarrow_p, l{:}0$$
$$(\sigma, l{:}p(n)) \downarrow_p = \sigma \downarrow_p, l{:}n$$
$$(\sigma, l{:}p'(n)) \downarrow_p = \sigma \downarrow_p, l{:}0 \qquad \text{if } p \neq p'$$
$$(\sigma, o{:}C(\vec{v})) \downarrow_p = \sigma \downarrow_p .$$

Note the case where a lock l is held by a thread named p' different from the thread p we project onto, the projection makes l free, i.e., $l{:}0$. At first sight, it might look strange that the locks appears to be locally free where it is actually held by another thread. The reason is that the type system captures a *safety* property about the locks and furthermore that locks ensure *mutual exclusion* between threads. Safety means that the effect type system gives, as usual, no guarantee that the local thread can actually take the lock, it makes a statement about what happens after the thread has taken the lock. If the local thread can take the lock, the lock must be free right before that step. The other aspect, namely mutual exclusion, ensures that for the thread that has the lock,

---

[1] Cf. the technical report [10] for the standard definition of $\sigma \vdash ok$.

the effect system calculates the balance without taking the effect of other thread into account. This reflects the semantics as the locks of course guarantee mutual exclusion. As locks are manipulated *only* via $l.$ lock and $l.$ unlock, there is no interference by other threads, which justifies the local, *compositional* analysis.

Now to the rules of Table 4, formalizing judgments of the form

$$\sigma \vdash P : ok , \tag{7}$$

where P is given as in Equation 1. In the rules, we assume that σ is well-formed, i.e., $\sigma \vdash ok$. The empty set of threads or processes $\mathbf{0}$ is well-formed (cf. T-EMPTY). Well-typedness is a "local property" of threads, i.e., it is compositional: a parallel composition is well-typed if both sub-configurations are (cf. T-PAR). A process $p\langle t \rangle$ is well-typed if its code t is (cf. T-THREAD). As precondition Δ_1 for that check, the projection of the current heap σ is taken. . As for the post-condition Δ_2, we require that the thread has given back all the locks, postulated by $\Delta_2 \vdash free$. The remaining rules do not deal with run-time configurations $\sigma \vdash P$, but with the static code as given in the class declarations/definitions. Rule T-METH deals with method declarations. The first premise looks up the *declaration* of method m in the class table. The declaration contains, as usual, the argument types and the return type of the method. Beside that, the effect specification $\Delta_1 \to \Delta_2$ specifies the pre- and post-condition on the lock parameters. We assume that the domain of Δ_1 and Δ_2 correspond exactly to the lock parameters of the method. The second premise then checks the code of the method body against that specification. So t is type-checked, under a type and effect context extended by appropriate assumptions for the formal parameters $\vec{x}$ and by assuming type C for the self-parameter this. Note that the method body t is checked with an empty heap $\bullet$ as assumption. As for the post-condition Δ_2, Δ_2' of the body, Δ_2' contains lock variables *other* than the formal lock parameters (which are covered by Δ_2). The last premise requires that the lock counters of Δ_2' must be free after t. The role of the lock contexts as pre- and post-conditions for method specifications and the corresponding premises of rule T-CALL are illustrated in Figure 2. Assume two methods m and n, where m calls n, i.e., m is of the form $m()\{\ldots;x.n()\ldots\}$. Let's assume the methods operate on one single lock, whose behavior is illustrated by the first two sub-figures of Figure 2.

The history in Figure 2(a) is supposed to represent the lock behavior m up to the point where method n is called, and Figure 2(b) gives the behavior of n in isolation. The net effect of method n is to decrease the lock-count by one (indicated by the dashed arrow), namely by unlocking the lock twice but locking it once afterwards again. It is not good enough as a specification for method n to know that the overall effect is a decrease by one. It is important that at the point where the method is called, the lock balance must be *at least* 2. Thus, the effect specification is $\Delta_1 \to \Delta_2$, where Δ_1 serves as precondition for all formal lock parameters of the method, and T-CALL requires current lock balances to be larger or equal to the one specified. The type system requires that the locks are handed over via parameter passing and the connection between the lock balances of the actual parameters with those of the formal ones is done by the form of substitution given in Definition 2. The actual value of the lock balances after the called method n is then determined by the lock balances before the call plus the net-effect of that method. See Figure 2(c) for combining the two histories of Figures 2(a) and 2(b). Finally, a class definition class $C(\vec{f}:\vec{T})\{\vec{f}:\vec{T};\vec{M}\}$ is dealt with in rule T-CLASS, basically checking that all method definitions are well-typed. For a program (a sequence of class definitions) to be well-typed, all its classes must be well-typed (we omit the rule).

5 Correctness

We prove the correctness of our analysis. A crucial part is subject reduction, i.e., the preservation of well-typedness under reduction. (The full proofs can be found in [10].)

Next we prove subject reduction for the effect part of the system of Tables 3 and 4.

Lemma 1 (Substitution). *Let x be a variable of type L and l be a lock reference If $\Delta_1 \vdash t :: \Delta_2 \& v$, then $\Delta_1[l/x] \vdash t[l/x] :: \Delta_2[l/x] \& v[l/x]$.*

The next lemma expresses that given a lock environment Δ_1 as precondition for an expression e such that the effect of e leads to a post-condition of Δ_2, e is still well-typed if we assume a Δ_1' where the lock balances are increased, and the corresponding post-condition is then increased accordingly.

Lemma 2 (Weakening). *If $\Delta_1 \vdash e :: \Delta_2$, then $\Delta_1 + \Delta \vdash e :: \Delta_2 + \Delta$.*

Lemma 3 (Subject reduction (local)). *Let $\sigma \vdash t$ be well-typed. Assume further $\Delta_1 \vdash t :: \Delta_2 \& v$ where $\Delta_1 = \sigma \downarrow_p$ for a thread identifier p and $\Delta_2 \vdash free$. If $\sigma \vdash t \to \sigma' \vdash t'$, then $\Delta_1' \vdash t' :: \Delta_2' \& v'$, with $\Delta_1' = \sigma \downarrow_p$ and with $\Delta_2' \vdash free$.*

Lemma 4 (Subject reduction (global)). *If $\sigma \vdash P : ok$ and $\sigma \vdash P \to \sigma' \vdash P'$ where the reduction step is* not *one of the two* R-ERROR-*rules, then $\sigma' \vdash P' : ok$.*

Lemma 5. *Let $P = P' \parallel p\langle t \rangle$. If $\sigma \vdash P : ok$ then $\sigma \vdash P \not\to \sigma \vdash P' \parallel p\langle \text{error} \rangle$.*

The next result captures one of the two aspects of correct lock handling, namely that never an exception is thrown by inappropriately unlocking a lock.

Theorem 1 (Well-typed programs are lock-error free). *Given a program in its initial configuration $\bullet \vdash P_0 : ok$. Then it's not the case that $\bullet \vdash P_0 \longrightarrow^* \sigma' \vdash P \parallel p\langle \text{error} \rangle$.*

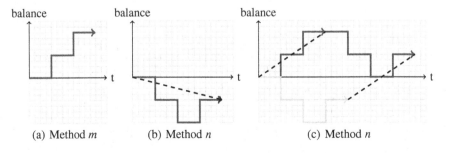

Fig. 2. Lock balance of methods m and n

The second aspect of correct lock handling means that a thread should release all locks before it terminates. We say, a configuration $\sigma \vdash P$ has a *hanging lock* if $P = P' \parallel p\langle \texttt{stop} \rangle$ where $\sigma(l) = p(n)$ with $n \geq 1$, i.e., one thread p has terminated but there exists a lock l still in possession of p.

Theorem 2 (Well-typed programs have no hanging locks). *Given a program in its initial configuration $\bullet \vdash P_0 : ok$. Then it's not the case that $\bullet \vdash P_0 \longrightarrow^* \sigma' \vdash P'$, where $\sigma' \vdash P'$ has a hanging lock.*

6 Related Work

Our static type and effect system ensures proper usage of non-lexically scoped locks in a concurrent object-oriented calculus to prevent run-time errors and unwanted behaviors. As mentioned, the work presented here extends our previous work [12], dealing with transactions as a concurrency control mechanism instead of locks. The extension is non-trivial, mainly because locks have user-level identities. This means that, unlike transactions, locks can be passed around, can be stored in fields, and in general aliasing becomes a problem. Furthermore, transactions are not "re-entrant". See [11] for a more thorough discussion of the differences. There are many type systems and formal analyses to catch already a compile time various kinds of errors. For multi-threaded Java, static approaches so far are mainly done to detect data races or to guarantee freedom of deadlocks, of obstruction or of livelocks, etc. There have been quite a number of type-based approaches to ensure proper usage of resources of different kinds (e.g., file access, i.e., to control the opening and closing of files). See [6] for a recent, rather general formalization for what the authors call the resource usage analysis problem (the paper discusses approaches to safe resource usage in the literature). Unlike the type system proposed here, [6] considers type *inference* (or type reconstruction). Their language, a variant of the λ-calculus, however, is sequential. [15] uses a type and effect system to assure deadlock freedom in a calculus quite similar to ours in that it supports thread based concurrency and a shared mutable heap. On the surface, the paper deals with a different problem (deadlock freedom) but as *part* of that it treats the same problem as we, namely to avoid releasing free locks or locks not owned, and furthermore,

Table 4. Type and effect system (global)

$$\frac{}{\sigma \vdash \mathbf{0} : ok} \text{ T-EMPTY} \qquad \frac{\sigma \vdash P_1 : ok \qquad \sigma \vdash P_2 : ok}{\sigma \vdash P_1 \parallel P_2 : ok} \text{ T-PAR} \qquad \frac{\forall i. \ \vdash M_i : ok}{\vdash C(\vec{f}{:}\vec{T})\{\vec{f}{:}\vec{T};\vec{M}\} : ok} \text{ T-CLASS}$$

$$\frac{\Delta_1 = \sigma \downarrow_p \qquad \sigma;\bullet;\Delta_1 \vdash t : T :: \Delta_2 \qquad t \neq \texttt{error} \qquad \Delta_2 \vdash free}{\sigma \vdash p\langle t\rangle : ok} \text{ T-THREAD}$$

$$\frac{\vdash C.m : \vec{T} \to T :: \Delta_1 \to \Delta_2 \qquad \bullet;\vec{x}{:}\vec{T},\texttt{this}{:}C;\Delta_1 \vdash t : T :: \Delta_2,\Delta_2' \qquad \Delta_2' \vdash free}{\vdash C.m(\vec{x}{:}\vec{T})\{t\} : ok} \text{ T-METH}$$

do not leave any locks hanging. The language of [15] is more low-level in that it supports pointer dereferencing, whereas our object-oriented calculus allows shared access on mutable storage only for the fields of objects and especially we do not allow pointer dereferencing. Pointer dereferencing makes the static analysis more complex as it needs to keep track of which thread is actually responsible for lock-releasing in terms of read and write permissions. We do not need the complicated use of ownership-concepts, as our language is more disciplined dealing with shared access: we strictly separate between *local* variables (not shared) and shared fields. In a way, the content of a local variable is *"owned"* by a thread; therefore there is no need to track the current owner across different threads to avoid bad interference. Besides that, our analysis can handle *re-entrant locks,* which are common in object-oriented languages such as Java or $C^\sharp$, whereas [15] covers only binary locks. The same restriction applies to [16], which represents a type system assuring race-freedom. Gerakios et.al. [5] present a uniform treatment of region-based management and locks. A type and effect system guarantees the absence of memory access violations and data races in the presence of region aliasing. The main subject in their work is regions, however, not locks. Re-entrant locks there are just used to protect regions, and they are implicit in the sense that each lock is associated with a region and has no identity. The regions, however, have an identity, they are non-lexically scoped and can be passed as arguments. The safety of the region-based management is ensured by a type and effect system, where the effects specify so-called region *capabilities*. Similar to our lock balances, the capabilities keep track of the "status" of the region, including a count on how many times the region is accessed and a *lock* count. As in our system, the static analysis keeps track of those capabilities and the soundness of the analysis is proved by subject reduction (there called "preservation"). [4] uses "flow sensitive" type qualifiers to statically correct resource usage such as file access in the context of a calculus with higher-order functions and mutable references. Also the Vault system [3] uses a type-based approach to ensure safe use of resources (for C-programs).

Laneve et. al. [2] develop a type system for statically ensuring proper lock handling also for the JVM, i.e., at the level of byte code as part of Java's bytecode verifier. Their system ensures what is known as *structured locking*, i.e., (in our terminology), each method body is balanced as far as the locks are concerned, and at no point, the balance reaches below 0. As the work does not consider non-lexical locking as in Java 5, the conditions apply *per method* only. Extending [14], Iwama and Kobayashi [8] present a type system for multi-threaded Java programs on the level of the JVM which deals with non-lexical locking. Similar to our system, the type system guarantees absence of lock errors (as we have called it), i.e., that when a thread is terminated, it has released all its acquired locks and that a thread never releases a lock it has not previously acquired. Unlike our system, they cannot deal with method calls, i.e., the system analyses method bodies in isolation. However, they consider type *inference*.

7 Conclusion

We presented a static type and effect system to prevent certain errors for non-lexical lock handling as in Java 5. The analysis was formalized in an object-oriented calculus in the style of FJ. We proved the soundness of our analysis by subject reduction. Challenges for the static analysis addressed by our effect system are the following: with dynamic lock creation and passing of lock references, we face *aliasing* of lock references, and due to dynamic thread creation, the effect system needs to handle concurrency.

Aliasing is known to be tricky for static analysis; many techniques have been developed to address the problem. Those techniques are known as alias or pointer analyses, shape analyses, etc. With dynamic lock creation and since locks are *meant* to be shared, one would expect that a static analysis on lock-usage relies on some form of alias analysis. Interestingly, aliasing poses no real challenge for the specific problem at hand, under suitable assumptions on the use of locks and lock variables. The main assumption restricts passing the lock references via instance fields. Note that to have locks *shared between threads,* there are basically only two possible ways: hand over the identity of a lock via the thread constructor or via an instance field: it's not possible to hand the lock reference to another thread via method calls, as calling a method continues executing in the *same* thread. Our core calculus does not support thread constructors, as they can be expressed by ordinary method calls, and because passing locks via fields is more general and complex: passing a lock reference via a constructor to a new thread means locks can be passed only from a parent to a child thread. The effect system then enforces a *single-assignment* policy on lock fields. The analysis also shows that this restriction can be relaxed in that one allows assignment concerning fields whose lock status corresponds to a *free* lock. Concerning passing lock references within *one* thread, parameter passing must be used. The effect specification of the formal parameters contains information about the effect of the lock parameters. We consider the restriction *not* to re-assign a lock-variable as a natural programming guideline and common practice.

Like aliasing, concurrency is challenging for static analysis, due to interference. Our effect system checks the effect of interacting locks, which are some form of shared variables. An interesting observation is that locks are, of course not just shared variables, but they synchronize threads for which they ensure mutual exclusion. Ensuring absence of lock errors is thus basically a *sequential* problem, as one can ignore interference; i.e., a parallel program can be dealt with *compositionally*. See the simple, compositional rule for parallel composition in Table 4. The treatment is similar to the effect system for TFJ dealing with transactions instead of locks. However, in the transactional setting, the local view works for a different reason, as transactions are *not shared* between threads.

The treatment of the locks here is related to type systems governing *resource usage*. We think that our technique in this paper and a similar one used in our previous work could be applied to systems where run-time errors and unwanted behaviors may happen due to improperly using syntactical constructs for, e.g., opening/closing files, allocating/deallocating resources, with a non-lexical scope. Currently, the exceptional behavior due to lock-mishandling is represented as one single `error`-expression. Adding a more realistic exception mechanism including exception handling and finally-clauses to the calculus is a furthrer step in our research. Furthermore we plan to implement the system for empirical results. The combination of our two type and effect systems, one for TFJ [12] and one for the calculus in this paper, could be a step in setting up an integrated system for the applications where locks and transactions are reconciled.

Acknowledgements. We are grateful to the very thorough anonymous reviewers for giving helpful and critical feedback and useful pointers to the literature.

References

1. Amtoft, T., Nielson, H.R., Nielson, F.: Type and Effect Systems: Behaviours for Concurrency. Imperial College Press (1999)
2. Bigliardi, G., Laneve, C.: A type system for JVM threads. In: Proceedings of 3rd ACM SIGPLAN Workshop on Types in Compilation, TIC 2000, p. 2003 (2000)
3. DeLine, R., Fähndrich, M.: Enforcing high-level protocols in low-level software. In: Proceedings of the 2001 ACM Conference on Programming Language Design and Implementation, pp. 59–69 (June 2001)
4. Foster, J.S., Terauchi, T., Aiken, A.: Flow-sensitive type qualifiers. In: Proceedings of the ACM SIGPLAN Conference on Programming Language Design and Implementation (2002)
5. Gerakios, P., Papaspyrou, N., Sagonas, K.: A concurrent language with a uniform treatment of regions and locks. In: Programming Language Approaches to Concurrency and Communication-eCentric Software. EPTCS, vol. 17, pp. 79–93 (2010)
6. Igarashi, A., Kobayashi, N.: Resource usage analysis. ACM Transactions on Programming Languages and Systems 27(2), 264–313 (2005)
7. Igarashi, A., Pierce, B.C., Wadler, P.: Featherweight Java: A minimal core calculus for Java and GJ. In: Object Oriented Programming: Systems, Languages, and Applications, OOPSLA 1999, pp. 132–146. ACM (1999); SIGPLAN Notices
8. Iwama, F., Kobayashi, N.: A new type system for JVM lock primitives. In: ASIA-PEPM 2002: Proceedings of the ASIAN Symposium on Partial Evaluation and Semantics-Based Program Manipulation, pp. 71–82. ACM, New York (2002)
9. Jagannathan, S., Vitek, J., Welc, A., Hosking, A.: A transactional object calculus. Science of Computer Programming 57(2), 164–186 (2005)
10. Johnsen, E.B., Tran, T.M.T, Owe, O., Steffen, M.: Safe locking for multi-threaded Java. Technical Report (revised version) 402, University of Oslo, Dept. of Computer Science (January 2011), www.ifi.uio.no/~msteffen/publications.html#techreports; A shorter version (extended abstract) has been presented at the NWPT 2010
11. Tran, T.M.T., Owe, O., Steffen, M.: Safe typing for transactional vs. lock-based concurrency in multi-threaded Java. In: Pham, S.B., Hoang, T.-H., McKay, B., Hirota, K. (eds.) Proceedings of the Second International Conference on Knowledge and Systems Engineering, KSE 2010, pp. 188-193. IEEE Computer Society (October 2010)
12. Tran, T.M.T., Steffen, M.: Safe Commits for Transactional Featherweight Java. In: Méry, D., Merz, S. (eds.) IFM 2010. LNCS, vol. 6396, pp. 290–304. Springer, Heidelberg (2010); An earlier and longer version has appeared as UiO, Dept. of Comp. Science Technical Report 392, October 2009 and appeared as extended abstract in the Proceedings of NWPT 2009
13. Oaks, S., Wong, H.: Java Threads, 3rd edn. O'Reilly (September 2004)
14. Stata, R., Abadi, M.: A type system for Java bytecode subroutines. ACM Transactions on Programming Languages and Systems 21(1), 90–137 (1999)
15. Suenaga, K.: Type-Based Deadlock-Freedom Verification for Non-Block-Structured Lock Primitives and Mutable References. In: Ramalingam, G. (ed.) APLAS 2008. LNCS, vol. 5356, pp. 155–170. Springer, Heidelberg (2008)
16. Terauchi, T.: Checking race freedom via linear programming. In: Proceedings of the 2008 ACM SIGPLAN Conference on Programming Language Design and Implementation, PLDI 2008, pp. 1–10. ACM, New York (2008)

Analysing the Control Software
of the Compact Muon Solenoid Experiment
at the Large Hadron Collider

Yi-Ling Hwong[1,*], Vincent J.J. Kusters[1,2], and Tim A.C. Willemse[2]

[1] CERN, European Organization for Nuclear Research,
CH-1211 Geneva 23, Switzerland
[2] Department of Mathematics and Computer Science,
Eindhoven University of Technology
P.O. Box 513, 5600 MB Eindhoven, The Netherlands

Abstract. The control software of the CERN Compact Muon Solenoid experiment contains over 30,000 finite state machines. These state machines are organised hierarchically: commands are sent down the hierarchy and state changes are sent upwards. The sheer size of the system makes it virtually impossible to fully understand the details of its behaviour at the macro level. This is fuelled by unclarities that already exist at the micro level. We have solved the latter problem by formally describing the finite state machines in the mCRL2 process algebra. The translation has been implemented using the *ASF+SDF meta-environment*, and its correctness was assessed by means of simulations and visualisations of individual finite state machines and through formal verification of subsystems of the control software. Based on the formalised semantics of the finite state machines, we have developed dedicated tooling for checking properties that can be verified on finite state machines in isolation.

1 Introduction

The Large Hadron Collider (LHC) experiment at the European Organization for Nuclear Research (CERN) is built in a tunnel 27 kilometres in circumference and is designed to yield head-on collisions of two proton (ion) beams of 7 TeV each. The Compact Muon Solenoid (CMS) experiment is one of the four big experiments of the LHC. It is a general purpose detector to study the wide range of particles and phenomena produced in the high-energy collisions in the LHC. The CMS experiment is made up of 7 subdetectors, with each of them designed to stop, track or measure different particles emerging from the proton collisions. Early 2010, it achieved its first successful 7 TeV collision, breaking its previous world record, setting a new one.

The control, configuration, readout and monitoring of hardware devices and the detector status, in particular various kinds of environment variables such as temperature, humidity, high voltage, and low voltage, are carried out by the Detector Control System

* This work has been supported in part by a Marie Curie Initial Training Network Fellowship of the European Community's Seventh framework program under contract number (PITN-GA-2008-211801-ACEOLE).

F. Arbab and M. Sirjani (Eds.): FSEN 2011, LNCS 7141, pp. 174–189, 2012.

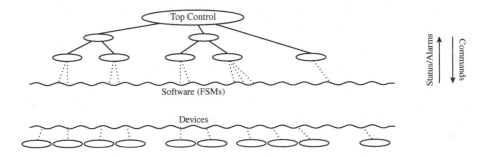

Fig. 1. Architecture of the real-time monitoring and control system of the CMS experiment, running at the LHC

(DCS). The control software of the CMS detector is implemented with the Siemens commercial Supervision, Control And Data Acquisition (SCADA) package PVSS-II and the CERN Joint Controls Project (JCOP) framework [9]. The architecture of the control software for all four big LHC experiments is based on the SMI++ framework [5,6]. Under the SMI++ framework, the real world is viewed as a collection of objects behaving as finite state machines (FSMs). These FSMs are described using the State Manager Language (SML). A characteristic of the used architecture is the regularity and relatively low complexity of the individual FSMs and device drivers that together constitute the control software; the main source of complexity is in the cooperation of these FSMs. Cooperation is strictly hierarchical, consisting of several layers; see Figure 1 for a schematic overview. The FSMs are organised in a tree structure where every node has one parent and zero or more children, except for the top node, which has no parent. Nodes communicate by sending commands to their children and state updates to their parents, so commands are refined and propagated down the hierarchy and status updates are sent upwards. Hardware devices are typically found only at the bottom-most layer.

The FSM system in the CMS experiment contains over 30,000 nodes. On average, each FSM contains 5 logical states. Based on our early experiments with some subsystems, we believe that $10^{30,000}$ states is a very conservative estimate of the size of the state space for the full control system. The sheer size of the system significantly contributes to its complexity. Complicating factors in understanding the behaviour of the system are the diversity in the development philosophies in subgroups responsible for controlling their own subdetectors, and the huge amount of parameters to be monitored. In view of this complexity, it is currently impossible to trace the root cause of problems when unexpected behaviours manifest themselves. A single badly designed FSM may be sufficient to lead to a livelock, resulting in non-responsive hardware devices, potentially ruining expensive and difficult experiments. Considering the scientific importance of these experiments, this justifies the use of rigorous methods for understanding and analysing the system.

Our contributions are twofold. First, we have formalised SML by mapping its language constructs onto constructs in the process algebraic language mCRL2 [7]. Second, based on our understanding of the semantics of SML, we have identified properties that can be verified for FSMs in isolation, and for which we have developed dedicated verification tooling.

Using the ASF+SDF meta-environment [13], we have developed a prototype translation implementing our mapping of SML to mCRL2. This allowed us to quickly assess the correctness of the translation through simulation and visualisation of FSMs in isolation, and by means of formal verification of small subsystems of the control software, using the mCRL2 toolset. The feedback obtained by the verification and simulation enabled us to further improve the transformation. The use of the ASF+SDF meta-environment allowed us to repeat this cycle in quick successions, and, at the same time, maintain a formal description of the translation. Although the ASF+SDF Meta Environment development was discontinued in 2010, we chose it over similar products as ATL because we were already familiar with it and because its syntax-driven, functional approach results in very clear translation rules.

Our dedicated verification tools allow the developers at CERN to quickly perform behavioural sanity checks on their design, and use the feedback of the tools to further improve on their designs in case of any problems. Results using these tools so far are favourable: with only a fraction of the total number of FSMs inspected so far, several problems have surfaced and have been fixed.

Outline. We give a cursory overview of the core of the SML language in Section 2. The mCRL2 semantics of this core are then explained in Section 3, and we briefly elaborate on the methodology we used for obtaining this semantics. Our dedicated verification tools for SML, together with some of the results obtained so far, are described in further detail in Section 4. We summarise our findings and suggestions in Section 5.

2   The State Manager Language

The finite state machines used in the CMS experiment are described in the State Manager Language (SML) [5,6]. We present the syntax and the suggested meaning of the core of the language using snapshots of a running example; we revisit this example in our formalisation in Section 3. Note that in reality, SML is larger than presented here, but the control system is made up largely of FSMs employing these core constructs only.

Listing 1 shows part of the definition of a *class* in SML. Conceptually, this is the same kind of class known from object-oriented programming: the class is defined once, but can be instantiated many times. An instantiation is referred to as a Finite State Machine. A class consists of one or more *state clauses*; Listing 1 only shows the state clause for the OFF state. Intuitively, a state clause describes how the FSM should behave when it is in a particular state. Every state clause consists of a list of *when clauses* and a list of *action clauses*, either of which may be empty.

A *when clause* has two parts: a *guard* which is a Boolean expression over the states of the children of the FSM and a *referer* which describes what should happen if the guard evaluates to true. The base form of a guard is P in_state S, where S is the name of a state (or a set of state names) and P is a *child pattern*. A child pattern consists of two parts: the first part is either ANY or ALL and the second part is the name of a class or the literal FwCHILDREN. The intended meaning is straightforward:

```
class: $FWPART_$TOP$RPC_Chamber_CLASS
    state: OFF
        when ( ( $ANY$FwCHILDREN in_state ERROR ) or
               ( $ANY$FwCHILDREN in_state TRIPPED ) )  move_to ERROR

        when ( $ANY$RPC_HV in_state {RAMPING_UP,
                                     RAMPING_DOWN} ) move_to RAMPING
        when ( ( $ALL$RPC_LV in_state ON ) and
               ( $ALL$RPC_HV in_state STANDBY ) )  move_to STANDBY

        when ( ( $ALL$RPC_HV in_state ON ) and
               ( $ALL$RPC_LV in_state ON ) )  move_to ON

        when ( ( $ALL$FwCHILDREN in_state ON ) and
               ( $ALL$RPC_T in_state OK ) )  move_to ON

        action: STANDBY
            do STANDBY $ALL$RPC_HV
            do ON $ALL$RPC_LV
        action: OFF
            do OFF $ALL$FwCHILDREN
        action: ON
            do ON $ALL$FwCHILDREN
```

Listing 1: Part of the definition of the *Chamber* class in SML

```
$ALL$FwCHILDREN in_state ON
```

means "all children are in the ON state", and:

```
$ANY$RPC_HV in_state {RAMPING_UP, RAMPING_DOWN}
```

evaluates to true if "some child of class RPC_HV is either in state RAMPING_UP or state RAMPING_DOWN".

A referer is either of the form move_to S, indicating that the finite state machine changes its state to S, or of the form do A, indicating that the action with name A should be executed next. If the guards of more than one *when clause* evaluate to true, the topmost enabled referer is executed. Whenever the FSM moves to a new state, it executes the *when clauses*, starting from the top *when clause*, to see if it should stay in this state (all guards are false) or if it should go to another state (some guard is true). It is therefore possible that a single move_to referer or statement (see below) triggers a series of state changes.

An *action clause* consists of a *name* and a list of *statements*. When an FSM receives a command while in a state S, it looks inside the state clause of state S for an *action clause* with the same name as the command and if such an *action clause* exists, it executes its statement list. If no such action exists, the command is ignored. For example, if the *Chamber* finite state machine from Listing 1 is in state OFF and it receives an ON command, it will execute the last *action clause*.

The most commonly used statement is do C P, which means that the command C is sent to all children which match the child pattern P. After a command is sent, the child is marked *busy*. When a child sends its new state back, this *busy* flag is removed. The do statement is non-blocking, *i.e.*, it does not wait for the children to respond with their new state. The child pattern always starts with ALL in this context. SML also provides if and move_to statements, as we illustrated in Listing 2.

```
action: STANDBY
    do STANDBY $ALL$RPC_HV
    do ON $ALL$RPC_LV
    if ( $ALL$RPC_LV in_state ON ) then
        do ON $ALL$RPC_HV
        do ON $ALL$RPC_LV
        if ( $ALL$RPC_HV in_state ON ) then
            do ON $ALL$RPC_HV
            move_to ON
        endif
    else
        do STANDBY $ALL$RPC_LV
        do STANDBY $ALL$RPC_HV
        do STANDBY $ALL$FwCHILDREN
    endif
```

Listing 2: An example of a more complex *action clause*

The move_to S statement immediately stops execution of the *action clause* and causes the FSM to move to the S state. The if G then S1 else S2 endif statement blocks as long as there is a child, referred to in G, that has a busy flag. If the guard G evalutates to true, then S1 is executed and otherwise S2 is executed. The else clause is optional.

3 A Formal Semantics for SML

We use the process algebra mCRL2 [7] to formalise the semantics of programs written in SML. The formal translation of SML into mCRL2 can be found in [10].

Our choice for mCRL2 is motivated largely by the expressive power of the language, its rich data language rooted in the theory of Abstract Data Types, its available tool support, and our understanding of the advantages and disadvantages of mCRL2. Before we address the translation of SML to mCRL2, we briefly describe the mCRL2 language.

3.1 A Brief Overview of mCRL2

The mCRL2 language consists of two distinct parts: a *data language* for describing the data transformations and data types, and a *process language* for specifying system behaviours. For a comprehensive language tutorial, we refer to http://mcrl2.org.

The data language, which is rooted in the theory of *abstract data types*, includes built-in definitions for many of the commonly used data types, such as Booleans, Integers, Natural numbers, *etc.*, and allows users to specify their own data sorts. In addition, container sorts, such as *lists*, *sets* and *bags* are available.

The process specification language of mCRL2 consists of only a small number of basic operators and primitives. The language is inspired by process algebras such as ACP [1], and has both an axiomatic and an operational semantics.

A set of (parameterised) actions are used to model atomic, observable events. Processes are constructed compositionally: the non-deterministic choice between processes p and q is denoted p+q; their sequential composition is denoted p.q, and their parallel composition is denoted p | q. In addition, there are facilities to enforce communication between different actions and abstracting from actions.

The main feature of the process language is that processes can depend on data. For instance, b->p<>q denotes a conditional choice between processes p and q: if b evaluates to *true*, it behaves as process p, and otherwise as process q. In a similar vein, sum d:D.p(d) describes a (possibly infinite) choice between processes p with different values for variable d.

3.2   From SML to mCRL2

We next present our formalisation of SML in mCRL2. Every SML class is converted to an mCRL2 process definition; the behaviour of an FSM is then described by the behaviour of a process instance. Each FSM maintains a state and a pointer to the code it is currently executing. In addition, an FSM is embedded in a global tree-like configuration that identifies its parent, and its children. In order to faithfully describe the behaviour of an FSM, we therefore equip each mCRL2 process definition for a class X with this information as follows:

```
proc X_CLASS(self: Id, parent: Id, s: State, chs: Children,
             phase: Phase, aArgs: ActPhaseArgs)
```

Parameter self represents a unique identifier for a process instance, and parent is the identifier of self's parent in the tree. Parameter s is used to keep track of the state of the FSM. The state information of self's children is stored in chs of sort Children, which is a list of sort Child, a structured sort:

```
Children = List(Child);
Child = struct child(id:Id, state:State, ptype:PType, busy:Bool);
```

The above structured sort Child can be thought of as a named tuple; id represents the unique identifier of a child, state is the state that this child sent to X in its last state-update message, ptype maintains the FSM class of this child, and busy is the flag that indicates that the child is still processing the last command X sent to it. This flag is set after sending a message to the child, and reset when it responds with its new state. Whenever X receives a state-update message from one of its children, the chs structure is updated accordingly. This structure is used to evaluate the *when clauses* and to determine to which processes commands have to be sent.

The phase parameter has value WhenPhase if the FSM is executing the *when clauses* and ActionPhase otherwise; Phase is a simple structured sort containing these two values. The phases will be explained in detail in the following section. Finally, aArgs is a structure that contains information we only need in the *action phase*. It is defined as follows:

```
ActPhaseArgs = struct actArgs(cq: CommandQueue, nrf: IdList,
                              pc: Int, rsc: Bool)
```

We forego a discussion of the nrf and rsc parameters, which are solely used during an intialisation phase. The command queue cq contains messages that are to be sent to an FSM's children. Specifically, when executing a do C P statement, we add a pair with the child's id and the command C to cq, for every child matching the child pattern P. The command queue is subsequently emptied by sending the messages stored in cq.

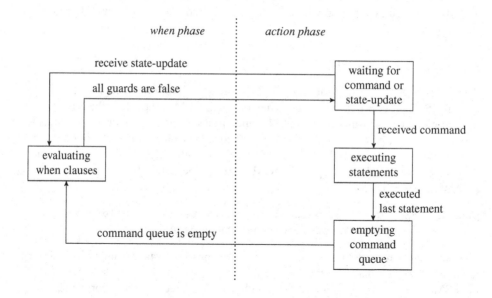

Fig. 2. Overview of the *when phase* and the *action phase*

Phases. During the *when phase*, a process executes *when clauses* until it reaches a state in which none of the guards evaluate to true. It then moves to the *action phase*. In the *action phase*, a process can receive a command from its parent or a state-update message from one of its children. This process is illustrated in Figure 2. After handling the command or message, it returns to the *when phase*.

Translating the *when phase* turns out to be rather straightforward: for each state a process term consisting of nested if-then-else statements is introduced, formalised by mCRL2 expressions of the form b->p<>q (if b, then act as process p, otherwise as q). Each if-clause represents exactly one *when clause*. The else-clause of the last *when clause* sends a state-update message (represented by the mCRL2 action send_state) with the current state to the parent of this FSM and moves to the *action phase*. An example is given in Translation 1.

SML	mCRL2

state: OFF
  when G1 move_to S1
  . . .
  when Gn move_to Sn
	instate_OFF(s) && isWhenPhase(phase) -> (
	  translation_of_G1 ->
	    move_state(self,S1).
	    X_CLASS(self,parent,S1,chs,phase,aArgs) <>
	  . . .
	  translation_of_Gn ->
	    move_state(self,Sn).
	    X_CLASS(self,parent,Sn,chs,phase,aArgs) <>
	  send_state(self,parent,s).
	  move_phase(self,ActionPhase).
	  X_CLASS(self,parent,s,chs,ActionPhase,
	                reset(aArgs)))

Translation 1: Simplified translation of the *when clauses* of a state OFF. Note that p.q describes the process p that, upon successful termination, continues to behave as process q.

The move_state action indicates that the process changes its state. The send_state action communicates with the receive_state action to a comm_state action, representing the communication of the new state to the parent. Note that the state is sent only if none of the guards are true. Upon sending the new state, the process changes to the *action phase*, signalled by a move_phase action.

Modelling the *action phase* is more involved as we need to add some terms for initialisation and sending messages. We will focus on the translation of the *action clauses* and the code which handles state-update messages.

SML allows for an arbitrary number of statements and an arbitrary number of (nested) if-statements in every *action clause*. We uniquely identify the translation of every statement with an integer label. After executing a statement, the pc(aArgs) program counter is set to the label of the statement which should be executed next. There are two special cases here:

- Label 0, the clause selector. When entering the *action phase*, the program counter is set to 0. Upon receiving a command, the clause selector sets the program counter to the label of the first statement of the *action clause* that should handle the command.
- Label -1, end of action. After executing an action, the program counter is set to -1, signalling that the command queue must be emptied and the process must change to the *when phase*.

An example is given in Translation 2. The `receive_command` action models the reception of a command that was sent by the FSM's parent. Such a command is ignored if no *action clause* handles it. In the example, observe that both after ignoring a command and after completing the execution of the STANDBY action handler, the program counter is set to -1. A process term not shown here then empties the command queue by issuing a sequence of `send_command` actions, and subsequently returns to the *when phase*. Note that these `send_command` actions and `receive_command` actions are meant to synchronise, resulting in a `comm_command` action. This is enforced at a higher level in the specification.

SML	mCRL2

`state: OFF`
  `action: STANDBY`
    `do STANDBY $ALL$Y`
    `do ON $ALL$Z`
  `action: OFF`
    `do OFF $ALL$Y`
  `action: ON`
    `do ON $ALL$Y`
	`instate_OFF(s) && isActPhase(phase) -> (`
	  `pc(aArgs) == 0 ->`
	    `sum c:Command.(`
	      `receive_command(parent,self,c).`
	      `isC_STANDBY(c) ->`
	        `X_CLASS(self,parent,s,chs,phase,`
	               `update_pc(aArgs,1)) <>`
	      `isC_OFF(c) ->`
	        `X_CLASS(self,parent,s,chs,phase,`
	               `update_pc(aArgs,3)) <>`
	      `isC_ON(c) ->`
	        `X_CLASS(self,parent,s,chs,phase,`
	               `update_pc(aArgs,4)) <>`
	      `send_state(self,parent,s).`
	      `ignored_command(self,c).`
	      `X_CLASS(self,parent,s,chs,phase,`
	            `update_pc(aArgs,-1))) +`
	
	  `pc(aArgs) == 1 ->`
	    `RPC_Chamber_CLASS(self,parent,s,chs,phase,`
	      `add_HV_STANDBY_commands(`
	        `update_pc(aArgs,2))) +`
	
	  `pc(aArgs) == 2 ->`
	    `RPC_Chamber_CLASS(self,parent,s,chs,phase,`
	      `add_LV_ON_commands(`
	        `update_pc(aArgs,-1)) + ...`

Translation 2: Simplified translation of the *action clauses* of a state OFF

Since a do statement is asynchronous, the children can send their state-update at any time during the *action phase*. This is dealt with as follows. Suppose a state-update message is received. If this precedes the reception of a command in this *action phase*, we simply process the state-update and move to the *when phase*. If we are in the middle of executing an *action clause*, we process the state-update, but do not move to the *when clause*.

3.3 Validating the Formalisation of SML

The challenge in formalising SML is in correctly interpreting its language constructs. We combined two strategies for assessing and improving the correctness of our semantics: informal discussions with the development team of the language and applying formal analysis techniques on sample FSMs taken from the control software.

The discussions with the SML development team were used to solidify our initial understanding of SML and its main constructs. Based on these discussions, we manually translated several FSMs into mCRL2, and validated the resulting processes manually using the available simulation and visualisation tools of mCRL2. This revealed a few minor issues with our understanding of the semantics of SML, alongside many issues that could be traced back to sloppiness in applying the translation from SML to mCRL2 manually.

In response to the latter problem, we eliminated the need for manually translating FSMs to mCRL2. To this end, we utilised the ASF+SDF meta-environment (see [13,11]) to rapidly prototype an automatic translator that, ultimately, came to implement the translation scheme we described in the previous section. The *Syntax Definition Formalism* (SDF) was used to describe the syntax of both SML and mCRL2, whereas the *Algebraic Specification Formalism* (ASF) was used to express the term rewrite rules that are needed to do the actual translation. Apart from the gains in speed and the consistency in applying the transformations that were brought about by the automation, the automation also served the purpose of formalising the semantics of SML.

The final details of our semantics were tested by analysing relatively well-understood subsystems of the control software in mCRL2. We briefly discuss our findings using a partly simplified subsystem, colloquially known as the *Wheel*, see Figure 3. The Wheel subsystem is a component of the Resistive Plate Chamber (RPC) subdetector of the CMS experiment. It belongs to the barrel region of the RPC subdetector. Each Wheel subsystem contains 12 sectors, each sector is equipped with 4 muon stations which are made of Drift Tube chambers. We forego a detailed formal discussion of this subsystem (for details, we refer to [12]), but only address our analysis of this subsystem using formal analyses techniques, and the impact this had on our understanding of the semantics and the transformation. It is important to keep in mind that the analysis was conducted primarily to assess the quality of our translation, the correctness of the subsystem being only secondary.

The mCRL2 specification of the *Wheel* subsystem was obtained by combining the mCRL2 processes obtained by running our prototype implementation on each involved FSM. Generating the state space of the *Wheel* subsystem takes roughly one minute using the symbolic state space generation tools offered by the LTSmin tools [4]. This toolset can be integrated in the mCRL2 toolset. For the discussed configuration, the state space is still of modest proportions, measuring slightly less than 5 million states and 24 million transitions. Varying the amount of children of class *Sector* causes a

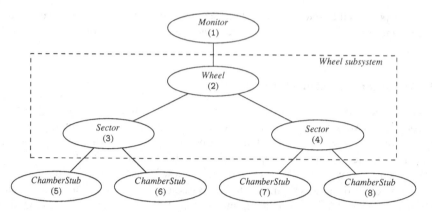

Fig. 3. A schematic overview of our model of the *Wheel* subsystem, and its used FSMs. The identifiers of the processes representing the FSMs are given between parentheses; these were used in our analyses.

dramatic growth of the state space. Using 3 instead of 2 children of class *Sector* yields roughly 800 million states; using 4 children of class *Sector*, leads to 120 billion states, and requires half a day.

Apart from repeating the simulations and visualisations, at this stage we also applied *model checking* to systematically probe the translation. Together with the development team of the *Wheel* subsystem, a few basic requirements were formalised in the first-order modal μ-calculus [8], see Table 1. The first-order modal μ-calculus is the default requirement specification language in the mCRL2 toolset.

The studied subsystem was considered to satisfy all stated properties. While smoothing out details in the translation of SML to mCRL2, the deadlock-freedom property was violated every now and then, indicating issues with our interpretation of SML. These were mostly concerned with the semantics of the blocking and non-blocking constructs of SML, and the complex constructs used to model the message passing between FSMs and their children.

The absence of intermediate states in the *when phase* was violated only once in our verification efforts. A more detailed scrutiny of the run revealed a problem in our translation, which was subsequently fixed.

The third requirement, stating the inevitability of a state change by a child once such a state change has been commissioned, failed to hold. The violation is caused by the overriding of commands by subsequent commands that are issued immediately. Discussions with the development teams revealed that the violations are real, *i.e.*, they are within the range of real behaviour, suggesting that our formalisation was adequate. The property was modified to ignore the spurious runs, resulting in the following property:

```
nu X. [true]X &&
    [comm_command(i,i_c,c)](mu Y. <true>true &&
        [!(comm_state(i_c,i,c2s(c)) ||
            exists c':Command. comm_command(i,i_c,c'))]Y)
```

Table 1. Basic requirements for the *Wheel* subsystem; `i:Id` denotes an identifier of an FSM; `i_c:Id` denotes a child of FSM `i`; `c:Command` denotes a command;`c2s(c)` denotes the state with the homonymous command name, *e.g.*, `c2s(ON)` = `ON`.

---

1. Absence of deadlock:

    ```
    nu X. [true]X && <true>true
    ```

2. Absence of intermediate states in the *when phase*:

    ```
    nu X. [true]X &&
            [exists s:State. move_state(i,s)](nu Y.
                [(!move_phase(i,ActionPhase))]Y
            && [exists s:State. move_state(i,s)]false)
    ```

3. Responsiveness:

    ```
    nu X. [true]X &&
            [comm_command(i,i_c,c)](mu Y.
                <true>true && [!comm_state(i_c,i,c2s(c))]Y)
    ```

4. Progress:

    ```
    nu X. [true]X &&
            mu Y. <exists s:State. move_state(i,s)>true
    ||
                (<true>true && [true]Y)
    ```

The final requirement also failed to hold. The violation is similar spirited to the violation of the third requirement, and, again found to comply to reality. The weakened requirement that was subsequently agreed upon expresses the attainability of some state change:

```
nu X. [true]X &&
    mu Y. <exists s:State. move_state(i,s)>true || <true>Y
```

Neither visual inspection of the state space using 2D and 3D visualisation tools, nor simulation using the mCRL2 simulators revealed any further incongruences in our final formalisation of SML, sketched in the previous section.

4 Dedicated Tooling for Verification

Some desired properties, such as the absence of loops within the *when phase*, can be checked by analysing an FSM in isolation, using the transformation to mCRL2. However, the verifications using the modal μ-calculus currently require too much overhead to serve as a basis for lightweight tooling that can be integrated in the SML development environment.

In an attempt to improve on this situation, we explored the possibilities of using *Bounded Model Checking* (BMC) [3,2]. The basic idea of BMC is to check for a counterexample in bounded runs. If no bugs are found using the current bound, then the bound is increased until either a bug is found, the problem becomes intractable, or some pre-determined upper bound is reached upon which the verification is complete. The BMC problem can be efficiently reduced to a propositional satisfiability problem, and can therefore be solved by SAT methods. SAT procedures do not necessarily suffer from the space explosion problem, and a modern SAT solver can handle formulas with hundreds of thousands of variables or more, see *e.g.* [2].

We have applied BMC techniques for the detection of move_to loops and the detection of unreachable states and trap states. As an example of a move_to loop, consider the excerpt of the ECALfw_CoolingDee FSM class in Listing 3, which our tool found to contain issues. If an instance of ECALfw_CoolingDee has one child in state ERROR and one in state NO_CONNECTION, it will loop indefinitely between these two states. Once this happens, an entire subsystem may enter a livelock and become unresponsive.

```
state: ERROR
  when ( $ANY$FwCHILDREN in_state NO_CONNECTION ) move_to NO_CONNECTION
  when ( $ALL$FwCHILDREN in_state OK ) move_to OK

state: NO_CONNECTION
  when ( $ALL$FwCHILDREN in_state OK ) move_to OK
  when ( $ANY$FwCHILDREN in_state ERROR ) move_to ERROR
```

Listing 3: An excerpt from the ECALfw_CoolingDee FSM that exhibits a loop within the *when phase*.

We first convert this problem into a graph problem as follows. Let $\mathcal{F}$ be an FSM and $\mathcal{M}$ be a Kripke structure. A state in $\mathcal{M}$ corresponds to the combined state of $\mathcal{F}$ and its children, *e.g.*, if $\mathcal{F}$ is in state ON and has two children which are in state OFF, then the corresponding state in $\mathcal{M}$ is (ON, OFF, OFF). There is a transition between two states s_1 and s_2 in $\mathcal{M}$ if and only if s_1 can do a move_to action to s_2 in $\mathcal{F}$. Moreover, every state in $\mathcal{M}$ is an initial state. It thus suffices to inspect $\mathcal{M}$ instead of $\mathcal{F}$, as stated by the following lemma:

Lemma 1. $\mathcal{F}$ *contains a loop of* move_to *actions if and only if* $\mathcal{M}$ *contains a loop.*

We next translate the problem of detecting a loop in $\mathcal{M}$ into a SAT problem. First, we consider executions of length k; afterwards, we show that we can statically choose k such that we can find every loop.

Let the predicate *in_state* be defined as follows: $in\_state(s, p, i)$ holds if and only if the process with identifier p is in state s after i steps. We assign the identifier zero to the FSM under consideration and the numbers $1, 2, 3, \ldots$ to its children. The resulting formula will have three components: the *state constraints*, the *transition relation* and the *loop condition*.

Using the state constraints, we ensure the FSM to always be in exactly one state. Moreover, the states of the children should not change during the execution of the *when phase*, per the semantics in the previous section. This is straigthforwardly expressed as a boolean formula on the *in_state* predicate.

Next, we encode the transition relation: the relation between $in\_state(s, 0, i)$ and $in\_state(s', 0, i + 1)$ for every i. In other words: the move_to steps the parent process is allowed to take. This involves converting the *when clauses* for each state of the parent FSM, taking care the semantics as outlined in the previous section is reflected. The last ingredient is the loop condition: if $in\_state(s, 0, 0)$ holds, then $in\_state(s, 0, i)$ must hold for some $i > 1$, indicating that the parent returned to the state in which it started.

The final SAT formula is obtained by taking the conjunction of the state constraints, the transition relation and the loop condition. It is not hard to see that if this formula is satisfiable, then there is a loop in $\mathcal{M}$ and hence in $\mathcal{F}$. It is more difficult to show that if there is a loop, then the formula is satisfiable. Let n be the total number of states of the FSM and let n_t be the total number of states of each child class t. We then have the following result:

Theorem 1. *All possible loops in $\mathcal{F}$ can be found by considering paths of length at most n in an FSM configuration $\mathcal{F}$ having n_t children for each child class t.*

Proof (sketch). Since $\mathcal{F}$ only has n states, the longest possible loop also contains n states. Since every state in $\mathcal{M}$ is an initial state, every possible loop can by found by doing n steps from an initial state.

It remains to show that all loops can be found by considering a configuration with n_t children for each child class t. This follows from the fact that SML guards are restricted to check for *any* or *all* children in a particular state.   □

A second desirable behavioural property of an FSM is that all states should remain reachable during the execution of an FSM. While we can again easily encode this property into the modal μ-calculus, we use a more direct approach to detect violations of this property by constructing a graph that captures all potential state changes. For this, we determine whether there is a configuration of children such that $\mathcal{F}$ can execute a move_to action from a state s to a state s'. Doing so for all pairs (s, s') of states of $\mathcal{F}$ yields a graph encoding all possible state changes of $\mathcal{F}$.

Computing the strongly connected components (SCCs) of the thusly obtained graph gives sufficient information to pinpoint violations to the reachability property: the presence of more than a single SCC means that one cannot move back and forth these SCCs (by definition of an SCC), and, therefore, their states. Note that this is an under-approximation of all errors that can potentially exist, as the actual reachability dynamically depends on the configuration of the children of an FSM. Still, as the state change graph of the ESfw_Endcap FSM class in Figure 4 illustrates, issues can be found in production FSMs: the OFF state can never be reached from any of the other states. Using the graphs generated by our tools, such issues are quickly explained and located.

Results. The results using our dedicated tools for performing these behavioural sanity checks on isolated FSMs are very satisfactory: of the several hundreds of FSM classes contained in the control system, we so far analysed 40 FSM classes and found 6 to contain issues. In 4 of these, we found logical errors that could give rise to livelocks in the system due to the presence of loops in the *when phase*; an example thereof is given in Listing 3. Somewhat unexpectedly, all loops were found to involve two states. Note that the size of the average FSM class (in general more than 100 lines of SML

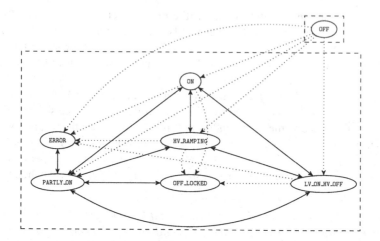

Fig. 4. The state change graph for the `ESfw_Endcap` FSM class. The solid lines are bidirectional; the dotted lines are unidirectional state changes. The SCCs are indicated by the dashed frames.

code, and at least two children) means that even short loops such as the ones identified so far remain unnoticed and are hard to pinpoint. The remaining two FSM classes were found to violate the required reachability of states, see *e.g.* Figure 4. The speed at which the errors can be found (generally requiring less than a second) means that the sanity checks could easily be incorporated in the design cycle of the FSMs.

5   Conclusion

We discussed and studied the State Machine Language (SML) that is currently used for programming the control software of the CMS experiment running at the Large Hadron Collider. To fully understand the language, we formalised it using the process algebraic language mCRL2. The quality of our formalisation was assessed using a combination of simulation and visualisation of the behaviour of FSMs in isolation and formally verifying small subsystems using model checking. To facilitate, among others, the assessment, the translation of SML to mCRL2 was implemented using the ASF+SDF meta-environment. Based on our understanding of the semantics of SML, we have built dedicated tools for performing sanity checks on isolated FSMs. Using these tools we found several issues in the control system. These tools have been well-received by the engineers at CERN, and are considered for inclusion in the development environment.

Our formalisation of SML opens up the possibility of verifying realistically large subsystems of the control system; clearly, it will be one of the most challenging verification problems currently available. In our analysis of the *Wheel* subsystem, we have only used a modest set of tools for manipulating the state space; symmetry reduction, partial order reduction, parallel exploration techniques, abstractions and abstract interpretation were not considered at this point. It remains to be investigated how such techniques fare on this problem.

Acknowledgments. We thank Giel Oerlemans, Dennis Schunselaar and Frank Staals from the Eindhoven University of Technology for their contribution to a first draft of the ASF+SDF translation. We also thank Frank Glege and Robert Gomez-Reino Garrido from the CERN CMS DAQ group for their support and advice, and Clara Gaspar for discussions on SML. Jaco van de Pol is thanked for his help with the LTSmin toolset.

References

1. Baeten, J.C.M., Basten, T., Reniers, M.A.: Process Algebra: Equational Theories of Communicating Processes. Cambridge Tracts in Theoretical Computer Science, vol. 50. Cambridge University Press (2010)
2. Biere, A., Cimatti, A., Clarke, E.M., Strichman, O., Zhu, Y.: Bounded Model Checking. Advances in Computers 58, 118–149 (2003)
3. Biere, A., Cimatti, A., Clarke, E., Zhu, Y.: Symbolic Model Checking without BDDs. In: Cleaveland, W.R. (ed.) TACAS 1999. LNCS, vol. 1579, pp. 193–207. Springer, Heidelberg (1999)
4. Blom, S., van de Pol, J., Weber, M.: LTSMIN: Distributed and Symbolic Reachability. In: Touili, T., Cook, B., Jackson, P. (eds.) CAV 2010. LNCS, vol. 6174, pp. 354–359. Springer, Heidelberg (2010)
5. Franek, B., Gaspar, C.: SMI++ object-oriented framework for designing and implementing distributed control systems. IEEE Transactions on Nuclear Science 52(4), 891–895 (2005)
6. Gaspar, C., Franek, B.: SMI++—Object-oriented framework for designing control systems for HEP experiments. Computer Physics Communications 110(1–3), 87–90 (1998)
7. Groote, J.F., Mathijssen, A.H.J., Reniers, M.A., Usenko, Y.S., van Weerdenburg, M.J.: Analysis of distributed systems with mCRL2. In: Process Algebra for Parallel and Distributed Processing, pp. 99–128. Chapman and Hall (2009)
8. Groote, J.F., Willemse, T.A.C.: Model-checking processes with data. Science of Computer Programming 56(3), 251–273 (2005)
9. Holme, O., González-Berges, M., Golonka, P., Schmeling, S.: The JCOP Framework. Technical Report CERN-OPEN-2005-027, CERN, Geneva (September 2005)
10. Hwong, Y.-L., Kusters, V.J.J., Willemse, T.A.C.: Analysing the control software of the Compact Muon Solenoid experiment at the Large Hadron Collider. arxiv.org/abs/1101.5324 (2011)
11. Klint, P.: A meta-environment for generating programming environments. ACM Trans. Softw. Eng. Methodol. 2(2), 176–201 (1993)
12. Paolucci, P., Polese, G.: The detector control systems for the cms resistive plate chamber, CERN-CMS-NOTE-2008-036 (2008) see, http://cdsweb.cern.ch/record/1167905
13. van den Brand, M.G.J., van Deursen, A., Heering, J., de Jong, H.A., de Jonge, M., Kuipers, T., Klint, P., Moonen, L., Olivier, P.A., Scheerder, J., Vinju, J.J., Visser, E., Visser, J.: The ASF+SDF Meta-Environment: A Component-Based Language Development Environment. In: Wilhelm, R. (ed.) CC 2001. LNCS, vol. 2027, pp. 365–370. Springer, Heidelberg (2001)

A Distributed Logic
for Networked Cyber-Physical Systems

Minyoung Kim, Mark-Oliver Stehr, and Carolyn Talcott

SRI International
{mkim,stehr,clt}@csl.sri.com

Abstract. A distributed logical framework designed to serve as a declarative semantic foundation for Networked Cyber-Physical Systems provides notions of facts and goals that include interactions with the environment via external goal requests, observations that generate facts, and actions that achieve goals. Reasoning rules are built on a partially ordered knowledge-sharing model for loosely coupled distributed computing. The logic supports reasoning in the context of dynamically changing facts and system goals. It can be used both to program systems and to reason about possible scenarios and emerging properties.

The underlying reasoning framework is specified in terms of constraints that must be satisfied, making it very general and flexible. Inference rules for an instantiation to a specific local logic (Horn clause logic) are given as a concrete example. The key novel features are illustrated with snippets from an existing application—a theory for self-organizing robots performing a distributed surveillance task. Traditional properties of logical inference and computation are reformulated in this novel context, and related to features of system design and execution. Proofs are outlined for key properties corresponding to soundness, completeness, and termination. Finally, the framework is compared to other formal systems addressing concurrent/distributed computation.

Keywords: Distributed declarative logic, partially ordered knowledge, networked cyber-physical systems.

1   Introduction

We present a novel distributed logic framework intended to serve as a semantic foundation for Networked Cyber-Physical Systems (NCPS). NCPS present many challenges that are not suitably addressed by existing distributed computing paradigms. They must be reactive and maintain an overall situation awareness that emerges from partial distributed knowledge. They must achieve system goals through local, asynchronous actions, using (distributed) control loops through which the environment provides essential feedback. NCPS should be resilient to failures of individual elements, readily adapt to changing situations, and often need to be rapidly instantiated and deployed for a given mission.

To address these challenges, we are developing a logical framework for NCPS that combines distributed reasoning and asynchronous control in space and time.

F. Arbab and M. Sirjani (Eds.): FSEN 2011, LNCS 7141, pp. 190–205, 2012.
© Springer-Verlag Berlin Heidelberg 2012

The purpose of logic in this context is many-fold. First of all, it provides a language to express and communicate system goals. Dually, it allows expressing and communicating facts about the current system state. In both cases, communication includes communication with the users but also communication among the system components themselves. At the level of an individual cyber-physical component, the logic provides a declarative interface for goal-oriented control and feedback through observations that are represented as logical facts. Finally, it provides a framework for inference and computation, which allows facts and goals to interact with each other and form new facts or goals. Our aim is a solution to declarative control that covers the entire spectrum between cooperation and autonomy, makes opportunistic use of networking resources, and adapts to changing resource constraints.

In the following we present a distributed inference system that is a significant step toward this goal. Our logical framework is based on partially ordered knowledge sharing, a distributed computing paradigm for loosely coupled systems that does not require continuous network connectivity. We use Horn clause logic to illustrate our approach, which we expect to generalize to more expressive logics. The features of the framework are illustrated using a theory of self-organizing robots. A simplified version of the inference system was presented in [11]. The main contributions of this paper are

- the fully general inference system with explicit derivations,
- the identification of conditions under which key properties such as soundness, completeness, termination, and confluence hold, and
- the application of our results to a theory for self-organizing robots

2   Case Study: Self-organizing Robots

We focus on networked cyber-physical systems S with a finite set of cyber-nodes. Two cyber-nodes have the capability to communicate whenever the network conditions permit. Each cyber-node can have sensors that can generate observations at arbitrary time points, and actuators driven by goals. S may operate under arbitrary conditions, so there is no guarantee that goals will be achieved. Consider a self-organizing network of mobile robots deployed in a building, e.g., for situational awareness during an emergency. In this paper, we use an abstract topological *mobility model* where a robot is located in some area and can move to any adjacent area. Each area is equipped with acoustic or motion sensors. The robots use a common logical theory that specifies a language (constants, functions, and predicates) and local inference rules based on Horn clause logic. A robot's local knowledge (state) consists of a set of facts and a set of goals. Facts are formulas derived by logical inference or by *observation* of the environment. Goals are formulas expressing what the system should achieve and drive the inference process. Goals can arrive from the environment at any time. They can also be generated as subgoals during local inference. Robots can exchange knowledge (i.e., facts and goals) opportunistically if they reside in the same or adjacent rooms.

Forward Clauses:

$F1 : Noise(T, A) \Rightarrow Trigger(T, A)$.
$F2 : Motion(T, A) \Rightarrow Trigger(T, A)$.
$F3 : Adjacent(A, B) \Rightarrow Adjacent(B, A)$.

Backward Clauses:

$B1 : Interest(T_I, I, R) \Leftarrow Result(T_I, T_T, 0, I), Deliver(T_I, T_T, 1, I, R)$.
$B2 : Deliver(T_I, T_T, N_D, I, R) \Leftarrow Delivered(T_I, T_T, N_D, I, R)$.
$B3 : Deliver(T_I, T_T, N_D, I, R) \Leftarrow$
$\quad\quad Position(T_P, R, A), Position(T'_P, R', A'), R' \neq R,$
$\quad\quad MoveTo(T_I, T_T, N_D, 0, \infty, R', A), Deliver(T_I, T_T, N_D, I, R)$.
$B4 : Result(T_I, T_T, N_D, I') \Leftarrow CompImage(T_I, T_T, N_D, I), I' = Extract(I)$.
$B5 : CompImage(T_I, T_T, N_D, I') \Leftarrow RawImage(T_I, T_T, N_D, I), I' = Compress(I)$.
$B6 : RawImage(T_I, T_T, N_D, I) \Leftarrow Trigger(T_T, A), T_I \leq T_T,$
$\quad\quad MoveTo(T_I, T_T, N_D, 0, T_T + \Delta t_{sd}, R, A),$
$\quad\quad TakeSnapshot(T_I, T_T, N_D, T_T + \Delta t_{sd}, A, I)$.
$B7 : TakeSnapshot(T_I, T_T, N_D, D, A, I) \Leftarrow$
$\quad\quad Snapshot(T_I, T_T, N_D, T_S, A, I), T_T \leq T_S, T_S \leq D$.
$B8 : MoveTo(T_I, T_T, N_D, W', D, R, B) \Leftarrow Position(T_P, R, B), T_P \leq D$.
$B9 : MoveTo(T_I, T_T, N_D, W', D, R, B) \Leftarrow Adjacent(A, B), W' > -b_w, W = W' - 1,$
$\quad\quad MoveTo(T_I, T_T, N_D, W, D, R, A), Move(T_I, T_T, N_D, W', D, R, A, B)$.

Replacement Ordering: (f denotes a fact and g a goal and x denotes either)

$O1 : f : Position(t_P, r, \ldots) \prec f : Position(t'_P, r, \ldots)$ if $t_P < t'_P$.
$O2 : x : X(t_I, \ldots) \prec g : Interest(t'_I, \ldots)$ if $t_I < t'_I$.
$O3 : x : X(t_I, t_T, 0, \ldots) \prec f : Result(t_I, t_T, 0, \ldots)$ if $x : X \neq f : Result$.
$O4 : x : X(t_I, t_D, 1, \ldots) \prec f : Deliver(t_I, t_D, 1, \ldots)$ if $x : X \neq f : Deliver$.

Variables: T: time, D: snapshot deadline, A and B: area, R: robot,
$\quad\quad\quad\quad$ I: image or derived information, N: identifier, W: weight
Constants: Δt_{sd}: relative snapshot deadline (max. delay from trigger event),
$\quad\quad\quad\quad$ b_w: bound for weight (diameter of the floor plan)

Fig. 1. Logical Theory for Self-Organizing Robots

Figure 1 shows the logical theory that is used to specify the possible behaviors of our self-organizing robots. The clauses are partitioned into forward and backward rules, providing a means for controlling inference/execution. Forward clauses such as the trigger conditions $F1$ and $F2$ can be applied at any time when the conditions are met. Backward clauses are applied only when the conclusion formula matches (unifies with) an existing goal. Goal atoms appearing as premises in forward or backward clauses generate new goals to be satisfied in an execution. The primary goal is delivery of images I to a node r, $Interest(T_I, I, r)$. Figure 2, shows a possible execution of the theory of Figure 1 achieving an instance of the $Interest$ goal. The variables (T_I, T_T, N_D) are suppressed, as they are fixed for an execution solving primary goal instance. For example, $Result(I)$ abbreviates $Result(t_I, t_T, n_D, I)$ where t_I is the session value of T_I and so on. At the top of Figure 2, the user injects a cyber-goal $Interest(I, r)$ at the root node r. Backward reasoning with clause $B1$ is used to add the first subgoal, $Result(I)$, to the local knowledge base. Then clauses $B4, B5$ for solving $Result$ goals, are used to add subgoals, $CompImage(I)$ and $RawImage(I)$.

Meanwhile, at the bottom of Figure 2, the cyber-fact $Noise(0.0, a)$ is observed by the sensor in area a, and forward reasoning using clause $F1$ leads to the fact $Trigger(0.0, a)$. Clause $B6$ for $RawImage(I)$ has three subgoals involving $Trigger$, $MoveTo$, and $TakeSnapshot$. The leftmost subgoal can be matched with the fact $Trigger(0.0, a)$. Suppose the above reasoning is carried out by robot r in area a and further that a camera robot, x, is in adjacent area b. Then by communication with r, x can learn the $RawImage$ goal, and the $Trigger$ fact and use $B6$ to add a $MoveTo$ goal to its knowledge base and $B8, B9$ to satisfy the goal. Then using its cam-

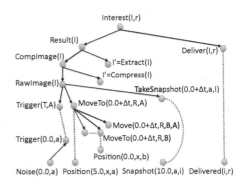

Fig. 2. Example Robot Execution

era, robot x can take a snapshot adding $Snapshot(10.0, a, i)$ to the set of facts and apply $B7, B6$ to realize the $TakeSnapshot(t_D, a, I)$, and the $RawImage(I)$ goals. The goals $CompImage(I)$ and $Result(I)$ can be solved by the robot x, since it has the fact $RawImage(i)$. Alternatively, it could be satisfied by another robot, possibly r, depending on available computational resources. The backward clause $B3$ is used to steer a robot toward the root node r to deliver the image, and $B2$ can be applied once a $Delivered$ fact is available. Then $Interest(I, r)$ can be satisfied.

Unlike traditional logics, new facts and/or goals can arrive at any time, interleaved with local inference processes. For example, a robot can observe its position at different times, and possibly get different answers. Two features of the logical framework help to avoid potential confusion. Certain predicates, called *cyber-predicates*, have time stamps as part of their argument list. For example, position readings are time stamped and thus different readings can be distinguished logically by their time stamp. In addition, the logical theory is augmented by a partial ordering on facts and goals, called the *replacement ordering*. A fact or goal can be replaced by one that is higher in the ordering. This provides a means of removing outdated knowledge from the distributed system state, without any need for synchronization.

The clauses (O1-4) at the end of Figure 1 axiomatize the replacement ordering of the robot theory. Suppose some robot has a fact $Position(0.0, r, b)$ in its knowledge base, stating that robot r is in area b at time 0.0, and later the robot receives the fact $Position(1.0, r, a)$. The replacement rule can be used to remove $Position(0.0, r, b)$ from its set of facts since $Position(0.0, r, b) \prec Position(1.0, r, a)$.

3   The Distributed Logical Framework

Constraints on the Local Theory. Let Σ be a signature, $\mathcal{V}$ a countably infinite set of variables, and Ω a fixed finite theory of Horn clause logic over Σ. The sets of *terms* $\mathcal{T}(\Sigma, \mathcal{V})$, and *atoms* $\mathcal{A}(\Sigma, \mathcal{V})$, ground terms $\mathcal{T}(\Sigma)$ and ground atoms $\mathcal{A}(\Sigma)$ are defined as usual. We use P and Q to range over atoms. A (ground) substitution is a mapping from variables to (ground) terms. We let σ range over substitutions, and $\sigma(e)$ denotes the application of a substitution, that is the result of replacing variables in e by their image under σ.

Σ contains built-in constants for natural numbers and names of cyber-nodes. Additional *built-in functions*, and *built-in predicates* can be included in Σ, and the application of a built-in predicate cannot be the conclusion of a clause in Ω. Σ also contains a distinguished set of predicates (distinct from built-ins) called *cyber-predicates*. These predicates define the interface of the logic with the outside world. We use p_c to range over such predicates. The first argument of a cyber-predicate is a natural number interpreted as a timestamp. In the robot theory, $\leq$, *Compress* and *Extract* are built in, while *Snapshot* and *Position* are cyber-predicates. Clauses in Ω are assigned unique labels, for example $l : P_1, \ldots, P_n \Rightarrow Q$ is a clause with label l. In addition $\Omega = \Omega_f \cup \Omega_b$, where Ω_f and Ω_b are sets of clauses that we refer to as *forward and backward clauses*, respectively. We use $\vdash$ to denote the *standard derivability* in Horn clause logic with all the built-ins in Σ.

A *fact* is a ground atom. The definition of *goal* is more complex. A subset of the predicates, designated as *goal predicates*, includes at least the built-in predicates and all predicates that appear in the conclusion of a clause from Ω_b. The set of *goals* can be any set of (not necessarily ground) atoms that are applications of goal predicates satisfying the following closure properties: **(1)** If G is a goal then $\sigma(G)$ is a goal. **(2)** If $l : P_1, \ldots, P_n \Rightarrow Q \in \Omega_f$, $j \in 1, \ldots, n$, P_j is the application of a goal predicate, and $\sigma(P_i)$ is a fact for $i \leq 1 < j$, then $\sigma(P_j)$ is a goal. **(3)** If $l : P_1, \ldots, P_n \Rightarrow Q \in \Omega_b$, P_j is the application of a goal predicate, $\sigma(P_i)$ is a fact for all $1 \leq i < j \leq n$, and $\sigma(Q)$ is a goal, then $\sigma(P_j)$ is a goal. In the robot theory, $Interest(t_I, I, R)$ is a goal only for ground terms t_I, and $MoveTo(t_I, t_T, n_D, W, D, R, B)$ is a goal for ground terms t_I, t_T, n_D. The capitalized arguments are variables.

We further require the *variable restriction*: **(1)** For $l : P_1, \ldots, P_n \Rightarrow Q \in \Omega_f$, each variable in Q appears in at least one of $P_1, \ldots, P_n$. **(2)** For $l : P_1, \ldots, P_n \Rightarrow Q \in \Omega_b$, if $\sigma(Q)$ is a goal, then each variable in $\sigma(Q)$ appears in at least one of $\sigma(P_1), \ldots, \sigma(P_n)$. It is easy to check that our example satisfies this restriction.

Derived Atoms as Knowledge. Derived facts and derived goals are objects of the form $f : F$ and $g : G$ that constitute units of knowledge, atoms equipped with an indication of their role and an explanation of their origin. The set of *(atomic) derived facts* and *(atomic) derived goals* together is inductively defined as follows: **(1)** $\mathsf{B}_\sigma(g) : \sigma(G)$ is a derived fact if G is a built-in goal, $\vdash \sigma(G)$, and $g : G$ is a derived goal. **(2)** $\mathsf{O}(F) : F$ is an atomic derived fact, also called an *observation*, for each cyber-fact F, **(3)** $\mathsf{C}(G) : G$ is an atomic derived goal, also called a *control*, for each cyber-goal G; **(4)** $l_\sigma(f_1, \ldots, f_n) : \sigma(Q)$ is a derived fact if $l : P_1, \ldots, P_n \Rightarrow Q \in \Omega_f$, $\sigma(Q)$ is a fact, and $f_i : \sigma(P_i)$ are derived facts; **(5)** $l_\sigma^{-1}(f_1, \ldots, f_{j-1}) : \sigma(P_j)$ is a derived goal if $l : P_1, \ldots, P_n \Rightarrow Q \in \Omega_f$, $j \in 1, \ldots, n$, $\sigma(P_j)$ is a goal, and $f_i : \sigma(P_i)$ are derived facts; **(6)** $l_\sigma(f_1, \ldots, f_n; g') : \sigma(Q)$ is a derived fact if $l : P_1, \ldots, P_n \Rightarrow Q \in \Omega_b$, $\sigma(Q)$ is a fact, $f_i : \sigma(P_i)$ are derived facts, and $g' : G'$ is a derived goal with $\sigma(G') = \sigma(Q)$; and **(7)** $l_\sigma^{-1}(f_1, \ldots, f_{j-1}; g') : \sigma(P_j)$ is a derived goal if $l : P_1, \ldots, P_n \Rightarrow Q \in \Omega_b$, $j \in 1, \ldots, n$, $\sigma(P_j)$ is a goal, $f_i : \sigma(P_i)$ are derived facts, $g' : G'$ is a derived goal, and $\sigma(G') = \sigma(Q)$.

A *derived atom* is either a derived fact or a derived goal. This is different from standard approaches to explicit proof objects where derivations of goals are not considered. We let $f : F$ range over derived facts with derivation f and underlying fact F. Similarly $g : G$ ranges over derived goals and $d : P$ ranges over derived atoms. Goals may have variables, and we consider two derived goals that differ only by renaming of the variables to be the same. Given a derived atom $d : P$, it is easy to see that P is uniquely determined by d. We write $at(d : P)$ to denote the atom of $d : P$, i.e., P.

We say that $d : P$ is an *immediate subderivation* of $d' : P'$, written $d : P \rhd d' : P'$, iff d' is of the form $L(\ldots, d, \ldots)$, where L represents any of the above constructors of derivations. $\rhd^+$ and $\rhd^*$ denote the transitive and reflexive transitive closure of $\rhd$, respectively. We let K range over derived atoms and $\mathcal{K}$ range over sets of derived atoms. The *knowledge entailment* relation $\vdash$ is defined inductively by: **(1)** $K \in \mathcal{K}$ implies $\mathcal{K} \vdash K$, and **(2)** $\mathcal{K}' \vdash_1 K''$ and $\mathcal{K} \vdash K'$ for all $K' \in \mathcal{K}'$ implies $\mathcal{K} \vdash K''$, where $\mathcal{K} \vdash_1 K'$ is defined by $K \rhd K'$ for some $K \in \mathcal{K}$.

We assume that the set of derived atoms is equipped with a quasi-order $\leq$, the so-called *subsumption order*, and a strict partial order $\prec$, the so-called *replacement order*. These relations must not make use of the structure of the derivations other than distinguishing between facts and goals, they must not relate distinct built-in derived atoms, and $\leq$ must not relate derived facts and derived goals. For derived goals $g : G$ and $g' : G'$ with $G = \sigma(G')$ we require $g : G \leq g' : G'$. The induced *subsumption equivalence* $K \equiv K'$ is defined as $K \leq K' \wedge K' \leq K$ and strict subsumption is defined by $K < K'$ iff $K \leq K'$ and $K' \not\leq K$. We require that the replacement order is a *compatible extension* of strict subsumption, that is, **(1)** $K < K'$ implies $K \prec K'$, and **(2)** $K \leq K'$, $K' \prec K''$, and $K'' \leq K'''$ implies $K \prec K'''$. In addition, the relations must satisfy the *ordering consistency* requirements, that is, **(1)** $K \prec K'$ implies $K \not\equiv K'$, and **(2)** $K_1' \leq K_1 \prec K_2 \leq K_2'$ and $K_1' < K_2'$ implies $K_1 < K_2$.

Distributed Proofs as Interactive Executions. The local state of a cyber-node is of the form $\Gamma \vdash \Delta @ t, x$, where x is the unique name of the node, t is a natural number representing its local time, and Γ, Δ constitutes the knowledge at the node. Γ is a finite set of derived facts, and Δ is a finite set of derived goals. A configuration of a cyber-physical system S is a set of local states $\Gamma \vdash \Delta @ t, x$, one for each cyber-node x of S. Given a configuration c containing $\Gamma \vdash \Delta @ t, x$, we write $\mathcal{F}_x(c)$ and $\mathcal{G}_x(c)$ to denote Γ and Δ, respectively.

Figure 3 gives the proof rules of our logic. The rule (Control) represents the addition of a new user-level objective to the set of system goals. The rule

$$\frac{\Gamma \vdash \Delta \ @ \ t, x}{\Gamma \vdash \Delta, \mathsf{C}(G) : G \ @ \ t', x} \quad \text{if } G = p_c(t, \ldots) \text{ is a cyber-goal} \qquad \text{(Control)}$$

$$\frac{\Gamma \vdash \Delta \ @ \ t, x}{\Gamma, \mathsf{O}(F) : F \vdash \Delta \ @ \ t', x} \quad \text{if } F = p_c(t, \ldots) \text{ is a cyber-fact} \qquad \text{(Observation)}$$

$$\frac{\Gamma, f : F \vdash \Delta \ @ \ t, x}{\Gamma \vdash \Delta \ @ \ t', x} \quad \text{if } f : F \prec \Gamma, \Delta \qquad \text{(Replacement1)}$$

$$\frac{\Gamma \vdash \Delta, g : G \ @ \ t, x}{\Gamma \vdash \Delta \ @ \ t', x} \quad \text{if } g : G \prec \Gamma, \Delta \qquad \text{(Replacement2)}$$

$$\frac{\Gamma_x \vdash \Delta_x \ @ \ t_x, x \quad \Gamma_y, f : F \vdash \Delta_y \ @ \ t_y, y}{\Gamma_x, f : F \vdash \Delta_x \ @ \ t'_x, x} \qquad \text{(Communication1)}$$
if $x \neq y$, $t'_x \geq t_y$, and $f : F$ is fresh at x.

$$\frac{\Gamma_x \vdash \Delta_x \ @ \ t_x, x \quad \Gamma_y \vdash \Delta_y, g : G \ @ \ t_y, y}{\Gamma_x \vdash \Delta_x, g : G \ @ \ t'_x, x} \qquad \text{(Communication2)}$$
if $x \neq y$, $t'_x \geq t_y$, and $g : G$ is fresh at x

$$\frac{\Gamma \vdash \Delta, g : G \ @ \ t, x}{\Gamma, \mathsf{B}_\sigma(g) : \sigma(G) \vdash \Delta, g : G \ @ \ t', x} \qquad \text{(Built-in)}$$
if G is a built-in goal with a solution $\sigma(G)$ such that $\mathsf{B}_\sigma(g) : \sigma(G)$ is fresh.

$$\frac{\Gamma, f_1 : \sigma(P_1), \ldots, f_n : \sigma(P_n) \vdash \Delta \ @ \ t, x}{\Gamma, f_1 : \sigma(P_1), \ldots, f_n : \sigma(P_n), f : \sigma(Q) \vdash \Delta \ @ \ t', x} \qquad \text{(Forward1)}$$
if $l : P_1, \ldots, P_n \Rightarrow Q$ is a clause from Ω_{f},
$f = l_\sigma(f_1, \ldots, f_n)$, $\sigma(Q)$ is a fact, and $f : \sigma(Q)$ is fresh.

$$\frac{\Gamma, f_1 : \sigma(P_1), \ldots, f_{j-1} : \sigma(P_{j-1}) \vdash \Delta \ @ \ t, x}{\Gamma, f_1 : \sigma(P_1), \ldots, f_{j-1} : \sigma(P_{j-1}) \vdash \Delta, g : \sigma(P_j) \ @ \ t', x} \qquad \text{(Forward2)}$$
if $l : P_1, \ldots, P_n \Rightarrow Q$ is a clause from Ω_{f},
$g = l_\sigma^{-1}(f_1, \ldots, f_{j-1})$, $\sigma(P_j)$ is a goal, and $g : \sigma(P_j)$ is fresh.

$$\frac{\Gamma, f_1 : \sigma(P_1), \ldots, f_n : \sigma(P_n) \vdash \Delta, g' : G' \ @ \ t, x}{\Gamma, f_1 : \sigma(P_1), \ldots, f_n : \sigma(P_n), f : \sigma(Q) \vdash \Delta, g' : G' \ @ \ t', x} \qquad \text{(Backward1)}$$
if $l : P_1, \ldots, P_n \Rightarrow Q$ is a clause from Ω_{b},
$f = l_\sigma(f_1, \ldots, f_n; g')$, $\sigma(Q) = \sigma(G')$, $\sigma(Q)$ is a fact, and $f : \sigma(Q)$ is fresh.

$$\frac{\Gamma, f_1 : \sigma(P_1), \ldots, f_{j-1} : \sigma(P_{j-1}) \vdash \Delta, g' : G' \ @ \ t, x}{\Gamma, f_1 : \sigma(P_1), \ldots, f_{j-1} : \sigma(P_{j-1}) \vdash \Delta, g' : G', g : \sigma(P_j) \ @ \ t', x} \qquad \text{(Backward2)}$$
if $l : P_1, \ldots, P_n \Rightarrow Q$ is a clause from Ω_{b},
$g = l_\sigma^{-1}(f_1, \ldots, f_{j-1}; g')$, $\sigma(Q) = \sigma(G')$, $\sigma(P_j)$ is a goal, and $g : \sigma(P_j)$ is fresh.

$$\frac{\Gamma \vdash \Delta \ @ \ t, x}{\Gamma \vdash \Delta \ @ \ t', x} \qquad \text{(Sleep)}$$

Notes. An implicit side condition $t < t'$ is omitted in all proof rules ($t_x < t'_x$ in the communication rules). In the context of a proof rule that has a premise $\Gamma \vdash \Delta \ @ \ t, x$ we say that K is *fresh* (at x) if there is no $K' \in \Gamma, \Delta$ such that $K \equiv K'$ or $K \prec K'$. In the condition of proof rules we use σ to range over all most general (not necessarily ground) substitutions that satisfy the condition of the proof rule.

Fig. 3. Proof Rules of our Distributed Logical Framework for NCPS

(Observation) captures the generation of information from the environment, spontaneously or triggered by a goal. The (Replacement) rules are used to overwrite subsumed and obsolete facts and goals. The (Communication) rules allow cyber-nodes to exchange facts or goals by means of asynchronous communication. The time constraints in the rule achieve a minimal level of temporal consistency. The forward and backward rules implement forward and backward reasoning. The rule (Forward1) is the usual Horn clause rule. The rule (Forward2) covers the case where the available facts are not sufficient to apply the clause so that a new subgoal $\sigma(P_j)$ needs to be generated for a missing fact. The backward rules are analogous to the two forward rules, but in addition require the Horn clause conclusion to unify with an existing goal. Finally, the (Sleep) rule allows the system to be inactive, for example to save energy or wait for new knowledge.

The proof rules determine a labeled transition relation $\rightarrow_r$ on configurations of the cyber-physical system S: For configurations c and c', we have $c \rightarrow_r c'$ iff there exists an instance of proof rule r such that c contains the premises of the instance, and c' is obtained by an update of c with the conclusion, i.e., by replacing $\Gamma \vdash \Delta$ @ t, x by the conclusion $\Gamma' \vdash \Delta'$ @ t', x. In this case, we also say that r is *applicable* at x in c. An execution of the networked cyber-physical system S is a finite or infinite sequence $\pi = c_0, r_0, c_1, r_1, c_2, \ldots$ of configurations such that $c_i \rightarrow_{r_i} c_{i+1}$ for all i, and we say that $c_i \rightarrow_{r_i} c_{i+1}$, or briefly r_i, is the ith step of π. We say that a rule r is *applied* in π at j iff $r = r_j$.

For a given execution π, we denote by $\mathcal{F}^O(\pi)$ all derived facts of the form $\mathsf{O}(F) : F$ generated in π by the observation rule and by $\mathcal{G}^C(\pi)$ all derived goals of the form $\mathsf{C}(G) : G$ generated in π by the control rule.

4 Properties of the Logical Framework

For a logical framework to be a useful semantic foundation it is important that we understand the guarantees provided by the framework. Here we discuss properties of executions, $\pi = c_0, r_0, c_1, r_1, c_2, \ldots$, where c_0 is an initial configuration in which each node has an empty set of facts and goals. Most of these properties are independent of the underlying communication system. Several of the properties only require the Horn clause theory and/or the execution strategy to satisfy additional conditions. Specifically, we consider notions of *Monotonicity*, *Soundness*, *Completeness*, *Termination*, and *Confluence*. These are analogs of properties of traditional inference and computation systems and important for ensuring desired properties of specific cyber-physical systems. In the following, $\pi_{|i}$ denotes the prefix $c_0, r_0, c_1, r_1, c_2, \ldots, c_i$ of π, and $\mathcal{K} \vdash Q$ denotes $at(\mathcal{K}) \vdash Q$ where $at(\mathcal{K})$ is the set of atoms of the derived facts of $\mathcal{K}$ (i.e., ignoring derivations).

Monotonicity is the property that for all steps $i \leq j$ of π and for every cyber-node x, $\mathcal{F}_x(c_i) \subseteq \mathcal{F}_x(c_j)$ and $\mathcal{G}_x(c_i) \subseteq \mathcal{G}_x(c_j)$. *Monotonicity* holds if no replacement rules are applied in π, because only replacement rules remove facts or goals from a node's state.

Soundness expresses that any derived fact appearing in an execution π is provable in Horn clause logic (with built-ins) from the previous observations. It holds because derived atoms that appear in π are entailed by previous observations and controls of π, and entailment on derived atoms implies entailment in Horn clause logic.

Theorem 1 (Soundness). *For every step i of π, and for each $f : F \in \mathcal{F}(c_i)$, we have $\mathcal{F}^O(\pi_{|i}), \mathcal{G}^C(\pi_{|i}) \vdash f : F$, which in turn implies $\mathcal{F}^O(\pi_{|i}) \vdash F$.*

Proof. By Lemmas 1 and 2 below.   □

Lemma 1 (Derivability implies provability). *If $f : F$ is a derived fact and $\mathcal{F}$ is the set of facts underlying the atomic subderivations of $f : F$ then $\mathcal{F} \vdash F$*

Proof. We show $\mathcal{F} \vdash F$ by cases on f. If $f : F$ is $B_\sigma(g) : \sigma(G)$, then $\vdash \sigma(G)$ by definition of derived facts. If $f : F$ is $O(F) : F$ we have $O(F) \vdash O(F)$. If $f : F$ is $l_\sigma(f_1, \ldots, f_n, [g']) : \sigma(Q)$, with $l : P_1, \ldots, P_n \Rightarrow Q$ in Ω, then by induction we have $\mathcal{F} \vdash f_i : \sigma(P_i), 1 \leq i \leq n$ and $\mathcal{F} \vdash \sigma(Q)$, applying clause l.   □

Lemma 2 (Derivations are derivable). *If $f : F \in \mathcal{F}(c_i)$ and $g : G \in \mathcal{G}(c_i)$, then $\mathcal{F}^O(\pi_{|i}), \mathcal{G}^C(\pi_{|i}) \vdash f : F$ and $\mathcal{F}^O(\pi_{|i}), \mathcal{G}^C(\pi_{|i}) \vdash g : G$.*

Proof. The proof is by induction on i. Note that $\mathcal{F}^O(\pi_{|i-1}), \mathcal{G}^C(\pi_{|i-1}) \vdash f : F$ implies $\mathcal{F}^O(\pi_{|i}), \mathcal{G}^C(\pi_{|i}) \vdash f : F$ (monotonicity of $\vdash$). We only need to consider rules r_i that introduce a new derived fact $f : F$ or goal $g : G$ at some cyber-node x. There are five cases for facts and four for goals. Here we show a few cases to illustrate the arguments (see [8] for the full proof).

(Observation) $f : F$ is $O(F) : F$, which is in $\mathcal{F}^O(\pi_{|i})$.

(Forward1) $f : F$ is $l_\sigma(f_1, \ldots, f_n) : \sigma(Q)$, $l : P_1, \ldots, P_n \Rightarrow Q \in \Omega_f$, $f_j : \sigma(P_j) \in \mathcal{F}(c_{i-1})$, $1 \leq j \leq n$. By induction $\mathcal{F}^O(\pi_{|i-1}), \mathcal{G}^C(\pi_{|i-1}) \vdash f_j : F_j$ for $1 \leq j \leq n$ and so $\mathcal{F}^O(\pi_{|i}), \mathcal{G}^C(\pi_{|i}) \vdash f : F$.

(Forward2) $g : G$ is $l_\sigma^{-1}(f_1, \ldots, f_{j-1}) : \sigma(P_j)$, $l : P_1, \ldots, P_n \Rightarrow Q \in \Omega_f$, and $f_k : \sigma(P_k) \in \mathcal{F}(c_{i-1})$, $1 \leq k < j$. By induction $\mathcal{F}^O(\pi_{|i-1}), \mathcal{G}^C(\pi_{|i-1}) \vdash f_k : F_k$ for $1 \leq k < j$ and thus $\mathcal{F}^O(\pi_{|i}), \mathcal{G}^C(\pi_{|i}) \vdash g : G$.   □

Note that *Monotonicity* and *Soundness* are independent of the specific theory; in particular, they hold for the robot theory.

Completeness gives conditions under which a fact provable in the logic will eventually be covered (either directly or by subsumption). These conditions include fairness conditions on executions and consistency conditions between the theory and the subsumption and replacement orderings.

Definition 1 (Weak Fairness). *A rule instance contains the parameters that determine whether a rule applies in a configuration and if so, what the result is. It is given by the rule name, the node(s), the clause label, substitution, and all derived facts or goals involved in the application. For example, $\mathsf{Forward1}(x, l, \sigma, f_1 :$*

$\sigma(P_1), \ldots, f_n : \sigma(P_n), l_\sigma(f_1, \ldots, f_n) : \sigma(Q))$ *represents an instance of the first forward rule. A rule instance ρ is* permanently applicable *in π at i iff ρ is applicable to c_j for $j \geq i$. An execution is* logically fair *iff each instance of a* reasoning rule, *i.e., either a built-in, forward, or backward rule, that is permanently applicable at i is applied at some $j \geq i$. Similarly, an execution is* replacement fair *iff each instance of a* replacement rule *that is permanently applicable at i is applied at some $j \geq i$. An execution is* communication fair *iff each instance of a* communication rule *that is permanently applicable at i is applied at some $j \geq i$. An execution is* globally fair *iff it is logically, replacement, and communication fair.*

Definition 2 (Subsumption Preservation). *We say subsumption is preserved iff whenever $K_i \leq K_i'$ and $K_1, \ldots, K_n \vdash_1 K$, then there exists K' such that $K_1', \ldots, K_n' \vdash_1 K'$ and $K \leq K'$ (recall that K ranges over derived atoms).*

Definition 3 (Replacement Conditions). *Replacement is* restricted *iff the following conditions hold: (1) If $K_1 \prec K_2$, then $K_2 \not\rhd^+ K_1$. (2) If $K_1 \prec K_2$, $K_1 \not\rhd^+ K_2$ and $K_1 \not\leq K_2$, then there exists atomic K_1', K_2' such that $K_1' \rhd^* K_1$, $K_2' \rhd^* K_2$ and $K_1' \prec K_2'$. (3) If $K_1 \prec K_2$, $K_1 \rhd^+ K_2$, $K_1 \rhd^+ K_3$, $K_3 \not\rhd^+ K_2$, and $K_2 \not\rhd^+ K_3$, then $K_3 \leq K_2$. (4) If $K_1 \leq K_2$ and there is an atomic $K_2' \rhd^* K_2$ with $K_2' \prec K$, then there is an atomic $K_1' \rhd^* K_1$ with $K_1' \prec K$.*

We say that a derived fact $f : F$ is *eventually covered in* π there is some i and $f' : F' \in \mathcal{F}(c_i)$ such that $f : F \leq f' : F'$. The essence of completeness is that if $\mathcal{F} \vdash F$ for a subset of the observed facts of an execution, then some derivation of F will be eventually covered in the execution. The completeness theorem statement refines this, beginning with sufficient constraints for completeness to hold. The statement is broken into two parts, first showing provability implies derivability, and second showing that if a derived fact $f : F$ is entailed by subset of the observations of an execution, $f : F$ will eventually be covered. This is further split into two cases depending whether the final rule in the Horn clause derivation is a forwards or backwards rule. This is needed to account for the requirement that there must be a goal that unifies with a backwards rule conclusion before the rule can be applied, and thus in the backwards case, the theorem only applies to instances of goals.

Theorem 2 (Completeness). *Let π be a logically and communication fair execution, and let $\mathcal{F} \subseteq \mathcal{F}^O(\pi)$ and $\mathcal{G} \subseteq \mathcal{G}^C(\pi)$ be such that each element in $\mathcal{F} \cup \mathcal{G}$ is maximal in $\mathcal{F}^O(\pi) \cup \mathcal{G}^C(\pi)$ w.r.t. the replacement ordering. Assume subsumption is preserved, upward well-founded, and that replacement is restricted. If $at(\mathcal{F}) \vdash_f F$ then there exists a derived fact $f : F$ such that $\mathcal{F} \vdash f : F$, which in turn implies that $f : F$ is eventually covered in π. If $G \in at(\mathcal{G})$ and $at(\mathcal{F}) \vdash_b \sigma(G)$ then there exists a derived fact $f : \sigma(G)$ such that $\mathcal{F}, \mathcal{G} \vdash f : \sigma(G)$, which in turn implies that $f : \sigma(G)$ is eventually covered in π. Here $\vdash_f$ ($\vdash_g$) denote Horn clause derivability where the last clause applied is from Ω_f (Ω_g).*

Proof. As for soundness the proof has two parts: (a) showing that entailment in the Horn logic sense implies entailment in derived-atom sense, and (b) showing that a derived-atom derivable from the observed facts and injected (control) goals will eventually be covered in an execution. The proof of (a) is similar to the proof of Lemma 1. The proof of (b) is structured using cases from the definition of replacement restriction. Maximality of the observed facts is needed as part of dealing with replacement rules. For details we refer to [8].   □

Completeness implies that all solutions for a goal are eventually generated, which is not always a desirable property in practice. For instance, in our robot example, the specification states that the user interest is satisfied as soon as one suitable snapshot is available, and further snapshots (and related activities) can be suppressed by means of the replacement ordering. Specifically, consider a situation where one goal $TakeSnapshot(t_I, t_T, n_D, t_D, A, I)$ leads to multiple $Snapshot(t_I, t_T, n_D, t_S, a, i)$ facts. Suppose there are two $Snapshot$ facts; the logic will solve the $Result$ goal with the first and discard both using replacement. In this execution one $Snapshot$ fact will be ignored, but there is another execution where it is not.

Termination constrains the local inference system to avoid infinite regression in the attempt to achieve a goal. To state the theorem we need to define the finite closure property for a set of derived atoms, which by the correspondence between Horn clause derivability and the derivability relation on derived atoms is in fact a constraint on the Horn clause theory. We use a special case of the general definition for simplicity.

Definition 4 (Finite Closure). *We say that a set $\mathcal{F} \cup \mathcal{G}$ of derived facts and goals has the* finite closure property *iff there exists a well-founded quasi-order $(\mathcal{K}, \leq)$ such that $\mathcal{F} \cup \mathcal{G} \subseteq \mathcal{K}$, for each induced equivalence class $\mathcal{K}'$ the projection on atoms $at(\mathcal{K}')$ is finite, and the following conditions are satisfied: (0) If $g:G \in \mathcal{K}$ is a built-in goal and $\vdash \sigma(G)$ then $\mathsf{B}_\sigma(g):\sigma(G) \in \mathcal{K}$ and $\mathsf{B}_\sigma(g):\sigma(G) \leq g:G$. (1) If $l:P_1,\ldots,P_n \Rightarrow Q$ in Ω_f and $\mathcal{K} \vdash f_1:\sigma(P_1),\ldots,f_n:\sigma(P_n)$, then $l_\sigma(f_1,\ldots,f_n):\sigma(Q) \in \mathcal{K}$, and $f_i:\sigma(P_i) \in \mathcal{K}$ implies $l_\sigma(f_1,\ldots,f_n):\sigma(Q) \leq f_i:\sigma(P_i)$ for $1 \leq i \leq n$. (2) If $l:P_1,\ldots,P_n \Rightarrow Q$ in Ω_f with a goal $\sigma(P_j)$ and $\mathcal{K} \vdash f_1:\sigma(P_1),\ldots,f_{j-1}:\sigma(P_{j-1})$, then $l_\sigma^{-1}(f_1,\ldots,f_{j-1}):\sigma(P_j) \in \mathcal{K}$, $f_i:\sigma(P_i) \in \mathcal{K}$ implies $l_\sigma^{-1}(f_1,\ldots,f_{j-1}):\sigma(P_j) \leq f_i:\sigma(P_i)$ for $1 \leq i < j$. (3) If $l:P_1,\ldots,P_n \Rightarrow Q$ in Ω_b and $\mathcal{K} \vdash f_1:\sigma(P_1),\ldots,f_n:\sigma(P_n)$, and $g':G' \in \mathcal{K}$ with $\sigma(Q) = \sigma(G')$, then $l_\sigma(f_1,\ldots,f_n;g'):\sigma(Q) \in \mathcal{K}$, and $f_i:\sigma(P_i) \in \mathcal{K}$ implies $l_\sigma(f_1,\ldots,f_n;g'):\sigma(Q) \leq f_i:\sigma(P_i)$ for $1 \leq i \leq n$. (4) If $l:P_1,\ldots,P_n \Rightarrow Q$ in Ω_b with a goal $\sigma(P_j)$ and $\mathcal{K} \vdash f_1:\sigma(P_1),\ldots,f_{j-1}:\sigma(P_{j-1})$, and $g':G' \in \mathcal{K}$ with $\sigma(Q) = \sigma(G')$, then $l_\sigma^{-1}(f_1,\ldots,f_{j-1};g'):\sigma(P_j) \in \mathcal{K}$, $l_\sigma^{-1}(f_1,\ldots,f_{j-1};g'):\sigma(P_j) \leq g':G'$, and $f_i:\sigma(P_i) \in \mathcal{K}$ with $i < j$ implies $l_\sigma^{-1}(f_1,\ldots,f_{j-1};g'):\sigma(P_j) \leq f_i:\sigma(P_i)$ for $1 \leq i < j$.*

Intuitively, the set $\mathcal{K}$ over-approximates the set of all derived facts and goals that could be generated in response to an element from this set. Condition (0) corresponds to the built-in rule, conditions (1) and (2) correspond to the forward rules (which can be applied to solutions of goals), and conditions (3) and (4) correspond to the backward rules. We note that $\mathcal{K}$ may be infinite, but due to the use of most general substitutions σ in the proof rules, only a finite subset of $\mathcal{K}$ will be generated in any actual execution.

Theorem 3 (Termination). *If $\mathcal{F}^O(\pi) \cup \mathcal{G}^C(\pi)$ is finite and has the finite closure property then π is terminating, that is, either π is finite or there is some n such that r_i is the sleep rule for all $i > n$.*

Proof. Define depth $d(K)$ of a derived fact or goal K such that if $K \in \mathcal{K}$ then there is a descending $\lessdot$-chain in $\mathcal{K}$ of length $d(K)$, where $\lessdot$ is the relation inductively generated by the conditions (0)–(4) above (replacing $\leq$ by $<$). We then argue (a) that if π is nonterminating then due to the freshness condition of the proof rules the set of derived facts and goals grows without bound; and (b) that there is a finite bound on the set of facts and goals of a given finite depth. This means that in a nonterminating proof there is a descending $\lessdot$-chain and hence a descending $<$ chain that grows without bound, which contradicts well-foundedness. For details we refer to [8].   □

Our robot theory does satisfy the conditions for termination. Intuitively, the cases to check involve recursive calls: F3, B3, B9. Recursive calls using the clause F3, axiomatizing commutativity, lead to cycles with two facts in the equivalence class for any pair of areas. Calls to B9 will terminate because the argument W decreases on each until it reaches the lower bound b_w. The recursive call in B3 will never happen, by freshness constraints, but even without freshness the recursive call results in an equivalent derived fact.

Theorem 4 (Confluence). *If π is a globally fair and terminating execution then π is* confluent, *i.e., there exists a suffix π' such that $\mathcal{F}_x(c) = \mathcal{F}_y(c)$ and $\mathcal{G}_x(c) = \mathcal{G}_y(c)$ for all cyber-nodes x, y and $c \in \pi'$.*

Proof. It is easy to see that in a globally fair and terminating system, the replacement and communication rules will eventually ensure that all cyber-nodes will reach the same logical state (disregarding time and name) after no new knowledge is produced by reasoning rules.

5 Related Work

Knowledge sharing is a well-known idea that has been investigated by Halpern in [6] and in much subsequent work. Understanding knowledge sharing in distributed environments has led to a complementary view providing new insights into distributed algorithms and a logical justification for their fundamental limitations. For instance, attaining common knowledge, i.e., complete knowledge about the knowledge of other agents (and hence about the global state) in a distributed system is not feasible in a strict sense, and hence problems such as coordinated attack are unsolvable in asynchronous systems. In practice, approximations of common knowledge can be used by making assumptions of (sufficient) synchrony, but the fundamental problem in asynchronous systems remains. Halpern's concept of knowledge is based on modal logic, which expresses facts and the state of knowledge of individual agents. A key axiom is the knowledge axiom, which states that if an agent knows a fact, it must be true. Such an axiom is problematic in a distributed setting without a global view of the world. Furthermore, such logics do not deal with changes in the facts during the reasoning process, or the ability to discard facts that are no longer useful, nor do they take goals into account.

The idea of applying declarative techniques in communication and networking is not new. A large body of work exists in the areas of specification, analysis, and synthesis of networking policies and protocols, e.g., in the context of security, routing, or dynamic spectrum access. Declarative querying of sensor networks has been studied through several approaches, for instance in [13], which composes services on the fly and in a goal-driven fashion using a concept of semantic streams. Declarative techniques to specify destinations have been used in disruption-tolerant networking [2]. A variant of Datalog has been applied to the declarative specification of peer-to-peer protocols [9]. Based on this work, [3] develops a very interesting approach to declarative sensor networks that can transmit generated facts to specific neighbors and can also utilize knowledge about neighbors to specify, e.g., routing algorithms. The idea of providing an abstraction that views a system as a single asset (an ensemble) rather then programming its individual components has been explored in several projects. Most interesting, the approach in Meld [1] extends the ideas from declarative sensor networks to modular robots, i.e., ensembles of robots with inter-robot communication limited to immediate neighbors. As an example, the movement of a composite robot emerges as a result of the coordinated interaction between its homogeneous robot modules. Most of the existing work focuses not on the theoretical foundations, but on efficient compilation into a conventional programming language. Another approach is the use of an efficient reasoning engine in embedded systems such as software-defined radios [5] or routers [12] as explored in the context of disruption-tolerant networking.

6   Conclusion and Future Directions

We have presented first steps toward combining local forward and backward reasoning in a fully distributed fashion with knowledge that is transparently shared. A fixed or known neighborhood is not assumed in our more abstract approach, and the use and dissemination of both facts and goals aims at general cyber-physical systems with distributed actuation, and hence leads us beyond sensor networks, in particular to dynamic sensor/actuator networks that are, unlike ensembles, inherently heterogeneous.

The partial order structure of knowledge enables distributed knowledge sharing and replacement. The subsumption relation has a logical interpretation, which in a sufficiently expressive logic can be defined in terms of a logical implication. The replacement ordering, on the other hand, allows the user to specify when knowledge becomes obsolete. The use of knowledge is not limited to facts; knowledge can also represent goals. We do not use a modal logic, which means that knowledge about knowledge must be explicitly represented if needed.

We have developed a prototype of our distributed logical framework based on an implementation of the partially ordered knowledge-sharing model and an application programming interface (API) for cyber-physical devices that enables interaction with the physical world [7]. Our framework provides a uniform abstraction for a wide range of NCPS applications, especially those concerned with distributed sensing, optimization, and control. Key features of our framework are that (i) it provides a generic service to represent, manipulate, and share knowledge across the network under minimal assumptions on connectivity, (ii) it enables the same application code to be used in various environments including simulation models and real-world deployments, (iii) it adapts to a wide range of operating points between autonomy and cooperation to overcome limitations in connectivity and resources, as well as uncertainties and failures.

The proof system that we have presented in this paper focuses on a few core ideas, but the work can be generalized in many directions. One step is the generalization of the underlying logic, for example, incorporation of equational features as in Maude [4]. Another possibility is introducing stochastic events and/or probablistic reasoning.

The logical framework should be thought of as a means of expressing the space of logically sound behaviors, which can be further constrained by more quantitative techniques. Our inference rules force a proof strategy that proceeds according to the ordering of atoms in the conditions of a Horn clause. More general proof strategies are possible, and could potentially lead to a higher degree of parallelism. Solved or unsolved goals that cannot generate further solutions could be removed — for example, by equipping goals with an expiration time to allow removal in a controlled manner. Several conflicting goals can be active at the same time, and strategies guided by prioritization and more generally distributed optimization techniques need to be developed.

This paper presents an interleaving semantics, but a true concurrency semantics, such as the semantics of rewriting logic [10], where the concurrent application of proof rules is represented explicitly, might be more appropriate.

In this paper derivations are used for meta-level reasoning. However, the explicit representation of derivations could be made available to applications. Possible uses include the following.

(1) *Faulty Facts Elimination.* If the initial sensor data (e.g., noise detected in area A) is wrong — for example, due to a faulty or malicious sensor — and is detected, this (meta) fact should be disseminated to other robots and the inference system should exclude reasoning based on faulty data.

(2) *Situation Awareness.* Noise was correctly detected, but ceases when one of the robots arrives in area A. In this case, new facts will be disseminated and decisions based on the obsolete facts might need to be canceled.

(3) *Uncertainty Management.* Derivations can be used to indicate whether a decision was made based on reliable information. If a decision is made based on an uncertain observation (e.g., a sensor with some error margin), the degree of uncertainty needs to be propagated through the derivation so that decisions can be based on the quality of derivations as well as the conclusions.

(4) *Post-Examination.* After a goal is satisfied, one can examine whether further optimization is possible (e.g., in terms of delay, energy consumption). For example, one can examine why a certain robot decided to move in a certain direction. This can be related to (3) if the less optimal decision was made due to data uncertainty that was not correctly evaluated (e.g., data fusion from two sensors with equal weight is suboptimal if one of the sensors has a larger error).

Acknowledgments. Support from National Science Foundation Grant 0932397 (A Logical Framework for Self-Optimizing Networked Cyber-Physical Systems) and Office of Naval Research Grant N00014-10-1-0365 (Principles and Foundations for Fractionated Networked Cyber-Physical Systems) is gratefully acknowledged. Any opinions, findings, and conclusions or recommendations expressed in this material are those of the author(s) and do not necessarily reflect the views of NSF or ONR.

References

1. Ashley-Rollman, M.P., Goldstein, S.C., Lee, P., Mowry, T.C., Pillai, P.: Meld: A declarative approach to programming ensembles. In: Proc. of the IEEE International Conference on Intelligent Robots and Systems (IROS 2007) (October 2007)
2. Basu, P., Krishnan, R., Brown, D.W.: Persistent delivery with deferred binding to descriptively named destinations. In: Proc. of IEEE MILCOM (2008)
3. Chu, D., Popa, L., Tavakoli, A., Hellerstein, J.M., Levis, P., Shenker, S., Stoica, I.: The design and implementation of a declarative sensor network system. In: SenSys 2007: Proc. of the 5th International Conference on Embedded Networked Sensor Systems, pp. 175–188 (2007)
4. Clavel, M., Durán, F., Eker, S., Lincoln, P., Martí-Oliet, N., Meseguer, J., Talcott, C.L. (eds.): All About Maude - A High-Performance Logical Framework, How to Specify, Program and Verify Systems in Rewriting Logic. LNCS, vol. 4350. Springer, Heidelberg (2007)
5. Elenius, D., Denker, G., Stehr, M.-O.: A Semantic Web Reasoner for Rules, Equations and Constraints. In: Calvanese, D., Lausen, G. (eds.) RR 2008. LNCS, vol. 5341, pp. 135–149. Springer, Heidelberg (2008)
6. Halpern, J.Y., Moses, Y.: Knowledge and common knowledge in a distributed environment. Journal of the ACM 37, 549–587 (1984)
7. Kim, M., Stehr, M.-O., Kim, J., Ha, S.: An application framework for loosely coupled networked cyber-physical systems. In: 8th IEEE Intl. Conf. on Embedded and Ubiquitous Computing, EUC 2010 (2010)
8. Kim, M., Stehr, M.-O., Talcott, C.: A distributed logic for networked cyber-physical systems (extended version) (in preparation)
9. Loo, B.T., Condie, T., Garofalakis, M., Gay, D.E., Hellerstein, J.M., Maniatis, P., Ramakrishnan, R., Roscoe, T., Stoica, I.: Declarative networking. Commun. ACM 52(11), 87–95 (2009)
10. Meseguer, J.: Conditional Rewriting Logic as a unified model of concurrency. Theoretical Computer Science 96(1), 73–155 (1992)

11. Stehr, M.-O., Kim, M., Talcott, C.L.: Toward Distributed Declarative Control of Networked Cyber-Physical Systems. In: Yu, Z., Liscano, R., Chen, G., Zhang, D., Zhou, X. (eds.) UIC 2010. LNCS, vol. 6406, pp. 397–413. Springer, Heidelberg (2010)
12. Stehr, M.-O., Talcott, C.: Planning and learning algorithms for routing in disruption-tolerant networks. In: Proc. of IEEE MILCOM (2008)
13. Whitehouse, K., Zhao, F., Liu, J.: Semantic Streams: A Framework for Composable Semantic Interpretation of Sensor Data. In: Römer, K., Karl, H., Mattern, F. (eds.) EWSN 2006. LNCS, vol. 3868, pp. 5–20. Springer, Heidelberg (2006)

Reachability Analysis
of Non-linear Planar Autonomous Systems

Hallstein Asheim Hansen[1], Gerardo Schneider[2,3], and Martin Steffen[3]

[1] Buskerud University College, Kongsberg, Norway
[2] Chalmers University of Gothenburg, Sweden
[3] University of Oslo, Norway

Abstract. Many complex continuous systems are modeled as *non-linear autonomous systems,* i.e., by a set of differential equations with one independent variable. Exact *reachability,* i.e., whether a given configuration can be reached by starting from an initial configuration of the system, is undecidable in general, as one needs to know the solution of the system of equations under consideration.

In this paper we address the reachability problem of planar autonomous systems approximatively. We use an approximation technique which "hybridizes" the state space in the following way: the original system is partitioned into a finite set of polygonal regions where the dynamics on each region is approximated by constant differential inclusions. Besides proving soundness, completeness, and termination of our algorithm, we present an implementation, and its application into (classical) examples taken from the literature.

1 Introduction

Many complex continuous systems can be modeled as *non-linear autonomous systems,* i.e., as a set of differential equations over one independent variable (typically interpreted as the time). Such systems can be found in the fields of mechanics, electrical engineering, etc., with typical textbook examples such as the damped pendulum, and oscillations in an electrical circuit as captured by the van der Pol oscillator equation.

Reachability analysis addresses the question whether, starting from an initial state or configuration, a system can evolve into another given state, i.e., whether it can reach that state. In this paper we investigate how to automate the approximation of non-linear dynamics in order to answer reachability questions for non-linear planar autonomous systems. The technique is based on *hybridizing*[1] the state space: the original system is partitioned into a finite set of polygonal regions where the dynamics on each region is approximated by constant differential inclusions. The resulting abstraction is called a Generalized Polygonal Hybrid System (GSPDI for short), for which reachability has been proved decidable [19]; the tool GSPeeDI [11] is a reachability-checker for such systems.

---

[1] A *hybrid system* combines both discrete and continuous behaviour.

F. Arbab and M. Sirjani (Eds.): FSEN 2011, LNCS 7141, pp. 206–220, 2012.
© Springer-Verlag Berlin Heidelberg 2012

A well-known, major difficulty in the analysis of differential equations are *critical points* such as sinks and attractors, i.e., objects of the so-called phase portrait. In their absence, our refinement may iteratively be of arbitrary precision (at least in theory). In regions containing critical points, however, the approximating GSPDI may lose precision quite drastically. We introduce an error measure, and an algorithm which allows us to choose the bound on the error arbitrarily small to obtain a practical and useful refinement.

Working on an abstraction of the original system gives a semi-test algorithm: a negative answer to reachability on the approximated system is indeed negative in the real system, whereas a positive answer is inconclusive. Obviously, a recurrent 'yes' answer is not useful unless we can iteratively refine the approximation to arrive, in some cases, at a definite 'no' with our technique, or 'yes' by other techniques.

Our algorithm takes as input a non-linear planar autonomous system S, an initial configuration given as set X_0 of points on the plane, and a final configuration X_f. Our approach performs reachability analysis by abstraction refinement: (1) Obtain a first (coarse) GSPDI H from S; (2) Check whether X_f is reachable from X_0; (3) If not, the algorithm terminates with a negative answer. (4) Otherwise, the situation is inconclusive, so refine the partition to obtain a better approximation H' and repeat from (2). The algorithm terminates after the error measure has been reached.

We prove that the above algorithm terminates and that it is sound and complete. Soundness, as usual, means that the result of the analysis can be relied on, i.e., the resulting GSPDI is indeed an abstraction of the original autonomous system in that it includes all the original behavior. Completeness states that if some state is reachable in the original system, the analysis provides evidence of that. We cannot expect completeness in that strict form, as the obtained GSPDIs will always over-approximate the real system, no matter how much we iterate the refinement procedure sketched above. Each refinement step, which corresponds to a finer partition of the plane, results in a GSPDI representing a more precise over-approximation, and by completeness we mean that we can approximate the original behavior up-to a given margin of error. We have incorporated a proof-of-concept prototype of the theory into the tool GSPeeDI. The prototype uses readily available local optimization libraries, and while this does not ensure that the test results are conservative in all cases, they give a good indication of what a real implementation of the theory would provide. We furthermore show the feasibility of the approach on a number of classical examples taken from the literature, and compare our results to those of related work.

The rest of the paper is organized as follows. Section 2 introduces notation and some mathematical results needed in the subsequent text. Section 3 gives the approximation from the dynamics of an autonomous systems to that of a GSPDI, presents our reachability analysis, and proves soundness, completeness, and termination. We discuss the implementation in Section 4, related work in section 5, and conclude in Section 6.

2   Background

In this section we present notations and definitions needed in the rest of the paper. We assume familiarity with Euclidean geometry, in particular vector operations. In the following we assume that, unless stated otherwise, vectors are normalized, so that two vectors are equal iff their directions are equal. A *unit circle* is a circle with radius 1, and vector $\mathbf{x}$ specifies a point on a unit circle. Henceforth, $\mathbf{x}$ refers to a vector as well as to the corresponding point on the unit circle.

An *arc* $\angle_{\mathbf{a}}^{\mathbf{b}}$ is a portion of the circumference of a unit circle, bounded by its endpoints, $\mathbf{a}$ and $\mathbf{b}$, where $\mathbf{a}$ is assumed located clockwise of $\mathbf{b}$. On the unit cycle, the length of an arc, written $|\angle_{\mathbf{a}}^{\mathbf{b}}|$ is also the angle between $\mathbf{a}$ and $\mathbf{b}$, measured in the interval $[0, 2\pi)$. We write $\mathbf{x} \in \angle_{\mathbf{a}}^{\mathbf{b}}$, if vector $\mathbf{x}$ is located clockwise of $\mathbf{b}$ and counter-clockwise of $\mathbf{a}$. If both $\mathbf{x} \in \angle_{\mathbf{a}}^{\mathbf{b}}$ and $\mathbf{y} \in \angle_{\mathbf{a}}^{\mathbf{b}}$ then we say that $\angle_{\mathbf{x}}^{\mathbf{y}} \subseteq \angle_{\mathbf{a}}^{\mathbf{b}}$ (if $\mathbf{x}$ is located clockwise with respect to $\mathbf{y}$), and so forth.

Many physical systems are modeled by one or more differential equations. Often the behavior of the system describes the development over time, so that the independent variable represents the time t.

Definition 1 (Autonomous system). *A non-linear planar, autonomous, system of first-order ordinary differential equations (ODEs) [5] is a system of the form*

$$\frac{dx}{dt} = f(x, y) \tag{1}$$

$$\frac{dy}{dt} = g(x, y). \tag{2}$$

The functions f and g may be non-linear, but neither depend on the independent variable t.

The functions f and g from Equations (1) and (2) represent derivatives of x and y w.r.t. t. The length of that vector gives the rate of change at that point and thus the vector $(f(x, y), g(x, y))$ describes the system's momentary *dynamic* at state (x, y). An *equilibrium point* is a point where the dynamic is the null vector; a system will remain in an equilibrium point forever.

For reachability, it is relevant only whether, not when, some point is reached. Thus we can normalize the dynamic as follows:

Definition 2 (Normalization). *The normalized dynamics of an autonomous system S is given by the function $h : \mathbb{R}^2 \to \mathbb{R}^2$:*

$$h(x, y) = (f(x, y)/r(x, y), g(x, y)/r(x, y))$$

where

$$r(x, y) = (\sqrt{f(x, y)^2 + g(x, y)^2}) \ .$$

The function is undefined when both $f(x, y) = 0$ and $g(x, y) = 0$. If $p = (x, y)$ is the input to h, we write $\dot{p}$ for $h(x, y)$.

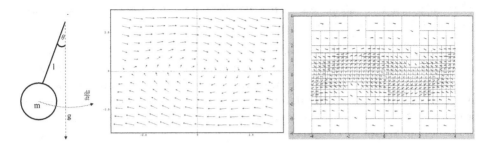

Fig. 1. On the left, the pendulum, with mass m, length l, gravitational acceleration g, angle θ, and angular velocity $\frac{d\theta}{dt}$. In the middle, the phase plane of the pendulum, with $m = 1, c = 2.5, l = 10, g = 10$. On the right, a corresponding GSPDI

Example 1 (Pendulum). The *damped pendulum* of Fig. 1 can be described by the second-order ODE

$$ml^2 \frac{d^2\theta^2}{dt^2} + cl\frac{d\theta}{dt} + mgl \sin \theta = 0$$

where constant c is the magnitude of the damping. Setting $x = \theta$ and $y = \frac{d\theta}{dt}$ allows us to transform the equation into the following autonomous system of two first-order ODEs:

$$\frac{dx}{dt} = y \ , \tag{3}$$

$$\frac{dy}{dt} = -\frac{c}{ml}y - \frac{g}{l} \sin x \ . \tag{4}$$

The associated phase plane is shown in Fig. 1 (middle), for the particular values $m = 1$, $l = 10$, $c = 2.5$, and $g = 10$. That is, $\frac{dx}{dt} = y$, and $\frac{dy}{dt} = -0.25y - \sin x$ and the picture illustrates the vector $\dot{p} = (y_i, -0.25y_i - \sin x_i)$ for several points (x_i, y_i). The equilibrium points are clearly visible, at $(0, 0)$ in the middle and furthermore $(-\pi, 0)$ and $(\pi, 0)$ to the left, respectively to the right.   □

We will not consider reachability for autonomous systems directly, but rather by abstracting them into a special form of hybrid systems, known as *generalized polygonal hybrid systems* [4, 19]. The discretization is given by a finite partitioning of the plane into separate regions, and the behavior inside each region is governed by a differential inclusion. More specifically, the dynamics is given by two vectors restricting the direction of the system's behavior.

Definition 3 (GSPDI). *A* Generalized Polygonal Hybrid System *(GSPDI) is a pair $H = \langle \mathbb{P}, \ \mathbb{F} \rangle$, where $\mathbb{P}$ is a finite partition of the plane. Each $P \in \mathbb{P}$, called a* region, *is a convex polygon with area P_A. The union $\bigcup \mathbb{P}$ of all regions is called the* domain *of the GSPDI and assumed to be a convex polygon of finite area itself. $\mathbb{F}$ is a function associating a pair of vectors to each region, i.e., $\mathbb{F}(P) = (\mathbf{a}_P, \mathbf{b}_P)$. Every point on the plane has its dynamics defined according* *to which polygon it belongs to: if $p \in P$, then $\dot{p} \in \angle_{\mathbf{a}_P}^{\mathbf{b}_P}$. In the following we assume all polygons are convex.*

A trajectory is a "path" through the state space, given as a function on the independent variable, which is often interpreted as time. In case of an autonomous system, possible trajectories are given by the differential equations; for the hybrid representation of GSPDIs, trajectories are determined by their direction of movement, in particular the tangent vector at any point should stay within the bounding angles (per region).

Definition 4 (Trajectory). *Let $I = [0, t]$ be a sub-interval of $\mathbb{R}_{\geq 0}$ (possibly identical to $\mathbb{R}_{\geq 0}$).*

1. *A trajectory ξ of an autonomous system S, written $\xi \in S$, is an almost-everywhere differentiable function $\xi : I \to \mathbb{R}^2$ which solves S for a given initial condition $\xi(t_0) = p$.*
2. *A trajectory of a GSPDI H, written $\xi \in H$, is an almost-everywhere differentiable function $\xi : I \to \mathbb{R}^2$ s.t. the following holds: whenever $\xi(t) \in P$ for some $P \in \mathbb{P}$, then its derivative $\dot{\xi}(t) \in \angle_{\mathbf{a}_P}^{\mathbf{b}_P}$.*

We now relate autonomous systems and GSPDIs through an *approximation* relation.

Definition 5 (Approximation). *A GSPDI H approximates an autonomous system S (written $H \geq S$) if $\xi \in S$ implies $\xi \in H$.*

Example 2 (Pendulum). Reconsider the damped pendulum from Example 1 given in Equations (3) and (4). An approximating GSPDI of the pendulum is shown in Fig. 1 (right). □

To abstract an autonomous system successfully into a GSPDI, it is crucial to expect a certain "smoothness" of the behavior. This is formulated as a continuity condition, stipulating that if two points p and q are located close to each other, then their dynamics, $\dot{p}$ and $\dot{q}$, do not differ too much.

Definition 6 (Lipschitz continuity.). *A function f is* Lipschitz continuous *(or just* Lipschitz, *for short) on a polygon P if, for all points $p, q \in P$, there exists a constant K such that $\frac{\|\dot{p} - \dot{q}\|}{\|p - q\|} \leq K$. The smallest such K is called the* Lipschitz constant *of the function f on P. The maximum distance $\|p - q\|$ between any two points p and q in P, the* diameter *of P, is denoted $diam(P)$.*

In the following we assume that the normalized function h describing the dynamics of the system (cf. Definition 2) is Lipschitz continuous on all subsets of $\mathbb{R}^2$ except for arbitrarily small neighborhoods around a finite number of points. Under this assumption, the partition $\mathbb{P}$ of the plane falls into two separate groups of regions, those which are Lipschitz and those which are not, i.e., $\mathbb{P} = \mathbb{P}_L \cup \mathbb{P}_N$.

3   Refinement Algorithm

This section presents the algorithm that over-approximates a given autonomous system by a GSPDI.

According to Definition 5, a GSPDI approximates the underlying autonomous system if its trajectories form a superset of the trajectories of the underlying autonomous system. The following lemma spells out a straightforward condition that tells us when that approximation holds.

Lemma 1 (Approximation). *Let S be an autonomous system with domain restricted to $\bigcup \mathbb{P}$, and H a GSPDI. If for all trajectories $\xi \in S$ and all points $\xi(t)$ on those trajectories, it is the case that $\xi(t) \in P$ and $\dot{\xi}(t) \in \angle_{\mathbf{a}_P}^{\mathbf{b}_P}$ (for some $P \in \mathbb{P}$), then $H \geq S$.*

Proof. The lemma follows directly from the Definitions 4 and 5.   □

Unavoidably, by going from the autonomous system to the GSPDI, we lose precision. To determine how good the approximation is we measure the precision of the approximating GSPDI by considering the angles that bound the trajectories. More precisely, we use the *maximal* angle of all the regions of the GSPDI. Clearly, the smaller that angle, the better the approximation. We use those angles to *order* GSPDIs and write $H' \leq H$ ("H' refines H" or "H over-approximates H'") for the corresponding order. With regions being convex, an angle of π or larger does not restrict trajectories at all inside a region. Thus π is the maximal angle to consider. Definition 8 formalizes the corresponding *strict* refinement relation $H' < H$, which treats *non-Lipschitz* regions specially: In a non-Lipschitz region, e.g., containing an equilibrium point, one cannot reduce the bounding angle. The only way to strictly refine the system is to partition the region into smaller regions.

We define two numerical parameters to measure the precision of a GSPDI, one using the maximal angle that bounds the behavior in a set X of regions, which will in general be the Lipschitz regions, $\mathbb{P}_L$, and the second one to measure the relative "weight" of the remaining regions Y, in general all the non-Lipschitz regions of the system $\mathbb{P}_N$, compared to the overall domain. In what follows P_A will denote the area of a region P.

Definition 7 (Measures for precision). *Assume an autonomous system S and a GSPDI $H = \langle \mathbb{P}, \mathbb{F} \rangle$, $H \geq S$, and two disjoint sets X, Y such that $\mathbb{P} = X \cup Y$.*

1. *$\theta(X)$ is the maximum angle $|\angle_{\mathbf{a}_P}^{\mathbf{b}_P}|$ of all $P \in X$.*
2. *$\delta(Y)$ is the relative weight of the regions of Y, $\frac{\sum_{P \in Y} P_A}{(\bigcup \mathbb{P})_A}$.*

We can order GSPDIs by how precise they model the system dynamics. A GSPDI *refines* another if its partition is more fine-grained and, in particular, the bounding angles get smaller. For the same reason as in Definition 7, the latter condition applies for Lipschitz regions, only. In abuse of notation, we use $\leq$ to denote the corresponding refinement relation:

Definition 8 (Refinement). *Given two GSPDIs $H = \langle \mathbb{P}, \mathbb{F} \rangle$ and $H' = \langle \mathbb{P}', \mathbb{F}' \rangle$, H' refines H properly, written $H' < H$, if $\mathbb{P}'$ is a sub-partition of $\mathbb{P}$, and furthermore $|\angle_{\mathbf{b}_{P'}}^{\mathbf{a}_{P'}}| < |\angle_{\mathbf{a}_P}^{\mathbf{b}_P}|$, where P and P' with $P' \subseteq P$ are Lipschitz regions for H, resp. of H', i.e., $P \in \mathbb{P}_L$ and $P' \in \mathbb{P}'_L$.*

The following lemma states that we can choose our approximating GSPDIs as precise as we want them.

Lemma 2 (Bounds). *Given an autonomous system S, an angle θ with $0 < \theta \leq \pi$, and a number $\delta > 0$. Then there exists an approximating GSPDI H such that 1) $\theta(\mathbb{P}_L) \leq \theta$, and 2) $\delta(\mathbb{P}_N) \leq \delta$.*

Proof. The lemma imposes two conditions on the precision of H. 1) For the first one, Definition 6 of Lipschitz continuity gives $\|\dot{p} - \dot{q}\| \leq K\|p - q\|$ for some K, for all points $p, q \in P$, and where K is the Lipschitz constant for P. Thus, $\|\dot{p} - \dot{q}\| \leq K * diam(P)$. Since there is a one-to-one correspondence between the distance $\|\dot{p} - \dot{q}\|$ and the angle $|\angle_{\dot{p}}^{\dot{q}}|$, we can always partition Q such that all $P \in \mathbb{P}$ have a small enough $diam(P)$ such that $\|\dot{p} - \dot{q}\| \leq K * diam(P)$ implies $|\angle_{\dot{p}}^{\dot{q}}| \leq \theta$.

2) The second condition is a direct consequence of the earlier assumption that h is Lipschitz on all subsets of $\mathbb{R}^2$ except for arbitrarily small neighborhoods around a finite number of (isolated) points: we can partition Q such that each region P from $\mathbb{P}_N$, the non-Lipschitz regions, contains exactly one such point and is arbitrarily small, which in turn renders the ratio arbitrarily small. □

Lemma 2 guarantees that there is always a GSPDI with $\theta(X)$ and $\delta(Y)$ arbitrarily small, for sets X, Y, trivially by letting $\mathbb{P}_L = X$ and $\mathbb{P}_N = Y$. To actually arrive at such a GSPDI, one can iteratively partition the domain finer and finer. For that purpose, we assume a function `partition`, which when applied to a partition of Q produces a sub-partition, for instance by splitting one particular polygon of the current partition. That, of course, leaves open which particular polygon or polygons are split, i.e., iterating the function `partition` is *non-deterministic*. It should be intuitively clear, that certain strategies for resolving the non-determinism will not improve the quality of the GSPDI, for instance by splitting only one half of the domain, but not improving on the other half, leaving the overall precision unchanged. The next lemma states, however, that there *exist* strategies of applying `partition` "smarter" than the one just mentioned, which eventually lead to partitions such that the corresponding GSPDI is below any predefined measure of precision.

Lemma 3. *Assume an autonomous system S, a polygon Q, an angle θ with $0 < \theta \leq \pi$, and a number $\delta > 0$. Then there exists a strategy to successively apply the `partition` function on Q that in a finite number of steps generates a partition $\mathbb{P}$ such that there exists a GSPDI $H = \langle \mathbb{P}, \mathbb{F} \rangle$ with Q as its domain, and where $\theta(\mathbb{P}_L) \leq \theta$ and $\delta(\mathbb{P}_N) \leq \delta$, such that $H \geq S$.*

Proof. The lemma requires application of `partition` iteratively such that $\theta(\mathbb{P}_L)$ and $\delta(\mathbb{P}_N)$ get smaller than the given upper bounds. This can be guaranteed, if

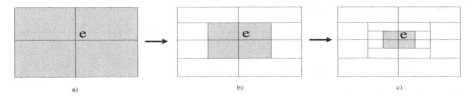

Fig. 2. Using `partition` on a rectangular initial polygon which contains an equilibrium point e. $\mathbb{P}_N$ is colored, $\mathbb{P}_L$ is white.

the strategy assures that all partitions of the domain of H get arbitrarily small (by Lemma 2). This can be achieved by splitting the polygons "uniformely", for instance, by always splitting (one of the) the largest into halves. □

In order to illustrate how one would realize `partition` we present an example. Here partitioning is done by simply splitting rectangles into two, along the rectangle's longest side. In particular the example shows that the number of non-Lipschitz regions remain constant under the chosen partitioning strategy.

Example 3. Consider an initial rectangle with an equilibrium point e at the exact center, see Figure 2. By partitioning twice we get four (colored) regions where the Lipschitz condition does not hold as they all contain e, Figure 2-a). Continuing to partition colored regions we can get a situation like in Figure 2-b), and later like in Figure 2-c). □

Applying the `partition` function as in (the proof of) the lemma above gives an algorithm which takes as input an autonomous system S, an initial polygon Q of finite area as domain of the intended GSPDI, and two bounds Θ and Δ as input. The iteration yields as output a partition $\mathbb{P}$ which forms part of a GSPDI $H = \langle \mathbb{P}; \mathbb{F} \rangle$ with $H \geq S$ and where furthermore $\mathbb{P}$ can be divided into two sets, $\mathbb{P}_{OK}$ and $\mathbb{P}_{BAD}$, such that $\theta(\mathbb{P}_{OK}) \leq \Theta$ and $\delta(\mathbb{P}_{BAD}) \leq \Delta$ (cf. Algorithm 1).

To maintain the successively finer partitioning of the given domain Q, the algorithm uses two collections of regions $\mathbb{P}_{OK}$ and $\mathbb{P}_{BAD}$. As loop invariant of the central iteration, the union of $\mathbb{P}_{OK}$ and $\mathbb{P}_{BAD}$ is a partition of the initial polygon Q. The collection $\mathbb{P}_{OK}$ contains regions P where $|\angle_{\mathbf{a}P}^{\mathbf{b}P}|$ is less than or equal to Θ. The collection $\mathbb{P}_{BAD}$, on the other hand, contains those regions whose angles are yet to be computed.

The collection $\mathbb{P}_{BAD}$ keeps the regions in a queue, which entails a form of "breadth-first" strategy: during each iteration, the first region P is removed from the head of the queue. If the corresponding bounding angle is small enough, i.e., if $|\angle_{\mathbf{a}P}^{\mathbf{b}P}| \leq \Theta$, then P is considered finished and moved to $\mathbb{P}_{OK}$. Otherwise, P is partitioned, and the subpolygons $P_1, \ldots, P_n$ are placed at the back of the queue $\mathbb{P}_{BAD}$. The while loop is executed until the area of $\mathbb{P}_{BAD}$ is less than or equal to the desired threshold, $\Delta * Q_A$. The return value is the union of $\mathbb{P}_{OK}$ and $\mathbb{P}_{BAD}$, which is a valid partition of Q, satisfying both Θ and Δ.

Note that the algorithm does not compute sets of polygons where underlying autonomous system is Lipschitz or not. Instead, these properties are implicitly

---

Algorithm 1. Construct a GSPDI on polygon Q on the plane, with precision parameters Δ and Θ.

Input: Convex polygon Q, $\Delta \in (0,1]$, $\Theta \in (0,\pi]$

Empty queue $\mathbb{P}_{BAD}$, and empty collection $\mathbb{P}_{OK}$

$\mathbb{P}_{BAD}.\text{insert}(Q)$
while $(\mathbb{P}_{BAD})_A > \Delta * Q_A$ **do**
  $P := \mathbb{P}_{BAD}.\text{remove}()$
  if $|\angle_{\mathbf{a}_P}^{\mathbf{b}_P}| \leq \Theta$ **then**
    $\mathbb{P}_{OK}.\text{insert}(P)$
  else
    $\{P_1,\ldots,P_n\} := \text{partition}(P)$
    $\mathbb{P}_{BAD}.\text{insert}(P_1,\ldots,P_n)$
  end if
end while
return $\mathbb{P}_{OK} \cup \mathbb{P}_{BAD}$

---

used to allow the computation of two sets $\mathbb{P}_{OK}$ and $\mathbb{P}_{BAD}$ where $|\angle_{\mathbf{a}_P}^{\mathbf{b}_P}| \leq \Theta$ for all $P \in \mathbb{P}_{OK}$ and where the area of $\bigcup \mathbb{P}_{BAD} \leq \Delta * Q_A$ (cf. also Definition 7 which gives the measures of precision).

One of the precision measures used in the iteration is the angle which bounds the dynamics of the system, per partition: For the termination condition of the refinement process, we rely that for a given polygon P, the minimal bound can be calculated, i.e., the smallest arc $\angle_{\mathbf{a}_P}^{\mathbf{b}_P}$ such that $\dot{p} \in \angle_{\mathbf{a}_P}^{\mathbf{b}_P}$ for all $p \in P$. In the implementation, we use external, numerical routines to implement a corresponding function `getArc` that calculates the value of $\angle_{\mathbf{a}_P}^{\mathbf{b}_P}$ (cf. Section 4 later about the implementation).

By the properties of $\angle_{\mathbf{a}_P}^{\mathbf{b}_P}$, i.e., with help of `getArc`, Algorithm 1 ensures that all the trajectories of the autonomous system are also trajectories of the generated approximating GSPDI (Lemma 1), that is the algorithm is sound It also satisfies that $\theta(H) \leq \Theta$ and $\delta(H) \leq \Delta$ (Lemma 3), which guarantees completeness, and also termination of the algorithm.

Theorem 1. *Algorithm 1 is sound, complete, and it terminates.*

Proof. The *soundness* of the algorithm is a direct consequence of the approximation Lemma 1: As an invariant, the domain Q is partitioned into regions $\mathbb{P}$ (split into $\mathbb{P}_{BAD}$ and $\mathbb{P}_{OK}$). Initially, the partition consists of one polygon, Q, and the loop either keeps the partition or refines it by replacing one polygon by sub-polygons. Each iteration/partition corresponds to a GSPDI, which approximates the autonomous system by Lemma 1.

As for *completeness:* the algorithm works by successively partitioning the polygons of $\mathbb{P}_{BAD}$. For each P considered, there are two options: Either $|\angle_{\mathbf{a}_P}^{\mathbf{b}_P}| \leq \Theta$, in which case it is moved from $\mathbb{P}_{BAD}$ to $\mathbb{P}_{OK}$, or not.

The question is whether the area of $\mathbb{P}_{BAD}$ eventually will be less that $\Delta * Q_A$. By Lemma 3 and its proof we know that our strategy for applying `partition` will generate two sets $\mathbb{P}_L$ and $\mathbb{P}_N$, the area of the latter which can be made arbitrarily small, and that we can find an arbitrarily small upper bound on the angle $|\angle_{\mathbf{a}P}^{\mathbf{b}P}|$ for each $P \in \mathbb{P}_L$. So we let Θ be an upper bound of these $|\angle_{\mathbf{a}P}^{\mathbf{b}P}|$, eventually forcing $\mathbb{P}_{BAD} \subseteq \mathbb{P}_N$. By having the upper bound of $(\cup \mathbb{P}_N)_A$ as $\Delta * Q_A$, we have that $\theta(\mathbb{P}_{OK}) \leq \Theta$ and $\delta(\mathbb{P}_{BAD}) \leq \delta(\mathbb{P}_N) \leq \Delta$.

Finally, the algorithm *terminates* when the area of $\mathbb{P}_{BAD}$ is less than $\Delta * Q_A$. The proof of completeness shows that this is always possible to achieve. In addition, Lemma 3 guarantees that there exists as strategy that generates a $\mathbb{P}_N$ with a sufficiently small area in a finite number of steps. Such a strategy is used in the implementation.   □

4   Prototype Implementation

The tool GSPeeDI contains an implementation of the results introduced in the previous section [10]. The tool answers 'maybe' or 'no' when asked to investigate safety properties. Graphics are also produced, and all the figures of GSPDIs in this paper are screen-shots from the tool. An overview of an older version of the tool has been published in [11].

A key issue was the implementation of the oracle `getArc`, which should return the extremal vectors $\mathbf{a}$ and $\mathbf{b}$ on polygon P, to create the arc $\angle_{\mathbf{a}P}^{\mathbf{b}P}$. We extracted the angle of a vector by using the function `atan2`, which is commonly implemented in many programming languages. It gives the angle of a vector with respect to the vector $(1, 0)$ in the interval $(-\pi, \pi]$. Since there is a discontinuity at the point $(-1, 0)$ we also used the function `atan2b` which gives the same angle, though in the interval $[0, 2\pi)$. Extremal vectors were thus obtained by maximizing and minimizing `atan2`, alternatively `atan2b`.

Note that due to the experimental nature of the prototype it does not strictly enforce the conservativeness of the theory presented in the previous sections. We used external, numerical routines for finding the extremal values of these two functions from the extensive Python scientific library Scipy [1]. This library includes a implementation of the limited memory Broyden-Fletcher-Goldfarb-Shanno method with bounds (L-BFGS-B) for non-linear optimization [24]. The bounds in question are box-constraints, which restrict us to rectangular regions.

The empirical results appear correct, as illustrated in figures 3 and 4, but an implementation that guarantees conservative answers should include global optimization methods [23].

A very real scenario when using optimization tools of any kind is that they may fail, depending on starting points, constraints, or the function to be optimized. The ratio of such failures, and their consequences, obviously determines the usability of the tool.

In the event of failure, we also implemented a backup routine that produced arcs that preserved the soundness of Algorithm 1. If that also fails we ultimately give up and declare the offending region to be reach-all.[2] We included a cut-off

---

[2] A *reach-all* region is one where every point is reachable from any other point.

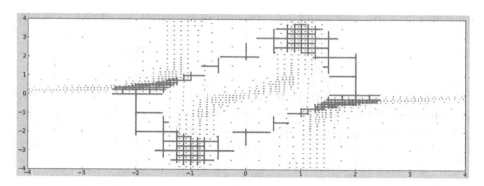

Fig. 3. Reach-set for van der Pol equation with $\Theta = 0.45$ and $\Delta = 5\%$. The parameter $\mu = 1.5$.

parameter to the algorithm implementation to ensure termination, should such failures should prove abundant.

The implementation was restricted to produce only rectangular regions, and the `partition` function is realized as simply splitting a rectangle P with length l and width w, $l \geq w$, into two rectangles with length $l/2$ and width w.

We are interested in assessing the performance of the prototype when applied to real non-linear autonomous systems, as means to decide whether to write a full, conservative implementation of the theory, and so we have performed some case studies.

4.1   Case Studies

We present results produced by our prototype when used on models of the damped pendulum (cf. Example 1) and the van der Pol oscillator.

Example 4. The equation of the van der Pol oscillator [6], are used in electrical engineering, neurology, and seismology. The second-order ODE

$$x''(t) = -\mu(x(t) - 1)x'(t) - x(t)$$

can be transformed into a first-order non-linear autonomous system:

$$x'(t) = y(t)$$
$$y'(t) = -\mu(x(t) - 1)y(t) - x(t).$$

The above equation, where the positive constant μ represents the amount of damping in the system, is interesting because it includes a limit cycle: All trajectories in the system converge towards that cycle.

We executed our tool on a laptop with a 1.33 Ghz Intel Atom processor, generating GSPDIs with different values of Θ and Δ, with initial area $Q = [-4, 4] \times [-4, 4]$. The results are shown in table 1. Also, some results are shown graphically in figures 3 and 4. The desired Δ was attained in all cases. Not

Table 1. Results obtained by running GSPeeDI on the damped pendulum and the van der Pol oscillator with different precision parameters

System	Θ	Δ	Refinement	Graph building	Reach set	Remark
Pendulum	0.125	20%	403s	90s	62s	
Pendulum	0.2	2.5%	298s	69s	41s	Fig. 4
Pendulum	0.5	5%	10s	12s	6s	Fig. 4
Pendulum	0.5	0.1%	33s	28s	58s	
Van der Pol	0.45	5%	36s	32s	485s	Fig. 3
Van der Pol	0.75	5%	12s	17s	2s	

shown in the table are the results we got concerning the failure ratio of the getArc function: For the van der Pol system it failed only on the initial rectangle Q, and for the pendulum only on Q and the two rectangles Q was split into, independently of Δ or Θ. We did not observe any failures of the backup routine.

5   Related Work

In this section we briefly survey related work, both with respect to our theoretical development as well as to our implementation.

5.1   Refinement

The idea of over-approximating systems having complex, often non-linear, dynamics by systems with simpler dynamics in order to investigate safety properties is not novel, and neither is the technique of creating finer and finer partitions to verify safety properties [14]. Our approach aims at a *fully automated* process to answer the reachability question for any non-pathological planar autonomous system by working on adjusting the precision up to a desirable level.

Defining an upper limit on the approximation error (the Θ parameter in our approach) is quite standard and used in many other approaches. However, for non-linear dynamics using only this upper limit is not enough as we cannot guarantee that $|\angle_{\mathbf{a}P}^{\mathbf{b}P}| \leq \Theta$ for non-Lipschitz regions P. The Δ parameter is used to put an upper limit to the area of these regions.

We presently consider the autonomous systems as 'black boxes' that are fed to the optimization software, while other related works (e.g., [16, 14, 17]) require manual analysis to find good partitions. Automatic partitioning has been implemented in [8], but not for systems with non-linear dynamics.

5.2   Approximation

As mentioned above the purpose of refinement is to replace complex, possibly non-linear, dynamics with simpler yet less precise dynamics. This can be done by techniques such as rate translation [14], the result of which is a rectangular hybrid automata [8], or linear phase-portrait approximation, generating linear

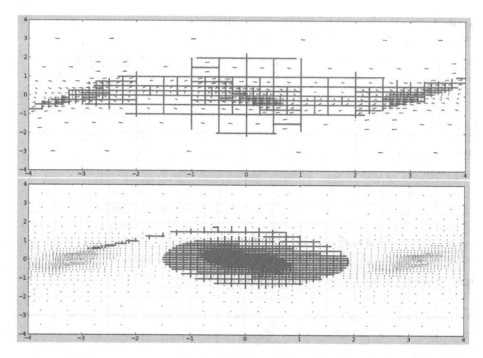

Fig. 4. Pendulum example: Above a coarse GSPDI and reach-set with parameters $\Theta = 0.5$ and $\Delta = 5\%$, and below a finer GSPDI with parameters $\Theta = 0.2$ and $\Delta = 2.5\%$

hybrid automata [15]. In both cases the method and resulting approximation are motivated by what automata are accepted by their tools, Hytech [12], and PHAVer [9], respectively. This is also true for our work: we produce approximations in the form of constant differential inclusions (GSPDIs), which can then be analyzed using our tool GSPeeDI [11]. Our method, realized through the getArc function, is optimal for any given region provided the external routines succeed in finding the extremal vectors of the function h.

5.3   Comparison with Other Tools

Known tools that do not directly analyze non-linear autonomous systems (automatically) are HyTech [12], based on linear hybrid automata [13], PHAVer [9], that approximates piece-wise affine dynamics into polyhedral automata, and d/dt [3], which is based on linear differential inclusions. A comparable tool is HSolver [21], which can analyze systems with non-linear dynamics (based on interval constraint propagation). HSolver is based on RSolver, a program for solving quantified inequality constraints [20], which guarantees conservative results.

We have formulated and run HSolver on the examples mentioned earlier, the damped pendulum, and the van der Pol equation. While our prototype shows promising results in terms of execution time, we will postpone any discussion of this until we have a conservative implementation.

6   Conclusion

In this paper we presented an approach for reachability for non-linear planar autonomous systems by hybridizing the system into a GSPDI using abstraction refinement.

Exploiting Lipschitz continuity for reachability checking and simulation is not new in itself. It is for instance inherent in the *hybridization* approach of [2], and is also used for hybrid computation [7]. A main difference is that we consider systems that may be Lipschitz continuous only in parts of the plane. A Lipschitz continuous system has an upper bound, the Lipschitz constant, on how fast the system's dynamics changes. We exploit the phenomenon that a system may be Lipschitz continuous almost everywhere, and have different Lipschitz constants for different areas of the plane. We minimize the area where the system is not Lipschitz continuous, and treat areas where the Lipschitz constant is large more thoroughly than areas where it is small, to get as good an approximation as possible. This comes with a computational price, as we must identify the Lipschitz constant for each area we consider, using non-linear optimization tools. We need, however, to identify these areas only once, and then we can perform multiple reachability computations based without needing to perform the task again.

Approximation of complex, possibly non-linear, dynamics by simpler, yet less precise, dynamics is a well-studied field [14, 16, 8]. Our work demonstrates a strategy by which, using optimizations tools, we can automate the approximation of non-linear dynamics, using an optimal approximation for GSPDIs.

We are currently working on a conservative implementation based on the current prototype. In the future, also we intend to expand the class of systems that can be analyzed by GSPDIs. Our approach may be used to approximate differential inclusions and switched continuous systems [22], as well. Applying the techniques on more general systems with an arbitrary numbers of variables, different modes, jumps, etc., is also an interesting topic, despite that this will cause loss of decidability in the approximated system. In addition, since we now are able to create GSPDIs with a large number of regions, we will work in improving the tool's performance and furthermore incorporate the theoretical improvements investigated in [18].

References

[1] The Scipy library, http://www.scipy.org
[2] Asarin, E., Dang, T., Girard, A.: Reachability Analysis of Nonlinear Systems Using Conservative Approximation. In: Maler, O., Pnueli, A. (eds.) HSCC 2003. LNCS, vol. 2623, pp. 20–35. Springer, Heidelberg (2003)
[3] Asarin, E., Bournez, O., Dang, T., Maler, O.: Approximate Reachability Analysis of Piecewise-Linear Dynamical Systems. In: Lynch, N.A., Krogh, B.H. (eds.) HSCC 2000. LNCS, vol. 1790, pp. 20–31. Springer, Heidelberg (2000)
[4] Asarin, E., Schneider, G., Yovine, S.: Algorithmic analysis of polygonal hybrid systems, part I: Reachability. TCS 379(1-2), 231–265 (2007)

[5] Boyce, W., DiPrima, R.: Elementary differential equations and boundary value problems, 8th edn. Wiley, New York (2004)

[6] Van der Pol, B., Van der Mark, J.: Frequency Demultiplication. Nature 120 (1927)

[7] Dora, J.D., Maignan, A., Mirica-Ruse, M., Yovine, S.: Hybrid computation. In: ISSAC, pp. 101–108 (2001)

[8] Doyen, L., Henzinger, T.A., Raskin, J.-F.: Automatic Rectangular Refinement of Affine Hybrid Systems. In: Pettersson, P., Yi, W. (eds.) FORMATS 2005. LNCS, vol. 3829, pp. 144–161. Springer, Heidelberg (2005)

[9] Frehse, G.: PHAVer: Algorithmic verification of hybrid systems past hyTech. In: Morari, M., Thiele, L. (eds.) HSCC 2005. LNCS, vol. 3414, pp. 258–273. Springer, Heidelberg (2005)

[10] Hansen, H.A.: GSPeeDI, http://heim.ifi.uio.no/hallstah/gspeedi/

[11] Hansen, H.A., Schneider, G.: GSPeeDI – A Verification Tool for Generalized Polygonal Hybrid Systems. In: Leucker, M., Morgan, C. (eds.) ICTAC 2009. LNCS, vol. 5684, pp. 343–348. Springer, Heidelberg (2009)

[12] Henzinger, T.A., Ho, P.-H., Wong-toi, H.: Hytech: A model checker for hybrid systems. Software Tools for Technology Transfer 1(1) (1997)

[13] Henzinger, T.A.: The theory of hybrid automata. In: LICS 1996, pp. 278–292. IEEE Computer Society (1996)

[14] Henzinger, T.A., Ho, P.-H.: Algorithmic Analysis of Nonlinear Hybrid Systems. In: Wolper, P. (ed.) CAV 1995. LNCS, vol. 939, pp. 225–238. Springer, Heidelberg (1995)

[15] Henzinger, T.A., Wong-Toi, H.: Linear phase-portrait approximations for nonlinear hybrid systems. In: Proceedings of the DIMACS/SYCON Workshop on Hybrid systems III: Verification and Control, pp. 377–388. Springer-Verlag New York, Inc., Secaucus (1996)

[16] Ho, P.-H.: Automatic analysis of hybrid systems. PhD thesis, Ithaca, NY, USA (1995)

[17] Ho, P.-H., Wong-toi, H.: Automated Analysis of an Audio Control Protocol. In: Wolper, P. (ed.) CAV 1995. LNCS, vol. 939, pp. 381–394. Springer, Heidelberg (1995)

[18] Pace, G., Schneider, G.: A Compositional Algorithm for Parallel Model Checking of Polygonal Hybrid Systems. In: Barkaoui, K., Cavalcanti, A., Cerone, A. (eds.) ICTAC 2006. LNCS, vol. 4281, pp. 168–182. Springer, Heidelberg (2006)

[19] Pace, G.J., Schneider, G.: Relaxing Goodness is Still Good. In: Fitzgerald, J.S., Haxthausen, A.E., Yenigun, H. (eds.) ICTAC 2008. LNCS, vol. 5160, pp. 274–289. Springer, Heidelberg (2008)

[20] Ratschan, S.: Efficient solving of quantified inequality constraints over the real numbers. ACM Transactions on Computational Logic 7(4), 723–748 (2006)

[21] Ratschan, S., She, Z.: Safety Verification of Hybrid Systems by Constraint Propagation Based Abstraction Refinement. ACM Transactions in Embedded Computing Systems 6(1), 573–589 (2007)

[22] Stursberg, O., Kowalewski, S.: Approximating switched continuous systems by rectangular automata. In: European Control Conference (1999)

[23] Weise, T.: Global Optimization Algorithms Theory and Application. E-book, 2nd edn (2009), http://www.it-weise.de/

[24] Zhu, C., Byrd, R.H., Lu, P., Nocedal, J.: Algorithm 78: L-BFGS-B: Fortran subroutines for large-scale bound constrained optimization. ACM Trans. Math. Softw. 23(4), 550–560 (1997)

Attacking the Dimensionality Problem of Parameterized Systems via Bounded Reachability Graphs*

Qiusong Yang[1], Bei Zhang[1,3], Jian Zhai[1], and Mingshu Li[1,2]

[1] National Engineering Research Center of Fundamental Software
[2] State Key Laboratory of Computer Science,
Institute of Software, Chinese Academy of Sciences, Beijing 100190, China
[3] Graduate University of Chinese Academy of Sciences, Beijing 100039, China
{qiusong,zhangbei,zhaijian,mingshu}@nfs.iscas.ac.cn

Abstract. Parameterized systems are systems that involve numerous instantiations of finite-state processes, and depend on parameters which define their size. The verification of parameterized systems is to decide if a property holds in its every size instance, essentially a problem with an infinite state space, and thus poses a great challenge to the community. Starting with a set of undesired states represented by an upward-closed set, the backward reachability analysis will always terminate because of the well-quasi-orderingness. As a result, backward reachability analysis has been widely used in the verification of parameterized systems. However, many existing approaches are facing with the dimensionality problem, which describes the phenomenon that the memory used for storing the symbolic state space grows extremely fast when the number of states of the finite-state process increases, making the verification rather inefficient. Based on bounded backward reachability graphs, a novel abstraction for parameterized systems, we have developed an approach for building abstractions with incrementally increased dimensions and thus improving the precision until a property is proven or a counterexample is detected. The experiments show that the verification efficiencies have been significantly improved because conclusive results tend to be drawn on abstractions with much lower dimensions.

1 Introduction

In various application domains, there is a kind of concurrent systems that is commonly seen. In these systems, numerous instantiations of one or more than one finite-state process need to be dynamically created during an application's execution to manipulate outer requests or do some background computations. In addition, it is difficult or impossible to precisely predict the maximum number of

---

* The work was partially supported by the National Natural Science Foundation of China under grant No. 60903051, as well as the Knowledge Innovation Program of the Chinese Academy of Sciences under grant No. ISCAS2009-DR09.

F. Arbab and M. Sirjani (Eds.): FSEN 2011, LNCS 7141, pp. 221–235, 2012.

instantiations to be created in each execution. As an example, a communication protocol is presented in Fig. 1. In the protocol, a server process, shown in Fig. 1(a), is responsible for manipulating incoming requests from an *arbitrary* number instances of the client process, shown in Fig. 1(b). In each communication, one head and at least one packet containing data will be sent. For the verification of such systems, a widely adopted strategy is to find errors in a system with a smaller size, by limiting the number of instances, without ensuring the full correctness.

```
 1: task body server is          1: task body client is
 2:    h,p: integer := 0;        2:    h,p: integer := 0;
 3: begin                        3: begin
 4: loop                         4: server.acquire;
 5:    exit when done;           5: server.header(h);
 6:    accept acquire;           6: server.packet(p);
 7:    accept header(h: in integer);   7: loop
 8:    accept packet(p: in integer);   8:    exit when done;
 9:    loop                      9:    server.packet(p);
10:       exit when done;       10: end loop
11:       accept packet(p: in integer);  11: server.release;
12:    end loop                 12: end client;
13:    accept release;
14: end loop;
15: end server;
```

(a) Server   (b) Client

Fig. 1. A Simple Communication Protocol

Instead of verifying systems with a limited number of instances, the verification of parameterized systems, which involve numerous instantiations of finite-state processes and depend on parameters defining their *size* [1], is to decide if a property holds in its every size instance. In essence, the verification problem has an infinite state space. In general, the verification of parameterized systems is undecidable [2]. However, a special class of systems consisting of many identical and finite-state processes proves to be decidable [3–5]. One class of decision procedures is based on the algorithm presented in [6, 7], computing backward reachability graphs of a parameterized system. It outperforms those variants of forward reachability analysis [4] in the sense that the latter does not terminate for certain systems and the former does because of the *well-quasi-orderingness* of parameterized systems[5].

As in the finite-state case, the verification of parameterized systems also faces the state space explosion problem and an algorithm's effectiveness largely depends on data structures used for representing infinite sets of states. To counter the state space explosion problem, several symbolic approaches based on constraints have been investigated [8–11]. The basic idea is to use a set of generators to represent an upward-closed set, the most widely adopted type of set in the backward reachability analysis of parameterized systems, where each generator is the conjunction of a set of linear constraints. However, the memory used for storing the symbolic state space will grow exponentially in the *dimension* of a parameterized system, defined as the number of states of the instantiated finite state processes, as the number of constraints in each symbolic state is normally closely related to the parameterized system's dimension. As a result, the *dimensionality problem* arises. For example, the *NA-constraints* in [8] and the *sharing trees* in [10] both face an exponential blow-up in size. What makes things worse is that the containment problem, deciding if a set of concrete states represented by one set of constraints is a subset of the set of states represented by another set of constraints, is sometimes co-NP complete (for example, the containment problem for constraints with additions and *DV-constraints* in [8] and the subsumption problem for *sharing trees* in [10]). As a result, those examples investigated in the literature, such as those in [8] and [10], would be considered of small size in finite-state model checking.

Based on bounded backward reachability graphs, a novel abstraction for parameterized systems, we have developed an approach for incrementally increasing the dimension of abstract states and thus improving the precision until a property is proven or a counterexample is detected. The experiments show that the verification efficiencies have been significantly improved because conclusive results might be drawn on abstractions with lower dimensions. The sequel of this paper is organized as follows. Preliminary definitions of parameterized systems are presented in Section 2. In Section 3, the overview of our approach is given. Section 4 develops the bounded backward reachability graphs for the verification of parameterized systems. The experiment results are given in Sections 5 and the related work is presented in Section 6. Section 7 concludes this paper.

2 Parameterized Systems

Let $\mathbb{N}$ denote the set of non-negative integers, $\mathbb{N}^+$ the set of positive integers, and $\mathbb{Z}$ the set of all integers, including negative and non-negative ones. Let $\mathbb{N}^m$ ($\mathbb{Z}^m$) denote the set of m-dimensional vectors in which each component belongs to the set $\mathbb{N}$ ($\mathbb{Z}$). In the sequel, an operation on vectors is interpreted as applying the operation's scalar version component-wise unless otherwise stated. For example, the operation $\mathbf{v_1} + \mathbf{v_2}$ results in a vector in which each component is equal to the addition of corresponding components of $\mathbf{v_1}$ and $\mathbf{v_2}$. For a given vector $\mathbf{v}$, $\mathbf{v}(i)$ denotes the i-th component of the vector and $\mathbf{v}(i : n_i')$ is equal to $\mathbf{v}$ except for substituting $\mathbf{v}(i)$ with n_i'. In addition, $\mathbf{0}$ denotes a vector whose entries are all equal to zero.

2.1 Definition

Following the terminologies in [3], the *communication alphabet* $\mathcal{A}$ is a set $\Sigma \times \{!, ?\}$ consisting of: a subset of $\Sigma \times \{?\}$ of rendezvous input actions and a subset of $\Sigma \times \{!\}$ of rendezvous output actions. A *process* is a tuple $A = \langle S, \mathcal{A}, \delta, s_0 \rangle$ where S denotes a finite set of *states*, $\delta \subseteq S \times \Sigma \times S$ a finite set of *transitions* and s_0 an *initial state*.

A *parameterized system* is a total function P over nonnegative integers that generates a finite transition system for each n, using a *control process* $\mathcal{C}$ and a *user process* $\mathcal{U}$. The processes $\mathcal{C}$ and $\mathcal{U}$ are defined as $\mathcal{C} = \langle S_{\mathcal{C}}, \mathcal{A}, \delta_{\mathcal{C}}, s_{\mathcal{C}}^0 \rangle$ and $\mathcal{U} = \langle S_{\mathcal{U}}, \mathcal{A}, \delta_{\mathcal{U}}, s_{\mathcal{U}}^0 \rangle$, respectively. The system $P(n)$, standing for $\mathcal{C} \times \mathcal{U}^n$, is a concurrent combination of $\mathcal{C}$ and n instances of $\mathcal{U}$ which communicate through complementary rendezvous actions. In essence, a parameterized system defines an infinite family of concurrent systems containing an arbitrary number of instances of $\mathcal{U}$, which can be thought of as a single infinite-state system [12].

A global state of a parameterized system P, denoted as $G = \langle s_{\mathcal{C}}, n_1, n_2, \cdots, n_m \rangle$, consists of a state $s_{\mathcal{C}}$ and an m-dimensional counter vector $\langle n_1, n_2, \cdots, n_m \rangle$ where $s_{\mathcal{C}} \in S_{\mathcal{C}}$ records $\mathcal{C}$'s current state, m is the dimension of the parameterized system and equal to $|S_{\mathcal{U}}|$, the number of states of $\mathcal{U}$, and each component n_i ($1 \leq i \leq m$) counts instances of $\mathcal{U}$ in the state $s_i \in S_{\mathcal{U}}$. The initial state of a parameterized system is $G_P^0 = \langle s_{\mathcal{C}}^0, 0, \cdots, \omega, \cdots, 0 \rangle$ where ω is greater than any integer and it appears in the component corresponding to the initial state of $s_{\mathcal{U}}^0$ (Without loss of generality, we assume that a parameterized system has only one initial state). A transition of a parameterized system P, denoted as δ_P, describes a communication either between the process $\mathcal{C}$ and an instance of $\mathcal{U}$ or between two instances of $\mathcal{U}$, by executing a pair of complementary rendezvous actions. A parameterized system will move from a global state G to another state G' through a communication c, denoted as $G \to^c G' \in \delta_P$, such that: a) $G' = G$ except that $G'(i+1) = G(i+1) - 1$, $G'(j+1) = G(j+1) + 1$, $G'(k+1) = G(k+1) - 1$ and $G'(l+1) = G(l+1) + 1$ when $G(i+1) \geq 1$ and $G(k+1) \geq 1$ and a pair of complementary rendezvous actions in two different instances of $\mathcal{U}$, $s_{\mathcal{U}}^i \to^{c?(c!)} s_{\mathcal{U}}^j$ and $s_{\mathcal{U}}^k \to^{c!(c?)} s_{\mathcal{U}}^l$, are executed; b) $G' = G$ except that $G'(1) = s_{\mathcal{C}}'$, $G'(i+1) = G(i+1) - 1$ and $G'(j+1) = G(j+1) + 1$ when $G(1) = s_{\mathcal{C}}$ and $G(i+1) \geq 1$ and a pair of complementary rendezvous actions between the process $\mathcal{C}$ and an instance of $\mathcal{U}$, $s_{\mathcal{C}} \to^{c?(c!)} s_{\mathcal{C}}'$ and $s_{\mathcal{U}}^i \to^{c!(c?)} s_{\mathcal{U}}^j$, are executed.

A computation, represented as C, of a parameterized systems defined as a sequence of communication events $c_0 c_1 \cdots c_{k-1}$ such that there is a *path* $G_P^0 \to^{c_0} G_1 \to^{c_1} \cdots \to^{c_{k-1}} G_k$. The projection of a computation C on the control process, denoted as $C_{\mathcal{C}}$, is a sequence of transitions obtained by orderly picking up those events in C in which the control process participates by executing a rendezvous action. Similarly, we can define C's projections on one or more instance of the user process, such as $C_{\mathcal{U}_i}, C_{\mathcal{U}_i, \mathcal{U}_j}$ where $\mathcal{U}_i$ and $\mathcal{U}_j$ are the ith and jth instance of $\mathcal{U}$, respectively.

2.2 Verification of Parameterized Systems

As stated in [2], the general verification of parameterized systems is not semi-decidable. However, a special class of systems consisting of many identical and finite-state processes, as those parameterized systems defined above, proves to be decidable [3–5]. What we are interested here is to use the automata-theoretic approach [13, 14] to verify parameterized systems against safety properties. Let ϕ be a finite *property automaton* $\langle S_\phi, \Sigma \cup \Sigma \times \{!, ?\}, \delta_\phi, s_\phi^0, F_\phi \rangle$, where F_ϕ is a set of accepting states. A property automaton essentially defines a set of undesired behaviors of a system. Once a state in F_ϕ is reached during a reachability analysis of the synchronous product $P \times \phi$, the property ϕ is said to be violated in the system P. We also use L_ϕ to denote the language accepted by the automaton ϕ.

In this paper, we consider the following four types of property automata: a) Automata regulating the universal behavior of a parameterized system, ϕ is said to be violated if there is a computation C of the parameterized system whose prefix belongs to L_ϕ; b) Automata regulating the behavior of the control process, ϕ is said to be violated if there is a computation C in the parameterized system such that a prefix of C_C belongs to L_ϕ; c) Automata regulating the behavior of the ith instance of the user process, ϕ is said to be violated if there is a computation C in the parameterized system such that a prefix of $C_{\mathcal{U}_i}$ belongs to L_ϕ; d) Automata regulating the behavior of two instances of the user process, ϕ is said to be violated if there is a computation C in the parameterized system such that a prefix of $C_{\mathcal{U}_i, \mathcal{U}_j}$ belongs to L_ϕ.

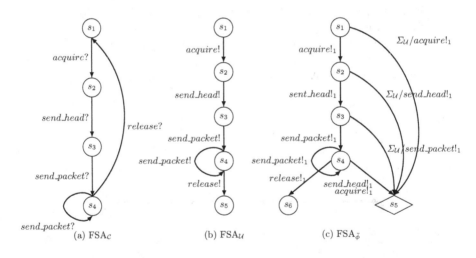

Fig. 2. Example Verification Problem in FSMs

The server and client processes in the example problem presented in Fig. 1 are represented by finite automata and they are given in Fig. 2(a) and Fig. 2(b), respectively. The property given in Fig. 2(c) corresponds to an automaton of the third type, stating that no orphan packets, which contains only data packets or the head, will be sent by the instance indexed with 1, that is to say no user instance will send orphan packets. The state s_5 with a diamond shape stands for a violating state and the notation $\Sigma_{\mathcal{U}}/a$ denotes the alphabet of the process $\mathcal{U}$ except for the action a.

3 Overall Approach

In this section, an overall view of our approach is presented. To start with, we first need to give the definition of an *extended parameterized system*, essentially the synchronous product of a parameterized system and the property automaton to be verified against. Given a property automaton ϕ and a parameterized system $P(n) = \mathcal{C} \times \mathcal{U}^n$, an *extended parameterized system*, denoted as P_e, is defined as $P_e(n) = \phi \times \mathcal{C} \times \mathcal{U}^n$. A global state of an extended parameterized system is a vector $\langle s_\phi, s_\mathcal{C}, \mathbf{v} \rangle$ where s_ϕ is ϕ's current state and $\langle s_\mathcal{C}, \mathbf{v} \rangle$ is the global state of the original parameterized system. The initial state corresponding to G_P^0 is represented as $G_{P_e}^0$. The set of transitions of an extended parameterized systems, denoted as δ_{P_e}, is defined as follows:

- If ϕ is a property automaton regulating the universal behavior of a parameterized system, then $\langle s_\phi, G \rangle \rightarrow^c \langle s'_\phi, G' \rangle \in \delta_{P_e}$ if and only if $s_\phi \rightarrow^c s'_\phi \in \delta_\phi$ and $G \rightarrow^c G' \in \delta_P$.
- If ϕ is a property automaton regulating the behavior of the control process, an instance or a pair of instances of the user process, then we will have the following two rules:
  - If c is a communication event in which none of those processes regulated by the property automaton ϕ participates, then $\langle s_\phi, G \rangle \rightarrow^c \langle s_\phi, G' \rangle \in \delta_{P_e}$ if and only if $G \rightarrow^c G' \in \delta_P$.
  - If c is a communication event in which some process regulated by the property automaton ϕ participates, then $\langle s_\phi, G \rangle \rightarrow^c \langle s'_\phi, G' \rangle \in \delta_{P_e}$ if and only if $s_\phi \rightarrow^c s'_\phi \subset \delta_\phi$ and $G \rightarrow^c G' \in \delta_P$.

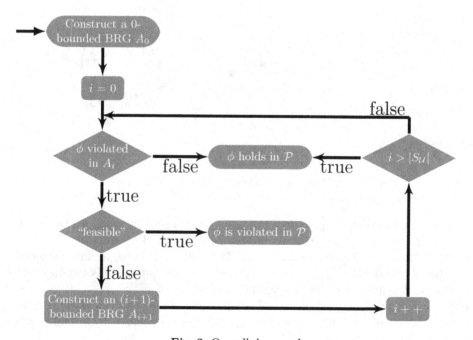

Fig. 3. Overall Approach

According to the overall approach presented in Fig. 3, the decision procedure will start with constructing the coarsest abstraction of the backward reachability graph (BRG) of an extended parameterized system, i.e. 0-bounded BRG A_0. More details about bounded BRGs will be presented in the next section and, at this point, we only need to know that an i-bounded BRG is an conservative abstraction of an j-bounded BRG for any $i < j \leq |S_\mathcal{U}|$ and the BRG of the original extended parameterized system is actually the $|S_\mathcal{U}|$-bounded BRG. In each iteration, a conclusion will be drawn if the property has been proved to hold or a feasible counter-example has been detected in the abstraction A_i. Otherwise, a refined abstraction will be constructed and the decision procedure will move into the next iteration.

The essence of the approach is to turn the original verification problem into a series of sub verification problems with lower dimensions, which tend to have a much smaller state space. In each sub-problem, the backward reachability analysis starts with an upward-closed set, constructed from the extended parameterized system. For a set D with a quasi-order, i.e. reflexive and transitive, relation $\preceq$, a subset $S \subseteq D$ is *upward-closed* if every $x \preceq y$ ($x \in S$) entails $y \in S$. For any $x \in D$, let $\uparrow x = \{y \mid x \preceq y \text{ and } y \in D\}$ and, for a set S, $\uparrow S = \bigcup_{s \in S} \uparrow s$. A *basis* of an upward-closed set S is a set $S_b \subseteq S$ such that $S = \uparrow S_b$. The quasi-order relation $(\preceq, P_e)$ over an extended parameterized system is defined as: $\langle s_\phi, s_\mathcal{C}, \mathbf{v} \rangle \preceq \langle s'_\phi, s'_\mathcal{C}, \mathbf{v}' \rangle$ if and only if $s_\phi = s'_\phi$, $s_\mathcal{C} = s'_\mathcal{C}$ and $\mathbf{v} \leq \mathbf{v}'$, meaning that $\mathbf{v}$ is componentwise less than or equal to $\mathbf{v}'$. Then, $\langle s_\phi, s_\mathcal{C}, \mathbf{v} \rangle$ is called a quasi predecessor of $\langle s'_\phi, s'_\mathcal{C}, \mathbf{v}' \rangle$. Then, the starting upward-closed set will be defined as $\uparrow \{F_\phi \times S_\mathcal{C} \times \{\langle 0, \cdots, 0 \rangle\}\}$, containing all the global states with ϕ being in an accepting state.

A *well-quasi-order* (a wqo) is any quasi-order relation $\preceq$ over some set X such that, for any infinite sequence $x_0, x_1, x_2, \cdots$, consisting of elements of X, there exists indexes $i < j$ with $x_i \preceq x_j$. As for the relation $(\preceq, P_e)$ defined previously, it is a well-quasi-order. To prove that, we need the *Dickson Lemma*, [15]: Let $v_1, v_2, \cdots$ be an infinite sequence of elements of $\mathbb{N}^k$, there exists $i < j$ such that $v_i \preceq v_j$ (pointwise order). In addition, the sets S_ϕ and $S_\mathcal{C}$ are finite. As a result, it is impossible to find an infinite sequence of states in an extended parameterized system (and bounded BRGs) in which there are no two states G_1 and G_2 such that $G_1 \preceq G_2$. Each path, starting from the undesired state, will ends with either the initial state of the verified system, meaning that the property does not hold, or a state G_1 such that another state G_2, satisfying $G_2 \preceq G_1$, is reachable from G_1. If no paths leading to the initial state exist in a bounded BRG, it indicates the property does hold in the corresponding abstraction. As a result, each sub-problem has a finite state space.

As it is also shown in Fig. 3 that a positive conclusion is drawn when $i > |S_U|$, at most $(|S_\mathcal{U}| + 1)$ iterations are needed in the overall approach. The whole decision procedure will certainly terminate and return conclusive results on whether a property holds in the given parameterized system. In the next section, the detailed definition of bounded BRGs and associated theorems will be presented.

4 Bounded Backward Reachability Graphs

A vector $v \in \mathbb{Z}^{|S_\mathcal{U}|}$ (remember that $|S_\mathcal{U}|$ is the number of states of the user process $\mathcal{U}$) is said to be *i-bounded* if $v(j) \geq 0$ for all $1 \leq j \leq i \leq |S_\mathcal{U}|$. As required in the definition of extended parameterized systems, the counter vector of each state visited during a backward reachability analysis has to be $|S_\mathcal{U}|$-bounded as the number of instances at each state of $\mathcal{U}$ has to be not less than zero. However, a series of upward abstractions for an extended parameterized system can be constructed if each state is only required to be i-bounded and only partial entries of counter vectors are considered.

An *i-bounded BRG* is defined as the abstraction of a given system's BRG, where each state is only required to be i-bounded. The dimension of i-bounded BRG is equal to i. The intuition behind the abstraction is rather straightforward. Assume that the execution of a communication c requires the participation of the user process, by executing a transition $s_l \rightarrow s_m$. In the original extended parameterized system, the communication is enabled only if the component of the counter vector, corresponding to the state s_l, of the current global state is greater than zero. However, the condition will not be necessary in an i-bounded BRG if the component corresponding to s_l is not included in the first i components being taken into account. In essence, an i-bounded BRG simulates an j-bounded BRG with $i < j$.

More specifically, the construction of an i-bounded BRG starts with an upward-closed set of undesired states. Because of the well-quasi-orderingness, an upward-closed set has a finite basis. At the same time, the set of immediate predecessors of an upward-closed set is also upward-closed and has a finite basis. In a bounded BRG, only the states contained in the bases of backwardly reachable upward-closed sets are needed to stored. Let $G = \langle s_\phi, s_C, \mathbf{v} \rangle$ be an i-bounded state already added to the i-bounded BRG. Then we have the following rules for adding additional states and transitions:

- If ϕ is a property automaton regulating the universal behavior of the system, a transition $G' \rightarrow^c G$ belongs to the i-bounded BRG, where $G' = \langle s'_\phi, s'_C, \mathbf{v}' \rangle$, if and only if $s'_\phi \rightarrow^c s_\phi \in \delta_\phi$, $s'_C \rightarrow^{c!(c?)} s_C \in \delta_C$, $s_k \rightarrow^{c?(c!)} s_j \in \delta_\mathcal{U}$, $\mathbf{v}' = \mathbf{v} + \mathbf{0}(k:1, j:-1)$ and $\mathbf{v}'$ is i-bounded;
- If ϕ is a property automaton regulating only partial behavior of the system, $G' \rightarrow^c G$ belongs to the i-bounded BRG if and only if
  - none of the processes regulated by ϕ are participating, $s_\phi = s'_\phi$, $s_C = s'_C$, $s_k \rightarrow^{c?(c!)} s_j \in \delta_\mathcal{U}$, $s_l \rightarrow^{c!(c?)} s_m \in \delta_\mathcal{U}$, $\mathbf{v}' = \mathbf{v} + \mathbf{0}(k:1, j:-1) + \mathbf{0}(l:1, m:-1)$ and $\mathbf{v}'$ is i-bounded;
  - none of the processes regulated by ϕ are participating, $s_\phi = s'_\phi$, $s'_C \rightarrow^{c?(c!)} s_C \in \delta_C$, $s_k \rightarrow^{c!(c?)} s_j \in \delta_\mathcal{U}$, $\mathbf{v}' = \mathbf{v} + \mathbf{0}(k:1, j:-1)$ and $\mathbf{v}'$ is i-bounded;
  - $s'_\phi \rightarrow^c s_\phi \in \delta_\phi$, $s'_C \rightarrow^{c?(c!)} s_C \in \delta_C$, $s_k \rightarrow^{c!(c?)} s_j \in \delta_\mathcal{U}$, $\mathbf{v}' = \mathbf{v} + \mathbf{0}(k:1, j:-1)$ and $\mathbf{v}'$ is i-bounded;
  - $s'_\phi \rightarrow^c s_\phi \in \delta_\phi$, $s_C = s'_C$, $s_k \rightarrow^{c?(c!)} s_j \in \delta_\mathcal{U}$, $s_l \rightarrow^{c!(c?)} s_m \in \delta_\mathcal{U}$, $\mathbf{v}' = \mathbf{v} + \mathbf{0}(k:1, j:-1) + \mathbf{0}(l:1, m:-1)$ and $\mathbf{v}'$ is i-bounded.

The above construction procedure will definitely terminate also because of the Dickson lemma. In addition, as each state in every path of an i-bounded BRG is i-bounded, they are also called i-*bounded paths*. Given two states G_1 and G_2, G_1 is said to be an i-quasi-predecessor of G_2 if their local states for the property automata and the control process are the same and $\mathbf{v}_1(j) \leq \mathbf{v}_2(j)$ for all $1 \leq j \leq i$, where $\mathbf{v}_1$ and $\mathbf{v}_2$ are the counter vectors of G_1 and G_2, respectively.

From the above construction procedure, we also have the following observations:: a) During the construction of an i-bounded BRG, a new state will be discarded if some state that has been added to the BRG is an i-quasi-predecessor of it. However, the new state might be added to an $(i+1)$-bounded BRG because the $(i+1)$th entry of the counter vector might make a difference to break the quasi-order; b) A path in an i-bounded BRG ends with either a state leading to no new i-bounded states, or a state that is an i-quasi-predecessor of $G^0_{P_e}$ (then the path is also called an i-*bounded counter-example*). However, the state may not be an $(i+1)$-quasi-predecessor of $G^0_{P_e}$ and backward leads to new $(i+1)$-bounded states.

As a result, we can learn that an i-bounded BRG normally has a smaller state space than a k-bounded BRG with $i < k$. That's the most important intuition behind our approach. More importantly, we have the following theorem to decide when the whole decision procedure can be terminated at an intermediate iteration and draw a conclusive positive conclusion.

Theorem 1. *Given an i-bounded BRG and an $(i+1)$-bounded BRG of an extended parameterized system. If there is an $(i+1)$-bounded counter-example p in the $(i+1)$-bounded BRG, there must exist an i-bounded counter-example p' in the i-bounded BRG.*

Proof. To construct an i-bounded path from $(i+1)$-bounded one, we need to remove those possible loops and redundant transitions resulted from abstracting an $(i+1)$-bounded path as an i-bounded one. Let p' be the resulted path and then it is proved that p' is an enabled i-bounded counter-example.

For every transition $G \rightarrow^c G'$ sequentially appeared in p', being an enabled transition of p, they are also sequentially enabled in the i-bounded BRG: a) if no user processes are involved in the transition, because the transition is enabled in p and its transition does not involve counter vectors of G and G'; b) if one or two user processes are involved in the transition, because the first $(i+1)$ entries of G''s counter vector are ensured to be non-negative, otherwise the transition being not enabled in p.

In addition, the first state of p is also an i-quasi-predecessor of $G^0_{P_e}$ if it is contained in p'; otherwise the state's i-quasi-predecessor in p' is also an i-quasi-predecessor of $G^0_{P_e}$. $\qquad \square$

In summary, we will have the following algorithm, shown in Fig. 4, for an Iterative and Backward Reachability Analysis (IBRA) of parameterized systems. A series of BRGs from 0-bounded to $|S_\mathcal{U}|$-bounded are sequentially constructed as the abstractions of the original verification problems. A negative conclusion will be drawn if a concrete counter-example is found during an iteration, while a positive conclusion is drawn when no counter-examples are found during an iteration.

IBRA // Decides if a property holds;
1: Graph T; // Records the BRGs created during the analysis
2: **boolean** b_1 = **false**; // True if a feasible i-bounded counter-example is found
3: **for int** i **from** 0 **to** m **do**
      // Remember m is the number of states of the user process
4:   **if** $i = 0$ **then**
5:      Add the set of undesired states to T;
6:   **end if**
7:   Remove those prefixes from T that starts with a non i-bounded state;
8:   Backward extend each path in T with i-bounded states that can be backward reached until all i-bounded paths have been explored or a state that is an i-quasi-predecessor of $G_{P_e}^0$ is reached;
9:   **if** A state that is an i-quasi-predecessor of $G_{P_e}^0$ is reached **then**
10:     **if** The i-bounded counter-example is feasible **then**
11:        let b_1 = **true**;
12:        **break**; // A negative conclusion is drawn
13:     **end if**
14:   **else**
15:     let b_1 = **false**;
16:     **break**; // A positive conclusion is drawn
17:   **end if**
18: **end for**
19: **if** b_1= **true then**
20:   The property does not hold;
21: **else**
22:   The property does hold;
23: **end if**

Fig. 4. IBRA

5   Experimental Results

5.1   Experiment Setup

For the sake of simplicity, we have only considered parameterized systems composed of one control process and one user process so far, although an arbitrary number of instances of the user process can be created. However, it is rather straightforward to extend the algorithm to parameterized systems consisting of a finite number of control processes and user processes. The algorithm remains exactly the same except that new local states and counter vectors are introduced to cover those additional processes in the global states.

Those systems used in the following experiments are listed in Table 1[1]. For each example problem, the details, such as the control processes and user

---

[1] Further details about those systems and the raw data collected during the following experiments can be seen from http://124.16.139.190/qiusongyang/systems.htm

Table 1. List of Example Problems Used in the Experiments

Index	Systems		ϕ	$|\phi|$	$\mathcal{C}$	$|\mathcal{C}|$	$\mathcal{U}$	$|\mathcal{U}|$	m
P_1	Bin Example		Inverse Dependency (Type 1, F)	24	Control	6	User	9	4
P_2	Loop Example		Looped Dependency (Type 1, F)	32	Control	4	User	7	4
P_3	Simple Protocol		Mutual Exclusive (Type 4, T)	36	Server	9	Client	10	5
P_4			No Orphan Packets (Type 3, T)	20					
P_5		Size=50	Produce First (Type 1, T)	15	Buffer	151	Producer	6	6
P_6	Producer&		Produce First (Type 2, T)	15			Consumer	6	
P_7	Consumer	Size=100	Produce First (Type 1, T)	15	Buffer	301	Producer	6	6
P_8			Produce First (Type 2, T)	15			Consumer	6	
P_9	Gas Station		Start Pumping First (Type 2, T)	19	Pump$_1$	12	Client	23	11
P_{10}			Start Pumping First (Type 3, T)	52	Pump$_2$	12			

processes of a parameterized system, the property to be verified, and their sizes are presented. Here, the size of an FSA is the sum of the numbers of states and transitions. In addition, the property's type information indicates the type of property automaton to be verified as discussed in Section 2.2. The indicator "T" or "F" shows whether or not the property actually holds in the system being verified. The last column, m, gives the dimension of counter vectors of each parameterized system.

The algorithm IBRA and existing typical algorithms for verification of parameterized systems are implemented in JAVA. Each data sample collected during the experiments consists of the execution time in milliseconds, the storage space needed to restore the global states reached during the verification. The algorithms are run on a Lenovo desktop with a Dual E2140@1.60GHz CPU and 1GB of memory running Windows XP.

5.2   Experiment Results

We tested the algorithm IBRA on the example problems listed in Table 1. For each example problem, the iterations for deciding if a property holds in the corresponding parameterized system are given in Table 2. The boolean variable B_1 indicates whether an i-bounded counter-example is encountered during the ith iteration (assume that the index starts with zero), while B_2 is true if the counter-example is feasible in the original system. The number of states visited during each iteration is recorded in S_i. IBRA's average execution time on each example problem is presented in the last column.

From Table 2, we can make the following observations. As for the problems from P_3 to P_{10}, it returns the decision result after the first iteration because B_1 is false, indicating that there is no counter-examples in the most coarsest upward abstraction. It should be also noted that the algorithm returns conclusive results in the second iteration of the problem P_1. B_1 and B_2 are simultaneously being true only if a feasible counter-example has been found.

To demonstrate the effectiveness of IBRA, we also implemented the Backward Reachability Analysis (BRA) algorithm proposed in [6, 7], from which many

Table 2. Experiment Results of IBRA

Index	B_1	B_2	S_i	T(ms)	Index	B_1	B_2	S_i	T(ms)	Index	B_1	B_2	S_i	T(ms)
$P_1\ i=0$	T	F	4	35.8	$P_2\ i=0$	T	F	5	89.1	$P_5\ i=0$	F		202	109.3
$i=1$	T	T	4		$i=1$	T	F	5		$P_6\ i=0$	F		202	89.2
$i=2$	T	F	4		$i=2$	T	F	5		$P_7\ i=0$	F		402	271.6
$i=3$	T	F	7		$i=3$	T	F	47		$P_8\ i=0$	F		402	297.1
$i=4$	T	T	15		$i=4$	T	F	47		$P_9\ i=0$	F		42	21.9
$P_3\ i=0$	F		64	34.1	$P_4\ i=0$	F		732	206.3	$P_{10}\ i=0$	F		1044	390.6

variants, such as [5, 7–10, 15], have been derived. The comparison between the two algorithms is presented in Fig. 5. We use the ratio of IBRA's average running time (visited states) to BRA's average running time (visited states) as the *y-axis* of the figure. On the *x-axis*, those example problems are orderly listed. The larger a ratio is, the better IBRA performs than BRA in an example problem.

From Fig. 5, it is confirmed that the number of states visited in IBRA will not be more than those visited by BRA. The worst case is that IBRA has to visit all states reached in BRA. Only partial state space reached in BRA is visited by IBRA for all the example problems except for P_1, P_2, and P_9. As for the average running time, the algorithm BRA outperforms IBRA in P_1 and P_2. However, the time ratio is very close to one because the number of states visited during the first several iterations of IBRA is relatively small. Although their sets of visited states are the same, the algorithm IBRA outperforms BRA somewhat in P_9, because each operation deciding if one state is a 0-quasi-predecessor of the other does not involve counter vectors in IBRA's 0th iteration. The data from other example problems demonstrates that an algorithm's execution time strongly depends on the number of states visited and a reduction in number of states often results in a greater gain in the execution time due to such factors as garbage collection [16].

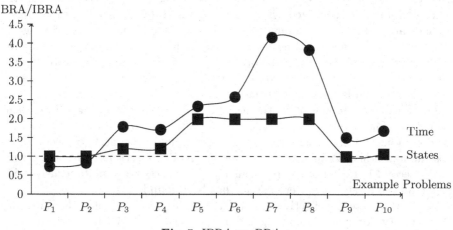

Fig. 5. IBRA vs. BRA

6   Related Work

An abstract algorithm based on backward reachability analysis is proposed in [6, 7] to verify concurrent systems with an infinite-state space. Several variants of the algorithm have been devised for verification of parameterized systems. Although the common idea is to calculate a least fixed-point, the data structures used for symbolically representing infinite sets of states are different. In [8], the authors use *additive constraints*, linear arithmetic constraints with additions, to represent collections of upward-closed sets. In [9, 10], *sharing trees*, in which a path corresponds to a generator (an element of the basis), are used in a compact way to represent an upward-closed set. In [11], *NA-constraints* and *DV-constraints* are used for representing upward-closed sets encountered during the backward reachability analysis of broadcast protocols. When implementing our approach, we actually used NA-constraints to represent an upward-closed set. The basic idea of our approach, building increasingly precise abstractions by taking more and more local states into account, is orthogonal to the works mentioned above. Our approach can be extended to other symbolic methods for representing upward-closed sets.

In [17], the author also uses an iterative approach based on BDDs to verify parameterized systems through iteratively computing the backward reachability for constituent systems of increasing size until a certain convergence condition is reached. A property is first verified in a system with n instances of the user process and, if the property does hold, the property will be checked against a system with $n + 1$ instances. Instead of an upward-abstraction as used in our approach, the author actually uses a downward abstraction of the original system. At the same time, the termination of the approach depends on a very restrictive condition, i.e. δ-deflectable DWS (Discrete Well Structured), and thus it is only applicable to a very small subset of parameterized systems.

An incrementally refinement approach for the verification of parameterized systems is also introduced in [18]. Based on forward reachability analysis, the authors proposed an approach for the verification of parameterized systems based on an inductively calculated cut-off on the maximum length of paths needed to be explored. However, that kind cut-offs do not exist for the backward reachability analysis of parameterized systems conducted in this paper. The finiteness of state space has to completely depend on the well-quasi-orderingness of parameterized systems. The work given in [19] is also highly related to ours. The authors present a symbolic exploration algorithm that avoids the dimensionality problem by carefully scheduling which counters to track at any moment during the search. However, they only consider the concurrent software with a finite number of processes.

7   Conclusion

Based on bounded backward reachability graphs, n novel approach is proposed for the verification of parameterized systems. A verification problem deciding if a property specified by an automata, regulating a set of undesired behaviors, holds in a parameterized system, is turned into a series of sub verification problems with low dimensions, which tend to have much smaller state spaces. Experiment results show that the algorithm outperforms typical backward reachability analysis algorithms in many of the example problems.

Although only safety properties are discussed in this paper, the approach can be extended to liveness properties in Büchi Automata. In addition, we used a random order to decide which state of the user process should be considered next. It might be possible to heuristically find an optimal ordering to further improve verification efficiencies.

References

1. Zuck, L.D., Pnueli, A.: Model checking and abstraction to the aid of parameterized systems (a survey). Computer Languages, Systems & Structures 30(3-4), 139–169 (2004)
2. Apt, K.R., Kozen, D.C.: Limits for automatic verification of finite-state concurrent systems. Inf. Process. Lett. 22(6), 307–309 (1986)
3. German, S.M., Sistla, A.P.: Reasoning about systems with many processes. J. ACM 39(3), 675–735 (1992)
4. Emerson, E.A., Namjoshi, K.S.: On model checking for non-deterministic infinite-state systems. In: Logic in Computer Science, pp. 70–80 (1998)
5. Esparza, J., Finkel, A., Mayr, R.: On the verification of broadcast protocols. In: LICS 1999: Proceedings of the 14th Annual IEEE Symposium on Logic in Computer Science, p. 352. IEEE Computer Society, Washington, DC (1999)
6. Abdulla, P.A., Cerans, K., Jonsson, B., Tsay, Y.K.: General decidability theorems for infinite-state systems. In: LICS 1996: Proceedings of the 11th Annual IEEE Symposium on Logic in Computer Science, pp. 313–321. IEEE Computer Society, Washington, DC (1996)
7. Finkel, A., Schnoebelen, P.: Well-structured transition systems everywhere? Theor. Comput. Sci. 256(1-2), 63–92 (2001)
8. Delzanno, G.: Constraint-Based Model Checking for Parameterized Synchronous Systems. In: Armando, A. (ed.) FroCos 2002. LNCS (LNAI), vol. 2309, pp. 72–318. Springer, Heidelberg (2002)
9. Delzanno, G., Raskin, J.-F., Van Begin, L.: Attacking Symbolic State Explosion. In: Berry, G., Comon, H., Finkel, A. (eds.) CAV 2001. LNCS, vol. 2102, pp. 298–310. Springer, Heidelberg (2001)
10. Delzanno, G., Raskin, J.-F.: Symbolic Representation of Upward-Closed Sets. In: Graf, S. (ed.) TACAS 2000. LNCS, vol. 1785, pp. 426–440. Springer, Heidelberg (2000)
11. Delzanno, G., Esparza, J., Podelski, A.: Constraint-Based Analysis of Broadcast Protocols. In: Flum, J., Rodríguez-Artalejo, M. (eds.) CSL 1999. LNCS, vol. 1683, pp. 50–66. Springer, Heidelberg (1999)
12. Esparza, J.: Verification of Systems with an Infinite State Space. In: Cassez, F., Jard, C., Rozoy, B., Dermot, M. (eds.) MOVEP 2000. LNCS, vol. 2067, pp. 183–186. Springer, Heidelberg (2001)
13. Vardi, M.Y., Wolper, P.: An automata-theoretic approach to automatic program verification (preliminary report). In: Meyer, A. (ed.) Proceedings of the First Annual IEEE Symp. on Logic in Computer Science, LICS 1986, pp. 332–344. IEEE Computer Society Press (1986)

14. Dwyer, M.B., Clarke, L.A., Cobleigh, J.M., Naumovich, G.: Flow analysis for verifying properties of concurrent software systems. ACM Trans. Softw. Eng. Methodol. 13(4), 359–430 (2004)
15. Delzanno, G.: Constraint-based verification of parameterized cache coherence protocols. Form. Methods Syst. Des. 23(3), 257–301 (2003)
16. Dwyer, M.B., Person, S., Elbaum, S.G.: Controlling factors in evaluating path-sensitive error detection techniques. In: Young, M., Devanbu, P.T. (eds.) SIGSOFT FSE, pp. 92–104. ACM (2006)
17. Bingham, J.D.: A new approach to upward-closed set backward reachability analysis. Electr. Notes Theor. Comput. Sci. 138(3), 37–48 (2005)
18. Yang, Q., Li, M.: A cut-off approach for bounded verification of parameterized systems. In: Proceedings of the 32nd ACM/IEEE International Conference on Software Engineering, ICSE 2010, vol. 1, pp. 345–354. ACM, New York (2010)
19. Basler, G., Mazzucchi, M., Wahl, T., Kroening, D.: Symbolic Counter Abstraction for Concurrent Software. In: Bouajjani, A., Maler, O. (eds.) CAV 2009. LNCS, vol. 5643, pp. 64–78. Springer, Heidelberg (2009)

Refinement-Based Modeling of 3D NoCs

Maryam Kamali[1,2], Luigia Petre[1], Kaisa Sere[1], and Masoud Daneshtalab[3]

[1] Åbo Akademi University, Finland
[2] Turku Centre for Computer Science (TUCS), Finland
[3] University of Turku, Finland

Abstract. Three-dimensional Networks-on-Chip (3D NoC) have recently emerged essentially via the stacking of multiple layers of two-dimensional NoCs. The resulting structures can support a very high level of parallelism for both communication and computation as well as higher speeds, at the cost of increased complexity. To address the potential problems due to the highly complex NoCs, we study them with formal methods. In particular, we base our study on the *refinement* relation between models of the same system. We propose three abstract models of 3D NoCs, M_0, M_1, and M_2 so that $M_0 \sqsubseteq M_1 \sqsubseteq M_2$, where '$\sqsubseteq$' denotes the refinement relation. Each of these models provides templates for communication constraints and guarantees the communication correctness. We then show how to employ one of these models for reasoning about the communication correctness of the XYZ-routing algorithm.

1 Introduction

The Network-on-Chip (NoC) architecture paradigm, based on a modular packet-switching mechanism, can address many of the on-chip communication design issues such as performance limitations of long interconnects and the integration of high numbers of Intellectual Property (IP) cores on a chip. However, the 2D-chip fabrication technology faces many challenges in the deep submicron regime even when employing NoC architectures, e.g, the design of the clock-tree network for large chips, limited floor-planning choices, the increase of both the wire delay and power consumption, the integration of various components that are digital, analog, MEMS and RF, etc. Three Dimensional Integrated Circuits (3D ICs) have been emerging as a viable candidate to achieve better performance and package density as compared to traditional Two Dimensional (2D) ICs. In addition, combining the benefits of 3D ICs and NoC schemes provides a significant performance gain for 3D architectures [13,27,22].

Three dimensional Networks-on-Chip (3D NoCs) [13] provide more reliable interconnections due to the increased number of links between components. Due to their promise of parallelism and efficiency, 3D NoCs have a critical role in leading towards reliable computing platforms. However, the majority of their evaluation approaches are simulation-based tools, such as XMulator [25], Noxim [26], etc. Simulation-based approaches are usually applied in the late stages of design and are limited, e.g., by the length of time that a system is simulated.

F. Arbab and M. Sirjani (Eds.): FSEN 2011, LNCS 7141, pp. 236–252, 2012.
© Springer-Verlag Berlin Heidelberg 2012

This means that exhaustive checking of all the system states is impossible in practice for complex 3D NoCs and thus, simulation is not suitable for verifying the correctness of a NoC design.

Another approach to address this problem is via formal methods. Formal methods refer to the application of mathematical techniques to the design and implementation of computer hardware and software. Prominent examples of applying formal methods are provided by, e.g., Intel [16,19] and IBM [21] for formally verifying hardware or systems-on-chip (SoC) [15]. By using rigorous mathematical techniques, it is possible to deliver *provably correct* systems. Formal methods are based on the capture of system requirements in a specific, precise format. Importantly, such a format can be analyzed for various properties and, if the formal method permits, also stepwise developed until an implementation is formed. By following such a formal development, we are *sure* that the final result correctly implements the requirements of the system.

Much of the research concerning the 3D NoC design is concentrated on various bottom-up approaches, such as the study of routing algorithms [6,20] or the design of dedicated 3D NoC architectures [29] where parameters such as hop count or power consumption are improved. Here we are concerned with a reverse, top-down approach where we start from simple models and add complexity later. There are already research results regarding the detection of faults as well as debugging in the early stages of NoC design. A generic model for specifying and verifying NoC systems is presented in [10] where the formal verification is addressed with the ACL2 theorem prover, a mechanized proof tool. This tool produces a set of proof obligations that should be discharged for particular NoC instances. This generic model has been used for verification of functionality features in 2D-NoC systems. Another formal approach to the development of the NoC systems employing the B-action systems formalism has been described in [28], where the focus is on the formal specification of communication routers. A framework for modeling 2D-NoC systems by composing more advanced routing components out of simpler ones, is proposed there.

In this paper, we go one step further and propose a top-down formalization of the early *3D* NoC design. The formal method we employ is Event-B [2] which comes with the associated tool Rodin [1,30]. One of the main features of Event-B is that the system development is done in a stepwise manner that eventually leads to a system implementation. The stepwise development is captured by the *refinement* [4,5] relation between models of the same system, so that a high-level model of a system is transformed by a sequence of correctness-preserving steps into a more detailed and efficient model that satisfies the original specification. We specify here the general structure of a 3D NoC at a high level of abstraction in Event-B. The specification formulates the main constraints of the communication model, needed to prove its correctness. Our definition for correctness at this abstract level of modeling is to show that a package injected in the network is eventually received at the destination. We propose three different abstract models M_0, M_1, and M_2 for a 3D NoC so that $M_0 \sqsubseteq M_1 \sqsubseteq M_2$, where '$\sqsubseteq$' denotes the refinement relation. Furthermore, each of these models can be refined into more concrete models to define specific 3D NoC designs in the early stages of the system development. When the concrete models preserve the correctness properties of the abstract models, we guarantee the correctness of the concrete 3D NoC designs. As an application of the general 3D NoC designs, we model the XYZ routing algorithm by refining the M_2 abstract model. To verify the XYZ routing algorithm, we generate the proof obligations using the Rodin tool and discharge them automatically or interactively.

We proceed as follows. In Section 2 we overview the Event-B formal method to the extent needed in this paper. In Section 3 we propose three increasingly more detailed formal models for a 3D NoC together with the constraints for proving correctness. In Section 4 we illustrate the formal modeling of the XYZ routing algorithm as a case study. In Section 5 we discuss the proof obligations while in Section 6 we present concluding remarks and future work.

2   Preliminaries

Event-B [2,1] is an extension of the B formalism [3,28] for specifying distributed and reactive systems. A system model is gradually specified on increasing levels of abstraction, always ensuring that a more concrete model is a *correct implementation* of an abstract model. The language and proof theory of Event-B are based on logic and set theory. The correctness of the stepwise construction of formal models is ensured by discharging a set of proof obligations: if these obligations hold, then the development is mathematically shown to be correct. Event-B comes with the associated tool Rodin [1,30], which automatically discharges part of the proof obligations and also provides the means for the user to discharge interactively the remaining proofs.

Each Event-B model consists of two components called *context* and *machine*. A context describes the static part of the model, i.e., it introduces new types and constants. The properties of these types and constants are gathered as a list of axioms. A machine represents the dynamic part of the model, consisting of variables that define the *state* of the model and operations called *events*. The system properties that should be preserved during the execution are formulated as a list of *invariant* predicates over the state of the model.

An event, modeling state changes, is composed of a *guard* and an *action*. The guard is the necessary condition under which an event might occur; if the guard holds, we call the event *enabled*. The action determines the way in which the state variables change when the event occurs. For initializing the system, a sequence of actions is defined. When the guards of several events hold at the same time, then only one event is non-deterministically chosen for execution. If some events have no variables in common and are enabled at the same time, then they can be considered to be executed in parallel since their sequential execution in any order gives the same result. For all practical purposes, this execution model is parallel and can be implemented as such when the model is refined to code. Events can be declared as *anticipated*, meaning that in the future refinements we need to set out a natural number expression called *variant* and prove that it is decreased by this event. Events can also be *convergent*, meaning that in the current machine there is a variant that decreases when this event is chosen for execution. Thus, an anticipated event is not convergent in the current machine but should become so in a future refinement of that machine.

A model can be developed by a number of correctness preserving steps called *refinements* [4,5]. One form of model refinement can add new data and new events on top of the already existing data and behavior but in such a way that the introduced behavior does not contradict or take over the abstract machine behavior. This form of stepwise construction is referred to as *superposition* refinement [18,9]. We may also use other refinement forms, e.g., *algorithmic* refinement [8]. In this case, an event of an abstract machine can be refined by several corresponding events in a refined machine. This will model different branches of execution, that can, for instance, take place in parallel and thus can improve the algorithmic efficiency. In this paper, we use only superposition refinement.

3   Three Abstract Models for the 3D NoC: M_0, M_1, M_2

In this section we formally develop three high-level models M_0, M_1, and M_2 for the 3D NoC. Our models are at three increasing levels of detail so that each model is a refinement of the previous one: $M_0 \sqsubseteq M_1 \sqsubseteq M_2$. In the initial model, we specify a network of nodes and define the correctness properties of this network based on a specific data structure called *pool*, as suggested by [2]. In the second model, we add new data and events to model the 3D mesh-based NoC architecture; besides, we specify the channels between nodes. In the third model, we model buffers for nodes and refine the communication model.

By starting from an initial model that is rather abstract, i.e., without detailing the communication topology, we obtain a rather general starting point that can later be refined to various topologies. Moreover, adding channels and ports only in the second model leads to a clean modelling of the basic communication mechanism (via routing and switching) in the initial model; the required detail (of channels and ports) are not needed for understanding the communication mechanism. Adding buffers in the third model illustrates an extra level of detail. Networks where the nodes have no buffers for communication will, therefore, employ the second model as their abstraction and not the third.

3.1   The Initial Model M_0

The first model M_0 that we construct is rather abstract: we do not consider the numerous parts of the network such as channels or buffers; they will be introduced in subsequent refinements. M_0 will thus allow us to reason about the system very abstractly [2]. The model M_0 is formed of the static part and the dynamic part, as follows.

The Static Part. The static part of our model is described in Fig. 1 and contains the sets *MESSAGES*, *ROUTER*, *DATA* and the constants *data*, *des*, *src* and *Neigh*. The message identifiers are modeled by the non-empty and finite

MESSAGES set. We use the following modeling idea for messages. A message id in the *MESSAGES* set relates to a triple *(data, source, destination)* where *data* is an element of the *DATA* set, *source* models the source node where a message is injected, and *destination* models the destination node where a message should be received. A message should not be destined to its source node. The set of network nodes and data are modeled by the sets *ROUTER* (finite and non-empty) and *DATA* (finite and non-empty), respectively. The relation *Neigh* (non-empty, symmetric, and non-reflexive) models the neighbor structure i.e., which node can communicate with which node.

```
SETS MESSAGES  ROUTER  DATA
CONSTANTS data  des  src    Neigh
AXIOMS
     MESSAGES ≠ ∅ ∧ finite(MESSAGES)
     ROUTER ≠ ∅ ∧ finite(ROUTER)
     DATA ≠ ∅ ∧ finite(DATA)
     data ∈ MESSAGES → DATA
     src ∈ MESSAGES → ROUTER ∧ des ∈ MESSAGES → ROUTER
     ∀m, sp, dp·m ∈ MESSAGES ∧ sp ∈ ROUTER ∧ dp ∈ ROUTER
          ∧m ↦ sp ∈ src ∧ m ↦ dp ∈ des ⇒ sp ≠ dp
     Neigh ∈ ROUTER ↔ ROUTER
     Neigh ≠ ∅ ∧ Neigh = Neigh⁻¹ ∧ dom(Neigh) ◁ id ∩ Neigh = ∅
```

Fig. 1. M_0: the static part

To define structure types such as records in Event-B, we use functions to represent attributes. Therefore, our modeling idea translates to the functions *data*, *src* and *des* with ranges *DATA*, *ROUTER*, and *ROUTER*, respectively.

The Dynamic Part. In our network model we use the following condition for modeling the communication correctness: the messages in the network will eventually reach their destinations. For this, we define two message subsets and one partial message-to-node map as machine variables: *sent_pool* ⊆ *MESSAGES*, *received_pool* ⊆ *MESSAGES* and *moving_pool* ∈ *sent_pool* ⇸ *ROUTER*.

The *sent_pool* subset denotes the list of messages injected into the network. The *sent_pool* subset is updated whenever a new message is injected into the network, while the *moving_pool* subset denotes the current position of traveling messages. All the messages injected into the network are added to the *moving_pool* and whenever a message is routed from a node to another one, the current position of that message is updated in the *moving_pool*. The *received_pool* subset denotes the list of messages received from the network by destination nodes. Whenever a message is received at its destination, it will be added to *received_pool* and removed from *moving_pool*. The behavior of message pools is illustrated in Fig. 2.

To model the communication and the message pool functions, we define three events as explained below. The *sent_message* event described in Fig. 3(a) handles the injection of a new message into the network. Whenever a message is injected into the network both *sent_pool* as well as *moving_pool* are updated.

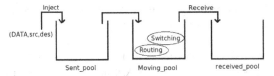

Fig. 2. Message Pools

Event $routing \; \widehat{=}$
   begin
     skip
   end
Event $switching \; \widehat{=}$
Status anticipated
   any
     $current\_msg \quad new\_position$
   where
     $current\_msg \in dom(moving\_pool)$
     $des(current\_msg) \neq$
       $moving\_pool(current\_msg)$
     $new\_position \mapsto moving\_pool(current\_msg)$
       $\in Neigh$
     $new\_position \neq src(current\_msg)$
   then
     $moving\_pool(current\_msg) := new\_position$
   end

Event $sent\_message \; \widehat{=}$
   any
     $current\_msg$
   where
     $current\_msg \in MESSAGES$
     $current\_msg \notin sent\_pool$
   then
     $sent\_pool := sent\_pool \cup \{current\_msg\}$
     $moving\_pool := moving\_pool$
       $\cup \{current\_msg \mapsto src(current\_msg)\}$
   end

(a) Message Injection   (b) Routing and Switching

Fig. 3. M_0 Events

A message in *moving_pool* should be routed toward its destination. This is composed of two actions, one for deciding which node would be the next one (routing) and the other for transferring the message to that node (switching). These two actions are available for all the nodes, including the source, the destination as well as all the intermediate nodes and are modeled respectively by the *routing* and *switching* events shown in Fig. 3(b). In this abstract model we do not have any routing decisions, hence, the *routing* event is modeled by *skip*. The *switching* event in the M_0 model only transfers a message from the current node to one of its neighbors nondeterministically and updates the *moving_pool* by changing the current position of a message. To avoid cycling, we do not allow a message to return to its source. The reason for not considering a specific routing algorithm is that it makes our initial model more general and reusable for a wide variety of routing algorithms implementations. The *switching* event has the status *anticipated*.

Event $received\_message \; \widehat{=}$
Status convergent
   any
     $current\_msg$
   where
     $current\_msg \in dom(moving\_pool)$
     $des(current\_msg) = moving\_pool(current\_msg)$
   then
     $moving\_pool := \{current\_msg\} \lhd moving\_pool$
     $received\_pool := received\_pool \cup \{current\_msg\}$
   end

Fig. 4. M_0: Received_message Event

The *received_message* event shown in Fig. 4 adds a message received at its destination to *received_pool* and removes the message from *moving_pool*. This event is convergent: if new messages are not injected to the network for a certain time, all the messages will be received at their destinations. This is proved by means of the (*sent_pool* \ *received_pool*) variant denoting the difference between the sets *sent_pool* and *received_pool*.

In order to prove the communication correctness, we need to prove that the *sent_pool* subset eventually becomes equal with the *received_pool* subset and the *moving_pool* subset is empty when all the messages are received at their destinations. These properties are formulated in Fig. 5 as invariants.

INVARIANTS
$dom(moving\_pool) \subseteq sent\_pool$
$received\_pool \cap dom(moving\_pool) = \varnothing$
$sent\_pool = received\_pool \Leftrightarrow moving\_pool = \varnothing$
$\forall msg \cdot msg \notin sent\_pool \Rightarrow msg \notin received\_pool$
$sent\_pool \setminus dom(moving\_pool) = received\_pool$
$sent\_pool \setminus received\_pool = dom(moving\_pool)$

Fig. 5. M_0: Invariants (Pool Modeling)

M_0 is a general specification of a general network and will be refined to model 3D NoC communication designs in the following. Moreover, the model provides the necessary properties that should be preserved by refinement. These properties, that guarantee the overall communication correctness, are defined as the list of invariants.

3.2   The Second Model M_1

Transferring a message from a node to its neighbor in the model M_0 is achieved simply by copying the message from a node to another. In this section we refine the initial model M_0 to also specify channels specific to the 3D NoCs. To specify channels, we need a 3D NoC architecture. There are a number of 3D NoC architectures, e.g., mesh-based [13], tree-based [14]. We consider here NoCs with 3D mesh topologies. The 3D mesh-based NoC (Fig. 6(a)) consists of $N = m * n * k$ nodes; each node has an associated integer *coordinate triple* (x, y, z), $0 < x \leq m$, $0 < y \leq n$, $0 < z \leq k$.

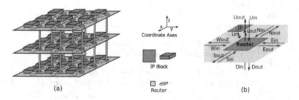

Fig. 6. (a) 3D Mesh-based NoC architecture   (b) Router channels

Our 3D NoC architecture employs seven-port routers: one port to the IP block, one port to above and below routers, and one in each cardinal direction (North, South, East and West), as shown in Fig. 6(b).

The Static Part. We extend the static part of the initial model M_0 in three ways: we map routers to coordinate triples, we add new properties for the *neigh* relation based on the coordinate triples, and we model ports and channels for the 3D NoC. In order to map routers to the coordinate triples, we define four constants: *coordX*, *coordY*, *coordZ* and *mk_position* as shown in Fig. 7. The *coordX*, *coordY* and *coordZ* constants represent coordinate triples (x, y, z) and the *mk_position* constant is a map associating each router to a position in space given by the coordinates. The *crossbarX*, *crossbarY* and *crossbarZ* constants model the number of nodes in X, Y and Z coordinate in the network, respectively.

Two nodes with coordinates (x_i, y_i, z_i) and (x_j, y_j, z_j) are connected by a communication channel if and only if $|x_i - x_j| + |y_i - y_j| + |z_i - z_j| = 1$. To model this neighbor structure, the *Neigh* relation in the initial model M_0 is restricted in this model by adding the axiom in Fig. 8.

```
SETS   CHANNEL   PORTS
CONSTANTS   coordX   coordY   coordZ   mk_position
              crossbarX   crossbarY   crossbarZ   mk_channel
AXIOMS
    crossbarX ∈ ℕ₁ ∧ crossbarY ∈ ℕ₁ ∧ crossbarZ ∈ ℕ₁
    mk_position ∈ (1 .. crossbarX) × (1 .. crossbarY) × (1 .. crossbarZ) ↣ ROUTER
    coordX ∈ ROUTER ↠ (1 .. crossbarX)
    coordY ∈ ROUTER ↠ (1 .. crossbarY)
    coordZ ∈ ROUTER ↠ (1 .. crossbarZ)
    ∀xx, yy, zz·xx ∈ 1 .. crossbarX ∧ yy ∈ 1 .. crossbarY ∧ zz ∈ 1 .. crossbarZ
        ⇒ coordX(mk_position(xx ↦ yy ↦ zz)) = xx
        ∧ coordY(mk_position(xx ↦ yy ↦ zz)) = yy
        ∧ coordZ(mk_position(xx ↦ yy ↦ zz)) = zz
    ∀pos1, pos2·pos1 ∈ ROUTER ∧ pos2 ∈ ROUTER ∧ pos1 ≠ pos2
        ⇒ coordX(pos1) ≠ coordX(pos2) ∨ coordY(pos1) ≠ coordY(pos2)∨
          coordZ(pos1) ≠ coordZ(pos2)
```

Fig. 7. M_1: Static Part 1

We define the $CHANNEL$ set to model the communication channels between routers and we define the $PORTS$ set to define the input and output ports of nodes in the static part of the second model. To show how two neighbors are connected to each other through channels, we define the *def_channel* and *mk_channel* relations with the help of axioms, as shown in Fig. 8. The *def_channel* relation models the relation of a port of a node to the corresponding port of its neighbor and the *mk_channel* relation maps the port relations to channels.

```
AXIOMS
    ∀r1, r2·r1 ↦ r2 ∈ Neigh ⇔ abs(coordX(r1) − coordX(r2)) + abs(coordY(r1)
        − coordY(r2)) + abs(coordZ(r1) − coordZ(r2)) = 1
    def_channel ∈ (ROUTER × PORTS) → (ROUTER × PORTS)
    partition(PORTS, {Ein}, {Eout}, {Win}, {Wout}, {Nin}, {Nout}, {Sin}
        , {Sout}, {Uin}, {Uout}, {Din}, {Dout}, {Lin}, {Lout})
    mk_channel ∈ def_channel ↣ CHANNELS
```

Fig. 8. M_1: Static Part 2

East and west ports of neighbor nodes with different X coordinate are related to each other through a channel. For instance, as shown in Fig. 9, Ein and $Eout$ ports of node $(1, 1, 1)$ are connected to $Wout$ and Win ports of node $(2, 1, 1)$ through a channel $((1, 1, 1) \mapsto Eout) \mapsto ((2, 1, 1) \mapsto Win)$ and $((2, 1, 1) \mapsto Wout) \mapsto ((1, 1, 1) \mapsto Ein)$ relations in $def\_channel$. This connection of the ports of the neighboring nodes on the X coordinate is modeled by the axiom shown in Fig. 10. The port relation between neighbors on other coordinates is defined by similar axioms which are not shown here due to lack of space.

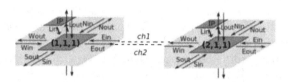

Fig. 9. Channels in 3D Mesh-Based NoCs

The Dynamic Part. In the static part of the model M_1, we define the 3D mesh NoC architecture with the triple coordinate of nodes and their channels. In the dynamic part of the model M_1, we refine the dynamic part of the model M_0 to specify the transferring of data through the communication channels, so that the overall correctness of communication holds.

The communication channels between routers are considered asynchronous channels, transferring data upon request. Each channel propagates data as well as control values. In our case, a control value models the fact that a channel is occupied by a message. When a message is injected to a channel, the control value of that channel is set to *busy* and when the message is received at the other side of channel, the control value of that channel is set to *free*.

AXIOMS
$\forall n, m, i, j \cdot (n \mapsto i) \mapsto (m \mapsto j) \in def\_channel \wedge i = Wout \wedge j = Ein$
$\Leftrightarrow coordX(n) - coordX(m) = 1 \wedge coordY(n) = coordY(m) \wedge coordZ(n) = coordZ(m)$
$\forall n, m, i, j \cdot (n \mapsto i) \mapsto (m \mapsto j) \in def\_channel \wedge i = Eout \wedge j = Win$
$\Leftrightarrow coordX(n) - coordX(m) = -1 \wedge coordY(n) = coordY(m) \wedge coordZ(n) = coordZ(m)$

Fig. 10. M_1: Static Part 3

In order to model the transferring of messages through the communication channels, the variables $channel\_state$ and $channel\_content$ are defined in the second model to represent the control and the data value on each channel. Each channel can have the *busy* or *free* state. When the channel receives data, its state switches from *free* to *busy* and the message is added to the $channel\_content$. When the channel transfers data to the end, $channel\_state$ changes to *free* and the channel is released by removing the message from $channel\_content$. The invariants of M_1 model that, when a channel is released, then its content is empty and can thus receive the next message; when a channel is busy, the message is in the channel. We illustrate these invariants in Fig.11.

VARIABLES
    channel_content   channel_state
INVARIANTS
    $channel\_content \in CHANNELS \rightarrowtail MESSAGES$
    $dom(channel\_content) = channel\_state^{-1}[\{busy\}]$
    $channel\_state \in CHANNELS \rightarrow state$
    $dom(channel\_state) = ran(mk\_channel)$
    $ran(channel\_content) \subseteq dom(moving\_pool)$
    $\forall msg \cdot msg \in dom(moving\_pool) \wedge des(msg) = moving\_pool(msg)$
        $\Rightarrow msg \notin ran(channel\_content)$

Fig. 11. M_1: Invariants (channels)

The *switching* event is now refined to transfer a message to the next router through channels. In order to model this, we add a new event *out_to_channel* as shown in Fig.15 (Appendix) to model pushing a message in the channel. This event is enabled when there is a message for transferring in a node and the channel between the node and the next node is free. In addition, we refine the *switching* event as shown in Fig.16 (Appendix) to model releasing the channel by receiving the message at the end of the channel. This event is enabled when a message is in the channel.

3.3   The Third Model M_2

In this model, we define buffers for the ports of the nodes and refine the second model to model the communication in 3D NoCs by considering these buffers.

The Static Part. The context of the third model contains a single constant $buffer\_size \in \mathbb{N}_1$, which is a strict natural number denoting the maximum number of messages allowed in a buffer.

The Dynamic Part. Each node has fourteen buffers, each assigned to node ports; those assigned to output ports are called *output buffers* and those assigned to input ports are called *input buffers*. When there is a message in an output buffer of a node, the node can transfer it to the channel provided that the channel is free. If in the other side of the channel the input buffer has an empty place, the message is transferred to the input buffer of the next node and the channel is released; otherwise, the channel will be busy until an empty place appears in the input buffer. To model the buffer structure in the third model we add a new machine variable *buffer_content* that models the current content of all buffers. Indeed, adding and removing messages in/from buffers is modeled by the *buffer_content* variable.

In order to guarantee the correctness of the buffer modeling, we need the invariants shown Fig.12. They model that the content of a buffer never becomes more than its size. In addition, while a message is in the *moving_pool*, i.e., it has not reached to its destination, it must be either in a channel or in a buffer.

```
VARIABLES
    buffer_content
INVARIANTS
    buffer_content ∈ MESSAGES ⇸ (ROUTER × PORTS)
    dom(buffer_content) ∪ ran(channel_content) = dom(moving_pool)
    dom(buffer_content) ∩ ran(channel_content) = ∅
    ∀b·b ∈ ran(buffer_content) ⇒ card(buffer_content ▷ {b}) ∈ 1 .. buffer_size
```

Fig. 12. M_2: Invariants (buffer)

The *switching* event, as shown in Fig.17 (Appendix), is refined to be enabled when there is an input buffer with at least one empty place at the end of the channel. Then, besides releasing the channel, the message in the channel is transfered to the input buffer. The status of the *switching* event is still anticipated since we do not store. The *out_to_channel* event, as shown in Fig.17, is refined to be enabled when there is a message in an output buffer meaning that the message is removed from buffer. The *sent_message* and *received_message* events are refined so that they update the $buffer\_content$ variable as shown in Fig. 18 (Appendix).

```
Event   routing ≙
extends  routing
    any
        msg   router   in_p   out_p
    where
        in_p ∈ {Win, Ein, Sin, Nin, Uin, Din, Lin}
        out_p ∈ {Wout, Eout, Sout, Nout, Uout, Dout, Lout}
        (in_p = Win ∧ out_p ≠ Wout) ∨ (in_p = Ein ∧ out_p ≠ Eout)
          ∨(in_p = Sin ∧ out_p ≠ Sout) ∨ (in_p = Nin ∧ out_p ≠ Nout)
          ∨(in_p = Uin ∧ out_p ≠ Uout) ∨ (in_p = Din ∧ out_p ≠ Dout)
          ∨(in_p = Lin ∧ out_p ≠ Lout)
        msg ↦ (router ↦ in_p) ∈ buffer_content
        card(buffer_content ▷ {router ↦ out_p}) < buffer_size
    then
        buffer_content(msg) := router ↦ out_p
    end
```

Fig. 13. M_2: Routing Event

At this level of abstraction, we refine the *routing* event (modeled as *skip* in the previous models) as shown in Fig.13. A routing algorithm decides on choosing an output channel for a message in an input channel. As we present a general model, we do not consider any specific routing algorithm and we model routing decision nondeterministically. That is, when there is a message in an input buffer of a node, it can be routed to any output buffer of the node except the output buffer in the same direction with the input buffer e.g., a message in the northern input buffer cannot be routed to the northern output buffer. We also check that there is enough space in the chosen buffer. We have this constraint to prevent a cycling problem in the communication that would lead to deadlock in the interconnection network.

We do not change the status of the *switching* event in this refinement step. Thus, its status is still anticipated. In order to have it convergent, we need to define a variant based on some ordering relation of the message identifiers. This can be achieved by modeling a channel dependency graph but is not part of this paper.

A more concrete 3D NoC design can be modeled by refining one or more of these three general models and by verifying whether the design can guarantee the overall communication correctness. In the following, we model the XYZ routing algorithm by refining the third model M_2 and verifying whether it guarantees the overall communication correctness.

4   Case Study: The XYZ Routing Algorithm

In this section, we formally develop a dimension-order routing (DOR) algorithm which is a deterministic routing scheme widely used for NoCs [24]. To make the best use of the regularity of the topology, the dimension-order routing transfers packets along minimal paths in the traversing of the low dimension first until no further move is needed in this dimension. Then, they go along the next dimension and so forth until they reach their destination. For example, the dimension-order routing in the 3D NoC called the *XYZ routing algorithm* uses Z dimension channels after using Y and X dimension channels. Packets travel along the X dimension, then along the Y dimension and finally along the Z dimension. Thus, if $current\_node = (c_x, c_y, c_z)$ is a node containing a message addressed to node $destination = (d_x, d_y, d_z)$, then the XYZ routing function $R_{xyz}(,)$ is defined as follows:

$$R_{xyz}((c_x, c_y, c_z), (d_x, d_y, d_z)) \quad = \quad \begin{cases} (c_{x-1}, c_y, c_z) & \text{iff} \quad c_x > d_x \\ (c_{x+1}, c_y, c_z) & \text{iff} \quad c_x < d_x \\ (c_x, c_{y-1}, c_z) & \text{iff} \quad c_x = d_x \wedge c_y > d_y \\ (c_x, c_{y+1}, c_z) & \text{iff} \quad c_x = d_x \wedge c_y < d_y \\ (c_x, c_y, c_{z-1}) & \text{iff} \quad c_x = d_x \wedge c_y = d_y \wedge c_z > d_z \\ (c_x, c_y, c_{z+1}) & \text{iff} \quad c_x = d_x \wedge c_y = d_y \wedge c_z < d_z \end{cases}$$

In order to model the XYZ routing algorithm based on the third general model, we have to refine the routing event which is nondeterministically defined. As shown in the above formula, a message can be transfered to six different directions based on its current position and destination. Therefore, we refine the *routing* event in the previous model to six *routing* events so that their guards are based on the routing formula. As an example of the *routing* event, we show in Fig.14 the situation where c_x is greater than d_x. All the correctness properties defined for the abstract models are proved. Hence, the XYZ routing algorithm guarantees the overall communication correctness.

```
Event   routing_X_dec ≙
extends  routing
    where
        coordX(router) > coordX(des(msg)) ∧ out_p = Wout
    then
        buffer_content(msg) := router ↦ out_p
    end
```

Fig. 14. The XYZ Model: Routing Event $(c_x > d_x)$

5   Verification of the Models

In order to prove that the models satisfy their correctness properties we have to check that they respect their invariants, i.e., the pool properties for our models. To prove this, we have generated the proof obligations for all the models using the Rodin tool: part of the proof obligations were automatically discharged and the rest of could be proved interactively. The proof statistics for our models are shown in Table 1. These figures express the number of proof obligations generated by the Rodin platform as well as the number of obligations automatically discharged by the platform and those interactively proved. A high number of interactive proofs were due to reasoning about set comprehension and unions, not currently supported automatically in Rodin. In addition, the interactive proving often involved manually suggesting values to discharging various properties containing logical disjunctions or existential quantifiers. Extra proving was due to the fact that currently, we cannot create proof scripts and reuse them whenever needed in RODIN. Thus, in some cases we had to manually repeat very similar or almost identical proofs.

Table 1. Proof Statistics

Model	Number of Proof Obligations	Automatically Discharged	Interactively Discharged
Context	21	6(28%)	15(72%)
M_0 Model	38	34(89%)	4(11%)
M_1 Model	33	11(33%)	22(67%)
M_2 Model	33	7(21%)	26(79%)
XYZ Model	13	0(0%)	13(100%)
Total	144	64(45%)	80(55%)

6   Conclusions

In this paper, we have proposed the abstract models M_0, M_1, and M_2 at three increasing levels of detail for 3D NoCs. These can be used for modeling and verifying 3D NoC-designs in the early stages of the system development. We have also shown how to apply such an abstract model to verify a concrete 3D NoC routing algorithm. Most importantly, the overall correctness of the communication models (expressed using a special data structure called pool [2]) is guaranteed for the 3D NoCs. We have achieved this by modeling the correctness condition via invariants; as each model added detail to the previous model, the invariant needed to reflect these added details in a consistent manner. In order for the invariant to be satisfied by a model, a number of proof obligations needs to be discharged. Moreover, in order for the models to respect the refinement relation $M_0 \sqsubseteq M_1 \sqsubseteq M_2$, i.e., to develop each other in a provably correct manner, some other proof obligations need to be generated. As we have employed the RODIN platform to specify our 3D NoC modeling, many of these proof obligations have been automatically discharged, while for the rest it was possible to discharge them interactively. We note an interesting property of our communication correctness condition, that essentially reduces to the fact that all the messages will eventually reach their destinations. This is a typical liveness property that we model here as an invariant, also based on the variant expression ensuring that our models will eventually terminate. The liveness property can also be verified via a model checker, for instance Pro-B [31], that is associated to the RODIN platform.

The NoC communication can be either unicast or multicast [23]. In the unicast communication a message is sent from a source node to a single destination node, while in the multicast communication a message is sent from a source node to an arbitrary set of destination nodes. We have considered here sending a message from a source to a single destination, hence modeled unicast communication. One of our future plans is to extend the abstract models M_0, M_1, and M_2 to also specify multicast communication and as a case study we target a novel routing protocol for multicast traffic called HAMUM [12], based on the extended 3D NoC model. HAMUM, Hamiltonian Adaptive path for both the Multicast and Unicast Model, is a new adaptive routing model based on Hamiltonian path for both the multicast and unicast traffic. An interesting property that we expect out of the multicast modeling is to have the case study reusing the M_2 model via an algorithmic refinement instead of a superposition one like we now have. This is because we can have several messages that could be routed in parallel using different events via several channels. Our XYZ routing employs already several events for the routing instead of the abstract routing event of the model M_2, but only one of them is enabled at all moments.

By strengthening the invariants we can verify more diverse properties of the 3D NoC designs, for instance we could prove deadlock-freedom for routing algorithms - currently, one of the most challenging properties for the 3D NoCs. For this, we envision an extension of the abstract 3D NoC models with an extra channel dependency graph to reason about deadlock-freedom; the HAMUM algorithm can then be shown as deadlock-free.

References

1. Abrial, J.R.: A System Development Process with Event-B and the Rodin Platform. In: Butler, M., Hinchey, M.G., Larrondo-Petrie, M.M. (eds.) ICFEM 2007. LNCS, vol. 4789, pp. 1–3. Springer, Heidelberg (2007)
2. Abrial, J.R.: Modeling in Event-B: System and Software Design. Cambridge University Press (2010)
3. Abrial, J.R.: The B-Book: Assigning Programs to Meanings. Cambridge University Press (1996)
4. Abrial, J.R., Cansell, D., Mery, D.: Refinement and Reachability in Even-B. In: 4th International Conference of B and Z Users, pp. 129–148 (2005)

5. Abrial, J.R., Hallerstede, S.: Refinement, Decomposition and Instantiation of Discrete Models: Application to Event-B. In: Fundamenta Informaticae, pp. 1–28 (2007)
6. Andreasson, D., Kumar, S.: Slack-Time Aware-Routing in NoC Systems. In: IEEE International Symposium on Circuits and Systems, pp. 2353–2356. IEEE (2005)
7. Arditi, L., Berry, G., Kishinevsky, M.: Late Design Changes (ECOs) for Sequentially Optimized Esterel Designs. In: Hu, A.J., Martin, A.K. (eds.) FMCAD 2004. LNCS, vol. 3312, pp. 128–143. Springer, Heidelberg (2004)
8. Back, R.J., Sere, K.: Stepwise Refinement of Action Systems. In: van de Snepscheut, J.L.A. (ed.) MPC 1989. LNCS, vol. 375, pp. 115–138. Springer, Heidelberg (1989)
9. Back, R.J., Sere, K.: Superposition Refinement of Reactive Systems. Formal Aspects of Computing 8(3), 324–346 (1996)
10. Borrione, D., Helmy, A., Pierre, L., Schmaltz, J.: A Formal Approach to the Verification of Networks on Chip. EURASIP Journal on Embedded Systems 2009(1), 1–14 (2009)
11. Duan, X., Zhang, D., Sun, X.: A Condition of Deadlock-free Routing in Mesh Network. In: Second International Conference on Intelligent Networks and Intelligent Systems, pp. 242–245 (2009)
12. Ebrahimi, M., Daneshtalab, M., Liljeberg, P., Tenhunen, H.: HAMUM A Novel Routing Protocol for Unicast and Multicast Traffic in MPSoCs. In: The 18th Euromicro Conference on Parallel, Distributed and Network-Based Computing (2010)
13. Feero, B.S., Pande, P.: Networks-on-Chip in a Three-Dimensional Environment: A Performance Evaluation. IEEE Transactions on Computers, 32–45 (2009)
14. Grecu, C., et al.: A Scalable Communication-Centric SoC Interconnect Architecture. In: 5th International Symposiom Quality Electronic Design (ISQED 2004), pp. 343–348 (2004)
15. Gupta, R., Guernic, P.L., Skuhla, S.K.: Formal methods and models for system design: a system level perspective. Kluwer Academic Publishers (2004)
16. Harrison, J.: Formal Verification at Intel. In: Symposium on Logic in Computer Science (2003)
17. Jerger, N.E., Peh, L.S., Lipasti, M.H.: Virtual Circuit Tree Multicasting: A Case for On-Chip Hardware Multicast Support. In: International Conference Computer Architecture, China, pp. 229–240 (2008)
18. Katz, S.: A Superimposition Control Construct for Distributed Systems. ACM Transactions on Programming Languages and Systems, 337–356 (1993)
19. Kaivola, R., Ghughal, R., Narasimhan, N., Telfer, A., Whittemore, J., Pandav, S., Slobodová, A., Taylor, C., Frolov, V., Reeber, E., Naik, A.: Replacing Testing with Formal Verification in Intel® CoreTM i7 Processor Execution Engine Validation. In: Bouajjani, A., Maler, O. (eds.) CAV 2009. LNCS, vol. 5643, pp. 414–429. Springer, Heidelberg (2009)
20. Kim, Y.B., Kim, Y.-B.: Fault-Tolerant Source Routing for Networks-on-Chip. In: 22nd IEEE International Symposium on Defect and Fault Tolerance in VLSI Systems, pp. 12–20. IEEE Computer Society (2007)
21. Liao, W., Hsiung, P.: Creating a Formal Verification Platform for IBM CoreConnect-based SoC. In: The 1st International Workshop on Automasted Technology for Verificatin and Analysis (ATVA 2003), pp. 7–18 (2003)
22. Loi, I., Benini, L.: An Efficient Distributed Memory Interface for Many-Core Platform with 3D Stacked DRAM. In: Proc. of the DATE Conference, Germany, pp. 99–104 (2010)

23. Lu, Z., Yin, B., Jantsch, A.: Connection-Oriented Multicasting in Wormhole-Switched Networks on Chip. In: Emerging VLSI Technologies and Architectures, pp. 205–211 (2006)

24. Montaana, J.M., Koibuchi, M., Matsutani, H., Amano, H.: Balanced Dimension-Order Routing for k-ary n-cubes. In: International Conference on Parallel Processing (2009)

25. Nayebi, A., Meraji, S., Shamaei, A., Sarbazi-azad, H.: XMulator: A listener-Based Integrated Simulation Platform for Interconnection Networks. In: Asia International Conference on Modeling and Simulation, pp. 128–132 (2007)

26. Palesi, M., Holsmark, R., Kumar, S., Catania, V.: Application Specific Routing Algorithms for Networks on Chip. IEEE Transactions on Parallel and Distributed Systems, 316–330 (2009)

27. Park, D., et al.: Mira, A Multi-Layered On-Chip Interconnect Router Architecture. In: ISCA 2008, pp. 251–261 (2008)

28. Tsiopoulos, L., Walden, M.: Formal Development of NoC Systems in B. Nordic Journal of Computing, 127–145 (2006)

29. Yan, S., Lin, B.: Design of Application-Specific 3D Networks-on-Chip Architectures. In: IEEE International Conference on Computer Design (ICCD 2008), pp. 142–149 (2008)

30. RODIN Tool Platform, http://www.event-b.org/platform.html

31. ProB Model Checker, http://www.stups.uni-duesseldorf.de/ProB/overview.php

Appendix

Event $out\_to\_channel\_ \;\widehat{=}$
any $new\_position \quad current\_msg \quad out\_p \quad in\_p$
where

$\quad current\_msg \in dom(moving\_pool) \wedge new\_position \in POSITION$
$\quad moving\_pool(current\_msg) \mapsto new\_position \in Neigh$
$\quad out\_p \in \{Nout, Sout, Wout, Eout, Uout, Dout\} \wedge in\_p \in \{Nin, Sin, Win, Ein, Uin, Din\}$
$\quad (moving\_pool(current\_msg) \mapsto out\_p) \mapsto (new\_position \mapsto in\_p) \in dom(mk\_channel)$
$\quad channel\_state(mk\_channel((moving\_pool(current\_msg) \mapsto out\_p) \mapsto (new\_position \mapsto in\_p))) = free$
$\quad moving\_pool(current\_msg) \neq des(current\_msg) \wedge current\_msg \notin ran(channel\_content)$
then

$\quad channel\_state(mk\_channel((moving\_pool(current\_msg) \mapsto out\_p) \mapsto (new\_position \mapsto in\_p))) := busy$
$\quad channel\_content(mk\_channel((moving\_pool(current\_msg) \mapsto out\_p) \mapsto (new\_position \mapsto in\_p)))$
$\qquad := current\_msg$
end

Fig. 15. M_1: Out_to_Channel Event

Event $switching \;\widehat{=}$
Status anticipated
extends $switching$
any $current\_msg \quad new\_position \quad p1 \quad p2$
where

$\quad p1 \in \{Nout, Sout, Wout, Eout, Uout, Dout\} \wedge p2 \in \{Nin, Sin, Win, Ein, Uin, Din\}$
$\quad (moving\_pool(current\_msg) \mapsto p1) \mapsto (new\_position \mapsto p2) \in dom(mk\_channel)$
$\quad channel\_state(mk\_channel((moving\_pool(current\_msg) \mapsto p1) \mapsto (new\_position \mapsto p2))) = busy$
$\quad current\_msg =$
$\qquad channel\_content(mk\_channel((moving\_pool(current\_msg) \mapsto p1) \mapsto (new\_position \mapsto p2)))$
then

$\quad moving\_pool(current\_msg) := new\_position$
$\quad channel\_state(mk\_channel((moving\_pool(current\_msg) \mapsto p1) \mapsto (new\_position \mapsto p2))) := free$
$\quad channel\_content := channel\_content \rhd \{current\_msg\}$
end

Fig. 16. M_1: Switching Event

Event $switching \;\widehat{=}$
Status anticipated
extends $switching$
$\quad$**where**
$\qquad card(buffer\_content \rhd \{new\_position \mapsto p2\}) < buffer\_size$
$\quad$**then**
$\qquad buffer\_content := buffer\_content \cup \{current\_msg \mapsto (new\_position \mapsto p2)\}$
$\quad$**end**
Event $out\_to\_channel \;\widehat{=}$
extends $out\_to\_channel\_$
$\quad$**where**
$\qquad card(buffer\_content \rhd \{new\_position \mapsto in\_p\}) > 0$
$\quad$**then**
$\qquad buffer\_content := buffer\_content \setminus \{current\_msg \mapsto (moving\_pool(current\_msg) \mapsto out\_p)\}$
$\quad$**end**

Fig. 17. M_2: Switching and Out_to_Channel Events

Event $sent\_message \;\widehat{=}$
extends $sent\_message$
$\quad$**where**
$\qquad current\_msg \notin dom(buffer\_content)$
$\quad$**then**
$\qquad buffer\_content := buffer\_content \cup \{current\_msg \mapsto (src(current\_msg) \mapsto Lin)\}$
$\quad$**end**
Event $received\_message \;\widehat{=}$
extends $received\_message$
$\quad$**where**
$\qquad current\_msg \mapsto (des(current\_msg) \mapsto Lout) \in buffer\_content$
$\quad$**then**
$\qquad buffer\_content := buffer\_content \setminus \{current\_msg \mapsto (des(current\_msg) \mapsto Lout)\}$
$\quad$**end**

Fig. 18. M_2: Sent_message and Received_message Events

Towards Model-Based Testing
of Electronic Funds Transfer Systems

Hamid Reza Asaadi[1,2], Ramtin Khosravi[1,2],
MohammadReza Mousavi[3], and Neda Noroozi[2,3]

[1] School of ECE, University of Tehran, Tehran, Iran
[2] Software Quality Lab., Fanap Co., Tehran, Iran
[3] Department of CS, TU/Eindhoven, Eindhoven, The Netherlands

Abstract. We report on our first experience with applying model-based testing techniques to an operational Electronic Funds Transfer (EFT) switch. The goal is to test the conformance of the EFT switch to the standard flows described by the ISO 8583 standard. To this end, we first make a formalization of the transaction flows specified in the ISO 8583 standard in terms of a Labeled Transition System (LTS). This formalization paves the way for model-based testing based on the formal notion of Input-Output Conformance (IOCO) testing. We adopt and augment IOCO testing for our particular application domain. We develop a prototype implementation and apply our proposed techniques in practice. We discuss the encouraging obtained results and the observed shortcomings of the present approach. We outline a roadmap to remedy the shortcomings and enhance the test results.

1 Introduction

Electronic Funds Transfer (EFT) systems provide the infrastructure for online financial transactions such as money transfer between bank accounts, electronic payments, balance enquiries, and bill payments. A central part of an EFT system is the *EFT Switch* (also known as *Payment Switch*, or simply *Switch*), which provides a communication mechanism among different components of an EFT system such as Automated Teller Machine (ATM) and Point-of-Sale (POS) terminals, e-Payment applications, and core banking systems.

The EFT system components communicate in the form of transactions consisting of several messages passed through the switch. For example, during a simple *purchase transaction* originated by a POS terminal, the switch forwards the purchase request to the core banking system (to charge the card holder's account) and forwards the response back to the POS terminal. In the real setting however, possible failures in the components and asynchrony in the communication media may give rise to more complicated transaction flows. For example, if a POS terminal sends a purchase request and it does not receive the response from the switch in time, it will time-out and send a reversal message to the switch, requesting to cancel the previous transaction. It is also possible that when the

F. Arbab and M. Sirjani (Eds.): FSEN 2011, LNCS 7141, pp. 253–267, 2012.
© Springer-Verlag Berlin Heidelberg 2012

time-out occurs, the purchase response is on the way back to the POS terminal. In this case, the POS terminal receives a purchase response after it sends a reversal request (which of course must be responded too, by the switch). This way, each transaction may comprise a complex combination of different possible interaction scenarios among the components of the EFT system.

In the presence of such complicated transaction flows, a thorough testing of EFT switches is essential, as presence of errors may lead to inconsistencies among different accounts (particularly among accounts at different banks). This calls for a reconciliation process, possibly requiring manual checks which are very costly for the banks.

The correct behavior of a typical EFT system is specified in the ISO 8583 standard [2] at a high level of abstraction. Since the nature of the system is concurrent and distributed, generating test cases manually with a high coverage is practically impossible, as the number of (combinations of) transaction flows is very large. To solve this, we use *model-based testing* [5,12] as a systematic method to automatically generate test cases from the specification.

Our testing method is mainly based on a formalization of the ISO 8583 standard in terms of Labeled Transition Systems (LTSs). Our formal specification captures the behavior of an ISO-compliant EFT switch as well as its environment, i.e., the terminals and the core banking system. We have also performed model-checking on our formal model to make sure that our formalization of the ISO 8583 standard meets the intuitive requirements set forth by the standard as well as by the switch designers. This formalization paves the way to exploit a formal conformance testing method called IOCO (for Input Output Conformance) testing [18,19] to automatically generate test-cases and perform online conformance testing. We combine IOCO testing with functional testing techniques, à la category-partition method, to capture the data-related aspects of switch functionality. Moreover, we interface the test-case generator, with our own test-case analysis and execution tool to evaluate, store, and prioritize test cases; the test-cases are executed and their outcomes are also stored by the same tool. Our test selection technique combines the black-box nature of IOCO (focusing on model-coverage criteria) with white-box coverage metrics in order to choose an effective test-suite. We developed a prototype tool implementing the above mentioned functionality. Using our tool, we can generate a prioritized test-suite for off-line and regression testing, without any need to explore the formal model any more. Furthermore, during the execution of test cases, our tool also validates various business rules which could not be captured in the formal model.

We applied our prototype implementation to an operational switch, developed by Fanap Co., interacting with POS terminals and a core banking system as its environment. We have covered a number of major transaction types and related business rules and have detected some defects in the switch, which are reported in the remainder of this paper. The defects have been reported to development team and have been fixed subsequently. The initial results obtained from our prototype, presented in this paper, were very encouraging. Hence, Fanap decided to embark on the development of a proprietary test-case generation tool which automatically combines the behavioral and functional models outlined in this paper.

The rest of this paper is organized as follows. Section 2 provides a background on the switch specification as described in the ISO 8583 standard. Section 3 covers our testing approach in addition to a quick overview of the IOCO theory. The way we model the system in terms of Input Output Transition Systems is described in Section 4. Various aspects of our testing method including test case execution, and generation and prioritization of off-line test suites, as well as checking business rules are presented in Section 5. The test results and code coverage are given in Section 6. Discussion of the merits and demerits of the current approach are discussed in Section 7. Section 8 presents a brief overview of related work. Finally, we conclude the paper and present some directions for future work in Section 9.

2   EFT Switch Functionality

Typical functionality of an EFT Switch include performing a purchase, balance enquiry, withdrawal, bill payment, refund, and money transfer. All these functions are composed of a few transaction flows introduced below. Apart from financial functions, there are also features for switch administration, monitoring and auditing that are out of the scope of this study.

As the components of an EFT system are usually provided by different vendors, the ISO 8583 standard [2] is defined to determine the type and format of the messages exchanged among the components of an EFT system. The standard also defines message and transaction flows at a high level of abstraction. For example, Fig. 1 shows the flow of a financial transaction as depicted in the standard [2]. According to the described flow, the acquirer sends a request to the card issuer, followed by zero or more request repeat messages, until it receives a response from the issuer. The data format of the messages (e.g., 1200 - financial request) has been defined elsewhere in the standard [2, Chapter 4]. Note that each typical functionality of an EFT switch, e.g., a purchase or a balance enquiry, is composed of a number of transaction flows, such as the one depicted in Fig. 1. There are eleven more transaction flows specified in the standard. We refer to [2, Chapter 5] for a detailed presentation of all transaction flows.

3   Testing Approach

3.1   IOCO Testing

IOCO testing [18,19] is a formal approach to *model-based black-box* testing of *functional* requirements. The approach relies on a formal model of system behavior, a specification typically called *s*, which captures the observable input and output interactions of the system with its environment in terms of a Labeled Transition System (LTS). Based on the specification, IOCO testing generates

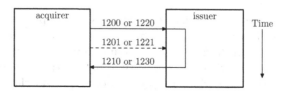

1200/1201 financial request/financial request repeat
1210   financial request response

1220/1221 financial advice/financial advice repeat
1230   financial advice response

Fig. 1. Message flow for financial transactions [2]

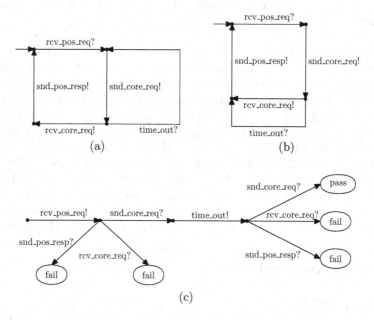

Fig. 2. IOCO testing of (b) an implementation against (a) a specification results in (c) a tree presenting test cases based on transaction flows

test-cases in order to establish whether the implementation under test, typically denoted by i, *conforms* to its specification, written as i conf s. The basic concepts of IOCO testing is illustrated next using the specification LTS depicted in Fig. 2. In an LTS specification of (an extremely simplistic view of) a transaction's life-cycle in an ideal switch is given. The IOCO testing is aimed at checking whether a particular implementation, e.g., the one depicted in Fig. 2.(b), conforms to its specification depicted in Fig. 2.(a). (Note that the LTS of the implementation is not available to the tester, and the LTS is only used here to illustrate possible patterns of interaction with the system.) To this end, the IOCO testing tech-nique uses the specification LTS and generates test-cases, e.g., those depicted in Fig. 2.(c), to test whether the (black-box) implementation conforms to the specification. In this figure, input and output actions are affixed with a question and an exclamation mark, respectively. In Fig. 2.(a), each path of the depicted tree presents a pattern of interaction (i.e., providing input- and observing output messages) eventually leading to a pass or a fail verdict. In particular, executing the test-case corresponding to the path rcv_pos_req! . snd_core_req? . time_out! . snd_pos_resp? reveals a bug in the implementation. (Note that inputs in the model become outputs of the test-case and outputs of the model become inputs of the test-case.)

3.2   The Testing Infrastructure

An overview of our test infrastructure is given in Fig. 3. We have made an LTS model of the EFT switch system with a POS terminal and a simplified core banking system as its environment. Details of this explanation are described in Section 4.

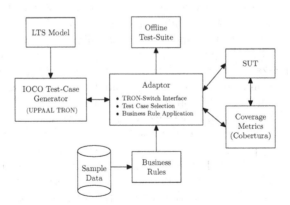

Fig. 3. An overview of the test infrastructure

For this experiment, we used the timed-automata language of UPPAAL [4] as our modeling language and UPPAAL TRON [11] as our test-case generation tool. (UPPAAL TRON implements a variant of IOCO, called RTIOCO; see [17] for a formal comparison of the notions). For the commercial use, we plan to implement the test-case generation algorithm in our in-house tool and integrate it with our test infrastructure described below. We have also developed an adaptor to translate and augment abstract interactions of the model to concrete network messages sent to the switch, on one side, and strip down network messages from EFT to model interactions, on the other side.

We have developed tools for storing test-cases and their outcomes, prioritizing them and executing off-line test-suites and have placed it around the test infrastructure. For the test prioritization and selection, we have implemented our heuristics and combined them with the code coverage metrics from Cobertura [1]. This allows us to re-use the information resulting from an online test campaign in future tests and also use the generated test-suite for regression testing.

4   Modeling the EFT Switch

Our LTS formalization of the ISO 8583 standard is specified in terms of the input language of UPPAAL in order to benefit from several modeling, simulation, verification and test-case generation tools available in its tool-set. A model in UPPAAL is in the form of a network of timed automata. A timed automaton is a finite-state machine (FSM), i.e., a set of *locations* which are connected via *edges*, extended with (constraints on and assignments to) clock variables [4]. An edge in an UPPAAL timed-automata can be annotated by four types of labels: *selections*, *guards*, *synchronizations* and *updates*.

When taking a transition specified by an edge, an automaton may send or receive a *signal* in the synchronization part. Synchronization in UPPAAL can be either a handshaking or a broadcast synchronization. Common to our previous examples, a send signal in UPPAAL is annotated by an exclamation mark and its receive counterpart is annotated by a question mark.

The behavior of an EFT switch and its environment is specified in terms of a number of transaction flows. Combining all of these flows into a single model (a timed-automaton) would compromise readability and maintainability; it is also very difficult, if not impossible, to check whether the specified automaton is a correct formalization of the flow specified by the ISO standard. Hence, we break the specification into several timed automata, each modeling the behavior of EFT system components in a specific transaction flow (see Fig. 4).

It is possible to have multiple instances of the same transaction flow executing concurrently. So, we need to have multiple instances of the corresponding FSMs in our model. This is possible in UPPAAL, since we can declare multiple instances of the same FSM "template". In fact, the number of declared instances of an FSM determines the maximum number of concurrent instances of the corresponding transaction type. To generate various combination of transaction flows, we use a coordinator automaton. The coordinator non-deterministically selects the next flow to start and sends it the start signal and repeats this continuously as long as a parallel instance is ready to receive the start signal. For example, when the switch is ready to accept another Reversal request, it sends a rev_ready signal to the coordinator. Then, the coordinator sends a rev_start to the POS FSM to start the Reversal (Fig. 4).

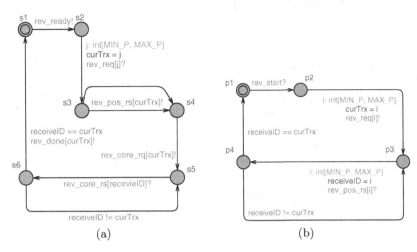

Fig. 4. Simplified models of the behavior of Switch (a) and POS (b) in Reversal transaction flow

During development of the model, human mistakes may introduce errors in the model. To discover such errors, we take a model-checking approach to verify the model against correctness properties before the testing process. We first formalized a few intuitive correctness based on the ISO standard and the intuition of the designer in the temporal-logic-based verification language provided by UPPAAL TRON (for some properties, we had to augment the model with observer automata in order to compensate for the limited expressiveness of the logic). For example, the following formula is used to verify that every transaction started must eventually be finished.

```
A[] forall (i : int[0, MAX_TX])
  TransFlow[i].start->TransFlow[i].finish
```

Subsequently, we use UPPAAL verifier to model check the formalized correctness properties.

Due to the combinatorial explosion of the state space, the performance of the UPPAAL TRON test-case generator was extremely low, when it tried to generate test-cases for the whole EFT system. To alleviate the state-space explosion problem, we implemented the abstract model of the core-banking system as a separate Java program and ran it in parallel with UPPAAL TRON and its adaptor. With this simple improvement, we were able to increase the performance of the test-case generation by a factor of 10. This way, we could generate test-cases for hundreds of concurrent transaction flows for each instance of UPPAAL TRON.

5   Testing the EFT Switch

5.1   Interfacing Switch and TRON

UPPAAL TRON continuously interacts with the system under test while exploring the LTS model. In other words, on-the-fly test-case generation is combined with online testing, so that the next step in the test-case generation can be determined by the response from the system under test [14]. Hence, to interface UPPAAL TRON with the system under test, an *adaptor* has to be implemented, which in its simplest form, communicates the messages between UPPAAL TRON and the system under test (possibly after converting them to the right format for each side). We implemented such an adaptor which translates the rather plain signals of UPPAAL TRON to (from) the elaborate format of financial messages specified by the ISO 8583 standard. In order to perform the translation to the ISO 8583 messages several details (concerning financial data of a transaction) have to be added to the message, which are selected from representative data stored in our sample database (more explanation about this to follow). Besides the format conversion and the addition/removal of financial data, we developed several other components in the adaptor which store and prioritize the test-cases in order to re-use them in regression testing. This way, a prioritized test suite is obtained, which can be run efficiently, without the overhead of exploring the formal model. Finally, there are some types of business rules that are hard to capture in UPPAAL TRON models and hence, are applied and verified by a separate component in the adaptor. The functionality of our extended adaptor is explained in [3] in more details.

5.2   Classifying and Covering Data Domains

Common to many reactive systems in the financial domain, the EFT switch exhibits complex reactive behavior while also having a data-dependent nature. An effective test method must address and integrate both of these facets.

So, we must set the fields of the messages generated by TRON to different combination of values. This results in multiple sequences of messages made from the single sequence of messages generated by TRON.

To manage the complexity of the data domain, we have used the *classification tree method* [10] (as an extension of the original category-partition method) to organize the test-case generation process. According to the method, we should select an aspect relevant to the test and partition the input domain into disjoint subsets called *classes*. The resulting classes will be subsequently classified according to some other aspect recursively, resulting in a tree of classifications and classes. This way, we specify representative elements for the content of data elements present in the structure of financial messages.

We divide the ongoing pattern of interaction into discrete pieces. We define each of these pieces (with some re-use of terminology) as a *test-case*. Hence, a test-case is a combination of transaction flows (possibly of different types) with specified values for the data items in the messages passed. For example, a test case may comprise a purchase transaction succeeded by a reversal. To specify discrete test-cases, in addition to the content of the financial messages, we should also specify the type and the number of transaction flows to be executed successively in the test-case.

In our prototype implementation, we used the domain and the implementation knowledge of the EFT switch to classify the following set of data domains:

- Transaction flow types,
- PIN validity,
- Purchase amount, and
- Transaction count.

For each aspect, we select a suitable set of discriminating values by using the domain knowledge. For *Transaction type* we consider five different classes: Purchase only (P), Balance Inquiry only (B), Purchase and Balance Inquiry (PB), Purchase with Reversal (PR), and Purchase with Reversal and Balance Inquiry (PRB). The *PIN validity* classification shows whether the transaction is authorized to be executed according to the PIN number input parameter. The domain of *Purchase amount* is the set of positive integers. The negative and zero cases are also included to test invalid cases. Finally, the *Transaction count* parameter is the number of transaction to be executed in the test case. A part of the resulting classification tree is shown in Fig. 5. Note that the classification tree is not supposed to be a balanced tree and hence, some parameters may not apply to all cases. For example, a Balance Inquiry transaction does not have a purchase amount as an input parameter.

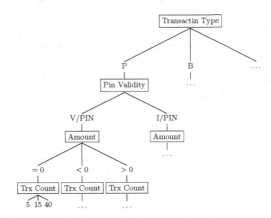

Fig. 5. A part of test-case classification tree

The transaction type parameter is applied to the coordinator machine (see Sec. 4) which affects the sequence of transactions generated by TRON. The other parameter values are set by the adaptor. The data selection tree is currently hard-coded in the adaptor, but we plan to make this generic and include it in the test specification model (see Section 7).

Table 1. Statement coverage results in percent

	Trx No.		
	5	15	40
B	0.614	0.622	0.620
B(Invalid PIN)	0.487	0.487	0.487
P	0.589	0.589	0.594
P(Invalid PIN)	0.487	0.487	0.487
PB	0.596	0.596	0.592
PB(Invalid PIN)	0.487	0.487	0.487
PR	0.630	0.671	0.671
PRB(Invalid PIN)	0.529	0.529	0.529
PRB	0.712	0.710	0.712
PRB(Invalid PIN)	0.529	0.529	0.529

6   Test Results

Apart from online testing, which has been very helpful in revealing defects in the product, defining suitable test-cases enabled us to measure test coverage for each test-case and prioritize the test-cases according to our test plan (in this case: full statement coverage of functional components, i.e., components involved in the realization of functionality in the main transaction flows). This prioritized set is used for off-line and regression testing, particularly when running the whole test-infrastructure is not feasible and the testers have to choose some of test-cases to get the most coverage. In this work, our test plan is to cover different flows as much as we can, instead of trying to cover all features of the switch.

We have selected the test cases based on our category-partitioning analysis. Due to some obstacles in the implementation, in this work we have just used positive values for the *Amount* parameter. Though, other parameters are tested as described in the resulted classification tree (Fig. 5). We have measured the statement coverage using Cobertura [1]. To reduce measurement errors, each test case has been repeated four times (with the same configuration) and the average coverage is reported in percents in Table 1.

Early analysis showed that there is a considerable amount of common code between the purchase and balance enquiry implementation because of inherent common logic. This hypothesis can also be proven by measuring the relative coverage of adding a test-case of former type to a test-case of the latter type (or vice versa); namely, the addition of each type of test-case to the other does not significantly increase the statement coverage measure. Hence, combining these two tests (i.e., the PB row in Table 1) did not result in any considerable improvement in coverage.

Further analysis shows that a significant amount of code for processing a transaction is devoted to common tasks such as authorization and packet routing. This justifies why there is not much difference between the coverage results of the cases.

Note that the increase in the size of transactions beyond 15 messages did not increase the coverage considerably, since apparently this does not lead to any new behavior in the EFT switch and the same logic is executed repeatedly. However, in our experience, having a large number of parallel transaction instances does increase the chance of catching errors caused by concurrency issues or (thread-pool) overflow problems.

Another point is that test-cases with exceptions have lower coverage among other combinations, yet they are deemed very important by domain experts. This is true because the switch drops unauthorized messages in early stages, so a big part of the code will never run. This is justified by developers' insight that the code for handling exceptional cases has little overlap with the code for the normal transaction flows. Hence, despite their individual low coverage, these test-cases should be appeared with high priority in the final priority list.

7   Discussion

Our system under test is inherently a mixture of reactive and functional behavior: it implements a high-level protocol for exchanging messages for a financial transaction, while its detailed implementation is very much dependent on the functional and data-related aspects. This mixture, if not structured properly, makes the generated models overly cluttered and complicated and unfortunately, most of the existing IOCO-based tools, including UPPAAL TRON and TorX [20] do not provide proper facilities for orthogonalizing, structuring and relating reactive and functional behavior. Hence, we plan to make a high-level specification language (inspired by prior effort in UML Testing Profile [15], TTCN3 [23]) as a front-end for our proprietary IOCO-based engine in order to solve the following issues:

1. Specification of abstract data types and their partitions: a specification language is needed to specify the data types used in the functional domain, different partitioning and the representative elements of partitions.
2. Full support of data parameters in the behavioral model: the support for data parameter in UPPAAL TRON is limited; it is not possible to define the representative data values of each data type attached to messages of the behavioral model. Being able to attach different data types and their different partitionings is an essential ingredient for improving our test results.
3. Support for asynchronous message passing: Thus far, we have experimented with different additions to our model in order to cater for the asynchronous nature of communication in our domain. We first tried adding input/output queues as one option which immediately led to drastic performance drawbacks. Then, we have experimented with abstracting from the asynchronous delays in our protocols, which does lead to better performance. However, such an abstraction results in fictitious sequences of messages that are not expected by the SUT. To overcome this, we had to add several guards to guarantee that the model will only be triggered with appropriate signals.

This last modification has led to a complicated specification. An inherent support for asynchronous message passing may be considered as an option, along the lines of the initial proposal in [22].

4. Specifying a more dynamic notion of test goal and model coverage: Uppaal Tron does not allow for specifying a notion of test goal. Apart from traditional notions of test goal, e.g., hitting certain states in the model, we need to specify test goals that refer to the coverage of the functional model. For example, it is essential to cover all (combinations of) representative elements of a certain partitioning of data types, a la the equivalence-class testing method.

Despite the above-mentioned shortcomings, UPPAAL TRON can still be considered for prototyping a test-bed for similar systems, however, our experience shows that the following issues need to be considered:

1. Performance issues: Due to the very complex and mixed nature of the system, we soon reached the boundaries of possibilities with UPPAAL TRON. To overcome this problem we had to distribute our test-case generation among a number of parallel instances of UPPAAL TRON. A challenge imposed by this solution is how to pass the received messages to the right instance of UPPAAL TRON. This problem is intensified by the lack of appropriate support of data-type-handling. To solve the latter problem, we annotated the messages in the underlying model of each UPPAAL TRON instance with a unique identifier which can be recognized and distinguished by our adapter.

2. Data-related behavior: UPPAAL natively supports data types and variables in the definition of its machines. Despite its limited flexibility (e.g., in defining customized data types), the specification language can still be used to implement basic data-dependent behaviors. The problem is, the UPPAAL engine generates a state-space which is suitable for model-checking purposes (i.e., the whole state-space). UPPAAL TRON uses this state-space to infer applicable test-cases, while a non-exhaustive state-space exploration algorithm could be sufficient to generate test-cases. Some of the above-mentioned performance issues, are also rooted in this problem. Additionally, not all UP-PAAL data structures are also supported in TRON. For instance, passing data arrays from the test engine to the SUT (or more precisely the adapter) or vice versa is not possible. It turns out that the performance deteriorates drastically when the specification makes use of UPPAAL variables, in comparison to hardcoded values in signal names (i.e., completely unfolding the model). Due to this, we decided to implement a *specification generator*, i.e., a script which creates multiple copies of the system behavior with all data fields embedded in signal names. These complex signals must be decoded by the adapter to get access to the actual values. A similar operation should be done with the SUT outgoing signals (i.e., the adapter should encode the data values appropriately in the signal name and pass it to the tester). Although we succeeded to reach an acceptable performance using this method, we soon reached the limit of defining automata in UPPAAL.

We have so far experimented with few types of transactions. We plan to include other types of transaction (such as special POS services) and other EFT devices (e.g., Automatic Teller Machines – ATMs) in our future test infrastructure.

Our test-case prioritization policy is now based on absolute statement coverage of test-cases. This can be extended in two ways: *first*, other coverage measure, particularly coverage metrics on the model should be taken into account and *second*, more complex and mature prioritization techniques can be exploited (e.g., incremental analysis of test-case coverage and assigning weights to the covered scenarios or components [7]).

Our approach to check the validity of performed transactions inside our test service layer may extend in the future to incorporate checking more business rules. However, in order to keep our adaptor still manageable we would like to add another layer of abstraction for specifying models of such business rules and an independent component which can perform the necessary checks based on the rules.

8   Related Work

GAST [13] implements an FSM-based conformance testing algorithm close to IOCO. The FSM model in GAST is specified in the functional programming language Clean. One can define abstract data types and use the generic function definition in Clean to use them in generating test-cases. In [21], GAST is used to test Java Card applet implementing an electronic purse application. The applicability of their test-technique is then demonstrated by manually injecting a number of bugs (creating mutations) and applying the automated test technique to find them. The work reported in [21] is essentially based on the same principles as our work (modulo some technical, e.g., the differences in the definition of conformance relation). We improve upon the trajectory proposed in [21] by integrating domain knowledge and code coverage metric in prioritizing test-cases.

The model-based testing environment of Microsoft called *Spec Explorer* to design and run automatic tests [24]. Their modeling language combines scenario-based modeling with state-based modeling [8,9]. This prevents complicated conversion from the developed code (which are scenario-based) to an FSM model (which is state-based) by test designers. This can make the learning curve for model-based testing less steep. For our application domain, however, a more elaborate model of both behavior and data domain seems indefensible and hence, we believe that it pays off to spend an extra effort to build a separate model for testing purposes. The ISO 8583 standard as a reference model facilitates making this model and keeps it relatively orthogonal to the changes in implementation.

Our prioritization method is based on the work of Elbaum et al. [7,6] in which they have analyzed and compared different test-case prioritizing techniques which helps test designers to select appropriate techniques according to their needs. We used category-partitioning in order to organize our test-case generation process. The technique was originally introduced by Ostrand and Balcer [16]. In particular, this method is more effective when enormous variety of test-cases can be generated but only some of them have real testing value.

9 Conclusions and Future Work

In this work, we developed a formal model of a high-risk financial system, called an Electronic Fund Transfer (EFT) switch, in terms of Labeled Transition Systems (LTSs). The formal model is then exploited to apply model based testing techniques in order to test such a system automatically and systematically. We used an existing test-case generator, called UPPAAL TRON, and extend it with several components, to augment the test-cases with financial data and to store, evaluate and prioritize the generated test-cases. Also, to enhance the performance and to prevent state-space explosion in our testing infrastructure, we implemented the formal model of some components in the environment as a separate Java component running in parallel with our test infrastructure.

Hitherto, we have only covered few transaction types (e.g., purchase, reversal and balance enquiry) and only used POS terminals to send messages to the EFT switch. Despite this limited scope of our current implementation, the test results both in terms of coverage and detected bugs are encouraging. However, we need to overcome the limitations in the present approach in order to replace the current manual testing techniques with the model-based approach presented in this paper. Hence, we would like to extend the approach along the lines presented in Section 7 and build an in-house tool to support it.

Acknowledgments. The authors would like to thank Marius Mikucionis for his helpful hints on the UPPAAL TRON engine. Tim Willemse provided useful comments on an earlier draft of this paper. This work is partially sponsored by Fanap IT corporation.

References

1. Cobertura project, http://cobertura.sourceforge.net/
2. ISO 8583 standard for financial transaction card originated messages - interchange message specifications – part 1: Messages, data elements and code values (2003)
3. Asadi, H.R., Khosravi, R., Mousavi, M.R., Noroozi, N.: Towards Model-Based Testing of Electronic Funds Transfer Systems. Technical Report CSR-10-04, Department of Computer Science, Eindhoven University of Technology (May 2010)
4. Behrmann, G., David, A., Larsen, K., Håkansson, J., Pettersson, P., Yi, W., Hendriks, M.: UPPAAL 4.0. In: Proc. of QEST 2006, pp. 125–126. IEEE CS (2006)
5. Broy, M., Jonsson, B., Katoen, J.-P., Leucker, M., Pretschner, A. (eds.): Model-Based Testing of Reactive Systems. LNCS, vol. 3472. Springer, Heidelberg (2005)
6. Elbaum, S., Malishevsky, A., Rothermel, G.: Prioritizing test cases for regression testing. In: Proceedings of the International Symposium on Software Testing and Analysis, pp. 102–112. ACM Press (2000)

7. Elbaum, S., Rothermel, G., Kanduri, S., Malishevsky, A.: Selecting a cost-effective test case prioritization technique. Software Quality Journal 12 (2004)
8. Grieskamp, W.: Multi-Paradigmatic Model-Based Testing. In: Havelund, K., Núñez, M., Roşu, G., Wolff, B. (eds.) FATES 2006 and RV 2006. LNCS, vol. 4262, pp. 1–19. Springer, Heidelberg (2006)
9. Grieskamp, W., Tillmann, N., Veanes, M.: Instrumenting scenarios in a model-driven development environment. Information & Software Technology 46(15), 1027–1036 (2004)
10. Grochtmann, M., Grimm, K.: Classification trees for partition testing. Softw. Test., Verif. Reliab. 3(2), 63–82 (1993)
11. Hessel, A., Larsen, K., Mikucionis, M., Nielsen, B., Pettersson, P., Skou, A.: Testing Real-Time Systems using UPPAAL. In: Hierons, R.M., Bowen, J.P., Harman, M. (eds.) FORTEST. LNCS, vol. 4949, pp. 77–117. Springer, Heidelberg (2008)
12. Hierons, R., Bogdanov, K., Bowen, J., Cleaveland, R., Derrick, J., Dick, J., Gheorghe, M., Harman, M., Kapoor, K., Krause, P., Lüttgen, G., Simons, A.J.H., Vilkomir, S.A., Woodward, M., Zedan, H.: Using formal specifications to support testing. ACM Computing Surveys 41(2) (2009)
13. Koopman, P., Plasmeijer, R.: Testing reactive systems with GAST. In: Post-Proceedings of TFP 2003, pp. 111–129, Intellect (2004)
14. Mikucionis, M., Nielsen, B., Larsen, K.: Real-time system testing on-the-fly. In: Proceedings of NWPT 2003, pp. 36–38 (2003)
15. Object Management Group, UML Testing Profile Version 1.0 (2005)
16. Ostrand, T., Balcer, M.: The category-partition method for specifying and generating functional tests. Commun. ACM 31(6), 676–686 (1988)
17. Schmaltz, J., Tretmans, J.: On Conformance Testing for Timed Systems. In: Cassez, F., Jard, C. (eds.) FORMATS 2008. LNCS, vol. 5215, pp. 250–264. Springer, Heidelberg (2008)
18. Tretmans, J.: A formal approach to conformance testing. In: Proceedings of the IFIP International Workshop on Protocol Test systems VI, pp. 257–276. North-Holland (1994)
19. Tretmans, J.: Model Based Testing with Labelled Transition Systems. In: Hierons, R.M., Bowen, J.P., Harman, M. (eds.) FORTEST. LNCS, vol. 4949, pp. 1–38. Springer, Heidelberg (2008)
20. Tretmans, J., Brinksma, E.: TorX: Automated Model-Based Testing. In: Proceedings of the European Conference on Model-Driven Software Engineering (2003)
21. van Weelden, A., Oostdijk, M., Frantzen, L., Koopman, P., Tretmans, J.: On-the-fly formal testing of a smart card applet. In: Security and Privacy in the Age of Ubiquitous Computing. IFIP, vol. 181, pp. 565–576. Springer, Heidelberg (2005)
22. Weiglhofer, M., Wotawa, F.: Asynchronous Input-Output Conformance Testing. In: Proceedings of COMPSAC 2009, vol. 1, pp. 154–159. IEEE CS (2009)
23. Willcock, C., Deiß, T., Tobies, S., Keil, S., Engler, F., Schulz, S.: An Introduction to TTCN-3. Wiley (2005)
24. Veanes, M., Campbell, C., Grieskamp, W., Schulte, W., Tillmann, N., Nachmanson, L.: Model-Based Testing of Object-Oriented Reactive Systems with Spec Explorer. In: Hierons, R.M., Bowen, J.P., Harman, M. (eds.) FORTEST. LNCS, vol. 4949, pp. 39–76. Springer, Heidelberg (2008)

Relating Modal Refinements, Covariant-Contravariant Simulations and Partial Bisimulations*

Luca Aceto[1], Ignacio Fábregas[2], David de Frutos Escrig[2], Anna Ingólfsdóttir[1], and Miguel Palomino[2]

[1] ICE-TCS, School of Computer Science, Reykjavik University, Iceland
[2] Departamento de Sistemas Informáticos y Computación, Universidad Complutense de Madrid, Spain

Abstract. This paper studies the relationships between three notions of behavioural preorder that have been proposed in the literature: refinement over modal transition systems, and the covariant-contravariant simulation and the partial bisimulation preorders over labelled transition systems. It is shown that there are mutual translations between modal transition systems and labelled transition systems that preserve, and reflect, refinement and the covariant-contravariant simulation preorder. The translations are also shown to preserve the modal properties that can be expressed in the logics that characterize those preorders. A translation from labelled transition systems modulo the partial bisimulation preorder into the same model modulo the covariant-contravariant simulation preorder is also offered, together with some evidence that the former model is less expressive than the latter. In order to gain more insight into the relationships between modal transition systems modulo refinement and labelled transition systems modulo the covariant-contravariant simulation preorder, their connections are also phrased and studied in the context of institutions.

1 Introduction

Modal transition systems (MTSs) have been proposed in, e.g., [11,12] as a model of reactive computation based on states and transitions that naturally supports a notion of *refinement* that is akin to the notion of implication in logical specification languages. (See the paper [3] for a thorough analysis of the connections between specifications given in terms of MTSs and logical specifications in the setting of a modal logic that characterizes refinement.) In an MTS, transitions come in two flavours: the *may* transitions and the *must* transitions, with the

---

* Research supported by Spanish projects DESAFIOS10 TIN2009-14599-C03-01, TESIS TIN2009-14321-C02-01 and PROMETIDOS S2009/TIC-1465, the project 'Processes and Modal Logics' (project nr. 100048021) of the Icelandic Fund for Research, and the Abel Extraordinary Chair programme within the NILS Mobility Project.

F. Arbab and M. Sirjani (Eds.): FSEN 2011, LNCS 7141, pp. 268–283, 2012.

requirement that each must transition is also a may transition. The idea behind the notion of refinement over MTSs is that, in order to implement correctly a specification, an implementation should exhibit all the transitions that are required by the specification (these are the must transitions in the MTS that describes the specification) and may provide the transitions that are allowed by the specification (these are the may transitions in the MTS that describes the specification).

The formalism of modal transition systems is intuitive, has several variants with varying degrees of expressive power and complexity—see, e.g., the survey paper [1]—and has recently been used as a suitable model for the specification of service-oriented applications. In particular, results on the supervisory control (in the sense of Ramadge and Wonham [15]) of systems whose specification is given in that formalism have been presented in, e.g., [4,8].

The very recent development of the notion of *partial bisimulation* in the setting of labelled transition systems (LTSs) presented in [2] has been explicitly motivated by the desire to develop a process-algebraic model within which one can study topics in the field of supervisory control. A partial bisimulation is a variation on the classic notion of bisimulation [13,14] in which two LTSs are only required to fulfil the bisimulation conditions on a subset B of the collection of actions; transitions labelled by actions not in B are treated as in the standard simulation preorder. Intuitively, one may think of the actions in B as corresponding to the uncontrollable events—see [2, page 4]. The aforementioned paper offers a thorough development of the basic theory of partial bisimulation.

Another recent proposal for a simulation-based behavioural relation over LTSs, called the *covariant-contravariant simulation preorder*, has been put forward in [5], and its theory has been investigated further in [6]. This notion of simulation between LTSs is based on considering a partition of their set of actions into three sets: the collection of covariant actions, that of contravariant actions and the set of bivariant actions. Intuitively, one may think of the covariant actions as being under the control of the specification LTS, and transitions with such actions as their label should be simulated by any correct implementation of the specification. On the other hand, the contravariant actions may be considered as being under the control of the implementation (or of the environment) and transitions with such actions as their label should be simulated by the specification. The bivariant actions are treated as in the classic notion of bisimulation.

It is natural to wonder whether there are any relations among these three formalisms. In particular, one may ask oneself whether it is possible to offer mutual translations between specifications given in those state-transition-based models that preserve, and reflect, the appropriate notions of behavioural preorder as well as properties expressed in the modal logics that accompany them—see, e.g., [2,3,6]. The aim of this study is to offer an answer to this question.

In this paper, we study the relationships between refinement over modal transition systems, and the covariant-contravariant simulation and the partial bisimulation preorders over labelled transition systems. We offer mutual translations between modal transition systems and labelled transition systems that preserve, and reflect, refinement and the covariant-contravariant simulation preorder, as well as the modal properties that can be expressed in the logics that characterize those preorders. We also give a translation from labelled transition systems modulo the partial bisimulation preorder into the same model modulo the covariant-contravariant simulation preorder, together with some evidence that the former model is less expressive than the latter. Finally, in order to gain more insight into the relationships between modal transition systems modulo refinement and labelled transition systems modulo the covariant-contravariant simulation preorder, we phrase and study their connections in the context of institutions [9].

The developments in this paper indicate that the formalism of MTSs may be seen as a common ground within which one can embed LTSs modulo the covariant-contravariant simulation preorder or partial bisimilarity. Moreover, there are some interesting, and non-obvious, corollaries that one may infer from the translations we provide. See Section 5, where we use our translations to show, e.g., that checking whether two states in an LTS are related by the covariant-contravariant simulation preorder can always be reduced to an equivalent check in a setting without bivariant actions, and provide a more detailed analysis of the translations. The study of the relative expressive power of different formalisms is, however, an art as well as a science, and may yield different answers depending on the conceptual framework that one adopts for the comparison. For instance, at the level of institutions [9], we provide an institution morphism from the institution corresponding to the theory of MTSs modulo refinement into the institution corresponding to the theory of LTSs modulo the covariant-contravariant simulation preorder. However, we conjecture that there is no institution morphism in the other direction. The work presented in the study opens several interesting avenues for future research, and settling the above conjecture is one of a wealth of research questions we survey in Section 8.

The remainder of the paper is organized as follows. Section 2 is devoted to preliminaries. In particular, in that section, we provide all the necessary background on modal and labelled transition systems, modal refinement and the covariant-contravariant simulation preorder, and the modal logics that characterize those preorders. In Section 3, we show how one can translate LTSs modulo the covariant-contravariant simulation preorder into MTSs modulo refinement. Section 4 presents the converse translation. We discuss the mutual translations between LTSs and MTSs in Section 5. Section 6 offers a translation from LTSs modulo partial bisimilarity into LTSs modulo the covariant-contravariant simulation preorder. In Section 7, we study the relationships between modal transition systems modulo refinement and labelled transition systems modulo the covariant-contravariant simulation preorder in the context of institutions. Section 8 concludes the paper and offers a number of directions for future research that we plan to pursue.

The proofs of all the results in the paper and further developments may be found in the full version of this study, which is available at http://www.ru.is/faculty/luca/PAPERS/mts-cc.pdf.

2   Preliminaries

We begin by introducing modal transition systems, with their associated notion of (modal) refinement, and labelled transition systems modulo the covariant-contravariant simulation preorder. We refer the reader to, e.g., [3,11,12] and [5,6] for more information, motivation and examples.

Modal Transition Systems and Refinement.

Definition 1. *For a set of actions A, a* modal transition *system (MTS) is a triple $(P, \to_\diamond, \to_\square)$, where P is a set of states and $\to_\diamond, \to_\square \subseteq P \times A \times P$ are transition relations such that $\to_\square \subseteq \to_\diamond$.*
  An MTS is image finite *iff the set $\{p' \mid p \xrightarrow{a}_\diamond p'\}$ is finite for each $p \in P$ and $a \in A$.*

The transitions in $\to_\square$ are called the *must transitions* and those in $\to_\diamond$ are the *may transitions*. In an MTS, each must transition is also a may transition, which intuitively means that any required transition is also allowed.

   In what follows, we often identify an MTS, or a transition system of any of the types that we consider in this paper, with its set of states. In case we wish to make clear the 'ambient' transition system in which a state p lives, we write (P, p) to indicate that p is to be viewed as a state in P.

   The notion of (modal) refinement $\sqsubseteq$ over MTSs that we now proceed to introduce is based on the idea that if $p \sqsubseteq q$ then q is a 'refinement' of the specification p. In that case, intuitively, q may be obtained from p by possibly turning some of its may transitions into must transitions.

Definition 2. *A relation $R \subseteq P \times Q$ is a* refinement relation *between two modal transition systems if, whenever $p \, R \, q$:*

 - *$p \xrightarrow{a}_\square p'$ implies that there exists some q' such that $q \xrightarrow{a}_\square q'$ and $p' \, R \, q'$;*
 - *$q \xrightarrow{a}_\diamond q'$ implies that there exists some p' such that $p \xrightarrow{a}_\diamond p'$ and $p' \, R \, q'$.*

We write $\sqsubseteq$ for the largest refinement relation.

Example 1. Consider the MTS U over the set of actions A with u as its only state, and transitions $u \xrightarrow{a}_\diamond u$ for each $a \in A$. It is well known, and not hard to see, that $u \sqsubseteq p$ holds for each state p in any MTS over action set A. The state u is often referred to as the *loosest (or universal) specification.*

Definition 3. *Given a set of actions A, the collection of* Boudol-Larsen's modal formulae [3] *is given by the following grammar:*

$$\varphi ::= \bot \mid \top \mid \varphi \land \varphi \mid \varphi \lor \varphi \mid [a]\varphi \mid \langle a \rangle \varphi \qquad (a \in A).$$

The semantics of these formulae with respect to an MTS P and a state $p \in P$ is defined by means of the satisfaction relation $\models$, which is the least relation satisfying the following clauses:

$$(P, p) \models \top.$$

$(P,p) \models \varphi_1 \wedge \varphi_2$ if $(P,p) \models \varphi_1$ and $(P,p) \models \varphi_2$.
$(P,p) \models \varphi_1 \vee \varphi_2$ if $(P,p) \models \varphi_1$ or $(P,p) \models \varphi_2$.
$(P,p) \models [a]\varphi$ if $(P,p') \models \varphi$ for all $p \xrightarrow{a}_\diamond p'$.
$(P,p) \models \langle a \rangle \varphi$ if $(P,p') \models \varphi$ for some $p \xrightarrow{a}_\Box p'$.

For example, the state U from Example 1 satisfies neither the formula $\langle a \rangle \top$ nor the formula $[a]\bot$. Indeed, it is not hard to see that U satisfies a formula φ if, and only if, φ is a tautology.

The following result stems from [3].

Proposition 1. *Let p, q be states in image-finite MTSs over the set of actions A. Then $p \sqsubseteq q$ iff the collection of Boudol-Larsen's modal formulae satisfied by p is included in the collection of formulae satisfied by q.*

Labelled Transition Systems and Covariant-contravariant Simulation. A labelled transition system (LTS) is just an MTS with $\rightarrow_\diamond = \rightarrow_\Box$. In what follows, we write $\rightarrow$ for the transition relation in an LTS.

Definition 4. *Let P and Q be two LTSs over the set of actions A, and let $\{A^r, A^l, A^{bi}\}$ be a partition of A^1. An (A^r, A^l)-simulation (or just a covariant-contravariant simulation when the partition of the set of actions A is understood from the context) between P and Q is a relation $R \subseteq P \times Q$ such that, whenever $p \, R \, q$, we have:*

- *For all $a \in A^r \cup A^{bi}$ and all $p \xrightarrow{a} p'$, there exists some $q \xrightarrow{a} q'$ with $p' \, R \, q'$.*
- *For all $a \in A^l \cup A^{bi}$ and all $q \xrightarrow{a} q'$, there exists some $p \xrightarrow{a} p'$ with $p' \, R \, q'$.*

We will write $p \lesssim_{cc} q$ if there exists a covariant-contravariant simulation R such that $p \, R \, q$.

The actions in the set A^r are sometimes called *covariant*, those in A^l are *contravariant* and the ones in A^{bi} are *bivariant*. When working with covariant-contravariant simulations, we shall sometimes refer to the triple (A^r, A^l, A^{bi}) as the *signature* of the corresponding LTS.

Example 2. Assume that $a \in A^r$ and $b \in A^l$. Consider the LTSs described by the CCS [13] terms $p = a + b$, $q = a$ and $r = b$. Then $r \lesssim_{cc} p \lesssim_{cc} q$, but none of the converse relations holds.

Definition 5. *Covariant-contravariant modal logic has almost the same syntax as the one for modal refinement:*

$$\varphi ::= \bot \mid \top \mid \varphi \wedge \varphi \mid \varphi \vee \varphi \mid [b]\varphi \mid \langle a \rangle \varphi \qquad (a \in A^r \cup A^{bi}, b \in A^l \cup A^{bi}).$$

The semantics differs for the modal operators, since we interpret formulae over ordinary LTSs:

$$(P,p) \models [b]\varphi \text{ if } (P,p') \models \varphi \text{ for all } p \xrightarrow{b} p'.$$

---

[1] Note that any of the sets A^r, A^l and A^{bi} may be empty.

$(P,p) \models \langle a \rangle \varphi$ if $(P,p') \models \varphi$ for some $p \xrightarrow{a} p'$.

For example, both p and q from Example 2 satisfy the formula $\langle a \rangle \top$, while r does not. On the other hand, q satisfies the formula $[b]\bot$, but neither p nor r do.

The following result stems from [6].

Proposition 2. *Let p, q be states in image-finite LTSs with the same signature. Then $p \lesssim_{cc} q$ iff the collection of covariant-contravariant modal formulae satisfied by p is included in the collection of covariant-contravariant modal formulae satisfied by q.*

3   From Covariant-Contravariant Simulations to Modal Refinements

We are now ready to begin our study of the connections between MTSs modulo refinement and LTSs modulo the covariant-contravariant simulation preorder. First we show that, perhaps surprisingly, LTSs modulo $\lesssim_{cc}$ may be translated into MTSs modulo $\sqsubseteq$. Such a translation preserves, and reflects, those preorders and the satisfaction of modal formulae.

Definition 6. *Let P be an LTS with the set of actions A partitioned into A^r, A^l, and A^{bi}. The MTS $\mathcal{M}(P)$ is constructed as follows:*

- *The set of actions of $\mathcal{M}(P)$ is A.*
- *The set of states of $\mathcal{M}(P)$ is the same as the one of P plus a new state u.*
- *For each transition $p \xrightarrow{a} p'$ in P, add a may transition $p \xrightarrow{a}_\diamond p'$ in $\mathcal{M}(P)$.*
- *For each transition $p \xrightarrow{a} p'$ in P with $a \in A^r \cup A^{bi}$, add a must transition $p \xrightarrow{a}_\Box p'$ in $\mathcal{M}(P)$.*
- *For each a in A^r and state p, add the transition $p \xrightarrow{a}_\diamond u$ to $\mathcal{M}(P)$, as well as transitions $u \xrightarrow{a}_\diamond u$ for each action $a \in A$.*

The following proposition essentially states that the translation $\mathcal{M}$ is correct.

Proposition 3. *Let P and Q be two LTSs with the same signature, and let $p \in P$ and $q \in Q$. Then $(P,p) \lesssim_{cc} (Q,q)$ iff $(\mathcal{M}(P),p) \sqsubseteq (\mathcal{M}(Q),q)$.*

Proof. We prove the two implications separately.

($\Rightarrow$) Assume that R is a covariant-contravariant simulation. We shall prove that $\mathcal{M}(R) = R \cup \{(u,q) \mid q$ a state of $\mathcal{M}(Q)\}$ is a refinement.

Suppose that $p \, R \, q$ and $q \xrightarrow{a}_\diamond q'$ in $\mathcal{M}(Q)$. By the definition of $\mathcal{M}(Q)$, the transition $q \xrightarrow{a} q'$ is in Q. If $a \in A^l \cup A^{bi}$, since $p \, R \, q$ and R is a covariant-contravariant simulation, we have that $p \xrightarrow{a} p'$ in P for some p' such that $p' \, R \, q'$. By the construction of $\mathcal{M}(P)$, it holds that $p \xrightarrow{a}_\diamond p'$ and we are done. If $a \in A^r$, then $p \xrightarrow{a}_\diamond u$ and $u \, \mathcal{M}(R) \, q'$, as required.

Assume now that $p \, R \, q$ and $p \xrightarrow{a}_\Box p'$ in $\mathcal{M}(P)$. Then $p \xrightarrow{a} p'$ in P with $a \in A^r \cup A^{bi}$. As R is a covariant-contravariant simulation, it follows that $q \xrightarrow{a} q'$

in Q for some q' such that $p' \, R \, q'$. Since $a \in A^r \cup A^{bi}$, there is a must transition $q \xrightarrow{a}_\square q'$ in $\mathcal{M}(Q)$, and we are done. To finish the proof of this implication, recall that, as shown in Example 1, q is a refinement of u for each q.

($\Leftarrow$) Assume that $\mathcal{M}(R)$ is a refinement. We shall prove that R is a covariant-contravariant simulation.

Suppose that $p \, R \, q$ and $q \xrightarrow{a} q'$ in Q with $a \in A^l \cup A^{bi}$. Then $q \xrightarrow{a}_\diamond q'$ in $\mathcal{M}(Q)$. Since $\mathcal{M}(R)$ is a refinement, in $\mathcal{M}(P)$ we have that $p \xrightarrow{a}_\diamond p'$ for some p' (different from u, because $a \notin A^r$) such that $p' \, R \, q'$. By the construction of $\mathcal{M}(P)$, it follows that $p \xrightarrow{a} p'$ in P and we are done.

Suppose now that $p \, R \, q$ and $p \xrightarrow{a} p'$ in P with $a \in A^r \cup A^{bi}$. Then $p \xrightarrow{a}_\square p'$ in $\mathcal{M}(P)$. Since $\mathcal{M}(R)$ is a refinement, there is some q' (again, different from u) such that $q \xrightarrow{a}_\square q'$ in $\mathcal{M}(Q)$ and $p' \, R \, q'$. By the construction of $\mathcal{M}(Q)$, it follows that $q \xrightarrow{a} q'$ in Q and we are done. $\square$

Definition 7. *Let us extend $\mathcal{M}$ to translate formulae over the modal logic that characterizes the covariant-contravariant simulation preorder to the modal logic for modal transition systems by simply defining $\mathcal{M}(\varphi) = \varphi$.*

Proposition 4. *If P is an LTS and φ is a formula of the logic that characterizes covariant-contravariant simulation, then for each $p \in P$:*

$$(P, p) \models \varphi \iff (\mathcal{M}(P), p) \models \mathcal{M}(\varphi).$$

4   From Modal Refinements to Covariant-Contravariant Simulations

We now show that MTSs modulo $\sqsubseteq$ may be translated into LTSs modulo $\lesssim_{cc}$. As the one studied in the previous section, our translation preserves, and reflects, those preorders and the satisfaction of modal formulae.

Definition 8. *Let M be an MTS with set of actions A. The LTS $\mathcal{C}(M)$, with signature $A^r = \{cv(a) \mid a \in A\}$, $A^l = \{ct(a) \mid a \in A\}$ and $A^{bi} = \emptyset$, is constructed as follows:*

- *The set of states of $\mathcal{C}(M)$ is the same as that of M.*
- *For each transition $p \xrightarrow{a}_\diamond p'$ in M, add $p \xrightarrow{ct(a)} p'$ to $\mathcal{C}(M)$.*
- *For each transition $p \xrightarrow{a}_\square p'$ in M, add $p \xrightarrow{cv(a)} p'$ to $\mathcal{C}(M)$.*

Observe that the LTSs obtained as a translation of an MTS have the following properties:

1. $A^{bi} = \emptyset$ and
2. there is a bijection $h : A^r \to A^l$ such that if $p \xrightarrow{a} p'$ with $a \in A^r$ then $p \xrightarrow{h(a)} p'$.

The following proposition essentially states that the translation $\mathcal{C}$ is correct.

Proposition 5. *Let P and Q be two MTSs with the same action set, and let $p \in P$ and $q \in Q$. Then $(P, p) \sqsubseteq (Q, q)$ iff $(\mathcal{C}(P), p) \lesssim_{cc} (\mathcal{C}(Q), q)$.*

Proof. We prove the two implications separately.

($\Rightarrow$) Assume that $p \; R \; q$ for some refinement R. If $p \overset{cv(a)}{\to} p'$ in $\mathcal{C}(P)$ then, by construction, $p \overset{a}{\to}_\Box p'$ in P. Since R is a refinement, there is some q' in Q with $q \overset{a}{\to}_\Box q'$ and $p' \; R \; q'$. Since $q \overset{cv(a)}{\to} q'$ is in $\mathcal{C}(Q)$ by construction, we are done. Now, assume that $q \overset{ct(a)}{\to} q'$ in $\mathcal{C}(Q)$. Then $q \overset{a}{\to}_\diamond q'$ in Q and, since R is a refinement, $p \overset{a}{\to}_\diamond p'$ in P for some p' with $p' \; R \; q'$. By construction, $p \overset{ct(a)}{\to} p'$ is in $\mathcal{C}(P)$ and we are done.

($\Leftarrow$) Assume that $p \; R \; q$ for some covariant-contravariant simulation R. If $q \overset{a}{\to}_\diamond q'$ in Q then $q \overset{ct(a)}{\to} q'$ in $\mathcal{C}(Q)$ and, since R is a covariant-contravariant simulation, $p \overset{ct(a)}{\to} p'$ for some p' in $\mathcal{C}(P)$ such that $p' R q'$; hence $p \overset{a}{\to}_\diamond p'$ in P as required. Now, if $p \overset{a}{\to}_\Box p'$ in P then $p \overset{cv(a)}{\to} p'$ in $\mathcal{C}(P)$. Since R is a covariant-contravariant simulation, there is some q' in $\mathcal{C}(Q)$ with $q \overset{cv(a)}{\to} q'$ and $p' \; R \; q'$, and therefore $q \overset{a}{\to}_\Box q'$ in Q. $\qquad\square$

Definition 9. *Let us extend $\mathcal{C}$ to translate formulae over the modal logic for modal transition systems with set of actions A to the modal logic that characterizes covariant-contravariant simulation with signature $A^r = \{cv(a) \mid a \in A\}$, $A^l = \{ct(a) \mid a \in A\}$ and $A^{bi} = \emptyset$.*

- $\mathcal{C}(\bot) = \bot$.
- $\mathcal{C}(\top) = \top$.
- $\mathcal{C}(\varphi \wedge \psi) = \mathcal{C}(\varphi) \wedge \mathcal{C}(\psi)$.
- $\mathcal{C}(\varphi \vee \psi) = \mathcal{C}(\varphi) \vee \mathcal{C}(\psi)$.
- $\mathcal{C}(\langle a \rangle \varphi) = \langle cv(a) \rangle \mathcal{C}(\varphi)$.
- $\mathcal{C}([a]\varphi) = [ct(a)]\mathcal{C}(\varphi)$.

Proposition 6. *If P is an MTS and φ a modal formula, then for each $p \in P$:*

$$(P, p) \models \varphi \iff (\mathcal{C}(P), p) \models \mathcal{C}(\varphi).$$

5 Discussion of the Translations

In Sections 3–4, we saw that it is possible to translate back and forth between the world of LTSs modulo the covariant-contravariant simulation preorder and MTSs modulo refinement. The translations we have presented preserve, and reflect, the preorders and the relevant modal formulae. There are, however, some interesting, and non-obvious, corollaries that one may infer from the translations.

To begin with, assume that P and Q are two LTSs with the same signature with $A^{bi} \neq \emptyset$. Let $p \in P$ and $q \in Q$ be such that $(P, p) \lesssim_{cc} (Q, q)$. By Proposition 3, we know that this holds exactly when $(\mathcal{M}(P), p) \sqsubseteq (\mathcal{M}(Q), q)$. Using Proposition 5, we therefore have that checking whether $(P, p) \lesssim_{cc} (Q, q)$ is equivalent to verifying whether $(\mathcal{C}(\mathcal{M}(P)), p) \lesssim_{cc} (\mathcal{C}(\mathcal{M}(Q)), q)$. Note now that A^{bi} is empty in the signature for the LTSs $\mathcal{C}(\mathcal{M}(P))$ and $\mathcal{C}(\mathcal{M}(Q))$. Therefore checking whether two states are related by the covariant-contravariant simulation preorder can always be reduced to an equivalent check in a setting without bivariant actions.

It is also natural to wonder whether there is any relation between a state p in an LTS P and the equally-named state in $\mathcal{C}(\mathcal{M}(P))$. Similarly, one may wonder whether there is any relation between a state p in an MTS P and the equally-named state in $\mathcal{M}(\mathcal{C}(P))$. In both cases, we are faced with the difficulty that the transition systems resulting from the compositions of the translations are over actions of the form $\{\mathrm{cv}(a), \mathrm{ct}(a) \mid a \in A\}$ whereas the original systems had transitions labelled by actions in A. In order to overcome this difficulty, let $\rho : \{\mathrm{cv}(a), \mathrm{ct}(a) \mid a \in A\} \to A$ be the renaming that, for each $a \in A$, maps both $\mathrm{cv}(a)$ and $\mathrm{ct}(a)$ to a. For any transition system P over the set of actions $\{\mathrm{cv}(a), \mathrm{ct}(a) \mid a \in A\}$, we write $\rho(P)$ for the transition system that is obtained from P by renaming the label of each transition in P as indicated by ρ.

Proposition 7.

1. Let P be an MTS and let $p \in P$. Then $(\rho(\mathcal{M}(\mathcal{C}(P))), p) \sqsubseteq (P, p)$.
2. Let P be an LTS and let $p \in P$. Then $(P, p) \lesssim_{cc} (\rho(\mathcal{C}(\mathcal{M}(P))), p)$.
3. In general, $(P, p) \sqsubseteq (\rho(\mathcal{M}(\mathcal{C}(P))), p)$ does not hold for an MTS P and a state $p \in P$, nor does $(\rho(\mathcal{C}(\mathcal{M}(P))), p) \lesssim_{cc} (P, p)$ for an LTS P and a state $p \in P$.

Definition 10. Let P be an LTS with the set of actions partitioned into A^r and A^l. The LTS $\overline{P}$ is obtained from P by renaming every $a \in A^r$ as $\mathrm{cv}(a)$ and every $a \in A^l$ as $\mathrm{ct}(a)$.

Proposition 8. Let P be an LTS over a set of actions $A^r \cup A^l$ and let Q be an MTS over the same actions. Then the following statements hold.

1. If a relation R is a covariant-contravariant simulation between $\overline{P}$ and $\mathcal{C}(Q)$ then R is a refinement between $\mathcal{M}(P)$ and Q.
2. If $(\overline{P}, p) \lesssim_{cc} (\mathcal{C}(Q), q)$ then $(\mathcal{M}(P), p) \sqsubseteq (Q, q)$, for all states $p \in P$ and $q \in Q$.
3. The converse implication of the above statement fails.

6   Partial Bisimulation

The partial bisimulation preorder has been recently proposed in [2] as a suitable behavioural relation over LTSs for studying the theory of supervisory control [15] in a concurrency-theoretic framework. Formally, the notion of partial bisimulation is defined over LTSs with a set of actions A and a so-called *bisimulation set* $B \subseteq A$. The LTSs considered in [2] also include a termination predicate $\downarrow$ over states. For the sake of simplicity, since its role is orthogonal to our aims in this paper, instead of extending MTSs and their refinements or covariant-contravariant simulations with such a predicate, we simply omit it in what follows.

Definition 11. *A partial bisimulation with bisimulation set B between two LTSs P and Q is a relation $R \subseteq P \times Q$ such that, whenever $p \, R \, q$:*

- *For all $a \in A$, if $p \xrightarrow{a} p'$ then there exists some $q \xrightarrow{a} q'$ with $p' \, R \, q'$.*
- *For all $b \in B$, if $q \xrightarrow{b} q'$ then there exists some $p \xrightarrow{b} p'$ with $p' \, R \, q'$.*

We write $p \lesssim_B q$ if $p \, R \, q$ for some partial bisimulation with bisimulation set B.

It is easy to see that partial bisimulation with bisimulation set B is a particular case of covariant-contravariant simulation.

Proposition 9. *Let P be an LTS. A relation R is a partial bisimulation with bisimulation set B iff it is a covariant-contravariant simulation when the LTS P has signature $A^r = A \setminus B$, $A^l = \emptyset$ and $A^{bi} = B$. Therefore, $p \lesssim_B q$ iff $p \lesssim_{cc} q$ with respect to that partition of A, for each $p, q \in P$.*

As a corollary of the above proposition, we immediately obtain the following result, to the effect that, instead of the modal logic used in [2] to characterize the partial bisimulation preorder with bisimulation set B, one can use the simpler, negation-free logic for the covariant-contravariant simulation preorder.

Corollary 1. *Let p, q be states in some image-finite LTS. Then $p \lesssim_B q$ iff the collection of formulae in Definition 5 over signature $A^r = A \setminus B$, $A^l = \emptyset$ and $A^{bi} = B$ satisfied by p is included in the collection of formulae satisfied by q.*

Note also that, as a corollary of Proposition 9, the translations of LTSs and formulae defined in Section 3 can be applied to embed LTSs modulo the partial bisimulation preorder into modal transition systems modulo refinement. In this case, however, there is an easier transformation that does not require the extra state u.

Definition 12. *Let P be an LTS over a set of actions A with a bisimulation set $B \subseteq A$. The MTS $\mathcal{N}(P)$ is constructed as follows:*

- *The set of states is that of P.*
- *For each transition $p \xrightarrow{a} p'$ in P, add a may transition $p \xrightarrow{a}_\diamond p'$ in $\mathcal{N}(P)$.*
- *For each transition $p \xrightarrow{b} p'$ in P with $b \in B$, add a must transition $p \xrightarrow{b}_\square p'$ in $\mathcal{N}(P)$.*

Proposition 10. *R is a partial bisimulation with bisimulation set B between P and Q iff R^{-1} is a refinement between $\mathcal{N}(Q)$ and $\mathcal{N}(P)$.*

Proof. ($\Rightarrow$) Assume that R is a partial bisimulation with bisimulation set B and suppose that $q \, R^{-1} \, p$. If $p \xrightarrow{a}_\diamond p'$ in $\mathcal{N}(P)$ then $p \xrightarrow{a} p'$ in P. Since R is a partial bisimulation, there is some $q \xrightarrow{a} q'$ in Q with $p' \, R \, q'$ and, by construction, $q \xrightarrow{a}_\diamond q'$ in $\mathcal{N}(Q)$ with $q' \, R^{-1} \, p'$. Now, if $q \xrightarrow{a}_\square q'$ in $\mathcal{N}(Q)$ then $q \xrightarrow{a} q'$ in Q with $a \in B$. Since R is a partial bisimulation and $p \, R \, q$, there is some $p \xrightarrow{a} p'$ in P with $p' \, R \, q'$ and hence $p \xrightarrow{a}_\square p'$ in $\mathcal{N}(P)$, as required.

($\Leftarrow$) Analogous. $\qquad\square$

Remark 1. In the special case $B = \emptyset$, the partial bisimulation preorder is just the standard simulation preorder. Therefore, letting 0 denote a one-state LTS with no transitions, $0 \lesssim_B p$ for each state p in any LTS P. Since $B = \emptyset$, all the modal transition systems $\mathcal{N}(P)$ that result from the translation of an LTS P will have no must transitions; for such modal transition systems, $\mathcal{N}(P) \sqsubseteq 0$ always holds. Indeed, in that case $\sqsubseteq$ coincides with the inverse of the simulation preorder over MTSs.

The drawback of the direct transformation presented in Definition 12, as compared to that in Section 3, is that it does not preserve the satisfiability of modal formulae. The problem lies in the fact that, while the existential modality $\langle a \rangle$ allows any transition with $a \in A$ in the partial bisimulation framework, it requires a must transition in the setting of MTSs.

As we have seen, it is easy to express partial bisimulations as a special case of covariant-contravariant simulations. It is therefore natural to wonder whether the converse also holds. We shall present some indications that the partial bisimulation framework is strictly less expressive than both modal refinements and covariant-contravariant simulations.

Let us assume, by way of example, that the set of actions A is partitioned into $A^r = \{a\}$ and $A^l = \{b\}$—so the set of bivariant actions is empty. In this setting, there cannot be a translation $\mathcal{T}$ from LTSs modulo $\lesssim_{cc}$ into LTSs modulo $\lesssim_B$ that satisfies the following natural conditions (by abuse of notation, we identify an LTS P with a specific state p):

1. For all p and q, $p \lesssim_{cc} q \iff \mathcal{T}(p) \lesssim_B \mathcal{T}(q)$.
2. $\mathcal{T}$ is a homomorphism with respect to $+$, that is, $\mathcal{T}(p + q) = \mathcal{T}(p) + \mathcal{T}(q)$, where $+$ denotes the standard notion of nondeterministic composition of LTSs from CCS [13]. (Intuitively, this compositionality requirement states that the translation is based on 'local information'.)
3. There is an n such that $\mathcal{T}(b^n)$ is not simulation equivalent to $\mathcal{T}(0)$, where b^n denotes an LTS consisting of n consecutive b-labelled transitions.

Indeed, observe that, by condition 2,

$$\mathcal{T}(p) = \mathcal{T}(p + 0) = \mathcal{T}(p) + \mathcal{T}(0) \quad \text{for each } p,$$

and therefore $\mathcal{T}(p) + \mathcal{T}(0) \lesssim_B \mathcal{T}(p)$. This means that $\mathcal{T}(0) \lesssim \mathcal{T}(p)$ for each p, where $\lesssim$ is the simulation preorder. In particular, $\mathcal{T}(0) \lesssim \mathcal{T}(\bot)$ where $\bot$ is the process consisting of a b-labelled loop with one state, which is the least element with respect to $\lesssim_{cc}$.

Note now that $\bot \lesssim_{cc} b^{n+1} \lesssim_{cc} b^n \lesssim_{cc} 0$ for each $n > 0$. Therefore, by condition 1,

$$\mathcal{T}(\bot) \lesssim_B \mathcal{T}(b^{n+1}) \lesssim_B \mathcal{T}(b^n) \lesssim_B \mathcal{T}(0) \quad \text{for each } n > 0.$$

Hence,

$$\mathcal{T}(\bot) \lesssim \mathcal{T}(b^n) \lesssim \mathcal{T}(0) \lesssim \mathcal{T}(\bot) \quad \text{for each } n > 0.$$

This yields that, for each $n > 0$, $\mathcal{T}(b^n)$ is simulation equivalent to $\mathcal{T}(0)$, which contradicts condition 3. (Note that we have only used the soundness of the transformation $\mathcal{T}$.)

This indicates strongly that any $\mathcal{T}$ that is compositional with respect to $+$ and is sound, in the sense of condition 1, would have to be very odd indeed, if it exists at all. Modulo simulation equivalence, such a translation would have to conflate a non-well-founded descending chain of LTSs into a point modulo simulation equivalence.

We end this section with a companion result.

Proposition 11. *Assume that $a \in A^r$ and $b \in A^l$. Suppose furthermore that $B = \emptyset$. Then there is no translation $\mathcal{T}$ from LTSs modulo $\lesssim_{cc}$ into LTSs modulo $\lesssim_B$ that satisfies conditions 1 and 2 above.*

7 Institutions and Institution Morphisms

In order to gain more insight into the relationships between modal transition systems modulo refinement and labelled transition systems modulo the covariant-contravariant simulation preorder, we will now study their connections at a more abstract level in the context of institutions [9]. When compared at the level of institutions it turns out that the correspondence between these models is, in a sense, not one-to-one.

Definition 13. *The institution $\mathcal{I}_{cc} = (\mathbf{Sign}_{cc}, sen_{cc}, \mathbf{Mod}_{cc}, \models_{cc})$, associated to the logic for the covariant-contravariant simulation preorder, is defined as follows.*

- *$\mathbf{Sign}_{cc}$ has as objects triples (A, B, C) of pairwise disjoint sets and morphisms $f : A \cup B \cup C \longrightarrow A' \cup B' \cup C'$ with $f(A) \subseteq A'$, $f(B) \subseteq B'$, and $f(C) \subseteq C'$.*
- *$sen_{cc}(A, B, C)$ is the set of formulae in the logic characterizing the covariant-contravariant simulation preorder, with A the set of covariant actions, B the set of contravariant actions, and C the set of bivariant actions. $sen(f)(\varphi)$ is obtained from φ by replacing each action a with $f(a)$.*
- *$\mathbf{Mod}_{cc}(A, B)$ is the category of LTS over the set of actions $A \cup B \cup C$, with a distinguished state; a morphism from (P, p) to (Q, q) is a covariant-contravariant simulation R such that $(p, q) \in R$.*
  Now, if $f : A \cup B \cup C \longrightarrow A' \cup B' \cup C'$, then

$$\mathbf{Mod}_{cc}(f) : \mathbf{Mod}_{cc}(A', B', C') \longrightarrow \mathbf{Mod}_{cc}(A, B, C)$$

  maps P to $P|_f$ and $R : P \longrightarrow Q$ to $R_f : P|_f \longrightarrow Q|_f$, where:
  - *The set of states of $P|_f$ is the same as that of P, and the distinguished state remains the same.*
  - *$p \xrightarrow{a} p'$ in $P|_f$ if $p \xrightarrow{f(a)} p'$ in P.*
  - *$R|_f$ coincides with R.*

- $(P, s) \models_{cc} \varphi$ if $(P, s) \models \varphi$ using the notion of satisfaction associated to the logic for the covariant-contravariant simulation preorder given in Definition 5.

Proposition 12. $\mathcal{I}_{cc}$ is an institution.

Definition 14. The institution $\mathcal{I}_{mts} = (\mathbf{Sign}_{mts}, sen_{mts}, \mathbf{Mod}_{mts}, \models_{mts})$, associated to the logic for refinement over modal transition systems, is defined as follows.

- $\mathbf{Sign}_{mts}$ is the category of sets.
- $sen_{mts}(A)$ is the set of formulae over A in the logic presented in Definition 3. The formula $sen_{mts}(f)(\varphi)$ is obtained from φ by replacing each action a with $f(a)$.
- $\mathbf{Mod}_{mts}(A)$ is the category of MTSs over the set of labels A, with a distinguished state. A morphism from (M, m) to (N, n) is a refinement R such that $(m, n) \in R$.
  If $f : A \longrightarrow B$ in $\mathbf{Sign}_{mts}$, then $\mathbf{Mod}_{mts}(f) : \mathbf{Mod}_{mts}(B) \longrightarrow \mathbf{Mod}_{mts}(A)$ maps an MTS M to $M|_f$ and a morphism R to $R|_f$, where:
  - $M|_f$ has the same set of states as M and the same distinguished state.
  - $p \xrightarrow{a}_\diamond p'$ in $M|_f$ if $p \xrightarrow{f(a)}_\diamond p'$ in M.
  - $p \xrightarrow{a}_\square p'$ in $M|_f$ if $p \xrightarrow{f(a)}_\square p'$ in M.
  - $R|_f$ coincides with R.
- $\models_{mts}$ is the notion of satisfaction presented in Definition 3.

Proposition 13. $\mathcal{I}_{mts}$ is an institution.

As the following result shows, one can translate $\mathcal{I}_{mts}$ into $\mathcal{I}_{cc}$ using an institution morphism. (The intuition for institution morphisms is that they are truth preserving translations from one logical system into another.)

Proposition 14. $(\Phi, \alpha, \beta) : \mathcal{I}_{mts} \longrightarrow \mathcal{I}_{cc}$ is an institution morphism, where:

- $\Phi : \mathbf{Sign}_{mts} \longrightarrow \mathbf{Sign}_{cc}$ maps A to the triple $(\mathrm{cv}(A), \mathrm{ct}(A), \emptyset)$, with:
  - $\mathrm{cv}(A) = \{\mathrm{cv}(a) \mid a \in A\}$ and
  - $\mathrm{ct}(A) = \{\mathrm{ct}(a) \mid a \in A\}$.
  For $f : A \longrightarrow B$, we define $\Phi(f)(\mathrm{cv}(a)) = \mathrm{cv}(f(a))$ and $\Phi(f)(\mathrm{ct}(a)) = \mathrm{ct}(f(a))$.
- The natural transformation $\alpha : sen_{cc} \circ \Phi \Rightarrow sen_{mts}$ translates a formula φ in $sen_{cc}(\mathrm{cv}(A), \mathrm{ct}(A), \emptyset)$ as follows:
  - $\alpha(\top) = \top$, $\alpha(\bot) = \bot$.
  - $\alpha(\varphi_1 \wedge \varphi_2) = \alpha(\varphi_1) \wedge \alpha(\varphi_2)$.
  - $\alpha(\varphi_1 \vee \varphi_2) = \alpha(\varphi_1) \vee \alpha(\varphi_2)$.
  - $\alpha(\langle \mathrm{cv}(a) \rangle \varphi) = \langle a \rangle \alpha(\varphi)$.
  - $\alpha([\mathrm{ct}(a)]\varphi) = [a]\alpha(\varphi)$.
- The natural transformation $\beta : \mathbf{Mod}_{mts} \Rightarrow \mathbf{Mod}_{cc} \circ \Phi$ maps an MTS (M, s) in $\mathbf{Mod}_{mts}(A)$ to $(\mathcal{C}(M), s)$, and a morphism R to itself.

The import of the above result is that MTSs modulo refinement and its accompanying modal logic can be 'translated in a truth preserving fashion' into LTSs modulo the covariant-contravariant simulation preorder and its companion modal logic. It is natural to ask oneself whether one can consider $\mathcal{I}_{mts}$ a 'subinstitution' of $\mathcal{I}_{cc}$. There are several related notions of subinstitution that have in common the requirement that the functor β, which is used to translate the models between the institutions, is an equivalence of categories.

Recall that an object in a category is weakly final if any other object has at least one arrow into it.

Proposition 15. $\mathbf{Mod}_{cc}(A, B, \emptyset)$ *has weakly final objects but* $\mathbf{Mod}_{mts}(A)$ *does not.*

In other words, in the absence of bivariant actions, there is a universal implementation in the setting of LTSs modulo the covariant-contravariant simulation preorder. Within that framework, there is also a universal specification, namely the LTS (I, s) where I is the LTS with a single state s and transitions $s \xrightarrow{b} s$ for every $b \in B$. On the other hand, there is a universal specification with respect to modal refinements, namely the MTS U from Example 1, but no universal implementation.

Proposition 16. *There is no embedding from* $\mathcal{I}_{mts}$ *into* $\mathcal{I}_{cc}$.

A natural question to ask is whether there is an embedding from $\mathcal{I}_{cc}$ into $\mathcal{I}_{mts}$. The following proposition answers this question negatively.

Proposition 17. *There exists no embedding from* $\mathcal{I}_{cc}$ *into* $\mathcal{I}_{mts}$.

We conjecture that there is not even an institution morphism from $\mathcal{I}_{cc}$ to $\mathcal{I}_{mts}$. (Compare with Proposition 14.)

8   Conclusions and Future Work

In this paper we have studied the relationships between three notions of behavioural preorders that have been proposed in the literature: refinement over modal transition systems, and the covariant-contravariant simulation and the partial bisimulation preorders over labelled transition systems. We have provided mutual translations between modal transition systems and labelled transition systems that preserve, and reflect, refinement and the covariant-contravariant simulation preorder, as well as the the modal properties that can be expressed in the logics that characterize those preorders. We have also offered a translation from labelled transition systems modulo the partial bisimulation preorder into the same model modulo the covariant-contravariant simulation preorder, together with some evidence that the former model is less expressive than the latter. Finally, in order to gain more insight into the relationships between modal transition systems modulo refinement and labelled transition systems modulo the covariant-contravariant simulation preorder, we have also phrased and studied their connections in the context of institutions.

The work presented in the study opens several interesting avenues for future research. Here we limit ourselves to mentioning a few research directions that we plan to pursue in future work.

First of all, it would be interesting to study the relationships between the LTS-based models we have considered in this article and variations on the MTS model surveyed in, for instance, [1]. In particular, the third author recently contributed in [7] to the comparison of several refinement settings, including modal and mixed transition systems. The developments in that paper offer a different approach to the comparison and application of the formalisms studied in this article.

In [6], three of the authors gave a ground-complete axiomatization of the covariant-contravariant simulation preorder over the language BCCS [13]. It would be interesting to see whether the translations between MTSs and LTSs we have provided in this paper can be used to lift that axiomatization result, as well as results on the nonexistence of finite (in)equational axiomatizations, to the setting of modal transition systems modulo refinement, using the BCCS-like syntax for MTSs given in [3]. We also intend to study whether our translations can be used to obtain characteristic-formula constructions [3,10,16] for one model from extant results on the existence of characteristic formulae for the other.

The existence of characteristic formulae allows one to reduce checking the existence of a behavioural relation between two processes to a model checking question. Conversely, the main result from [3] offers a complete characterization of the model checking questions of the form $(M, m) \models \varphi$, where M is an MTS and φ is a formula in the logic for MTSs considered in this paper, that can be reduced to checking for the existence of a refinement between (M_φ, m_φ) and (M, m), where (M_φ, m_φ) is an MTS with a distinguished state that 'graphically represents' the formula φ. In future work, we plan to offer a characterization of the logical specifications that can be 'graphically represented' by LTSs modulo the covariant-contravariant simulation preorder and partial bisimilarity. Such characterizations may shed further light on the relative expressive power of the two formalisms and may give further evidence of the fact that LTSs modulo the covariant-contravariant simulation preorder are, in some suitable formal sense, more expressive than LTSs modulo partial bisimilarity.

From the theoretical point of view, it would also be satisfying to settle our conjecture that there is no institution morphism from $\mathcal{I}_{cc}$ to $\mathcal{I}_{mts}$.

Last, but not least, the development of the notion of partial bisimulation in [2] has been motivated by the desire to develop a process-algebraic model within which one can study topics in the field of *supervisory control* [15]. Recently, MTSs have been used as a suitable model for the specification of service-oriented applications, and results on the supervisory control of systems whose specification is given in that formalism have been presented in, e.g., [4,8]. It is a very interesting area for future research to study whether the mutual translations between MTSs modulo refinement and LTSs modulo the covariant-contravariant simulation preorder can be used to transfer results on supervisory control from MTSs to LTSs. One may also wish to investigate directly the adaptation of the supervisory control theory of Ramadge and Wonham to the enforcement of specifications given in terms of LTSs modulo the covariant-contravariant simulation preorder.

References

1. Antonik, A., Huth, M., Larsen, K.G., Nyman, U., Wąsowski, A.: 20 years of modal and mixed specifications. Bull. Eur. Assoc. Theor. Comput. Sci. EATCS 95, 94–129 (2008)
2. Baeten, J., van Beek, D., Luttik, B., Markovski, J., Rooda, J.: Partial bisimulation. SE Report 2010-04, Systems Engineering Group, Department of Mechanical Engineering, Eindhoven University of Technology (2010)
3. Boudol, G., Larsen, K.G.: Graphical versus logical specifications. Theoretical Comput. Sci. 106(1), 3–20 (1992)
4. Darondeau, P., Dubreil, J., Marchand, H.: Supervisory control for modal specifications of services. In: Proceedings of WODES 2010, Berlin, Germany, August 30–September 1 (2010) (to appear)
5. Fábregas, I., de Frutos Escrig, D., Palomino, M.: Non-Strongly Stable Orders also Define Interesting Simulation Relations. In: Kurz, A., Lenisa, M., Tarlecki, A. (eds.) CALCO 2009. LNCS, vol. 5728, pp. 221–235. Springer, Heidelberg (2009)
6. Fábregas, I., de Frutos Escrig, D., Palomino, M.: Logics for Contravariant Simulations. In: Hatcliff, J., Zucca, E. (eds.) FMOODS/ FORTE 2010. LNCS, vol. 6117, pp. 224–231. Springer, Heidelberg (2010)
7. Fecher, H., de Frutos-Escrig, D., Lüttgen, G., Schmidt, H.: On the Expressiveness of Refinement Settings. In: Arbab, F., Sirjani, M. (eds.) FSEN 2009. LNCS, vol. 5961, pp. 276–291. Springer, Heidelberg (2010)
8. Feuillade, G., Pinchinat, S.: Modal specifications for the control theory of discrete event systems. Discrete Event Dynamical Systems 17, 211–232 (2007)
9. Goguen, J.A., Burstall, R.M.: Institutions: Abstract model theory for specification and programming. J. ACM 39(1), 95–146 (1992)
10. Graf, S., Sifakis, J.: A modal characterization of observational congruence on finite terms of CCS. Information and Control 68(1–3), 125–145 (1986)
11. Larsen, K.G.: Modal Specifications. In: Sifakis, J. (ed.) CAV 1989. LNCS, vol. 407, pp. 232–246. Springer, Heidelberg (1990)
12. Larsen, K.G., Thomsen, B.: A modal process logic. In: Proceedings of 3rd Annual Symposium on Logic in Computer Science, Edinburgh, pp. 203–210. IEEE Computer Society Press (1988)
13. Milner, R.: Communication and Concurrency. Prentice-Hall International, Englewood Cliffs (1989)
14. Park, D.: Concurrency and automata on infinite sequences. In: Deussen, P. (ed.) GI-TCS 1981. LNCS, vol. 104, pp. 167–183. Springer, Heidelberg (1981)
15. Ramadge, P., Wonham, W.: Supervisory control of a class of discrete event processes. SIAM Journal of Control and Optimization 25, 206–230 (1987)
16. Steffen, B., Ingólfsdóttir, A.: Characteristic formulae for processes with divergence. Information and Computation 110(1), 149–163 (1994)

Decidability of Behavioral Equivalences in Process Calculi with Name Scoping*

Chaodong He, Yuxi Fu, and Hongfei Fu

BASICS, Department of Computer Science,
Shanghai Jiao Tong University, Shanghai 200240, China,
MOE-MS Key Laboratory for Intelligent Computing and Intelligent Systems

Abstract. Local channels and their name scoping rules play a significant role in the study of the expressiveness of process calculi. The paper
contributes to the understanding of the expressiveness in the context
of CCS by studying the decidability issues of the bisimilarity/similarity
checking problems. The strong bisimilarity for a pair of processes in
the calculi with only static local channels is shown Π_1^0-complete. The
strong bisimilarity between those processes and the finite state processes
is proved decidable. The strong similarity between the finite state processes and the processes without name-passing capability is also shown
decidable.

1 Introduction

Process calculi are usually Turing complete. The known proofs of Turing completeness share the same guideline that counting is represented as the nesting of
suitable components [4,6,20]. In the name-passing calculi [24,26], the encodings
of counter [4,6] depend on the existence of *local channels* and some degrees of
name-passing capabilities. In the setting of CCS-like calculi, there are several
Turing complete variants in which local channels are provided by the localization operation while name-passing capabilities are partly obtained by an explicit
operation such as *parametric definition* [23,11] or *relabeling* [22], or by an implicit
dynamic-scoping recursion [28,4].

A fundamental problem in the area of system verification is that of *equivalence (or preorder) checking* [3]. In concurrency theory these are the problems
of deciding whether two given processes are behaviorally equal, or whether one
process is behavioral close to the other. Among these equivalences (or preorders),
bisimilarity (or similarity) plays a prominent role.

This paper explores the decidability issues of bisimilarity/similarity checking
problems for various subcalculi of CCS classified by different name scoping rules,
in which the capability of producing and manipulating local channels becomes
weaker and weaker. These decidability results contribute to the understanding
of the way productions and mobilities of local channels affect the expressiveness.

---

* The work is supported by NSFC (60873034, 61033002).

F. Arbab and M. Sirjani (Eds.): FSEN 2011, LNCS 7141, pp. 284–298, 2012.

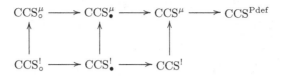

Fig. 1. CCS Hierarchy

The seven subcalculi of CCS studied in this paper are given in Fig. 1. In the diagram an arrow ' $\longrightarrow$ ' indicates the sub-language relationship. These seven subcalculi are further divided into four classes in which the scoping rules of local channel names are weakened gradually.

The first class contains CCS^{Pdef}, the full CCS with parametric definition (but without relabeling), which is known to be Turing complete [11]. In CCS^{Pdef} process copies can be nested at arbitrary depth by the name-passing capability offered by parametric definition. Turing completeness implies that all behavioral equivalences and preorders for CCS^{Pdef} are undecidable.

The second class contains CCS^{μ} and $CCS^{!}$. These two subcalculi have the power of producing new local channels but do not have the power of passing names around. In both models the infinite behaviors are specified by (static scoping) recursion and replication respectively. They are not Turing complete because they are not expressive enough to define the process *Counter* in the sense of Section 2.5 of [10]. For the readers unfamiliar with the static scoping recursion, we give the following illustration. Static scoping and dynamic scoping are different ways of manipulating local names when unfolding recursions [11,10]. When a process is defined as $P \stackrel{\text{def}}{=} \mu X.(a \,|\, (a)(\overline{a} \,|\, X))$, the static scoping requires that the local a and the global a must be distinguished before unfolding. That is, $\mu X.(a \,|\, (a)(\overline{a} \,|\, X))$ is understood the same as $\mu X.(a \,|\, (a')(\overline{a'} \,|\, X))$. The recursion used in [4,6] admits dynamic scoping, meaning that P should be understood as $a \,|\, (a)(\overline{a} \,|\, a \,|\, (a)(\overline{a} \,|\, P))$, which induces the infinite computation $P \stackrel{\tau}{\longrightarrow} a \,|\, (a)(\mathbf{0} \,|\, \mathbf{0} \,|\, (a)(\overline{a} \,|\, P)) \stackrel{\tau}{\longrightarrow} \ldots$. It is pointed out in [11] that the dynamic scoping recursion can be encoded via parametric definition. For this reason we shall only consider the parametric definition in this paper.

The third class contains $CCS^{\mu}_{\bullet}$ and $CCS^{!}_{\bullet}$. They are the subcalculi of CCS^{μ} and $CCS^{!}$ which have only static local names. Here 'static' means that no local channels can be produced during the evolution of a process. In these situations, localizations can only act as the outermost constructors, and processes in $CCS^{\mu}_{\bullet}$ and $CCS^{!}_{\bullet}$ can be assumed in the form $(\widetilde{a})P$ where the inner process P is localization-free. In this paper the word 'static' is only used in the context of 'static local names' in order to avoid confusion with the 'static scoping recursion'.

The fourth class contains $CCS^{\mu}_{\circ}$ and $CCS^{!}_{\circ}$, where the localization operator are removed completely. For those subcalculi, strong bisimilarity is decidable [7].

$\mathcal{L}$	$\mathcal{L} \sim \mathcal{L}$	$\mathcal{L} \sim \mathbf{FS}$	$\mathbf{FS} \precsim \mathcal{L}$	$\mathcal{L} \precsim \mathbf{FS}$
$\mathrm{CCS}_{\circ}^{!}$	✓ [7]	✓ [7]	?	?
$\mathrm{CCS}_{\circ}^{\mu}$	✓ [7]	✓ [7]	?	?
$\mathrm{CCS}_{\bullet}^{!}$	?	?	?	?
$\mathrm{CCS}_{\bullet}^{\mu}$	?	?	?	?
$\mathrm{CCS}^{!}$	?	?	?	?
CCS^{μ}	?	?	?	?
$\mathrm{CCS}^{\mathrm{Pdef}}$	× [4,11]	× [4,11]	× [4,11]	× [4,11]

"$\sim$": strong bisimilarity
"$\precsim$": strong similarity

"✓": known decidable
"×": known undecidable
"?": unknown

Fig. 2. Problems to Explore

We will use notation $\mathcal{L}_1 \sim \mathcal{L}_2$ (or $\mathcal{L}_1 \precsim \mathcal{L}_2$) to indicate the problem of checking strong bisimilarity (or strong similarity) between an $\mathcal{L}_1$ process and an $\mathcal{L}_2$ process. These problems are indicated by the question marks in the table of Fig. 2. The notation **FS** stands for the class of the finite state processes. The contributions of this paper are summarized as follows.

- We show the undecidability (Π_1^0-hardness) of $\mathrm{CCS}_{\bullet}^{\mu} \sim \mathrm{CCS}_{\bullet}^{\mu}$ by a reduction from the halting problem of Minsky Machine. The relevant technique is called 'Defender's Forcing' [14,18], which is widely used in undecidability proofs for bisimilarity checking. Typical examples of this technique can also be found in [17,18]. The reduction is then modified to show the undecidability (Π_1^0-hardness) of $\mathrm{CCS}_{\bullet}^{!} \sim \mathrm{CCS}_{\bullet}^{!}$. This resolves the four problems in the first column of the table.
- Busi, Gabbrielli and Zavattaro establish in [5] the undecidability (Σ_1^0-hardness) of the weak bisimilarity of $\mathrm{CCS}^{!}$. By modifying the proof of Busi et al., $\mathrm{CCS}^{!} \sim \mathbf{FS}$ is shown undecidable (Π_1^0-hard), which immediately implies the undecidability (Π_1^0-hardness) of $\mathrm{CCS}^{\mu} \sim \mathbf{FS}$.
- By constructing a translation from $\mathrm{CCS}_{\bullet}^{!}$ to the Labeled Petri Net, we demonstrate the decidability of $\mathrm{CCS}_{\bullet}^{!} \sim \mathbf{FS}$, $\mathrm{CCS}_{\bullet}^{!} \precsim \mathbf{FS}$ and $\mathbf{FS} \precsim \mathrm{CCS}_{\bullet}^{!}$, making use of Jančar and Moller's decidability result [16] on the Labeled Petri Nets. The same approach applies to $\mathrm{CCS}_{\bullet}^{\mu}$.
- We show that $\mathbf{FS} \precsim \mathrm{CCS}^{!}$ is decidable. The technique used in the proof is *simulation base*, originated from the technique of *bisimulation base* pioneered by Caucal and widely used in decidability proofs of bisimilarity. Our proof also makes use of expansion tree presented in [17] and the *well-structured transition system* [8] for $\mathrm{CCS}^{!}$ [4,10]. In literature there are examples of formalisms [19] in which bisimilarity is decidable while similarity is not. We are not aware of any examples showing that the opposite situation happens. This result is more or less surprising.

The finite branching property guarantees that the bisimilarity can be approximated in the sense that $P \not\sim Q$ if and only if $P \not\sim_n Q$ for some n. The approximation can also be applied to the similarity relation. It necessarily implies that all the problems in Fig. 2 are actually in Π_1^0. So we only need to show Π_1^0-hardness to get Π_1^0-completeness. We remark that a relation $R(x)$ is in Σ_1^0 (resp. Π_1^0) in arithmetic hierarchy if it can be expressed by $\exists y. S(x, y)$

Choice $\dfrac{}{\sum_{i=1}^n \lambda_i.E_i \xrightarrow{\lambda_i} E_i}$ Composition $\dfrac{E \xrightarrow{\lambda} E'}{E\,|\,F \xrightarrow{\lambda} E'\,|\,F}$ $\dfrac{E \xrightarrow{l} E' \quad F \xrightarrow{\bar{l}} F'}{E\,|\,F \xrightarrow{\tau} E'\,|\,F'}$

Localization $\dfrac{E \xrightarrow{\lambda} E' \quad a \text{ not appear in } \lambda}{(a)E \xrightarrow{\lambda} (a)E'}$ Fixpoint $\dfrac{E\{\mu X.E/X\} \xrightarrow{\lambda} E'}{\mu X.E \xrightarrow{\lambda} E'}$

Fig. 3. Semantics of CCS^μ

(resp. $\forall y.S(x,y)$) for some decidable relation $S(x,y)$. Clearly $R(x)$ is in Σ_1^0 if and only if its complement is in Π_1^0.

The rest of the paper is organized as follows. Section 2 lays down the preliminaries. Section 3 investigates the problems of deciding the strong bisimilarity on the CCS^μ processes and the $\text{CCS}^!$ processes. Section 4 considers the problem of deciding the strong bisimilarity/similarity between a $\text{CCS}^!/\text{CCS}^\mu$ process and a finite state process. Section 5 gives concluding remarks.

Most proofs and technical details are omitted. See [13] for complete coverage.

2   Basic Definition and Notation

To describe the interactions between systems, we need channel names. The set of the names $\mathcal{N}$ is ranged over by $a, b, c, \ldots$, and the set of the names and the conames $\mathcal{N} \cup \overline{\mathcal{N}}$ is ranged over by $l, \ldots$. The set of the action labels $\mathcal{A} = \mathcal{N} \cup \overline{\mathcal{N}} \cup \{\tau\}$ is ranged over by λ. To define the fixpoint operator and we need a set of *process variables* $\mathcal{V}$ ranged over by X, Y, Z.

The set $\mathcal{E}_{\text{CCS}^\mu}$ of CCS^μ terms is generated by the following grammar.

$$E ::= \mathbf{0} \quad | \quad X \quad | \quad \sum_{i=1}^n \lambda_i.E_i \quad | \quad E\,|\,E' \quad | \quad (a)E \quad | \quad \mu X.E.$$

A name a appeared in a localization term $(a)E$ is *local*. A name is *global* if it is not local. The variable X in the fixpoint term $\mu X.E$ is *bound*. A variable is *free* if it is not bound. A CCS^μ term containing no free variables is a CCS^μ *process*.

In $\mu X.E$ it is not required that X be guarded in E because unguarded recursion can be encoded by guarded recursion in CCS^μ [10]. With guarded recursion and guarded choice $\sum_{i=1}^n \lambda_i.E_i$, finite branching property is guaranteed. Once unguarded recursion is admitted, replication $!P$ can be defined by the recursion $\mu X.(X\,|\,P)$.

The standard semantics of CCS^μ is given by the *labeled transition system* $(\mathcal{E}_{\text{CCS}^\mu}, \mathcal{A}, \longrightarrow)$, where the elements of $\mathcal{E}_{\text{CCS}^\mu}$ are often referred to as *states*. The relation $\longrightarrow \subseteq \mathcal{E}_{\text{CCS}^\mu} \times \mathcal{A} \times \mathcal{E}_{\text{CCS}^\mu}$ is the *transition* relation. The membership $(E, \lambda, E') \in \longrightarrow$ is always indicated by $E \xrightarrow{\lambda} E'$. The relation $\longrightarrow$ is generated inductively by the rules defined in Fig. 3. The symmetric rules are omitted.

Standard notations and conventions in process calculi will be used throughout the paper. The inactive process $\mathbf{0}$ is omitted in most occasions. For instance

$a.b.\mathbf{0}$ is abbreviated to $a.b$. A finite sequence (or set) of names $a_1, \ldots, a_n$ is often abbreviated to $\tilde{a}$. The guarded choice term $\sum_{i=1}^{n} \lambda_i.E_i$ is usually written as $\lambda_1.E_1 + \cdots + \lambda_n.E_n$. Processes are not distinguished syntactically up to the commutative monoid generated by '$+$' and '$|$'. We shall write $\prod_{i=1}^{n} P_i$ for $P_1 | \ldots | P_n$. The notation '$\equiv$' is used to indicate syntactic congruence. We shall write $\mathcal{P}_\mathcal{L}$ for the set of the processes definable in $\mathcal{L}$. The set of the *derivatives* of a process P, denoted by $\mathtt{Drv}(P)$, is the set of the processes P' such that $P \xrightarrow{\lambda_1} \cdots \xrightarrow{\lambda_n} P'$ for some $n \geq 0$ and $\lambda_1, \ldots, \lambda_n \in \mathcal{A}$.

CCS$^!$ is obtained from CCS$^\mu$ by using the *replication* instead of the fixpoint operation. The grammar is defined as follows:

$$P ::= \mathbf{0} \quad | \quad \sum_{i=1}^{n} \lambda_i.P_i \quad | \quad P \,|\, P' \quad | \quad (a)P \quad | \quad !P.$$

The operational semantics of the replication stated below is from [4,5], which enjoys the finite branching property.

$$\text{Replication} \quad \frac{P \xrightarrow{\lambda} P'}{!P \xrightarrow{\lambda} P' \,|\, !P} \qquad \frac{P \xrightarrow{l} P' \quad P \xrightarrow{\bar{l}} P''}{!P \xrightarrow{\tau} P' \,|\, P'' \,|\, !P}$$

The advantage of the replication is that one could give a first order presentation of CCS. There is no need for process variables. This is why the above grammar and rules are defined on the set of the processes, not on the set of the terms.

A binary relation $\mathcal{R}$ on $\mathcal{P}_\mathcal{L}$ is a *strong simulation* if, for each pair $(P, Q) \in \mathcal{R}$, P can be simulated by Q in the following sense:

If $P \xrightarrow{\lambda} P'$, then $Q \xrightarrow{\lambda} Q'$ for some Q' such that $(P', Q') \in \mathcal{R}$.

A binary relation $\mathcal{R}$ is a *strong bisimulation* if both $\mathcal{R}$ and its inverse $\mathcal{R}^{-1}$ are strong simulations. The *strong similarity* $\precsim$ is the largest strong simulation, and the *strong bisimilarity* $\sim$ is the largest strong bisimulation. The former is a preorder and the latter is an equivalence.

Strong bisimilarity has a game theoretic characterization known as the *bisimulation game*. It is a complete-information dynamic game played by two players named 'attacker' and 'defender'. The labeled transition system $(\mathcal{P}_\mathcal{L}, \mathcal{A}, \longrightarrow)$ is perceived as a game-board. During the play the current position is described by a pair of states $(P_1, P_{-1}) \in \mathcal{P}_\mathcal{L} \times \mathcal{P}_\mathcal{L}$. The game is played in rounds. In each round the players change the position according to the following rules:

1. The attacker chooses a state $i \in \{1, -1\}$, an action $\lambda \in \mathcal{A}$, and some $P_i' \in \mathcal{P}_\mathcal{L}$ such that $P_i \xrightarrow{\lambda} P_i'$.
2. The defender responds by choosing some $P_{-i}' \in \mathcal{P}_\mathcal{L}$ such that $P_{-i} \xrightarrow{\lambda} P_{-i}'$; and then (P_1', P_{-1}') becomes the current position of the next round.

If the defender never gets stuck, it wins. Otherwise the attacker wins. It is easy to see that the defender has a winning strategy in the bisimulation game starting from the position (P, Q) if and only if $P \sim Q$.

3   Undecidability of Strong Bisimilarity

This section aims at the undecidability of $CCS^\mu \sim CCS^\mu$ and $CCS^! \sim CCS^!$. In fact, by many-one reductions from the halting problem of Minsky Machines, it can be shown that both $CCS^\mu_\bullet \sim CCS^\mu_\bullet$ and $CCS^!_\bullet \sim CCS^!_\bullet$ are Π^0_1-complete.

Two-register *Minsky Machine* is a well-known Turing complete computational model [25]. A Minsky Machine $\mathbb{R}$ has two registers r_1 and r_2 that can hold arbitrary large natural numbers. The behavior of $\mathbb{R}$ is specified by a sequence of instructions $\{(1 : I_1), (2 : I_2), \ldots, (n-1 : I_{n-1}), (n : \texttt{halt})\}$. For each $i \in \{1, \ldots, n-1\}$, the i-th instruction may be in one of two forms:

- $(i : Succ(r_j))$: The instruction adds 1 to the content of the register r_j and $i+1$ becomes the value of the program counter.
- $(i : Decjump(r_j, s))$: If the content of the register r_j is not zero, the instruction decreases it by 1 and $i+1$ becomes the value of the program counter; otherwise s becomes the value of the program counter.

The configuration of $\mathbb{R}$ is given by the tuple $(i; c1, c2)$ where i is the program counter indicating the instruction to be executed, and $c1, c2$ are the current contents of the registers. The computation of $\mathbb{R}$ is defined in a natural way via a (finite or infinite) sequence of configurations starting from a certain initial configuration. Whenever the n-th instruction (known as the halting state) is reached, the computation terminates.

The halting problem of Two-register Minsky Machines, whose undecidability is well-known, is formally stated as follows:

Problem:	HALTINGMINSKYMACHINE
Instance:	A Two-register Minsky Machine $\mathbb{R}$.
Question:	Does the computation of $\mathbb{R}$ terminate when $\mathbb{R}$ starts from the initial configuration $(1; 0, 0)$?

Lemma 1. HALTINGMINSKYMACHINE *is undecidable. It is Σ^0_1-complete in the arithmetic hierarchy.*

If a process calculus $\mathcal{L}$ is able to encode the computation of a Minsky Machine faithfully, undecidability of $\mathcal{L} \sim \mathcal{L}$ can be obtained by a straightforward reduction from HALTINGMINSKYMACHINE, which confirms that the i-th Minsky Machine $\mathbb{R}_i$ does not halt if and only if the interpretation $P_{\mathbb{R}_i}$ of $\mathbb{R}_i$ is strongly bisimilar to $!\tau$. Recall that there is no such reduction for any calculi in Fig. 1 except for CCS^{Pdef}.

In the rest of this section, we outline the reductions that demonstrate the undecidability of $CCS^\mu_\bullet \sim CCS^\mu_\bullet$ and $CCS^!_\bullet \sim CCS^!_\bullet$.

3.1   Undecidability of $CCS^\mu_\bullet \sim CCS^\mu_\bullet$

The idea is to construct a $CCS^\mu_\bullet$ process which models a given Minsky Machine $\mathbb{R}$ in a nondeterministic fashion. The encoding is nondeterministic because it introduces unfaithful computations which do not follow the expected behavior of $\mathbb{R}$.

Two slightly modified copies of the constructed process are taken for bisimilarity checking. The modifications guarantee that in the bisimulation game, whenever the attacker takes the 'unfaithful' move at some round, the defender have the ability to punish the attacker by moving to a pair of trivially bisimilar states. Thus the attacker are 'forced' to take the 'faithful' move at each round and the defender will lose the game if $\mathbb{R}$ ever halts. This technique is known as 'Defender's Forcing' [14,18].

The construction is motivated by a construction in [17]. For convenience constant definitions are used instead of μ-operations. Since localization operator must not appear underneath any μ-operations, no confusion will arise. Two slightly modified copies are given directly instead of describing the encoding in advance.

Let $\mathbb{R}$ be an instance of HALTINGMINSKYMACHINE whose instruction set is $\{(1 : I_1), (2 : I_2), \ldots, (n-1 : I_{n-1}), (n : \texttt{halt})\}$. Without using the localization operator the processes $\{P_i\}_{i=1}^n$ and $\{Q_i\}_{i=1}^n$ are defined as follows:

- $P_i \overset{\text{def}}{=} \overline{\text{inc}_j}.P_{i+1}$ and $Q_i \overset{\text{def}}{=} \overline{\text{inc}_j}.Q_{i+1}$ if the i-th instruction is $(i : Succ(r_j))$.
- If the i-th instruction is $(i : Decjump(r_j, s))$, then let

$$P_i \overset{\text{def}}{=} \overline{\text{dec}_j}.d.P_{i+1} + \overline{\text{zero}_j}.(\overline{\text{tt}}.z.P_s + \overline{\text{ff}}.z.Q_s),$$

$$Q_i \overset{\text{def}}{=} \overline{\text{dec}_j}.d.Q_{i+1} + \overline{\text{zero}_j}.(\overline{\text{tt}}.z.Q_s + \overline{\text{ff}}.z.P_s).$$

- $P_n \overset{\text{def}}{=} \overline{\text{halt}}.\mathbf{0}$ and $Q_n \overset{\text{def}}{=} \mathbf{0}$ for the n-th instruction $(n : \texttt{halt})$.

The processes $\{P_i\}_{i=1}^n$ and $\{Q_i\}_{i=1}^n$ are two families of slightly different processes that interpret the instructions of $\mathbb{R}$. Special attention should be paid to the gadget $\overline{\text{ff}}.z.Q_s$ (or $\overline{\text{ff}}.z.P_s$) in the defining equation of P_i (or Q_i) for instruction $(i : Decjump(r_j, s))$. This gadget is designed to 'force' the attacker to stick to the faithful moves. Also notice that the only asymmetry between P_i's and Q_i's is that P_n can perform a special action $\overline{\text{halt}}$ whereas Q_n cannot.

The processes $PseudoCounter_j(k)$, for $j \in \{1, 2\}$, introduced below are used to partially model the registers of $\mathbb{R}$.

$$PseudoCounter_j(k) \overset{\text{def}}{=} \underbrace{C_j \mid C_j \mid \ldots \mid C_j}_{k} \mid O_j,$$

where O_j and C_j are defined as follows without using the localization operation:

$$O_j \overset{\text{def}}{=} \text{inc}_j.(C_j \mid O_j) + \text{zero}_j.\text{tt}.O_j,$$

$$C_j \overset{\text{def}}{=} \text{dec}_j.\mathbf{0} + \text{zero}_j.\text{ff}.C_j.$$

The process $PseudoCounter_j$'s are the weak forms of the counter, for they lack the ability to zero-test — they can make a 'zero' move while the actual value of the counters are positive. However $PseudoCounter_j$'s are good enough for the purpose of deriving the undecidability results we want.

Finally every configuration of $\mathbb{R}$ is modeled by the following two slightly different processes.

$$Config_P(i; c_1, c_2) \stackrel{\text{def}}{=} (\widetilde{\mathsf{inc}})(\widetilde{\mathsf{dec}})(\widetilde{\mathsf{zero}})(\mathsf{tt})(\mathsf{ff})$$
$$(P_i \mid PseudoCounter_1(c_1) \mid PseudoCounter_2(c_2)),$$
$$Config_Q(i; c_1, c_2) \stackrel{\text{def}}{=} (\widetilde{\mathsf{inc}})(\widetilde{\mathsf{dec}})(\widetilde{\mathsf{zero}})(\mathsf{tt})(\mathsf{ff})$$
$$(Q_i \mid PseudoCounter_1(c_1) \mid PseudoCounter_2(c_2)).$$

The correctness of the above encoding is guaranteed by Lemma 2, Lemma 3, and Lemma 4, which eventually lead to Theorem 1.

Lemma 2. *Let $(i; c1, c2)$ be a configuration of $\mathbb{R}$ and $(i : Succ(r_j))$ be the i-th instruction. Then there is a unique continuation of the bisimulation game from the pair of processes $Config_P(i; c_1, c_2)$ and $Config_Q(i; c_1, c_2)$ such that, after one round, the players reach the pair $Config_P(i; c_1', c_2')$ and $Config_Q(i; c_1', c_2')$ where $c_j' = c_j + 1$ and $c_{3-j}' = c_{3-j}$.*

Lemma 3. *Let $(i; c1, c2)$ be a configuration of $\mathbb{R}$ and $(i : Decjump(r_j, s))$ be the i-th instruction. Assume that a bisimulation game is played from the pair $Config_P(i; c_1, c_2)$ and $Config_Q(i; c_1, c_2)$. The followings hold:*

(a) *If $c_j = 0$, then there is a unique continuation of the game such that after three rounds, the players reach the pair $Config_P(s; c_1, c_2)$ and $Config_Q(s; c_1, c_2)$.*
(b) *If $c_j > 0$ and the attacker chooses the τ action induced by the synchronization via channel dec_j, then the defender has a way to continue the game such that, after two rounds, $Config_P(i; c_1', c_2')$ and $Config_Q(i; c_1', c_2')$ are reached, where $c_j' = c_j - 1$ and $c_{3-j}' = c_{3-j}$. If the defender does not play in this way, there is a way for the attacker to win the game.*
(c) *If $c_j > 0$ and the attacker chooses the τ action induced by the synchronization via channel zero_j, then there is a way for the defender to win the game.*

Lemma 4. *The execution of $\mathbb{R}$ from the configuration $(1; 0, 0)$ terminates if and only if $Config_P(1; 0, 0) \not\sim Config_Q(1; 0, 0)$.*

Theorem 1. *Both $\mathrm{CCS}_\bullet^\mu \sim \mathrm{CCS}_\bullet^\mu$ and $\mathrm{CCS}^\mu \sim \mathrm{CCS}^\mu$ are Π_1^0-complete.*

3.2   Undecidability of $\mathrm{CCS}_\bullet^! \sim \mathrm{CCS}_\bullet^!$

The result established in Section 3.1 does not immediately imply the same result for $\mathrm{CCS}^!/\mathrm{CCS}_\bullet^!$. A well known fact is that recursion can be turned into replication [26,11] by the encoding $[\![\_]\!]$ whose nontrivial part is given by $[\![X_i]\!] = \overline{a_i}.0$ and $[\![\mu X_i.E]\!] = (a_i)(\overline{a_i} \mid !a_i.[\![E]\!])$, where names a_i's are fresh. However this encoding does not give rise to a strong bisimulation. Another problem is that an encoding from CCS^μ to $\mathrm{CCS}^!$ would not always produce an encoding from $\mathrm{CCS}_\bullet^\mu$ to $\mathrm{CCS}_\bullet^!$ automatically since they introduce additional local names.

Undecidability of $\mathrm{CCS}_\bullet^! \sim \mathrm{CCS}_\bullet^!$ does not rely on the existence of such an encoding. The basic idea and the construction in Section 3.1 can be repeated with subtle modifications. The intuition of the next encoding is to interpret every instruction of a Minsky Machine $\mathbb{R}$ by a process of the form $!addr.opr$, where $addr$ should be understood as the address of the instruction and opr the operation of the instruction. The difficulty is to guarantee that only a finite number of local channels are necessary. In the following definition $2n$ extra static local channels $\{\mathsf{inst}_P^i, \mathsf{inst}_Q^i\}_{i=1}^n$ are used.

- If the i-th instruction is $(i : Succ(r_j))$, let

$$P_i \stackrel{\text{def}}{=} !\mathsf{inst}_P^i.\overline{\mathsf{inc}_j}.\overline{\mathsf{inst}_P^{i+1}}, \qquad Q_i \stackrel{\text{def}}{=} !\mathsf{inst}_Q^i.\overline{\mathsf{inc}_j}.\overline{\mathsf{inst}_Q^{i+1}}.$$

- If the i-th instruction is $(i : Decjump(r_j, s))$, let

$$P_i \stackrel{\text{def}}{=} !\mathsf{inst}_P^i.(\overline{\mathsf{dec}_j}.d.\overline{\mathsf{inst}_P^{i+1}} + \overline{\mathsf{zero}_j}.(\overline{\mathsf{tt}}.\tau.\tau.z.\overline{\mathsf{inst}_P^s} + \overline{\mathsf{ff}}.\mathsf{ack}.z.\overline{\mathsf{inst}_Q^s})),$$

$$Q_i \stackrel{\text{def}}{=} !\mathsf{inst}_Q^i.(\overline{\mathsf{dec}_j}.d.\overline{\mathsf{inst}_Q^{i+1}} + \overline{\mathsf{zero}_j}.(\overline{\mathsf{tt}}.\tau.\tau.z.\overline{\mathsf{inst}_Q^s} + \overline{\mathsf{ff}}.\mathsf{ack}.z.\overline{\mathsf{inst}_P^s})).$$

- For the n-th instruction $(n : \mathtt{halt})$, let

$$P_n \stackrel{\text{def}}{=} !\mathsf{inst}_P^n.\overline{\mathsf{halt}}.\mathbf{0}, \qquad Q_n \stackrel{\text{def}}{=} !\mathsf{inst}_Q^n.\mathbf{0}.$$

In the following modification of $PseudoCounter_j(k)$, $\{\mathsf{m}_j\}_{j=1}^2$ and ack are the only extra local channels introduced.

$$PseudoCounter_j(k) \stackrel{\text{def}}{=} \underbrace{C_j \mid C_j \mid \ldots \mid C_j}_{k} \mid O_j \mid !\mathsf{m}_j.\overline{\mathsf{ack}}.C_j,$$

where $O_j \stackrel{\text{def}}{=} !(\mathsf{inc}_j.C_j + \mathsf{zero}_j.\mathsf{tt})$, and $C_j \stackrel{\text{def}}{=} \mathsf{dec}_j + \mathsf{zero}_j.\mathsf{ff}.\overline{\mathsf{m}_j}$. When zero_j is triggered on some C_j, channel m_j is used to require a new copy of C_j from the resource $!\mathsf{m}_j.\overline{\mathsf{ack}}.C_j$, and after that, the channel ack ais used to inform the process that triggers the action zero_j. Such treatment will make the whole system sequential. As a side-effect it will take two more computation steps when the zero-testing is unfaithfully chosen by the attacker, and for the defender, two extra τ's are introduced into the definition of P_i and Q_i. The configuration $(i; c_1, c_2)$ of $\mathbb{R}$ is interpreted by the following two processes:

$$Config_P^!(i; c_1, c_2) \stackrel{\text{def}}{=} (\widetilde{\mathsf{inst}})(\widetilde{\mathsf{inc}})(\widetilde{\mathsf{dec}})(\widetilde{\mathsf{zero}})(\widetilde{\mathsf{m}})(\mathsf{tt})(\mathsf{ff})(\mathsf{ack})$$
$$\left(\overline{\mathsf{inst}_P^i} \mid \prod_{i=1}^n P_i \mid \prod_{i=1}^n Q_i \mid \prod_{j=1}^2 PseudoCounter_j(c_j)\right),$$

$$Config_Q^!(i; c_1, c_2) \stackrel{\text{def}}{=} (\widetilde{\mathsf{inst}})(\widetilde{\mathsf{inc}})(\widetilde{\mathsf{dec}})(\widetilde{\mathsf{zero}})(\widetilde{\mathsf{m}})(\mathsf{tt})(\mathsf{ff})(\mathsf{ack})$$
$$\left(\overline{\mathsf{inst}_Q^i} \mid \prod_{i=1}^n P_i \mid \prod_{i=1}^n Q_i \mid \prod_{j=1}^2 PseudoCounter_j(c_j)\right).$$

Using the same argument as in Section 3.1 we can prove the following.

Theorem 2. *Both* $\mathrm{CCS}_\bullet^! \sim \mathrm{CCS}_\bullet^!$ *and* $\mathrm{CCS}^! \sim \mathrm{CCS}^!$ *are* Π_1^0-*complete.*

4   Strong (Bi)similarity on Finite State Processes

We investigate in this section the decidability of strong bisimilarity/similarity between a $\mathrm{CCS}^!/\mathrm{CCS}^\mu$ process and a finite state process.

4.1   Undecidability of $\mathrm{CCS}^! \sim \mathbf{FS}$

The general problem $\mathrm{CCS}^! \sim \mathbf{FS}$ is undecidable. This result depends on the construction of Busi *et al* in Section 3 of [5], where Minsky Machines are encoded by $\mathrm{CCS}^!$ processes in a nondeterministic fashion. Using this encoding, one can show that if a Minsky Machine $\mathbb{R}$ does not halt, the encoding of $\mathbb{R}$ is a $\mathrm{CCS}^!$ process strongly bisimilar to $!\tau$, which cannot perform any visible actions and is divergent in every computation branch. If $\mathbb{R}$ does halt, the encoding of $\mathbb{R}$ has at least one divergent computation branch. This fact leads to Theorem 3.

Theorem 3. *The strong bisimilarity between a process* $P \in \mathcal{P}_{\mathrm{CCS}^!}$ *(or* $P \in \mathcal{P}_{\mathrm{CCS}^\mu}$*) and a fixed finite state process* $F \in \mathcal{P}_{\mathbf{FS}}$ *is* Π_1^0-*complete.*

It is worth noting that Theorem 1 of [5] confirms that the Minsky Machine $\mathbb{R}$ halts if and only if $\mathbb{R}$ is interpreted as a $\mathrm{CCS}^!$ process P satisfying $P \approx \tau.P + \overline{\mathsf{halt}}$, which establishes the Σ_1^0-hardness of the weak bisimilarity checking problem of $\mathrm{CCS}^!$. An interesting question is how to establish the Π_1^0-hardness of $\mathrm{CCS}^! \approx \mathbf{FS}$. It is widely believed that checking weak bisimilarity is harder than checking the strong bisimilarity. However the above construction does not immediately offer an answer to the latter problem.

4.2   Decidability of $\mathrm{CCS}^!_\bullet \sim \mathbf{FS}$

Although both $\mathrm{CCS}^! \sim \mathbf{FS}$ and $\mathrm{CCS}^\mu \sim \mathbf{FS}$ are undecidable in the general case, their restricted versions, $\mathrm{CCS}^!_\bullet \sim \mathbf{FS}$ and $\mathrm{CCS}^\mu_\bullet \sim \mathbf{FS}$, turn out to be decidable. These results are motivated by the following observations. Suppose $P \in \mathcal{P}_{\mathrm{CCS}^!_\bullet}$ or $P \in \mathcal{P}_{\mathrm{CCS}^\mu_\bullet}$. We may assume that P is of the form $(\tilde{a}) \prod_{i \in I} P_i$ in which $\tilde{a}$ are all the local names of P and every P_i is localization free and is not a composition. We call $(\tilde{a}) \prod_{i \in I} P_i$ a *concurrent normal form* of P, and every P_i a *concurrent component* of P. The key opoint is that no local names can be produced during the evolution of P, and the number of the possible concurrent components of all derivatives of P must be finite.

Based on the above observations, a strongly bisimilar encoding from $\mathrm{CCS}^!_\bullet$ (or $\mathrm{CCS}^\mu_\bullet$) to the Labeled Petri Net is constructed. With the help of the results of Jančar *et al.* [16], we know that the same problem for the Labeled Petri Net is decidable. Hence the decidability of $\mathrm{CCS}^!_\bullet \sim \mathbf{FS}$ and $\mathrm{CCS}^\mu_\bullet \sim \mathbf{FS}$.

Definition 1. *A Petri Net is a tuple* $N = (Q, T, F, M_0)$ *and a Labeled Petri Net is a tuple* $N = (Q, T, F, L, M_0)$, *where* Q *and* T *are finite disjoint sets of places and transitions respectively,* $F : (Q \times T) \cup (T \times Q) \to \mathbb{N}$ *is a flow function and* $L : T \to \mathcal{A}$ *is a labeling.* M_0 *is the initial marking, where a marking* M *is a function* $Q \to \mathbb{N}$ *assigning the number of tokens to each place.*

A transition $t \in T$ *is* enabled *at a marking* M, *denoted by* $M \xrightarrow{t}$, *if* $M(p) \geq F(p, t)$ *for every* $p \in Q$. *A transition* t enabled *at* M *may* fire *yielding the marking* M', *denoted by* $M \xrightarrow{t} M'$, *where* $M'(p) = M(p) - F(p, t) + F(t, p)$ *for all* $p \in Q$. *For each* $\lambda \in \mathcal{A}$, *we write* $M \xrightarrow{\lambda}$, *respectively* $M \xrightarrow{\lambda} M'$ *to mean that* $M \xrightarrow{t}$, *respectively* $M \xrightarrow{t} M'$ *for some* t *with* $L(t) = \lambda$.

In the above definition $\mathcal{A}$ is the set of the action labels. A Labeled Petri Net N can be viewed as a labeled transition system $(\mathbb{M}, \mathcal{A}, \longrightarrow)$ with $\mathbb{M}$ being the markings of N. Strong bisimilarity is defined accordingly. Suppose $Q = \{S_1, S_2, \ldots, S_n\}$ is the finite set of places. Labeled transition rules of the form $S_1^{m_1} S_2^{m_2} \ldots S_n^{m_n} \xrightarrow{\lambda} S_1^{m_1'} S_2^{m_2'} \ldots S_n^{m_n'}$ are used to indicate that there is a transition t whose label is λ and the flow function for t is defined by $F(S_i, t) = m_i$ and $F(t, S_i) = m_i'$ for every $i = 1, \ldots, n$. A marking M is denoted by $S_1^{M(S_1)} S_2^{M(S_2)} \ldots S_n^{M(S_n)}$, which can be viewed as a multiset over Q. Thus N is specified by $(Q, \mathcal{A}, \mathrm{Tr}, M_0)$, where Tr is the set of the labeled transition rules.

The next lemma is due to Jančar and Moller [16].

Lemma 5. *The strong bisimilarity between a marking* M_0 *of a Labeled Petri Net* N *and a finite state process* $F \in \mathcal{P}_{\mathbf{FS}}$ *is decidable.*

To describe the encoding from $\mathrm{CCS}_\bullet^!$ to the Labeled Petri Net, we need the following definitions and lemma, borrowed from [10].

Definition 2. *Suppose the* $\mathcal{P}_{\mathrm{CCS}^!}$ *process* P *does not contain any local names. The* concurrent subprocesses of P, *notation* $\mathrm{Csub}(P)$, *is defined inductively by*

$$\mathrm{Csub}(\mathbf{0}) \stackrel{\text{def}}{=} \emptyset,$$

$$\mathrm{Csub}(P' \mid P'') \stackrel{\text{def}}{=} \mathrm{Csub}(P') \cup \mathrm{Csub}(P''),$$

$$\mathrm{Csub}(\sum_{i=1}^{n} \lambda_i.P_i) \stackrel{\text{def}}{=} \{\sum_{i=1}^{n} \lambda_i.P_i\} \cup \bigcup_{i \in I} \mathrm{CSub}(P_i),$$

$$\mathrm{Csub}(!P') \stackrel{\text{def}}{=} \{!P'\} \cup \mathrm{Csub}(P').$$

Clearly if $P \equiv (a)P'$ is in concurrent normal form, then $\mathrm{Csub}(P) \stackrel{\text{def}}{=} \mathrm{Csub}(P')$.

Lemma 6. *For every process* P *of* $\mathrm{CCS}_\bullet^!$ *in concurrent normal form,* $\mathrm{Csub}(P)$ *is finite, and for every* $P' \in \mathrm{Drv}(P)$, $\mathrm{Csub}(P') \subseteq \mathrm{Csub}(P)$.

By letting $\mathrm{Csub}(\mu X.E) \stackrel{\text{def}}{=} \{\mu X.E\} \cup \mathrm{Csub}(E\{\mu X.E/X\})$, the counterpart of Lemma 6 for $\mathrm{CCS}_\bullet^\mu$ can be established. Now an encoding from the concurrent normal forms of $\mathrm{CCS}_\bullet^!$ or $\mathrm{CCS}_\bullet^\mu$ to the Labeled Petri Net is given in the proof of Lemma 7.

Lemma 7. *There is an algorithm such that, given process* $P \in \mathcal{P}_{\mathrm{CCS}^!_\bullet}$ *(or* $P \in \mathcal{P}_{\mathrm{CCS}^\mu}$*) in concurrent normal form, it outputs a Labeled Petri Net* N_P *with the same set of the action labels and* $P \sim N_P$.

Proof. Let $\mathrm{Csub}(P) = \{C_i \mid i \in I\}$ and $P = (\tilde{a})(\prod_{i \in I} C_i^{n_i})$. The Labeled Petri Net $N_P = (Q, \mathcal{A}, \longrightarrow, M_0)$ is defined as follows. The set of the places is $Q \stackrel{\text{def}}{=} \{[C_i] \mid i \in I\}$ and the initial marking is $M_0 \stackrel{\text{def}}{=} \prod_{i \in I}[C_i]^{n_i}$. The transition rules are defined inductively:

- If $C_i \stackrel{\lambda}{\longrightarrow} \prod_{j \in I} C_j^{n_j}$, then $[C_i] \stackrel{\lambda}{\longrightarrow} \prod_{j \in I}[C_j]^{n_j}$ is a rule provided that $\lambda \notin \tilde{m}$.
- If $C_{i_1} \stackrel{l}{\longrightarrow} \prod_{j \in I} C_j^{m_j}$ and $C_{i_2} \stackrel{\bar{l}}{\longrightarrow} \prod_{j \in I} C_j^{n_j}$, then $[C_{i_1}][C_{i_2}] \stackrel{\tau}{\longrightarrow} \prod_{j \in I}[C_j]^{m_j + n_j}$ is a rule.

The remaining work is to confirm that

$$\{((\tilde{a})(\prod_{i \in I} C_i^{n_i}), \prod_{i \in I}[C_i]^{n_i}) \mid n_i \geq 0 \text{ for } i \in I)\}$$

is a bisimulation. □

The combination of Lemma 7 and Lemma 5 produces the following.

Theorem 4. *The strong bisimilarity between a process* $P \in \mathcal{P}_{\mathrm{CCS}^!_\bullet}$ *(or* $P \in \mathcal{P}_{\mathrm{CCS}^\mu_\bullet}$*) and a finite state process* $F \in \mathcal{P}_{\mathbf{FS}}$ *is decidable.*

4.3 Decidability Results of Simulation Preorder

This part focuses on the problems $\mathcal{L} \precsim \mathbf{FS}$ and $\mathbf{FS} \precsim \mathcal{L}$. In the case that $\mathcal{L}$ is $\mathrm{CCS}^!_\bullet$ or $\mathrm{CCS}^\mu_\bullet$, the decidability result can be obtained via the same encoding provided in Section 4.2 with the help of the results already known for the Labeled Petri Net stated in Theorem 3.2 and Theorem 3.5 of [16].

Theorem 5. $\mathbf{FS} \precsim \mathrm{CCS}^!_\bullet$, $\mathbf{FS} \precsim \mathrm{CCS}^\mu_\bullet$, $\mathrm{CCS}^!_\bullet \precsim \mathbf{FS}$, $\mathrm{CCS}^\mu_\bullet \precsim \mathbf{FS}$ *are decidable.*

Now let's turn to $\mathrm{CCS}^!$ or CCS^μ. It has been suggested that the similarity checking is computational harder than the bisimilarity checking. This point is supported by two general proof methods applied to many process classes in a paper by Kučera and Mayr [19]. These two proof methods however cannot be used to show similar results for $\mathrm{CCS}^!$ or CCS^μ. As a matter of fact we will prove that $\mathbf{FS} \precsim \mathrm{CCS}^!$ is decidable, despite of the fact that $\mathbf{FS} \sim \mathrm{CCS}^!$ is undecidable by Theorem 3.

Our proof makes use of *simulation bases*. A simulation base is a finite subset of $\precsim$ consisting only of 'crucial' similar pairs from which a possibly infinite simulation relation can be produced algorithmically. Similarity will be decidable if simulation bases can be effectively constructed. For more on this technique, the reader is referred to [3,17,18].

In order to get a simulation base, we shall make good use of the *well-structured transition system* [8] of $\mathcal{P}_{\mathrm{CCS}^!}$, which was first pointed out by Busi *et al* in [4]. Here we follow the definition from [10] with slight amendment.

Definition 3. *A* well quasi order *$(X, \leq)$ is a preorder such that, for every infinite sequence $x_0, x_1, x_2, \ldots$ in X, there exist indexes $i < j$ such that $x_i \leq x_j$.*

Definition 4. *The* structural expansion $\preccurlyeq$ *on the* $\text{CCS}^!$ *processes is defined inductively as follows:*

- $P \preccurlyeq Q$ *whenever* $Q \equiv P \mid R$ *for some* R;
- $(a)P \preccurlyeq (a)Q$ *whenever* $P \preccurlyeq Q$;
- $P \preccurlyeq Q$ *whenever* $P \equiv P_1 \mid P_2$, $Q \equiv Q_1 \mid Q_2$, $P_1 \preccurlyeq Q_1$ *and* $P_2 \preccurlyeq Q_2$.

Notice that Definition 4 works up to structural congruence. Intuitively $P \preccurlyeq Q$ means that Q contains at least as many possible individual processes running concurrently as P. The relation $\preccurlyeq$ is transitive. Due to the syntactical nature of the definition, $\preccurlyeq$ is decidable. The next two technical lemmas, due to Busi *et al*, are crucial to the effective production of the simulation bases. The proof of Lemma 8 is straightforward. For a detailed proof of Lemma 9, one may consult [10].

Lemma 8 (Compatibility Lemma). *Suppose that P,Q are $\text{CCS}^!$ processes. If $P \preccurlyeq Q$ and $P \xrightarrow{\lambda} P'$, then Q' exists such that $Q \xrightarrow{\lambda} Q'$ and $P' \preccurlyeq Q'$.*

Lemma 9 (Expansion Lemma). *Let $P \in \mathcal{P}_{\text{CCS}^!}$, then $(\text{Drv}(P), \preccurlyeq)$ is a well quasi order.*

Using the techniques and lemmas discussed above, one can infer the following main result of the section.

Theorem 6. $\text{FS} \precsim \text{CCS}^!$ *is decidable.*

5   Concluding Remark

Summary. We have studied several decidability and undecidability issues on the bisimilarity and similarity checking problems of some subcalculi of CCS. We have concentrated on the question of how the solutions are affected when the capability of producing and manipulating local channels becomes weaker. An instance is identified that similarity checking is decidable while bisimilarity checking is not. Fig. 4 summarizes the status quo of our understanding of the decidability property. These results offer a different angle to look at the relative expressiveness of the subcalculi of CCS.

Related Work. The relative expressiveness of CCS is studied in [4,5,11,6,10,2]. It is proved in [5,11] that $\text{CCS}^!$ and CCS^μ are less expressive than CCS^{Pdef}. Two problems are left open in [11,2]. Both are answered in [10]. One answer is given by an encoding from CCS^μ to $\text{CCS}^!$ that is codivergent and branching bisimilar. The other is by an encoding from CCS^μ to itself with only guarded recursion. A more formal approach to the expressiveness study is proposed in [9]. In [15] the bisimilarity checking problem between the infinite-state processes and the finite-state ones is reduced to the model checking problem of *reachability of Hennessy-Milner property*. A recent survey on the decidability and complexity results of bisimilarity checking for the processes defined in Process Rewrite Systems [21] is given in [27]. A surprising result is pointed out in [20] that strong bisimilarity

$\mathcal{L}$	$\mathcal{L} \sim \mathcal{L}$	$\mathcal{L} \sim \mathbf{FS}$	$\mathbf{FS} \precsim \mathcal{L}$	$\mathcal{L} \precsim \mathbf{FS}$
$\mathrm{CCS}^!_\circ$	✓ [7]	✓ [7]	✓	✓
$\mathrm{CCS}^\mu_\circ$	✓ [7]	✓ [7]	✓	✓
$\mathrm{CCS}^!_\bullet$	× (Th.2)	✓ (Th.4)	✓ (Th.5)	✓ (Th.5)
$\mathrm{CCS}^\mu_\bullet$	× (Th.1)	✓ (Th.4)	✓ (Th.5)	✓ (Th.5)
$\mathrm{CCS}^!$	×	× (Th.3)	✓ (Th.6)	?
CCS^μ	×	× (Th.3)	?	?
$\mathrm{CCS}^{\mathrm{Pdef}}$	× [4,11]	× [4,11]	× [4,11]	× [4,11]

"$\sim$": strong bisimilarity
"$\precsim$": strong similarity

"✓": known decidable
"×": known undecidable
"?": unknown

Fig. 4. Summary of the Results

is decidable for a higher-order calculus. The Petri Net semantics is proposed in [12] for $\mathrm{CCS}^\mu_\circ$ with guarded recursion. In [2] a similar encoding of $\mathrm{CCS}^!_\circ$ into the Petri Nets is presented. Our results assert the nonexistence of reasonable encodings from $\mathrm{CCS}^!/\mathrm{CCS}^\mu$ to the Labeled Petri Net. The interplay between $\mathrm{CCS}^!$ and the Chomsky Hierarchy are studied in [1].

Future Work. Recently we have attempted to set up an expansion order for CCS^μ, which we hope would help us prove the decidability of $\mathbf{FS} \precsim \mathrm{CCS}^\mu$. The problem $\mathrm{CCS}^! \precsim \mathbf{FS}$ is interesting. It appears undecidable, but nothing seems to indicate that a positive answer is unlikely. Finally notice that the number of the static local channels used to show Theorem 1 is bounded, whereas we have not got such a bound for Theorem 2. This may suggest that $\mathrm{CCS}^\mu_\bullet$ cannot be encoded into $\mathrm{CCS}^!_\bullet$.

Acknowledgements. The authors are indebted to all the anonymous referees for their detailed reviews on the previous version of the paper. Their criticisms, questions and suggestions have led to a significant improvement of the paper.

References

1. Aranda, J., Di Giusto, C., Nielsen, M., Valencia, F.: CCS with Replication in the Chomsky Hierarchy: The Expressive Power of Divergence. In: Shao, Z. (ed.) APLAS 2007. LNCS, vol. 4807, pp. 383–398. Springer, Heidelberg (2007)
2. Aranda, J., Valencia, F.D., Versari, C.: On the Expressive Power of Restriction and Priorities in CCS with Replication. In: de Alfaro, L. (ed.) FOSSACS 2009. LNCS, vol. 5504, pp. 242–256. Springer, Heidelberg (2009)
3. Burkart, O., Caucal, D., Moller, F., Steffen, B.: Verification on infinite structures. In: Handbook of Process Algebra, pp. 545–623 (2001)
4. Busi, N., Gabbrielli, M., Zavattaro, G.: Replication vs. Recursive Definitions in Channel Based Calculi. In: Baeten, J.C.M., Lenstra, J.K., Parrow, J., Woeginger, G.J. (eds.) ICALP 2003. LNCS, vol. 2719, pp. 133–144. Springer, Heidelberg (2003)
5. Busi, N., Gabbrielli, M., Tennenholtz, M.: Comparing Recursion, Replication, and Iteration in Process Calculi. In: Díaz, J., Karhumäki, J., Lepistö, A., Sannella, D. (eds.) ICALP 2004. LNCS, vol. 3142, pp. 307–319. Springer, Heidelberg (2004)
6. Busi, N., Gabbrielli, M., Zavattaro, G.: On the expressive power of recursion, replication and iteration in process calculi. Mathematical Structures in Computer Science 19(6), 1191–1222 (2009)

7. Christensen, S., Hirshfeld, Y., Moller, F.: Decidable subsets of CCS. Comput. J. 37(4), 233–242 (1994)
8. Finkel, A., Schnoebelen, P.: Well-structured transition systems everywhere? Theor. Comput. Sci. 256(1-2), 63–92 (2001)
9. Fu, Y.: Theory of interaction (2010), http://basics.sjtu.edu.cn/~yuxi/
10. Fu, Y., Lu, H.: On the expressiveness of interaction. Theor. Comput. Sci. 411 (11-13), 1387–1451 (2010)
11. Giambiagi, P., Schneider, G., Valencia, F.: On the Expressiveness of Infinite Behavior and Name Scoping in Process Calculi. In: Walukiewicz, I. (ed.) FOSSACS 2004. LNCS, vol. 2987, pp. 226–240. Springer, Heidelberg (2004)
12. Goltz, U.: CCS and Petri Nets. In: Guessarian, I. (ed.) LITP 1990. LNCS, vol. 469, pp. 334–357. Springer, Heidelberg (1990)
13. He, C., Fu, Y., Fu, H.: Decidability of behavioural equivalences in process calculi with name scoping (2010), http://basics.sjtu.edu.cn/~chaodong/
14. Jancar, P., Srba, J.: Undecidability of bisimilarity by defender's forcing. J. ACM 55(1) (2008)
15. Jančar, P., Kučera, A., Mayr, R.: Deciding bisimulation-like equivalences with finite-state processes. Theor. Comput. Sci. 258(1-2), 409–433 (2001)
16. Jančar, P., Moller, F.: Checking Regular Properties of Petri Nets. In: Lee, I., Smolka, S.A. (eds.) CONCUR 1995. LNCS, vol. 962, pp. 348–362. Springer, Heidelberg (1995)
17. Jančar, P., Moller, F.: Techniques for Decidability and Undecidability of Bisimilarity. In: Baeten, J.C.M., Mauw, S. (eds.) CONCUR 1999. LNCS, vol. 1664, pp. 30–45. Springer, Heidelberg (1999)
18. Kučera, A., Jancar, P.: Equivalence-checking on infinite-state systems: Techniques and results. TPLP 6(3), 227–264 (2006)
19. Kučera, A., Mayr, R.: Why is simulation harder than bisimulation? In: Brim, L., Jančar, P., Křetínský, M., Kučera, A. (eds.) CONCUR 2002. LNCS, vol. 2421, pp. 594–609. Springer, Heidelberg (2002)
20. Lanese, I., Pérez, J.A., Sangiorgi, D., Schmitt, A.: On the expressiveness and decidability of higher-order process calculi. In: LICS, pp. 145–155 (2008)
21. Mayr, R.: Process rewrite systems. Inf. Comput. 156(1-2), 264–286 (2000)
22. Milner, R.: Communication and concurrency. Prentice-Hall (1989)
23. Milner, R.: Communicating and Mobile Systems: the π-calculus. Cambridge University Press (1999)
24. Milner, R., Parrow, J., Walker, D.: A calculus of mobile processes. Inf. Comput. 100(1), 1–77 (1992)
25. Minsky, M.L.: Computation: finite and infinite machines. Prentice-Hall (1967)
26. Sangiorgi, D., Walker, D.: PI-Calculus: A Theory of Mobile Processes. Cambridge University Press (2001)
27. Srba, J.: Roadmap of Infinite results. Formal Models and Semantics, vol. 2. World Scientific Publishing Co. (2004)
28. Taubner, D.A.: Finite Representations of CCS and TCSP Programs by Automata and Petri Nets. LNCS, vol. 369. Springer, Heidelberg (1989)

Rewriting Approximations for Properties Verification over CCS Specifications

Roméo Courbis

INRIA/CASSIS
LIFC/University of Franche-Comté
16 route de Gray
F-25030 Besançon Cedex
rcourbis@lifc.univ-fcomte.fr

Abstract. This paper presents a way to verify CCS (without renaming) specifications using tree regular model checking. From a term rewriting system and a tree automaton representing the semantics of CCS and equations of a CCS specification to analyse, an over-approximation of the set of reachable terms is computed from an initial configuration. This set, in the framework of CCS, represents an over-approximation of all states (modulo bisimulation) and action sequences the CCS specification can reach. The approach described in this paper can be fully automated. It is illustrated with the Alternating Bit Protocol and with hardware components specifications.

1 Introduction

Model-checking techniques [20, 21] are commonplace in computer aided verification. Model checking refers to the following problem: given a desired property, expressed as a temporal logic formula φ, and a structure M with initial state s, decide if $M, s \models \varphi$. The use of model-checking techniques and tools is however limited to systems whose state space can be finitely and concisely represented.

Recently, reachability analysis turned out to be a very efficient verification technique for proving properties on infinite systems modeled by term rewriting systems (TRSs for short). In the rewriting theory, the reachability problem is the following: given a TRS $\mathcal{R}$ and two terms s and t, can we decide whether $\mathcal{R}^*(\{s\}) \cap \{t\} = \emptyset$ or not? This problem, which can easily be solved on strongly terminating TRSs, is undecidable on non terminating TRSs. However, on the one hand, there exist several syntactic classes of TRSs for which this problem becomes decidable [13, 18, 26]. On the other hand, in addition to classical proof tools of rewriting, given a set $\mathsf{E} \subseteq \mathcal{T}(\mathcal{F})$ of initial terms, provided that $s \in \mathsf{E}$, one can prove $\mathcal{R}^*(\{s\}) \cap \{t\} = \emptyset$ by using over-approximations of $\mathcal{R}^*(\mathsf{E})$ [13, 19] and proving that t does not belong to these approximations.

Motivations. Recently, some of the most successful experiments using reachability analysis were done on cryptographic protocols, [6, 16], and on Java byte code programs [5]. For example, Java MIDLet applications security properties

F. Arbab and M. Sirjani (Eds.): FSEN 2011, LNCS 7141, pp. 299–315, 2012.

are verified through $\mathcal{R}^*(\mathsf{E})$ over-approximations. To this end, following works on CEGAR [8], an over-approximations refinement depending on a security property to be verified is developed in [4]. As TRSs and tree automata are powerful tools to express specifications, it is possible to perform reachability analysis on those. This paper fits in line with this context by adapting reachability analysis to verification of CCS (without renaming) specifications. Note that the reachability problem for this fragment of CCS is undecidable [7].

Contributions. This paper address the following problem : *Is it easy to adapt approximation rewriting to the verification of infinite state systems specified in CCS ?* The solution presented in this paper consists in a translation of a CCS specification into a TRS and a tree automaton. Then it is possible to verify properties using reachability analysis. This solution is illustrated with the Alternating Bit Protocol and with specifications of hardware components.

Structure of the Paper. This paper is organised as follows. Section 2 introduces basic definitions of terms, TRSs, tree automata completion and CCS. Then Section 3 explains how to translate a CCS specification into a TRS and a tree automaton, and then how to verify properties on sequences of actions. Section 4 and Section 5 show applications of the technique presented in Section 3. Finally, Section 6 presents related works and the conclusion.

2   Preliminaries

Comprehensive surveys can be found in [1, 12] for TRSs, in [10, 17] for tree automata and tree language theory, and in [22] for CCS.

2.1   Terms and TRSs

Let $\mathcal{F}$ be a finite set of symbols, associated with an arity function $ar : \mathcal{F} \to \mathbb{N}$, and let $\mathcal{X}$ be a countable set of variables. $\mathcal{T}(\mathcal{F}, \mathcal{X})$ denotes the set of terms, and $\mathcal{T}(\mathcal{F})$ denotes the set of ground terms (terms without variables). The set of variables of a term t is denoted by $\mathcal{V}ar(t)$. A substitution is a function σ from $\mathcal{X}$ into $\mathcal{T}(\mathcal{F}, \mathcal{X})$, which can be extended uniquely to an endomorphism of $\mathcal{T}(\mathcal{F}, \mathcal{X})$. A position p for a term t is a word over $\mathbb{N}$. The empty sequence ϵ denotes the top-most position. The set $\mathcal{P}os(t)$ of positions of a term t is inductively defined by $\mathcal{P}os(t) = \{\epsilon\}$ if $t \in \mathcal{X}$ and by $\mathcal{P}os(f(t_1, \ldots, t_n)) = \{\epsilon\} \cup \{i.p \mid 1 \leq i \leq n \text{ and } p \in \mathcal{P}os(t_i)\}$ otherwise. If $p \in \mathcal{P}os(t)$, then $t|_p$ denotes the subterm of t at position p and $t[s]_p$ denotes the term obtained by replacement of the subterm $t|_p$ at position p by the term s. We also denote by $t(p)$ the symbol occurring in t at position p. Given a term $t \in \mathcal{T}(\mathcal{F}, \mathcal{X})$, we denote $\mathcal{P}os_A(t) \subseteq \mathcal{P}os(t)$ the set of positions of t such that $\mathcal{P}os_A(t) = \{p \in \mathcal{P}os(t) \mid t(p) \in A\}$. Thus $\mathcal{P}os_{\mathcal{F}}(t)$ is the set of functional positions of t. A TRS $\mathcal{R}$ is a set of *rewrite rules* $l \to r$, where $l, r \in \mathcal{T}(\mathcal{F}, \mathcal{X})$ and $l \notin \mathcal{X}$. A rewrite rule $l \to r$ is *left-linear* (resp. right-linear) if each variable of l (resp. r) occurs only once within l (resp. r). A TRS $\mathcal{R}$ is left-linear (resp. right-linear) if every rewrite rule $l \to r$ of $\mathcal{R}$ is left-linear (resp. right-linear). A TRS $\mathcal{R}$ is linear if it is right and left-linear. The TRS $\mathcal{R}$ induces a rewriting relation $\rightarrow_{\mathcal{R}}$ on terms whose reflexive transitive closure is written $\rightarrow_{\mathcal{R}}^{*}$. The set of $\mathcal{R}$-descendants of a set of ground terms E is $\mathcal{R}^{*}(\mathsf{E}) = \{ t \in \mathcal{T}(\mathcal{F}) \mid \exists s \in \mathsf{E} \text{ s.t. } s \rightarrow_{\mathcal{R}}^{*} t \}$.

2.2 Tree Automata Completion

Note that $\mathcal{R}^{*}(\mathsf{E})$ is possibly infinite: $\mathcal{R}$ may not terminate and/or E may be infinite. The set $\mathcal{R}^{*}(\mathsf{E})$ is generally not computable [17]. However, it is possible to over-approximate it [13] using tree automata, i.e. a finite representation of infinite (regular) sets of terms. We next define tree automata.

Let $\mathcal{Q}$ be a finite set of symbols, of arity 0, called *states* such that $\mathcal{Q} \cap \mathcal{F} = \emptyset$. $\mathcal{T}(\mathcal{F} \cup \mathcal{Q})$ is called the set of *configurations*.

Definition 1 (Transition and normalised transition). *A transition is a rewrite rule* $c \rightarrow q$, *where* $c \in \mathcal{T}(\mathcal{F} \cup \mathcal{Q})$ *is a configuration and* $q \in \mathcal{Q}$. *A normalised transition is a transition* $c \rightarrow q$ *where* $c = f(q_1, \ldots, q_n)$, $f \in \mathcal{F}$, $ar(f) = n$, *and* $q_1, \ldots, q_n \in \mathcal{Q}$.

Definition 2 (Bottom-up non-deterministic finite tree automaton). *A bottom-up non-deterministic finite tree automaton (tree automaton for short) is a quadruple* $\mathcal{A} = (\mathcal{F}, \mathcal{Q}, \mathcal{Q}_f, \Delta)$, $\mathcal{Q}_f \subseteq \mathcal{Q}$ *and* Δ *is a finite set of normalised transitions.*

The *rewriting relation* on $\mathcal{T}(\mathcal{F} \cup \mathcal{Q})$ induced by the transition set Δ of $\mathcal{A}$ is denoted $\rightarrow_{\Delta}$. When Δ is clear from the context, $\rightarrow_{\Delta}$ is also written $\rightarrow_{\mathcal{A}}$.

Definition 3 (Recognised language). *The tree language recognised by* $\mathcal{A}$ *in a state* q *is* $L(\mathcal{A}, q) = \{ t \in \mathcal{T}(\mathcal{F}) \mid t \rightarrow_{\mathcal{A}}^{*} q \}$. *The language recognised by* $\mathcal{A}$ *is* $L(\mathcal{A}) = \bigcup_{q \in \mathcal{Q}_f} L(\mathcal{A}, q)$. *A tree language is regular if and only if it is recognised by a tree automaton.*

Let us now recall how tree automata and TRSs can be used for term reachability analysis. Given a tree automaton $\mathcal{A}$ and a TRS $\mathcal{R}$, the tree automata completion algorithm proposed in [13] computes a tree automaton $\mathcal{A}_{\mathcal{R}}^{k}$ such that $L(\mathcal{A}_{\mathcal{R}}^{k}) = \mathcal{R}^{*}(L(\mathcal{A}))$ when it is possible (for the classes of TRSs where an exact computation is possible, see [13]), and such that $L(\mathcal{A}_{\mathcal{R}}^{k}) \supseteq \mathcal{R}^{*}(L(\mathcal{A}))$ otherwise.

The tree automata completion works as follows. From $\mathcal{A} = \mathcal{A}_{\mathcal{R}}^{0}$ the completion builds a sequence $\mathcal{A}_{\mathcal{R}}^{0}, \mathcal{A}_{\mathcal{R}}^{1} \ldots \mathcal{A}_{\mathcal{R}}^{k}$ of automata such that if $s \in L(\mathcal{A}_{\mathcal{R}}^{i})$ and $s \rightarrow_{\mathcal{R}} t$ then $t \in L(\mathcal{A}_{\mathcal{R}}^{i+1})$. If there is a fix-point automaton $\mathcal{A}_{\mathcal{R}}^{k}$ such that $\mathcal{R}^{*}(L(\mathcal{A}_{\mathcal{R}}^{k})) = L(\mathcal{A}_{\mathcal{R}}^{k})$, then $L(\mathcal{A}_{\mathcal{R}}^{k}) = \mathcal{R}^{*}(L(\mathcal{A}_{\mathcal{R}}^{0}))$ (or $L(\mathcal{A}_{\mathcal{R}}^{k}) \supseteq \mathcal{R}^{*}(L(\mathcal{A}))$ if $\mathcal{R}$ is in no class of [13]). To build $\mathcal{A}_{\mathcal{R}}^{i+1}$ from $\mathcal{A}_{\mathcal{R}}^{i}$, a *completion step* is achieved. It consists of finding *critical pairs* between $\rightarrow_{\mathcal{R}}$ and $\rightarrow_{\mathcal{A}_{\mathcal{R}}^{i}}$. To define the notion of critical pair, the substitution definition is extended to terms in $\mathcal{T}(\mathcal{F} \cup \mathcal{Q})$. For a substitution $\sigma : \mathcal{X} \mapsto \mathcal{Q}$ and a rule $l \rightarrow r \in \mathcal{R}$ such that $Var(r) \subseteq Var(l)$, if there exists $q \in \mathcal{Q}$ satisfying $l\sigma \rightarrow_{\mathcal{A}_{\mathcal{R}}^{i}}^{*} q$ then $l\sigma \rightarrow_{\mathcal{A}_{\mathcal{R}}^{i}}^{*} q$ and $l\sigma \rightarrow_{\mathcal{R}} r\sigma$ is a critical pair. Note that since $\mathcal{R}$ and $\mathcal{A}_{\mathcal{R}}^{i}$ are finite, there is only a finite number of critical pairs.

Thus, for every critical pair detected between $\mathcal{R}$ and $\mathcal{A}_{\mathcal{R}}^i$ such that $r\sigma \not\rightarrow_{\mathcal{A}_{\mathcal{R}}^i}^* q$, the tree automaton $\mathcal{A}_{\mathcal{R}}^{i+1}$ is constructed by adding a new transition $r\sigma \rightarrow q$ to $\mathcal{A}_{\mathcal{R}}^i$. Consequently, $\mathcal{A}_{\mathcal{R}}^{i+1}$ recognises $r\sigma$ in q, i.e. $r\sigma \rightarrow_{\mathcal{A}_{\mathcal{R}}^{i+1}} q$.

However, the transition $r\sigma \rightarrow q$ is not necessarily a normalized transition of the form $f(q_1, \ldots, q_n) \rightarrow q$ and so it has to be normalized first. For example, to normalize a transition of the form $f(g(a), h(q')) \rightarrow q$, we need to find some states q_1, q_2, q_3 and replace the previous transition by a set of normalized transitions: $\{a \rightarrow q_1, g(q_1) \rightarrow q_2, h(q') \rightarrow q_3, f(q_2, q_3) \rightarrow q\}$.

If q_1, q_2, q_3 are new states, then adding the transition itself or its normalized form does not make any difference. On the opposite, if we identify q_1 with q_2, the normalized form becomes $\{a \rightarrow q_1, g(q_1) \rightarrow q_1, h(q') \rightarrow q_3, f(q_1, q_3) \rightarrow q\}$. This set of normalized transitions represents the regular set of non-normalized transitions of the form $f(g^*(a), h(q')) \rightarrow q$ which contains the transition we want to add but also many others. Hence, this is an over-approximation. We could have made an even more drastic approximation by identifying q_1, q_2, q_3 with q, for instance.

When always using a new states to normalize the transitions, completion is as precise as possible. However, without approximation, completion is likely not to terminate (because of general undecidability results [17]). To enforce termination, and produce an over-approximation, the completion algorithm is parametrized by a set N of *approximation rules*. When the set N is used during completion to normalize transitions, the obtained tree automata are denoted by $\mathcal{A}_{N,\mathcal{R}}^1, \ldots, \mathcal{A}_{N,\mathcal{R}}^k$. Each such rule describes a context in which a list of rules can be used to normalize a term. For all $s, l_1, \ldots, l_n \in \mathcal{T}(\mathcal{F} \cup \mathcal{Q}, \mathcal{X})$ and for all $x, x_1, \ldots, x_n \in \mathcal{Q} \cup \mathcal{X}$, the general form for an approximation rule is: $[s \rightarrow x] \rightarrow [l_1 \rightarrow x_1, \ldots, l_n \rightarrow x_n]$. The expression $[s \rightarrow x]$ is a pattern to be matched with the new transition $t \rightarrow q'$ obtained by completion. The expression $[l_1 \rightarrow x_1, \ldots, l_n \rightarrow x_n]$ is a set of rules used to normalize t. to normalize a transition of the form $t \rightarrow q'$, we match s with t and x with q', obtain a substitution σ from the matching and then we normalize t with the rewrite system $\{l_1\sigma \rightarrow x_1\sigma, \ldots, l_n\sigma \rightarrow x_n\sigma\}$. Furthermore, if $\forall i = 1 \ldots n : x_i \in \mathcal{Q}$ or $x_i \in Var(l_i) \cup Var(s) \cup \{x\}$ then $x_1\sigma, \ldots, x_n\sigma$ are necessarily states. If a transition cannot be fully normalized using approximation rules N, normalization is finished using some new states.

The main property of the tree automata completion algorithm is that, whatever the state labels used to normalize the new transitions, if completion terminates then it produces an over-approximation of reachable terms [13]. In other words, approximation safety does not depend on the set of approximation rules used. Since the role of approximation rules is only to select particular states for normalizing transitions, the safety theorem of [13] can be reformulated in the following way.

Theorem 1. *Let $\mathcal{A}$ be a tree automaton, N be a set of approximation rules and $\mathcal{R}$ be a left-linear TRS such that for every $l \rightarrow r \in \mathcal{R}$, $Var(r) \subseteq Var(l)$. If completion terminates on $\mathcal{A}_{N,\mathcal{R}}^k$ then*

$$L(\mathcal{A}_{N,\mathcal{R}}^k) \supseteq \mathcal{R}^*(L(\mathcal{A}))$$

Here is a simple example illustrating completion and the use of approximation rules when the language $\mathcal{R}^*(E)$ is not regular.

Example 1. Let $\mathcal{R} = \{g(x,y) \rightarrow g(f(x), f(y))\}$ and let $\mathcal{A}$ be a tree automaton such that $\mathcal{Q}_f = \{q_f\}$ and $\Delta = \{a \rightarrow q_a, g(q_a, q_a) \rightarrow q_f\}$. Hence $L(\mathcal{A}) = \{g(a,a)\}$ and $R^*(L(\mathcal{A})) = \{g(f^n(a), f^n(a)) \mid n \geq 0\}$. Let $N = [g(f(x), f(y)) \rightarrow z] \rightarrow [f(x) \rightarrow q_1 \; f(y) \rightarrow q_1]$. During the first completion step, we find a critical pair $g(q_a, q_a) \rightarrow_\mathcal{R} g(f(q_a), f(q_a))$ and $g(q_a, q_a) \rightarrow_\mathcal{A}^* q_f$. We thus have to add the transition $g(f(q_a), f(q_a)) \rightarrow q_f$ to $\mathcal{A}$. To normalize this transition, we match $g(f(x), f(y))$ with $g(f(q_a), f(q_a))$ and match z with q_f and obtain $\sigma = \{x \mapsto q_a, y \mapsto q_a, z \mapsto q_f\}$. Applying σ to $[f(x) \rightarrow q_1 f(y) \rightarrow q_1]$ gives $[f(q_a) \rightarrow q_1 f(q_a) \rightarrow q_1]$. This last system is used to normalize the transition $g(f(q_a), f(q_a)) \rightarrow q_f$ into the set $\{g(q_1, q_1) \rightarrow q_f, f(q_a) \rightarrow q_1\}$ which is added to $\mathcal{A}$ to obtain $\mathcal{A}_{N,\mathcal{R}}^1$. The completion process continues for another step and ends on $\mathcal{A}_{N,\mathcal{R}}^2$ whose set of transition is $\{a \rightarrow q_a, g(q_a, q_a) \rightarrow q_f, g(q_1, q_1) \rightarrow q_f, f(q_a) \rightarrow q_1, f(q_1) \rightarrow q_1\}$. We have $L(\mathcal{A}_{N,\mathcal{R}}^2) = \{g(f^n(a), f^m(a)) \mid n, m \geq 0\}$ which is an over-approximation of $\mathcal{R}^*(L(\mathcal{A}))$.

2.3   The Calculus of Communicating Systems

Syntax. Let $A = \{a, b, c, \ldots\}$ be the set of names and $\bar{A} = \{\bar{a}, \bar{b}, \bar{c}, \ldots\}$ be the set of co-names. Let $L = A \cup \bar{A}$ be a set of labels, and let τ be the invisible action such that $\tau \notin L$. Let $Act = L \cup \{\tau\}$ be the set of actions. Let $\mathcal{P}$ be a set of process names, and let $\mathbf{0} \in \mathcal{P}$ be the inactive process. Let $\mathcal{E}$ be the set of restricted CCS expressions defined according to the following syntax:
$E, E_1, E_2 := \alpha.E \mid E_1 + E_2 \mid E_1 \parallel E_2 \mid E \setminus \ell \mid \mathbf{0} \mid P$
where $\alpha, \ell \in Act$, $E, E_1, E_2 \in \mathcal{E}$ and $P \in \mathcal{P}$. Process names $P \in \mathcal{P}$ are defined such that for all P and $E \in \mathcal{E}$, one has : $P \stackrel{def}{=} E$. The set $Action(E)$ of actions is inductively defined by $Action(\alpha.E) = \{\alpha\} \cup Action(E)$, $Action(\mathbf{0}) = \emptyset$, $Action(P) = Action(E)$ (with $P \stackrel{def}{=} E$) and $Action(E_1 + E_2) = Action(E_1 \parallel E_2) = Action(E_1) \cup Action(E_2)$. The set of actions $ResAction(E)$ is inductively defined by: $ResAction(E \setminus \ell) = ResAction(E) \cup \{\ell\}$ and $ResAction(\alpha.E) = ResAction(E)$, $ResAction(\mathbf{0}) = \emptyset$, $ResAction(P) = ResAction(E)$ (with $P \stackrel{def}{=} E$) and $ResAction(E_1 + E_2) = ResAction(E_1 \parallel E_2) = ResAction(E_1) \cup ResAction(E_2)$. The set $Subterm(E)$ of CCS expressions is inductively defined by $Subterm(\alpha.E) = \{\alpha.E\} \cup Subterm(E)$, $Subterm(\mathbf{0}) = \emptyset$, $Subterm(P) = Subterm(E)$ (with $P \stackrel{def}{=} E$), $Subterm(E_1 + E_2) = \{E_1 + E_2\} \cup Subterm(E_1) \cup Subterm(E_2)$ and $Subterm(E_1 \parallel E_2) = \{E_1 \parallel E_2\} \cup Subterm(E_1) \cup Subterm(E_2)$. A CCS expression E' is a sub-term of E, or E contains E', if $E' \in Subterm(E)$.

CCS Programs. A CCS program S is a 3-tuple $S = (\Lambda, \Gamma, P_0)$ where $\Lambda \subseteq Act$, $\Gamma \subseteq \mathcal{P} \times \mathcal{E}$ is a finite set of equations, denoted by (P, E) or by $P \stackrel{def}{=} E$, and $P_0 \in dom(\Gamma)$ is the head process name, which usually builds the complete system. For example if we have : $A \stackrel{def}{=} a.B$, $B \stackrel{def}{=} b.B$, $S = (\{a, b\}, \{(A, a.B), (B, b.B)\}, A)$ is a CCS program.

Semantics. A CCS program $S = (\Lambda, \Gamma, P_0)$ defines the labeled transition system (LTS) $T_{CCS} \subseteq \mathcal{E} \times \Lambda \times \mathcal{E}$, built according to inference rules in Fig. 1. A transition $E \stackrel{\alpha}{\to} E'$ will denote the 3-uplet $(E, \alpha, E') \in T_E$. In this context, CCS expressions E and E' can be called states.

$$\textbf{Act} \; \frac{}{\alpha.E \stackrel{\alpha}{\to} E} \qquad \textbf{Com}_1 \; \frac{E_1 \stackrel{\alpha}{\to} E_1'}{E_1 \parallel E_2 \stackrel{\alpha}{\to} E_1' \parallel E_2}$$

$$\textbf{Sum}_1 \; \frac{E_1 \stackrel{\alpha}{\to} E_1'}{E_1 + E_2 \stackrel{\alpha}{\to} E_1'} \qquad \textbf{Com}_2 \; \frac{E_2 \stackrel{\alpha}{\to} E_2'}{E_1 \parallel E_2 \stackrel{\alpha}{\to} E_1 \parallel E_2'}$$

$$\textbf{Sum}_2 \; \frac{E_2 \stackrel{\alpha}{\to} E_2'}{E_1 + E_2 \stackrel{\alpha}{\to} E_2'} \qquad \textbf{Com}_3 \; \frac{E_1 \stackrel{a}{\to} E_1' \; E_2 \stackrel{\bar{a}}{\to} E_2'}{E_1 \parallel E_2 \stackrel{\tau}{\to} E_1' \parallel E_2'}$$

$$\textbf{Res} \; \frac{E \stackrel{\alpha}{\to} E'}{E \setminus \ell \stackrel{\alpha}{\to} E' \setminus \ell} \; \text{if } \alpha, \bar{\alpha} \neq \ell \in \mathrm{L}$$

$$\textbf{Con} \; \frac{E \stackrel{\alpha}{\to} E'}{P \stackrel{\alpha}{\to} E'} \; \text{if } (P, E) \in \Gamma$$

Fig. 1. Inference rules of CCS

As a CCS program $S = (\Lambda, \Gamma, P_0)$ has a head process, the initial state of the corresponding LTS is the state (or process) P_0.

A CCS expression E can perform an action α and becomes a CCS expression E' if the transition $E \stackrel{\alpha}{\to} E'$ can be inferred by the rules of Fig. 1. For example, the transition $(a.b.\mathbf{0} + c.\mathbf{0}) \parallel d.\mathbf{0} \stackrel{a}{\to} b.\mathbf{0} \parallel d.\mathbf{0}$, can be inferred by rules $\textbf{Com}_1$, $\textbf{Sum}_1$ and $\textbf{Act}$.

Derivatives. If $E \stackrel{\alpha}{\to} E'$, the pair (α, E') is called the *immediate derivative* of E. If $E \stackrel{\alpha_0}{\to} \ldots \stackrel{\alpha_n}{\to} E'$, the pair $(\alpha_0 \ldots \alpha_n, E')$ is called a *derivative* of E, where $\alpha_0 \ldots \alpha_n$ is an action sequence.

Let $deriv(E)$ be the set of all derivatives of E such that $deriv(E) = \{(\alpha_0 \ldots \alpha_n, E') \mid E' \in \mathcal{E}, \; E \stackrel{\alpha_0}{\to} \ldots \stackrel{\alpha_n}{\to} E'\}$.

3   Rewriting Approximations for CCS

Section 3 shows how to encode a CCS program into a TRS $\mathcal{R}$ and an initial automaton $\mathcal{A}$. The aim is to compute an over-approximation of $\mathcal{R}^*(L(\mathcal{A}))$ representing an over-approximation of all derivatives of a CCS program and, then, to verify properties such as absence of specific succession of actions.

3.1 Representation of a CCS Program and Semantics with Terms and TRS

Terms for CCS Expressions. A term corresponding to a CCS expression in $\mathcal{E}$ is built by induction on the structure of the CCS expression. Let $\mathcal{F}_{CCS}$ be an alphabet such that $\mathcal{F}_{CCS} = \mathcal{F}_0 \cup \mathcal{F}_1 \cup \mathcal{F}_2 \cup \mathcal{F}_3$, where $\mathcal{F}_0 = \{\mathbf{0}\}$, $\mathcal{F}_1 = \{bar\} \cup Act$, $\mathcal{F}_2 = \{Pre, Sum, Com, Res, Sys\}$. Let $\Phi : \mathcal{E} \to \mathcal{T}(\mathcal{F}_{CCS})$ be the function such that:

$$\Phi(\alpha.E) = Pre(\Phi(\alpha), \Phi(E))$$
$$\Phi(E_1 + E_2) = Sum(\Phi(E_1), \Phi(E_2))$$
$$\Phi(E_1 \parallel E_2) = Com(\Phi(E_1), \Phi(E_2))$$
$$\Phi(P) = P, \text{ if } P \in \mathcal{P}$$
$$\Phi(E \setminus \ell) = Res(\Phi(E), \ell)$$
$$\Phi(\mathbf{0}) = \mathbf{0}$$
$$\Phi(\alpha) = \begin{cases} \alpha & \text{if } \alpha \in A \\ bar(a) & \text{if } \alpha = \bar{a} \text{ and } \alpha \in \bar{A} \end{cases}$$

Example 2. Let $E = (a.b.\mathbf{0} + c.\mathbf{0}) \parallel d.\mathbf{0}$ be in $\mathcal{E}$. The term corresponding to this expression is:

$$\begin{aligned}
\Phi(E) &= Com(\Phi(a.b.\mathbf{0} + c.\mathbf{0}), \Phi(d.\mathbf{0}) \\
&= Com(Sum(\Phi(a.b.\mathbf{0}), \Phi(c.\mathbf{0})), Pre(d, \Phi(\mathbf{0}))) \\
&= Com(Sum(Pre(a, \Phi(b.\mathbf{0})), Pre(c, \Phi(\mathbf{0}))), Pre(d, \mathbf{0})) \\
&= Com(Sum(Pre(a, Pre(b, \Phi(\mathbf{0}))), Pre(c, \mathbf{0})), Pre(d, \mathbf{0})) \\
&= Com(Sum(Pre(a, Pre(b, \mathbf{0})), Pre(c, \mathbf{0})), Pre(d, \mathbf{0}))
\end{aligned}$$

Terms for Derivatives. Let E be in $\mathcal{E}$. A derivative $(\alpha_0 \ldots \alpha_n, E)$ is encoded into a term of the type $Sys(\alpha_0, Sys(\ldots, Sys(\alpha_n, \Phi(E))))$. Formally, the encoding function $\Psi : deriv(E) \times \mathcal{T}(\mathcal{F}_{CCS})$ is defined by:

$$\Psi((\alpha, E)) = Sys(\alpha, \Phi(E))$$
$$\Psi((\alpha_0 \ldots \alpha_n, E)) = Sys(\alpha_0, \Psi((\alpha_1 \ldots \alpha_n, E)))$$

Rewriting Rules for CCS Semantics. Rewriting rules corresponding to CCS semantic are in Figure 2.

ρ_1	$Pre(x, p)$	$\to Sys(x, p)$
ρ_2	$Sum(Sys(x, p), r)$	$\to Sys(x, p)$
ρ_3	$Sum(r, Sys(x, p))$	$\to Sys(x, p)$
ρ_4	$Com(Sys(x, p), r)$	$\to Sys(x, Com(p, r))$
ρ_5	$Com(r, Sys(x, p))$	$\to Sys(x, Com(r, p))$
ρ_6	$Com(Sys(x, p), Sys(bar(x), r))$	$\to Sys(\tau, Com(p, r))$
ρ_7	$Com(Sys(bar(x), p), Sys(x, r))$	$\to Sys(\tau, Com(p, r))$
ρ_8	$Res(Sys(x, p), y)$	$\to Sys(x, Res(p, y))$

Fig. 2. Rewriting rules for CCS semantics

Let $\mathcal{R}_{sem}^{\vartheta}$ denote the TRS defined by $\mathcal{R}_{sem}^{\vartheta} = \{\rho_1, \ldots, \rho_5\} \cup \{l\sigma \to r\sigma \mid \sigma = (x, \alpha), \alpha \in \vartheta, l \to r \in \{\rho_6, \rho_7\}\}$, where $\vartheta \subseteq Act$. Let $\mathcal{R}_{res}^{\Theta_1, \Theta_2}$ be the TRS defined by $\mathcal{R}_{res}^{\Theta_1, \Theta_2} = \{\rho_8 \sigma \mid \sigma(x) = \alpha, \sigma(y) = \beta, \alpha \in \Theta_1, \beta \in \Theta_2, \alpha \neq \beta\}$, where $\Theta_1, \Theta_2 \subseteq Act$. The right part of the union in $\mathcal{R}_{sem}^{\vartheta}$ is made to have a left-linear TRS (as rewriting rules ρ_6 and ρ_7 are not left-linear) because completion algorithm requires a left-linear TRS to be correct. And, let $\mathcal{R}_{Con}^{\theta}$ denotes the TRS defined such that $\mathcal{R}_{Con}^{\theta} = \{\Phi(P) \to \Phi(E) \mid (P, E) \in \theta\}$, where $\theta \subseteq \mathcal{P} \times \mathcal{E}$.

Now, we can define a TRS and a tree automaton corresponding to a CCS program.

Given a CCS program $S = (\Lambda, \Gamma, P_0)$, let us denote by L_S the tree language defined such that $L_S = \{\Phi(P_0)\}$, and let us denote by $\mathcal{R}_S$ the TRS defined such that $\mathcal{R}_S = \mathcal{R}_{sem}^{\Lambda} \cup \mathcal{R}_{Con}^{\Gamma} \cup \mathcal{R}_{res}^{\Lambda, \Lambda'}$, where $\Lambda' = ResAction(E) \cup ResAction(P)$ for all $(P, E) \in \Gamma$. The TRS $\mathcal{R}_{Con}^{\Gamma}$ corresponds to the **Con** inference rule. The set of actions Λ' is the set of all actions ℓ used for the restriction in the definition of S. Thereafter, we will use the TRS $\mathcal{R}_{sr}^{\Lambda, \Lambda'} = \mathcal{R}_{sem}^{\Lambda} \cup \mathcal{R}_{res}^{\Lambda, \Lambda'}$.

The main idea is to compute the set $\mathcal{R}_S^*(L_S)$, representing all derivatives of P_0, and, then, compute the intersection between $\mathcal{R}_S^*(L_S)$ and a set of derivatives. Intuitively, the TRS $\mathcal{R}_{sem}^{\vartheta}$ rewrites a term $\Phi(E)$ into a term $Sys(\alpha, \Phi(E'))$, if it is possible, by rewriting leafs to the root. This process can be viewed as a derivation of a transition $E \xrightarrow{\alpha} E'$ by inference rules, but, in a reversed way. Moreover, the TRS $\mathcal{R}_{Con}^{\theta}$ corresponds to equation(s) of a CCS program and handles recursion in equations.

Example 3. Let $E = (a.b.\mathbf{0} + c.\mathbf{0}) \parallel d.\mathbf{0}$ be in $\mathcal{E}$. According to CCS semantics we have the transition $E \xrightarrow{a} b.\mathbf{0} \parallel d.\mathbf{0}$, justified by inference rules **Com$_1$**, **Sum$_1$** and **Act**. With the help of the TRS $\mathcal{R}_{sem}^{Action(E)}$ rules, the term $\Phi(E)$ is rewritten $Sys(a, (Com(Pre(b, \mathbf{0}), Pre(d, \mathbf{0}))))$. More precisely we have :

$$Com(Sum(Pre(a, Pre(b, \mathbf{0})), Pre(c, \mathbf{0})), Pre(d, \mathbf{0}))$$
$$\to_{\rho_1} Com(Sum(Sys(a, Pre(b, \mathbf{0})), Pre(c, \mathbf{0})), Pre(d, \mathbf{0}))$$
$$\to_{\rho_2} Com(Sys(a, Pre(b, \mathbf{0})), Pre(d, \mathbf{0}))$$
$$\to_{\rho_4} Sys(a, Com(Pre(b, \mathbf{0}), Pre(d, \mathbf{0})))$$

As we can see, it is possible to draw a parallel between proving that one has $E \xrightarrow{a} b.\mathbf{0} \parallel d.\mathbf{0}$ with inference rules of Fig. 1, and rewriting $\Phi(E)$ into $\Psi((a, b.\mathbf{0} \parallel d.\mathbf{0}))$: rule ρ_1 matches with the inference rule **Act**, rule ρ_2 with **Sum$_1$**, and rule ρ_4 with **Com$_1$**.

Lemma 1. *Let α be in Act and E_s, E be in $\mathcal{E}$. If $\alpha.E_s \in Subterm(E)$ then $Pre(\alpha, \Phi(E_s))$ is a sub-term of $\Phi(E)$.*

Proof. We will show that there exists a position $p \in \mathcal{P}os(\Phi(E))$ such that $\Phi(E)|_p = Pre(\alpha, \Phi(E_s))$ by structural induction on E and on p:

Case 1: $E = \beta.E'$

    Case 1.1: $\beta = \alpha$ and $E' = E_s$

        According to definition of Φ we have $\Phi(E) = \Phi(\alpha.E_s) = Pre(\alpha, \Phi(E_s))$ and $p = \epsilon$.

Case 1.2: $\beta \neq \alpha$ or $E' \neq E_s$

One has $\Phi(\beta.E') = Pre(\beta, \Phi(E'))$ with $\alpha.E_s$ is a sub-term of E' and, by induction hypothesis, there exists a position $p = 2.p'$ such that $\Phi(E')|_{p'} = Pre(\alpha, \Phi(E_s))$. Then, the proof is by induction on E', thus $p = 2.p'$ satisfies the requirement.

Case 2: $E = E_1 + E_2$

Case 2.1: $\alpha.E_s$ is a sub-term of E_1

According to the definition of Φ we have :

$\Phi(E) = \Phi(E_1 + E_2) = Sum(\Phi(E_1), \Phi(E_2))$ with $\alpha.E_s$ a sub-term of E_1. By induction hypothesis, one has $p = 1.p'$ such that $\Phi(E_1)|_{p'} = Pre(\alpha, \Phi(E_s))$. Then, the proof is by induction on E_1.

Case 2.2: $\alpha.E_s$ is a sub-term of E_2

Similar to case 2.1.

Case 3: $E = E_1 \parallel E_2$

Similar to case 2.

Case 4: $E = E' \setminus \ell$

According to definition of Φ we have $\Phi(E) = Res(\Phi(E'), \ell)$ with $\alpha.E_s$ a sub-term of E', and one has $p = 1.p'$ such that $\Phi(E')|_{p'} = Pre(\alpha, \Phi(E_s))\}$. Then, the proof is by induction on E'.

There are no cases $E = \mathbf{0}$ or $E = P$ with $P \in \mathcal{P}$, because the condition of lemma 1 $\alpha.E_s \in Subterm(E)$ is not verified. $\square$

Proposition 1. *Let E and E' be two CCS expressions, let $\alpha \in Act$, let $A_E = Action(E)$ and $A'_E = ResAction(E)$. If $E \xrightarrow{\alpha} E'$ then*

$$Sys(\alpha, \Phi(E')) \in \mathcal{R}_{sr}^{A_E A'_E *}(\Phi(E))$$

Proof. Assuming that $E \xrightarrow{\alpha} E'$, we will show there exists a sequence of rewriting rules $r_0, \ldots, r_n \in \mathcal{R}_{sr}^{A_E A'_E *}$ and a sequence of terms $t_0, \ldots, t_n \in \mathcal{T}(\mathcal{F}_{CCS})$ such that $\Phi(E) = t_0 \to_{r_0} \ldots \to_{r_n} t_n = Sys(\alpha, \Phi(E'))$. (1)

We begin by proving that $r_0 = \rho_1$. In fact, as $\mathcal{P}os_{\{Sys\}}(t_0) = \emptyset$, only rule ρ_1 can be applied to t_0. As $E \xrightarrow{\alpha} E'$, E contains a sub-term of the form $\alpha.E_s$, then, according to Lemma 1, there exists a position $p \in \mathcal{P}os(\Phi(E))$ such that $\Phi(E)|_p = Pre(\alpha, \Phi(E_s))$. We can conclude that there exists a substitution $\sigma : \mathcal{X} \to \mathcal{T}(\mathcal{F}_{CCS})$ such that $t_0 \to_{\rho_1} t_0[r_{\rho_1}\sigma]_p$ (with $\rho_1 = l_{\rho_1} \to r_{\rho_1}$). (2)

Now we have to show (1) using (2) by transition induction on the depth of the inference by which the action $E \xrightarrow{\alpha} E'$ is inferred. We argue by cases on the form of E and its sub-terms:

Case 1: $E = \beta.E_1$

As $E \xrightarrow{\alpha} E'$, one has $\beta = \alpha$ and $E_1 = E'$. Then, using (2), we have $\Phi(E) = Pre(\alpha, \Phi(E'))$ and $\Phi(E) \to_{\rho_1} Sys(\alpha, \Phi(E'))$. One can conclude that $Sys(\alpha, \Phi(E')) \in \mathcal{R}_{sr}^{A_E A'_E *}(\Phi(E))$.

Case 2: $E_3 = E_1 + E_2$, where E_3 is a sub-term of E

Case 2.1: (α, E_1') is a derivative of E_1

According to the definition of Φ, one has $\Phi(E_3) = Sum(\Phi(E_1), \Phi(E_2))$. As $\Phi(E_1) = Sys(\alpha, \Phi(E_1'))$, and by induction hypothesis (1), there exists a substitution $\sigma_1 : \mathcal{X} \to \mathcal{T}(\mathcal{F}_{CCS})$ such that $l_{\rho_2}\sigma_1 \to_{\rho_2} r_{\rho_2}\sigma_1$. We obtain $\Phi(E_3) \to_{\rho_2} Sys(\alpha, \Phi(E_1'))$. If $E_3 = E$ then Proposition 1 is proved, else the proof continues by induction on a sub-term of E containing E_3.

Case 2.2: (α, E_2') is a derivative of E_2

Similar to case 2.1.

Case 3: $E_3 = E_1 \parallel E_2$

Similar to case 2.

Case 4: $E_2 = E_1 \setminus \ell$, where E_2 is a sub-term of E such that (α, E_1') if a derivative of E_1.

According to the Φ definition, one has $\Phi(E_2) = Res(\Phi(E_1), \Phi(\ell))$. As $\Phi(E_1) = Sys(\alpha, \Phi(E_1'))$, one has $\Phi(E_2) = Res(Sys(\alpha, \Phi(E_1')), \Phi(\ell))$.

One obtains $\Phi(E_2) \to_{\rho_8} Sys(\alpha, Res(\Phi(E_1'), \Phi(\ell)))$. If $E_2 = E$ then Proposition 1 is proved, else the proof continues by induction on a sub-term of E containing E_2.

$\square$

Directly from Proposition 1, we can deduce that for all $D \in Deriv(E)$ one has $\Psi(D) \in \mathcal{R}_{sr}^{A_E A_E'*}(\Phi(E))$. Moreover, for CCS programs (and not only CCS expressions as in Proposition 1) we have the following proposition:

Proposition 2. *Let* $S = (\Lambda, \Gamma, P_0)$ *be a CCS program. If* $d \in Deriv(P_0)$ *then* $\Psi(d) \in \mathcal{R}_S^*(L_S)$.

Proof. We will show that $\Psi(P_0) \to_{\mathcal{R}_S}^* \Psi(d)$. As $d \in Deriv(P_0)$, one has $d = (\alpha_0 \ldots \alpha_n, E_n)$ and by definition one has $P_0 \xrightarrow{\alpha_0} E_1 \ldots \xrightarrow{\alpha_n} E_n$. As $P_0 \in \mathcal{P}$ and $P_0 \xrightarrow{\alpha_0} E_1$, there exists $(P_0, E_0) \in \Gamma$ such that $E_0 \xrightarrow{\alpha_0} E_1$. Let $\Lambda' = ResAction(E) \cup ResAction(P)$ for all $(P, E) \in \Gamma$. According to Proposition 1, one has $\Phi(E_0) \to_{\mathcal{R}_{sr}^{\Lambda\Lambda'}}^* Sys(\alpha_0, \Phi(E_1))$. In addition, one has

$\Phi(E_0) \to_{\mathcal{R}_{sr}^{\Lambda\Lambda'}}^* Sys(\alpha_0, \Phi(E_1)) \to_{\mathcal{R}_{sr}^{\Lambda\Lambda'}}^*$
$\ldots \to_{\mathcal{R}_{sr}^{\Lambda\Lambda'}}^* Sys(\alpha_0, Sys(\ldots, Sys(\alpha_{n-1}, \Phi(E_{n-1}))\ldots)) \to_{\mathcal{R}_{sr}^{\Lambda\Lambda'}}^*$
$Sys(\alpha_0, Sys(\ldots, Sys(\alpha_n, \Phi(E_n))\ldots))$.

It remains to prove that $\Phi(P_0) \to_{\mathcal{R}_S}^* \Phi(E_0)$. By definition, there exists a rewriting rule $\Phi(P_0) \to \Phi(E_0) \in \mathcal{R}_{Con}^\Gamma$. From this we obtain that $\Phi(P_0) \to_{\mathcal{R}_S}^* \Phi(E_0)$. Finally we can conclude $\Phi(P_0) \to_{\mathcal{R}_S}^* \Phi(E_0) \to_{\mathcal{R}_{sr}^{\Lambda\Lambda'}}^* Sys(\alpha_0, \Phi(E_1)) \to_{\mathcal{R}_{sr}^{\Lambda\Lambda'}}^* \ldots \to_{\mathcal{R}_{sr}^{\Lambda\Lambda'}}^* \Psi((\alpha_0 \ldots \alpha_{n-1}, E_{n-1})) \to_{\mathcal{R}_{sr}^{\Lambda\Lambda'}}^* \Psi(d)$ which completes the proof. $\square$

4   The Alternating Bit Protocol Verification

This section shows that the Alternating Bit Protocol (ABP) CCS program is not able to perform a specific succession of actions represented by a set of derivatives.

Given the TRS $\mathcal{R}$ and the language L, corresponding to the ABP CCS program, the construction of the set $\mathcal{R}^*(L)$ is not possible, but an over-approximation $\mathcal{K}$ of this reachability set can be computed [14, 19]. Because of the over-approximation, we can only deduce that a language L_p is not reachable $(\mathcal{R}^*(L) \cap L_p = \emptyset)$ if $\mathcal{K} \cap L_p = \emptyset$. In our case, the language $\mathcal{K}$ recognises an over-approximation of all possible derivatives of the ABP CCS program, and the language L_p recognises a set of derivatives we do not want to be in $\mathcal{K}$. Then, if the intersection between $\mathcal{K}$ and L_p is empty, we can conclude that the set of all possible derivatives of the ABP CCS Program does not contain derivatives represented by L_p.

4.1   The Alternating Bit Protocol Description

The ABP is a protocol made to ensure the successful transmission of messages through a channel which may lose or duplicate data. More precisely, the ABP is composed of a Sender and a Receiver communicating via two channels (which may lose or duplicate messages) called Trans and Ack. The Sender sends a message with a bit b through the Trans channel, and sends it one or more times until the Receiver sends an acknowledgment with the bit b through the Ack channel. After the reception of this message by the Sender, it sends (once or more) another message with the bit $b - 1$ (also written $\hat{b}$) until it receives an acknowledgment with the bit $\hat{b}$, and so on.

4.2   Modeling the ABP

The CCS specification of ABP used in this article can be found in [22], and is represented by the CCS program $ABP = (\Lambda, \Gamma, AB)$ where :

- the set $\Lambda = \{accept, ack(b), deliver, reply(b), send(b), trans(b)\}$;
- the set Γ is composed of rules in Figures 3 and 4, where for each transition $A \xrightarrow{\alpha} B$ we have $(A, \alpha.B) \in \Gamma$, with $A, B \in \mathcal{E}$ and $\alpha \in \Lambda$.

The corresponding TRS $\mathcal{R}_{ABP}$ and tree language L_{ABP} is defined according to definition in Section 3. But also, we have to add rewriting rules to handle sequences of bits.

4.3   Verifying the ABP

In this section we will show how to verify, using the tool Tomedtimbuk [2], that the ABP can not send a message with the bit b after an acknowledgment with the bit b.

We proceed as follows: first, the property is modeled using patterns. Then, we have to find an abstraction function suitable for our analysis to ensure termination of the completion. Finally we use the Tomedtimuk tool to prove automatically that the ABP can not acknowledge and then send a message with the same bit.

$$Send(b) \quad \overset{def}{=} \quad \overline{send(b)}.Sending(b)$$

$$Sending(b) \overset{def}{=} \tau.Send(b) + ack(b).Accept(\hat{b}) + ack(\hat{b}).Sending(b)$$

$$Accept(b) \quad \overset{def}{=} \quad accept.Send(b)$$

$$Reply(b) \quad \overset{def}{=} \quad \overline{reply(b)}.Replying(b)$$

$$Replying(b) \overset{def}{=} \tau.Reply(b) + trans(\hat{b}).Deliver(\hat{b}) + trans(b).Replying(b)$$

$$Deliver(b) \quad \overset{def}{=} \quad \overline{deliver}.Reply(b)$$

$$AB \quad \overset{def}{=} \quad Accept(\hat{b}) \parallel Trans(\varepsilon) \parallel Ack(\varepsilon) \parallel Reply(b)$$

Fig. 3. System equations for ABP

$$Ack(bs) \overset{\overline{ack(b)}}{\longrightarrow} Ack(s) \qquad Trans(sb) \overset{\overline{trans(b)}}{\longrightarrow} Trans(s)$$

$$Ack(s) \overset{reply(b)}{\longrightarrow} Ack(sb) \qquad Trans(s) \overset{send(b)}{\longrightarrow} Trans(bs)$$

$$Ack(sbt) \overset{\tau}{\to} Ack(st) \qquad Trans(tbs) \overset{\tau}{\to} Trans(ts)$$

$$Ack(sbt) \overset{\tau}{\to} Ack(sbbt) \qquad Trans(tbs) \overset{\tau}{\to} Trans(tbbs)$$

$$\text{where } s, t \in \{0, 1\}^* \text{ and } b \in \{0, 1\}.$$

Fig. 4. System transitions for ABP

The property modelisation is very simple, one can use the following patterns:

Sys(s,Sys(bar(send(b)),Sys(ack(b),Sys(bar(send(b)),Sys(ss,p)))))
Sys(s,Sys(bar(send(inv(b))),Sys(ack(inv(b)),Sys(bar(send(inv(b))),Sys(ss,p)))))
Sys(s,Sys(bar(send(b)),Sys(ack(b),Sys(bar(send(b)),p))))
Sys(s,Sys(bar(send(inv(b))),Sys(ack(x,y,inv(b())),Sys(bar(send(inv(b))),p))))
Sys(bar(send(b)),Sys(ack0(b),Sys(bar(send(b)),p)))
Sys(bar(send(inv(b))),Sys(ack(inv(b)),Sys(bar(send(inv(b))),p)))

where s, ss and p can be anything in $\mathcal{T}(\mathcal{F}_{CCS})$. Those six patterns represent all possible derivatives of ABP where an action $\overline{send(b)}$ succeeds to an action $ack(b)$ (with $b \in \{0, 1\}$).

Concerning the abstraction function, the main idea is to abstract each action involved in the property in one state, and all other actions into one other state. Abstraction rules for the ABP actions, process names and bits are: $[x \to y] \to [b \to q_b, inv(q_b) \to q_b, send(q_b) \to q_{send}, bar(q_{send}) \to q_{\overline{send}}, ack(q_b) \to q_{ack}, accept(q_b) \to q_{rem}, reply(q_b) \to q_{rem}, trans(q_b) \to q_{rem}, deliver(q_b) \to q_{rem}, nil \to q_{rem}, bar(q_{rem}) \to q_{rem}, Send(q_b) \to q_{rem}, Sending(q_b) \to q_{rem}, Accept(q_b) \to q_{rem}, Reply(q_b) \to q_{rem}, Replying(q_b) \to q_{rem}, Deliver(q_b) \to q_{rem}]$. The $[x \to y]$ part matches any new transition which need to be normalized. The rules $b \to q_b$ and $inv(q_b) \to q_b$ merge all bit into one state q_b. The rules $send(q_b) \to q_{send}$, $bar(q_{send}) \to q_{\overline{send}}$ and $ack(q_b) \to q_{ack}$ merge all actions $\overline{send(b)}$ and $ack(b)$ into, respectively, states $q_{\overline{send}}$ and q_{ack}. All others actions and process names are merged into one state q_{rem}, according to the fact that those last actions and process names are not referenceed by the property.

Finally, given the initial automaton recognizing L_{ABP}, the TRS $\mathcal{R}_{ABP}$, the property and the abstraction function, the Tomedtimbuk tool computes a fixpoint automaton $\mathcal{A}_k$ over-approximating the set of all possibles derivatives of ABP. The intersection between $L(\mathcal{A}_k)$ and the property is empty, so we can conclude the ABP can not do an action $\overline{send(b)}$ after an action $ack(b)$, according to the following Proposition 3.

Proposition 3. *Let $S = (\Lambda, \Gamma, P_0)$ be a CCS program, let L_p be the language representing a derivative $(\alpha_0 \ldots \alpha_n, E)$ with $\alpha_0, \ldots, \alpha_n \in \Lambda$ and $E \in \mathcal{E}$ such that $L_p = \{\Psi((\alpha_0 \ldots \alpha_n, E))\}$. One has: $\mathcal{R}_S^*(L_S) \cap L_p = \emptyset$ if and only if $(\alpha_0 \ldots \alpha_n, E)$ is not a derivative of P_0.*

Proof. We have to prove that $(\mathcal{R}_S^*(L_S) \cap L_p = \emptyset) \Leftrightarrow ((\alpha_0 \ldots \alpha_n, E) \notin Deriv(P_0))$. The proof is divided into two parts: we will prove that $(\mathcal{R}_S^*(L_S) \cap L_p = \emptyset) \Rightarrow ((\alpha_0 \ldots \alpha_n, E) \notin Deriv(P_0))$ (1), and then that $((\alpha_0 \ldots \alpha_n, E) \notin Deriv(P_0)) \Rightarrow (\mathcal{R}_S^*(L_S) \cap L_p = \emptyset)$ (2).

(1) By contraposition of Proposition 2, one has $(\mathcal{R}_S^*(L_S) \cap L_p = \emptyset) \Rightarrow ((\alpha_0 \ldots \alpha_n, E) \notin Deriv(P_0))$.

(2) Suppose that $((\alpha_0 \ldots \alpha_n, E) \notin Deriv(P_0)) \Rightarrow (\mathcal{R}_S^*(L_S) \cap L_p = \emptyset)$ is false, we have the following hypothesis : $((\alpha_0 \ldots \alpha_n, E) \notin Deriv(P_0)) \wedge (\mathcal{R}_S^*(L_S) \cap L_p \neq \emptyset)$. If $\mathcal{R}_S^*(L_S) \cap L_p \neq \emptyset$ then $\Psi(P_0) \to_{\mathcal{R}_S}^* \Psi((\alpha_0 \ldots \alpha_n, E))$. We will prove that $(\alpha_0 \ldots \alpha_n, E) \in Deriv(P_0)$ which is in contradiction with the hypothesis. In order to succeed we have to prove the Lemma 2.

Lemma 2. *Let E and E' be two CCS expressions, let α be an action name and let $A_E = Action(E)$ and $A_E' = ResAction(E)$. If $\Phi(E) \to_{\mathcal{R}_{sr}^{A_E A_E'}}^* \psi((\alpha, E'))$ then $E \xrightarrow{\alpha} E'$.*

Proof. We have to show that E' can be built according to the inference rules of Figure 1 from E.

As $\mathcal{P}os_{\{Sys\}}(\Phi(E)) = \emptyset$, one has $\Phi(E) \to_{\rho_1} t_1 \to_{\mathcal{R}_{sr}^{A_E A_E'}}^* \Psi((\alpha, E'))$ such that there exists $p \in \mathcal{P}os(t_1)$ where $\Phi(E)|_p = Pre(\alpha, \Phi(E_1))$ and $t_1|_p = Sys(\alpha, \Phi(E_1))$. If $p = \epsilon$ then one has $\Phi(E) \equiv \Phi(\alpha.E')$, and we can deduce that $E \xrightarrow{\alpha} E'$ according to the **Act** inference rule. Else, one has $\alpha.E_1 \xrightarrow{\alpha} E_1$.

Then, we argue by cases of the term at a position p', such that $p = p'.1$ or $p = p'.2$:

Case 1: $t_1|_p = Sum(Sys(\alpha, \Phi(E_1)), t_2)$ (resp. $t_1|_p = Sum(t_2, Sys(\alpha, \Phi(E_1)))$)
According to rewriting rule ρ_2 (resp. ρ_3), it follows that $t_1|_p \to_{\rho_2} Sys(\alpha, \Phi(E_1))$ (resp. $t_1|_p \to_{\rho_3} Sys(\alpha, \Phi(E_1))$). As $\alpha.E_1 \xrightarrow{\alpha} E_1$, hence $\alpha.E_1 + E_2 \xrightarrow{\alpha} E_1$ (where $t_2 = \Phi(E_2)$), according to **Sum1** and **Sum2** inference rules.

Case 2: $t_1|_p = Com(Sys(\alpha, \Phi(E_1)), t_2)$ (resp. $t_1|_p = Com(t_2, Sys(\alpha, \Phi(E_1)))$)
Similar to Case 1.

Case 3: $t_1|_{p'.1} = Res(Sys(\alpha, \Phi(E_1)), \ell)$, with ℓ an action name. According to rewriting rule ρ_8, it follows that $t_1|_{p'.1} \to_{\rho_8} Sys(\alpha, Res(\Phi(E_1), \ell))$. As $\alpha.E_1 \xrightarrow{\alpha} E_1$, hence $\alpha.E_1 \setminus \ell \xrightarrow{\alpha} E_1 \setminus \ell$ according to **Res** inference rule.

$\square$

Consequently to Lemma 2, one has $(\alpha_0 \ldots \alpha_n, E) \in Deriv(P_0)$ if $\Psi(P_0) \to_{\mathcal{R}_S}^*$ $\Psi((\alpha_0 \ldots \alpha_n, E))$. This contradicts the hypothesis and proves (2).

Finally, from proofs of (1) and (2), one can conclude that $(\mathcal{R}_S^*(L_S) \cap L_p = \emptyset) \Leftrightarrow ((\alpha_0 \ldots \alpha_n, E) \notin Deriv(P_0))$. □

5   Hardware Components Verification

In this section we are going to verify properties over two hardware components specified with CCS [25].

5.1   The *Lockable* Component

The *Lockable* component is composed of two elements:

- one element with three inputs a, b and $free$, and one output z ;
- one element with two inputs $lock$ and $unlock$, and one output $free$.

We call *Lockable* the component including the parallelization of this two elements, while restricting the $free$ action. *Lockable* allows the lock and unlock effects on z output. Indeed, there is no output z when the $lock$ action is done, until the $unlock$ is done. And there is an output z only after a silent action. The CCS program corresponding to the *Lockable* component is defined in Figure 5, where LC is the initial process.

The property we want to verify is : *Is* Lockable *able to realize an action lock followed by an action $\overline{z}$?* To answer this question, we proceed in a same way that for ABP. A TRS $\mathcal{R}_{LC}$ and a tree automaton A_{LC} are constructed from the *Lockable* CCS program, the abstraction function is written following the principle used for ABP. Finally, a tree automaton A_p is build to recognize derivative of the form $(\alpha^*(lock\overline{z})\alpha^*, E)$ (where α is an action and E a CCS expression). Using Tomedtimbuk tools, one has $\mathcal{R}_{LC}^*(L(A_{LC})) \cap L(A_p) = \emptyset$, so we can answer *No* to the question.

$$LockC \stackrel{def}{=} (a.b + b.a).free.\overline{z}.C \qquad\qquad U_1 \stackrel{def}{=} r_1.gS.\overline{g_1}.d_1.\overline{pS}.\overline{a_1}.U_1$$

$$Lock \stackrel{def}{=} \overline{free}.Lock + lock.unlock.Lock \qquad U_2 \stackrel{def}{=} r_2.gS.\overline{g_2}.d_2.\overline{pS}.\overline{a_2}.U_2$$

$$LC \stackrel{def}{=} (LockC \parallel Lock) \setminus \{free\} \qquad\qquad S \stackrel{def}{=} (\overline{gS}.pS.S) \setminus \{gS, pS\}$$

Fig. 5. Equations for the *Lockable* component

Fig. 6. Equations for the *RGDA* component

5.2   The *RGDA* Component

The *RGDA* component (*Request Grant Done Acknowledgment*) is a component handling two users access to a critical section. It ensures that one user access to this section at a time. The CCS program corresponding to this component is composed by equations of Figure 6, where S is the initial process, U_1 and U_2 are users.

The property we want to verify is : *Is* RGDA *able to realize the actions* $\overline{g_1}$ *and* $\overline{g_2}$ *successively ?* As the *Lockable* component, a TRS $\mathcal{R}_{RGDA}$, a tree automaton A_{RGDA}, an abstraction function and a tree automaton A_p are defined. The tree automaton A_p recognizes derivatives of the form $(\alpha^*(\overline{g_1g_2})\alpha^*, E)$ (where α is an action and E a CCS expression). With the help of Tomedtimbuk, one can compute that $\mathcal{R}^*_{RGDA}(L(A_{RGDA})) \cap L(A_p) = \emptyset$, so we can answer *No* to the question.

6   Conclusion and Related Works

The paper describes a method of encoding CCS specifications into a TRS and a tree automaton. Using the completion algorithm, one can compute an over-approximation of reachable derivatives K, modulo bisimulation. It means that the set K do not contain CCS expressions bisimilar to CCS expressions of derivatives in K. Then, it is possible to semi-decide if derivatives, encoded into a tree automaton, are reachable or not. So, bisimilar CCS expressions have to belong to those derivatives in order to get a correct answer by the semi-decision procedure.

For other existing process algebras like CSP, BPP, BPA, PA, SDL, LOTOS, ..., sharing syntax and semantics elements with CCS, it could be insteresting to adapt the over-approximation rewriting to those process algebras.

Furthermore, to build this over-approximation, a pertinent abstraction function is needed i.e. the abstraction function allows the termination of the over-approximation computation without introducing spurious counter-examples which prevent the verification to conclude. In sections 4 and 5, abstraction functions can easily be generated automatically according to a property. However, it is not always possible. Note that the automatic generation of abstraction function has already been used for the protocol verification [3].

Related Works. It exists some tools made for the verification of CCS programs, as the Edinburgh Concurrency Workbench [23], the Concurrency Workbench North Carolina [9] and XMC [24], which are finite-state model-checkers while our technique deals with infinite-state systems. Also, verification of CCS programs can be done with Maude [27], where the CCS semantics is represented by conditional rewriting rules, while our method uses rewriting rules.

In [15], authors present a semi-decision procedure allowing verification of ACTL properties [11] (action based temporal properties) for infinite states systems. The method presented in this article does not handle CTL properties, but allows to verify reachability properties, based on actions and on CCS expressions. This property is represented by a tree automaton, instead of a temporal property. This can be similar to the proof by bisimulation, where behaviors of two CCS expressions are compared from the action point of view.

References

1. Baader, F., Nipkow, T.: Term Rewriting and All That. Cambridge University Press (1998)
2. Balland, E., Boichut, Y., Genet, T., Moreau, P.-E.: Towards an Efficient Implementation of Tree Automata Completion. In: Bevilacqua, V., Roşu, G. (eds.) AMAST 2008. LNCS, vol. 5140, pp. 67–82. Springer, Heidelberg (2008)
3. Boichut, Y.: Approximations pour la vérification automatique de protocoles de sécurité. Thèse de doctorat, Laboratoire Informatique de l'université de Franche-Comté, Université de Franche-Comté, Besançon, France (2006), http://www.irisa.fr/lande/boichut/publications.html
4. Boichut, Y., Courbis, R., Héam, P.C., Kouchnarenko, O.: Finer is Better: Abstraction Refinement for Rewriting Approximations. In: Voronkov, A. (ed.) RTA 2008. LNCS, vol. 5117, pp. 48–62. Springer, Heidelberg (2008)
5. Boichut, Y., Genet, T., Jensen, T., Le Roux, L.: Rewriting Approximations for Fast Prototyping of Static Analyzers. In: Baader, F. (ed.) RTA 2007. LNCS, vol. 4533, pp. 48–62. Springer, Heidelberg (2007)
6. Boichut, Y., Héam, P.C., Kouchnarenko, O.: Approximation-based tree regular model-checking. Nordic Journal of Computing (2009) (to appear)
7. Busi, N., Gabbrielli, M., Zavattaro, G.: Replication vs. Recursive Definitions in Channel Based Calculi. In: Baeten, J.C.M., Lenstra, J.K., Parrow, J., Woeginger, G.J. (eds.) ICALP 2003. LNCS, vol. 2719, pp. 133–144. Springer, Heidelberg (2003)
8. Clarke, E.M.: Counterexample-guided abstraction refinement. In: TIME-ICTL, p. 7. IEEE Computer Society (2003)
9. Cleaveland, R., Sims, S.: The NCSU Concurrency Workbench. In: Alur, R., Henzinger, T.A. (eds.) CAV 1996. LNCS, vol. 1102, pp. 394–397. Springer, Heidelberg (1996)
10. Comon, H., Dauchet, M., Gilleron, R., Jacquemard, F., Lugiez, D., Tison, S., Tommasi, M.: Tree Automata Techniques and Applications (2002), http://www.grappa.univ-lille3.fr/tata/
11. De Nicola, R., Vaandrager, F.: Action Versus State Based Logics for Transition Systems. In: Guessarian, I. (ed.) LITP 1990. LNCS, vol. 469, pp. 407–419. Springer, Heidelberg (1990)
12. Dershowitz, N., Jouannaud, J.P.: Handbook of Theoretical Computer Science. In: Rewrite Systems, vol. B, ch.6, pp. 244–320. Elsevier Science Publishers B. V (1990)
13. Feuillade, G., Genet, T., VietTriemTong, V.: Reachability analysis over term rewriting systems. Journal on Automated Reasoning 33 (3-4) (2004)
14. Feuillade, G., Genet, T., Tong, V.V.T.: Reachability analysis over term rewriting systems. Journal of Automated Reasoning 33(3-4), 341–383 (2004)
15. Francesco, N.D., Fantechi, A., Gnesi, S., Inverardi, P.: Model checking of non-finite state processes by finite approximations. In: Brinksma, E., Steffen, B., Cleaveland, W.R., Larsen, K.G., Margaria, T. (eds.) TACAS 1995. LNCS, vol. 1019, pp. 195–215. Springer, Heidelberg (1995)
16. Genet, T., Klay, F.: Rewriting for Cryptographic Protocol Verification. In: McAllester, D. (ed.) CADE 2000. LNCS, vol. 1831, pp. 271–290. Springer, Heidelberg (2000)
17. Gilleron, R., Tison, S.: Regular tree languages and rewrite systems. Fundamenta Informatica 24(1/2), 157–174 (1995)
18. Gyenizse, P., Vágvölgyi, S.: Linear Generalized Semi-Monadic Rewrite Systems Effectively Preserve Recognizability. Theoretical Computer Science 194(1-2), 87–122 (1998)

19. Jacquemard, F.: Decidable Approximations of Term Rewriting Systems. In: Ganzinger, H. (ed.) RTA 1996. LNCS, vol. 1103, pp. 362–376. Springer, Heidelberg (1996)
20. Lamport, L.: A temporal logic of actions. ACM Transactions On Programming Languages And Systems, TOPLAS 16(3), 872–923 (1994)
21. Manna, Z., Pnueli, A.: The Temporal Logic of Reactive and Concurrent Systems: Specification. SV (1992)
22. Milner, R.: Communication and Concurrency. Prentice Hall (1989)
23. Cleaveland, R., Parrow, J., Steffen, B.: The concurrency workbench: A semantics based tool for the verification of concurrent systems. ACM Transactions on Programming Languages and Systems 15 (1994)
24. Ramakrishna, Y.S., Ramakrishnan, C.R., Ramakrishnan, I.V., Smolka, S.A., Swift, T., Warren, D.S.: Efficient Model Checking Using Tabled Resolution. In: Grumberg, O. (ed.) CAV 1997. LNCS, vol. 1254, pp. 143–154. Springer, Heidelberg (1997)
25. Stevens, K., Aldwinckle, J., Birtwistle, G., Liu, Y.: Designing parallel specifications in ccs. In: Proceedings of Canadian Conference on Electrical and Computer Engineering, pp. 983–986 (1993)
26. Takai, T., Kaji, Y., Seki, H.: Right-Linear Finite-Path Overlapping Term Rewriting Systems Effectively Preserve Recognizability. In: Bachmair, L. (ed.) RTA 2000. LNCS, vol. 1833, pp. 246–260. Springer, Heidelberg (2000)
27. Verdejo, A., Martí-Oliet, N.: Two case studies of semantics execution in Maude: CCS and LOTOS. Formal Methods in System Design 27, 113–172 (2005)

Type Checking Cryptography Implementations

Manuel Barbosa[1], Andrew Moss[2], Dan Page[3],
Nuno F. Rodrigues[1,4], and Paulo F. Silva[1]

[1] Departamento de Informática, Universidade do Minho, Portugal
[2] School of Computing, Blekinge Institute of Technology, Sweden
[3] Department of Computer Science, University of Bristol, United Kingdom
[4] DIGARC, Instituto Politécnico do Cávado e do Ave, Portugal

Abstract. Cryptographic software development is a challenging field: high performance must be achieved, while ensuring correctness and compliance with low-level security policies. CAO is a domain specific language designed to assist development of cryptographic software. An important feature of this language is the design of a novel type system introducing native types such as predefined sized vectors, matrices and bit strings, residue classes modulo an integer, finite fields and finite field extensions, allowing for extensive static validation of source code. We present the formalisation, validation and implementation of this type system.

1 Introduction

The development of cryptographic software is clearly distinct from other areas of software engineering. The design and implementation of cryptographic software draws on skills from mathematics, computer science and electrical engineering. Also, since security is difficult to sell as a feature in software products, cryptography needs to be as close to invisible as possible in terms of computational and communication load. As a result, cryptographic software must be optimised aggressively, without altering the security semantics. Finally, cryptographic software is implemented on a very wide range of devices, from embedded processors with very limited computational power and memory, to high-end servers, which demand high-performance and low-latency. Therefore, the implementation of cryptographic kernels imposes a specific set of challenges that do not apply to other system components. For example, direct implementation in assembly language is common, not only to guarantee a more efficient implementation, but also to ensure that low-level security policies are satisfied by the machine code.

THE CAO LANGUAGE. The CAO language aims to change this state of affairs, allowing natural description of cryptographic software implementations, which can be analysed by a compiler that performs security-aware analysis, transformation and optimisation. The driving principle behind the design of CAO is that the language should support cryptographic concepts as first-class language features. Unlike the languages used in mathematical software packages such as Magma or Maple, which allow the description of high-level mathematical constructions in

F. Arbab and M. Sirjani (Eds.): FSEN 2011, LNCS 7141, pp. 316–334, 2012.

their full generality, CAO is restricted to enabling the implementation of crypto-graphic components such as block ciphers, hash functions and sequences of finite field arithmetic for Elliptic Curve Cryptography (ECC).

CAO preserves some higher-level features to be familiar to an imperative pro-grammer, whilst focusing on the implementation aspects that are most critical for security and efficiency. The memory model of CAO is, by design, extremely simple to prevent memory management errors (there is no dynamic memory allocation and it has call-by-value semantics). Furthermore, the language does not support any input/output constructions, as it is targeted at implementing the core components in cryptographic libraries. In fact, a typical CAO program comprises only the definition of a global state and a set of functions that per-mit performing cryptographic operations over that state. Conversely, the native types and operators in the language are highly expressive and tuned to the spe-cific domain of cryptography. In short, the design of CAO allowed trading off the generality of a language such as C or Java, for a richer type system that permits expressing cryptographic software implementations in a more natural way.

CAO introduces as first-class features pure incarnations of mathematical types commonly used in cryptography (arbitrary precision integers, ring of residue classes modulo an integer, finite field of residue classes modulo a prime, finite field extensions and matrices of these mathematical types) and also bit strings of known finite size. A more expressive type system would be expected from any domain-specific language. However, in the case of CAO, the design of the type system was taken a step further in order not only to allow an elegant formali-sation of the type checking rules, but also to allow the efficient implementation of a type checking system that performs extensive preliminary validation of the code, and extracts a very rich body of information from it. This fact makes the CAO type checker a critical building block in the implementation of compilation and formal verification tools supporting the language.

CONTRIBUTIONS. This paper presents the formalisation, validation and imple-mentation of the CAO type system. Our main contribution is to show that the trade-offs in language features that were introduced in the design of CAO – specifically for cryptographic software implementation – enabled us to tame the complexity of formalising and validating a surprisingly powerful type system. We also show, resorting to practical examples, how this type system enforces strong typing rules and how these rules detect several common run-time errors. To support this claim, we outline our proof of soundness of the CAO type system.

More in detail, we describe a formalisation of the CAO type system and the corresponding implementation of a type checker[1] as a front-end of the CAO tool chain. One of the main achievements of our system is the enforcement of strong typing rules that are aware of type parameters in the data types of the language. The type checking rules permit determining concrete values for these parameters and, furthermore, resolving the consistency of these parameters inside CAO pro-grams. Concretely, the CAO type system explicitly includes as type parameters

---

[1] An implementation of a CAO interpreter (including the type system and semantics) is available via http://www.cace-project.eu.

the sizes of containers such as vectors, matrices and bit strings. In other words, CAO is dependently typed. Furthermore, typing of complex operations over these containers, including concatenation and extensional assignment, statically checks the compatibility of these parameters.

More interestingly, we are able to handle parameters in mathematical types in a similar way. Our type system maintains information for the concrete values of integer moduli and polynomial moduli, so that it is possible to validate the consistency of complex mathematical expressions, including group and finite field operations, the conversion between a finite field element and its polynomial representation, and other type conversions. Finally, the CAO type system also deals with language usability issues that include implicit (automatic) type conversions between bit strings and the integer value that they represent, and also between values within the same finite field extension hierarchy.

PAPER ORGANISATION. In Sect. 2 we expand on the relevant features of CAO. We then build some intuition for the subsequent formal presentation of the type system by introducing real-world examples of CAO code in Sect. 3. In Sect. 4 we present the CAO type system, including a detailed example of its operation. In Sect. 5 we describe our implementation. We conclude with a discussion of soundness and related work in Sect(s). 6 and 7.

2   A Closer Look at CAO

Real world examples of the most relevant CAO language features are presented in Sect. 3. We now provide an intuitive description of the CAO type system.

BIT STRINGS. The bits type represents a string of n bits (labelled $0 \ldots n - 1$, where the 0-th is the least-significant bit). This should not be seen as the "bit vector" type, as the get operator a[i] actually returns type bits[1]. The distinction between ubits and sbits concerns only the conversion convention to the integer type, which can be unsigned or two's complement respectively. The bits type is equipped with a set of C-like bit-wise operators, including the usual Boolean, shift and rotate operators, which are closed over the bit-length. The range selection/assignment (or slicing) operator (..), combined with the concatenation operator @ can be used to (de)construct bit strings of different sizes using a very concise syntax. For example, the following is a valid CAO statement over bit strings:

$$\texttt{a[3..8] := b[0..2] @ c[2..4];}$$

INTEGERS AND THE mod TYPE. Operations modulo some prime or composite integer are used extensively in cryptography [6]; for example, the ring[2] $\mathbb{Z}_n$ underlies the pervasively used RSA function [4], and the finite field[3] $\mathbb{F}_p$ is widely

---

[2] The ring of residue classes modulo an integer n can be seen as the set of numbers in the range 0 to n-1 with addition and multiplication modulo n.

[3] The ring of residue classes modulo an integer p is actually a field when p is prime: all non-zero elements have a multiplicative inverse.

used in ECC. Therefore, CAO includes not only arbitrary precision integers as a native type (int), but also a mod[n] type. For example, the mod[7] type is an instance of mod with modulus 7. In this case the modulus is prime, and hence inhabitants of this type are actually elements of a finite field. More generally, the modulus can be prime or composite, provided it is fixed at compile-time. Algebraic operations over the mod type are closed over the modulus parameter.

INTERNAL REPRESENTATION AND CASTS. The internal representation of mathematical types is deliberately undefined. The CAO semantics ensures that arithmetic with such values is valid, but makes no guarantee about (and hence disallows access to) their physical representation. Nevertheless, the CAO type system includes the necessary functionality to access the conceptually natural representation of algebraic types, by supporting appropriate cast operators. For example, to obtain the representation of a finite field element in mod[p] as an integer value of the appropriate range, one simply casts it into the int type. To obtain the representation of an arbitrary precision integer, one can cast it into a bit string of a predetermined size, and so on. Hence, compared to C, a CAO cast is more explicitly a conversion. Aside from this nuance, the syntax of casts is similar to C: one specifies the target type in parenthesis, e.g. y := (int) x.

GENERAL MODULI. An alternative form of the mod type allows defining finite field extensions, as shown below:

```
typedef a := mod[ 2 ];
typedef b := mod[ a<X> / X**8 + X**4 + X**3 + X + 1 ];
```

The type synonym a represents a mod type whose modulus is 2; this is simply the field $\mathbb{F}_2$. This is used as the base type for a second type synonym b which represents the field $\mathbb{F}_{2^8}$. In addition to the base type one also specifies an indeterminate symbol (in this case X), and an irreducible polynomial in the ring of polynomials with coefficients in the base type (in this case $P(X) = X^8 + X^4 + X^3 + X + 1$). Intuitively, this declaration defines an implementation of the field based on the referred polynomial ring, with arithmetic defined via standard polynomial algebra with reductions modulo $P(X)$. To access the coefficients in this representation, one can cast the value into a vector of elements in the base type.

MATRICES. The matrix type represents a 2-dimensional algebraic matrix over which one can perform addition and multiplication. For this reason, there are some restrictions on what the base type can be. The matrix type also has an undefined representation; its size must be fixed at compile-time, but the ordering of elements in memory (e.g. row-major or column-major order) is a choice that can be made by the compiler. The matrix type also supports get and range selection/assignment operations that permit easily (de)constructing matrices of different sizes.

VECTORS. The vector type represents a 1-dimensional generic container of elements of homogeneous type, where each element is referred to by a single index in the range $0 \ldots n - 1$, offering selection/assignment, concatenation and rotate operations similar to the bits type.

3   CAO Type System in Action

In this section we present some examples of CAO code taken from the implementation of the NaCl cryptographic library[4] that illustrate the validation capacity of the type checker over real world examples.

The following program fragment was taken from the implementation of the poly1305 one-time message authentication mechanism [2]. The function receives two vectors ciu and ru of content type byte, which is an alias for type unsigned bits[8], and an integer q. It returns a value of type mod1305, an alias for type mod[2**130-5].

```
def polyStep(ciu:vector[17] of byte, ru:vector[16] of byte, q:int) : mod1305 {
    def r : unsigned bits[16*8]; def ci : unsigned bits[17*8];

    r := ru[0]@ru[1]@ru[2]@ru[3]@ru[4]@ru[5]@ru[6]@ru[7]@ru[8]@ru[9]@ru[10]@
         ru[11]@ru[12]@ru[13]@ru[14]@ru[15];

    ci:= ciu[0]@ciu[1]@ciu[2]@ciu[3]@ciu[4]@ciu[5]@ciu[6]@ciu[7]@ciu[8]@
         ciu[9]@ciu[10]@ciu[11]@ciu[12]@ciu[13]@ciu[14]@ciu[15]@ciu[16];

    return ((mod1305)ci * (mod1305)r**q); }
```

The type system must solve the following problems to type the function body. Firstly, the concatenation of several bit strings must be typed to a single bit string of the appropriate type and size (and fail if these do not match in assignment). Secondly, the type checker must recognise that the cast to type mod1305 requires the expression on the right to be coerced to type int.

The next program fragment is from the NaCl implementation of hsalsa20 [3].

```
seq i := 0 to 3 {
    x[i+1]  :=  from_littleendian( k[i*4..i*4+3]);
    x[i+6]  :=  from_littleendian(in[i*4..i*4+3]);
    x[i+11] :=  from_littleendian( k[i*4+16..i*4+19]); }
...
seq i := 0 to 3 {
    out[i*4..i*4+3]     := to_littleendian(x[5*i]);
    out[i*4+16..i*4+19] := to_littleendian(x[i+6]); }
```

This is a good example of how CAO was fine tuned to provide assistance to the programmer in what, at first sight, might seem like a surprisingly powerful validation procedure. Range selection and assignment operators in bit strings, vectors and matrices may depend on the value of integer expressions, which can only be formed by literals, constants and basic arithmetic operations that can be evaluated at compile-time. This might seem just like a pre-processing step of compilation, were it not for the fact that we are also able to include in these expressions locally defined constants. Our type system is able to validate that all range selections (resp. assignments) result in vectors that are compatible with calls to function from_littleendian (resp. return type of function to_littleendian).

Finally, the following code snippet is extracted from a CAO implementation of AES. It shows how our type system is capable of dealing with the complex mathematical types that arise in cryptographic implementations. In this case we have a matrix multiplication operation mix * s[0..3,i], where the contents of the matrices are elements of a finite field extension GF2N.

---

[4] http://nacl.cr.yp.to

$n : \mathbf{Num}$	Numerals	$pg : \mathbf{Progs}$	Programs
$x : \mathbf{Id}_V$	Variable Identifiers	$e : \mathbf{Exp}$	Expressions
$fp : \mathbf{Id}_{FP}$	Function and Procedure Identifiers	$c : \mathbf{Stm}$	Statements
$dv : \mathbf{Dec}_V$	Variable declarations	$l : \mathbf{Lv}$	LValues
$dfp : \mathbf{Dec}_{FP}$	Function and Procedure declarations	$pol : \mathbf{Poly}$	Polynomials
$ds : \mathbf{Dec}_S$	Struct declarations	$t : \mathbf{Types}$	Types

$$e ::= n \mid \mathsf{true} \mid \mathsf{false} \mid x \mid -e \mid e_1 \dagger e_2 \mid e.x \mid e_1[e_2] \mid e_1[e_2..e_3] \mid$$
$$\quad e_1[e_2, e_3] \mid e_1[e_2..e_3, e_4..e_5] \mid \sim e \mid (t)\, e \mid fp(e_1, ..., e_n) \mid\, !\, e$$
$$l ::= x \mid l.x \mid l[e] \mid l[e_1..e_2] \mid l[e_1, e_2] \mid l[e_1..e_2, e_3..e_4]$$
$$c ::= dv \mid l_1, ..., l_i := e_1, ..., e_j \mid c_1; c_2 \mid \mathsf{if}\ (e)\ \{\ c_1\ \} \mid \mathsf{if}\ (e)\ \{\ c_1\ \}\ \mathsf{else}\ \{\ c_2\ \} \mid$$
$$\quad \mathsf{while}\ (e)\ \{\ c\ \} \mid \mathsf{seq}\ x := e_1\ \mathsf{to}\ e_2\ \mathsf{by}\ e_3\ \{\ c\ \} \mid \mathsf{seq}\ x := e_1\ \mathsf{to}\ e_2\ \{\ c\ \} \mid$$
$$\quad \mathsf{return}\ e_1, ..., e_n \mid fp(e_1, ..., e_n)$$
$$dv ::= \mathsf{def}\ x_1, ..., x_n : t_1, ..., t_n \mid \mathsf{def}\ x_1, ..., x_n : t_1, ..., t_n := e_1, ..., e_n$$
$$ds ::= \mathsf{typedef}\ x := t; \mid \mathsf{typedef}\ x_1 := \mathsf{struct}\ [\ \mathsf{def}\ x_2 : t_1; ...; \mathsf{def}\ x_n : t_n\ ];$$
$$dfp ::= \mathsf{def}\ fp\ (x_1 : t_1, ..., x_n : t_n) : rt\ \{\ c\ \}$$
$$rt ::= \mathsf{void} \mid t_1, ..., t_n$$
$$t ::= x \mid \mathsf{int} \mid \mathsf{bool} \mid \mathsf{signed\ bits}\ [e] \mid \mathsf{unsigned\ bits}\ [e] \mid \mathsf{mod}\ [e] \mid \mathsf{mod}\ [\ t\, x\ /\ pol\ ] \mid$$
$$\quad \mathsf{vector}\ [n]\ \mathsf{of}\ t \mid \mathsf{matrix}\ [n_1, n_2]\ \mathsf{of}\ t$$
$$pg ::= dv; \mid ds \mid dfp \mid pg_1\ pg_2$$

Fig. 1. Formal syntax of CAO

```
typedef GF2  := mod[ 2 ];
typedef GF2N := mod[ GF2<X> / X**8 + X**4 + X**3 + X + 1 ];
typedef S    := matrix[4,4] of GF2N;

def mix : matrix[4,4] of GF2N  :=
  {[X],[X+1],[1],[1],[1],[X],[X+1],[1],[1],[1],[X],[X+1],[X+1],[1],[1],[X]};

def MixColumns( s : S ) : S {
  def r : S;
  seq i := 0 to 3 { r[0..3,i] := mix * s[0..3,i]; }
  return r; }
```

In addition to resolving the matrix size restrictions imposed by the matrix multiplication operation, our type system is able to individually type the finite field literals in the matrix initialisation, and check that these types are compatible with the type of the matrix contents. Note that this implies recognising that a literal of type mod[2] is coercible to GF2N.

4   Formalisation of the **CAO** Type System

In this section, we will overview our formalisation of the CAO type system. Since CAO is a relatively large language, only the most interesting features will be covered. A full description of the CAO formalisation can be found in [1].

CAO SYNTAX. The formal syntax of CAO is presented in Fig. 1. To simplify presentation we use $\dagger$ to represent a set of traditional binary operators, namely

$$\dagger \in \{+, -, *, /, \%, **, \&, \char`\^, |, \gg, \ll, @, ==, !\,=, <, >, <=, >=, ||, \&\&, \char`\^\char`\^\}$$

Most of the binary operators are the same as their C equivalents, although they are overloaded for multiple types. Worth mentioning are the multiplicative exponentiation operator for integers, residue class groups and fields (**); the bit-wise conjunction (AND), inclusive- (IOR) and exclusive-disjunction (XOR) operators (&, | and ^ respectively); the shift operators for bit strings and vectors (≫ and ≪); the concatenation operator for bit strings and vectors @; and the boolean logic exclusive-disjunction (XOR) operator (^^).

Most of the language syntactic entities, and the accompanying syntax rules, are also similar to C. Additional domains have been added to this basic set: some for the sake of a clearer presentation, and others because they are part of CAO's domain specific character for cryptography.

4.1 CAO Type System

FUNCTION CLASSIFICATION. The type checker is able to automatically classify CAO functions with respect to their interaction with global variables. The type checking rules classify functions as either of the following three types:

Pure Functions. Do not depend on global variables in any way and can only call other pure functions. These functions are, not only side-effect free, but also return the same result in every invocation with the same input. This property is often called referential transparency.

Read-Only Functions. Can read values from global variables, but they cannot assign values to them. They can call pure functions and other read-only functions, but not procedures. These functions are side-effect free.

Procedures. Can read and assign values from/to global variables. They can call pure functions, read-only functions and other procedures.

For the CAO type checker, the most important distinction is that between procedures and other functions. Procedures are only admitted in restricted contexts, such as simple assignment constructions. This distinction is completely automated in the type-checking rules that associate the following total order of classifiers to CAO constructions: Pure < ReadOnly < Procedure

Put simply, the type checking system enforces the following rules: 1) A construction depending only on local variables is classified as Pure; 2) When reading the value of a global variable, the classifier is set to Read-only; 3) When a global variable is used in an assignment target, the classifier is set to Procedure; 4) Expressions and statements procedures are classified with respect to their sub-elements using the *maximum operator* defined over the total order specified above. Note that this classification system is conservative in the sense that, for example, it will fail to correctly classify a function as pure when it reads a global variable but does not use its value.

ENVIRONMENTS, TYPE JUDGEMENTS AND CONVENTIONS. We use symbol τ (possibly with subscripts) to represent an arbitrary (fixed) data type. We write $x :: \tau$ to denote that x has type τ. We use two distinct environments in our type rules: the type environment relation Γ, which collects all the declarations (e.g. variables, function, procedures) together with their associated types; and the constant environment relation Δ, which records the values associated with integer constants. The Γ environment is partitioned into two relations: Γ_G for global definitions and Γ_L for local definitions. This distinction is important to deal with symbol scoping and visibility when typing, for example function declarations. Whenever this distinction is not important we will just write Γ to abbreviate Γ_G, Γ_L. Notation $\Gamma[x :: \tau]$ is used to extend the environment Γ with a new variable x of type τ, providing that x is not in the original environment (i.e., $x \notin dom(\Gamma)$). Similarly, $\Delta[x := n]$ is used to extend the environment Δ with a new constant x with value n, also provided that x is not in the domain of environment Δ. Notation $\Gamma(x)$ and $\Delta(x)$ represent, respectively, the type and the integer value associated with identifier x, assuming that x belongs to the domain of the respective environment. Environments are built by order of declaration in source code, implying that recursive declarations are not possible and that function classifiers are already known when the functions are called.

We use symbol $\vdash$ for type judgement of expressions of the form $\Gamma, \Delta \vdash e :: (\tau, c)$, retrieving type τ and functional classifier c associated to an expression. Operator $\Vdash_\beta$ denotes type judgements of statements that may modify the type environment relation: it retrieves not only a typed statement, but also a new type environment relation. Subscript β (seen as a place-holder) in operator $\Vdash_\beta$ represents the return type of the function in which the statement was defined. This information is particularly useful, allowing the type checker to guarantee that the several return statements that may appear in a function are always in accordance with the return type of the corresponding function declaration.

EVALUATION OF INTEGER EXPRESSIONS. We define a partial function ϕ_Δ to deal with type parameters such as vector sizes that must be determined at compile time. This function is used in typing rules to compute the integer value of a given expression e in context Δ. If this value cannot be determined, then typing will fail. This function is defined as follows

$$
\begin{aligned}
\phi_\Delta(n) &= n & \phi_\Delta(x) &= \Delta(x), \ x \in dom \ \Delta \\
\phi_\Delta(-e) &= -\phi_\Delta(e) & \phi_\Delta(e_1 \dagger e_2) &= \phi_\Delta(e_1) \dagger \phi_\Delta(e_2) \\
\phi_\Delta(e_1 \mathbin{**} e_2) &= (\phi_\Delta(e_1))^{(\phi_\Delta(e_2))} & \phi_\Delta(e_1 \mathbin{\%} e_2) &= \phi_\Delta(e_1) \mod \phi_\Delta(e_2)
\end{aligned}
$$

for $\dagger \in \{+, -, *, /\}$. When evaluating integer expressions in typing rules, we write

$$
\frac{\dots \quad \phi_\Delta(e) = n \quad \dots}{\Gamma, \Delta \vdash \dots} \quad \text{to mean} \quad \frac{\dots \quad \Gamma, \Delta \vdash e :: (\mathsf{Int}, \mathsf{Pure}) \quad \phi_\Delta(e) = n \quad \dots}{\Gamma, \Delta \vdash \dots}
$$

which implicitly implies that expression e is of integer type.

DATA TYPES. In Sect. 2, types were informally described using CAO syntax for type declarations. Here we will distinguish between a type declaration and the type it refers to in our formalisation. We use upper case to indicate the CAO

Table 1. CAO data types

Bool	Booleans
Int	Arbitrary precision integers
UBits $[i]$	Unsigned bit strings of length i
SBits $[i]$	Signed bit strings of length i
Mod $[n]$	Rings or fields defined by integer n
Mod $[\tau/pol]$	Extension field defined by τ/pol
Vector $[i]$ of τ	Vectors of i elements of type τ
Matrix $[i,j]$ of α	Matrices of $i \times j$ elements of type $\alpha \in \mathcal{A}$

$$\mathcal{A} = \{\mathsf{Int}, \mathsf{Mod}\ [m], \mathsf{Matrix}\ [i,j]\ \text{of}\ \alpha\ \mid \alpha \in \mathcal{A}\}$$

data types shown in Table 1. An important difference is that the CAO grammar allows any expression as a parameter of a type declaration, while CAO types must have parameters of the correct type and with a fully determined value, e.g., sizes must be integer values. In Table 1, $\mathcal{A}$ denotes the set of algebraic types, which are the only ones that can be used to construct matrices. These are types for which addition, multiplication and symmetric operators are closed. In order to emphasise occurrences where the type must be algebraic, we will use α (possibly with subscripts) instead of τ.

TYPE TRANSLATION. To deal with the type parameters informally described in Sect. 1, we introduce a new judgement that makes the translation between type declaration in the CAO syntax and types used in the type checking process. This judgement, of the form $\Delta \vdash_t t \rightsquigarrow \tau$, depends only on the environment Δ, which can in turn be used to determine the values of expressions that only depend on constants. This accounts for the fact that, during type checking, types must have their parameters fully determined, while type declarations in CAO can depend on arithmetic expressions using constants stored in the environment Δ. Hence the translation judgement uses evaluation function ϕ_Δ to compute parameter expressions in the declaration of bit string, vector and matrix sizes, ensuring that no negative or zero sizes are used. The evaluation function is also used in modular types with integer modulus to determine its value and ensure that it is meaningful (i.e., greater than 1). We present only part of this definition below.

$$\frac{\phi_\Delta(e) = n}{\Delta \vdash_t \text{unsigned bits } [e] \rightsquigarrow \mathsf{UBits}[n]}\, n \geq 1 \qquad \frac{\phi_\Delta(e) = n}{\Delta \vdash_t \text{mod } [e] \rightsquigarrow \mathsf{Mod}[n]}\, n \geq 2$$

$$\frac{\phi_\Delta(e) = n \quad \Delta \vdash_t t \rightsquigarrow \tau}{\Gamma, \Delta \vdash_t \text{vector } [e] \text{ of } t \rightsquigarrow \mathsf{Vector}\ [n] \text{ of } \tau}\, n \geq 1$$

$$\frac{\phi_\Delta(e_1) = n \quad \phi_\Delta(e_2) = m \quad \Delta \vdash_t t \rightsquigarrow \alpha}{\Delta \vdash_t \text{matrix } [e_1, e_2] \text{ of } t \rightsquigarrow \mathsf{Matrix}\ [n,m] \text{ of } \alpha}\, \alpha \in \mathcal{A}, n \geq 1, m \geq 1$$

TYPE COERCIONS. Type coercions are essentially implicit (typically data preserving) type conversions, whereby the programmer is allowed to use terms of some type whenever another type is expected. In CAO, this mechanism is remarkably useful, for example when dealing with field extensions (cf. the third

Table 2. Type coercion relation, $\vdash_\leq t_1 \leq t_2$

t_1	t_2	Condition
UBits$[n]$	Int	
SBits$[n]$	Int	
τ	Mod$[\tau'/pol]$	$\vdash_\leq \tau \leq \tau'$
Vector$[n]$ of τ_1	Vector$[n]$ of τ_2	$\vdash_\leq \tau_1 \leq \tau_2$
Matrix $[i,j]$ of α_1	Matrix $[i,j]$ of α_2	$\vdash_\leq \alpha_1 \leq \alpha_2$ and $\alpha_1, \alpha_2 \in \mathcal{A}$

Table 3. A few cases for the cast relation, $\vdash_c t_1 \Rightarrow t_2$

t_1	t_2	Condition
Int	Bits $[i]$	
Int	Mod $[n]$	
Vector $[i]$ of τ_1	Mod $[\tau_2/pol]$	$\vdash_c \tau_1 \Rightarrow \tau_2$ and $i = degree(pol)$
Mod $[\tau_1/pol]$	Vector $[i]$ of τ_2	$\vdash_c \tau_1 \Rightarrow \tau_2$ and $i = degree(pol)$
Matrix $[1,j]$ of α	Vector $[j]$ of τ	$\vdash_c \alpha \Rightarrow \tau$ and $\alpha \in \mathcal{A}$
Vector $[i]$ of τ	Matrix $[i,1]$ of α	$\vdash_c \tau \Rightarrow \alpha$ and $\alpha \in \mathcal{A}$
Vector $[i]$ of τ_1	Vector $[i]$ of τ_2	$\vdash_c \tau_1 \Rightarrow \tau_2$
Matrix $[i,j]$ of α_1	Matrix $[i,j]$ of α_2	$\vdash_c \alpha_1 \Rightarrow \alpha_2$ and $\alpha_1, \alpha_2 \in \mathcal{A}$

rule in Table 2), since a field can be seen as a subtype of all its field extensions. In general, when a CAO type τ_1 is coercible to another type τ_2, then the set of values in τ_1 can be seen as a subset of the values in τ_2. For example, all bit-strings of a given size can be coerced to the integer type. We define a coercion relation $\leq$, associated with a new kind of judgement $\vdash_\leq$. Coercions are naturally reflexive, and Table 2 summarises the other possible coercions.

Often the arguments of an operation have different types but are coercible to a common type, or one is coercible to the other. In order to capture this situation, we define the $\uparrow$ operator on types, which returns the least upper bound of the types to which its arguments are coercible:

$$\tau_1 \uparrow \tau_2 = \min\{\tau \mid \vdash_\leq \tau_1 \leq \tau \text{ and } \vdash_\leq \tau_2 \leq \tau\}$$

This requires that the coercion relation $\leq$ is regarded as a partial order on types, thus requiring the reflexivity, transitivity and anti-symmetry properties to hold. As we have seen before, the coercion relation is reflexive; the transitivity and anti-symmetry requirements are also easy to add and well suited to our intuitive notion of coercion. With these properties in place, and for the particular set of coercions allowed in CAO, we have that $\tau_1 \uparrow \tau_2$ is always uniquely defined. In typing rules, we therefore abbreviate the following pattern

$$\frac{\ldots \quad \Gamma, \Delta \vdash e :: \tau_1 \quad \vdash_\leq \tau_1 \leq \tau_2 \quad \ldots}{\Gamma, \Delta \vdash \ldots} \quad \text{by} \quad \frac{\ldots \quad \Gamma, \Delta \vdash e \leq \tau_2 \quad \ldots}{\Gamma, \Delta \vdash \ldots}.$$

CASTS. The CAO language includes a cast mechanism that allows for explicitly converting values from one type to another. However, not all casts are possible:

the set of admissible type cast operations has been carefully designed to account for those conversions that are conceptually meaningful in the mathematical sense and/or are important for the implementation of cryptographic software in a natural way. We define a type cast relation $\Rightarrow$, which is associated with a new kind of judgment $\vdash_c$. Table 3 shows the part of the definition of the cast relation. Using the cast relation, we only have to provide one typing rule for cast expressions.

$$\frac{\vdash_\leq \tau_1 \leq \tau_2}{\vdash_c \tau_1 \Rightarrow \tau_2} \qquad \frac{\Delta \vdash_t t \rightsquigarrow \tau \quad \Gamma, \Delta \vdash e :: (\tau', \mathsf{c}) \quad \vdash_c \tau' \Rightarrow \tau}{\Gamma, \Delta \vdash (t)\, e :: (\tau, \mathsf{c})}$$

The additional rule on the left is needed so that coercions can be made explicit, which also implies that a certain type can be cast to itself.

SIZES OF BIT STRINGS, VECTORS AND MATRICES. Since type declarations are mandatory and container types have explicit sizes, we can verify if operations deal consistently with these sizes. Furthermore, the type system can feed this information to subsequent components in the CAO tool chain.

For instance, the operation that concatenates two vectors should return a new vector whose size is the sum of the sizes of the individual vectors, and whose type is the least upper bound of the types of the two vectors, with respect to the coercion ordering $\leq$:

$$\frac{\Gamma, \Delta \vdash e_1 :: (\mathsf{Vector}[i] \text{ of } \tau_1, \mathsf{c}_1) \quad \Gamma, \Delta \vdash e_2 :: (\mathsf{Vector}[j] \text{ of } \tau_2, \mathsf{c}_2) \quad \tau_1 \uparrow \tau_2 = \tau}{\Gamma, \Delta \vdash e_1 @ e_2 :: (\mathsf{Vector}[i+j] \text{ of } \tau, \max(\mathsf{c}_1, \mathsf{c}_2))}$$

The concatenation of bit strings is similar. Moreover, in the case of matrix algebraic operations, e.g. multiplication, the dimension of the matrices can be checked for correctness.

When range selection is used over bit strings, vectors or matrices, we require that the integer expressions must be evaluated at compile-time so that the size of the expression, and therefore its type can be determined. In this case, the limits of the range are compared against the bounds of the associated type. For instance, for a range access to a vector we have:

$$\frac{\Gamma, \Delta \vdash e :: (\mathsf{Vector}[k] \text{ of } \tau, \mathsf{c}) \quad \phi_\Delta(e_1) = i \quad \phi_\Delta(e_2) = j}{\Gamma, \Delta \vdash e[e_1..e_2] :: (\mathsf{Vector}[j - i + 1] \text{ of } \tau, \mathsf{c})} k > j, j \geq i \geq 0$$

This is also a limited form of dependent typing since the type associated with the expression depends on the expression itself.

RINGS, FINITE FIELDS AND EXTENSIONS. One of the most unusual features of the CAO language is the support for ring and finite field types and their possible extensions. Our type checking rules allow us to ensure that operations over values of these types are well-defined and that values from different (instances of these) types are not being erroneously mixed due to programming errors. For instance, the typing rule for division is:

$$\frac{\Gamma, \Delta \vdash e_1 :: (\mathsf{Mod}\,[m_1], \mathsf{c}_1)}{\Gamma, \Delta \vdash e_2 :: (\mathsf{Mod}\,[m_2], \mathsf{c}_2) \quad \mathsf{Mod}\,[m_1] \uparrow \mathsf{Mod}\,[m_2] = \mathsf{Mod}\,[m]}{\Gamma, \Delta \vdash e_1 / e_2 :: (\mathsf{Mod}\,[m], \max(\mathsf{c}_1, \mathsf{c}_2))}$$

The use of the least upper bound captures the fact that the types may be equal, or one may be an extension of the other.

VARIABLES AND FUNCTION CALLS. The classification of expressions depends on the environment accessed when retrieving the value of a variable. If a local variable is accessed, the code is considered pure; if a global variable is read, the code is classified as read-only.

$$\frac{\Gamma_G(x) = \tau}{\Gamma_G, \Gamma_L, \Delta \vdash x :: (\tau, \mathsf{ReadOnly})} \quad x \in dom(\Gamma_G)$$

$$\frac{\Gamma_L(x) = \tau}{\Gamma_G, \Gamma_L, \Delta \vdash x :: (\tau, \mathsf{Pure})} \quad x \in dom(\Gamma_L)$$

Since in expression, we can only use functions that do not cause side-effects, the typing rule for function application has a side condition to ensure that the body of the function is not a procedure (i.e., it does not modify a global variable):

$$\frac{\Gamma_G(f) = ((\tau_1, \ldots, \tau_n) \to \tau, \mathsf{c}) \quad \Gamma_G, \Gamma_L, \Delta \vdash e_1 \leq (\tau_1, \mathsf{c}_1) \quad \ldots \quad \Gamma_G, \Gamma_L, \Delta \vdash e_n \leq (\tau_n, \mathsf{c}_n)}{\Gamma_G, \Gamma_L, \Delta \vdash f(e_1, \ldots, e_n) :: (\tau, \max(\mathsf{c}, \mathsf{c}_1, \ldots, \mathsf{c}_n))}$$

$$\max(\mathsf{c}, \mathsf{c}_1, \ldots, \mathsf{c}_n) < \mathsf{Procedure} \text{ and } f \in dom(\Gamma_G)$$

FUNCTIONS, PROCEDURES AND STATEMENTS. We introduce symbol • as a possible (empty) return type to detect misuses of the return statement. We distinguish the cases when a block has explicitly executed a return statement from the cases where no return statement has been executed. In the former case we take the type of the parameter passed to the return statement or • if no such parameter exists. In the latter case we also use the • symbol. Thus, a return statement is typed with the same type as its argument, which must coincide with the expected return type for the block.

$$\frac{\Gamma, \Delta \vdash e_1 \leq (\tau_1, \mathsf{cc}_1) \quad \ldots \quad \Gamma, \Delta \vdash e_n \leq (\tau_n, \mathsf{cc}_n)}{\Gamma, \Delta \Vdash_{(\tau_1, \ldots, \tau_n)} \mathsf{return} \; e_1, \ldots, e_n :: ((\tau_1, \ldots, \tau_n), \max(\mathsf{cc}_1, \ldots, \mathsf{cc}_n), \Gamma)}$$

Since CAO has a call-by-value semantics, returning multiple values is allowed in order to make references or additional structures unnecessary.

The typing rule for a function definition therefore verifies if the type of its body is not • to ensure that a return statement was used to exit the function. Moreover, the returned type has to be equal (or coercible) to the declared type (recall the use of judgement $\Vdash_\tau$).

The seq statement permits iterating over an integer variable varying between two statically determined bounds. The index starts with the value of the lower (resp. upper) bound and at each step is incremented (resp. decremented) by the amount of the step value until it reaches the upper (resp. lower) bound. The interesting feature of this mechanism is that the iterator is regarded as a constant at each iteration step. In the typing rules, this allows us to add the index and its respective value to the environment Δ at each iteration:

$$\frac{\phi_\Delta(e_1) = i \quad \phi_\Delta(e_2) = j \quad \forall_{n \in \{i \ldots j\}} \Gamma_G, \Gamma_L[x :: \mathsf{Int}], \Delta[x := n] \Vdash_\tau c :: (\rho, \mathsf{cc}, \Gamma_G', \Gamma_L')}{\Gamma_G, \Gamma_L, \Delta \Vdash_\tau \mathsf{seq}\ x := e_1\ \mathsf{to}\ e_2\ \{\ c\ \} :: (\bullet, \mathsf{cc}, \Gamma_G, \Gamma_L)}$$

$\rho \in \{\tau, \bullet\}$, $x \notin dom\ \Gamma_L$, $i \leq j$

Therefore, declarations and access expressions inside the body of the sequence statement may depend on the index but may still be statically typeable. As highlighted in Sect. 3, the combination of range selection and assignment operators for bit strings, vectors and matrices with this simplified loop construction is a good example of how the CAO language design allowed us to fine tune the type checker to provide extra assistance to the programmer. Note, however, that sequential statements can make the type checking process slow, as sequences must be explicitly unfolded and typed for each possible value of the iterator.

A DETAILED EXAMPLE. We now present a detailed example of the how our type system handles the hsalsa20 fragment introduced in Sect. 3. The syntactic form of the program is

```
seq i := 0 to 3 {
    x[i+1]  :=  from_littleendian( k[i*4..i*4+3]);
    x[i+6]  :=  from_littleendian(in[i*4..i*4+3]);
    x[i+11] :=  from_littleendian( k[i*4+16..i*4+19]); }
```

where we desire type annotations for each node in the parse tree. The inference process traverses the tree matching rules against syntax. This traversal highlights aspects of the inference at three levels in the tree. Before reaching this fragment the declarations have already been produced and thus the initial environment is

$\Gamma_L = \{\mathsf{k} :: \mathsf{Vec}[32]\ \mathsf{of}\ \mathsf{UBits}[8], \mathsf{in} :: \mathsf{Vec}[16]\ \mathsf{of}\ \mathsf{UBits}[8], \mathsf{x} :: \mathsf{Vec}[8]\ \mathsf{of}\ \mathsf{UBits}[32]\}$

$\Gamma_G = \{\mathsf{to\_littleendian} :: \mathsf{UBits}[32] \to \mathsf{Vec}[4]\ \mathsf{of}\ \mathsf{UBits}[8],$

$\quad\quad \mathsf{from\_littleendian} :: \mathsf{Vec}[4]\ \mathsf{of}\ \mathsf{UBits}[8] \to \mathsf{UBits}[32]\}$

$\Delta = \{\}$

The first step matches the entire fragment against $\mathsf{seq}\ \mathsf{i} := 0\ \mathsf{to}\ 3\ \{s_1; s_2; s_3\}$

$$\frac{\forall_{n \in \{0 \ldots 3\}} \Gamma_G, \Gamma_L[\mathsf{i} :: \mathsf{Int}], \Delta[\mathsf{i} := n] \Vdash_\tau c :: (\rho, \mathsf{cc}, \Gamma_G', \Gamma_L')}{\Gamma_G, \Gamma_L, \Delta \Vdash_\tau \mathsf{seq}\ \mathsf{i} := 0\ \mathsf{to}\ 3\ \{s_1; s_2; s_3\} :: (\bullet, \mathsf{cc}, \Gamma_G, \Gamma_L)}$$

This entails, for each of the $n \in \{0, 1, 2, 3\}$ cases, that for assignments $(l_i := r_i) = s_i$ in each of the s_1, s_2, s_3 preconditions, each statement is matched by

$$\frac{\Gamma_n, \Delta_n \vdash l_i :: (\tau, \mathsf{cl}) \quad \Gamma_n, \Delta_n \vdash r_i \leq (\tau, \mathsf{c})}{\Gamma_n, \Delta_n \Vdash_\tau l_i := r_i :: (\bullet, \max(\mathsf{cl}, \mathsf{c}), \Gamma)}$$

Here $\Gamma_n = \Gamma_G, \Gamma_L[\mathsf{i} :: \mathsf{Int}]$ and $\Delta_n = \Delta[\mathsf{i} := n]$. Now, for each of the l_i we obtain something of the form $\mathsf{x}[\mathsf{i} + 1]$ where $\Gamma_L(\mathsf{x}) = \mathsf{Vec}[8]\ \mathsf{of}\ \mathsf{UBits}[32]$ and an index expression $\mathsf{i} + 1 :: (\mathsf{Int}, \mathsf{Pure})$, thus we can match

$$\frac{\Gamma_n, \Delta_n \vdash \mathsf{x} :: (\mathsf{Vec}[8] \text{ of } \mathsf{UBits}[32], \mathsf{Pure}) \quad \Gamma_n, \Delta_n \vdash \mathsf{i} + 1 \leq (\mathsf{Int}, \mathsf{Pure})}{\Gamma_n, \Delta_n \vdash \mathsf{x}[\mathsf{i} + 1] :: (\mathsf{UBits}[32], \max(\mathsf{Pure}, \mathsf{Pure}))}$$

Finally, for each of the r_i the function parameter e_i is either $\Gamma_G[\mathsf{k}]$ or $\Gamma_G[\mathsf{in}]$ :: $\mathsf{Vec}[16]$ of $\mathsf{UBits}[8]$, Furthermore, the index expression is defined only over i, whose value is known, and integer literals. Thus each expression of the form $\mathsf{k}[\mathsf{i} * 4..\mathsf{i} * 4 + 3]$ becomes a slice over determined indices after application of ϕ_Δ and $\mathsf{k}[\mathsf{i} * 4..\mathsf{i} * 4 + 3] :: (\mathsf{Vec}[4] \text{ of } \mathsf{UBits}[8], \mathsf{Pure})$. Hence

$$\frac{\Gamma_G(\mathsf{from\_littleendian}) = (\mathsf{Vec}[4] \text{ of } \mathsf{UBits}[8] \rightarrow \mathsf{UBits}[32], \mathsf{Pure})}{\Gamma_G, \Gamma_L, \Delta_1 \vdash \mathsf{k}[\mathsf{i} * 4..\mathsf{i} * 4 + 3] \leq (\mathsf{Vec}[4] \text{ of } \mathsf{UBits}[8], \mathsf{Pure})}$$
$$\frac{}{\Gamma_G, \Gamma_L[\mathsf{i} :: \mathsf{Int}], \Delta_1 \vdash \mathsf{from\_littleendian}(\mathsf{k}[\mathsf{i} * 4..\mathsf{i} * 4 + 3]) :: (\mathsf{UBits}[32], \max(\mathsf{Pure}, \mathsf{Pure}))}$$

5   Implementation

The CAO type-checker was fully implemented in the Haskell functional language, which provides a plethora of libraries and built-in features. Among these, we found some to be particularly useful, such as *classes*, specific syntax for handling monadic data types and the *monad Error* data type. These Haskell assets, not only simplified the implementation process, but also helped improving substantially the readability of the code and its comparison with the formal specification of the type checking rules described in the previous section.

To generally illustrate Haskell's ability to deal with the formal type checking rules, consider the following code snippet, which implements the rule for type checking while statements.

```
tcStatement s@(WhileStatement info cond wstms) h rt =
  do (cond', condt, cb) <- tcExp cond h
     checkMatchType info condt Boolean
     (wstms', wst, cc, h') <- tcStatements wstms h rt
     return (mkWhileStatement (buildTcNodeInfo info Bullet)
                     cond' wstms', Bullet, max cb cc ,h)
```

The interpretation of the above code is quite immediate. Function tcStatement is our formal statement type checking function ⊩, rt represents the expected return type, which in the formal definition subscripts ⊩ and h corresponds to the type environments Γ and Δ. Note that, even though we have made clear the distinction between Γ and Δ in the formal rules, this was mainly justified by presentation reasons. Still on the arguments side, one finds (WhileStatement info cond wstms), trivially matching while b $\{c\}$, except for the info identifier, which is an add-on of the implementation for storing the exact place where the CAO code being analysed appears in the input file.

Regarding the function body, in accordance to the formal rule, which relies on premises referring to ⊢ and ⊩, so does the implementation, referring to functions tcExp and tcStatements respectively. Here, however, one resorts to Haskell's monadic operator <- over the monad Error data type. In this way we combine calls to different type checking functions that may return type checking errors, ensuring that if an error occurs in one of the calls, the error is propagated down to the end of the type checker execution, without interfering with any other type checking rule in between.

Function checkMatchType corresponds to our order comparison operator $\leq$ over data types, while Bullet is our functional representation of symbol •. Function max ensures that type classifiers, which allow the type system to recognise various types of functions, are properly propagated. Instead of returning the type of the expression being evaluated, the implementation returns the expression received annotated with its type, to be used by subsequent compilation steps. Nevertheless, the above rule implementation illustrates how we have kept the implementation reasonably close to the formal definition, therefore favoring a direct validation by inspection of the implementation.

6   Soundness of the Type System

As usual, the CAO type system aims to ensure that *"well-typed programs do not go wrong"* [7]. This is formalised as a soundness theorem relating static (typing) and dynamic semantics. For the moment, our result only ensures that the evaluation of well-typed program does not fall into a certain class of errors: formally, we are proving a *weak soundness theorem*. Concretely, we have shown that only a well-defined set of run-time errors (trapped errors, denoted by ϵ in the semantic domain $\mathbf{V}$) can occur when evaluating a correctly typed program. These are explicitly captured in the semantics of the language, and they are limited to divisions by zero and out of bounds accesses to containers. In this section, we first shortly present some aspects of our formalization of the CAO semantics necessary to provide support to the subsequent discussion of our soundness theorem and proof sketch. The complete description of both can be found in [1].

CAO Semantics. Evaluation of a CAO program is defined by an *evaluation relation* that relates an initial configuration (a CAO program together with a description of the initial state) with a final configuration (a semantic value and a final state). The domain of *semantic values* is defined as a solution of the domain equation $\mathbf{V} = \mathbb{Z} + \mathbf{V}^* + \mathcal{E}$, where $\mathbb{Z}$ denotes the domain of integers, $\mathbf{V}^*$ denotes sequences of values of type $\mathbf{V}$ of the form $[v_0, \ldots, v_{n-1}]$ and $\mathcal{E}$ is the type of the trapped error value ϵ. A *trapped error* is an execution error that results in an immediate fault (run-time error); an *untrapped error* is an execution error that does not immediately result in a fault, corresponding to an unexpected behavior. We denote such an error by $\perp$.

We define three mutually recursive evaluation relations, each of them responsible for characterising the evaluation of different syntactic classes: *expressions*, *statements* and *declarations*:

  $-\ \langle\, e \mid \rho \,\rangle \rightarrow r$ evaluates expression e in state ρ to the value r. Expression evaluation is side-effect free, and hence the state is not changed.

- $\langle\, c \mid \rho\,\rangle \Rightarrow \langle\, r\,,\,\rho'\,\rangle$ means that the evaluation of statement c in state ρ transforms the state into ρ', and (possibly) produces result r.
- $\langle\, d \mid \rho\,\rangle \Rightarrow \langle\, \rho'\,\rangle$ means that the evaluation of declaration d in state ρ transforms the state into ρ'.

CAO has a *call by value* semantics, where there are no references and each variable identifier denotes a value. Assignments mean that old values are replaced by the new ones in the state. Since expressions are effect-free, simultaneous value assignments are possible (however, here we will stick to the simpler single-assignment version of the evaluation rule). In CAO, a run-time trapped error can occur only in three cases: 1) accessing a vector, matrix or bit string out of the bounds; 2) division (or remainder of division) by zero; and 3) assigning a value to a vector, matrix or bit string out of bounds. We present example rules for the latter two cases below, noting that the frame update operator is defined to return ϵ when l identifies an update to an invalid index in a container representation.

$$\text{ASSIGN-ERR} \quad \frac{\langle\, e \mid \rho\,\rangle \to v}{\langle\, l \,:=\, e \mid \rho\,\rangle \Rightarrow \langle\, \epsilon\,,\,\_\,\rangle} \quad \rho[v/l] = \epsilon$$

$$\text{ASSIGN} \quad \frac{\langle\, e \mid \rho\,\rangle \to v}{\langle\, l \,:=\, e \mid \rho\,\rangle \Rightarrow \langle\, \bullet\,,\, \rho[r/l]\,\rangle} \quad \rho[v/l] \neq \epsilon$$

$$\text{DIV} \quad \frac{\langle\, e_1 \mid \rho\,\rangle \to v_1 \quad \langle\, e_2 \mid \rho\,\rangle \to v_2}{\langle\, e_1 \,/\, e_2 \mid \rho\,\rangle \to [\![/]\!][v_1, v_2]}$$

$$\text{DIV-ZERO} \quad \frac{\langle\, e_1 \mid \rho\,\rangle \to v_1 \quad \langle\, e_2 \mid \rho\,\rangle \to 0}{\langle\, e_1 \,/\, e_2 \mid \rho\,\rangle \to \epsilon}$$

where function at returns the n-th element of a sequence. Range accesses actually cannot cause trapped errors, as the type system enforces that the limits must be statically defined in order to determine the size of the result, which means that such errors can be detected. Trapped errors are propagated throughout evaluation rules, i.e., whenever a premiss evaluates to ϵ the overall rule also evaluates to ϵ. All cases that fall outside of our semantic rules are implicitly evaluated to untrapped errors ($\bot$ value).

Soundness Theorem and Proof Sketch. Our result is stated in the following theorem, where $\vdash \rho :: \Gamma_G$ denotes consistency and $\circ$ denotes empty store/state.

Theorem 1. *Given a program p if $\circ, \circ, \circ \vdash p :: (\bullet, \Gamma_G)$ and $\langle\, p \mid \circ\,\rangle \Rightarrow \langle\, \rho\,\rangle$ terminates, then $\vdash \rho :: \Gamma_G$ or ρ is an error state.*

Proof (Sketch). The full proof is presented in [1]. The proof is by induction on typing derivations. The base case for induction is that prior to execution, every type-checked program has an initial evaluation environment that is (trivially) consistent with the typing environment. Here, consistency means that all variables in the evaluation environment have associated values compatible with their corresponding type in the typing environment. The inductive cases are considered for each transition defined in the semantics of the language. In each case we show that one of two cases can occur: 1) either a consistent environment is produced at the end of each transition; or 2) a trapped error has been generated and is returned by the program. We present two cases, illustrating how the proof proceeds for division expressions and assignment statements that may raise trapped errors.

DIVISION EXPRESSIONS. We have to prove that if $\langle\, e_1 \,/\, e_2 \mid \rho \,\rangle \to v$ terminates then $v \in \mathbf{V}$. Two semantic rules can be applied for each operator, one in the case of division by 0; the other in the general case:

- If $\langle\, e_1 \mid \rho \,\rangle \to v_1$ and $\langle\, e_2 \mid \rho \,\rangle \to 0$ terminate, then $\langle\, e_1/e_2 \mid \rho \,\rangle$ evaluates to $\epsilon \in \mathbf{V}$ by semantic DIV-ZERO.
- If $\langle\, e_1 \mid \rho \,\rangle \to v_1$ and $\langle\, e_2 \mid \rho \,\rangle \to v_2$ terminate, with $v_2 \neq 0$, then $\langle\, e_1/e_2 \mid \rho \,\rangle$ evaluates to $[\![/]\!][v_1, v_2]$ by semantic rule DIV. Here $[\![/]\!]$ gives the interpretation of the $/$ operator with respect to the values v_1 and v_2. By induction hypothesis, v_1 and v_2 are in the semantic domain $\mathbf{V}$, corresponding to representations of integer values. Since division is well-defined for integer representations, then $[\![/]\!][v_1, v_2]$ evaluates to another value v which is again a representation of an integer and $v \in \mathbf{V}\backslash\mathcal{E}$.

ASSIGNMENT STATEMENTS. We have to prove that if $\langle\, l := e \mid \rho \,\rangle \Rightarrow \langle\, v \,,\, \rho' \,\rangle$ terminates then, either the statement raises a trapped error due to an invalid access on the left value, or the returned environment ρ' is consistent with the typing environment. Two semantic rules are applicable, ASSIGN and ASSIGN-ERR, the latter only when the target is an invalid position in a container. If $\langle\, e \mid \rho \,\rangle \to v$ terminates, then $v \in \mathbf{V}\backslash\mathcal{E}$ and v represents a value of type τ. The semantic rule to apply depends on the result of the frame update operation $\rho[v/l]$. If this returns ϵ, then semantic rule ASSIGN-ERR is applied, and the statement evaluates to $\langle\, \epsilon \,,\, \_ \,\rangle$. Otherwise it will return an updated state ρ', in which case semantic rule ASSIGN is applied, and the statement evaluates to $\langle\, \bullet \,,\, \rho[v/l] \,\rangle$. It remains to prove that this resulting evaluation environment is consistent with the typing environment. Here we resort to the induction hypothesis $\vdash \rho :: \Gamma$, which guarantees the value currently stored for l represents a value of type τ. Since v also represents a value of type τ, the update of left value l for value v preserves consistency.

7   Related Work

Cryptol [5] is a domain-specific language and tool suite developed for the specification and implementation of cryptographic algorithms. It is a functional DSL without global state or side-effects, which was developed with the main purpose of producing formally verified hardware implementations of symmetric cryptographic primitives such as block ciphers and hash functions. CAO is an imperative language that targets a wider application domain, although also restricted to cryptography. Indeed, the CAO language features have been designed to permit expressing, not only symmetric but also asymmetric cryptographic primitives, in a natural way. Furthermore, CAO tools are released under an open-source policy.

Dependent types offer a powerful approach to ensure program properties. However, this power in not incorporated in any of the mainstream languages, while the prototypical languages that do it are mostly functional. The first prototype of an imperative language to use dependent types was Xanadu [9], allowing, e.g., to statically verify that accesses to arrays are within bounds. So far, CAO offers a modest form of dependent types, where all type parameters values must be statically known. Ongoing work aims extend CAO with a more powerful approach to dependent types inspired by [9]. This new version of the type system allows for symbolic parametrisation, dropping the requirement that all sizes are known at compilation, using an SMT solver to handle associated constraints.

The use of Generalized Algebraic Data Types (GADTs) in Haskell, together with type families and existential types, allows the implementation of embedded DSL's with some dependent typing features. Moreover, since this approach relies on Haskell's type system, this permits avoiding the full implementation of a type checker. CAO does not follow this embedded approach because it would make it harder to preserve characteristics of the language that pre-dated formal work on the type system. For example, the CAO syntax tries to follow the cryptographic specification standards, and GADTs would impose their own syntax, which is more suitable for building combinator systems. One could of course try to use a GADT-based intermediate representation, but it is not clear that this would pay out in terms of the global implementation effort. In particular, we anticipate that dealing with coercions and casts would complicate the type checking apparatus [8]. Moreover, it would probably be difficult using an embedded approach to keep the implementation structure close to the formal specification.

The use of an embedded implementation in a dependently typed language, e.g. Coq or Agda, could also be an option for the implementation of our type system. However, this would suffer from the same drawbacks previously presented for GADTs, and would also require specific expertise that are not realistic to assume in the target audience for CAO. The need to reason about the correctness and termination of CAO programs at this level would also be an overkill for most applications. In the CAO tool-chain, this sort of analysis is enabled by an independent deductive formal verification tool called CAOVerif.

8   Conclusion

CAO is a language aimed at closing the gap between the usual way of specifying cryptographic algorithms and their actual implementation, reducing the possibility of errors and increasing the understanding of the source code. This language offers high-level features and a type system tailored to the implementation of cryptographic concepts, statically ruling out some important classes of errors. In this paper, we have presented a short overview of CAO and the specification, validation and implementation of a type-system designed to support the implementation of front-ends for CAO compilation and formal verification tools.

References

1. Barbosa, M., Moss, A., Page, D., Rodrigues, N.F., Silva, P.F.: Type checking cryptography implementations. Tech. Rep. DI-CCTC-11-01, CCTC, Univ. Minho (2011)
2. Bernstein, D.J.: The Poly1305-AES Message-Authentication Code. In: Gilbert, H., Handschuh, H. (eds.) FSE 2005. LNCS, vol. 3557, pp. 32–49. Springer, Heidelberg (2005)
3. Bernstein, D.J.: Cryptography in NaCl (2009), http://nacl.cr.yp.to
4. Jonsson, J., Kaliski, B.: Public-Key Cryptography Standards (PKCS) #1: RSA Cryptography Specification Version 2.1 (2003)
5. Lewis, J.: Cryptol: specification, implementation and verification of high-grade cryptographic applications. In: FMSE 2007, p. 41. ACM (2007)
6. Menezes, A.J., Vanstone, S.A., Oorschot, P.C.V.: Handbook of Applied Cryptography. CRC Press, Inc., Boca Raton (1996)
7. Milner, R.: A theory of type polymorphism in programming. Journal of Computer and System Sciences 17, 348–375 (1978)
8. Silva, P.F., Oliveira, J.N.: 'Galculator': functional prototype of a Galois-connection based proof assistant. In: PPDP 2008, pp. 44–55. ACM (2008)
9. Xi, H.: Imperative programming with dependent types. In: LICS 2000, pp. 375–387. IEEE Computer Society (2000)

Intentional Automata: A Context-Dependent Model for Component Connectors

(Extended Abstract)

David Costa[1,4], Milad Niqui[1], and Jan Rutten[1,2,3]

[1] CWI, Amsterdam
[2] VUA, Amsterdam
[3] RUN, Nijmegen
[4] Fredhopper, Amsterdam,
The Netherlands

1 Introduction

In recent years, a promising line of research on formal compositional models for component connectors [3–6, 8, 9] has demonstrated the merits of having connectors as first class concepts, and incrementally increased the expressiveness of the interaction protocols that can be captured compositionally. Typically, in these models connectors are entitled to have their own *specification* and *abstractions*. Through composition, just like components, connectors can be *combined* and yield more sophisticated connectors. The models provide an abstract semantic domain to express interaction protocols, provide operations on the domain, and a behavioural equivalence relation of interest that identifies elements of the domain. Special elements of the domain are chosen to specify *basic* interaction protocols and correspond to the behaviour of so-called *primitive connectors*. Bruni *et al.* [8] consider four rather simple stateless primitive connectors, that essentially model synchronisation, mutual exclusion and hiding. The obtained model allows to build a wide range of coordination connectors. For instance, they are expressive enough to model the multiple-action synchronisation mechanism of CommUnity [11] which uses complex architectural connectors. Arbab and Rutten [3] and Baier *et al.* [4] consider in their models three additional primitive connectors: FIFO buffers, non-deterministic merger, and lossy channel; and define elegant compositional operational semantics for a large class of Reo connectors. In particular, both these models are refined enough to differentiate the behaviour of non-deterministic Reo connectors that in dataflow models, such as Kahn networks, lead to the so-called Brock-Ackerman anomalies [7]. Clarke *et al.* [9] consider an additional primitive, the *LossySync* channel, and proposed the colouring semantics as the first compositional model for context-dependent connectors. Context-dependency is a feature that extends the class of dataflow behaviour that connectors can express by including behaviour that depends on the presence or absence of *pending* I/O operations—an I/O operation present on a port. The observation of pending I/O operations permits to express in the model non-monotonic behaviour such as precedence and blocking—referred to as context-dependent behaviour. More recently Bonsangue *et al.* [6] proposed

F. Arbab and M. Sirjani (Eds.): FSEN 2011, LNCS 7141, pp. 335–342, 2012.

an alternative model for context dependent-connectors based on guarded automata. The class of context-dependent behaviour captured compositionally by their models is similar to the colouring semantics, but because guarded automata can be *partial*, deficiencies identified in the colouring semantics that arise due to the totality of colouring tables not being preserved under composition, are avoided. In the context of service orchestration, Barbosa *et al.* [5] define a compositional calculus in the Bird and Meertens style where $\mathcal{R}eo$-like context-dependent connectors can be modelled compositionally and show that their expressiveness permits to capture non-trivial orchestration protocols.

In this paper we contribute to that same line of research, and propose models for context-dependent connectors that permit to capture compositionally a larger class of context-dependent behaviour. Our contributions are:

1) The definition of intentional automata, and an operational semantics based on observational equivalence à la Milner, to reason compositionally about context-dependent connectors. The semantics permit to express compositionally a class of *dataflow priority* and *dataflow blocking* behaviour that includes the intended behaviour of the *LossySyncFIFO$_1$* channel, and unlike all the previous models, includes context-dependent connectors constructed with multiple *FIFO$_1$* channels, like the *LossySyncFIFO$_2$* channel.

2) The identification of a particular class of intentional automata, called $\mathcal{R}eo$ automata, resulting from the axiomatisation of a $\mathcal{R}eo$ connector port.

3) A definition that captures the intentional automata that model context-dependent behaviour and characterises context-dependent connector.

These results have been obtained in the context of Costa's PhD research and recently detailed in his thesis [10]. In this paper due to size limitations, we skip the technical details and give an overview of the results, and for a detailed account we refer the reader to the thesis.

2   Preliminaries

We assume a set $\{A, B, C, \ldots\}$ of names that we denote by $\mathcal{N}ames$. A connector is viewed as a black box with a well-defined interface that corresponds to the collection of communication *ports*, $\Sigma \subseteq \mathcal{N}ames$, through which the connector interacts with its environment. Given a connector C with a set of ports Σ, the different ways that the environment can interact with C are given by the set of requests $\mathcal{R} = \mathcal{P}(\Sigma)$. For a *request-set* $R \in \mathcal{R}$, every port in R has a request, whereas there are no requests on ports in $\Sigma \backslash R$. For instance, consider a connector with a set of ports $\Sigma = \{A, B\}$. The set $\mathcal{P}(\{A, B\})$ contains all the request-sets the environment can perform on *Sync*. The empty request-set $\emptyset$ denotes that none of the ports of the connector receives a request from its environment. The request-set $\{A\}$ denotes that a request is present on port A, and no request is present on port B. The request-set $\{A, B\}$ denotes that a request is present on port A and another one is present on port B simultaneously. A connector C processes one *request-set* at a time, and in response produces a (possibly empty)

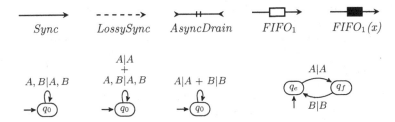

Fig. 1. Reo channel types and their intentional automata models

firing-set $F \subseteq \Sigma$. The set of all firing-sets $\mathcal{P}(\Sigma)$ is denoted by $\mathcal{F}$. For example, the empty firing-set $\emptyset$ denotes *quiescence*—no firing at any of the ports. The firing-set $\{A, B\}$ denotes the simultaneous firing of ports A and B. A (possibly empty) request-set is related to a (possibly empty) firing-set.

We use Reo as our reference language to build connectors. Reo is a coordination language based on a calculus of channel composition to construct component connectors. Due space limitations we refer the reader to the paper by Farhad [1] for an introduction on Reo.

Figure 1 contains some common Reo channel types. *Sync* denotes a synchronous channel. Data flows through this channel if and only if it is possible to synchronously accept data on one end and pass it out through the other end. *LossySync* denotes a lossy synchronous channel. If a *take* is pending on the sink end of this channel and a *write* is requested on its source end, then the channel behaves as a synchronous channel. However, if no *take* is pending, the *write* fires, and the data is lost. Observe that this channel has *context-dependent behaviour*, as it behaves differently depending upon whether there is a *take* pending on its sink end—if it were context independent, the data could be lost regardless of whether its sink end has or does not have a *take* pending. *AsyncDrain* denotes an asynchronous drain. Data can flow into only one end of this channel at the exclusion of data flow at the other end. $FIFO_1$ denotes an empty FIFO with one buffer cell. Data can flow into the source end of this buffer, but no flow is possible at its sink end (since its buffer is empty). After data flow into the buffer cell, it becomes a full FIFO. $FIFO_1(x)$ denotes a full FIFO with one buffer cell occupied by the data value x. Data value x can flow out of the sink end of this buffer, but no flow is possible at the source end (since its buffer is full). After x flows out of the buffer, it becomes an empty FIFO.

3   Intentional Automata

To model a connector with an intentional automaton one can think of an abstract state machine, where each *state* corresponds to a possible *configuration* of the connector and the *transitions* indicate the *experiments* that take the connector from one configuration to another, not necessarily different, configuration.

Definition 1 (intentional automata). *A non-deterministic intentional automaton over the set of ports* Σ *is a system* $\mathcal{A} = (Q, \Sigma, \delta, I)$, *with a set of states* Q; *a transition function* $\delta : Q \rightarrow \mathcal{P}(\mathcal{F} \times Q)^{\mathcal{R}}$ *that associates for every state* $q \in Q$, *a function* $\delta_q \in \mathcal{R} \longrightarrow \mathcal{P}(\mathcal{F} \times Q)$, *where* $\mathcal{R}$ *are the requests of* $\mathcal{A}$ *and* $\mathcal{F}$ *are the* firings *of* $\mathcal{A}$, *and a non-empty set of initial states* $I \subseteq Q$.

The transition function δ assigns to each state $q \in Q$ the behaviour given by a function $\delta_q : \mathcal{R} \longrightarrow \mathcal{P}(\mathcal{F} \times Q)$. For each request-set $R \in \mathcal{R}$, δ_q maps R to a set of responses in $\mathcal{P}(\mathcal{F} \times Q)$. Whenever the behaviour of a state q is undefined for a particular request-set R, $\delta_q(R) = \emptyset$, and we write $\delta_q \Uparrow R$. Whenever $I = Q$ we simply write $\mathcal{A} = (Q, \Sigma, \delta)$ to denote the intentional automaton $\mathcal{A} = (Q, \Sigma, \delta, I)$.

$\longrightarrow$ *Transition Relation.* The transition function of the non-deterministic intentional automata $\delta : Q \longrightarrow \mathcal{P}(\mathcal{F} \times Q)^{\mathcal{R}}$ can be equivalently represented by a relation $\longrightarrow \subseteq Q \times \mathcal{R} \times \mathcal{F} \times Q$ defined by: $q \xrightarrow{R|F} q' \equiv (F, q') \in \delta_q(R)$.

Internal Transitions. Internal steps (or internal activity) of a connector account for the non-observable activity of a connector and are modelled in the automata by *internal transitions*. Internal activity in the connector takes place without involving the ports of the connector. An internal transition allows the automaton to change from a state q to state q' when no requests are present in the ports of the connector and as a result no ports of the connector are fired.

Definition 2 (internal transition). *We call a transition of type* $q \xrightarrow{\emptyset|\emptyset} q'$, *with* $q \neq q'$, *an* internal transition.

Labelled Transition Diagram. A labelled transition diagram for an intentional automaton $\mathcal{A} = (Q, \Sigma, \delta, I)$ has its vertices labelled by the states $q \in Q$; there is a directed edge represented with an arrow labelled $R \mid F$ from the vertex labelled q to the vertex labelled q' precisely when $\delta_q(R) = (F, q')$ The initial states are distinguished by an inward-pointing arrow. If $R_1|F_1, \ldots, R_n|F_n$ label n edges from the state q to the state q' then we simply draw one arrow from q to q' labelled $R_1|F_1 + \ldots + R_n|F_n$ instead of n arrows labelled $R_1|F_1$ to $R_n|F_n$. We omit the delimiting set of brackets of the request-set R and firing-set F when labelling an edge. Irrespective of the direction of arrows, the label $R|F$ reads always from left to right: the two edges $q \xrightarrow{A,B|A} q'$ and $q' \xleftarrow{A,B|A} q$ both depict the transition $\delta_q(\{A, B\}) = (\{A\}, q')$.

Figure 1 contains the intentional automata models for some $\mathcal{R}$eo channel types.

3.1   Connector Equivalence and Operations on Automata

Like in constraint automata we use bisimulation as equivalence relation [10, Def. 4.2.2, p. 78]). Unlike constraint automata we use weak-bisimulation as observational equivalence [10, Def. 4.2.7, p. 79]) and show that it is a congruence with respect to the operations. The main reason to consider observational equivalence is because we consider internal transitions in the model. In constraint automata, all the transitions are observable and the hiding operation that removes hidden ports also eliminates what could be interpreted as internal transitions (transitions labeled with an empty set of ports).

We define three operations on intentional automata to model compositionally composite connectors [10, Section 4.3]): product, hiding, and internal transitions elimination. The product operation on intentional automata, like in constraint automata, follows the standard construction for building finite automata for intersection. It also has similarities with composition operators of process algebra, namely, the parallel composition of labelled transition systems with synchronisation over common actions and interleaving over other actions, as in TCSP [18]. The hiding operation on constraint automata performs two separate constructions: (a) it removes all information about the hidden port; (b) it performs the elimination of the transitions labelled only with the hidden port. The hiding operation on intentional automata performs also two separate constructions: (i) it removes all information about the hidden port; (ii) it prioritises the transitions in which the hidden port has a request and fires, over the transitions in which the hidden port has a request but does not fire. Construction (i) is similar to (a), whereas construction (ii) has no counterpart in constraint automata. Construction (b) is not performed by the hiding operation on intentional automata. In intentional automata, the transitions labelled only by hidden ports become internal transitions. The internal transition in intentional automata are eliminated by performing a construction similar to construction (b) on constraint automata; and both are similar to the elimination of ϵ-transitions in ordinary non-deterministic finite automata. Construction (ii) represents the main difference between the operations on the two automata models. In fact, construction (ii) uses information present only in intentional automata transitions regarding requested I/O operations, and based on this information, it prioritises the transitions. We opted for having a dedicated operation to eliminate the internal transitions and separate it from the hiding operation mainly because it makes the definition of the hiding operation easier to write, and makes more clear the parallel between the operation to eliminate internal transitions on intentional automata, with the operation to eliminate epsilon transitions from the classical theory of Finite Automata.

4   Reo Automata

Using properties that characterise how Reo ports interact with their environment we can restrict the large class of connectors that intentional automata models to the class of models that captures Reo connectors behaviour. In this particular class, it helps to think of states as having a structure according to the configuration of a Reo connector. A connector *configuration* is partitioned into two parts: the *internal configuration* and the *external configuration*. An *internal configuration* is an abstract representation of the internal memory of the connector. An internal configuration is denoted by an element $s \in S$, where S is the set of all internal configurations of the connector. The *external configuration* of a connector describes the status of the connector's interface and is denoted by a set $P \subseteq \Sigma$, where Σ is the set of ports of the connector. The intuition is that in a given configuration (s, P), the set P indicates the ports of the connector that have a *pending request*. We shall refer to these as *pending ports*. These are ports that have received a request in previous evaluation steps and for which the request has not been handled until now. Obviously, if a port is not in P, then this port has no pending requests.

Definition 3 (connector configuration). *Consider a connector with a set of internal configurations S and a set of ports Σ. A configuration is a pair (s, P) consisting of an internal configuration $s \in S$ and an external configuration $P \subseteq \Sigma$. The set of all configurations of the connector is given by $S \times \mathcal{P}(\Sigma)$. Given a configuration (s, P), we say p is a pending port or port p has a pending request if $p \in P$. All the configurations of a connector are initial, unless a subset of configurations $I \subseteq S \times \mathcal{P}(\Sigma)$ is defined as initial.*

Recall the transition relation of intentional automata, $\longrightarrow \subseteq Q \times \mathcal{R} \times \mathcal{F} \times Q$. We define the set of states Q as the set of configurations $S \times \mathcal{P}(\Sigma)$. A transition $(s, P) \xrightarrow{R|F} (s', P')$ models an *evaluation step* of a connector. The connector changes from configuration (s, P) to configuration (s', P') by evaluating the request-set R and producing the firing-set F.

Ports in $\mathcal{R}$eo connectors interact in a particular manner with the environment, which allows us to infer important axioms for the evaluation steps of automata models for $\mathcal{R}$eo connectors [10]:

♡ in a given configuration, a connector takes each pending port ($p \in P$) and requested port ($p' \in R$), and either fires it ($p \in F$ and/or $p' \in F$) or keeps it pending ($p \in P'$ and/or $p' \in P$, accordingly): $P \cup R = F \cup P'$.

♣ a port $p \in P$ (p is pending) implies $p \notin R$ (p cannot receive a request): $P \cap R = \emptyset$.

♢ a port that fires cannot become/remain pending: $F \cap P' = \emptyset$.

The $\mathcal{R}$eo connectors from the literature are expressive and constitute an interesting class to study. These connectors have an additional axiom: *None of the $\mathcal{R}$eo connector specifications distinguishes between the set of pending ports and the set of requested ports when deciding which ports to fire.* Considering an evaluation step of an automaton model for a $\mathcal{R}$eo connector, this translates to the following property: $\delta_{(s, P)}(R) = \delta_{(s, \emptyset)}(R \cup P)$. This property together with ♣ imply an additional property that characterises the transition function δ for automata models of $\mathcal{R}$eo connectors present in the literature:

$$\spadesuit \quad \delta_{(s,P)}(R) = \begin{cases} \delta_{(s,\emptyset)}(R \cup P) & \text{if } R \cap P = \emptyset \\ \emptyset & \text{otherwise} \end{cases}$$

Consider a firing-set that involves multiple ports. By property ♡, the environment must perform requests on these ports before they can fire. Property ♠ says that the firing is produced independently of the order in which the environment executes the requests on the ports that subsequently fire. Therefore we can identify the different ordering possibilities as a single one and reduce the complexity of the model. The $\mathcal{R}$eo connectors enjoy properties $\heartsuit$, $\spadesuit$, and $\diamondsuit$.

Definition 4 ($\mathcal{R}$eo automata). *Consider a connector C with ports Σ, internal configurations S, and a set of initial configurations $I \subseteq S \times \mathcal{P}(\Sigma)$. A $\mathcal{R}$eo automaton for C is a non-deterministic intentional automaton $\mathcal{A}_C = (Q, \Sigma, \delta, I)$ with states $Q = S \times \mathcal{P}(\Sigma)$ and transition function $\delta : Q \to \mathcal{P}(\mathcal{F} \times Q)^{\mathcal{R}}$ that associates with every state $q = (s, P)$ a function $\delta_q : \mathcal{R} \longrightarrow \mathcal{P}(\mathcal{F} \times Q)$ such that:*

$$\heartsuit \diamondsuit \; \langle F, (s', P') \rangle \in \delta_{(s, P)}(R) \implies P \cup R = F \cup P' \text{ and } F \cap P' = \emptyset$$

$$\spadesuit \quad \delta_{(s, P)}(R) = \begin{cases} \delta_{(s, \emptyset)}(R \cup P) & \text{if } R \cap P = \emptyset \\ \emptyset & \text{otherwise} \end{cases}$$

We write $C = (S, \Sigma, \mathcal{A}_C)$ to denote a connector with name C, ports Σ, internal configurations S, and semantics given $\mathcal{A}_C = (Q, \Sigma, \delta, I)$ where $Q = S \times \mathcal{P}\Sigma$.

In a $\mathcal{R}$eo automaton, it follows from properties $\heartsuit \diamondsuit$ and $\spadesuit$ that for each internal (memory) configuration s the transitions from the state $(s, \emptyset)$ are enough to characterise the transitions of all states of the form (s, P). Furthermore, for any transition of the form $(s, \emptyset) \xrightarrow{R|F} (s, P)$ we have that $R = F \cup P$ and $F \cap P = \emptyset$.

Properties $\heartsuit \diamondsuit$ and $\spadesuit$ make it possible to turn a partial intentional automaton that defines only the transition function for the states of the form $(s, \emptyset)$ into a fully specified intentional automaton. To represent a partial intentional automaton that specifies the transition function only for states of the form $(s, \emptyset)$ we define a concise tabular representation called *configuration table*.

$\mathcal{R}$eo automata encode in each transition the context in which a firing occurs. With this information in the model we can define and precisely characterise context-dependent connectors like the *LossySync*.

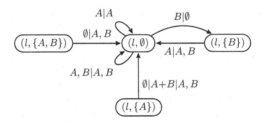

Fig. 2. The labelled transition diagram of $\mathcal{A}_{LossySync}$

Definition 5 (context-dependent connector). *Consider a $\mathcal{R}$eo connector $C = (S, \Sigma, \mathcal{A})$. For each state (s, P) in $\mathcal{A} = (Q, \Sigma, \delta)$ we calculate the set:*

$$\Phi_{(s, P)} = \{F \mid \exists R, q \text{ s.t. } (s, P) \xrightarrow{R|F}_\delta q, F \neq \emptyset\}.$$

C is a context-dependent *connector if for some $s \in S$, there is a pair of different states (s, P_1), and (s, P_2) such that $\Phi_{(s, P_1)} \neq \Phi_{(s, P_2)}$.*

Consider the *LossySync* $\Re$eo automata model depicted in Figure 2 we have $\Phi_{(l,\emptyset)} = \{\{A\}, \{A,B\}\}$ and $\Phi_{(l,\{B\})} = \{\{A,B\}\}$. Hence, because $\Phi_{(l,\emptyset)} \neq \Phi_{(l,\{B\})}$, by definition 5 *LossySync* is a context-dependent connector.

References

1. Arbab, F.: Reo: a channel-based coordination model for component composition. Mathematical Structures in Computer Science 14(3), 329–366 (2004)
2. Arbab, F., Chothia, T., van der Mei, R., Meng, S., Moon, Y.J., Verhoef, C.: From Coordination to Stochastic Models of QoS. In: Field, J., Vasconcelos, V.T. (eds.) COORDINATION 2009. LNCS, vol. 5521, pp. 268–287. Springer, Heidelberg (2009)
3. Arbab, F., Rutten, J.J.M.M.: A Coinductive Calculus of Component Connectors. In: Wirsing, M., Pattinson, D., Hennicker, R. (eds.) WADT 2003. LNCS, vol. 2755, pp. 34–55. Springer, Heidelberg (2003)
4. Baier, C., Sirjani, M., Arbab, F., Rutten, J.: Modeling component connectors in Reo by Constraint Automata. SCP 61(2), 75–113 (2006)
5. Barbosa, M.A., Barbosa, L.S.: A perspective on service orchestration. SCP 74(9), 671–687 (2009)
6. Bonsangue, M., Clarke, D., Silva, A.: Automata for Context-Dependent Connectors. In: Field, J., Vasconcelos, V.T. (eds.) COORDINATION 2009. LNCS, vol. 5521, pp. 184–203. Springer, Heidelberg (2009)
7. Brock, J.D., Ackerman, W.B.: Scenarios: A model of non-determinate computation. In: Díaz, J., Ramos, I. (eds.) Formalization of Programming Concepts. LNCS, vol. 107, pp. 252–259. Springer, Heidelberg (1981)
8. Bruni, R., Lanese, I., Montanari, U.: A basic algebra of stateless connectors. TCS 366(1-2), 98–120 (2006)
9. Clarke, D., Costa, D., Arbab, F.: Connector Colouring I: Synchronisation and Context Dependency. SCP 66(3), 205–225 (2007)
10. Costa, D.: Formal Models For Component Connectors. Ph.D. thesis, VUA (2010), http://dare.ubvu.vu.nl/handle/1871/16380
11. Fiadeiro, J.: Categories for Software Engineering. Springer, Heidelberg (2004)
12. Gelernter, D., Carriero, N.: Coordination languages and their significance. Commun. ACM 35(2), 97–107 (1992)
13. Hopcroft, J.E., Motwani, R., Ullman, J.D.: Introduction to Automata Theory, Languages, and Computation, 3rd edn. Addison-Wesley LP Co., Inc. (2006)
14. Milner, R.: Communication and Concurrency. Prentice-Hall, Inc. (1989)
15. Park, D.: Concurrency and Automata on Infinite Sequences. In: Deussen, P. (ed.) GI-TCS 1981. LNCS, vol. 104, pp. 167–183. Springer, Heidelberg (1981)
16. Perry, D.E., Wolf, A.L.: Foundations for the study of software architecture. SIG-SOFT Softw. Eng. Notes 17, 40–52 (1992)
17. Shaw, M.: Procedure Calls are the Assembly Language of Software Interconnection: Connectors Deserve First-Class Status. In: Lamb, D.A. (ed.) ICSE-WS 1993. LNCS, vol. 1078, pp. 17–32. Springer, Heidelberg (1996)
18. Brookes, S.D., Hoare, C.A.R., Roscoe, A.W.: A Theory of Communicating Sequential Processes. J. ACM 31(3), 560–599 (1984)

Nested Dynamic Condition Response Graphs

Thomas Hildebrandt, Raghava Rao Mukkamala, and Tijs Slaats*

IT University of Copenhagen, Rued Langgaardsvej 7, 2300 Copenhagen, Denmark
{hilde,rao,tslaats}@itu.dk

Abstract. We present an extension of the recently introduced declarative process model *Dynamic Condition Response Graphs* (DCR Graphs) to allow *nested sub-graphs* and a new *milestone relation* between events. The extension was developed during a case study carried out jointly with our industrial partner Exformatics, a danish provider of case and workflow management systems. We formalize the semantics by giving first a map from Nested to (flat) DCR Graphs with milestones, and then extending the previously given mapping from DCR Graphs to Büchi-automata to include the milestone relation.

1 Introduction

Declarative process models have been suggested by several research groups [1–5, 15, 16, 18, 19] as a good approach to describe case management and other non-rigid business and workflow processes where it is generally allowed to redo or skip activities, and even dynamically adapt the set of activities and constraints. The rationale is that if a strict sequencing is the exception, then the implicit specification of control flow in declarative models is more appropriate than notations based on explicit control flows such as the (typical use of) Business Process Model and Notation (BPMN) 2.0 [13].

A drawback of the declarative approaches in general, however, is that the implicit definition of the state and control flow makes it more complex to perceive the state and execute the process. To find out what are the next possible activities it is necessary to evaluate a set of constraints defined relatively to the history of the execution.

This motivates finding an expressive declarative process language that allows for a simple run-time scheduling which is easily visualized for the case worker. As a candidate for such a language we recently introduced in [7, 11] a declarative process model called Dynamic Condition Response Graphs (DCR Graphs). The model is a generalization of the classic event structure model for concurrency [20] and is inspired by the Process Matrix model [10, 12] developed by one of our industrial partners Resultmaker, a Danish provider of workflow and case-management systems.

The core DCR Graphs model consists of a set of events and four binary relations between the events: The *dynamic inclusion* and *dynamic exclusion* relations, and the *condition* and *response* relations. The dynamic inclusion and exclusion relations generalize the usual symmetric conflict relation of event structures by splitting it in two

---

* This research is supported by the Danish Research Agency through a Knowledge Voucher granted to Exformatics (grant #10-087067, www.exformatics.com), the Trustworthy Pervasive Healthcare Services project (grant #2106-07-0019, www.trustcare.eu) and the Computer Supported Mobile Adaptive Business Processes project (grant #274-06-0415, www.cosmobiz.dk).

F. Arbab and M. Sirjani (Eds.): FSEN 2011, LNCS 7141, pp. 343–350, 2012.

asymmetric relations: If an event A excludes an event B, written $A \rightarrow\% B$, then B can not happen until after the occurrence of an event C that includes event B, which is written $C \rightarrow+ B$. Similarly, the condition and response relations generalize the usual causal order relation of event structures by splitting it in two relations: If an event B has event A as condition, written $A \rightarrow\bullet B$, then event A must either be currently excluded or have happened for B to happen. Dually, if an event A has event B as response, written $A \bullet\rightarrow B$, then event B must eventually happen or always eventually be excluded after an occurrence of event A. To express that events are executed by actors with different roles the core model is extended with roles assigned to the events.

In [7] we show that the run-time state of DCR Graphs can be represented as a marking consisting of three sets of events, recording respectively the *executed events*, the *currently included events*, and the *pending response events*, i.e. events that must eventually happen or be excluded. From the marking, it is easy to evaluate if an event can happen (by checking if all its conditions are either executed or excluded) and to verify if the graph is in a completed state (by checking if the set of included pending responses is empty). It is also easy to update the state when executing an event by adding it to the set of executed events, remove the event from the pending response set and add new response events according to the response relation, and include/exclude events in the set of currently included events according to the include/exclude relations. In [7, 11] we express the acceptance condition for infinite runs (no pending response is continuously included without being executed) by giving a map to a Büchi automaton.

In the present paper we describe how to extend the model to allow for *nested subgraphs* as is standard in most state-of-the art modelling notations. The work was carried out during a case study, in which we are applied *Nested DCR Graphs* in the design phase of the development of a distributed, inter-organizational case management system carried out by our industrial partner, Exformatics, a company that specializes in solutions for knowledge sharing, workflows and document handling.

Fig. 1 shows the graphical notation for nested DCR graphs and illustrates the use of nested sub-graphs in a sub part of the model arising from our case study. The Arrange meeting event represents the arrangement of a meeting be-

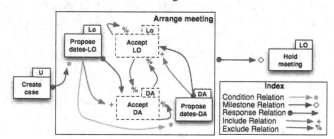

Fig. 1. Nested DCR Graphs with Arrange meeting sub-graph

tween two of the organizations (DA and LO) using the distributed case management system being developed. It has been refined to a sub-graph including four sub events for proposing and accepting dates for the meeting. The dashed boxes indicate that the events Accept DA and Accept LO for accepting meeting dates are initially excluded. Described briefly, when the organization (U) creates a case, it triggers as a response the event Propose dates-LO, representing LO proposing dates for a meeting. This event triggers as a response and includes the event Accept DA, representing DA accepting the dates. But it also enables that DA can propose other dates, represented by the event **Propose Dates-DA**. Now, this event triggers as a response and includes the event **Accept LO**, representing LO accepting the dates. Again, LO may do this, or again propose dates. The proposal of dates may continue forever, and as long as no one accepts there will be a pending response on at least one of the accept events. As soon as one of the accept events happen, they will both be excluded, and there will be none of the included events in the sub-graph having pending responses. This corresponds to the accepting condition for finite runs of DCR graphs [7], and thus intuitively reflects that the sub-graph is in a completed state. Now, we want to express that the event **Hold meeting** can only be executed when this is the case. To do this, we introduced a new core relation between events called the *milestone* relation. If an event A is a milestone for an event B, written $A \rightarrow\!\diamond B$, then B can not happen if A is included and required to be executed again (i.e. as a response). The new milestone relation allow us to define nesting as simply a tree structure on events that can be flattened to (flat) DCR Graphs by keeping all atomic events (i.e. events with no sub-events) and letting them inherit the relations defined for their super-events. In particular, the flattening does not introduce new events (in fact it removes all super events) and at most introduce an order of n^2 new relations. Thus, we need not define a new operational semantics for nested DCR Graphs, instead we can make the much simpler extension of the semantics for (flat) DCR Graphs to consider the new milestone relation. It is worth noting that while the milestone relation makes it very direct to express completion of subgraphs, we conjecture that it does not add expressiveness to DCR Graphs.

Related Work. Our approach is closely related to the work on ConDec [18, 19]. The crucial difference is that we allow nesting and a few core constraints making it possible to describe the state of a process as a simple marking. ConDec does not address nesting (nor dynamic inclusion/exclusion), but allows one to specify any relation expressible within Linear-time Temporal Logic (LTL). This offers much flexibility with respect to specifying execution constraints. In particular the condition and response relations are standard verification patterns and also considered in [18, 19] (the condition relation is called precedence), and we have used the same graphical notation. However, the execution of a process expressed as LTL (which typically involves a translation to a Büchi-automaton) is more complex and the run-time state is difficult to relate to the original ConDec specification. Moreover, we conjecture that DCR Graphs are as expressive as Büchi-automata, and thus more expressive than LTL. Finally, Nested DCR Graphs relates to the independent (so far unpublished) work on the declarative *Guard-Stage-Milestone* model by Hull, presented in invited talks at WS-FM 2010 and CASCON 2010.

Structure of Paper. In Sec. 2 we define Nested DCR Graphs formally, motivated by the case study, and define the mapping to flat DCR Graphs with milestones. In Sec. 3 we then define the lts semantics and the mapping from flat DCR Graphs with milestones to Büchi-automata. The two maps together define the semantics of Nested DCR Graphs. Due to space limitations we refer to [8] and the full version [9] for a detailed description of the case study and tool support. We conclude in Sec. 4 and give pointers to future work.

2   Nested DCR Graphs and Milestones

We now give the formal definition of the Nested DCR Graph model described informally above, which extends the model in our previous work [7] with nesting and the new milestone relation $\rightarrow\diamond$ between events.

Definition 1. *A* Nested Distributed dynamic condition response graph with milestones *is a tuple* $(E, \rhd, M, \rightarrow\bullet, \bullet\rightarrow, \rightarrow\diamond, \pm, \mathsf{Act}, l, R, P, \mathsf{as})$*, where*

(i) E *is the set of* events

(ii) $\rhd : E \rightharpoonup E$ *is a partial function mapping an event to its super-event (if defined), and we also write* $e \rhd e'$ *if* $e' = \rhd^k(e)$ *for* $0 < k$*, referred to as the* nesting relation

(iii) $M = (E, R, I) \subseteq \mathsf{atoms(E)} \times \mathsf{atoms(E)} \times \mathsf{atoms(E)}$ *is the* marking, *containing sets of currently executed events* (E)*, currently pending responses* (R)*, and currently included events* (I)*.*

(iv) $\rightarrow\bullet \subseteq E \times E$ *is the* condition *relation*

(v) $\bullet\rightarrow \subseteq E \times E$ *is the* response *relation*

(vi) $\rightarrow\diamond \subseteq E \times E$ *is the* milestone *relation*

(vii) $\pm : E \times E \rightharpoonup \{+, \%\}$ *is a partial function defining the* dynamic inclusion and exclusion *relations by* $e \rightarrow+ e'$ *if* $\pm(e, e') = +$ *and* $e \rightarrow\% e'$ *if* $\pm(e, e') = \%$

(viii) Act *is the set of* actions

(ix) $l : E \rightarrow \mathsf{Act}$ *is a* labeling *function mapping events to actions.*

(x) R *is a set of* roles,

(xi) P *is a set of* principals *(e.g. persons or processors) and*

(xii) $\mathsf{as} \subseteq (P \cup \mathsf{Act}) \times R$ *is the* role assignment *relation to principals and actions.*

where $\mathsf{atoms(E)} = \{e \mid \forall e' \in E . \rhd (e') \neq e\}$ *is the set of* atomic *events.*

We require that the nesting relation $\rhd \subset E \times E$ *is acyclic and that there are no infinite sequence of events* $e_1 \rhd e_2 \rhd \dots$ *We will write* $e \unrhd e'$ *if* $e \rhd e'$ *or* $e = e'$*, and* $e \unlhd e'$ *if* $e' \rhd e$ *or* $e = e'$*. We require that the nesting relation is consistent with respect to dynamic inclusion/exclusion in the following sense: If* $e \rhd e'$ *or* $e' \rhd e$ *then* $\pm(e, e'') = +$ *implies* $\pm(e', e'') \neq \%$ *and* $\pm(e, e'') = \%$ *implies* $\pm(e', e'') \neq +$*.*

The new elements are the nesting relation $\rhd \subset E \times E$ and the milestone relation $\rightarrow\diamond \subseteq E \times E$. The consistency between the nesting relation and the dynamic inclusion/exclusion is to ensure that when we map a nested DCR Graph to the corresponding flat DCR Graph as defined in Def. 2 below, no atomic event both includes and excludes another event. That is, if an event e includes (excludes) another event e'', then any of its super or sub events e' can not exclude (include) the event e''.

The new elements conservatively extend the DCR Graphs defined in [7] in the sense that given a Nested dynamic condition response graph as defined in Def. 1, the tuple $(\mathsf{atoms(E)}, M, \rightarrow\bullet, \bullet\rightarrow, \pm, \mathsf{Act}, l, R, P, \mathsf{as})$ is a (Distributed) dynamic condition response graph as defined in [7]. In particular, the semantics will be identical if both the $\rhd$ map and the milestone relation are empty.

A nested distributed dynamic condition response graph can be mapped to a flat distributed dynamic condition response graph with at most the same number of events and a quadratic growth of the relations . Essentially, all relations are extended to sub events, and then only the atomic events are preserved. The labelling function is extended by labelling an atomic event e by the sequence of labels labelling the chain of super events starting by the event itself: $e \rhd e_1 \ldots \rhd e_k \not\rhd$. The role assignment is extended to sequences of actions by taking the union of roles assigned to the actions.

Definition 2. *For a Nested DCR Graph $G = (\mathsf{E}, \rhd, \mathsf{M}, \rightarrow\bullet, \bullet\rightarrow, \rightarrow\diamond, \pm, \mathsf{Act}, l, \mathsf{R}, \mathsf{P}, \mathsf{as})$ define the underlying flat DCR Graph as*

$$G^\flat = (\mathsf{atoms}(\mathsf{E}), \mathsf{M}, \rightarrow\bullet^\flat, \bullet\rightarrow^\flat, \rightarrow\diamond^\flat, \pm^\flat, \mathsf{Act}^+, l^\flat, \mathsf{R}, \mathsf{P}, \mathsf{as}^\flat),$$

where

- $rel^\flat = \rhd rel \unlhd \ for \ rel \in \{\rightarrow\bullet, \bullet\rightarrow, \rightarrow\diamond\}$,
- $\pm(e, e')^\flat = \pm(e_s, e'_s) \ if \ \pm(e_s, e'_s) \ is \ defined, \ e \unrhd e_s \ and \ e' \unlhd e'_s$,
- $l^\flat(e_0) = a_0.a_1.a_2 \ldots a_k \ and \ \mathsf{as}^\flat(a_0.a_1.a_2 \ldots a_k) = \bigcup_{0 \le i \le k} \mathsf{as}(a_i), \ if \ e_0 \rhd e_1 \rhd e_2 \ldots \rhd e_k \not\rhd \ and \ l(e_i) = a_i, \ for \ 0 \le i \le k, \ and$
- $\mathsf{as}^\flat(p) = p \ for \ p \in \mathsf{P}$.

3   Semantics

Below we define the semantics of DCR Graphs with milestones by giving a labelled transition semantics and a mapping to Büchi-automata.

Notation. For a set A we write $\mathcal{P}(A)$ for the power set of A. For a binary relation $\rightarrow \subseteq A \times A$ and a subset $\xi \subseteq A$ of A we write $\rightarrow \xi$ and $\xi \rightarrow$ for the set $\{a \in A \mid (\exists a' \in \xi \mid a \rightarrow a')\}$ and the set $\{a \in A \mid (\exists a' \in \xi \mid a' \rightarrow a)\}$ respectively.

Definition 3. *For a dynamic condition response graph with milestones $G = (\mathsf{E}, \mathsf{M}, \rightarrow\bullet, \bullet\rightarrow, \rightarrow\diamond, \pm, l, \mathsf{Act}, \mathsf{R}, \mathsf{P}, \mathsf{as})$, we define the corresponding labelled transition systems $T(G)$ to be the tuple $(S, \mathsf{M}, \rightarrow \subseteq S \times \mathsf{Act} \times S)$ where $S = \mathcal{P}(\mathsf{E}) \times \mathcal{P}(\mathsf{E}) \times \mathcal{P}(\mathsf{E})$ is the set of markings of G and $\mathsf{M} = (R, I, E) \in S$ is the initial marking, $\rightarrow \subseteq S \times \mathsf{E} \times (\mathsf{P} \times \mathsf{Act} \times \mathsf{R}) \times S$ is the transition relation given by $\mathsf{M'} \xrightarrow{(e,(p,a,r))} \mathsf{M''}$ where*

- *(i) $\mathsf{M'} = (E', R', I')$ is the marking before transition*
- *(ii) $\mathsf{M''} = (E' \cup \{e\}, R'', I'')$ is the marking after transition*
- *(iii) $e \in I, l(e) = a, p \mathop{as} r, and \ a \mathop{as} r$,*
- *(iv) $\rightarrow\bullet e \cap I' \subseteq E'$,*
- *(v) $\rightarrow\diamond e \cap I' \cap R' = \emptyset$,*
- *(vi) $I'' = (I' \cup e\rightarrow+) \setminus e\rightarrow\%$,*
- *(vii) $R'' = (R' \setminus \{e\}) \cup e\bullet\rightarrow$,*
- *(viii) $E'' = E' \cup \{e\}$*

We define a run $(e_0, (p_0, a_0, r_0)), (e_1, (p_1, a_1, r_1)), \ldots$ of the transition system to be a sequence of labels of a sequence of transitions $\mathsf{M}_i \xrightarrow{(e_i,(p_i,a_i,r_i))} \mathsf{M}_{i+1}$ starting from the initial marking. We define a run to be accepting if $\forall i \ge 0, e \in R_i. \exists j \ge i.(e = e_j \vee e \notin I_j)$. In words, a run is accepting if no response event is included and pending forever, i.e. it must either happen at some later state or become excluded.

Condition *(iii)* in the above definition expresses that, only events e that are currently included, can be executed, and to give the label (p, a, r) the label of the event must be a, p must be assigned to the role r, which must be assigned to a. Condition *(iv)* requires that all condition events to e which are currently included should have been executed previously. Condition *(v)* states that the currently included events which are milestones to event e must not be in the set of pending responses (R'). Conditions *(vi)*, *(vii)* and *(viii)* are the updates to the sets of included events, pending responses and executed events respectively. Note that an event e' can not be both included and excluded by the same event e, but an event may trigger itself as a response.

If one considers only finite runs then the acceptance condition degenerates to requiring that no pending response is included at the end of the run. If infinite runs are also of interest (as e.g. for reactive systems and LTL) the acceptance condition can be captured by a mapping to a Büchi-automaton with τ-event defined as follows.

Definition 4. *A Büchi-automaton with τ-event is a tuple $(S, s, Ev_\tau, \rightarrow \subseteq S \times Ev_\tau \times S, F)$ where S is the set of states, $s \in S$ is the initial state, Ev_τ is the set of events containing the special event τ, $\rightarrow \subseteq S \times Ev_\tau \times S$ is the transition relation, and F is the set of accepting states. A (finite or infinite) run is a sequence of labels not containing the τ event that can be obtained by removing all τ events from a sequence of labels of transitions starting from the initial state. The run is accepting if the sequence of transitions passes through an accepting state infinitely often.*

Since we at any given time may have several pending responses we must make sure in the mapping to Büchi-automata that all of them are eventually executed or excluded. To do this we assume any fixed order of the finite set of events E of the given dynamic condition response graph. For an event $e \in E$ we write $rank(e)$ for its rank in that order and for a subset of events $E' \subseteq E$ we write $min(E')$ for the event in E' with the minimal rank.

Definition 5. For a finite distributed dynamic condition response graph $G = (E, M, \rightarrow\bullet, \bullet\rightarrow, \rightarrow\diamond, \pm, \mathsf{Act}, l, \mathsf{R}, \mathsf{P}, \mathsf{as})$ where $E = \{e_1, \ldots, e_n\}$, marking $M = (E, R, I)$ and $rank(e_i) = i$, we define the corresponding Büchi-automaton with τ-event to be the tuple $B(G) = (S, s, \rightarrow \subseteq S \times Ev_\tau \times S, F)$ where

- $S = \mathcal{P}(E) \times \mathcal{P}(E) \times \mathcal{P}(E) \times \{1, \ldots, n\} \times \{0, 1\}$ is the set of states,
- $Ev_\tau = (E \times (P \times \mathsf{Act} \times R)) \cup \{\tau\}$ is the set of events,
- $s = (M, 1, 1)$ if $I \cap R = \emptyset$, and $s = (M, 1, 0)$ otherwise
- $F = \mathcal{P}(E) \times \mathcal{P}(E) \times \mathcal{P}(E) \times \{1, \ldots, n\} \times \{1\}$ is the set of accepting states and
- $\rightarrow \subseteq S \times Ev_\tau \times S$ is the transition relation given by $(M', i, j) \xrightarrow{\;\tau\;} (M', i, j')$
  where

(a) $M' = (E', R', I')$ is the marking
(b) $j' = 1$ if $I' \cap R' = \emptyset$ otherwise $j' = 0$.

$$\text{and } (M', i, j) \xrightarrow{\;(e,(p,a,r))\;} (M'', i', j') \text{ where}$$

(i) $M' = (E', R', I') \xrightarrow{\;(e,(p,a,r))\;} (E'', R'', I'') = M''$ is a transition of $T(D)$.

(ii) For $M = \{e \in I' \cap R' \mid rank(e) \rangle i\}$ let $j' = 1$ if
   (a) $I'' \cap R'' = \emptyset$ or
   (b) $min(M) \in (I' \cap R' \backslash (I'' \cap R'')) \cup \{e\}$ or
   (c) $M = \emptyset$ and $min(I' \cap R') \in (I' \cap R' \backslash (I'' \cap R'')) \cup \{e\}$
   otherwise $j' = 0$.
(iii) $i' = rank(min(M))$ if $min(M) \in (I' \cap R' \backslash (I'' \cap R'')) \cup \{e\}$ or else
(iv) $i' = rank(min(I' \cap R'))$ if $M = \emptyset$ and $min(I' \cap R') \in (I' \cap R' \backslash (I'' \cap R'')) \cup \{e\}$
   or else
(v) $i' = i$ otherwise.

We prove that the mapping from the labelled transition semantics to Büchi-automata is sound and complete in the full version of the paper [9].

The formal semantics of DCR graphs mapped to Büchi-automata enabled us to perform model checking and formal verification of processes specified in DCR graphs. The prototype implementation allows us to perform verification of both safety and liveness properties using the SPIN [17] model checker and only verification of safety properties using the ZING [14] model checker. The prototype has also been extended to support runtime verification, for monitoring of properties specified using Property Patterns [6].

4   Conclusion and Future Work

We have given a conservative extension of the declarative process model Distributed DCR Graphs [7] to allow for nested sub-graphs motivated and guided by a case study carried out jointly with our industrial partner. A detailed description of the case study and tool support for DCR Graphs can be found in [8]. The main technical challenge was to formalize the execution and in particular *completion* of sub-graphs. We do this by introducing a new *milestone* relation $A \rightarrow\!\!\diamond B$, which blocks the event B as long as there are events in A required to be executed (i.e. required responses). We believe this is the right notion of completeness of nested sub-graphs. First of all, it coincides with the definition of acceptance of finite runs in DCR Graphs [7] recalled in Sec. 3 above. Secondly, its formalization is a simple extension of the labelled transition semantics given in [7, 11] since it is a condition on the set of pending responses already included in the states. Finally, it allows for a nested sub-graph to alternate between being completed and not completed, as is often the case in ad hoc case management. This is not possible in the related ad-hoc sub-process activity in BPMN 2.0. Future work within the Trust-Care and CosmoBiz projects, which are the context of the work, includes exploring the expressiveness of DCR Graphs, extending the theory and tools for analysis, verification and model-driven engineering, extending the model to be able to express other relevant features such as multi-instance sub-graphs, time, exceptions, data, types and run-time adaption, i.e. dynamic changes of the model.

References

1. Bhattacharya, K., Gerede, C., Hull, R., Liu, R., Su, J.: Towards Formal Analysis of Artifact-Centric Business Process Models. In: Alonso, G., Dadam, P., Rosemann, M. (eds.) BPM 2007. LNCS, vol. 4714, pp. 288–304. Springer, Heidelberg (2007)

2. Bussler, C., Jablonski, S.: Implementing agent coordination for workflow management systems using active database systems. In: Proceedings Fourth International Workshop on Research Issues in Data Engineering, 1994. Active Database Systems, pp. 53–59 (February 1994)
3. Cohn, D., Hull, R.: Business artifacts: A data-centric approach to modeling business operations and processes. IEEE Data Eng. Bull. 32(3), 3–9 (2009)
4. Davulcu, H., Kifer, M., Ramakrishnan, C.R., Ramakrishnan, I.V.: Logic based modeling and analysis of workflows. In: Proceedings of ACM SIGACT-SIGMOD-SIGART, pp. 1–3. ACM Press (1998)
5. Deutsch, A., Hull, R., Patrizi, F., Vianu, V.: Automatic verification of data-centric business processes. In: Proceedings of the 12th International Conference on Database Theory, ICDT 2009, pp. 252–267. ACM Press, New York (2009)
6. Dwyer, M.B., Avrunin, G.S., Corbett, J.C.: Property specification patterns for finite-state verification. In: Proceedings of the Second Workshop on Formal Methods in Software Practice, FMSP 1998, pp. 7–15. ACM (1998)
7. Hildebrandt, T., Mukkamala, R.R.: Declarative event-based workflow as distributed dynamic condition response graphs. In: Programming Language Approaches to Concurrency and Communication-cEntric Software, PLACES 2010, EPTCS (2010)
8. Hildebrandt, T., Mukkamala, R.R., Slaats, T.: Designing a cross-organizational case management system using dynamic condition response graphs. In: Accepted for IEEE International EDOC Conference (2011)
9. Hildebrandt, T., Mukkamala, R.R., Slaats, T.: Designing a cross-organizational case management system using nested dynamic condition response graphs. Technical Report TR-2011-141, IT University of Copenhagen (2011)
10. Lyng, K.M., Hildebrandt, T., Mukkamala, R.R.: From paper based clinical practice guidelines to declarative workflow management. In: Proceedings ProHealth 2008 Workshop (2008)
11. Mukkamala, R.R., Hildebrandt, T.: From dynamic condition response structures to büchi automata. In: Proceedings of 4th IEEE International Symposium on Theoretical Aspects of Software Engineering (TASE 2010) (August 2010)
12. Mukkamala, R.R., Hildebrandt, T., Tøth, J.B.: The resultmaker online consultant: From declarative workflow management in practice to LTL. In: Proceeding of DDBP (2008)
13. Object Management Group BPMN Technical Committee. Business Process Model and Notation, version 2.0 (2010),
    http://www.omg.org/cgi-bin/doc?dtc/10-06-04.pdf
14. Microsoft Research. Zing model checker. Webpage (2010),
    http://research.microsoft.com/en-us/projects/zing/
15. Senkul, P., Kifer, M., Toroslu, I.H.: A logical framework for scheduling workflows under resource allocation constraints. In: VLDB, pp. 694–705 (2002)
16. Singh, M.P., Meredith, G., Tomlinson, C., Attie, P.C.: An event algebra for specifying and scheduling workflows. In: Proceedings of DASFAA, pp. 53–60. World Scientific Press (1995)
17. Spin. On-the-fly, ltl model checking with spin. Webpage (2008),
    http://spinroot.com/spin/whatispin.html
18. van der Aalst, W.M.P., Pesic, M., Schonenberg, H.: Declarative workflows: Balancing between flexibility and support. Computer Science - R&D 23(2), 99–113 (2009)
19. Pesic, M., van der Aalst, W.M.P.: A Declarative Approach for Flexible Business Processes Management. In: Eder, J., Dustdar, S. (eds.) BPM 2006. LNCS, vol. 4103, pp. 169–180. Springer, Heidelberg (2006)
20. Winskel, G.: Event Structures. In: Brauer, W., Reisig, W., Rozenberg, G. (eds.) APN 1986. LNCS, vol. 255, pp. 325–392. Springer, Heidelberg (1987)

Efficient Verification
of Evolving Software Product Lines

Hamideh Sabouri and Ramtin Khosravi

School of Electrical and Computer Engineering,
University of Tehran, Karegar Ave., Tehran, Iran
{sabouri,rkhosravi}@ece.ut.ac.ir

Abstract. Software product line engineering represents a promising approach to achieve systematic reuse in development of families of software. Software product lines are intended to be used in a long period of time. As a result, they evolve over time, due to the changes in the requirements. Having several individual products in a software family, verification of the entire software family may take a considerable effort. In this paper, we present an idea for efficient verification of evolving software product lines, by reusing the result of verification and state space of the product family. To this end, we generate the state space of the product family once and verify the desired properties. The result of verification is the set of products satisfying the given properties. When the product line evolves, we may use the result of verification, and the state space to produce new results, and update the existing state space. We show the applicability of our approach by applying it on a small case study.

1 Introduction

Software product line engineering is a paradigm to develop software applications using platforms and mass customization. To this end, the commonalities and differences of the applications are modeled explicitly [1]. Feature models are usually used to specify the variability of software product lines. A product is defined by a combination of features. The set containing all of the valid feature combinations defines the set of products [2]. A feature model is a tree of features, containing mandatory, and optional features. It may also contain a number of constraints among the features. Feature models may evolve over time due to the changes in the requirements. This evolution may imply addition, removal, or replacement of some features. It also may add or remove some constraints.

Recently, several approaches have been developed for formal modeling and verification of product lines [3–7]. However, these works do not consider the evolution of the product line.

Software product lines are intended to be used in a long period of time. As a result, they evolve over time, due to the changes in the requirements [8]. The evolution may imply addition, removal, or replacement of some features. Moreover, it may add or remove some constraints. At the model level, adding and removing features result in adding a new behavior and eliminating an existing

F. Arbab and M. Sirjani (Eds.): FSEN 2011, LNCS 7141, pp. 351–358, 2012.

behavior from the model, and the model should be verified entirely again, after these changes. However, from the product line perspective, adding features to a product line, and removing features from a product line will cause adding a number of new products, and elimination of a number of products. Moreover, removing some of the constraints, and adding some new constraints, will cause a number of previously invalid products to be valid, and invalidation of a number of the valid products. Now, if we look at the problem again, we can see that re-verifying the entire product family after adding or removing features, leads to regeneration of the state spaces of products that are generated before, and re-verification of a number of products that are verified before.

As verification of the product family may take a considerable effort, in this work, we present an idea to verify evolving product lines efficiently, by reusing the state space of the product family and the result of verification. For this purpose, we generate the state space of the product family and verify it against the properties once. The result of verification of the product family against a given property is the set of products satisfying the property. When the product line evolves, it is not necessary to generate the state space of the product family from scratch and verify the entire product family against the set of properties again. The space and the result of verification are used to update the existing state space and produce the new results.

In this paper, we use a product family of coffee machines, as a running example. A coffee machine may serve one type of coffee, and may add fix or variable amount of sugar to the coffee.

This paper is structured as follows. Section 2 introduces product line modeling using PL-CCS. In Section 3, we explain our approach to reuse the existing state space and results of verification, to verify the evolved product line. In Section 4, we present the result of applying the proposed approach on the coffee machine case study, and Section 5 concludes the work.

2   Product Line Modeling

A product line can be modeled as a system including a number of *variation points*. Each variation point has a number of *variants* that are associated to it. Each variant represents a feature, and selection of a variant of a variation point corresponds to including a feature from the feature model, in the final product. Individual products can be obtained from a product line model by deciding about all of the variation points.

The Coffee Machine Example: Feature Model. The feature model of the coffee machine example is shown in Figure 1. A coffee machine may serve coffee or coffee with milk. Moreover it may add fix amount or adjustable amount of sugar to the coffee. In our paper, we use PL-CCS notation [6] to model a product line. PL-CCS supports modeling variation in the behavior of product families, by means of *optional* and *variants* operators.

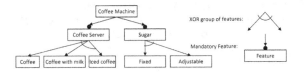

Fig. 1. The feature model of the coffee machine example

2.1 PL-CCS

The process algebra PL-CCS [6], is an extension of CCS [9], and is used to model the behavior of product families. PL-CCS extends CCS with the variants operator $\oplus$, and the optional operator $\langle\ \rangle$, to define variation points. The variants operator $\oplus$ defines a variation point that one and only one of its variants should be included in the final products. The optional operator $\langle\rangle$ defines a variation point where a variant may be included in the final products, but its inclusion is not mandatory. As the optional operator can be defined using the variants operator ($\langle P \rangle := P \oplus Nil$), we focus on the variants operator only.

In [6], the *configured-transition system* semantics is defined for a PL-CCS program. For a PL-CCS program with n variants, we associate to each variant a unique number, and keep track of inclusion or exclusion made for each variant using a *configuration vector* $\nu \in \{I, E, ?\}^n$, where I and E represent the inclusion and exclusion of the variants respectively, and ? denotes that it is not decided about the inclusion or exclusion of the variant yet. For simplicity, we assume that the ith element of the configuration vector represents the decision that is made for the ith variant.

The Coffee Machine Example: PL-CCS Model. The product family of coffee machines can be modeled using PL-CCS as:

$$S \stackrel{def}{=} coin.AddCoffee.AddSugar.S \qquad AddCoffee \stackrel{def}{=} coffee \oplus coffee.milk$$
$$AddSugar \stackrel{def}{=} sugar \oplus (sugar + sugar.sugar)$$

According to the above model, a coffee machine receives a coin, fills the cup with coffee (corresponding to the coffee feature) or coffee and milk (corresponding to the coffee with milk feature), and finally adds sugar. It may add one unit of sugar (corresponding to the fixed sugar feature), or select between one unit or two units of sugar (corresponding to the adjustable sugar feature).

3   Verification of Evolved Product Line

In this section, we describe our approach to reuse the state space and verification result of the product family, in verification of the evolved product line.

The Coffee Machine Example: Evolution. We assume that the coffee machine product line evolves by adding the new feature, *iced coffee*, to its feature model. The new model of the product family is:

$$S \stackrel{def}{=} coin.AddCoffee.AddSugar.S \quad AddCoffee \stackrel{def}{=} coffee \oplus coffee.milk \oplus coffee.ice$$
$$AddSugar \stackrel{def}{=} sugar \oplus (sugar + sugar.sugar)$$

3.1 Reusing the State Space

In our proposed approach for reuse, the state space of a product family is generated once and is updated as the product line evolves. A trivial way to reuse the state space is generating the state space of each product independently, and update the state space by adding or removing the state space of the new and eliminated products, respectively:

The state space:	$S = S_{p_1} \cup ... \cup S_{p_m}$
Adding a new product p_{m+1}:	$S' = S \cup S_{p_{m+1}}$
Removing a product p_k:	$S' = S_{p_1} \cup ... \cup S_{p_{k-1}} \cup S_{p_{k+1}} \cup ... \cup S_{p_m}$

In this way, we reuse the state space of the products that are verified before. However, we want to reuse state space that is common among products as well. For this purpose, we verify the whole product family, and store the state space. After the evolution of product line, we update the state space based on the evolution, as it is described in the following.

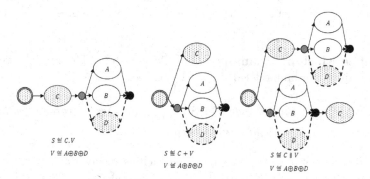

$$S \cong C.V$$
$$V \cong A \oplus B \oplus D$$

$$S \cong C+V$$
$$V \cong A \oplus B \oplus D$$

$$S \cong C \| V$$
$$V \cong A \oplus B \oplus D$$

Fig. 2. Updating the existing state space after adding a new variant D, for sequential, non-deterministic, and interleaved execution of two processes

Adding a New Feature. To update the state space after adding a new feature, we should mark the states where we are deciding about each variation point in the model. For simplicity, we add two special states to indicate where the behavior varies. In Figure 2, these states are shown using gray and black colors. A new feature, appears as a new operand of a variant operator. To update the state space, we add the states of the variant to the variant behaviors which are indicated by the special states, for the associated variation point. Figure 2, shows the updated state space after adding a new variant D to the variation point, for sequential, non-deterministic, and interleaved execution of a common behavior C and a variable behavior V. In this figure, only the dashed states are added to the state space and other states are reused.

Removing a Feature. To update the state space after eliminating an existing feature, we should keep track of the features that use each state. To update the state space, the states that are used only by the specific feature which is eliminated from the product line, are removed along with their outgoing and incoming transitions.

The Coffee Machine Example: Reusing the State Space. Figure 3, shows how the state space of the coffee machine example can be updated by adding the dashed states, after adding a new feature named *iced coffee* to the feature model of the product line.

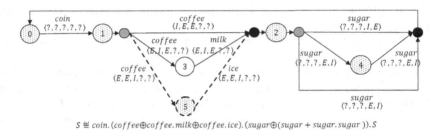

$S \overset{\text{def}}{=} coin.(coffee \oplus coffee.milk \oplus coffee.ice).(sugar \oplus (sugar + sugar.sugar)).S$

Fig. 3. Updating the existing state space of the coffee machine example after adding the new feature *iced coffee*

3.2 Reusing the Result of Verification

The result of verification of a product family is reused when new products are added to the product line, or some of the products are eliminated. The result of verification of a product family against a property φ, is the set of products that satisfy φ, and are valid according to the feature model:

$$R = \{p_i \mid (p_i \in \mathcal{V}) \wedge (p_i \vDash \varphi)\}$$

Adding a New Feature. After adding a new feature to the product line, we intend to only verify the set of new products that are added to the product family consequently. For this purpose, we initialize the configuration vector, to restrict the model checker to verify only the new products. Adding a new feature leads to adding a new variant in the configuration vector: $\nu \in \{I, E, ?\}^{n+1}$. Considering the fact that we verified all of the products that do not include the new feature before, we should only verify the new products which are the combinations of existing features with the new feature. To this end, the configuration vector is initialized as:

$$\nu = \langle \overbrace{?, ..., ?, I}^{n} \rangle$$

In this way, we only verify the new products against φ. Figure 2 shows that after adding the new variant D to the variation point, only the dotted states, which represent $C.D$, $C + D$, and $C \parallel D$ products, should be investigated for verification.

Eliminating a Feature. Elimination of a feature from the product line, causes the elimination of a number of products from the product family. In this case, we only need to update the result set, and there is even no need to re-verify the product family. Therefore, for each product p_k, that is eliminated from the product family, we remove it from the result set.

Adding a New Constraint. Adding a new constraint to the feature model leads to invalidation of some of the products that were valid before, and a new set of valid products $\mathcal{V}' \subseteq \mathcal{V}$. To obtain the new result set without re-verifying the product family, we check the validation of the products of the result set, and remove the products that are not valid according to the feature model anymore.

Removing a Constraint. Removing an existing constraint from the feature model makes some of the invalid products valid, and leads to a new set of valid products $\mathcal{V}'$ which $\mathcal{V} \subseteq \mathcal{V}'$. In this case, we avoid re-verification of the entire product family by initializing the configuration vector, to restrict the model checker to only verify the new products. To this end, we should consider the effect of each type of constraints on the validation of products, and define the binding constraints based on it. The *requires* constraint from feature f to feature f' ($f \rightarrow f'$) leads to invalidation of products that include f, but exclude f'. The *excludes* constraint between two features f and f' ($f \rightarrow \neg f', f' \rightarrow \neg f$), causes invalidation of products that include both features. We assume that f and f' correspond to the ith and j^{th} ($i < j$) variants of the configuration vector ν, and and initialize the configuration vectors ν_{req} and ν_{excl} to verify only the new products, after removing the *requires* and *excludes* constraints respectively:

$$\nu_{req} = \langle \overbrace{\overbrace{?, ..., ?}^{i-1}, I, ?, ..., ?}^{j-1}, E, ?, ..., ? \rangle \qquad \nu_{excl} = \langle \overbrace{\overbrace{?, ..., ?}^{i-1}, I, ?, ..., ?}^{j-1}, I, ?, ..., ? \rangle$$

By applying the above initializations, we only verify the new products against φ.

The Coffee Machine Example: Result Reuse. After adding the new feature, *iced coffee*, we only should verify the coffee machines that serve iced coffee and add a fixed or adjustable amount of sugar. For this purpose, we initialize the configuration vector to $\langle E, E, I, ?, ? \rangle$. The dotted states in Figure 3 show the states that should be investigated for verification. Therefore, practically we should only verify $\langle E, E, I, I, E \rangle$ and $\langle E, E, I, E, I \rangle$ products, and add them to the previous result set that we have, if they satisfy the property. If we add a new constraint to the feature model stating that "coffee with milk" feature requires the "adjustable sugar" feature, we simply remove the $\langle E, I, E, I, E \rangle$ product from the result set, as it is not valid according to the feature model anymore.

4   Results

We considered the product family of coffee machines as a case study to evaluate the proposed approach. The coffee machine presented in this paper as a running example, is a simplified version of this case study. We modeled the coffee machine using *Promela* and verified it with *Spin* model checker, as PL-CCS does not have tool support. We modeled the configuration vector, using global variables to be able to investigate our approach.

The first model of the coffee machine (M1) serves coffee which is a mandatory feature, and may serve tea, which is an optional feature, and there is one payment method, and a coffee and tea container. In the second model (M2) one more payment method is added as a new feature to the product family. In the next step, the product line of coffee machine evolves, by adding the capability of serving iced coffee (M3) and iced tea (M4). Finally, on the last two models (M5, M6), we can decide about using a small coffee/tea container or a large one, in a coffee machine. Table 1 shows the number of states generated for verification of a product family, the number of states generated for verification of single products, the number of states added to the existing state space after evolution, and the number of states investigated for verification of product family by reusing the existing results.

Table 1. The result of applying our method to the coffee machine case study

Model	Product Family	Single Products	New states	Investigated states
M1	774	854	774	774
M2	14,342	15,533	13,488	13,342
M3	26,179	44,548	10,646	26,179
M4	38,016	79,217	6,533	24,976
M5	96,682	191,493	17,465	52,126
M6	245,006	447,203	53,513	132,460

The result shows the effectiveness of our approach. For example, in the case of model M6, 447,203 states are generated to verify each product independently. By reusing the common states among products the number of states is reduced to 245,006. However, if we reuse the state space and the result of M5, we only need to add 53,513 new states to it, and investigate 132,460 states to verify the new products.

5   Conclusion

In this paper, we proposed an idea to reuse the state space and the result of verification of a product family, to verify the product line after evolution. Using this approach, we do not need to generate the state space of the product family from scratch, and verify the entire product family against the properties again. The result of applying our proposed approach on a coffee machine example shows the effectiveness of this approach.

References

1. Pohl, K., Böckle, G., van der Linden, F.J.: Software Product Line Engineering: Foundations, Principles and Techniques. Springer-Verlag New York, Inc., Secaucus (2005)
2. Kang, K.C., Cohen, S.G., Hess, J.A., Novak, W.E., Peterson, A.S.: Feature-oriented domain analysis (foda) feasibility study. Technical report, Carnegie-Mellon University Software Engineering Institute (November 1990)
3. Kishi, T., Noda, N., Katayama, T.: Design Verification for Product Line Development. In: Obbink, H., Pohl, K. (eds.) SPLC 2005. LNCS, vol. 3714, pp. 150–161. Springer, Heidelberg (2005)
4. Larsen, K.G., Nyman, U., Wasowski, A.: Modeling software product lines using color-blind transition systems. Int. J. Softw. Tools Technol. Transf. 9(5), 471–487 (2007)
5. Larsen, K.G., Nyman, U., Wąsowski, A.: Modal I/O Automata for Interface and Product Line Theories. In: De Nicola, R. (ed.) ESOP 2007. LNCS, vol. 4421, pp. 64–79. Springer, Heidelberg (2007)
6. Gruler, A., Leucker, M., Scheidemann, K.: Modeling and Model Checking Software Product Lines. In: Barthe, G., de Boer, F.S. (eds.) FMOODS 2008. LNCS, vol. 5051, pp. 113–131. Springer, Heidelberg (2008)
7. Sabouri, H., Khosravi, R.: An effective approach for verifying product lines in presence of variability models. In: FMSPLE: First International Workshop on Formal Methods in Software Product Line Engineering, pp. 113–120 (2010)
8. Svahnberg, M., Bosch, J.: Evolution in software product lines: Two cases. Journal of Software Maintenance 11, 391–422 (1999)
9. Milner, R.: A Calculus of Communicating Systems. Springer-Verlag New York, Inc., Secaucus (1982)

Extending Interface Automata with Z Notation[*]

Zining Cao[1,2,3] and Hui Wang[1]

[1] National Key Laboratory of Science and Technology
on Avionics System Integration,
Shanghai 200233, P.R. China
[2] Department of Computer Science and Technology,
Nanjing University of Aero. & Astro., Nanjing 210016, P.R. China
[3] Provincial Key Laboratory for Computer Information Processing Technology,
Soochow University, Suzhou 215006, P.R. China
caozn@nuaa.edu.cn

Abstract. In this paper, we propose a specification approach combining interface automata and Z language. This approach can be used to describe behavioural properties and data properties of software components. We also study the composition and refinement relation on ZIAs.

1 Introduction

Modern software systems are comprised of numerous components, and are made larger through the use of software frameworks. Such software systems exhibit various behavioural aspects such as communication between components, and state transformation inside components. Formal specification techniques for such systems have to be able to describe all these aspects. Unfortunately, a single specification technique that is well suited for all these aspects is yet not available. Instead one needs various specialised techniques that are very good at describing individual aspects of system behaviour. This observation has led to research into the combination and semantic integration of specification techniques. In this paper we combine two well researched specification techniques: Interface automata and Z.

An interface automaton (IA), introduced by de Alfaro and Henzinger in [1], is an automata-based model suitable for specifying component-based systems. IA is part of a class of models called interface models, which are intended to specify concisely how systems can be used and to adhere to certain well-formedness criteria that make them appropriate for modelling component-based systems.

Z [5] is a typed formal specification notation based on first order predicate logic and set theory. The formal basis for Z is first order predicate logic extended

---

[*] This work was supported by the Aviation Science Fund of China under Grant No. 20085552023, the National Natural Science Foundation of China under Grants No. 60873025, the Natural Science Foundation of Jiangsu Province of China under Grant No. BK2008389, and the Foundation of Provincial Key Laboratory for Computer Information Processing Technology of Soochow University under Grant No. KJS0920.

F. Arbab and M. Sirjani (Eds.): FSEN 2011, LNCS 7141, pp. 359–367, 2012.
© Springer-Verlag Berlin Heidelberg 2012

with type set theory. Using mathematics for specification is all very well for small examples, but for more realistically sized problems, things start to get out of hand. To deal with this, Z includes the schema notation to aid the structuring and modularization of specifications. A boxed notation called schemas is used for structuring Z specifications. This has been found to be necessary to handle the information in a specification of any size. In particular, Z schemas and the schema calculus enable a structured way of presenting large state spaces and their transformation.

In this paper, we combine interface automata with Z to describe both behavioural property and data property. We give the definition of ZIA. Roughly speaking, a ZIA is in a style of interface automata but its states and transitions are described by Z language. Then the composition of ZIA is defined. Furthermore, we define the refinement relation between ZIAs and prove some propositions of such refinement relation. This paper is organized as follows: Section 2 gives a specification language-ZIA. Section 3 proposes the composition for ZIA, and Section 4 presents refinement relation for ZIA. The paper is concluded in Section 5.

2   Interface Automata with Z Notation

An interface automaton (IA) [1], introduced by de Alfaro and Henzinger, is an automata-based model suitable for specifying component-based systems. An IA consists of states, initial states, internal actions, input actions, output actions and a transition relation. The composition and refinement of two IAs are proposed in [1]. Z was introduced in the early 80's in Oxford by Abrial as a set-theoretic and predicate language for the specification of data structure, state spaces and state transformations. A boxed notation called schemas is used for structuring Z specifications. Z makes use of identifier decorations to encode intended interpretations. A state variable with no decoration represents the current (before) state and a state variable ending with a prime ($'$) represents the next (after) state. A variable ending with a question mark (?) represents an input variable and a variable ending with an exclamation mark (!) represents an output variable. In Z, there are many schema operators. For example, we write $S \wedge T$ to denote the conjunction of these two schemas: a new schema formed by merging the declaration parts of S and T and conjoining their predicate parts. $S \Rightarrow T$ ($S \Leftrightarrow T$) is similar to $S \wedge T$ except connecting their predicate parts by $\Rightarrow$ ($\Leftrightarrow$). The hiding operation $S \backslash (x_1, ..., x_n)$ removes from the schema S the components $x_1, ..., x_n$ explicitly listed, which must exist. The hiding operation $S \backslash (x_1, ..., x_n)$ removes from the schema S the components $x_1, ..., x_n$ explicitly listed, which must exist. Formally, $S \backslash (x_1, ..., x_n)$ is equivalent to $(\exists x_1 : t_1; ...; x_n : t_n \bullet S)$, where $x_1, ..., x_n$ have types $t_1, ..., t_n$ in S. The notation $\exists x : a \bullet S$ states that there is some object x in a for which S is true. The notation $\forall x : a \bullet S$ states that for each object x in a, S is true. For the sake of space, more details of Z can be refereed to some books on Z [5]. Interface automata and Z seem in all ways to complement each other in their capabilities. Interface automata can characterise precisely the behavioural aspects of a system, whereas they are not suitable for modelling concisely (abstractly) the system data structures. On the other hand, Z has great expressive power to describe abstract data structures but lack the notion of operation evaluation order. This paper is based on ZIA, a specification language which integrates interface automata and Z. ZIA is defined such that apart from enabling one to deal with the behavioural and the data structure aspects of a system independently. In the original interface automata, states and operations are abstract atomic symbols. But in ZIA, states and operations are described by Z schemas.

In the rest of this paper, we use the following terminology: A state schema is a Z schema which does not contain any variable with decoration $'$. An input operation schema is a Z schema which contains input variables. An output operation schema is a Z schema which contains output variables. An internal operation schema is a Z schema which contains variables with decoration $'$. Let S to be a Z schema, we use $V^I(S)$ ($V^O(S)$, $V^H(S)$) to denote the set of input variables (output variables, internal variables) in S. In the following, given an assignment ρ and a Z schema A, we write $\rho \models A$ if ρ assigns every variable x in the declaration part of A to an element of its type set, which satisfies the predicate part of A; we write $\models A$ if $\rho \models A$ for any assignment ρ.

Definition 1. An interface automaton with Z notation (ZIA) $P = \langle S_P, S_P^i, A_P^I, A_P^O, A_P^H, V_P^I, V_P^O, V_P^H, F_P^S, F_P^A, G_P^{IA}, G_P^{OA}, T_P \rangle$ consists of the following elements:

(1) S_P is a set of states.

(2) $S_P^i \subseteq S_P$ is a set of initial states. If $S_P^i = \emptyset$ then P is called empty.

(3) A_P^I, A_P^O and A_P^H are disjoint sets of input, output, and internal actions, respectively. We denote by $A_P = A_P^I \cup A_P^O \cup A_P^H$ the set of all actions.

(4) V_P^I, V_P^O and V_P^H are disjoint sets of input, output, and internal variables, respectively. We denote by $V_P = V_P^I \cup V_P^O \cup V_P^H$ the set of all variables.

(5) F_P^S is a map, which maps any state in S_P to a state schema in Z language. Intuitively, for any state s, $F_P^S(s)$ specifies the data properties of all the variables in the state s.

(6) F_P^A is a map, which maps any input action in A_P^I to an input operation schema in Z language, and maps any output action in A_P^O to an output operation schema in Z language, and maps any internal action in A_P^H to an internal operation schema in Z language. Intuitively, for any action a, $F_P^A(a)$ specifies the data properties of all the variables before and after performing action a.

(7) G_P^{IA} is a map, which maps any input action in A_P^I to a set of input variables. Intuitively, an input action a inputs all the input variables in $G_P^{IA}(a)$. For any input action a, $G_P^{IA}(a) \subseteq V^I(F_P^A(a))$.

(8) G_P^{OA} is a map, which maps any output action in A_P^I to a set of output variables. Intuitively, an output action a outputs all the output variables in $G_P^{OA}(a)$. For any output action a, $G_P^{OA}(a) \subseteq V^O(F_P^A(a))$.

(9) T_P is the set of transitions between states, $T_P \subseteq S_P \times A_P \times S_P$. If $(s, a, t) \in T_P$ then $((F_P^S(s) \wedge F_P^A(a))\backslash(x_1, ..., x_m) \Leftrightarrow F_P^S(t)[y_1'/y_1, ..., y_n'/y_n])$ is a

tautology, where $\{x_1, ..., x_m\}$ is the set of the variables in $F_P^S(s)$, $\{y_1, ..., y_n\}$ is the set of the variables in $F_P^S(t)$, the set of variables in $F_P^A(a)$ is the subset of $\{x_1, ..., x_m\} \cup \{y_1', ..., y_n'\}$.

An action $a \in A_P$ is enabled at a state $s \in V_P$ if there is a step $(s, a, s') \in T_P$ for some $s \in S_P$. We indicate by $A_P^I(s)$, $A_P^O(s)$, $A_P^H(s)$ the subsets of input, output and internal actions that are enabled at the state s and we let $A_P(s) = A_P^I(s) \cup A_P^O(s) \cup A_P^H(s)$.

3   Composition

An interface automata is a specification of software component. A software system consists of several components. The specification of a software system can be modelled by the composition of ZIAs. In this section, we give the definition of composition of ZIAs.

We first define composablity of ZIAs. Intuitively, two ZIAs are composable if there is no conflict between their actions and between their variables.

Definition 2. Two ZIAs P and Q are composable if
$V_P^H \cap V_Q = \emptyset$, $V_P^I \cap V_Q^I = \emptyset$, $V_P^O \cap V_Q^O = \emptyset$, $V_Q^H \cap V_P = \emptyset$, and
$A_P^H \cap A_Q = \emptyset$, $A_P^I \cap A_Q^I = \emptyset$, $A_P^O \cap A_Q^O = \emptyset$, $A_Q^H \cap A_P = \emptyset$.
We let $SharedV(P, Q) = V_P \cap V_Q$, $SharedA(P, Q) = A_P \cap A_Q$.

Now we can define the product of two ZIAs if they are composable. The two automata will synchronize on the shared actions and asynchronously interleave all other actions.

Definition 3. If P and Q are composable ZIAs, their product $P \otimes Q$ is the automaton defined by:

(1) $S_{P \otimes Q} = S_P \times S_Q$.

(2) $S_{P \otimes Q}^i = S_P^i \times S_Q^i$.

(3) $A_{P \otimes Q}^I = (A_P^I \cup A_Q^I) - SharedA(P, Q)$.

(4) $A_{P \otimes Q}^O = (A_P^O \cup A_Q^O) - SharedA(P, Q)$.

(5) $A_{P \otimes Q}^H = A_P^H \cup A_Q^H \cup SharedA(P, Q)$.

(6) $V_{P \otimes Q}^I = (V_P^I \cup V_Q^I) - SharedV(P, Q)$.

(7) $V_{P \otimes Q}^O = (V_P^O \cup V_Q^O) - SharedV(P, Q)$.

(8) $V_{P \otimes Q}^H = V_P^H \cup V_Q^H \cup SharedV(P, Q)$.

(9) $F_{P \otimes Q}^S : F_{P \otimes Q}^S((s, t)) = F_P^S(s) \wedge F_Q^S(t)$.

(10) $F_{P \otimes Q}^A : F_{P \otimes Q}^A(a) = F_P^A(a) \wedge F_Q^A(a)$ if $a \in SharedA(P, Q)$, $F_{P \otimes Q}^A(a) = F_P^A(a)$ if $a \in A_P \backslash SharedA(P, Q)$, $F_{P \otimes Q}^A(a) = F_Q^A(a)$ if $a \in A_Q \backslash SharedA(P, Q)$.

(11) $G_{P \otimes Q}^{IA} : G_{P \otimes Q}^{IA}(a) = G_P^{IA}(a)$ if $a \in A_P^I \backslash SharedA(P, Q)$, $G_{P \otimes Q}^{IA}(a) = G_Q^{IA}(a)$ if $a \in A_Q^I \backslash SharedA(P, Q)$.

(12) $G_{P \otimes Q}^{OA} : G_{P \otimes Q}^{OA}(a) = G_P^{OA}(a)$ if $a \in A_P^O \backslash SharedA(P, Q)$, $G_{P \otimes Q}^{OA}(a) = G_Q^{OA}(a)$ if $a \in A_Q^O \backslash SharedA(P, Q)$.

(13) $T_{P \otimes Q} = \{((s,t), a, (s^*, t)) \mid (s, a, s^*) \in T_P \wedge a \notin SharedA(P, Q) \wedge t \in S_Q\} \cup \{((s,t), a, (s, t^*)) \mid (t, a, t^*) \in T_Q \wedge a \notin SharedA(P, Q) \wedge s \in S_P\} \cup \{((s,t), a, (s^*, t^*)) \mid (s, a, s^*) \in T_P \wedge (t, a, t^*) \in T_Q \wedge a \in SharedA(P, Q)\}.$

In the product $P \otimes Q$ of two ZIAs P and Q, one of the automata may produce an output (input) action that is an input (output) action of the other automaton, but is not responded. The set $IllegalA(P, Q)$ of states of $P \otimes Q$ where this happens are called the illegal states of the product with respect to actions.

Definition 4. Given two composable ZIAs P and Q, the set $IllegalA(P, Q) \subseteq S_P \times S_Q$ of illegal states of $P \otimes Q$ with respect to actions is defined by:
$\quad IllegalA(P, Q) = \{(s, t) \in S_P \times S_Q \mid \exists a \in SharedA(P, Q). ((a \in A_P^O(s) \wedge a \notin A_Q^I(t)) \vee (a \notin A_P^O(s) \wedge a \in A_Q^I(t)) \vee (a \in A_Q^O(t) \wedge a \notin A_P^I(s)) \vee (a \notin A_Q^O(t) \wedge a \in A_P^I(s)))\}.$

The definition of product should deal with not only the synchronization of the shared actions but also the shared variables, i.e., when one ZIA writes to a shared variable and the other should read this variable and etc. The set $IllegalV(P, Q)$ of states of $P \otimes Q$ where this is not satisfied are called the illegal states of the product with respect to variables.

Definition 5. Given two composable ZIAs P and Q, the set $IllegalV(P, Q) \subseteq S_P \times S_Q$ of illegal states of $P \otimes Q$ with respect to variables is defined by:
$\quad IllegalV(P, Q) = \{(s, t) \in S_P \times S_Q \mid \exists a. ((a \in A_P^O(s) \wedge a \in A_Q^I(t) \wedge G_P^{OA}(a) \neq G_Q^{IA}(a)) \vee (a \in A_P^I(s) \wedge a \in A_Q^O(t) \wedge G_P^{OA}(a) \neq G_Q^{IA}(a)) \vee (a \in A_P^I(s) \wedge a \notin A_Q^O(t) \wedge G_P^{IA}(a) \cap SharedV(P, Q) \neq \emptyset) \vee (a \notin A_P^I(s) \wedge a \in A_Q^O(t) \wedge G_Q^{OA}(a) \cap SharedV(P, Q) \neq \emptyset)) \vee (a \notin A_P^O(t) \wedge a \in A_Q^I(s) \wedge G_Q^{IA}(a) \cap SharedV(P, Q) \neq \emptyset) \vee (a \in A_P^O(t) \wedge a \notin A_Q^I(s) \wedge G_P^{OA}(a) \cap SharedV(P, Q) \neq \emptyset))\}.$

The following proposition states that the product of two ZIAs also satisfies the condition of the definition of ZIA.

Proposition 1. If P and Q are two composable ZIAs and $IllegalA(P, Q) \cup IllegalV(P, Q) = \emptyset$, then $P \otimes Q$ is a ZIA.

The product of ZIAs is associative, which is a ZIA extension version of Theorem 3.1 in [1].

Proposition 2. If P, Q and R are composable and $IllegalA(P, Q) \cup IllegalV(P, Q) = \emptyset$, $P \otimes Q$ and R are composable and $IllegalA(P \otimes Q, R) \cup IllegalV(P \otimes Q, R) = \emptyset$, then Q and R are composable and $IllegalA(Q, R) \cup IllegalV(Q, R) = \emptyset$, P and $Q \otimes R$ are composable and $IllegalA(P, Q \otimes R) \cup IllegalV(P, Q \otimes R) = \emptyset$, and $(P \otimes Q) \otimes R = P \otimes (Q \otimes R)$.

The existence of a legal environment indicates that there is a way to use the interfaces P and Q together without giving rise to incompatibilities. A legal environment for R needs to satisfy the following side conditions.

Definition 6. An environment for a ZIA R is a ZIA E such that (1) E is composable with R, (2) E is nonempty, (3) $A_R^O \subseteq A_E^I$, (4) $A_R^I \subseteq A_E^O$, (5) $V_R^O \subseteq V_E^I$, (6) $V_R^I \subseteq V_E^O$, (7) $IllegalA(R, E) = \emptyset$ and (8) $IllegalV(R, E) = \emptyset$.

Definition 7. Given two composable ZIAs P and Q, a legal environment E for the pair (P, Q) is an environment E for $P \otimes Q$ such that no state in $(IllegalA(P, Q) \cup IllegalV(P, Q)) \times S_E$ is reachable in $(P \otimes Q) \otimes E$.

We define compatibility as the existence of a legal environment:

Definition 8. Two ZIAs P and Q are compatible with respect to E if they are nonempty, composable, and there exists a legal environment E for (P, Q).

The composition of two ZIA is obtained by restricting the product of the two automata to the set of compatible states which are the states from which the environment can prevent entering illegal states.

Definition 9. Consider two composable ZIAs P and Q. A pair $(s, t) \in S_P \times S_Q$ of states is compatible with respect to environment E if there is an environment E for $P \otimes Q$ such that no state in $(IllegalA(P, Q) \cup IllegalV(P, Q)) \times S_E$ is reachable in $(P \otimes Q) \otimes E$ from the state $\{(s, t)\} \times S_E^i$. We write $Cmp_E(P, Q)$ for the set of compatible states of $P \otimes Q$ with respect to environment E.

Hence we can rephrase the definition of compatibility for ZIA as follows: two nonempty composable ZIAs P and Q are compatible with respect to environment E iff their initial states are compatible with respect to E.

Definition 10. Consider two composable ZIAs P and Q, and an environment E. The composition $P \parallel_E Q$ is a ZIA with the same action sets as $P \otimes Q$. The states are $S_{P \parallel_E Q} = Cmp_E(P, Q)$, the initial states are $S_{P \parallel_E Q}^i = S_{P \otimes Q}^i \cap Cmp_E(P, Q)$, and the steps are $T_{P \parallel_E Q} = T_{P \otimes Q} \cap (Cmp_E(P, Q) \times A_{P \otimes Q} \times Cmp_E(P, Q))$.

The composition of ZIAs is associative.

Proposition 3. For all ZIAs P, Q, R and E, either both $(P \parallel_E Q) \parallel_E R$ and $P \parallel_E (Q \parallel_E R)$ are undefined because some of the automata are not composable or $(P \parallel_E Q) \parallel_E R = P \parallel_E (Q \parallel_E R)$.

4   Refinement Relation

The refinement relation aims at formalizing the relation between abstract and concrete versions of the same component, for example, between an interface specification and its implementation.

Roughly, a ZIA P refines a ZIA Q if all the input or output actions of P can be simulated by Q. To define this concept, we need some preliminary notions.

In order to define the refinement relation between Z schemas, we need the following notation.

Definition 11. Consider two Z schemas A and B with $V^I(A) = V^I(B)$, $V^O(A) = V^O(B)$ and $V^H(A) = V^H(B) = \emptyset$, where $V^I(S)$ $(V^O(S), V^H(S))$ denotes the set of input variables (output variables, internal variables) in S. We use the notation $A \geq B$ if one of the following cases holds:

(1) If $V^I(A) \neq \emptyset$ and $V^O(A) \neq \emptyset$ then given an assignment ρ on $V^I(A)$, for any assignment σ on $V^O(A)$, $\rho \cup \sigma \models B$ implies $\rho \cup \sigma \models A$, and given an assignment σ on $V^O(A)$, for any assignment ρ on $V^I(A)$, $\rho \cup \sigma \models A$ implies $\rho \cup \sigma \models B$, where $\rho \models A$ means that A is true under assignment ρ, $\rho \cup \sigma$ is an assignment which the union of ρ and σ.

(2) If $V^I(A) \neq \emptyset$ and $V^O(A) = \emptyset$ then for any assignment ρ on $V^I(A)$, $\rho \models A$ implies $\rho \models B$.

(3) If $V^I(A) = \emptyset$ and $V^O(A) \neq \emptyset$ then for any assignment ρ on $V^O(A)$, $\rho \models B$ implies $\rho \models A$.

(4) $V^I(A) = \emptyset$ and $V^O(A) = \emptyset$.

Intuitively, $A \geq B$ means that schemas A and B have the same input variables and the same output variables, and schema B has bigger domains of input variables but smaller ranges of output variables than schema A.

Now we give the refinement relation between Z schemas, which describe the refinement relation between data structures properties of states.

Definition 12. Given two Z schemas A and B, we use the notation $A \trianglerighteq B$ if

(1) $V^I(A) \subseteq V^I(B)$, $V^O(A) \subseteq V^O(B)$.

(2) $A\backslash(x_1, ..., x_m) \geq B\backslash(y_1, ..., y_n)$, where $\{x_1, ..., x_m\} = V(A) - V^I(A) - V^O(A)$, $\{y_1, ..., y_n\} = V(B) - V^I(A) - V^O(A)$.

The precise definition of refinement relation between ZIAs must take into account the fact that the internal actions of P and Q are independent.

We now give the following definition which describes the set of states after performing a sequence of internal actions from a given state.

Definition 13. Given a ZIA P and a state $s \in S_P$, the set $\varepsilon - closure_P(s)$ is the smallest set $U \subseteq S_P$ such that (1) $s \in U$ and (2) if $t \in U$, $a \in A_P^H$, and $(t, a, t^*) \in T_P$ then $t^* \in U$.

The environment of a ZIA P cannot see the internal actions of P. Consequently if P is at a state s then the environment cannot distinguish between s and any state in $\varepsilon - closure_P(s)$.

The following definition describes the set of states after performing several internal actions and an external action from a given state.

Definition 14. Given a ZIA P, a state $s \in S_P$, and an action $a \in A_P$, we let $ExtDest_P(s, a) = \{s^* \mid \exists(t, a, t^*) \in T_P.\ t \in \varepsilon - closure_P(s)$ and $s^* \in \varepsilon - closure_P(t^*)\}$.

In the following, we give a refinement relation between ZIAs. For ZIAs, a state has not only behavioural properties but also data properties. Therefore this refinement relation involves both the refinement relation between behavioural properties and the refinement relation between data properties.

Definition 15. Consider two ZIAs P and Q. A binary relation $R \subseteq S_P \times S_Q$ is a refinement from Q to P if for all states $s \in S_P$, there exists $t \in S_Q$ such that $s\ R\ t$ the following conditions hold:

(1) $F_P^V(s) \trianglerighteq F_Q^V(t)$.

(2) For any $s^* \in \varepsilon - closure_P(s)$, there is a state $t^* \in \varepsilon - closure_Q(t)$, such that $F_P^S(s^*) \trianglerighteq F_Q^S(t^*)$, and $s^*\ R\ t^*$.

(3) For any $a \in A_P^I$, if $s^* \in ExtDest_P(s, a)$, there is a state $t^* \in ExtDest_Q(t, a)$, such that $G_P^{IA}(a) \subseteq G_Q^{IA}(a)$, $F_P^A(a) \trianglerighteq F_Q^A(a)$, $F_P^S(s^*) \trianglerighteq F_Q^S(t^*)$, and $s^*\ R\ t^*$.

(4) For any $a \in A_P^O$, if $s^* \in ExtDest_P(s, a)$, there is a state $t^* \in ExtDest_Q(t, a)$, such that $G_P^{OA}(a) \subseteq G_Q^{OA}(a)$, $F_P^A(a) \trianglerighteq F_Q^A(a)$, $F_P^S(s^*) \trianglerighteq F_Q^S(t^*)$, and $s^*\ R\ t^*$.

We write $s \succeq t$ if there is a refinement R such that $s\ R\ t$.

We say that ZIA P is refined by ZIA Q if for some initial states s in P and t in Q, s is refined by t.

Definition 16. The ZIA Q refines the ZIA P written $P \succeq Q$ if:

there are a state $s \in S_P^i$ and a state $t \in S_Q^i$ such that $s \succeq t$.

The above definitions of refinement relations can be extended to the definitions of bisimulation relations by adding the symmetric condition of relations.

The following proposition means that $\succeq$ is a partial order relation.

Proposition 4. For all ZIAs P, Q and R, the following claims hold:

(1) $P \succeq P$.

(2) If $P \succeq Q$ and $Q \succeq R$, then $P \succeq R$.

The following propositions state that the resulting specification can be refined independently, i.e., the approach to refinement is compositional in the sense that refining the components leads to the refinement of the whole specification.

Proposition 5. Consider three ZIAs P, Q and R such that P and R are composable, Q and R are composable, $IllegalA(P, R) \cup IllegalV(P, R) = \emptyset$, and $IllegalA(Q, R) \cup IllegalV(Q, R) = \emptyset$. If $P \succeq Q$, and for any $s \in S_P$, $t \in S_Q$

such that $s \succeq t$, $V^I(F_P^S(s)) \cap V_R^O = V^I(F_Q^S(t)) \cap V_R^O$, $V^O(F_P^S(s)) \cap V_R^I = V^O(F_Q^S(t)) \cap V_R^I$, $A_P^I(s) \cap A_R^O = A_Q^I(t) \cap A_R^O$, $A_P^O(s) \cap A_R^I = A_Q^O(t) \cap A_R^I$, and for any a in both P and Q, $V^I(F_P^A(a)) \cap V_R^O = V^I(F_Q^A(a)) \cap V_R^O$, $V^O(F_P^A(a)) \cap V_R^I = V^O(F_Q^A(a)) \cap V_R^I$, $G_P^{IA}(a) \cap V_R^O = G_Q^{IA}(a) \cap V_R^O$, $G_P^{OA}(a) \cap V_R^I = G_Q^{OA}(a) \cap V_R^I$, then $P \otimes R \succeq Q \otimes R$.

Proposition 6. Consider four ZIAs P, Q, R and E such that P and R are composable, Q and R are composable, E is an environment for $P \otimes R$ and $Q \otimes R$. If $P \succeq Q$, and for any $s \in S_P$, $t \in S_Q$ such that for any $s \succeq t$, $V^I(F_P^S(s)) \cap V_R^O = V^I(F_Q^S(t)) \cap V_R^O$, $V^O(F_P^S(s)) \cap V_R^I = V^O(F_Q^S(t)) \cap V_R^I$, $A_P^I(s) \cap A_R^O = A_Q^I(t) \cap A_R^O$, $A_P^O(s) \cap A_R^I = A_Q^O(t) \cap A_R^I$, and for any a in both P and Q, $V^I(F_P^A(a)) \cap V_R^O = V^I(F_Q^A(a)) \cap V_R^O$, $V^O(F_P^A(a)) \cap V_R^I = V^O(F_Q^A(a)) \cap V_R^I$, $G_P^{IA}(a) \cap V_R^O = G_Q^{IA}(a) \cap V_R^O$, $G_P^{OA} \cap V_R^I = G_Q^{OA}(a) \cap V_R^I$, then $P \parallel_E R \succeq Q \parallel_E R$.

5 Conclusions

This paper proposed a specification approach which is able to describe properties of both behaviour and data of systems. There are several other works for such topic. Some examples are LOTOS and Z [2], CSP-OZ [3], and Circus [4]. In this paper, we define a combination of interface automata and Z, called ZIA. The composition and refinement relation for ZIAs are also defined and studied. ZIA is well suited for specification of software components. It provides a techniques to specify both behaviour and data in a common framework.

References

1. de Alfaro, L., Henzinger, T.A.: Interface Automata. In: The Proceedings of the 9th Annual ACM Symposium on Foundations of Software Engineering (2001)
2. Derrick, J., Boiten, E., Bowman, H., Steen, M.: Viewpoint Consistency in Z and LOTOS: A case study. In: Fitzgerald, J.S., Jones, C.B., Lucas, P. (eds.) FME 1997. LNCS, vol. 1313, pp. 644–664. Springer, Heidelberg (1997)
3. Fischer, C.: CSP-OZ: A combination of Object-Z and CSP. In: FMODDS 1997 (1997)
4. Sampaio, A., Woodcock, J., Cavalcanti, A.: Refinement in *Circus*. In: Eriksson, L.-H., Lindsay, P.A. (eds.) FME 2002. LNCS, vol. 2391, pp. 451–470. Springer, Heidelberg (2002)
5. Spivey, J.M.: The Z Notation: A Reference Manual, 2nd edn. Prentice Hall International (UK) Ltd. (1998)

A Specification Language for Reo Connectors

Alexandra Silva

Centrum Wiskunde & Informatica

Abstract. Recent approaches to component-based software engineering employ coordinating connectors to compose components into software systems. Reo is a model of component coordination, wherein complex connectors are constructed by composing various types of primitive channels. Reo automata are a simple and intuitive formal model of context- dependent connectors, which provided a compositional semantics for Reo.

In this paper, we study Reo automata from a coalgebraic perspective. This enables us to apply the recently developed coalgebraic theory of generalized regular expressions in order to derive a specification language, tailor-made for Reo automata, and sound and complete axiomatizations with respect to three distinct notions of equivalence: (coalgebraic) bisimilarity, the bisimulation notion studied in the original papers on Reo automata and trace equivalence. The obtained language is simple, but nonetheless expressive enough to specify all possible finite Reo automata. Moreover, it comes equipped with a Kleene-like theorem: we provide algorithms to translate expressions to Reo automata and, conversely, to compute an expression equivalent to a state in a Reo automaton.

1 Introduction

The holy grail of component-based software engineering is to develop truly reusable software components that can be sold off-the-shelf and reused to build software systems [17]. Research on software composition plays a key role in this quest, as it offers flexible ways of plugging together components. Channel based-languages, where 'channels' or 'connectors' are used to compose components into a system [3,10,1,9], play a prominent in the world of software composition. These 'languages' express various coordination patterns exhibiting combinations of synchronisation, mutual exclusion, non-deterministic choice, context-dependent and state-dependent behaviour. A number of component connector models exist, including Reo [1], Ptolemy [11,12], MoCha [10], Manifold [2], BIP [4] and an algebra of stateless connectors [8].

In this paper, we focus on the coordination language Reo and in a particular semantic model thereof: Reo automata [6,7]. We present a specification language for Reo automata, together with a Kleene-like theorem and sound and complete axiomatizations with respect to three notions of equivalence which enable algebraic reasoning on specifications. In order to achieve this, we make use of the coalgebraic view on systems.

In the last decades, coalgebra has arisen as a prominent candidate for a mathematical framework to specify and reason about computer systems. Coalgebraic

F. Arbab and M. Sirjani (Eds.): FSEN 2011, LNCS 7141, pp. 368–376, 2012.

modeling works, on the surface, as follows: the basic features of a system, such as non-determinism or probability, are collected and combined in the appropriate way, determining the type of the system. This type (formally, a functor) is then used to derive a suitable equivalence relation and a universal domain of behaviors, which allow to reason about equivalence of systems. The strength of coalgebraic modeling lies in the fact that many important notions are parameterized by the type of the system. Recently, in [16] the coalgebraic view on systems enabled the development of a framework wherein specification languages and axiomatizations can uniformly be derived for a large class of systems.

In this paper, we apply the general coalgebraic framework of [16] to Reo automata. The main contributions of the paper are the following:

1. A coalgebraic characterization of Reo automata and of the bisimulation considered in [6].
2. A tailor-made language to specify Reo automata.
3. An analogue of Kleene's theorem for Reo automata, yielding algorithms to convert expressions to equivalent automata and vice-versa.
4. A sound and complete axiomatization of the language with respect to three different types of equivalence (bisimilarity, trace semantics and the bisimulation considered in [6]).

The items 2. − 4. partially stem from the general framework of [16]. However, the only axiomatization derived from the general framework of [16] is that of bisimilarity. The other two are completely new.

This is a short paper and therefore we omit proofs and discussion of related work, as well as preliminaries on Reo and Reo automata. This extra material can be found in the technical report [15].

2 A Specification Language for Reo

In this section, we instantiate the generic framework presented in [16] yielding a language to specify and to reason about Reo automata.

Definition 1 (Expressions for Reo automata). *Given sets of ports Σ and variables X, the set* Exp *of expressions for Reo automata is given by the closed expressions contained in the following BNF, for $g \in \mathcal{B}_\Sigma$, $f \in 2^\Sigma$ and $x \in X$:*

$$\varepsilon ::= \underline{\emptyset} \mid \varepsilon \oplus \varepsilon \mid \mu x.\gamma \mid x \mid g{\uparrow}f(\sigma)$$
$$\gamma ::= \underline{\emptyset} \mid \gamma \oplus \gamma \mid \mu x.\gamma \mid g{\uparrow}f(\sigma)$$
$$\sigma ::= \underline{\emptyset} \mid \sigma \cup \sigma \mid \{\varepsilon\}$$

The operator μ in the expression $\mu x.\gamma$ functions as a binder for all the occurrences of the variable x in γ. Note that the only difference between γ and ε is the occurrence of x (γ is an expression where x occurs guarded, *that is only inside an expression of the shape $g{\uparrow}f(-)$). An expression ε is* closed *if all variables $x \in X$ occurring in ε are bounded.*

Intuitively, the expressions $\emptyset$, $\oplus$ and $\mu x.\gamma$ are the counterpart of the empty expression, $+$ and star expressions in classical regular expressions, where they denoted the empty language, language union and iteration. In our context, the reader can think of $\emptyset$ as the specification of a deadlocked channel, of $\oplus$ as putting the specifications of two channels in parallel and of $\mu x.\gamma$ as the specification of a channel with recursive behavior (or in other words, a persistent channel).

Example 1. Even before providing semantics to the expressions above, in order to give the reader a feeling for which expressions specify Reo channels, we include in Figure 1 the expressions equivalent to the basic Reo automata.

$ab\|ab$	$ab\|ab$ $a\bar{b}\|a$	$ab\|ab$	$a\|a$ $b\|b$
Sync	LossySync	SyncDrain	FIFO1
$\mu x.ab{\uparrow}ab(\{x\})$	$\mu x.ab{\uparrow}ab(\{x\}) \oplus a\bar{b}{\uparrow}a(\{x\}))$	$\mu x.ab{\uparrow}ab(\{x\})$	$e = \mu x.a{\uparrow}a(b{\uparrow}b(\{x\}))$ $f = \mu x.b{\uparrow}b(a{\uparrow}a(\{x\}))$

Fig. 1. Expressions corresponding to the automata for basic Reo channels

We now proceed to provide the set of expressions with a coalgebraic structure, which will provide operational semantics to the expressions. More precisely, we will define below a function $\delta: \mathsf{Exp} \to \mathcal{P}(\mathsf{Exp})^{\mathcal{B}_\Sigma \times 2^\Sigma}$. This will allow us to determine when a state s of a system and an expression ε are bisimilar, $s \sim \varepsilon$, or trace equivalent $s \sim_{tr} \varepsilon$.

Definition 2 (Operational semantics). *We define* $\delta: \mathsf{Exp} \to \mathcal{P}(\mathsf{Exp})^{\mathcal{B}_\Sigma \times 2^\Sigma}$ *by induction on the number of nested ocurrences of* μ *(and structural induction) as follows:*

$$\delta(\emptyset)(\langle g, f \rangle) = \emptyset$$
$$\delta(\varepsilon_1 \oplus \varepsilon_2)(\langle g, f \rangle) = \delta(\varepsilon_1)(g, f) \cup \delta(\varepsilon_2)(g, f)$$
$$\delta(\mu x.\gamma) = \delta(\gamma[\mu x.\gamma/x])$$
$$\delta(g{\uparrow}f(\sigma))(\langle g', f' \rangle) = \begin{cases} \bar{\delta}(\sigma) & f = f' \& g = g' \\ \emptyset & otherwise \end{cases}$$
$$\bar{\delta}(\emptyset) = \emptyset \quad \bar{\delta}(\sigma_1 \cup \sigma_2) = \bar{\delta}(\sigma_1) \cup \bar{\delta}(\sigma_2) \quad \bar{\delta}(\{\varepsilon\}) = \{\varepsilon\}$$

Note that $\bar{\delta}$ simply interprets each σ, a syntactical representation of a set of specifications, as the corresponding set.

Having a coalgebra structure on the set of expressions has two advantages: it provides immediately a natural semantics, using the unique homomorphism into the final coalgebra (which can be thought of as the universe of behaviors), and it enables an easy definition on when a state s of a Reo automaton and an expression ε are bisimilar, $s \sim \varepsilon$, or trace equivalent $s \sim_{tr} \varepsilon$.

3 A Kleene Theorem for Reo Automata

In this section, we present the analogue of Kleene's theorem for Reo automata. More precisely, we show how to convert each expression into a Reo automaton and, conversely, how to compute an expression equivalent to a state of a Reo automaton.

From Reo Automata to Expressions. We start by proving that for each state of a Reo automaton it is possible to compute a bisimilar expression. The expression is built in a similar way as in the classical case of regular expressions and deterministic automata, by solving a system of equations describing the transition structure of each state.

Theorem 1 (Kleene's theorem for Reo automata (part I)). *For every Reo automaton* (S, ξ), *if S is* finite *then there exists for any $s \in S$ an expression* $\varepsilon_s \in \mathsf{Exp}$ *such that $s \sim \varepsilon_s$.*

In the proof of the above theorem (for details see [15]), a construction is presented, which we illustrate here by means of an example. We recall on the left one of the Reo automata presented in Figure 1. We associate with e and f the variables x_1 and x_2, respectively, and we define the expressions $A_1 = \mu x_1.\psi_1$ and $A_2 = \mu x_2.\psi_2$, where $\psi_1 = a{\uparrow}a(\{x_2\})$ and $\psi_2 = b{\uparrow}b(\{x_1\})$. Then, we solve the system of equations above by replacing x_1 in the second with the expression A_1, yielding a closed expression, which in turn can substitute x_2 in the first equation. This yields the closed expressions

$$\varepsilon_1 = \mu x_1.a{\uparrow}a(\{\mu x_2.b{\uparrow}b(\{\mu x_1.a{\uparrow}a(\{x_2\})\})\}) \qquad \varepsilon_2 = \mu x_2.b{\uparrow}b(\{\mu x_1.a{\uparrow}a(\{x_2\})\})$$

By construction we have $e \sim \varepsilon_1$ and $f \sim \varepsilon_2$. Note that the expression computed here is slightly different than the one presented in Figure 1. They are however equivalent as can be proved using the axioms we shall introduce later or by just directly constructing a bisimulation. Moreover, we note that computing all the A^i_j is not really needed. In general, one can solve the system of equations by eliminating variables in a more convenient way, but we decided in this example to follow exactly the formalization which we presented above.

All the Reo automata we have seen so far were deterministic. For the reader to get the intuition of what happens in the truly non-deterministic case expression-wise we show the construction above for the automaton on the right. We associate with s_1 and s_2 the variables x_1 and x_2, respectively, and we define $A_1 = \mu x_1.\psi_1$ and $A_2 = \mu x_2.\psi_2$, where ψ_1 and ψ_2 are given by

$$\psi_1 = a{\uparrow}a(\{x_1\} \cup \{x_2\}) \qquad \psi_2 = b{\uparrow}b(\{x_1\})$$

Again, we solve the system of two equations, yeilding the expressions

$$\varepsilon_1 = A_1^2 = \mu x_1.a{\uparrow}a(\{x_1\} \cup \{\varepsilon_2\})\}) \qquad \varepsilon_2 = A_2^2 = \mu x_2.b{\uparrow}b(\{\mu x_1.a{\uparrow}a(\{x_1\} \cup \{x_2\})\})$$

As before, we have, by construction, $s_1 \sim \varepsilon_1$ and $s_2 \sim \varepsilon_2$.

From Expressions to Reo Automata. The coalgebra structure (Exp, δ) also provides us with a way of constructing a Reo automaton from an expression $\varepsilon \in \mathsf{Exp}$, by considering the subcoalgebra $\langle \varepsilon \rangle$ (intuitively, $\langle \varepsilon \rangle$ denotes the unraveling of the automaton generated starting in ε by applying δ). The synthesis of a Reo automaton from an expression $\varepsilon \in \mathsf{Exp}$ is what we need to be able to state and prove the second half of Kleene's theorem for Reo automata.

Theorem 2 (Kleene's theorem for Reo automata (part II)). *For every expression $\varepsilon \in \mathsf{Exp}$, there exists a Reo automaton (S, ξ) with S finite and $s \in S$ such that $s \sim \varepsilon$.*

Consider the expression $\varepsilon_1 = \mu x.ab{\uparrow}ab(\{x\} \cup \{\mu y.ab{\uparrow}ab(\{y\})\})$. Applying δ we obtain the following:

$$\delta(\varepsilon_1)(\langle g, f \rangle) = \delta(ab{\uparrow}ab(\{\varepsilon_1\} \cup \{\mu y.ab{\uparrow}ab(\{y\})\}))(\langle g, f \rangle)$$
$$= \overline{\delta}(\{\varepsilon_1\} \cup \{\mu y.ab{\uparrow}ab(\{y\})\}))$$
$$= \{\varepsilon_1, \mu y.ab{\uparrow}ab(\{y\})\}$$

The first step of the unraveling then yields the automaton on the left below, where $\varepsilon_2 = \mu y.ab{\uparrow}ab(\{y\})$. Applying δ to the new state $\varepsilon_2 = \mu y.ab{\uparrow}ab(\{y\})$ then completes the automaton, which we depict below on the right.

4   Sound and Complete Axiomatizations

We present next an equational system for expressions in Exp. We define the relation $\equiv\, \subseteq \mathsf{Exp} \times \mathsf{Exp}$, written infix, as the least reflexive and transitive relation containing the following identities:

1. $(\mathsf{Exp}, \oplus, \emptyset)$ is a join-semilattice

$$\varepsilon \oplus \varepsilon \qquad\qquad \equiv \varepsilon \qquad (Idemp) \qquad \varepsilon_1 \oplus \varepsilon_2 \equiv \varepsilon_2 \oplus \varepsilon_1 \; (Commut)$$
$$\varepsilon_1 \oplus (\varepsilon_2 \oplus \varepsilon_3) \equiv (\varepsilon_1 \oplus \varepsilon_2) \oplus \varepsilon_3 \; (Assoc) \qquad \emptyset \oplus \varepsilon \qquad \equiv \varepsilon \qquad (Empty)$$

2. μ is the unique fixed-point.

$$\gamma[\mu x.\gamma/x] \equiv \mu x.\gamma \; (FP) \qquad \gamma[\varepsilon/x] \equiv \varepsilon \Rightarrow \mu x.\gamma \equiv \varepsilon \; (Unique)$$

3. The join-semilattice structure propagates through the expressions.

$$g{\uparrow}f(\emptyset) \equiv \emptyset \quad (Zero) \qquad g{\uparrow}f(\sigma_1 \cup \sigma_2) \equiv g{\uparrow}f(\sigma_1) \oplus g{\uparrow}f(\sigma_2) \quad (Dist)$$

4. $\equiv$ is a congruence.

$$\varepsilon_1 \equiv \varepsilon_2 \Rightarrow \varepsilon[\varepsilon_1/x] \equiv \varepsilon[\varepsilon_2/x] \qquad \text{if } x \text{ is free in } \varepsilon \; (Cong)$$

5. α-equivalence

$$\mu x.\gamma \equiv \mu y.\gamma[y/x] \qquad \text{if } y \text{ is not free in } \gamma \; (\alpha - equiv)$$

Theorem 3 (Soundness and Completeness (bisimilarity)). *The axiomatization presented above is sound and complete with respect to bisimilarity, that is:*
$$\varepsilon_1 \sim \varepsilon_2 \Leftrightarrow \varepsilon_1 \equiv \varepsilon_2$$

It is interesting to remark that in the axiomatization above one cannot derive $g{\uparrow}f(\varepsilon_1 \oplus \varepsilon_2) \equiv g{\uparrow}f(\varepsilon_1) \oplus g{\uparrow}f(\varepsilon_2)$. This is similarly to what happens in, for instance, CCS, where the axiom $a.(P + Q) = a.P + a.Q$ is not valid. It is also the key point in order to distinguish bisimilarity from trace equivalence.

An interesting observation, which was not at all considered in the general framework of [16], is that the axiomatization above can be extended with the axiom above and yield a sound and complete axiomatization for trace semantics. This is reminiscent of what Rabinovich [14] showed for a fragment of CCS, where adding to the axiomatization of Milner for bisimilarity the axiom $a.(P + Q) = a.P + a.Q$ resulted in a sound and complete axiomatization for trace semantics. The proof of the theorem below follows a similar structure to that of Rabinovich's and, for space reasons, we omit it here.

Theorem 4 (Soundness and Completeness (trace semantics)). *The axiomatization presented above, augmented with the axiom*

$$g{\uparrow}f(\{\varepsilon_1 \oplus \varepsilon_2\}) \equiv g{\uparrow}f(\{\varepsilon_1\}) \oplus g{\uparrow}f(\{\varepsilon_2\}) \qquad (D1)$$

is sound and complete with respect to trace semantics, that is:

$$\varepsilon_1 \sim_{tr} \varepsilon_2 \Leftrightarrow \varepsilon_1 \equiv \varepsilon_2$$

An interesting feature of the axiomatization(s) above is that $\oplus$ enables the definition of a natural order on expressions: $\varepsilon_1 \leq \varepsilon_2 \Leftrightarrow \varepsilon_1 \oplus \varepsilon_2 \equiv \varepsilon_2$. This opens the door to study refinement of specifications of Reo automata (or, at the automaton level notions of simulation).

4.1   Coalgebraic Characterization of $\sim_R$

The definition of bisimulation, which we denote $\sim_R$, considered in [6,7] is different than the notion of coalgebraic bisimilarity which one obtains from the functor of Reo automata. The definition of $\sim_R$ involved atoms and, in fact, in [7] they showed a two step construction, where in the first step the automaton is determinized (using the powerset construction, which we recalled in the preliminaries) and in the second step each transition labeled by $g|f$ in the automaton is replaced by n transitions labeled by $\alpha_i|f$, using the fact that each guard g is always equivalent to a disjunction of atoms $\alpha_1 \vee \ldots \vee \alpha_n$. The construction described above had as goal to show that the set $2^{(\mathbf{At}_\Sigma \times \Sigma)^*}$ of guarded strings is the counterpart of formal languages for Reo automata.

It is the aim of this section to show that the definition of $\sim_R$ can be recovered coalgebraically and that the axiomatization above (the one for trace semantics) can be augmented with two axioms yielding a sound and complete axiomatization with respect to the bisimulation of [6,7]. The key observation is that the bisimulation of [6,7] can be characterized coalgebraically by the following diagram

$$X \xrightarrow{\{\cdot\}} \mathcal{P}(X) \dashrightarrow^{L} 2^{(\text{At}_\Sigma \times \Sigma)^*}$$

$$2 \times \mathcal{P}(X)^{\mathcal{B}_\Sigma \times 2^\Sigma} \xrightarrow{2 \times c} 2 \times \mathcal{P}(X)^{\text{At}_\Sigma \times 2^\Sigma} \xrightarrow{2 \times L^A} 2 \times (2^{(\text{At}_\Sigma \times \Sigma)^*})^A$$

where c performs the replacement of $g|f$ by $\alpha_i|f$ as explained above. It is easy to show now that the bisimulation of [6,7] which is denoted by $\sim_R$ can be recovered from the above diagram

$$q_1 \sim_R q_2 \Leftrightarrow L(\{q_1\}) = L(\{q_2\})$$

Moreover, by analyzing the construction above we discovered which axioms we have to add to our previous axiomatization.

Theorem 5 (Soundness and Completeness). *The axiomatization presented in the previous section for trace semantics plus the axioms*

$$(b_1 \vee b_2)\uparrow f(\sigma) \equiv b_1\uparrow f(\sigma) \oplus b_2\uparrow f(\sigma) \quad (\vee) \qquad\qquad (\bot\uparrow f)(\sigma) \equiv \underline{\emptyset} \quad (\bot)$$

is sound and complete with respect to $\sim_R$, that is $\varepsilon_1 \sim_R \varepsilon_2 \Leftrightarrow \varepsilon_1 \equiv \varepsilon_2$.

To wrap up this section, we observe that the three equivalences considered in this paper are related by an inclusion: $\sim \subseteq \sim_{tr} \subseteq \sim_R$. This means that the Kleene theorem we presented above for bisimilarity is also valid for the other two equivalences.

5   Discussion

We have presented a framework to reason about Reo automata, a simple and compositional model of the coordination language Reo. The framework consists of (i) a specification language, together with (ii) a Kleene theorem or, more precisely, algorithms to translate expressions to automata and vice-versa and (iii) axiomatizations which enable equational reasoning on expressions. We considered three axiomatizations which are sound and complete with respect to, respectively, bisimilarity, trace equivalence and the bisimulation of [6,7].

The framework presented in this paper is still in its early stages: there are improvements needed to turn it into a practical language. However, we believe it sets the base of an interesting framework for Reo, which will allow the use of powerful existing tools, in order to perform verification, synthesis and model-checking of Reo circuits. For instance, the general framework of [16] was recently implemented in the automatic theorem prover `Circ` [13,5]. In [5], the authors proved that it is always possible to automatically decide if two expressions are bisimilar. This enables automatic reasoning on the language presented in this paper. We would like to (i) integrate the framework of [5] in the Eclipe tool-suite of Reo; (ii) extend the `Circ` framework of [5] in order to also automatically prove different equivalences of expressions, such as trace equivalence.

Another research direction is to investigate how to model composition of connectors at the expression level. We have preliminary results on this which suggest that this is not only possible but also not very difficult. Once the composition operator is part of the language it is a natural question whether it is possible to easily prove (algebraically or coalgebraically) interesting properties such as, for instance, that the Sync channel is an identity element for the composition. Further, casting the framework we presented in this paper in a bialgebraic setting would enable adding new operators, specified by structural operational semantic rules, to the language. Also introducing syntactic sugar would improve the usability of the language (for example, $b \ll a$ could denote b only fires if a also fires and would be translated to a long expression containing all the possible firings containing ab or only a).

Recently, Reo was extended with stochastic information and a quantitative version of Reo automata was proposed as an operational model. Extending the language in order to incorporate stochastic values is an interesting research path, as well as studying if Circ can be used to perform quantitative analysis or to model check quantitative Reo.

Encoding translation of other models into the language could also yield useful results. For instance, properties such as the one mentioned above, of Sync being identity in the composition, could then be automatically checked in Circ for several semantic models of Reo.

References

1. Arbab, F.: Reo: a channel-based coordination model for component composition. Mathematical Structures in Computer Science 14(3), 329–366 (2004)
2. Arbab, F., Herman, I., Spilling, P.: An overview of Manifold and its implementation. Concurrency - Practice and Experience 5(1), 23–70 (1993)
3. Barbosa, M.A., Barbosa, L.S., Campos, J.C.: Towards a coordination model for interactive systems. Electronic Notes in Theoretical Computer Science 183, 89–103 (2007)
4. Bliudze, S., Sifakis, J.: The algebra of connectors - structuring interaction in BIP. IEEE Trans. Computers 57(10), 1315–1330 (2008)
5. Bonsangue, M., Caltais, G., Goriac, E.-I., Lucanu, D., Rutten, J., Silva, A.: A Decision Procedure for Bisimilarity of Generalized Regular Expressions. In: Davies, J., Silva, L., Simão, A. (eds.) SBMF 2010. LNCS, vol. 6527, pp. 226–241. Springer, Heidelberg (2011)
6. Bonsangue, M.M., Clarke, D., Silva, A.: Automata for Context-Dependent Connectors. In: Field, J., Vasconcelos, V.T. (eds.) COORDINATION 2009. LNCS, vol. 5521, pp. 184–203. Springer, Heidelberg (2009)
7. Bonsangue, M.M., Clarke, D., Silva, A.: A model of context-dependent component connectors. Science of Computer Programming (2010)
8. Bruni, R., Lanese, I., Montanari, U.: A basic algebra of stateless connectors. Theor. Comput. Sci. 366(1-2), 98–120 (2006)
9. Fiadeiro, J.L., Lopes, A.: Community on the Move: Architectures for Distribution and Mobility. In: de Boer, F.S., Bonsangue, M.M., Graf, S., de Roever, W.-P. (eds.) FMCO 2003. LNCS, vol. 3188, pp. 177–196. Springer, Heidelberg (2004)

10. Scholten, J.V.G.: Mobile channels for exogenous coordination of distributed systems: semantics, implementation and composition. PhD thesis, LIACS, Faculty of Mathematics and Natural Sciences, Leiden University (January 2007)
11. Lee, B., Lee, E.A.: Hierarchical concurrent finite state machines in Ptolemy. In: ACSD, pp. 34–40. IEEE Computer Society (1998)
12. Liu, X., Xiong, Y., Lee, E.A.: The Ptolemy II framework for visual languages. In: HCC, pp. 50–51. IEEE Computer Society (2001)
13. Lucanu, D., Roşu, G.: CIRC: A Circular Coinductive Prover. In: Mossakowski, T., Montanari, U., Haveraaen, M. (eds.) CALCO 2007. LNCS, vol. 4624, pp. 372–378. Springer, Heidelberg (2007)
14. Rabinovich, A.M.: A Complete Axiomatisation for Trace Congruence of Finite State Behaviors. In: Brookes, S., Main, M., Melton, A., Mislove, M., Schmidt, D. (eds.) MFPS 1993. LNCS, vol. 802, pp. 530–543. Springer, Heidelberg (1994)
15. Silva, A.: A specification language for Reo connectors. Technical report, Centrum Wiskunde & Informatica (February 2011)
16. Silva, A., Bonsangue, M.M., Rutten, J.J.M.M.: Non-deterministic Kleene coalgebras. Logical Methods in Computer Science 6(3) (2010)
17. Szyperski, C.: Component Software: Beyond Object-Oriented Programming, 2nd edn. Addison-Wesley Professional (2002)

Author Index